QUANTITATIVE METHODS
for Decision Makers

Visit the *Quantitative Methods for Decision Makers, fifth edition* Companion Website at **www.pearsoned.co.uk/wisniewski** to find valuable **student** learning material including:

- Real-life data sets in Excel to accompany the exercises in the book

Fifth Edition

QUANTITATIVE METHODS
for Decision Makers

Mik Wisniewski

Senior Research Fellow, Department of Management Science,
University of Strathclyde Business School

FT Prentice Hall
FINANCIAL TIMES

An imprint of **Pearson Education**

Harlow, England • London • New York • Boston • San Francisco • Toronto • Sydney • Singapore • Hong Kong
Tokyo • Seoul • Taipei • New Delhi • Cape Town • Madrid • Mexico City • Amsterdam • Munich • Paris • Milan

Pearson Education Limited

Edinburgh Gate

Harlow

Essex CM20 2JE

England

and Associated Companies throughout the world

Visit us on the World Wide Web at:

www.pearsoned.co.uk

———————————

First published 1994

Second edition published under the Financial Times/Pitman Publishing imprint 1997

Third edition 2002

Fourth edition 2006

Fifth edition published 2009

© Mik Wisniewski 1994, 2009

ISBN: 978-0-273-71207-7

British Library Cataloguing-in-Publication Data

A catalogue record for this book is available from the British Library

Library of Congress Cataloging-in-Publication Data

Wisniewski, Mik.

Quantitative methods for decision makers / Mik Wisniewski. — 5th ed.

p. cm.

Includes bibliographical references and index.

ISBN 978-0-273-71207-7 (pbk. : alk. paper) 1. Decision making—Mathematical models. 2. Management science. I. Title.

HD30.23.W566 2009

658.4'03—dc22

2009000270

10 9 8 7 6 5 4 3

13 12 11 10

Typeset in 9.5/12.5 1Stone Serif by 73

Printed by Graficas Estella, Spain

Still dedicated to Hazel – to whom I promised after the last book that I'd never write another.

Contents

Supporting resources

Visit **www.pearsoned.co.uk/wisniewski** to find valuable online resources

Companion Website for students
• Data sets in Excel to accompany the exercises in the book

For instructors
• A downloadable Instructor's Manual, including full teaching notes and solutions to the exercises in the book

For more information please contact your local Pearson Education sales representative or visit **www.pearsoned.co.uk/wisniewski**

List of 'QMDM in Action' case studies

Preface

The contribution that quantitative techniques can make to management decision making is well researched. There is extensive empirical evidence that the relevant application of such techniques has resulted in significant improvements in efficiency – particularly at the microeconomic level – and has led to improvements in decision making in both profit and not-for-profit organisations. Numerous professional journals regularly provide details of successful applications of such techniques to specific business problems.

This is, arguably, one of the major reasons why in recent years there has been a considerable expansion of the coverage of such topics throughout business studies programmes in the higher education sector, not only in the UK but also across much of Western Europe. Not only postgraduate courses (such as MBAs) and professional courses (in finance, banking and related fields) but most, if not all, business undergraduate courses nowadays expose the student to basic quantitative techniques. It is no longer simply the statistical or mathematical specialist who is introduced to these topics but, in numerical terms far more importantly, a large number of students who go on to a career in general management.

Coupled with this development has been the revolution that has occurred in making available powerful and cost-effective computing power on the manager's desk top. Not only has this meant that the manager now has instant direct access to available business information but also that techniques which used to be the prerogative of the specialist can be applied directly by the manager through the use of appropriate – and relatively cheap and user-friendly – computer software such as Excel.

Because of these developments it is increasingly important for managers to develop a general awareness and understanding of the more commonly used techniques and it is because of this that this textbook was written. There is a plethora of textbooks covering the quantitative field and the author was reluctant simply to add another. However, MBA students – and those studying at equivalent levels – often have different needs and require a different appreciation of these techniques, and it was for this audience that this text primarily was written. The text aims to provide the reader with a detailed understanding of both the role and purpose of quantitative techniques in effective management and in the process of managerial decision making. This text focuses not only on the development of appropriate skills but also on the development of an understanding as to how such techniques fit into the wider management process. Above all, such techniques are meant to be of direct, practical benefit to the managers and decision makers of all organisations. By the end of the text the reader should be able to use the techniques introduced, should have an awareness of common areas of business application and should have developed sufficient confidence and understanding to commission appropriate applications of more complex techniques and contribute to the evaluation of the results of such analysis.

To assist in this each chapter includes:

- a fully worked example, usually with real data, applying each technique in a business context and evaluating the implications of the analysis for management decision making;
- short articles from the *Financial Times* illustrating the use of techniques in a variety of business settings;
- Quantitative methods in action (QMDM in Action) case studies illustrating how the techniques are used in practice.

There is also a comprehensive, fully-worked Instructors' Manual available for lecturers who adopt the text as the main teaching text for their class. The Manual is around 300 pages long, all end-of-chapter exercises have a full, worked solution together with supporting, explanatory text and there are suggestions for other related exercises that can be given to students. Diagrams and tables forming part of the solution are available in A4 size so they can be incorporated into PowerPoint presentations, copied onto acetate or photocopied for students. Further details are available on the website listed below.

Students can download, in spreadsheet format, many of the data sets used in the end-of-chapter exercises from www.pearsoned.co.uk/wisniewski

Guided Tour

Case studies and examples from sources such as the *Financial Times* bring the statistical concepts to life.

Longer **QMDM in Action** case studies appear throughout each chapter, exploring the application of quantitative methods in managerial decision making.

Worked examples are used throughout to illustrate key points and to make the text even easier to follow and understand.

Activities are scattered throughout the chapters, with solutions at the back of the book.

Online resources are provided at the end of every chapter.

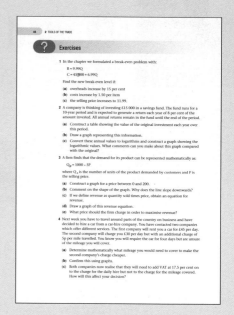

Exercises at the end of every chapter are supported by Excel data sets on the book's companion website.

The **companion website** at **www.pearsoned.co.uk/wisniewski** contains Excel data sets for students. A downloadable Instructor's Manual, with the solutions to the exercises in the text, is available for lecturers.

Acknowledgements

We are grateful to the following for permission to reproduce copyright material:

Figures
Figure 1.3 from You've got direct mail, *Significance* June 1, 2, pp. 78–80 (Mohamed, O. 2004); Figures 1.4, 1.5, 1.6 from Staffing the Front Office, *Operational Research Insight*, 4 (2) (Richardson, C. 1991), Palgrave Macmillan; Figure on pages 135–6 from Halifax plc, Halifax House Price Index; Figures 6.5, 6.6 from *Operations Research*, 39 (1) (1991), Copyright held by the Operations Research Society of America and the Institute of Management Sciences; Figure 8.12 from Employee Receptivity to Total Quality, *International Journal of Quality and Reliability Management*, 10 (1) (Kowalski, E. and Walley, P. 1993), MCB University Press; Figure 10.8 from Energy Forecasting Made Simple, *Operational Research Insight*, 1 (3) (Lang, P. 1988), Palgrave Macmillan; Figures 10.21, 10.22, 10.23, 10.24 from Corporate Modelling at RAC Motoring Services, *Operational Research Insight*, 9 (3), pp. 6–12 (Clarke, S., Hopper, A., Tobias, A. and Tomlin, D. 1996), Palgrave Macmillan; Figures 11.6, 11.7 from Blue Bell Trims its Inventory, *Interfaces*, 15 (1), pp. 34–52 (Edwards, J. R., Wagner, H.M. and Wood, W.P. 1985), Copyright held by the Operations Research Society of America and the Institute of Management Sciences; Figure 12.6 from Responsive delivery!, *Operational Research Insight*, 4 (2), pp. 14–18 (Taylor, T. 1991), Palgrave Macmillan; Figures 14.4a, 14.4b, 14.4c, 14.5, 14.6 from Patients, Parking and Paying, *Operational Research Insight*, 1 (2), pp. 9–13 (Moores, B., Bolton, C. and Fung, A. 1988), Palgrave Macmillan; Figures 15.1, 15.2 from Decision Analysis and its Application in the Choice Between Two Wildcat Adventures, *Interfaces*, 16 (2) (Hosseini, J. 1986), Copyright held by the Operations Research Society of America and the Institute of Management Sciences.

Tables
Table 1.1 from You've Got Mail, *Significance*, p. 80 (Mohamed, O. June 2004); Table 15.1 from Decision Analysis and its Application in the Choice Between Two Wildcat Adventures, *Interfaces*, 16 (2) (Hosseini, J. 1986), Copyright held by the Operations Research Society of America and the Institute of Management Sciences.

Text
Case Study on pages 11–13 from You've got direct mail, *Significance* June 1, 2, pp. 78–80 (Mohamed, O. 2004); Case Study on pages 16–18 adapted from Based on Staffing the Front Office, *Operational Research Insight*, 4 (2), pp. 19–22 (Richardson, C. 1991), Palgrave Macmillan; Case Study on pages 154–6 from The National Lottery, *Significance* pp. 28–29 (Haigh, J. March 2006); Case Study on pages 160–3 from Microsoft Research,

Significance pp. 69–72 (Goodman, J. and Heckerman, D. June 2004); Case Study on pages 300–1 from Fixing a forecasting model that ain't broke, *The Financial Times*, 20 February 2003, p. 17 (copyright: Chrystal, A.), copyright Alec Chrystal; Case Study on pages 398–403 adapted from Corporate Modelling at RAC Motoring Services, *Operational Research Insight*, 9 (3), pp. 6–12 (Clarke, S., Hopper, A., Tobias, A. and Tomlin, D. 1996), Palgrave Macmillan; Case Study on pages 465–6 adapted from Responsive Delivery!, *Operational Research Insight*, 4 (2), pp. 14–18 (Taylor, jT. 1991), Palgrave Macmillan; Case Study on pages 527–9 adapted from Patients, Parking and Paying, *Operational Research Insight*, 1 (2), pp. 9–13 (Moores, B., Bolton, C. and Fung, A. 1988), Palgrave Macmillan; Case Study on page 539 from Shareholders need better boards, not more regulation, *The Financial Times*, 11 January 2008, copyright Theo Vermaelen.

The Financial Times

Case Study on page 10 adapted from Cautious of creating too much complexity, *The Financial Times*, 16 June 2008 (Simon, B.); Case Study on pages 3–4 from Numbers man bridges the Gap, *The Financial Times*, 24 August 2004, p. 10 (Buckley, N.); Case Study on pages 6–7 from Mathematics offers business a formula for success, *The Financial Times* (Cookson, C.); Case Study on pages 27–28 from Multiple answers to Europe's maths problem, *The Financial Times*, 18 June 2007 (Munchau, W.); Case Study on pages 34–35 from Fixing cracks in the crystal ball, *The Financial Times*, 23 December 2008; Case Study on page 49 from A-levels are more profitable than arts degrees, *The Financial Times*, 6 March 2003 (Turner, D.); Case Study on page 54 from Brazil launches new cellular phone drive, *The Financial Times*, 4 October 2000 (Collitt, R.); Case Study on page 56 from Nintendo and Sony showdown in war of consoles, *The Financial Times*, 22 September 2004 (Nakamoto, M.); Case Study on page 57 from Piracy blamed for poor music sales, *The Financial Times*, 2 October 2003 (Burt, T.); Case Study on page 63 from Remuneration is exposed to glare of public scrutiny, *The Financial Times*, 31 January 1996, p. 11; Case Study on page 65 from McDonnell abandons plans for new jetliner, *The Financial Times*, 29 October 1996, p. 26; Case Study on pages 75–76 from Managers focus on right treatment for faked illness, *The Financial Times*, 24 August 2004 (Moules, J.); Screenshot on page 48 from Trading volumes reach new high in London, *The Financial Times*, 7–8 June 2003 (Johnson, S. and Wine, E.); Cartoon on page 49 from A-levels are more profitable than arts degrees, *The Financial Times*, 6 March 2003 (Turner, D.); Figure on page 54 from Brazil launches new cellular phone drive, *The Financial Times*, 4 October 2000 (Parks, C.); Figure on page 55 from Benefits to move from wallets to purses, *The Financial Times*, 8 March 2000; Figure on page 56 from Nintendo and Sony showdown in war of consoles, *The Financial Times*, 22 September 2004 (Nakamoto, M.); Figure on page 57 from Piracy blamed for poor music sales, *The Financial Times*, 2 October 2003 (Burt, T.); Figures on page 59 from Bush focuses on a burning issue, *The Financial Times*, 12 October 2000; Figures on page 59 from How the pies are sliced, *The Financial Times*, 31 January 2001; Figure on page 63 from Remuneration is exposed to glare of public scrutiny, *The Financial Times*, 31 January 1996, p. 11; Figure on page 65 from McDonnell abandons plans for new jetliner, *The Financial Times*, 29 October 1996, p. 26; Figures on page 75, page 76, page 77 from Managers focus on right treatment for faked illness, *The Financial Times*, 24 August 2004 (Moules, J.); Figure on page 77 from Through the demographic window of opportunity, *The Financial Times*, 25 September 2004 (Wolf, M.); Figure on page 78 from Stock markets shrug off central bankers' assurances, *The Financial Times*, 13 March 2001; Figures on page 83 from World Wide Web?, *The Financial Times*, 24 January 2001; Case Study on page 109 from Sarasin banks on its subtle speciality,

The Financial Times, 6 July 2008 (Wood, A.); Case Study on page 127 from Bank study puts underlying inflation at 1.2%, *The Financial Times*, 27 March 2001; Case Study on page 131 from Price of Big Mac shows the Miami-Nairobi gulf, *The Financial Times*, 21 August 2003 (Williams, F.); Case Study on pages 104–5 from The catch in using City earnings data, *The Financial Times*, 28 October 2006 (Giles, C.); Case Study on pages 137–8 from Confusing measures of house prices fall well short, *The Financial Times*, 25 August 2003 (Briscoe, S. and Swann, C.); Case Study on pages 139–40 from The perfect indicator moves closer, *The Financial Times*, 20 September 2003 (Briscoe, S.); Case Study on pages 103–104 from Investors beware of partisan promises, *The Financial Times*, 5 January 2001 (Roberts, D.); Case Study on pages 110–111 from Blue chip shares go the way of the white rhino, *The Financial Times*, 4 October 2000; Case Study on pages 114–115 from 'Unpalatable choices lie ahead' in quest for more equal society, *The Financial Times*, 22 October 2004 (Timmins, N.); Figure on page 103 from Investors beware of partisan promises, *The Financial Times*, 5 January 2001 (Roberts, D.); Figure on page 110 from Blue chip shares go the way of the white rhino, *The Financial Times*, 4 October 2000; Figures on page 115 from 'Unpalatable choices lie ahead' in quest for more equal society, *The Financial Times*, 22 October 2004 (Timmins, N.); Figures on page 124 from Motorola sets scene with strong results, *The Financial Times*, 14 October 2003 (Morgan, M.); Figure on page 137 from Confusing measures of house prices fall well short, *The Financial Times*, 25 August 2003 (Briscoe, S. and Swann, C.); Figure on page 139 from The perfect indicator moves closer, *The Financial Times*, 20 September 2003 (Briscoe, S.); Table 4.12 from Salaries in City of London finance, *The Financial Times*, 14 February 1996, p. 12; Case Study on pages 146–8 from Some ruminations on risk, *The Financial Times*, 11 April 1996, p. 12 (Brittan, S.); Case Study on pages 151–2 from Most of us are highly likely to get probability wrong, *The Financial Times*, 16 August 2005 (Kay, J.); Case Study on pages 182–3 from When it's time to ask for whom the bell curve tolls, *The Financial Times*, 4 May 2008 (Authers, J.); Case Study on pages 186–7 from Probability and distributions, *The Financial Times*, 3 November 1995, p. 12; Figure on page 182 from When it's time to ask for whom the bell curve tolls?, *The Financial Times*, 4 May 2008 (Authers, J.); Figures on page 187 from Probability and distributions, *The Financial Times, Mastering Management Part 2*, 3 November 1995; Case Study on page 206 from Initiative to boost business and research links, *The Financial Times*, 22 February 2005 (Hall, W.); Case Study on pages 196–7 from Game theory helps insurers to judge the risks of terror, *The Financial Times*, 8 September 2004 (Wiggins, J.); Case Study on pages 218–9 from Pollsters predict a shake-out, *The Financial Times*, 29 July 2003 (Burt, T.); Case Study on pages 221–2 from Every statistic tells a story, *The Financial Times*, 29 September 2003; Case Study on pages 259–63 from Taking samples, *The Financial Times: Mastering Management Part 3*, 10 November 1995 (van Ackere, A.); Figure on page 218 from Pollsters predict a shake-out, *The Financial Times*, 29 July 2003 (Burt, T.); Case Study on page 293 from Adventures in Six Sigma: how the problem-solving technique helped Xerox, *The Financial Times*, 23 September 2005; Case Study on pages 276–7 from Bad service 'costing companies millions', *The Financial Times*, 29 November 1996, p. 14 (Harverson, P.); Figure on page 276 from Bad service 'costing companies millions, *The Financial Times*, 29 November 1996, p. 14; Case Study on page 299 from Narrow-bodied jets to take 70% of market, *The Financial Times*, 7 March 1996, p. 5 (Skapinker, M.); Case Study on page 301 from Accuracy of analysts' profits forecasts hits record low, *The Financial Times*, 9 February 2004 (Roberts, D.); Case Study on page 309 from Baby store's boom might just have got ahead of itself, *The Financial Times*, 12 July 2003 (Smith, A.); Case Study on page 328 from Thorntons' chief hopes to taste seasonal success, *The Financial Times*, 14 December 2000; Case Study on page 331 from Sharp down turn in German job creation, *The Financial Times*, 1 July 2008 (Benoit, B.); Case Study on pages 318–9 from Technical analysis: How to identify your friend the trend, *The Financial Times*, 24 January 2003 (Heaney, V.); Case Study on pages 322–3 adapted from Learning to live with distortions, *The Financial Times*, 22 February 2003 (Briscoe, S.); Figures on page 299 from Narrow-bodied jets to take 70% of market, *The Financial Times*, 7 March 1996, p. 5 (Skapinker, M.); Figures on page 309 from Baby store's boom might just have got ahead of itself, *The Financial Times*, 12 July 2003 (Smith, A.); Figure on page 310 from *The Financial Times*, 29 June 2006; Case Study on page 369 from Bank lifts hopes on inflation target, *The Financial Times*, 15 February 1996, p. 1 (Chote, R.); Case Study on pages 354–5 from Why states must grow, *The Financial Times*, 6 November 1995, p. 25 (Flanders, S.); Case Study on pages 390–1 from Strategy by computer, *The Financial Times*, 17 April 1996, p. 24 (Griffith, V.); Figure on page 354 from Why states must grow, *The Financial Times*, 6 November 1995, p. 25 (Flanders, S.); Figure 10.22 from Bank lifts hopes on inflation target, *The Financial Times*, 15 February 1996, p. 1 (Chote, R.); Figures on page 432 from Getting the combination right, *FT Mastering Management Part 8*, 15 December 1995 p. 25 (Vlahos, K.); Tables on page 432 from Getting the combination right, *FT Mastering Management Part 8*, 15 December 1995 p. 25 (Vlahos, K.); Case Study on pages 411–3 from How shops use the information, *The Financial Times*, 7 October 2003 (Briscoe, S.); Case Study on pages 431–4 from Getting the combination right, *FT Mastering Management Part 8*, 15 December 1995 p. 25 (Vlahos, K.); Case Study on page 445 from Retailers hope tighter stock control will stem theft and fraud losses, *The Financial Times*, 21 November 2005 (Buckley, S.); Case Study on pages 457–8 from The challenge of changing everything at once, *The Financial Times*, 2 April 2008 (Pritchard, S.); Case Study on pages 458–61 from Systems are never good enough, *FT Mastering Management Part 3*, 10 November 1995 (Vollmann, T. E.); Case Study on page 472 adapted from Spiralling costs of big road schemes criticised, *The Financial Times*, 28 July 2006 (Adams, C.); Case Study on page 473 from Fines could help fill holes in the road, *The Financial Times*, 6 April 2000; Case Study on pages 471–2 adapted from European centre proves invaluable for project planning and liaising with customers, *The Financial Times*, 15 September 2005 (Palmer, M.); Case Study on pages 508–9 from Decision-making software in the fast lane, *The Financial Times*, 28 February 2007 (Cane, A.); Case Study on pages 525–6 from Hedge funds eye glamour of movie land, *The Financial Times*, 9 October 2006 (Garrahan, M.); Case Study on pages 530–3 from Taking the risk out of uncertainty, *FT Mastering Management Part 5*, 24 November 1995 (Vlahos, K.); Case Study on page 542 from Is money in my account mine?, *The Financial Times*, 7 April 2004 (Ross, S.); Case Study on page 548 from Terra Firma sued over 'modelling flaw', *The Financial Times*, 5 February 2008; Case Study on page 550 from Lex: Internal rate of return, *The Financial Times*, 1 June 2005; Case Study on pages 557–60 from Project approval: the key criteria, *FT Mastering Management Part 2*, 3 November 1995 (Farkas, A.).

In some instances we have been unable to trace the owners of copyright material, and we would appreciate any information that would enable us to do so.

1 Introduction

There's no getting away from it. Quantitative information is everywhere in business: share prices, costs, income and revenue levels, profit levels, cash flow figures, productivity figures, customer satisfaction ratings, market share figures. The list goes on and on. If you're in a public sector or not-for-profit organisation comparable information is also being generated. The trend seems to be: let's measure and quantify everything we can.

The problem this causes for managers is how to make sense of this mass of quantitative information. How do we use it to help make decisions and to help the organisation deal with the issues and pressures that it increasingly faces? Such decisions may be routine, day-to-day operational issues: deciding how much laser printer paper to order for the office. They may be longer-term strategic decisions which will have a critical impact on the success of the organisation: which products/services do we expand?

And – no great surprise here – this is why this textbook has been written: to help managers make sense of quantitative business information and understand how to use that quantitative information constructively to make business decisions. However, we're not looking to turn you into mathematical and statistical experts. We want to give you a reasonable understanding of how a variety of quantitative techniques can be used to help decision making in any organisation. We also want to convince you that these techniques are of real, practical benefit. That's why throughout the text we focus on the business application of the techniques rather than the theory behind them. We also illustrate how real organisations have used these techniques to improve their business performance.

We hope you find this textbook useful.

The Use of Quantitative Techniques by Business

Okay, let's start with a reality check.

You're *really* looking forward to the quantitative methods module on your MBA course. Right?

You *really* wish there could be more quantitative methods on your course. Right?

You *really* see quantitative methods as the key to a successful management career. Right?

I don't think so!

Like just about every other business degree student around the world you're probably approaching this course and this textbook with a mixture of concern, worry and misunderstanding.

Concern about your ability in statistics and mathematics, especially as these probably weren't your favourite subjects in school either.

Worry about whether you'll be able to pass the exam and assessments in this subject.

Misunderstanding about why you have to do a quantitative methods course on a business degree. After all, business is about strategy, about marketing, about finance, about human resource management, about IT and ecommerce. We know these are important to every business because company boards have directors in these areas. But whoever heard of a company with a director of quantitative methods?

One of the major reasons for writing this book was to provide business studies students at both undergraduate and postgraduate levels with a text that is relevant to their own studies, is easy to read and to understand and which demonstrates the practical application – and benefits – of quantitative techniques in the real business world. The book is *not* aimed at students whose main interest is in statistics, mathematics or computing. We assume that, like ourselves, students in the fields of management, accountancy, finance and business have no interest in these in their own right but rather are simply interested in the practical applications of such topics and techniques to business and to management decision making. The reason why all students in the business area nowadays need a working knowledge of these quantitative techniques is clear. In order to work effectively in a modern business organisation – whether the organisation is a private commercial company, a government agency, a state industry or whatever – managers must be able routinely to use quantitative techniques in a confident and reliable manner. Today's students are striving to become tomorrow's managers. Accountants will make decisions based on the information relating to the financial state of the organisation. Economists will make decisions based on the information relating to the economic framework in which the organisation operates. Marketing staff will make decisions based on customer response to products and design. Personnel managers will make decisions based on the information relating to the levels of employment in the organisation, and so on. Such information is increasingly quantitative and it is apparent that managers (both practising and intending) need a working knowledge of the procedures and techniques appropriate for analysing and evaluating such information. Such analysis and certainly the business evaluation cannot be delegated to the specialist statistician or mathematician, who, adept though they might be at sophisticated numerical analysis, will frequently have little overall understanding of the business relevance of such analysis.

Numbers man bridges the Gap

The US clothing group's chief ignores fashion intuition, using scientific analysis to woo alienated customers, writes Neil Buckley

The first few times Paul Pressler, chief executive of Gap, the US clothing group, reviewed the new season's products, the designers were baffled.

He would ask only a few basic questions – had they thought of this or that, why had they chosen a particular style – and he would not pass judgment. When he left the room, the designers "were, like, 'OK. Did he *like* it?' ", he says, recounting the story in Gap's design office in Chelsea, New York.

But for Mr Pressler, a former Disney theme park executive, "it didn't matter whether I liked it or not – what mattered was whether the consumer liked it". His refusal to air stylistic opinions was his way of showing his staff how he planned to manage the company. "I had to demonstrate to everyone that the general manager is here to lead people – not pick the buttons," he says.

Mr Pressler's anecdote illustrates how he runs Gap very differently from his predecessor, Millard "Mickey" Drexler, whom he succeeded two years ago. Whether Mickey Drexler liked things or not was very important indeed.

Popularly known as Gap's "Merchant Prince", Mr Drexler set the tone, designed products and even dictated what quantities of products buyers should order from the company's suppliers. The business was largely run on his instinct. Designers, jokes Mr Pressler, "relied on getting their blessing from the pope".

The approach was successful for 15 years, as Mr Drexler worked with Don Fisher, Gap's founder, to transform into an international fashion retailing giant what had started as a single store in counter-culture 1960s San Francisco.

Yet by 2002, when Mr Pressler arrived, Gap Inc – which now includes the lower priced Old Navy and upmarket Banana Republic chains in North America as well as international Gap stores – was in trouble. Comparable sales, or sales from stores open at least a year – an important indicator of a retailer's health – had fallen, year-on-year, for 29 straight months. It was clear Gap had lost touch with its customers.

Mr Drexler's genius had been to be absolutely in tune with the postwar baby boomers – those born between 1946 and 1964 – who were Gap's first customers. Gap grew and adapted with them; when they had children, it clothed them too, launching Gap Kids in 1986 and Baby Gap in 1990. It kept up their interest with quirky and distinctive advertising. By the late 1990s, as the boomers took over America's boardrooms, the internet took off and 'business casual' replaced suits and ties, Gap seemed unstoppable.

It increased the number of stores – and the amount of debt – tossing out Mr Fisher's previously cautious approach of opening just enough stores to ensure 15 per cent compound annual earnings growth.

But, like many of its customers, Gap was about to experience what Mr Pressler calls a mid-life crisis.

Gap's massive investment in expansion was not yielding a return.

Sassy, youth-orientated retailers such as Abercrombie & Fitch and American Eagle were coming on the scene, offering Gap stiff competition. "Everyone was looking at them and saying 'look how cool and hip they are' and 'Gap is now my father's brand,' " says Mr Pressler.

To address the problem, Mr Drexler decided Gap needed to go after a younger consumer. Out went the khakis and simple white shirts; in came turquoise low-rise jeans and tangerine cropped T-shirts. But the customers deserted the stores in droves. "Mickey took the fashion in a direction that was, to his credit, trying to be more hip and relevant," says Mr Pressler, "but it was too singular, too hip and youthful."

At this point, Mr Drexler left Gap, having served 19 years. Mr Pressler, then running Walt Disney's theme park division and considered a possible successor to Michael Eisner as Disney's CEO, says he did not have to think too long about accepting the Gap job. Like many businessmen of his generation – he is now 48 – he felt a personal connection.

"I thought about it first as a consumer and said: 'Damn! This brand is too good and too awesome'. Many of us went to [business] school on Gap: how it reinvented itself, how it did its marketing. And as consumers we were all a little pissed off that it had alienated us."

Once inside, he spent 90 days reviewing the business, interviewing the 50 most senior people in the company. He was shocked.

"A company that I had thought was this unbelievably consumer-centric company was not a consumer-centric company at all," he says. "The truth is that we made decisions in our head, not in the real world. The tool we used was yesterday's sales – which didn't give you consumer insights, or tell you why people didn't shop at our stores."

There were other problems. The technology system was, as Mr Pressler puts it: "massively, woefully, behind anything I had ever seen in my life for a company of our size." A $15bn-a-year business was run largely on Excel spreadsheets and inventory discipline was non-existent, with little account taken of how much working capital was being tied up.

Mr Pressler set about replacing intuition with science. He carried out a detailed "segmentation" study for each brand and introduced consumer research, interviews with customers and store managers, and focus groups.

The message that came back was clear. Prices aside, consumers could see little difference between Gap and its Old Navy sister chain.

In response, Old Navy was repositioned as more of a value chain and Banana Republic was taken upmarket and given a "designer" feel. That left the middle ground for Gap.

Mr Pressler stuck with Mr Drexler's strategy of waving goodbye to the boomers, though. "We have brought a more youthful style aesthetic," he says, "but it's a safe one, not a scary one."

"Instead of going to the 15- to 20-year-olds, we pushed the brand back to what it has always been, which is really a 20- to 30-year-olds' brand," says Mr Pressler.

The research also helped identify new product niches that could be added to stores – petite sizes in Banana Republic, so-called "plus" sizes in Old Navy and maternity wear in Gap.

It helped each chain segment its customers into types – mums, mums shopping for families, fashionable teens and more conservative "girl-next-door" teens – so designers had a clearer idea of their likely buyers.

In pursuit of what Mr Pressler calls fashion retailing's "Holy Grail" – women's trousers that fit right – Gap stopped using in-house "fit models" who were a perfect size 8. Instead, it organised "fit clinics" across the country, and designers got real people to try on their clothes.

Sizing initiatives did not stop there. Gap's chains used to ship identical proportions of different sizes of products to all stores. But in, say, fitness-obsessed San Francisco, it would be left with lots of surplus extra large sizes. In the Midwest, the surplus would be in extra small sizes.

Mr Pressler got mathematical experts to analyse Gap's electronic sales information. They divided its stores into seven different "clusters" according to the likely sizes of the customers in the local area. Each cluster now gets a different mixture of sizes. As a result, fewer products are out of stock, more customers are satisfied and fewer goods get left over to be marked down.

Meanwhile, systems were updated and sophisticated inventory management software introduced.

Mr Pressler admits that the company's designers were initially sceptical about his analytical approach. But once they saw what was happening to sales they became converts.

Comparable sales began growing again in late 2002 and continued until last month when sales fell 5 per cent year-on-year. This drop was largely attributable to poor weather and higher petrol prices. Operating margins are also getting back towards the mid-teens they reached in the 1990s.

However, at around $20, Gap's shares still remain well below their $50-plus peak in 1999 and the market is clamouring to hear where future growth will come from.

Mr Pressler says Gap is studying how to expand its core brand in its existing overseas markets – Japan, the UK and France – as well as in some other countries. It is also considering whether Old Navy and Banana Republic could work outside the US and Canada. He does not rule out departing from the existing model of company-run stores and using franchising, licensing arrangements or partnerships in these overseas markets.

In the US, Mr Pressler admits that he is contemplating a fourth brand. But he refuses to comment on speculation that Gap is considering a chain catering to boomer women – those aged 35–50 – for whom the core brand is too youthful.

If Gap is targeting the post-boomer generation now, Mr Pressler insists the brand will never lose sight of its 1960s counter-culture origins.

Its autumn advertising campaign, featuring *Sex and the City* star Sarah Jessica Parker, will, he says, affirm its cultural relevance.

"We were always right on the spot, on the cultural phenomenon happening at the moment. And we brought it to you, through our commercials, and through our product, in ways that were compelling," he says. "That piece of the DNA we still feel very strongly."

Source: *Financial Times*, 24 August 2004, p. 10.

Quantitative methods can make all the difference to business success or failure.

This text introduces the major mathematical and statistical techniques used to help decision making by managers of all types of business organisation: large and small, private sector, public sector, profit-oriented, not-for-profit, manufacturing, or service sector. In an increasingly complex business environment managers have to grapple with problems and issues which range from the relatively trivial – which make of photocopier will prove more reliable and cost effective – to the strategic – which products or services do we continue to deliver and which do we discontinue. As the article on Gap illustrates, managers are expected to be able to justify the decisions they reach on the basis of logic and hard analysis not just on judgement and experience. In such an environment the quantitative techniques we shall be examining have an important part to play. We do not pretend that these techniques offer the manager an instant solution to the problems faced. But they do offer a method of analysing a problem using proven techniques, of providing information about that problem and of assessing the potential outcomes from different decisions. This is not to say, however, that management decision making is simply about the application of such techniques. It clearly is not. However, such techniques can provide valuable information about a business problem that may not be available from any other source. But such information is only part of the problem. The manager must assess the information generated by techniques alongside that available from Finance, from Engineering, from Sales, from Marketing, from Personnel and so on. Like any piece of information the manager must be in a position to assess its reliability and its potential usefulness.

This is why, in this text, the focus is very much on an understanding of the general principles – from a management perspective – behind each technique. It is not the intention of the text to turn you into an 'expert' in the use of such techniques although you will develop skills in the practical aspects of many of these as we progress. Rather it is to enable you to appreciate when such techniques may be useful in your decision-making capacity and to provide you with an insight into how the information generated by such techniques can be evaluated and used.

But don't just take our word for this. Let's look at some documented examples (you'll find full details of each of these in the Further Reading section at the end of this chapter).

- An electricity company in the USA developed a computer-based planning system to help improve forecasts of demand. The result was a reduction of some US$140 million in fuel costs over a seven-year period.

- The UK Royal Air Force developed a simulation model to quantify the number of battle damage repair teams likely to be required to maintain aircraft capabilities in the event of hostilities.

- A computer-based simulation model was developed to help evaluate the strategic options in terms of transporting coal in Canada from its source to power stations – a distance of some 3000 km.

- In Canada the technique of linear programming was applied to the use of ambulances in health care and to the related shift systems. This generated annual savings of around CN$250 000.

- A farming cooperative in Holland implemented an interactive optimisation system to help plan bulk deliveries of its sugar beet crop with a resulting reduction of 7 per cent in its operating costs.

- A New Zealand utility company applied quantitative techniques to its car pooling procedures with the result that the number of vehicles required was reduced by 35 per cent, which generated annual savings of NZ$55 000.

● Quantitative techniques were applied to the problem of transporting mentally hand-icapped adults to a training centre in the UK. As a result travel time could be reduced by almost 16 per cent and distance travelled by 12 per cent.

● A quantitative model was developed to assist in the planning of transportation of blood from a regional centre to hospitals. The model generated a reduction of over 12 per cent in the number of units of blood which had reached their expiry date before use compared with the manual planning system.

● American Airlines has developed a number of quantitative models in relation to its airline seat reservation systems. The models are estimated to contribute around US$500 million per year to the company's revenue.

● Hewlett-Packard used quantitative techniques to forecast capacity and to determine locations of stocks and supplies in the context of one of its computer printers. As a result, productivity increased by 50 per cent and incremental revenues of US$280 mil-lion in sales were generated.

● Forecasting models are estimated to have saved the mail order company L.L. Bean US$300 000 each year through improved prediction of incoming calls and staffing requirements in its call centres.

● Delta Airlines uses mathematical programming models to help in its assignment of airplanes in its fleet to flight routes. The approach saved the company around US$300 million over a three-year period.

● Kentucky Fried Chicken (KFC) reduced waiting times for customers by half and improved productivity, sales and profit through the application of quality manage-ment techniques.

● DEC (Digital) saved an estimated US$100 million by applying linear programming to its global manufacturing and distribution strategy.

● Taco Bell, a chain of popular restaurants, used forecasting to help it predict arrivals of customers through the day and developed a simulation model for planning its per-sonnel requirements. The company saved an estimated US$53 million in labour costs in one year alone.

That made you sit up and take notice, didn't it?

The appropriate use of quantitative techniques can help the business 'bottom line' – whether that bottom line is increased profitability, reduced costs, improved efficiency, or better customer service. Quantitative techniques *work*! And they work best when used by managers.

Mathematics offers business a formula for success

FT

By Clive Cookson, Science Editor

Mathematicians have come up with an impressive multiplication formula for British commerce and industry: spend a few million pounds promot-ing the use of maths as a strategic tool, and add billions of pounds of value to businesses. That is the thinking about a new government–industry consortium, the Mathemat-ics Knowledge Transfer Network. The network aims to boost the use of maths throughout the economy from grocery distribution to banking, telecoms to manufacturing.

The Department of Trade and Industry will make a core invest-ment of £1.5m in the network's infrastructure over three years, with other partners contributing £3.5m. Industry is expected to increase research and development spending by a further £7m as a result of the project. But Robert Leese, the consortium manager, said the indirect benefits could be hundreds or thousands of times greater.

"It is already recognised that the use of mathematics in the R&D process adds billions of pounds of value to UK business," said Mr Leese, who directs the Smith Institute for Industrial Mathematics in Guildford. "I predict the newly-formed KTN will multiply that value by two, three or perhaps even four times." Mr Leese added: "I do not think many businesses are fully aware of the benefits that maths can bring. Few companies recognise that they have mathematical expertise in-house, and few universities are promoting their maths departments effectively to industry."

Lenny Smith, an American mathematician with academic appointments at the London School of Economics and Oxford University,

said: "The quality of mathematics and the ability to do ground-breaking research in the UK are second to none." But Prof Smith, who works with industry on both sides of the Atlantic, added that UK companies were slower than their US counterparts to apply mathematical ideas.

Huge savings can be made by applying algorithms – mathematical rules – to existing information, according to Prof Smith. For example, the retailing and logistics sectors could find more efficient ways to move goods around the country. "Maths can help Adnams brewery decide how best to collect its empty beer kegs or Sainsbury's decide where to sell two truckloads of lettuce in Birmingham," he said. Unilever, one of 12 companies on the network industrial steering committee, has recently made extensive use of maths. It says statistical analysis of the relationships between advertising campaigns,

sales and market share has made Unilever advertising campaigns 15 per cent more efficient. "We are also borrowing mathematical simulation methods used in the film industry and gaming world, such as agent-based methods, to model the psychology of how shoppers choose one brand over another," said Shail Patel, mathematical and psychological sciences leader for Unilever Research. "Mathematics is universal as, unlike most other disciplines, it can add value to any function within Unilever."

Mr Leese is most enthusiastic about the ability of maths to "shine a torch" down possible R&D routes so that managers can decide quickly which are dead ends and which should be pursued. "The whole concept of mathematics 'accelerating' the innovation process is simple to state," he said. "It both provides an earlier return on investment in R&D and cuts down on wasted R&D spend."

Source: Financial Times, 13 February 2006.

UK business has started to wake up to the benefits that quantitative methods can bring.

The Role of Quantitative Techniques in Business

It will be worthwhile at this stage considering the specific role of quantitative techniques in the wider business decision-making context. Although this text inevitably focuses on a number of common techniques, business decision making is more than simply the application of a technique to a problem. It is worth considering what the overall purpose of such techniques is in relation to the decision maker. Such techniques aim to improve decision making within an organisation.

Those of you with experience of management in an organisation will appreciate that life for any manager in any organisation is becoming increasingly difficult and complex. Although there are many factors contributing to this, Figure 1.1 illustrates some of the major pressures making decision making increasingly problematic. Organisations generally find themselves operating in an increasingly complex environment. Changes in government policy, privatisation, increasing involvement of the European Union, and political and economic changes in Eastern Europe all contribute to this complexity. At the same time, organisations face increasing competition from both home and abroad. Markets that were thought to be secure are lost to competitors. In the public sector,

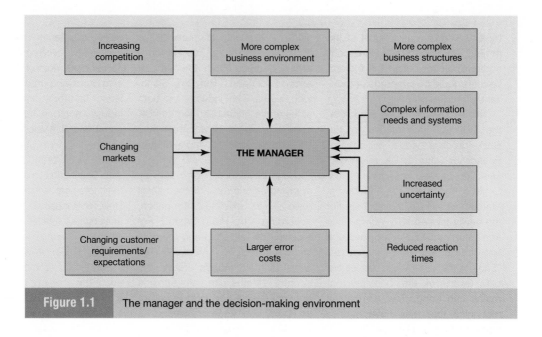

Figure 1.1   The manager and the decision-making environment

services – local authority, health care, emergency services – are increasingly required to operate in a competitive manner. Also, the markets and customers available to organisations are changing. This combines with increasing and constantly changing pressures from customers in terms of both their requirements and their expectations. The drive for quality and customer satisfaction gathers pace in both the public and private sectors.

Because of the increasing complexity of the business environment in which organisations have to function, the information needs of a manager become more complex and demanding also. With the pace of increasing competition – and with continual improvements in telecommunications – the time available to a manager to assess, analyse and react to a problem or opportunity is much reduced.

Managers, and their supporting information systems, need to take fast – and hopefully appropriate – decisions. Finally, to add to the problems, the consequences of taking wrong decisions become more serious and costly. Entering the wrong markets, producing the wrong products or providing inappropriate services will have major, and often disastrous, consequences for organisations.

All of this implies that anything which can help the manager of an organisation in facing up to these pressures and difficulties in the decision-making process must be seriously considered. Not surprisingly this is where quantitative techniques have a role to play. This is not to say that such techniques will automatically resolve such problems. But they can provide both information about a situation or problem and a different way of examining that situation that may well help. Naturally such quantitative analysis will produce information that must be assessed and used in conjunction with other sources. Business problems are rarely, if ever, tackled solely from the quantitative perspective. Much qualitative assessment must also take place. For example, consider a local authority considering the replacement of some of its refuse collection vehicles. We may well be able to apply a number of quantitative techniques to this situation – applying financial analysis principles, examining patterns and trends in refuse collection, comparing one vehicle's performance with other vehicles, forecasting the likely demand for refuse collection over the life of the vehicle and so on. However, before reaching a decision, other factors and information will need to be considered. Is this

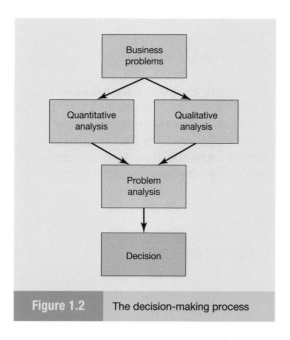

Figure 1.2   The decision-making process

the right time 'politically' to be making what may be a major capital investment? How will the workforce react to a new vehicle – given this may require some retraining – and to what may be new modes or methods of working? Will the management of this service be able to cope with the problems that such a change will bring? All of these factors and more will need to be taken into account by the manager before reaching a decision. Clearly, techniques have a potentially important role to play in helping reach a decision but they are not sufficient by themselves. This is illustrated – albeit simplistically – in Figure 1.2. A business situation – at the strategic or operational level – needs to be examined from both a quantitative and a qualitative perspective. Information and analysis from both these perspectives need to be brought together, assessed and acted upon.

However, the techniques we introduce in this text not only are valuable at corporate, strategic level, but they are also particularly useful at the operational level in day-to-day management (although use at this level is rarely publicly reported). We shall be introducing a number of illustrations of this level of use throughout the chapters. In short, knowledge of such techniques, the ability to know when to apply them and the ability to relate the quantitative outputs from such techniques to business decision making is critically important for every manager in every organisation. Not to develop such skills and knowledge will put your own organisation at a critical competitive disadvantage.

Models in Quantitative Decision Making

Throughout the text we shall be introducing what are known as *models* to help develop quantitative techniques in a business context. Models come in a variety of forms in business: they are not just quantitative. A scale model might be constructed of a new office development; a financial model may be developed to assess the impact of budget changes on product/service delivery; the marketing department may develop a model in terms of assessing customer response to product changes. However, any model, no matter what its form or purpose, has one distinctive feature: it is an attempt to represent a situation in a simplified form. Any model tries to represent the complex real-world situation in a more simplistic and potentially more easily understood form. This is achieved by developing the model so that it focuses on the key aspects of the situation and ignores the rest.

In this text we shall be developing a variety of statistical and mathematical models for use in business decision making. We shall be using such mathematics and statistics to help us make sense of a complex real-world problem, and we shall be utilising techniques to help us focus on what we believe to be the key aspects of the problem. Just as an architect uses a scale model of a new construction or an engineer of some machine, so a manager needs to be able to develop and use quantitative models to help in the decision-making process.

John Hull: Cautious of creating too much complexity

By Bernard Simon in Toronto

John Hull has a confession to make. As a professor of finance at the University of Toronto's Rotman School of Management, he has won international acclaim for designing and valuing complex financial tools such as options and other derivatives. But when it comes to managing his own money, Prof Hull has little use for such exotic instruments. His investment portfolio comprises mainly index funds. And while he keeps reminding his students about the importance of hedging risk, his own liabilities are heavily concentrated in Canadian dollars.

Seen from a different angle however, Prof Hull's financial strategy is entirely consistent with the message he hammers home as a teacher, author, consultant and expert witness in derivative-related lawsuits: that is, keep things as simple as possible.

"There's a danger, with all the people with PhDs in physics and maths who have moved into this area, that some of the models become too complicated", Prof Hull says. "There's a tendency for people with that sort of background

to just want a really difficult problem to solve. And that's not necessarily what's needed."

Quantitative analysis and analysts have made deep in-roads in trading rooms and financial research departments since two University of Chicago economists, Fischer Black and Myron Scholes, devised a mathematical model for pricing options and corporate liabilities in the early 1970s. However, the recent turmoil in financial markets has jolted faith in the so-called "quants".

Prof Hull agrees that "there's some ground for concern" that traders and analysts have relied too heavily on mathematical models in their decision-making. "We need a much more common-sense approach to risk management and must not let quants and traders run free-rein for short-term profits," he says.

The problem, in Prof Hull's view, has been an overdependence on models that are based chiefly on recent market trends. Over the past three years, for instance, "we were looking at a period when volatilities were very low", he says, "so values

at risk were lower". "To some extent, that model led to a false confidence on the part of the banks. Somebody should have been saying: 'Let's look at the big picture, what could go wrong? How well will we come out if it does go wrong?'

"In most institutions I don't think anybody was doing that. They were just relying on: 'We're making a lot of money, the value-at-risk model says we're okay'." But heavy losses since the onset of the US subprime mortgage crisis have prompted a good deal of soul-searching among quants, and those who employ them. "I don't think there is a substitute for sound managerial judgment," Prof Hull says. "In a few companies, however, rather than senior managers letting the traders run loose on this, they sat back and thought about the environment out there; about what could go wrong and how badly they would suffer if it did."

"It's more looking at a situation, coming up with the simplest model that captures the essence of it, and then writing it up in such a way that people will easily be able to understand it."

Source: Financial Times, 16 June 2008.

Models have a useful role to play in business decision making but they have to be used in combination with management judgement and experience.

QMDM IN ACTION
You've got direct mail: the Marks and Spencer "&More" credit card

Predictive modelling provides a way to increase profitability and customer satisfaction in the financial services sector. Following on from Career Story, **Omar Mohamed** *describes the successful use of this technique in recent marketing activities for the M&S "&More" credit card.*

Why use predictive modelling?

The financial services industry is fiercely competitive, with a constant stream of new entrants (e.g. Egg and Virgin) branching out into financial services, and companies must find ways of targeting customers effectively if they are to increase their market share. Knowing which customers are most likely to respond to a particular product offer is invaluable business information. By analysing customers' responses to past offers, businesses can gain insight into which offers individual customers are likely to respond to and decide whether they should be contacted in connection with a particular product offer in future marketing activities.

Effective targeting allows businesses to be extremely cost effective in activities such as direct mail, and also to maintain a good relationship with customers by not bombarding them with offers which do not interest them. This is particularly important because the number of pieces of direct mail the average household receives is constantly increasing.

Predictive modelling is key to effective targeting. Predictive models allow businesses to forecast customer behaviour by analysing the wealth of information stored on large customer databases. These models are used to produce forecasts of customer behaviour commonly known as *scores* or *propensities*, which are then used to decide which customers should be mailed to achieve the most profitable activity or financial target. Customers are usually ranked by their score and then the best customers are selected first until response targets are met.

The challenge

The marketing Credit Card Team wanted to carry out an offer mailing to existing M&S Money customers. The initial problem was to decide which customers were likely to take up the product, with the goal of reaching the desired number of responders at minimum cost. Since the cost per mailing piece is fairly constant, the only way to reduce the cost of the campaign was to send fewer pieces of mail.

However, since the Credit Card Team wanted to reach a target number of responders, the solution was not simply to send fewer mail pieces. If customers were selected for the offer at random from among all available customers, the number of mail pieces could not be reduced without the risk of falling short of the number of responders required to make the campaign successful. So we needed a targeting tool that could be used to select those customers who were most likely to respond to the offer.

Application of predictive modelling
Creating the model

The first step in producing the predictive model was data selection. This step was key, since a model is only as good as the underlying data. Selecting the best data for the development of the targeting model required a good understanding of the market and the objective, and, not surprisingly, this stage took up the most time and effort, identifying, locating and preparing the data. Since there were no previous campaigns offering this product, the data set was selected from customers who had, and who had not, taken up the product of their own accord.

The model's target variable was the probability that a customer would take up our offer. Customers who had taken up the product were given a value of 1 and customers who did not have the product were given a value of 0.

→

We then identified and located data, from sources both inside and outside the organisation, that could be used to build the model. This covered

- demographics, including gender, age, household income, marital status, home ownership and type of dwelling,
- behavioural information, including types and numbers of purchases,
- product holdings, including characteristics describing the products customers already held (e.g. "holds an M&S Money Mini Cash ISA, previously held an M&S Money loan"),
- third-party data, including products customers purchased, their attitudes, beliefs and opinions, geodemographic data, demographic and lifestyle data.

The next stage was the creation of new variables from these raw data. This is a critical element of good model building as data are often more predictive when transformed into descriptive and summary statistics. Behaviour and product data, such as monthly balances, monthly transactions and the loans a customer had in the past were used in the creation of new fields. For example, balances over the last 6 months were used to create a new field: 'average balance in the last 6 months'.

At this point we had generated a modelling data set with several hundred variables, including derived and raw data inputs. We next looked at reducing the number of modelling variables from several hundred to the 100 or so most predictive, by selecting those that were most correlated with the target variable. The tools used included descriptive statistics, crosstabs, χ^2-tests and cumulative modelling.

Next came the modelling stage, for which we separated the modelling data set into a training data set and a validation data set. The training data set was used to develop the model and the validation data set was held back to check that the model was robust.

Stepwise logistic regression was then used for the development of the response model, although other statistical techniques were also investigated. The hundred variables identified as being the most predictive in the previous stage were used for modelling the training data set. This was an iterative process, resulting in several variants of the final

model that all performed well. These were compared against each other using a variety of diagnostic tools in order to select the best performing model.

The final model was then validated by running fresh data through it to see how well it performed. The results were very consistent with the results seen in the training stage so we were confident that the model would perform well when implemented.

Implementing the model

The model was then used to produce scores for all available customers on the customer database (a score of 100 meaning that a customer was most likely to take up the product and a score of 1 meaning that the customer was least likely to take up the product).

Customers were then sorted into descending order according to their score. First a small random sample of customers was selected so that the model's performance could be compared against results for a non-targeted campaign, and then a group of the best customers was selected to achieve the required number of responders for the campaign.

The benefits

When the responses had come in, we could see how the predictive model performed.

The mailing carried out to a selection of our best customers achieved approximately three times the number of responders we would have received had we mailed a random selection of the same size.

Figure 1.3 shows the total mailed population, ranked according to their model score along the x-axis (highest likelihood to respond to lowest likelihood to respond from left to right). The y-axis shows the cumulative captured responses, as percentages of the total response to the campaign. The straight black line represents the results of a non-targeted campaign within the mailing population; the red curve shows the actual response to the campaign.

Table 1.1 further illustrates the efficiency of the model and the benefit to the business. The first column describes the mailing population split into deciles, the second the cumulative percentage of customers who responded, the third the cumulative

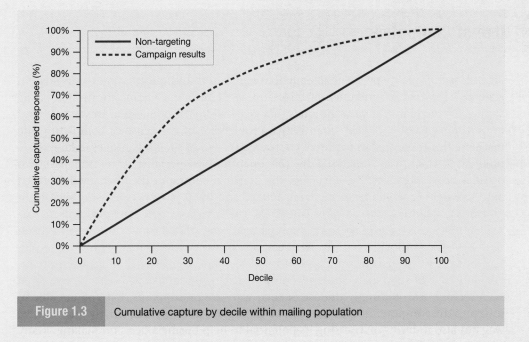

Figure 1.3   Cumulative capture by decile within mailing population

percentage of customers who did not respond, the fourth the cost per response relative to the overall cost per response and finally the model efficiency, this last being the rate at which responding customers are found in the targeted population.

It can be seen that the model was most efficient at the first decile and least efficient at the bottom decile. In the first decile the cost per response was only 36 percent of the overall cost per response for the targeted mailing, showing that the

cost of acquisition could have been further reduced if we had not needed to meet a target number of responders.

The development and successful implementation of the predictive model had two main benefits. The first was a cheaper and more effective campaign; the second was a reduction in mailing volume. Overall, the reduction in costs and number of customers mailed was good news from both a financial and a customer relationship perspective.

Source: *Significance* magazine, June 2004, pp. 78–80.

Table 1.1   Efficiency of the model

Cumulative decile	% of responding customers	% of non-responding customers	Cost per response as % of overall cost per response	Model efficiency
1	27.8	9.4	36	278
2	49.2	19.0	41	246
3	65.7	28.8	46	219
4	75.5	38.8	55	189
5	82.1	48.9	61	164
6	88.2	59.1	68	147
7	93.4	69.2	75	133
8	95.6	79.5	84	120
9	98.3	89.7	92	109
10	100.0	100.0	100	100

Use of Computers

Readers will probably be aware already that computers and information technology in general have had a fundamental effect on most business organisations. The same applies to the quantitative techniques that we shall be introducing in the text. It used to be the case that 'solving' quantitative problems – in the sense of completing the mathematics and statistics required – restricted the use of such techniques to large-scale problems, which were analysed by the quantitative specialist. Over the past two decades or so, however, the advent of the personal computer (PC) has revolutionised both the areas to which techniques are applied and the type of person using such techniques. PC facilities such as spreadsheets or the more common statistical and mathematical packages now make such analysis readily available to any business decision maker. In the author's view, this has been one of the major factors behind the explosion of interest in such techniques (mirrored of course by virtually all business undergraduate and postgraduate students being forced to undertake at least one course in such techniques). Naturally the use of such software presupposes that you are able to interpret the computer output that can be generated, not only in a strictly quantitative way but also in terms of assessing its potential to help business decision making. Many of the end-of-chapter exercises, however, are eminently suited for further analysis using either a spreadsheet package or some statistical software, and we would encourage both students and tutors to take advantage of this wherever possible.

The data sets used in the text are suitable for PC-compatible computers, relating to end-of-chapter exercises which are suitable for computer-based analysis. These files can also be used as direct input with many spreadsheet programs and with the more popular statistical packages such as Statgraphics and SPSSPC+. The files can be found on the website at www.pearsoned.co.uk/wisniewski.

Using the Text

The text is aimed primarily at those students who have a clear interest in management and business decision making but who also appreciate the potential that quantitative analysis brings to the management process (or at worst find themselves required to complete a course in this area). Deliberately we have kept the focus through the text on developing a conceptual, rather than a mathematical, understanding of the principles of each topic and on the potential application of the techniques to typical business problems.

At the same time we need to stress that one of the worst ways in which such techniques can be seen by a manager is in terms of the 'toolbox' approach, where the focus is often on finding a technique to fit the problem rather than on focusing on an appropriate solution method and methodology to help resolve the problem under investigation. It is all too tempting to look at a business problem briefly and assume that the problem is one of stock control, forecasting or whatever. Once designated as, for example, a stock-control problem, it is tempting then to ignore other quantitative – and qualitative – ways of examining the problem. This can result in the technique being forced to fit the problem and generating information and results that are at best incomplete and immediate and at worst downright misleading to the manager. Business problems rarely, if ever, fit into nice neat compartments labelled 'stock control' and the like. What may on the surface appear to be a problem in the stock department may well turn out to be a problem in production or sales or related to quality management.

Each chapter in the text follows a similar general format. First, we provide an introduction to the focus of that chapter. Then we introduce the relevant topics and place them in a typical business context. An example problem is then introduced and thoroughly investigated and discussed in terms of both determining a solution to the problem and the wider business applications of the technique. Within each chapter you will also find a number of Student Activities. These are tasks for you to complete at that point in your reading of that chapter. Although you may be tempted to 'skip over' an activity we would strongly encourage you not to do so. The activities are an integral part of the learning process and will typically lead you into the next part of that chapter. Solutions to these activities appear either in the next part of the chapter or in Appendix F. Most chapters conclude with a fully worked example showing how to approach a particular problem or question using the techniques introduced thus far. Finally, we present details of an actual business application, illustrating how the techniques introduced in that chapter are used in the real world to help business decision making. After the appendices at the end of the book, for many of the chapters, we have included a section on further reading. This details articles, cases and applications which will help develop your understanding of that chapter's topics in more detail.

Summary

It will by now be evident that the topics and techniques that we introduce in this text are not simply of academic interest. They are all techniques that are actively – and profitably – used by a variety of business organisations and, perhaps more importantly, they are being used by the managers of these organisations as well as the 'experts'. Developing your own awareness and understanding of these techniques as well as skills in their use will be a worthwhile investment, not only as part of your current studies but also in terms of your management career.

Useful online resources

Detailed below are some internet resources that may be useful. Many have further links to other sites. An updated version is available from the accompanying website (**www.pearsoned.co.uk/wisniewski**). In addition, I would be grateful for details of other websites that have been found to be useful.

exploringdata.cqu.edu.au – Exploring Data website

www.informs.org/Resources/ – INFORMS MS/OR resources page

www.informs.org – Institute for Operations Research and the Management Sciences

www.mathstore.ac.uk/ – Maths, Stats and OR Network

www.ruf.rice.edu/%7Elane/rvls.html – Rice University Virtual Lab in Statistics

www.statsoft.com/textbook/stathome.html – StatSoft Electronic Textbook

www.nationalstatistics.gov.uk – UK National Statistics

QMDM IN ACTION
British Telecom

British Telecom (BT) is one of the largest UK-based organisations both in terms of employees (over 200 000 at the time this application was undertaken) and in terms of financial size (a market capitalisation of over £30 billion in mid-2001). It is also an organisation that was one of the first to be converted from a state organisation controlled by the UK government to a private sector company. Along with other privatised organisations this has led to a fundamental change in attitudes and approaches to customers where customer care, responsiveness to customer requirements and high-quality customer service are seen as critical items on the organisation's strategic agenda.

At the time this application was being conducted, BT was looking at ways of improving the initial interface with customers, the so-called Front Office. This was seen as a single point of contact for the customer. So any customer telephoning the company to make enquiries, to seek assistance or just to obtain service information would be dealt with by the Front Office. The intention was that the customer experience of being transferred from one person in the organisation to another (something that most of us will have experienced at some time with some organisation) could be minimised and, potentially, removed. A specialist team within the company was given the task of looking at ways of delivering this service.

The first step – as is often the case – involved basic data collection and building up a picture of the situation under investigation. In this context, the team first needed to assess the typical pattern of calls received during the day and during the week, shown in Figures 1.4 and 1.5, in order to assess likely demand on the Front Office.

Using simple presentation techniques it can readily be seen that there are classic resource implications to the patterns exhibited. From Figure 1.4 we note that the maximum number of calls is around 300 in any one 30-minute period – an indication of current maximum demand on the Front Office.

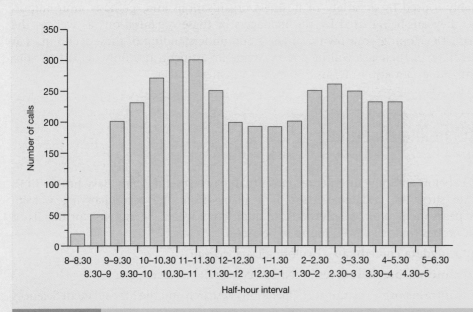

Figure 1.4   Calls by the half-hour throughout the day

Taken from 'Staffing the Front Office', C Richardson, *Operational Research Insight*, **4** (2), 1991. Copyright held by the Operational Research Society.

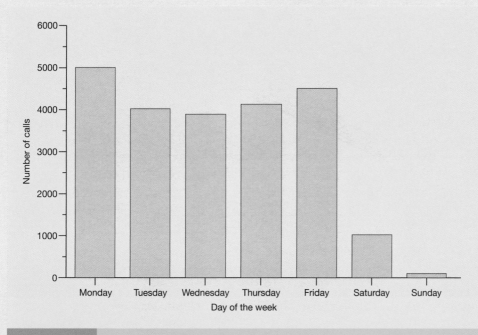

Figure 1.5   Number of calls by day of the week

Taken from 'Staffing the Front Office', C Richardson, *Operational Research Insight*, **4** (2), 1991. Copyright held by the Operational Research Society.

Similarly we see from Figure 1.5 that Monday is the peak day with around 5000 calls having to be dealt with in total. It is evident, though, that the number of calls not only fluctuates during each day, it varies considerably across days of the week. The obvious implication of this fluctuation is in terms of staffing – having people available to respond to the calls. The manager's dilemma is evident. On the one hand the company is keen to have prompt responses to customer calls so that customers will not be kept waiting for the phone call to be answered. From Figure 1.4 this implies a maximum capacity of about 300 calls in a 30-minute period and having enough staff available to deal with this capacity. On the other hand, the company will also want to minimise staff costs associated with this part of its activities, and it is evident that for most of the time this capacity will not be needed, as the number of calls will be less than 300. If the manager provides dedicated staff to deal with the maximum capacity they will not all be needed at other times of the day and will represent an unnecessary cost, unless the situation can somehow be managed in terms of rotas and shift patterns or ensuring these staff are multiskilled so that they can undertake other productive work

during a quiet period. As if this were not enough of a problem, such call patterns are not likely to remain static: they will change over time as the size of the business changes. As BT's customer base grows the demand on the Front Office is likely to increase also.

Accordingly, the team used a number of forecasting techniques to try to predict future call levels and also carried out some 'what if' analysis around these forecasts, recognising that any particular forecast cannot be 100 per cent guaranteed. In conjunction with this work the team also developed a computer simulation model to simulate staff workloads in a typical Front Office and to assess the impact on staffing levels and performance of different call levels occurring. The call level forecasts, the what-if analysis and the staffing simulation could then be put together to help assess the staff required to deal with particular call levels as shown in Figure 1.6. The team made great efforts to ensure the results of their analysis would be available in a readily accessible form to the managers taking the actual decisions. Managers in any organisation are, understandably, reluctant to act on information that they do not properly understand, and the team developed a user-friendly

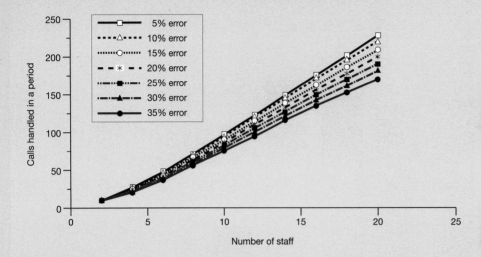

Figure 1.6   Maximum number of calls handled reduces as the forecast error increases

Taken from 'Staffing the Front Office', C Richardson, *Operational Research Insight*, **4** (2), 1991. Copyright held by the Operational Research Society.

computer program based around this analysis to help managers take decisions about staffing the Front Offices for which they were responsible. As the team concluded, '*[this] offers managers, for the first time, the ability to understand the full implications and potential consequences of staffing decisions*'.

This application is based on the article: 'Staffing the Front Office', C Richardson, Operational Research Insight, *4 (2), 1991, pp 19–22. Copyright is held by the Operational Research Society.*

2 Tools of the Trade

Learning objectives

By the end of this chapter you should be able to:

- deal with fractions, percentages and proportions
- understand the principles of rounding and significant figures
- understand common mathematical notation
- understand and be able to use mathematical symbols and simple equations
- construct and use simple graphs
- understand what is meant by the term 'real' value

As we said in Chapter 1, the main focus throughout the text is on the practical uses of quantitative techniques in business and management. However, before we can start introducing the more common techniques used by managers, we have to make sure that we have the basic quantitative knowledge and skills we will need from now on. So, in this chapter, we shall be covering the concepts and skills that form the 'tools of the trade' that we will be using throughout the text. For many of you, you will remember some, if not all, the material we are covering in this chapter. However, don't just skip over it because it looks familiar. Try one of the associated Activities just to make sure you do know how to do what that section is covering. Also, if later on in the text some of the basic calculations we're doing are causing you difficulty, come back to this chapter and re-read the relevant section.

Some Basic Terminology

The following sections introduce some of the basic terminology that we shall be using.

Variables

The term *variable* refers to the characteristic we are investigating or analysing. So, for example, the variable in question might relate to company profits, number of employees, salaries, length of service, customer attitudes and so on. In general, a variable may fall into one of three types.

Discrete

A discrete variable is one which can only take certain fixed numerical values. The number of cars sold by Ford in 2009 can only be a whole number.

Continuous

A continuous variable is one which – in principle at least – can take any numerical value. The length of a piece of sheet steel used in the vehicle manufacturing process can be measured to any required degree of accuracy – centimetres, millimetres, hundredths of a millimetre and so on.

Attribute

An attribute variable is one which is not normally expressed in numerical terms. The level of education achieved by MBA applicants or the gender of the applicant is not a variable that we can express sensibly in numerical form. For purposes of analysis, however, we may assign an arbitrary numerical value to such a variable. Many of you will have seen and completed personal questionnaires where you are asked to indicate your gender. You may recollect that there is often a numerical value printed alongside the possible responses – for example, Male = 1 Female = 2 – which will allow the computer system being used to quantify the number of responses in each category.

Activity 2.1

Consider the following and determine what type of variable each best represents:

(a) the number of private houses built last year
(b) the average price of a house
(c) the number of people employed in the construction industry
(d) the number of tonnes of concrete used in house construction
(e) the different types of houses constructed.

Solution is given on p 576.

Primary and secondary data

It is frequently important in business to assess the source of the data which is being analysed and upon which decisions might be based. We distinguish between *primary* data and *secondary* data. Primary data relates to that which has been collected at first hand and which has been collected for the purposes of analysis which is then undertaken. Secondary data, on the other hand, relates to data which has been collected for some purpose other than the analysis currently being undertaken. Consider the Finance Department of a local authority with the responsibility for collecting a local tax from residents in its area. It may well construct a database of those residents who have not paid the tax this year. Clearly for the department this will be primary data: collected by the department for its own use. This database, however, may then be used by the Economic Development Unit in the local authority, which is investigating income and poverty levels in the area and evaluating strategic options to try to alleviate these. Although the database may well be useful for their purposes, it is now a secondary source of data. In principle we would need to be more cautious about analysing and using such information on a secondary basis, since we would not have been involved in the initial data collection and may be uncertain about the precise logistics used to obtain this data. Its quality therefore on a secondary basis must be suspect.

Fractions, Proportions, Percentages

The use of, and relationship between, fractions, proportions and percentages give many students difficulty but with little reason if you take time to ensure you understand the relationship between them. Fractions are simply a way of expressing amounts which are, literally, less than one (in whatever units of measurement we are using). Consider monetary measurement. The pound sterling (£) is made up of 100 pence. If we insist on our units of measurement being pounds, however, then any amount less than this will need to be shown as part of a pound – a fraction. So, for example, 50p is less than one unit (£1) and since we are insisting on units of measurement being in pounds, it cannot be shown as 50p. Instead, it can be shown as a fraction: £$\frac{1}{2}$. Similarly, 25p would be £$\frac{1}{4}$ as a fraction of a pound. Any number can be shown as a fraction simply by taking that number and dividing by the number that makes up one unit. So for 50p we would have:

$$\frac{50}{100}$$

since 50 is the number we require the fraction for and there are 100p making up one unit (£1). Clearly this does not look like $\frac{1}{2}$. The reason is that 50/100 can be simplified through some basic arithmetic. We note that both numbers are in terms of 10s (five tens and ten tens respectively), so it can be rewritten:

$$\frac{5}{10}$$

These numbers are in turn seen to be in units of 5 (one on top, two on the bottom) so we have $\frac{1}{2}$ as the final fraction. It is important to realise that it really does not matter which of these fractions you use ($\frac{50}{100}, \frac{5}{10}, \frac{1}{2}$) since they are the same. Which you use is up to you in terms of whichever you find easiest.

The fraction we have, $\frac{1}{2}$, can also be expressed as a decimal proportion: 0.50. To add to the confusion, if we multiply a proportion by 100 we have a percentage:

$$0.50 \times 100 = 50\%$$

(that is, 50p is 50 per cent of £1). Although it does not matter whether we use fractions, proportions or percentages in terms of the calculations, it may well affect how we view the information that is generated. Perceptions differ, but consider what reactions you might get from employees if you told them that they would receive a salary increase next year of either 1/10, 0.10 or 10 per cent. Do you think that everyone would immediately view these as being identical in terms of the impact on their salary?

The 30 per cent struggle

In their book *The tiger that isn't: seeing through a world of numbers*, Michael Blastland and Andrew Dilnot (2007) comment on a survey that found that 30 per cent of people struggle to understand what "30%" actually means!

Source: Blastland, M. and Dilnot, D. (2007) *The tiger that isn't: seeing through a world of numbers.* London: Profile Books.

We must also be careful when using percentages in terms of how we comment on or explain the results. Consider the following example. We are told that inflation in the UK last year was 5 per cent (that is prices went up on average by 5 per cent). This year inflation is 6 per cent. A typical comment in the press might then be: 'the rate of inflation has increased by 1 per cent'. In fact it has not. To be technical, the rate of inflation has increased by 1 percentage *point* (since our initial unit of measurement is in percentage terms) and by 20 per cent (1/5). It is also easy to become confused over percentage increases and decreases. Consider the following. A manufacturer sells a product for £10 inclusive of a government tax. Because of cost pressures the company increases the price by 15 per cent. Some time later the government reduces the tax on this product, bringing the price down by 15 per cent. It is tempting to conclude that the price will once again be £10 but some simple arithmetic illustrates the error in this conclusion.

Original price: £10

Price increase: 15% = 15%(£10) = £1.50

New price: £11.50

Tax decrease: 15% = 15%(£11.50) = £1.72

New price: £9.78

We see that after these changes the new price is actually lower than the original.

Activity 2.2

Calculate the following percentages and fractions of 12 098 and 139.5:

25%, 33%, 90%, 5%, 1/3, 1/8, 3/8

Solutions are given on p 576.

Rounding and Significant Figures

It is often desirable to abbreviate – or round – numbers to make them easier to understand and use. When doing this, however, we must be cautious about the results and their implications. For example, if we are out shopping and we see some item on sale for £9.99 most of us would view this as £10 – mentally we round the original figure to the nearest whole number. Similarly, being told as a manager that you have a budget for a particular project of £126 784 doesn't really help you remember what your budget allocation is. If we rounded this to £127 000 however, or even £130 000, it becomes much easier to remember (although technically less accurate).

FirstBus pair to get 80% rise

By Geoff Dyer

Two directors of FirstBus, the bus and rail operator, will receive a pay rise of more than 80 per cent this year, according to the group's annual report.

FirstBus has taken the unusual step of disclosing directors' current salaries in the report, as well as payments for the previous year.

The report shows Mr Trevor Smallwood, chairman, is to be paid a basic salary of £150,000, up from £82,000 last year, Mr Moir Lockwood, chief executive, will also receive a salary of £150,000, a 95 per cent increase on last year's £77,000.

Source: *Financial Times*, 10 July 1996.

Get your calculator out. Can you figure out where the 80% headline comes from? We couldn't.

The principle of rounding numbers is based largely on common sense. First, we determine how many *significant figures* we require. The term significant figures relates to the number of digits in the number that are precise and accurate. So, our exact budget figure of £126 784 contains six significant digits (all six numbers are accurate). The second rounded number of £127 000 contains only three significant figures (the last three zeroes are not). Having decided we want the number to be rounded to three significant figures we then take the last four digits of the original number and round to the nearest whole number: thus 6784 becomes 7000. (The reason for taking the last four digits is that we start with six significant figures, we require only three, so that the last (3 + 1) digits need to be rounded.) The only slight note of caution comes when rounding the number five. For example if we had had 6500, should we round this to 7000 or to 6000? The answer is that it depends on which convention you use. Our preference is to round fives to the nearest *even* number – in this case to 6000, although we should note that it is just as acceptable to round upwards to the nearest whole number.

Activity 2.3

A company reports a profit figure for last year of £1 078 245.67. Show this figure with:

(a) 8 significant digits

(b) 6 significant digits

(c) 4 significant digits

(d) 2 significant digits.

Solutions are given on p 577.

What does matter, though, is the degree of accuracy you imply in any calculations you produce using rounded numbers. Consider the following two numbers: 3.4 and 6.23. We know that each number has been rounded to two and three significant digits respectively. If we multiply these two numbers we have:

$$3.4 \times 6.23 = 21.182$$

which appears to imply five significant digits (and a relatively high level of accuracy). However, the result of this arithmetic cannot be accurate to more than two significant digits (the lower of the two original numbers), hence we should report the result as 21. To see why, consider the two original numbers. 3.4 could originally be anywhere between 3.35 and 3.45, and 6.23 anywhere between 6.2251 and 6.2349. The smallest possible value from this multiplication would then be 20.854085 (3.35 × 6.2251) and the largest 21.510405 (3.45 × 6.2349). Hence only the first two digits should be seen as significant.

Let us illustrate with another example. Consider the company with an annual profit of £1 078 245.67. This may well have been reported in the local press as a profit of £1.1 million. The company has an agreement with the workforce that 10 per cent of the profit will be distributed equally among the firm's 100 employees. The arithmetic appears to be:

$$\frac{£1.1 \text{ million} \times 10\%}{100} = £1100$$

which is what each member of the workforce may well expect to see in their next pay packet. The actual amount, however, will be £1078.25. A simple misunderstanding may well lead to industrial relations tension. The message is clearly to round numbers *after* completing the arithmetic and not before and to ensure that results which have been rounded are acknowledged as such.

Common Notation

One of the most difficult aspects of quantitative analysis that many students encounter in the early stages of their studies relates to the use of mathematical 'shorthand' – the use of mathematical notation in analysing and presenting results. Tell people that the average salary of a group of employees is £13 500 and there is no problem. Tell them that the arithmetic mean for a random sample is 13 500 and the eyes glaze over and the mental shutters start to come down. Clearly this is a barrier we must break if we are to progress through the text, since we require this shorthand frequently.

Symbols

The first thing to get used to is the use of symbols rather than descriptive text. We might use the symbol S to represent the salary of an individual, for example. This makes it much more convenient when we require to indicate that S = 12 000 rather than having to spell out that 'the salary of an individual is £12 000'. Similarly we might use D to denote taxes and other salary deductions, with T representing take-home pay for the individual. A simple equation then becomes:

$$T = S - D$$

which is much easier to note and use than its verbal equivalent.

Arithmetic operators and symbols

You will already be familiar with the more common mathematical operators: $+ - \times \div$. Some of the other operators and symbols that we shall be using include:

> < less than
>
> <10 implies all numbers taking a value less than 10.

> \> greater than

> ⩽ less than or equal to
>
> So, for example, ⩽10 means any number up to and including 10 but excludes all numbers greater than 10.

> ⩾ greater than or equal to
>
> ⩾ 10 implies all numbers of 10 or more.

> ≠ not equal to
>
> So ≠10 implies all values which are different from 10.

The sequence of calculation when there are several operators in an expression is also important. For example, consider:

$$10 + 3 \times 6 - 3 \times 2$$

Arithmetic operators have an established order of priority and this order must be followed to obtain the correct numerical result. The logic is generally straightforward. We use the convention in terms of using different operators that we evaluate in the priority of: $\times \div + -$. That is, we perform:

- any multiplications
- then any divisions
- then any additions
- then any subtractions.

Multiplying (3×6) first, and then (3×2) we have:

$$10 + 18 - 6$$

and then we complete the arithmetic as:

$$28 - 6 = 22$$

We will frequently encounter expressions which also involve brackets. Consider the expression:

$$(10 + 3) \times 6 - (3 \times 2)$$

The approach is as before in terms of priority but we must first evaluate all expressions *inside* brackets. This gives:

$$(13) \times 6 - (6) = 78 - 6 = 72$$

It is also worth noting that computer logic acts in exactly the same way when it comes to undertaking some assigned calculation. Spreadsheets, for example, will tend to calculate the expression in the same way and same order as we do.

Note also that we may frequently omit the multiplication symbol, ×, in complex expressions. We might have, for example:

$$10 \times (6 - 4)$$

although this would normally be shown as:

10(6 − 4)

Powers and Roots

Frequently we may be involved in arithmetic that requires one number to be multiplied by itself some number of times. For example, we may want:

$3 \times 3 \times 3 \times 3 \times 3$

The shorthand way of writing this is as 3^5 (read as three to the power of five). The super-script number (5) is known as the *exponent* and simply shows that we take the actual number (3) and multiply it by itself five times. So, we would have:

$3^5 = 3 \times 3 \times 3 \times 3 \times 3 = 243$

As with most mathematics there is an opposite to taking the power of a number. This is known as taking the *root* of a number. For example, we might have:

$10^2 = 100$

and then require what is known as the root of 100, which we would denote as:

$\sqrt{100}$

where $\sqrt{}$ is the root symbol. A root implies that we require a number such that when we square the number (raise to the power 2) then we will obtain 100. Clearly in this case we have:

$\sqrt{100} = 10$ since $10^2 = 100$

This example is known as the square root of 100. Other roots – the third, fourth, etc. – are possible. So we might have:

$\sqrt[5]{243} = 3$

since as we saw earlier $3^5 = 243$. (We'll see how to work out the answer of 3 shortly.) To make matters worse, however, it is possible to denote roots as fractional powers. Thus:

$\sqrt{100}$ can be written as $100^{1/2}$ or $100^{0.5}$

and

$\sqrt[5]{243}$ as $243^{1/5}$ or $243^{0.2}$

It is worth remembering that whenever you see a number raised to a fractional power it is simply another way of writing a root expression. We should also note two special cases. Any number raised to the power 1 simply equals that number:

$$10^1 = 10$$

and any number raised to the power zero equals 1:

$$123^0 = 1$$

(Don't ask why! Just remember it!)

Multiple answers to Europe's maths problem

By Wolfgang Munchau

What is a fair voting system for the European Union? It looks as though, thanks to Poland, European leaders will be forced to debate this difficult question at their summit this week.

Since the simplified draft treaty is substantively identical to the old and rejected constitution – minus some cosmetics – the voting system proposed is going to be the same one: passage of legislation requires a coalition of countries representing at least 55 per cent of the member states and 65 per cent of the population. The Poles have threatened a veto unless the second of those two numbers is based on the square root of the population size – to reduce Germany's influence. It sounds arbitrary, but the Poles have a point. Mathematics is on the side of Poland.

To an uninitiated observer, this does not appear immediately obvious. Does it not seem fair that the voting power of a country in an international organisation should be proportional to its population size? The answer is no. In fact, it is totally unfair. The reason is that effective voting power in multi-nation settings such as the EU depends not on voting size but on the ability to form winning coalitions. Large countries are better placed than their relative population size would suggest. The original, six-member Community is a good example of this counter-

intuitive idea. Germany, France and Italy each had four votes in the council of ministers, the Netherlands and Belgium had two and Luxembourg one vote. Germany then had more than 100 times the population of Luxembourg, yet only four times the number of votes.

Intuition might suggest that tiny Luxembourg was surely over-represented. In truth, the opposite was the case. The threshold for a majority was set at 12 votes. Since every member except Luxembourg had an even number of votes, Luxembourg was never in a position to cast a make-or-break vote. Despite being numerically over-represented, Luxembourg in effect had zero voting power. That would have been different if, for example, an odd number had been chosen as the threshold.

So how do you measure effective voting power? Lionel Penrose, the British mathematician and psychiatrist who developed a theory of voting power in the 1940s, concluded that votes in international organisations should be based on the square root of the population. This is where the Poles got their idea. In the 1960s, John Banzhaf, a US attorney, established an index to measure a country's voting power. There are two versions of the Banzhaf index. The absolute Banzhaf index measures the ability

of a country to cast the decisive vote in a winning coalition as a proportion of all coalitions in which that country takes part. In the case of the pre-1973 EU, the absolute Banzhaf index for Luxembourg was precisely zero. For Germany it was 24 per cent. Germany, not Luxembourg, was over-represented.

What about the EU today? With 27 members, there are a total of 133m possible coalitions. The economists Richard Baldwin and Mika Widgrén have calculated the Banzhaf indices for each member state, both under the current regime, established by the treaty of Nice and in force since 2004, and the constitution [www.cepr.org/pubs/PolicyInsights/]. The results clearly support the Polish case. Germany's absolute Banzhaf index shoots up from about 5 per cent to more than 15 per cent (it would have gone up to 30 per cent under the original draft). The trouble is that everyone's absolute Banzhaf index also goes up, including Poland's. How could that be?

The reason is that the constitution dramatically improves the probability of legislation being passed. Mathematically, the passage probability can be defined as the ratio of "winning" coalitions to all coalitions. In the 15-member EU, this ratio was 8 per cent (this means that 8 per cent of all possible coalitions produce a

Yes vote). Under the Nice rules it has fallen to 3 per cent and will approach zero as the EU expands further. This is why the present voting system needs to be fixed.

The constitutional treaty raises this ratio to 13 per cent. But as the overall passage probability rises, so does a country's ability to cast a pivotal vote. This explains why the absolute Banzhaf index rises for everybody, including Poland. The Polish problem is that Germany's influence would be enormous in relative terms.

Is Poland's square root solution the only alternative? Of course not.

EU leaders could, for example, raise the threshold for population size and number of countries from their 55 and 65 per cent respectively or introduce some complicated new formula – perhaps with a square root in it. There is a quite a bit a leeway left without creating Nice-style gridlock. Professors Baldwin and Widgrén propose another simple and effective solution: drop the voting rules of the constitution and just repair the Nice rules by reducing some of the high thresholds.

The Poles have put their finger on an important issue, though their

own answer is not as compelling as they think. If and when EU leaders set out to amend the rules, they should heed the lessons of the past. Any new system needs to fulfil two parallel goals: it needs to make the voting system more effective and it needs to be fair. The Nice system is fair and ineffective. The constitution is effective but unfair.

If they get this wrong again, they will be back at the negotiating table not too long from now. But if they get it right, they will have managed to create the one and only substantive change from the original treaty.

Source: Financial Times, 18 June 2007.

Politics and a square root!

Logarithms

It may have occurred to you that using power and roots notation is all very well but how do we actually work out the answer? Consider:

$$\sqrt[4]{365.3}$$

How do we actually determine what the fourth root of 365.3 is? To obtain such a result we must turn to the use of logarithms. You will find it useful to have a calculator with logarithmic facilities available for this next section. We have already seen that the exponent of a number indicates the power to which it is to be raised. Let us consider the number 10. We then might write:

$$10^2 = 100$$
$$10^3 = 1000$$
$$10^4 = 10\ 000$$

and so on with the exponents being 2, 3 and 4 respectively. We can describe the logarithm of a number as the exponent of 10 which equates to that number. That is, we say that the logarithm of 100 is 2 (since $10^2 = 100$), the logarithm of 1000 is 3, of 10 000 is 4 and so on. In fact any number (not just those involving 10) can be expressed in logarithmic form. For example, from a pocket calculator:

$$\log(13) = 1.11394 \text{ since } 10^{1.11394} = 13$$
$$\log(540) = 2.73239 \text{ since } 10^{2.73239} = 540 \text{ and so on.}$$

Effectively with logarithms what we are doing is converting all numbers to a common base of 10 (with the exponent allowing us to use 10 raised to some power to denote any other number). But how do we use such logarithms? Suppose you were asked to calculate:

$$3^2 \times 3^4$$

With a little thought you might realise that this would actually be 3^6 (since it is actually $3 \times 3 \times 3 \times 3 \times 3 \times 3$). That is, if we require to multiply two numbers together that have a common base (3 in our example) we can simply *add* their exponent parts together to get the result. With logarithms that is exactly what we can do, given that logarithms use the base 10. So, for example, if we wanted:

$$13 \times 540$$

we use the principle of logarithms:

$$10^{1.11394} \times 10^{2.73239} = 10^{3.84633}$$

or just using the logarithms:

$$1.11394 + 2.73239 = 3.84633$$

But how do we get back to 'sensible' numbers (like 13 and 540)? The answer is that we reverse the logarithmic process and take the *antilog* of the logarithm (again using a pocket calculator, where the antilog key is often shown as 10^x). The antilog of 3.84633 is 7019.9, which, if you check the multiplication of 13×540 directly, is different from the 'true' answer of 7020 only because we rounded the logarithmic values. In fact we can generalise logarithmic arithmetic into some simple rules:

Multiplication of numbers

● Convert the numbers into logarithms.
● Add the logarithms together.
● Take the antilog of this total to get the answer to the original multiplication.

Division of numbers

● Take the logarithm of the number on top of the division.
● Take the logarithm of the number on the bottom.
● Subtract this second number from the first.
● Take the antilog of the result to get the answer to the original division.

Obtaining powers

● Take the logarithm of the number to be raised to some power.
● Multiply the logarithm by the exponent.
● Take the antilog of the result to obtain the answer to the original power.

Obtaining roots

● Take the logarithm of the number for which the root is required.
● Divide the logarithm by the required root.
● Take the antilog to obtain the required result.

We shall illustrate with our original example. We required the fourth root of 365.3. Following the rules we have:

$$\log(365.3) = 2.562648672$$

(Note the number of significant digits used to ensure accuracy.)

$$\frac{2.562648672}{4} = 0.640662418$$

$$\text{antilog}(0.640662418) = 4.3718 \text{ (rounded)}$$

which is the fourth root of 365.3. To check, multiply 4.3718 by itself four times and you will get 365.3. Logarithms are very useful ways of performing complex calculations.

Activity 2.5

Perform the following calculations using logarithms:

(a) 1098.2×34

(b) $345.6/23.7 \times 109.3$

(c) 12.569^5

(d) $156^{1/8}$

Solutions are given on p 578.

QMDM IN ACTION
Google and logarithms

Internet search engines. We all use them – searching for websites we're interested in, products that we want to buy, concerts that we want to go to. As users of a search engine like Google or Yahoo, we want the search to throw up the most relevant websites for our search. But if we're an advertiser or supplier of products or services on the web then we want a search engine to put our details and website at the top of the search results list.

For example, you might have used a search engine to search for quantitative methods textbooks. A Google search done when I was writing this edition revealed around 186 000 webpage hits.

So how do search engines like Google decide where to present each webpage in their results? The answer is – no-one really knows except a few people in the company! Search engines keep most of their methods – their algorithms – secret both for

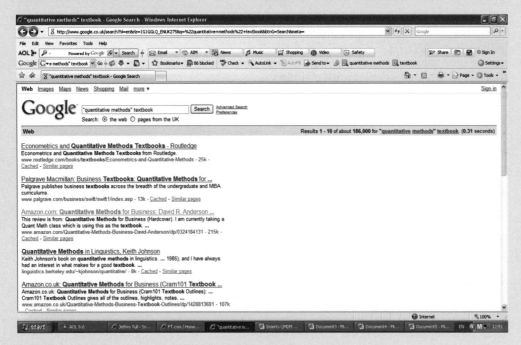

competitive reasons and also to try to prevent web-masters manipulating the system to put their page at the top of the list. However, some details of one of the algorithms are known publicly, for the PageRank algorithm invented by Google founders Larry Page and Sergey Brin when they were graduate students in Computer Science at Stanford University. Its details were published when they were granted a US patent. PageRank effectively measures the probability that you would end up on a given webpage if you clicked links randomly while surfing.

Google assigns a numeric weighting from 0–10 for each webpage on the internet, effectively showing a webpage's importance in the eyes of Google. This PageRank score is derived from a theoretical probability value on a logarithmic scale.

And when Google started planning to sell shares through an IPO (initial public offering) in 2004 it valued itself at $2 718 281 828. Some commentators realised that the value quoted was exactly 1 billion times the value of the natural logarithm base e, or 2.718281828!

Summation and Factorials

We frequently need to undertake repetitive calculations on a set of numbers and it is useful to be able to summarise such calculations in a shorthand manner. There are two such calculations that we shall require. The first of these is *summation*. Consider if we have the salary levels of a number of employees and we wish to add these together to get the total salary cost. Clearly we would add the first figure to the second to the third and so on. If we denote the salary figures with a suitable symbol such as S then we can summarise the required calculation as:

$$\Sigma S_i \quad \text{where} \quad i = 1, ..., n$$

This simply indicates that we have some number (n) of salary figures and that we are to add them together. The Σ symbol (pronounced sigma) is the conventional symbol for summation. Here we would simply say that we required the sum of all the S values, with the expression i = 1 to n indicating we take each S number in turn from the first in the data set to the nth. We may for convenience remove the i notation where it is clearly understood. Frequently we may want to use the symbol in more complex formulae and care must be taken to evaluate these properly. For example, suppose the organisation is adding a £50 Christmas bonus to everyone's salary. The corresponding total would then be:

$$\Sigma(S + 50)$$

That is, we would first add £50 to each of the individual S values and then we would add these together to give the total. This would be different from:

$$\Sigma S + 50$$

which implies we are adding £50 to the total salary cost. The second type of calculation for which we require a shorthand notation is the *factorial*. We shall see the uses of such a calculation later in the text, but assume that we require a calculation such as:

$$7 \times 6 \times 5 \times 4 \times 3 \times 2 \times 1$$

That is, a sequence of numbers multiplied together where the sequence changes by one each time. We would denote such a calculation as 7! (pronounced 7 factorial).

Activity 2.6

We have the following data:

Y: 10, 12, 14, 18
X: 2, 3, 7, 9

Calculate:

(a) ΣX (d) $(\Sigma X)^2$ (g) 10!

(b) ΣY (e) ΣYY (h) 3!

(c) ΣX^2 (f) ΣYX (i) 10! – 3!

Solutions are given on p 578.

Equations and Mathematical Models

We shall be expressing relationships between variables frequently in the form of an equation and using such equations to develop business mathematical models. An equation is simply any expression where we have an equals sign (=). Once again, to the uninitiated they seem more complex than they actually are. Consider a store selling some item for £9.99. For any given level of sales the firm can calculate its sales income. If the store sells 100 items then its income is readily calculated as £999. But if we are interested in a more general expression – allowing us to calculate income for any level of sales – we will benefit from an equation. The income, or revenue, the firm gets from selling this item can be expressed as a simple equation:

$$R = P \times Q \quad \text{or} \quad R = PQ$$

where R denotes the revenue from sales, P the selling price and Q the quantity, or number, of items sold. Clearly this is a generic equation (it will fit any such situation). For this firm the corresponding equation would be:

$$R = 9.99Q$$

since the selling price is fixed at £9.99. All this equation does is to define numerically the relationship between the two variables R and Q. In simple terms it allows us to calculate R for any value of Q. So, if Q = 1000, R will be 9990 (9.99 × 1000); if Q = 5000, R = 49 950 and so on. Such equations can be used with others to develop simple mathematical models. Equally, if R is known we can find the corresponding value for Q.

Let us expand the problem. The firm actually buys these items from a supplier at £6.99 and has calculated that, on an annual basis, its overheads are £45 000 (made up of rent and various fixed costs). In the same way as with revenue we can derive an equation showing the firm's costs:

$$C = 45\,000 + 6.99Q$$

where C is costs. These costs are made up of two elements: a fixed cost and a variable cost. We see clearly that fixed costs are independent of Q (that is, if Q changes, the fixed cost element will not). The variable cost *is* affected by Q, however. We can go one step further. The firm wishes to quantify the profit it will have earned for any level of sales.

In simple terms profit (F) will be the difference between revenue (R) and costs (C). So we have:

$$F = R - C$$

but we know that C = 45 000 + 6.99Q and R = 9.99Q, so substituting these for C and R we have:

$$F = 9.99Q - (45\ 000 + 6.99Q)$$

Note we have enclosed 45 000 + 6.99Q in brackets to make it clear that *all* of this must be subtracted from 9.99Q. If we multiply everything in the brackets by the minus sign in front of the bracket we get:

$$F = 9.99Q - 45\ 000 - 6.99Q$$

We now have two terms involving Q on the right-hand side of the equation and so to simplify we can bring them together. We have +9.99Q and −6.99Q. This gives an equation for profit of:

$$F = -45\ 000 + 3Q$$

Effectively, this equation allows us to determine the profit we would achieve for any given level of Q.

Activity 2.7

How many items must the firm sell before it breaks even (i.e. where its profit is exactly zero)?

Such an equation becomes useful when we wish to carry out some business analysis such as determining the break-even level of sales. It is evident that the profit equation consists of a negative element (−45 000) and a positive (+3Q). It will also be evident that when Q takes low values the calculation for F will turn out to be negative (since the −45 000 part will more than outweigh the +3Q part). This means that the firm will make a negative profit (i.e. it will make a loss). Conversely, if Q is sufficiently high, profit will become positive. The break-even point by definition is where we are about to move from a loss situation into one where we earn a positive profit. What we require is a value for Q where this will happen. Also, by definition, at the break-even point F = 0. So we have:

$$F = -45\ 000 + 3Q = 0$$

or

$$-45\ 000 + 3Q = 0$$

We now have just one (unknown) variable, Q, and should be able to work out its numerical value. To do this we use a simple procedure. We can alter the left-hand side (LHS) of the equation in some way, as long as we alter the right-hand side (RHS) in exactly the same way. This will mean we still have the exact relationship specified in the original equation, even though the resulting (new) equation might look different. Let us add 45 000 to the LHS. This gives:

$$-45\ 000 + 3Q + 45\ 000$$

which simplifies to 3Q since the two other numbers cancel out. But we must now alter the RHS in the same way to keep the relationship as per the original equation. This would then give a new equation:

$$3Q = 45\ 000$$

Let us now divide the LHS by 3, remembering that we must do the same to the RHS. This will give:

$$Q = \frac{45\ 000}{3} = 15\ 000$$

We have now 'solved' this equation. For the firm to break even it must sell 15 000 items. If it does this, profit will be exactly zero. The implication is that if it sells less, profit will be negative, if it sells more, profit will be positive. The potential use of such equations and the models they can be built into should now be clear. They offer a convenient way of both describing and analysing more complex situations – to those who can understand and use them. To expand on this, consider the following:

- The firm's overheads look as if they will increase by 15 per cent next year. How will this affect the break-even sales figure?
- The firm's supplier indicates that the cost of the item will increase by £1.50. How will this affect profit?
- The firm is considering increasing its selling price to £11.99. How will this affect profits and break-even?

All of these questions can readily be investigated through the use of the appropriate equations.

The equations we have examined in this section are all technically known as *linear* equations. They can be recognised as such since they involve only variables of the first power – they do not involve variables which are squared, cubed, rooted, etc. Such equations are referred to as linear because they can be represented as a straight line on a graph. Other types of equation are *non-linear*, since they will not show as a straight line.

Fixing cracks in the crystal ball   FT

Sir John Gieve, deputy governor of the Bank of England, has admitted that the Bank did not realise how serious the fall-out from the credit boom would be. He and his colleagues are hardly alone. While many economists saw trouble ahead – what economist does not? – the profession failed to put together the pieces of the puzzle to see the magnitude of the looming crisis.

This is not because of the unique incompetence of economists, but because of the inherent slipperiness of the task: as the psychologist, Philip Tetlock, has painstakingly demonstrated, most political experts barely outperform monkeys with darts when it comes to making meaningful forecasts. Whether we should blame the world for being too complicated, or human experts for being foolish, is not clear. Either way, as the saying goes, it's tough to make predictions, especially about the future.

Eighteen months of financial surprises have served to remind us of the risks of a seductive journey: from thinking about the future, which is essential; to forecasting the future, which is something of a parlour game; to believing that one has truly understood what the future holds, which is dangerous.

At times, it seems that the forecasting process has become so automated, and the underlying assumptions so well-hidden, that the first step on the journey has been skipped entirely, and we move to the hubris of believing we understand the future without ever having to go through the tiresome process of thinking about it.

This appears to have been one of the root causes of the credit crunch. Quantitative analysts produced sophisticated models of risk that were flawed in one way or another. The flaws in the models may not have occurred to the analysts who built them, and certainly not to the bosses who took the big decisions.

David Viniar, the chief financial officer of Goldman Sachs, and a man widely regarded as having done more than most to guard his institution against the credit crunch, complained of "25-standard deviation moves, several days in a row" back in August 2007. Such events are so impossibly unlikely that writing down the probability that they would occur would fill the rest of this paragraph with zeros. The implication should have been clear instantly:

the mathematical models on which so many trillions of dollars depended were simply wrong. The financial sector will never see a real "25-standard deviation move", but it will see plenty of modelling errors.

Yet it is no use complaining that it is impossible to see the future. Most people need to take a view, and sometimes large bets must be made on what the future might hold. But there are sensible ways and foolish ways to go about the task. Responsible soothsayers should explore different scenarios. They should work hard to understand the assumptions they are making. They should try reverse engineering, imagining some catastrophic loss and then trying to work out the sequence of events by which such a loss might have occurred.

These qualitative approaches are often far more helpful than the

quantitative forecasts the market demands. Two years ago, many economists successfully identified risks to the banking system. Such warnings were well worth studying, even if the numbers conjured by the same economists were not.

If pundits must be responsible, so, too, must those who listen to them. Sensible experts will try to obfuscate when asked for a prediction. They will explain the uncertainties involved; they will list a range of scenarios, or sketch an all-encompassing cloud of possibilities; they will make their predictions conditional rather than absolute. And when they do so, our response tends to be mockery. It should not be. When crossing unknown terrain, it is far more useful to pick up some survival tips than to be confidently pointed in the wrong direction.

Source: *Financial Times*, 23 December 2008.

Models are used extensively in business and have a useful role to play. However, as the 2008 credit crisis showed, an over-reliance on quantitative models can be very risky. The decision-makers also need the confidence – and understanding – to challenge those who've developed the models.

Graphs

We shall be exploring a number of methods of graphical presentation in more detail in the next chapter. Before doing so, however, we need to ensure that the basics of graph drawing are understood and appreciated, particularly for equations of the form we have been looking at. We shall use the profit equation we derived in the last section as our example. We want to show the equation in graphical form:

$$F = -45\,000 + 3Q$$

What we require is a diagram like that in Figure 2.1.

Given that a graph has two axes and two scales, this implies that we must plot one variable on the vertical axis and one on the horizontal. Typically, for an equation the vertical axis (often referred to as the Y axis) is used for the variable on the LHS of the equation (in this case profit), and the horizontal axis, referred to as the X axis, for the variable on the RHS. We can then follow a sequence of stages to construct the graph.

Step 1

Choose an appropriate numerical scale for the X axis. This can be somewhat arbitrary, depending on the context of the problem. Let us assume we wish to plot a graph for

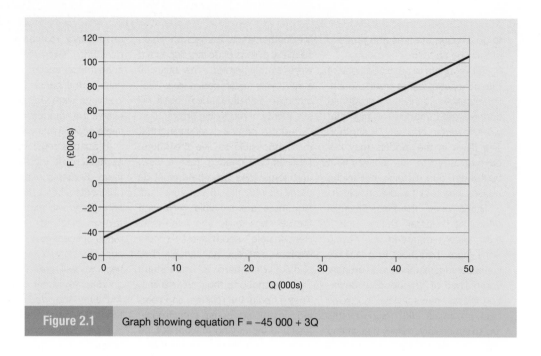

Figure 2.1   Graph showing equation F = −45 000 + 3Q

sales up to 50 000. Logically, the minimum value for the X scale is then 0. If you are drawing the graph manually (as opposed to using a computer package) then you will need to determine a suitable number of points to label on the scale. It seems sensible to show steps of 10 000 in this case (i.e. 0, 10 000, 20 000, 30 000, etc.). Where possible keep the number of steps shown on the graph to between 5 and 10.

Step 2

Calculate a suitable scale for the Y axis. Having chosen values for the X axis we can use these in the equation to calculate corresponding values for the Y axis. In fact, in our example we can take advantage of the type of equation we have derived to simplify this. Our profit equation is known as a linear equation, which will give a straight line on a graph. To obtain the straight line we need only two points to be able to draw it. Logically, we can determine the Y value corresponding to the minimum and maximum X values. We would then have:

X value	Y value
0	−45 000
50 000	105 000

Using these Y values we can again choose a suitable Y scale, say from −60 000 to 120 000 with intervals of say 20 000.

Step 3

Draw both axes on the graph and both scales. Label the axes with the variable it represents and the units of measurement on each scale.

Step 4

Take the first pair of coordinates (X = 0, Y = −45 000) and plot this as a single point on the graph. Take the second pair (X = 50 000, Y = 105 000) and plot this as a second point. Both points are shown in Figure 2.2 as points A and B.

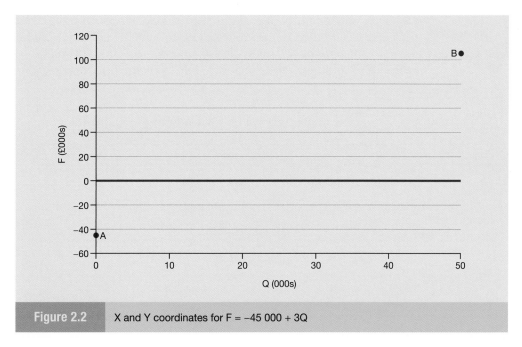

Figure 2.2 X and Y coordinates for F = –45 000 + 3Q

Step 5

Join both points together with a straight line. This line represents the linear equation F = –45 000 + 3Q as shown in Figure 2.1.

It is important to appreciate that the equation and its graph contain exactly the same information, and either or both can be used for analysis purposes. We can, for example, determine the break-even point on the graph, although because of the scale its accuracy is not as good.

Activity 2.8

A firm has assessed that sales of its products are linked to the price it charges:

Q = 100 – 5P

where Q is sales (in 000s of units) and P is the price charged in £s per unit sold.

Draw a graph of this equation, known as a demand equation, and from the graph determine the following:

(a) sales when the firm charges a price of £7

(b) the price that was charged if the firm sold 40 000 units.

Solutions are given on p 579.

Non-linear equations

Not all equations, however, will be linear. Many of the more useful quantitative business models involve non-linear equations, as these frequently more accurately represent business behaviour, or may be more useful in a decision-making context. Consider the linear equation in Activity 2.8:

Q = 100 – 5P

This shows the quantity of some product sold at any given price. From the company's perspective, it would also be interested in not just the quantity sold but the revenue or income earned from such sales. Clearly, in terms of simple arithmetic, its revenue (R) will be found by multiplying the quantity sold, Q, by the price charged per unit, P. That is:

$$R = Q \times P$$

but Q itself can be represented by the linear equation, giving:

$$R = Q \times P$$
$$R = (100 - 5P) \times P$$
$$R = 100P - 5P^2$$

This revenue equation is clearly not linear (it involves a variable which is not to the power 1 – we now have a P^2 term). At the same time it will frequently be useful to show such an equation on a graph. The procedure for graphing a non-linear equation is very similar to that of a linear equation.

Step 1

As before, choose an appropriate range for the X scale. Here, it makes sense to choose P = 0 to P = 20.

Step 2

For a linear equation we would now find two Y values and then the two points to be plotted to give the straight line. For a non-linear equation we must determine more than two such points, since we no longer have a simple straight line to draw. As a rule of thumb, if you are drawing such a graph manually then we need to find around 10 to 15 different Y values for the non-linear equation. (On a spreadsheet, of course, this can be done very easily and, indeed, you should take advantage of the spreadsheet to plot more points than this to give a more accurate graph.) In our example, it seems sensible to determine values for Y (Q) for P = 0, 2, 4, 6, 8, 10, 12, 14, 16, 18, 20. The results are as follows:

P	Q	Equation
0	0	$100 \times 0 - 5(0^2)$
2	180	$100 \times 2 - 5(2^2)$
4	320	$100 \times 4 - 5(4^2)$
6	420	$100 \times 6 - 5(6^2)$
8	480	$100 \times 8 - 5(8^2)$
10	500	$100 \times 10 - 5(10^2)$
12	480	$100 \times 12 - 5(12^2)$
14	420	$100 \times 14 - 5(14^2)$
16	320	$100 \times 16 - 5(16^2)$
18	180	$100 \times 18 - 5(18^2)$
20	0	$100 \times 20 - 5(20^2)$

So we have a total of 11 points of P and Q values that we can now plot on a graph. We can also determine from this series of Q values that the Q (Y) scale would need to cover 0 to 500.

Step 3

Labelling as before.

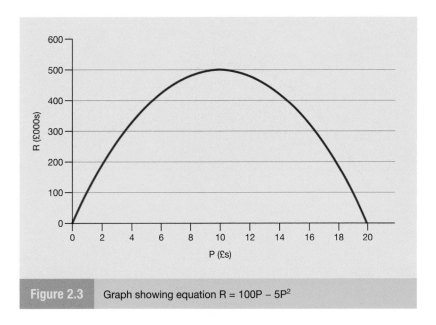

| Figure 2.3 | Graph showing equation R = 100P − 5P² |

Step 4

We can plot the 11 points we have but this time we join the points together with a curve rather than a straight line (since we know the equation will be non-linear). This produces the graph shown in Figure 2.3.

As with all such business diagrams it is always worthwhile spending a few moments studying the diagram to ensure the business implications are understood. Here, we see that R (revenue earned) starts from zero (after all setting a price of zero will give you zero revenue no matter what quantity you sell), gradually rises to a maximum of 500 (£000) and then falls away again to zero (since at a price of 20 we know from the demand equation that sales will be zero, hence revenue must be zero also). It is also clear that such a diagram reveals something that is not evident from the equation itself. Under such a situation there is clearly an optimal price for the firm to charge if it wishes to maximise the revenue it earns from sales. At a price of 10 the firm clearly will maximise its revenue at £500 000.

And if you think this sort of analysis looks too simplistic for the real business world take a look at the next case study.

QMDM IN ACTION

Cap Gemini Ernst & Young – an optimisation model

Cap Gemini Ernst & Young's client is the European corporate arm of one of the world's largest car manufacturers.

The company sells a large range of cars into distinct market sectors in most European countries with the client controlling the market spend budget for the national sales companies in each country.

One of the responsibilities of the client is to ensure that each budget is allocated effectively and that total profit across Europe is maximised. Historically, each national sales company would submit a base plan as the basis for its budget allocation. However, the corporate client was interested in seeing whether a model could be developed to suggest

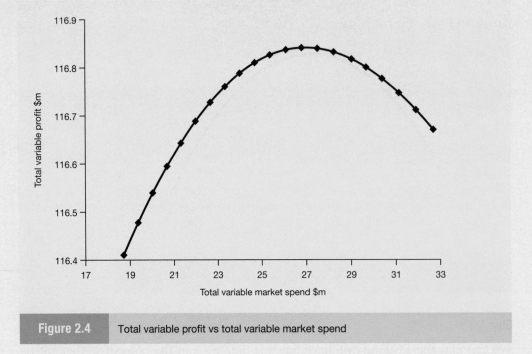

Figure 2.4   Total variable profit vs total variable market spend

alternative budget allocations that would deliver more profit than those submitted in each base plan. The model would need to be based on its understanding of the economic theory at work in its markets and on the practical constraints facing the business.

Cap Gemini Ernst & Young first developed a detailed understanding of the data which the client had available. A model to represent the economics of the business in Europe was then developed and agreed. This model was then used to underpin an optimisation model (we shall develop these ourselves in Chapter 11), which was solved using a specialist computer package. Input and output of the data required by the optimisation model was through Microsoft Excel and an interface created by Microsoft Access.

Cap Gemini Ernst & Young developed an optimisation model based on the agreed economic model for the client's business. The optimisation model was designed in part to allow the client to set constraints easily, such as the size of available production runs. The model found an optimal solution over three levels of the business: for the country being analysed, for the model of car being analysed and

for the market segment under review. The output for the model was written to a spreadsheet system to help in the easy analysis of results and to enable graphs of key relationships to be shown readily. The results from the model were also stored to allow what-if analysis to be undertaken easily.

Figure 2.4 shows the relationship between total variable profit and total variable market spend for a particular combination of country, car model and market segment. The graph illustrates clearly that there is an optimal market spend if profit is to be maximised.

The benefits are as follows:

- The model provides a rigorous basis for proposing alternative market spend allocations which deliver higher expected profits.

- The client can now easily run additional what-if optimisations, which allow the results of any further proposed actions to be seen easily.

- The client has gained an understanding of the importance of price elasticities in each of their market segments (price elasticity shows the percentage change in sales demand in response to a percentage change in price).

I am grateful to Cap Gemini Ernst & Young for permission to use this case study and to reproduce the figure shown. Further case study applications are available through their website: www.uk.capgemini.com/services/consulting/or/success_stories

Real and Money Terms

In most business organisations we will frequently have to deal with financial information that often covers some period of time. Consider an individual who had an income in 2009 of £25 000. In 2007 this individual's income was £20 000. On the face of it, it appears that the individual is better off (a 25 per cent increase in income over this two-year period). However, as we all know from personal experience, most economies are affected by inflation – the increase in the prices of goods and services that people buy. If over this same two-year period prices (inflation) had risen by more than 25 per cent, the individual would actually be worse off in terms of what the money could buy, even though – at face value – he or she appears to be better off. Accordingly we frequently make the distinction between a financial value being expressed in *money* terms and being expressed in *real* terms. The two figures we have so far are expressed in money terms. Let us suppose inflation over this period has actually been 10 per cent. The individual's income in money terms in 2009 is still £25 000. In real terms, however – in terms of what the money would buy compared with 2007 – we need to make an adjustment. Between 2007 and 2009 the individual would require a 10 per cent increase in income just to be able to buy the same quantity of products bought in 2007. So to see how the 2009 income really compares with that of 2007 we need to reduce the 2009 income by the amount of inflation. There are different ways we can perform the calculation but we shall do so by using what is known as an *index*.

An index effectively allows us to perform percentage comparisons and calculations. Some index variables may already be known to you: the Retail Price Index, the FT Share Index, the Dow Jones Index. We denote the price level in 2007 as an index with an arbitrary value of 100. The price index for 2009 must then be 110 (i.e. 10 per cent higher). The 2009 money income can then be adjusted for inflation:

$$25\ 000 \times \frac{100}{110} = £22\ 727$$

with the result of £22 727 referred to as real income. It can be seen that we have multiplied the 2009 income by a ratio of the two price index numbers: the 2007 figure on top and the 2009 figure below. Effectively the result of £22 727 is the value of the 2009 money income (£25 000) in terms of what it would have been worth in 2007 prices. We see that in real terms the individual's income has increased by £2727 after we have taken inflation into account. Such a result would often be reported as £22 727 in 2007 prices or as base 2007. The distinction between money and real values is a critical one for business analysis. The calculation is often referred to as deflating the money value.

Activity 2.9

In 2010 this individual's income rose to £26 000. Inflation between 2007 and 2010 was 15 per cent. Calculate the real income for 2010.

Solution is given on p 580.

Worked Example

To illustrate some of the ideas in this chapter – and to give you more practice – we'll introduce a small case study example and work through it fully. Table 2.1 shows data for the UK from 1995 to 2005. The data relates to the amount of money borrowed by individuals: total borrowing which is then divided between borrowing for mortgages and borrowing for other loans and credit card purchases. Also shown is the Retail Price Index for the period. We have been asked to put together a short report highlighting the key features of the data.

The first thing we might do is to show the borrowing data in a graph like that in Figure 2.5. (The graph has been produced in Excel which allows us to alter format, labelling, scales, etc. easily.) From this we see that total borrowing has increased every year but we also see that the increase itself is increasing year-on-year. We also see that mortgage borrowing follows the same trend and is a large proportion of total borrowing. Borrowing on loans and credit cards has also increased over this period but at a much steadier rate than the total. Further calculations also show that mortgage borrowing has been around 83 per cent of total borrowing. However, as we know from this chapter, all these figures are in money terms not real terms. Inflation over this period, as shown by the RPI, has been around 30 per cent. In money terms, total borrowing has increased by over £600 billion – an increase of around 150 per cent over this period. Table 2.2 shows the deflated borrowing data. Although the general patterns are the same (they must be since we have adjusted all the data series using the same RPI figures) we see that in real terms total borrowing has increased by around £270 billion – around a 90 per cent increase once inflation is taken into account.

Table 2.1	UK personal borrowing			
	Total borrowing (£ billion)	Mortgages (£ billion)	Loans and credit cards (£ billion)	RPI 1987 = 100
March 1995	442	380	62	147.5
March 1996	463	394	69	151.5
March 1997	495	416	79	155.4
March 1998	528	436	92	160.8
March 1999	571	465	106	164.1
March 2000	624	505	119	168.4
March 2001	677	548	129	172.2
March 2002	751	607	144	174.5
March 2003	853	697	156	179.9
March 2004	971	801	170	184.6
March 2005	1081	895	186	190.5

Source: Office of National Statistics and Bank of England

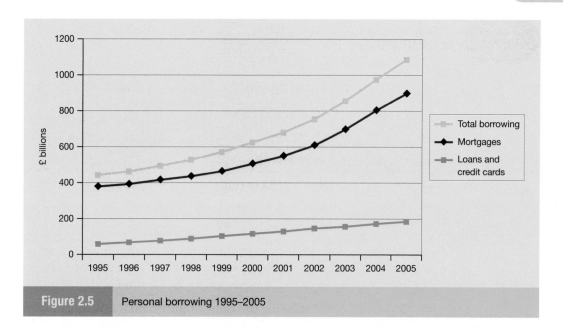

| Figure 2.5 | Personal borrowing 1995–2005 |

| Table 2.2 | UK personal borrowing. In real terms, deflated by RPI, 1987 = 100 |

	Total borrowing (£ billion)	Mortgages (£ billion)	Loans and credit cards (£ billion)
March 1995	300	258	42
March 1996	306	260	46
March 1997	319	268	51
March 1998	328	271	57
March 1999	348	283	65
March 2000	371	300	71
March 2001	393	318	75
March 2002	430	348	83
March 2003	474	387	87
March 2004	526	434	92
March 2005	567	470	98

✳ Summary

In this chapter we have introduced the basic mathematical tools that we shall need as we progress through the text. For your own benefit you should ensure you are competent in these before proceeding. If at a later stage in the text you find you are having difficulty with part of the topic consider returning to the relevant section in this chapter to ensure you understand the basics.

Exercises

1 In the chapter we formulated a break-even problem with:

$$R = 9.99Q$$
$$C = 45\,000 + 6.99Q$$

Find the new break-even level if:

(a) overheads increase by 15 per cent

(b) costs increase by 1.50 per item

(c) the selling price increases to 11.99.

2 A company is thinking of investing £15 000 in a savings fund. The fund runs for a 10-year period and is expected to generate a return each year of 8 per cent of the amount invested. All annual returns remain in the fund until the end of the period.

(a) Construct a table showing the value of the original investment each year over this period.

(b) Draw a graph representing this information.

(c) Convert these annual values to logarithms and construct a graph showing the logarithmic values. What comments can you make about this graph compared with the original?

3 A firm finds that the demand for its product can be represented mathematically as:

$$Q_d = 1000 - 5P$$

where Q_d is the number of units of the product demanded by customers and P is the selling price.

(a) Construct a graph for a price between 0 and 200.

(b) Comment on the shape of the graph. Why does the line slope downwards?

(c) If we define revenue as quantity sold times price, obtain an equation for revenue.

(d) Draw a graph of this revenue equation.

(e) What price should the firm charge in order to maximise revenue?

4 Next week you have to travel around parts of the country on business and have decided to hire a car from a car-hire company. You have contacted two companies which offer different services. The first company will rent you a car for £45 per day. The second company will charge you £30 per day but with an additional charge of 5p per mile travelled. You know you will require the car for four days but are unsure of the mileage you will cover.

(a) Determine mathematically what mileage you would need to cover to make the second company's charge cheaper.

(b) Confirm this using graphs.

(c) Both companies now realise that they will need to add VAT at 17.5 per cent on to the charge for the daily hire but not to the charge for the mileage covered. How will this affect your decision?

5 An airline company is considering providing a new daily service between Edinburgh and Copenhagen. The aircraft has a maximum capacity of 200 passengers and each flight incurs a fixed cost of £25 000 (regardless of the number of passengers). In addition, a cost is also incurred of £75 per passenger (to cover such things as catering, booking, baggage handling).

  (a) The company is thinking of charging £225 per ticket. How many passengers will the airline need on each flight to break even?

  (b) The company knows from previous experience that it is unlikely to sell more than 80 per cent of its seats on any one flight. Assuming it sells exactly this many, what price per seat should it charge to break even?

  (c) The company also has the option of accepting a cargo contract with a Danish company. Under this contract the airline will receive £5000 per flight for transporting cargo but, because of the extra weight, it will have to reduce its maximum number of passengers to 190. How will this affect the break-even ticket price?

6 Return to the worked example and Table 2.1 shown earlier in the chapter.

  (a) Obtain data showing the UK population over this period. Calculate per capita borrowing figures and comment on the result.

  (b) Obtain data for personal income and/or wealth over this period and compare it with borrowing. Comment on the results.

7 A firm has analysed its sales and profitability and found that its profit can be represented as:

$$F = -100 + 100Q - 5Q^2$$

where F is profit (£000s) and Q is units sold (in 000s).
It has also found that its costs are:

$$C = 100 + 2Q^2$$

where C is costs (£000s).

  (a) Obtain a third equation showing the firm's revenue, R.

  (b) Using a graph determine how many units the firm should sell to maximise profit.

  (c) What will the firm's costs be at the profit-maximising level of sales?

3 Presenting Management Information

Learning objectives

By the end of this chapter you should:

- appreciate the potential for using different methods of data presentation in business
- understand the major alternative methods of data presentation
- be able to choose between the major alternative methods
- appreciate the limitations of data presentation methods

In this chapter we will look at methods of data presentation typically used by business organisations. You may consider at this stage that such a topic appears somewhat elementary for a manager. After all, why should the busy manager spend valuable time on tables, charts, graphs and other pictorial representations? Why not get straight down to 'hard' analysis of the problem and the 'bottom line'? We shall be addressing this question through the chapter but suffice it to say for the moment that diagrammatic representation of information has over the past few years become increasingly important at middle and senior management level. The old adage that a picture is worth a thousand words is an appropriate one in this context. As we shall see, data presentation can provide a quick and concise insight into some business problem, allowing a manager to identify and focus upon the key elements of the problem. Thanks largely to the advances in personal computing, managers these days have a considerable facility to display information visually and to focus quickly on the key characteristics of a set of data. This is a particularly valuable skill when managers have more and more data coming their way and have to make sense of it quickly but accurately. One of the purposes of this chapter is to allow you to develop an awareness of what is possible and, equally, what is desirable in the context of business data presentation.

A Business Example

To illustrate the usefulness of diagrams at presenting management information in a concise and user-friendly way, let us consider the following situation. Over the past few years domestic consumers of gas and electricity in the UK have been able to select their energy supplier, unlike the previous arrangements where as a domestic customer you had to buy your gas or electricity from the single supplier operating in your area. A company – perhaps currently operating in the petrol and oil markets – is thinking of entering this business and has asked us to provide an overview of domestic gas sales in the UK over the last few years. Naturally, we could produce a variety of tables showing patterns and trends in terms of gas sales (and would certainly want to do so as part of a more detailed analysis). However, we can give a quick overview with Figure 3.1, which shows gas sales to UK domestic customers for the period 1992 to 2007 on a quarterly basis. We see clearly that domestic sales follow what we can refer to as a seasonal pattern through the year, with sales higher in quarters 1 and 4 (the winter period) and lower in the summer (quarters 2 and 3).

By calculating what is known as a sales trend (which we will look at in Chapter 9) and superimposing this on quarterly sales, we obtain Figure 3.2. The trend shows the long-term movement in domestic gas sales and some interesting patterns begin to emerge. We see that throughout this whole period the trend has shown some modest growth from around 80 000 gigawatt hours in 1992 to around 100 000 gigawatt hours in 2004. There has been some growth in the market therefore – around 25 per cent in total. However, we also notice that since 2004 sales have fallen back to their 1997 level.

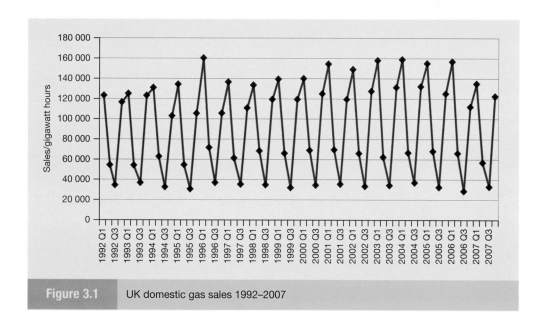

| Figure 3.1 | UK domestic gas sales 1992–2007 |

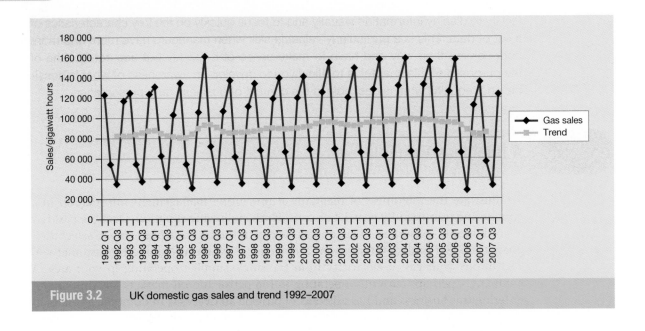

Figure 3.2   UK domestic gas sales and trend 1992–2007

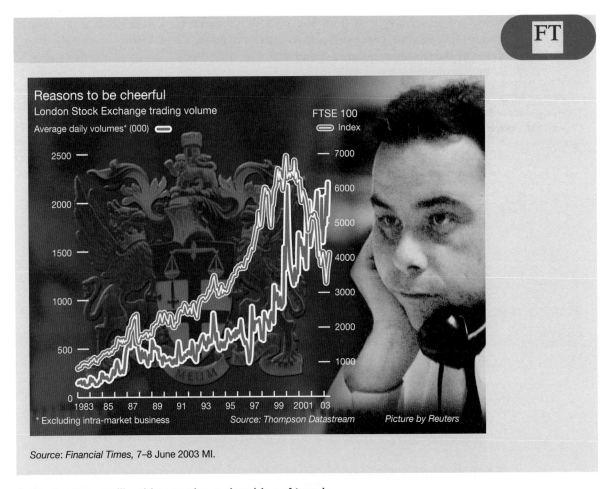

Source: *Financial Times*, 7–8 June 2003 MI.

A simple diagram like this can give a clear idea of trends.

A-levels are more profitable than arts degrees

By David Turner, Employment Correspondent

Effect of a degree on wages
compared to two or more A-levels, by degree subject*

Men

Women

Base: Graduates aged 25 and over

England and Wales 1993–2001

Source: Labour Force Survey

Arts graduates earn less than their friends who decided to give university a miss after gaining their A-levels, according to research from the government's official statisticians.

But law graduates enjoy the top position at the other end of the spectrum, earning more than 25 per cent above people whose education finished with A-levels.

The findings make grim reading for Britain's aesthetes, injecting new life into the old joke: What do you say to an arts graduate? "Burger and fries, please."

But they also provoked warnings from student and artistic circles that an arts degree was not just about earning money, despite the government's persistent attempts to justify its ambitious plans to increase student numbers on economic grounds.

Source: Financial Times, 6 March 2003.

The National Union of Students also used the research to attack the government's recent decision to force students to repay much of the cost of their university education after they enter working life. Mandy Telford, NUS president, said: "Quite clearly not all students will earn the graduate premiums that the government is using to sell its new proposals."

Lisa Roberts of the Poetry Society said: "Arts students know the money won't be brilliant, but the environment will be creative and inspiring."

The figures will also reinforce concerns that the arts degree is set to become a luxury consumer good, affordable only to students from well-heeled families.

The research, carried out by Ian Walker and Yu Zhu of Warwick University and published in the

Office for National Statistics' monthly *Labour Market Trends* journal, suggests that male graduates in English, history and other arts subjects earn about 7 per cent less than their peers whose educational achievement stretched only to two A-levels or more. Female graduates earn about 4 per cent less. The figures do not exclude the possibility that the artistically inclined may earn even less if they do not go to university. But Prof Walker said that at the very least, they suggested the financial return on an arts degree was low. Medicine and veterinary science follow law as the most financially productive degrees, followed by economics and business, maths and engineering. Males who took education degrees also earn less than A-level students who did not go to university.

Diagrams like this are often used to support more detailed analysis and to support arguments made in accompanying text.

Clearly, the diagram does not tell us what caused this phenomenon but it does provide a clear impression of the variable over time. In short, simple diagrams convey general patterns and trends in a way which has considerable impact. We can use such diagrams to convey key conclusions about some analysis that we have undertaken. Naturally, as part of the decision process, such diagrams would not be sufficient by themselves. We would need further detailed analysis and more information but such diagrams do help convey a message quickly and clearly. In part this explains why such business diagrams are both popular and common – appearing in many organisations' annual reports, in the financial and business press and in internal management reports. There are a considerable number of diagrams available and we shall look at some of the more common and useful.

It is also worth commenting at this stage that the production of such diagrams to help decision making is often a process of trial and error (fortunately made easier through the use of computer-based spreadsheet and graphics software). It is often difficult at the start of some analysis to know exactly which type of diagram will best convey the message you wish to put across. Through trial and error – and experience – it is often a matter of constructing one diagram and assessing whether this conveys the information you want it to. If it does not, then a different diagram can be tried. Realistically, you need to accept that this trial-and-error approach is inevitable.

Have a look at the two extracts on pages 48 and 49 taken from the *Financial Times*, which show how effective simple diagrams can be at getting key messages across.

Bar Charts

Bar charts are probably one of the most popular types of business diagram, examples of which are found in the annual report of almost every large public and private sector organisation. They come in a number of forms, all of which are relatively straightforward to produce and to interpret from a management perspective. Consider the data in Table 3.1, which shows UK consumers' expenditure in 2003 prices for a number of expenditure categories in 1995 and 2005. Note that not all expenditure categories are shown. We have selected four to analyse. The 'Total of 4 categories' figures refer to the

Table 3.1	UK consumers' expenditure on selected categories (£m at 2003 prices)	
	1995	*2005*
Alcoholic beverages and tobacco	25 666	27 279
Food and non-alcoholic beverages	54 483	65 690
Recreation and culture	46 302	98 910
Restaurants and hotels	67 562	83 840
Total of 4 categories	194 013	275 719
Total consumer's expenditure	521 694	719 514

Source: Annual Abstract of Statistics.

Activity 3.1

Why do you think a private sector retail organisation might be interested in such information? What comments can you make about the data?

Solution is given on p 580.

sum of the categories shown, whereas the 'Total consumers' expenditure' figures refer to all consumers' expenditure in that year.

Although the table contains detailed data, we want a quick overview of the data; we want to see quickly and easily key patterns, trends and features of the data set. Obviously the data could be examined further in a variety of ways: each year individually, both years together, the change between the two years, the percentage in each year, the percentage change between the two years and so on. There are a variety of bar graphs that we can produce to try to help provide this overview of the data. Once again, we reinforce the point that very often we produce a particular diagram on a trial-and-error basis – not knowing until we see it whether it will be helpful at providing this overview. Figure 3.3 shows a bar graph of the data. For each of the categories in each year we have simply drawn a bar, where the height of that bar represents consumers' expenditure on that category in that year. From the graph we can readily see that:

- The Restaurants and hotels category is the largest of those shown in 1995 but was overtaken by Recreation and culture in 2005.
- Alcoholic beverages and tobacco was the smallest category.
- All categories increased between 1995 and 2005 but by differing amounts.
- Recreation and culture showed the largest increase between 1995 and 2005.

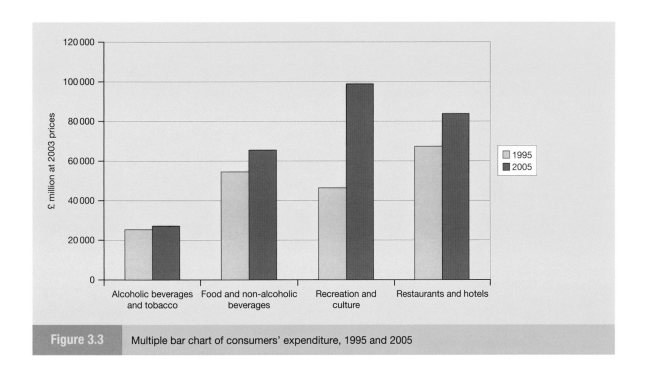

Figure 3.3   Multiple bar chart of consumers' expenditure, 1995 and 2005

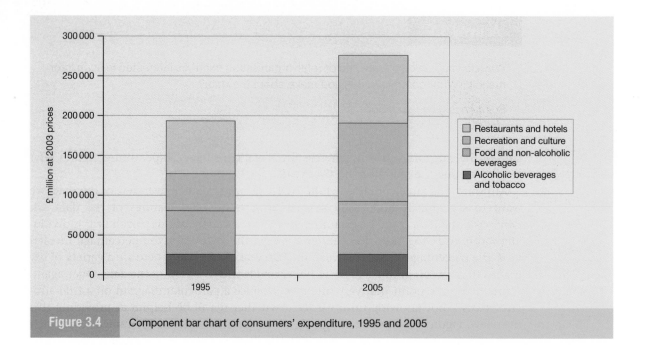

| **Figure 3.4** | Component bar chart of consumers' expenditure, 1995 and 2005 |

Once again, we have confirmation that a quick and ready overview of the data is easily obtained from an appropriate diagram. It is also worth noting that a number of different types of bar graph are available. The diagram we have produced is technically known as a *multiple* bar graph since it shows more than one bar in each category (one for each year in our case). *Simple* bar graphs, as the name suggests, show only one bar in each category, which would have been the case if we had graphed only the 2005 data, for example. A *component* bar chart (sometimes known as a *stacked bar*) for this data is shown in Figure 3.4.

It is evident that we now have a single bar for each year with the height of the bar representing the total of the four categories. The bar is then subdivided to show each element – or component – of this total as a proportion of the total. So, for 1995, for example, we see that the Alcoholic beverages and tobacco category made up almost £25 billion of the total of around £200 billion (note that throughout the text we are adopting the convention of denoting a billion as one thousand million or 1 000 000 000). From the diagram we readily confirm again that the total expenditure across these categories has increased between 1995 and 2005 in real terms by about £75 billion. We also confirm the earlier impression that the Recreation and culture category has seen a substantial increase, since this component increases in size between the 1995 bar and that for 2005. Although such component bar charts are common, they should be used with caution. They are typically useful only where we have a relatively small number of categories. It can be difficult to see the changes between categories if there are too many categories in the bar itself.

A related bar chart can be produced using the *percentage component bar chart*, as shown in Figure 3.5. In this case, each category is shown as a percentage of the total for that year and, accordingly, the height of each bar is the same – corresponding to 100 per cent. Although we lose any impression of the change in the total expenditure over this period, we gain a different comparison between the different categories. Between 1995 and 2005 we see changes in the relative importance of the four categories

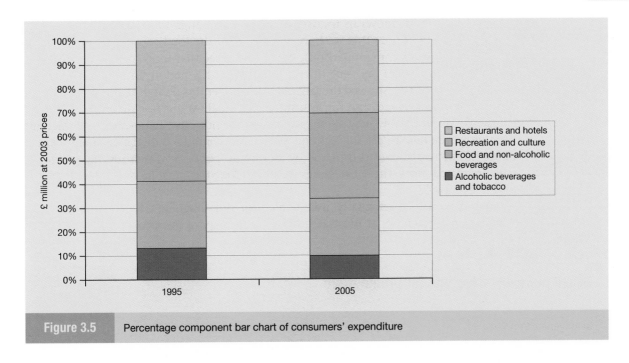

Figure 3.5   Percentage component bar chart of consumers' expenditure

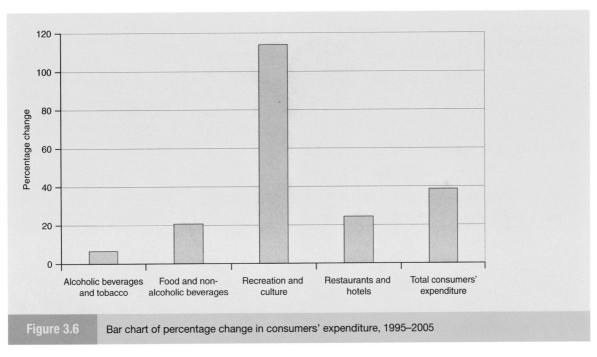

Figure 3.6   Bar chart of percentage change in consumers' expenditure, 1995–2005

with Recreation and culture taking a much larger share of the total expenditure at the expense of the other three categories. Finally, we might use a simple bar chart to show the percentage change in expenditure over these categories, as in Figure 3.6. The change in each category is calculated as a percentage of the 1995 figure (so for Food and non-alcoholic beverages, for example, the change between 2005 and 1995 is 11 207 and this is 20 per cent of the 1995 figure of 54 483).

Figure 3.6 readily allows us to assess the relative change in expenditure across the four categories (and note that we have also included the total consumers' expenditure as an extra yardstick for comparison). We can now see that total consumers' expenditure rose by almost 40 per cent in real terms over this period. In percentage terms, Recreation and culture showed the largest increase over this period, at around or 114 per cent. Alcoholic beverages and tobacco shows the smallest increase over this period. Of course, we do not know why such patterns and trends have happened, but diagrams like these often help us ask the right questions. For example, if total consumers' expenditure has increased over this period by around 40 per cent, which specific categories have increased most (three categories we have looked at have increased less than the overall average)?

Bar charts are a particularly useful management diagram. The same set of data can easily be presented, as illustrated here, in a variety of forms. A degree of trial and

Brazil launches new cellular phone drive

By Raymond Collitt

Raymond Collitt reports from São Paulo on the government's call for more operators

Government officials will launch tomorrow an international roadshow to try to convince domestic and foreign investors that Brazil needs more cellular telephone operators.

At first glance, that may seem an absurd proposition. There are already 21 companies offering cellular telephone services, more than in any other market of a similar size. Several of them have performed far below expectations.

Still, between January and March of next year, Anatel, the telecoms regulator, is to hold three tenders for a total of nine licences to operate mobile telephony using GMS technology. Currently the industry standard is TDMA and CDMA technology.

Analysts say that while the government is unlikely to match the $7bn it raised from the previous,

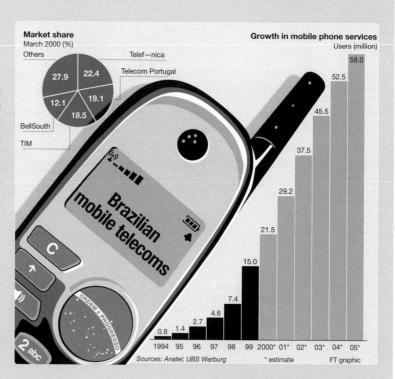

hugely successful, licensing round, it is likely to sell most, if not all, the licences.

Underlying such assumptions is the enormous growth potential of Brazil's mobile telephone market.

Source: Financial Times, 4 October 2000.

A simple bar chart like this can send a strong visual message.

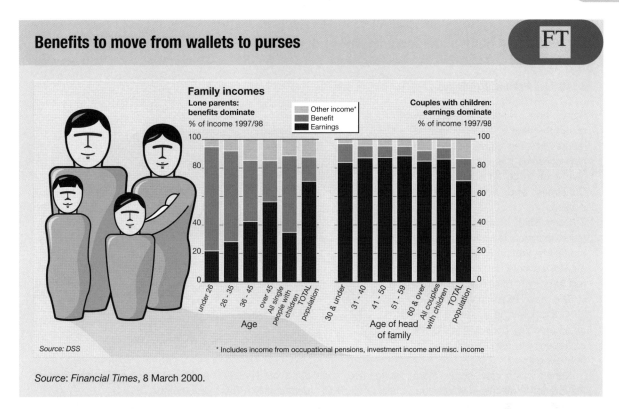

Benefits to move from wallets to purses

FT

Family incomes

Lone parents:
benefits dominate
% of income 1997/98

Other income*
Benefit
Earnings

Couples with children:
earnings dominate
% of income 1997/98

Age

Age of head
of family

Source: DSS

* Includes income from occupational pensions, investment income and misc. income

Source: *Financial Times*, 8 March 2000.

A percentage component bar chart like this can highlight differences very easily.

error – and caution – must be exercised, however. The temptation is often to produce the most sophisticated bar chart that your spreadsheet or graphics package will allow. Frequently, however, this is not appropriate, as a simpler diagram will often have far more impact. There are a number of points to note when constructing bar charts:

● Experiment with the various bar charts for the set of data you are analysing.

● For each chart consider the key points the chart illustrates for the data.

● Decide which charts best illustrate the points that you want to make and discard the other bar charts.

● As a generalisation, ensure that the numerical scale includes zero. Bar charts that do not include zero in the scale – or have what appears to be a carefully selected scale – are suspect in that they may give a distorted picture.

● Ensure that labels, titles and sources are all properly shown and are not open to mis-interpretation.

● Avoid using graphical enhancements available in your software package (3D diagrams, 57 colours, etc.) unless it is genuinely improving the diagram.

● Keep the bar charts as simple as possible. It is usually better to have two (or more) relatively simple bar charts rather than one more complex.

Above all, remember that you are using these diagrams to get a point across to the person who will be seeing them. In other words, you are using these diagrams to try to convey management information. Ensure, above all, that the user of these diagrams is correctly understanding the information you are trying to convey.

Nintendo and Sony showdown in war of consoles

By Michiyo Nakamoto in Tokyo

Sony and Nintendo yesterday raised the heat in the video games market as they unveiled plans for new consoles that each hopes will give it an edge during the crucial Christmas and year-end selling season.

Sony said it would hold the global launch in November of a new model PlayStation 2, its best-selling games console, which would be half the weight of its existing model.

The new PS2, priced at $149 (£84) and €149, is almost as small as a hardcover book and will come equipped with an Ethernet port for network gaming.

Sony, which has sold 73.6m PlayStation 2 machines worldwide, hopes the smaller version will further boost sales of the console.

Ken Kutaragi, president of Sony Computer Entertainment, which is responsible for the PlayStation, said: "We believe, from experience, that reducing the size [of the console] is one factor that can help expand the market."

Sony has also reduced the number of parts in the PS2 from 1,614 to 1,216 and Mr Kutaragi is looking to cut this further.

Nintendo, whose GameCube has struggled against the PS2, fought back yesterday, releasing details of the launch of its hand-held games machine, the Nintendo DS.

It said Nintendo DS would appear in US shops on November 21 and in Japan on December 2, with a

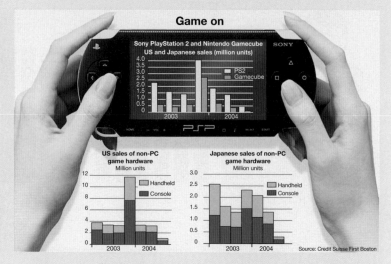

suggested retail price of $149.99 and Y15 000, respectively. The European release date has not yet been set but is expected to be between January and March.

The Nintendo DS will have two screens allowing users to experience games from different angles, as well as voice recognition and wireless communication capabilities.

Nintendo hopes the new portable player will reinforce its dominance of the handheld games market. It said it expected to sell 4 m consoles, up from an initial target of 3.5 m, by the end of March.

But Nintendo, which has sold just 15 m units of GameCube, faces a Sony offensive in the hand-held market as well. Sony said yesterday it had 105 software titles ready for its PSP portable games console, which is expected to appear in

shops in leading markets in the next few months.

Although Sony declined to specify a launch date or suggested retail price, Mr Kutaragi underlined that preparations were nearing completion.

"In terms of the timing of the PSP launch, the question is the software, not the hardware, which is ready," he said.

Sony yesterday also underlined its support for the next generation blu-ray disc format by announcing plans to use it as the software medium for the next generation PlayStation, which is expected to be launched in late 2005 or early 2006.

The blu-ray disc, which is competing with another next-generation disc format supported by Toshiba and NEC, has six times the data capacity of existing DVDs.

Source: Financial Times 22 September 2004.

Bar charts can be used effectively to show similarities and difference.

Piracy blamed for poor music sales

By Tim Burt, Media Editor

The troubled music industry yesterday suffered another blow as figures showed that global sales fell almost 11 per cent in the first half of the year.

The IFPI, representing more than 1500 recorded music companies, blamed internet piracy and illegal CD manufacturing as revenues fell to $12.7bn (£7.6bn) from $14.3bn in the six months to June 30.

The association warned that pirate sales and illegal downloading had overtaken legitimate retailing in several leading markets.

"Germany, Japan, the US and Canada have seen the numbers of unauthorised downloads of tracks and copied CDs reach, and in some cases exceed, the levels of legitimate track and CD album sales," according to the IFPI.

Continued price discounting also hampered industry revenues in spite of strong demand for albums by artists such as Christina Aguilera, Coldplay and Celine Dion.

Rampant piracy and intense competition could lead to further consolidation among the five music majors: Universal, Sony Music, EMI, Warner Music and BMG.

EMI, the British music group, earlier this month approached Warner Music, part of Time Warner, with a $1.6bn takeover proposal. Time Warner has also discussed a possible 50–50 merger with BMG, the music arm of Germany's Bertelsmann.

BMG, meanwhile, has also been named as a possible partner for Sony Music. But regulatory opposition in Brussels and Washington could prevent any deal proceeding.

Source: *Financial Times*; 2 October 2003.

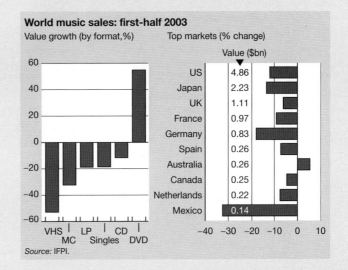

World music sales: first-half 2003
Value growth (by format,%)   Top markets (% change)

Source: IFPI.

Universal Music, part of Vivendi Universal of France, has reacted to the accelerating decline in sales by cutting wholesale CD prices by more than 20 per cent.

In the first half of the year the number of albums, music videos and singles sold in the US fell by 16.5 per cent compared with an 8.8 per cent drop in the first half of 2002.

By retail value, music sales fell from $5.53bn to $4.86bn in the US, the world's largest market. Other important markets including Germany, Japan and Brazil also registered double digit falls.

The IFPI hinted that sales would have fallen more sharply had it not been for strong demand for DVD music videos, which rose 55 per cent by value in the first six months of the year.

Warner Music and Sony are understood to be co-operating on the production of combined CDs and DVDs, dubbed "dual discs", in a

bid to exploit strong demand for music videos.

Music industry executives hope the arrival of legitimate online sales and more competitive pricing will boost demand in the second half of the year.

Jay Berman, chairman of the IFPI, said: "It's a very difficult landscape to fight back against but we are. We have gone through the worst period and we have enough positive signs about how online business models can go forward."

Several technology groups including Microsoft and Apple have launched music download services.

Apple's iTunes has sold 10m songs since its launch in April.

The IFPI also claimed that a "strong schedule of releases" in the second half could underpin some recovery in the sector. They include albums by artists such as Beyoncé, Dido, Bon Jovi, Kylie Minogue and REM.

Bar charts can be shown sideways as well.

Activity 3.2

The data below shows gas sales to different categories of customers in 2002 and in 2006. Use appropriate bar charts to highlight key changes over this period.

UK gas sales: gigawatt hours

	2002	*2006*
Electricity generators	326 218	309 760
Iron and steel industry	19 533	8 410
Other industries	161 456	135 539
Domestic	376 328	364 555
Other	101 304	105 224
Total	984 839	923 488

Source: Monthly Digest of Statistics.

Solution is given on p 580.

Pie Charts

Very often data shown in bar charts can also be shown in the form of a pie chart. Again, these are quite a common method of visually presenting some types of data, although actually quite limited in their ability to convey useful management information. Figure 3.7 shows a pie chart for the 2005 consumers' expenditure category data. A pie chart is readily – if somewhat tediously – constructed manually, although anyone in their right minds will use a spreadsheet instead which will do all of this automatically

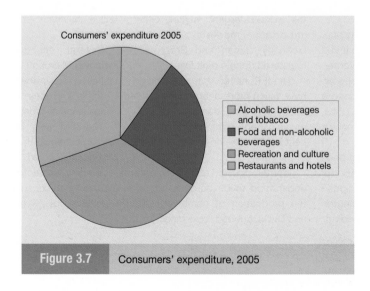

Consumers' expenditure 2005

- Alcoholic beverages and tobacco
- Food and non-alcoholic beverages
- Recreation and culture
- Restaurants and hotels

Figure 3.7	Consumers' expenditure, 2005

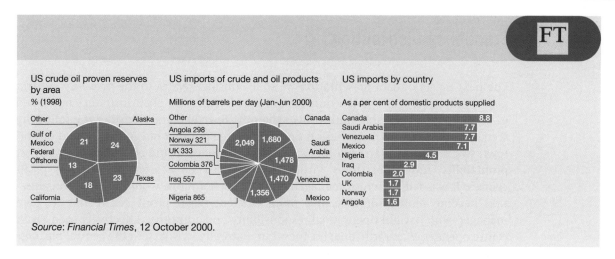

Pie charts can be used with other diagrams as well.

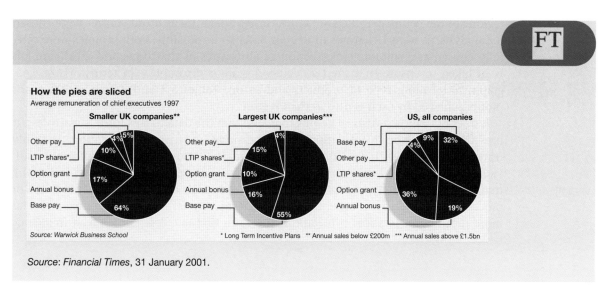

Or just by themselves.

for you. We draw a circle to represent the total expenditure for all categories then proportion the 'slices' of the pie to represent the percentage of this total made up by each category. Given that a circle (the pie) has 360 degrees, we simply apportion the circle to the component categories according to their relative importance. In 2005 the Food and non-alcoholic beverages category, for example, comprises 24 per cent of the total. Given that the total of the circle is 360 degrees, then this 'slice' has to cover 86 degrees (24 per cent of 360). A pie chart allows for a quick overall view of relative sizes of categories but offers little potential for comparison – with another year, for example. As with bar charts, pie charts should be constructed, and used, with caution, ensuring they provide useful information rather than simply looking pretty.

Frequency Distributions

The next aspect of data presentation we shall consider relates to the *frequency distribution*. To illustrate this – and a number of related areas – we shall introduce a detailed example to which we shall return over the next few chapters. Consider the following scenario. A large retail organisation operates a large number of high street and out-of-town stores. As part of an ongoing process to monitor costs and efficiency and to boost profitability, individual stores within the company have been organised as profit centres. It was felt by senior management that such a move would help the organisation become more profitable and more efficient. Each profit centre has its own manager, who has full operational responsibility and authority. Effectively each profit centre operates as an individual business but, naturally, is linked to the central business organisation.

As part of this strategic change in a number of these profit centres, performance-related pay (PRP) is being considered by senior management. In simple terms the more profit a store earns, the more PRP the manager responsible earns. To try to assist this decision it has been decided to examine a sample of profit centres in two different regions of the country. In Region A, 113 stores operating as profit centres were chosen for analysis, as were 121 stores in Region B. As far as possible, both samples were carefully chosen as a suitable cross-section of all centres of that type, and great care has been taken to ensure that the two categories are comparable – in terms of size, geographical location, type of products and so on. Tables 3.2 and 3.3 show last year's profits achieved by each centre in each region.

It does not take a statistical genius to realise that the data in this form is worthless. It provides little, or no, information about the situation we are investigating. The only features of any value that we note are that there is considerable variability in the individual data items and that some are positive and some negative (the latter indicating that a centre operated at a loss in that year). Clearly the data must be manipulated or processed in some way in order to be useful in managerial terms. It is, for example, far more meaningful to show this data in the form of Table 3.4, known as a frequency table.

Table 3.2	Annual profit for stores in Region A (£s)										
42 130	6 320	38 470	–320	3 650	7 770	4 310	4 530	–2 690	3 220	9 030	–2 590
6 390	84 330	47 230	11 780	4 310	5 270	9 730	5 480	62 480	–1 510	13 920	2 130
17 480	7 210	15 620	55 310	–1 160	12 620	–490	3 390	24 390	7 510	7 670	12 590
41 470	8 040	2 150	4 760	–1 570	10 800	5 530	14 730	14 970	15 170	16 070	13 310
93 050	5 460	6 610	33 610	5 300	8 560	–1 120	4 590	2 300	66 990	5 430	5 980
3 630	10 530	8 010	38 920	–740	3 530	32 070	42 200	13 820	17 730	4 760	1 450
5 200	9 860	11 350	–270	18 360	3 300	30 880	1 760	16 730	–13 070	9 060	2 440
7 230	1 270	–270	10 010	43 060	25 460	570	6 620	10 780	6 330	3 480	5 000
16 050	3 870	7 760	12 870	–3 850	4 740	21 110	29 070	3 570	1 760	4 720	6 600
3 160	6 840	34 100	–6 480	20 230							

Data available in file T32.

Table 3.3 Annual profit for stores in Region B (£s)

4 280	2 340	−2 470	3 400	9 170	46 620	560	−2 340	91 400	3 470	13 030	2 800
−4 130	1 800	8 690	28 000	36 240	21 300	8 580	82 880	11 680	3 930	13 140	1 710
7 360	2 610	5 350	5 040	7 540	9 760	12 980	67 780	5 490	38 210	4 600	38 360
−3 200	7 440	500	23 580	11 620	1 230	26 990	13 350	11 800	20 080	8 460	3 810
8 740	32 890	3 650	180	43 530	36 800	62 510	12 520	14 950	42 170	120	4 600
6 080	13 600	42 640	7 390	2 010	2 610	14 290	23 870	12 540	14 020	1 560	13 320
11 050	72 660	50 400	98 800	4 400	3 640	35 390	13 140	25 570	15 010	8 560	17 700
3 030	770	31 260	8 250	25 000	24 100	3 240	47 730	1 360	4 600	22 680	27 310
44 910	4 020	35 970	6 800	43 530	17 720	9 580	37 600	1 540	31 700	2 360	6 510
30 100	5 870	4 360	6 250	14 080	22 740	12 140	6 570	1 850	7 750	28 040	730
5 640											

Source: Company accounts.
Data available in file T33.

Table 3.4 Frequency table

Interval			Region A	Region B
Lower class limit (£s)		Upper class limit (£s)	No. of stores	No. of stores
less than		−10 000	1	0
−10 000	<	0	13	4
0	<	10 000	56	58
10 000	<	20 000	22	21
20 000	<	30 000	5	13
30 000	<	40 000	6	11
40 000	<	50 000	5	7
50 000 or over			5	7
Total			113	121

This frequency table shows the distribution of the individual data items in the two data sets, Region A and Region B. We have chosen a number of profit intervals (eight in this instance) and then counted the number of centres of each type falling into each interval. So, for example, we see that there was one Region A centre making a loss of more than £10 000 compared with none for the Region B group.

Activity 3.3

What observations can you now make about profits in the two years, based on Table 3.4?

Clearly such a tabulation allows us to begin the process of identifying the key characteristics of the two data sets, comparing and contrasting. We see that in both cases the bulk of stores fall into the profit category of £0 to £10 000. At the extremes of the distribution, however, the two regions appear to differ. At the lower end, Region B stores appear to be fewer in number, whilst there are more of them at the higher profit levels. Clearly, we shall wish to investigate the data in other ways, but the frequency table is a start in the process of examining a data set to determine its key features. The construction of such a table from a set of raw data is straightforward – particularly if using computer software to do the hard work. Like much of this chapter, the construction follows a set of 'rules' that are a mixture of common sense and things that have been found to work. We must make two decisions:

- the number of classes, or intervals, to be used
- the size of these intervals.

The two decisions are interrelated and typically subject to trial and error. Fortunately, with appropriate computer technology it is generally a matter of a few moments to 'experiment' with these two features to see which combination of those available gives the 'best' distribution. One useful rule of thumb is that between five and fifteen classes will usually prove suitable (with a smaller number of classes for a smaller set of data). In Table 3.4 we have eight classes. More than eight and we would find that a number of these would contain few, if any, observations. Fewer than eight and we would lose sight of some of the patterns becoming apparent. The class width(s) must then be chosen. Ideally, class widths should be the same for all the classes. Frequently, however, this is impractical and would lead to a large number of classes. Note also that we have two open-ended classes at the start and end of the table. Once again, this is quite a common way of dealing with one or two individual extreme values. Technically we could have 'closed' each of these classes by using, respectively, the minimum and maximum values in the data set. It is arguable, however, whether this would help our understanding of the data distribution. You should also note that the lower and upper limits of each of the classes are clearly and unambiguously defined. We know categorically into which class any one individual observation will have been placed. A common error is to present classes in the form:

> 0 to 10 000
> 10 000 to 20 000
> 20 000 to 30 000

and so on. This is inappropriate since it is not evident into which class an observation taking a value, say, of 10 000 would be placed. Having decided on the number of intervals to be used and their size, it is then a straightforward matter to count the number of data items falling into each interval.

Percentage and Cumulative Frequencies

It may also be appropriate to show the frequency distribution in the form of percentages of the total or of cumulative frequencies (or cumulative percentages). The reasons for this are self-evident. Percentage comparisons are frequently more revealing, whereas

Remuneration is exposed to glare of public scrutiny

KPMG's first annual report and accounts throws light on one of the murkiest areas of professional life – how much the partners of the Big Six accountancy firms earn. The answer is quite a lot.

Pay experts who have studied the accounts said the firm's 600 partners were paid more than the directors of companies in the FTSE Mid-250 with similar numbers of employees or turnover.

But they admitted that comparisons were difficult because KPMG's real competitors still guarded details of their remuneration policies behind the confidentiality afforded by partnerships. KPMG pointed to the earnings of partners in merchant banks and legal firms, which it said were higher than their own.

KPMG's partners are paid £125,000 on average. This "executive remuneration" is set by consultants Heidrick & Struggles who study the market and lay out a

series of "benchmark" notional salaries for each partner. But the overall average is £180,000 – this includes an extra £24,000 for pensions and £31,000 from "proprietorship profit" – the return on the partner's equity in the business.

But KPMG has more of a pyramid structure than its competitors. The real earnings are skewed. Senior partner Mr Colin Sharman takes £438,000 in executive remuneration – plus £125,000 from a pension, and £176,753 from proprietorship profit, making a total of £739,753.

Mr Steve Tatton, editor of Incomes Data Services management pay review, points to the IDS pay survey for 1994–95 of the FTSE Mid-250. He compares Mr Sharman's £614,000 (minus pension) with the average for the highest paid directors in companies with a turnover of £500m to £1bn, which is £305,000.

Source: Financial Times, 31 January 1996, p 11.

Accounting at the top

KPMG partners and staff remuneration

Band (£)	1994 number	1995 number
1–25,000	8	18
25,001–50,000	15	12
50,001–75,000	74	59
75,001–100,000	176	132
100,001–125,000	160	148
125,001–150,000	75	87
150,001–175,000	32	61
175,001–200,000	25	17
200,001–225,000	7	21
225,001–250,000	16	12
250,001–275,000	2	12
275,001–300,000	1	1
300,001–325,000	2	2
325,001–350,000	1	2
350,001–375,000	-	1
375,001–400,000	1	-
400,001–425,000	-	-
425,001–450,000	-	1

Colin Sharman, senior partner

Salary	£438,000
Pension	£125,000
Proprietorship profit	£176,753
Total	**£739,753**

Source: KPMG company report.

The frequency table provides more detail than the average of £125 000 quoted in the article and allows us to assess how 'good' the average is at representing the whole data set.

cumulative frequencies have their own special uses that we shall explore in more detail later in this chapter. In Table 3.5 a number of these calculations have been performed: the percentage of observations in each interval and the cumulative total up to and including that interval.

We can now see readily that for Region A some 12.4 per cent of stores were operating at a loss, compared with only 3.3 per cent of Region B stores. Similarly, some 8.8 per cent (100 – 91.2) of Region A stores had a profit of £40 000 or more compared with 11.6 per cent of Region B's. What the analysis does not reveal, of course, are the causes of such differences.

Table 3.5	Frequency table: percentages and cumulative figures

| Interval | | Region A | | | | Region B | | | |
Lower limit (£s)	Upper limit (£s)	Frequency no.	%	Cum. freq. no.	%	Frequency no.	%	Cum. freq. no.	%
less than	−10 000	1	0.9	1	0.9	0	0	0	0
−10 000 <	0	13	11.5	14	12.4	4	3.3	4	3.3
0 <	10 000	56	49.6	70	62.0	58	47.9	62	51.2
10 000 <	20 000	22	19.5	92	81.5	21	17.4	83	68.6
20 000 <	30 000	5	4.4	97	85.9	13	10.7	96	79.3
30 000 <	40 000	6	5.3	103	91.2	11	9.1	107	88.4
40 000 <	50 000	5	4.4	108	95.6	7	5.8	114	94.2
50 000 or over		5	4.4	113	100.0	7	5.8	121	100.0
Total		113				121			

Histograms

Naturally, given the orientation of this chapter, we would expect to be able to show the data from the frequency table in the form of a diagram. In fact a variety of these are available. The first is a simple representation of the frequency distribution in the form of a *histogram*. Such a diagram is shown for the Region A stores in Figure 3.8. Effectively,

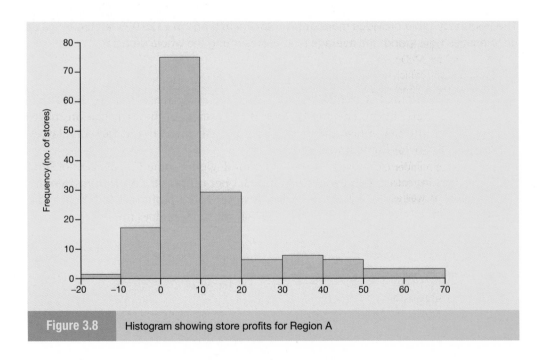

Figure 3.8	Histogram showing store profits for Region A

a histogram is a type of bar chart but where the bars are adjacent to each other rather than with a gap between as in a bar chart. The reason for this is that the histogram (and frequency table) shows data which is continuous, whereas a bar chart is dealing with data which is discrete.

For each interval in the table a bar has been drawn where the height represents the frequency of observations in that interval. The second interval, for example, stores making a loss of up to £10 000, has a frequency of 13, which corresponds to the height of the bar in the histogram. But what about the two open-ended intervals? Remember that we have two intervals: less than –£10 000 and £50 000 or over. To draw each interval on a histogram we must close these to give, respectively, lower and upper limits. Ideally, we could close these intervals to make them the same width (10 000) as

McDonnell abandons plans for new jetliner

FT

By Christopher Parkes in Los Angeles

McDonnell Douglas has scrapped plans to develop a large jetliner to compete with market leaders Boeing and Airbus. The decision will again raise questions about the aerospace group's future in the commercial sector.

After reviewing a six-month engineering study, the board decided the risks of the $3bn MD-XX project were too great, officials said.

The cancellation of the project, which included options to extend the flying range or increase the passenger capacity of the 300-seat MD-11, leaves McDonnell without an aircraft with which to compete effectively for a share of the fast-growing markets in Asia and Latin America.

Plans for the new MD-11 included a wider-bodied version with the same number of seats and a 20 per cent increase in range to 8,500 miles, as well as a stretched variant with 75 more seats.

Officials rebutted suggestions that the company, which has seen its share of the world commercial jet market shrink by half to 10 per cent

Aircraft demand, 1995 to 2014

Number of aircraft, '000

Source: Airbus.

since 1990, might be obliged to quit the business.

A spokesman refused to discuss the possibility of merger talks, such as the negotiations broken off earlier this year with Boeing.

"We will stay in the market with the MD-11 for now while we look at other options," an official said. Longer-term development work was still under way on a futuristic aircraft with a blended wind and body configuration, for example.

Production rates were increasing, and the MD-11, the biggest aircraft in the current range, had recently been boosted by an order from Lufthansa, the German flag carrier.

McDonnell's commercial aircraft unit, based in Long Beach, California, is still profitable. Operating income more than doubled to $90m in the first nine months of this year on revenues down from $3bn to $1.9bn.

Source: Financial Times, 29 October 1996, p 26.

Use of histogram to give a profile of estimated demand for aircraft of different sizes.

all the others. This would give a lower interval of –£20 000 < –£10 000. For the upper interval, however, this might seem a little misleading to set the upper limit at £60 000, since we know from visual inspection of Tables 3.2 and 3.3 that there are stores exceeding this. Obviously a compromise is necessary. We could set the upper limit at £100 000, which would ensure we properly include all values. The trouble is this would give us one interval much wider (five times) than any of the others, although it would include all the data. However, it is worthwhile remembering why we are bothering with a diagram at all. Its purpose is to give a quick – and reasonably accurate – overview of the data we are examining. We do not pretend the diagram allows us to see all the fine detail of the data. As long as it is not downright misleading it will have served its purpose. Let us choose, therefore, an upper limit of £70 000 as a compromise figure.

Effectively, this interval is now double the width of the others and it would not be 'fair' to show the height of this (extra wide) interval as five, the actual frequency. If we were to do this it would make this (wider) interval look too 'important' relative to the others. (If you are unsure of this point you should try drawing this last interval on the histogram without the adjustment we are about to calculate.) Accordingly, we must adjust the actual frequency of the observations in this interval to compensate for the different width. If we denote the standard interval as having width SW and the width of the interval we need to adjust as AW, then the actual frequency can be adjusted by:

$$\text{Adjusted frequency} = \frac{\text{Actual frequency}}{\text{AW/SW}}$$

$$= \frac{5}{20\,000/10\,000}$$

$$= \frac{5}{2} = 2.5$$

That is, the frequency to be plotted on the histogram for this interval is 2.5 not five. You will probably have realised that we have effectively scaled the actual frequency down by a factor of two (given the interval width is two times the standard). It is important to bear this point in mind when constructing histograms – either manually or using computer software – particularly as many commercial software programs do not automatically adjust the frequencies of unequal intervals. It reinforces the point that, wherever possible, we should construct frequency tables with equal class widths to avoid the problem.

However, leaving aside the technicalities, consider your own reaction to the diagram. As a manager wanting a quick and easy overview of profits from the region A stores, would you prefer the histogram or the frequency table?

Activity 3.4

Draw a comparable histogram for profits for Region B stores and compare it with Figure 3.8. What comments can you make about this distribution compared with that of Region A?

Solution is given on p 583.

Histograms in percentage form

We could just as well have drawn the histograms not in terms of frequency – the actual number of stores in each interval – but in terms of the percentage of the total of stores falling into each interval. A percentage histogram is often useful where the total number of observations makes direct comparison from one interval to another difficult: we might prefer to use percentages in our example given the (albeit slight) difference in total number of observations between the Region A and Region B groups.

Frequency Polygons

Although a histogram shows the overall distribution of the variable, it can be problematic when we wish to compare two, or more, such distributions. (You may have already experienced difficulty in making detailed comparisons in the last Activity.) An alternative method is to construct a *frequency polygon*. Such a diagram differs from a histogram only in that rather than drawing a bar for the frequency in each interval we use points. We mark the frequency in each interval with a point drawn at the appropriate frequency height in the middle of the interval width. These points are then joined using lines as in Figure 3.9, which shows a frequency polygon for Region A. There appears little benefit from showing the data in this way until we superimpose the data for Region B stores on to the same diagram, now shown in Figure 3.10. The polygons now make a visual comparison between the two sets of data much easier. We see that the two distributions follow a broadly similar profile and that the major differences in the two distributions occur at the two ends of the distribution – in the middle intervals the two groups of stores are more or less the same. The Region B polygon tends to be below that for Region A stores at low profit levels and above it for high profit levels, indicating fewer low-profit stores and more high-profit stores.

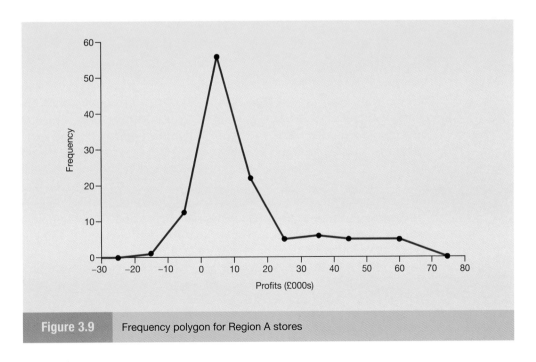

| Figure 3.9 | Frequency polygon for Region A stores |

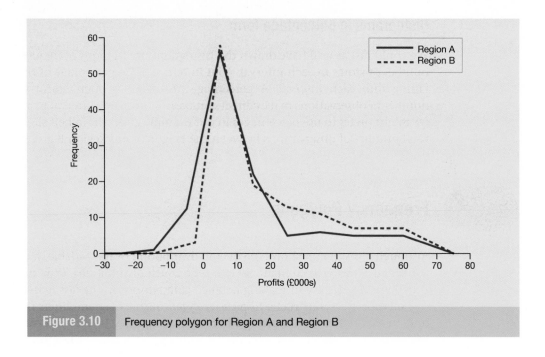

Figure 3.10   Frequency polygon for Region A and Region B

Ogives

You will remember that in Table 3.5 we calculated the cumulative frequencies as well as the individual. The visual presentation of these cumulative frequencies – either the actual values or the percentages – takes the form of an *ogive* (pronounced oh-jive). Such a diagram is easily constructed. We have the intervals as usual on the horizontal axis and the cumulative values on the vertical. We plot the cumulative value for each interval against the upper limit of each interval and then join the points together with straight lines.

To see how this is done – since it sounds more complicated than it is – let us return to the data in Table 3.5. Figure 3.11 shows the cumulative percentage frequencies for Region A stores, using the data in Table 3.5. So, for example, there are 0.9 per cent of stores with a profit less than –£10 000, 12.4 per cent of stores with a profit less than £0 (obviously including the 0.9 per cent in the previous interval) and so on. The ogive is now constructed by marking the right-hand end of each bar with a point (also shown in Figure 3.11) and then joining each pair of these points together with a straight line to give the ogive shown in Figure 3.12.

The diagram may take a little getting used to. Remember that the vertical scale shows the cumulative percentage frequencies. The figure of 30, for example, relates to 30 per cent of all stores in Region A. The ogive starts from 0 per cent and goes up to 100 per cent. Any point we choose on the line will show the percentage of stores falling below a given profit figure and, by default, the percentage lying above that profit figure. For example, assume management regard a profit of £25 000 as a critical performance

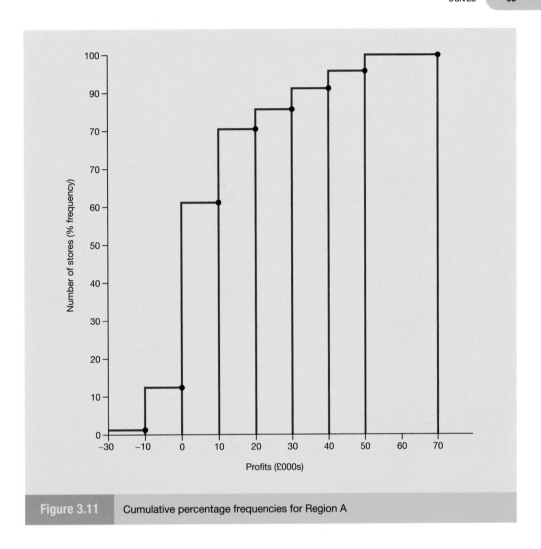

Figure 3.11   Cumulative percentage frequencies for Region A

measure. Locating this value on the horizontal axis, drawing a line upwards until it intersects the ogive and then extending the line along until we intersect the vertical axis will give 84 per cent. This implies that 84 per cent of stores in Region A have a profit of up to £25 000 while the remainder, 16 per cent (100 – 84), have a profit greater than £25 000. The ogive is readily used to examine the distribution of data over a given range and to compare one data set with another in terms of its distribution.

Activity 3.5

Draw an ogive showing profits for Region A and for Region B on the same diagram. Comment on the differences.

Solution is given on p 584.

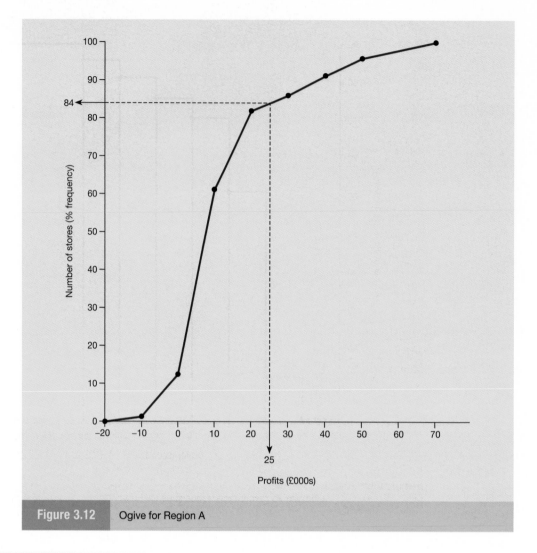

| Figure 3.12 | Ogive for Region A |

Lorenz Curves

Similar in principle to an ogive is the *Lorenz curve*, sometimes known as a *Pareto diagram*. The difference is that an ogive plots cumulative percentage frequencies against the class intervals. A Lorenz curve plots cumulative percentage frequencies against cumulative percentage class totals. This sounds far more complicated than it is. Let us return to the Region A stores. This time we shall consider only those which showed a profit greater than zero. The results we shall be using are shown in Table 3.6.

The table shows the distribution of stores (restricted to those earning a positive profit) in both frequency, percentage and cumulative percentage terms. Thus, of the 99 Region A stores making a positive profit, 56 of them – 56.6 per cent – earned a profit of up to £10 000, 22.2 per cent earned a profit between £10 000 and £20 000 and so on. In the final three columns, however, we have added new data. We now show – for the stores in each interval – the total profit that they earned. So, for example, these 56 stores earned a combined profit of £289 150, which in turn represents some 19 per cent of total profit for the 99 stores. You may begin to see where we are going. We have a situation where some 57 per cent of stores contribute only 19 per cent of total profit – a somewhat

| Table 3.6 | Region A stores with a positive profit | | | | | |

Profit up to (£s)	Freq.	%	Cum. %	Total profit (£s)	%	Cum. % profit
10 000	56	56.6	56.6	289 150	19.2	19.2
20 000	22	22.2	78.8	307 290	20.4	39.7
30 000	5	5.1	83.8	120 260	8.0	47.7
40 000	6	6.1	89.9	208 050	13.8	61.5
50 000	5	5.1	94.9	216 090	14.4	75.9
70 000	5	5.1	100.0	362 160	24.1	100.0
Total	99			1 503 000		

disproportionate result. On the other hand, we have (the top) 5 per cent of stores contributing some 24 per cent to total profit. Effectively, we are comparing the percentage distribution of stores against the percentage distribution of profit. If we do this visually with the cumulative values, we get a Lorenz curve as in Figure 3.13. On the diagram we have plotted the cumulative percentage values for the number of stores on the vertical axis and the cumulative percentage profit on the other to give the Lorenz curve. Also on the diagram is the line of equal distribution (LED). This is a line showing what the distribution would be if it were perfectly equal: if 10 per cent of stores earned 10 per cent of profit, 20 per cent of stores earned 20 per cent of profit and so on. The LED acts as a reference point to allow us to assess actual 'inequality' in the distribution. The further away the Lorenz curve is from the LED then the more unequal the distribution of profit. It will probably be evident that we could now compare inequality in the Region A group with that of the Region B group. While this is left as an exercise the potential importance of the diagram is evident. Given the relative importance of a small number of stores in terms of their profit contribution, management should be focusing attention on these

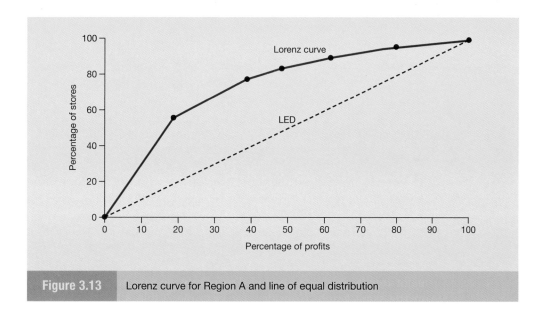

Figure 3.13   Lorenz curve for Region A and line of equal distribution

stores to ensure continuing profitability. Equally, the large number of stores which contribute relatively little to overall profit need to be examined in the context of the organisation's strategy. Would we be better merging some of these stores to make them more viable or even getting rid of some of them altogether?

Lorenz curves are a fairly specialist diagram but quite useful in those circumstances. Typical uses relate to income distribution, distribution of value among stock (inventory) items, distribution of earnings/profits and distribution of faults/failures in a manufacturing process. One local authority in the UK, for example, was investigating the outstanding debt owed by council house tenants in terms of rent on the properties. The total amount of such rent which had not been paid by tenants was around £2 million, a substantial sum given the financial restrictions under which local authorities operate. Management were considering a number of options in terms of trying to recover this debt, but the issue was a sensitive one given the economic recession and general levels of income of the tenants. However, the application of a Lorenz curve to the data revealed that around 72 per cent of the outstanding debt was owed by only 9 per cent of those in arrears. Rather than considering options to recover arrears from all tenants, management realised that by focusing effective measures on only a small group most of the outstanding debt could be recovered.

The man who helped Japan's quality revolution

FT

By Richard Donkin

Joseph Juran, who died last week at the age of 103, was the last of the great statistical gurus who established the quality movement in business and helped to transform Japanese production after the second world war.

Perhaps his best known contribution to the workplace – and not unrelated to this casino observation – was what he called the "Pareto Principle" now better known as the 80/20 rule. This holds that most effects come from relatively few causes. Later, he acknowledged that the influence for this rule had less to do with Vilfredo Pareto, the Italian economist after whom it was named, and more to do with the work of Max Otto Lorenz, whose "Lorenz curve" displayed the deviation of a sample from the standard. Juran used this observation when tackling waste, arguing that it was more important initially to concentrate on the "vital few" operations in manufacturing, rather than the "trivial many".

Source: Financial Times, 6 March 2008. www.richarddonkin.com

Time-Series Graphs

Frequently we may wish to examine the behaviour of some variable in which we are interested over a period of time. Our interest may lie in production figures, costs, manpower levels, sales, profits and the like, and we wish to gain some impression as to how the variable of interest has altered over a given period. A *time-series graph* tries to show such patterns.

In fact, we have already seen a time-series graph at the start of this chapter in Figure 3.1. Their construction is straightforward, with time being shown on the horizontal axis and the value of the variable on the vertical, and they are useful for showing major trends over some period. Frequently we may wish to show two or more series on the same graph. Consider, for example, Table 3.7, which shows motor vehicles

	Private cars	Motor cycles	All vehicles
1988	2154.7	90.1	2723.5
1989	2241.2	97.3	2828.9
1990	1942.3	94.4	2438.7
1991	1536.6	76.5	1921.5
1992	1528.0	65.6	1901.8
1993	1694.6	58.4	2074.0
1994	1809.1	64.6	2249.0
1995	1828.3	68.9	2306.5
1996	1888.4	89.6	2410.1
1997	2015.9	121.3	2597.2
1998	2123.5	143.3	2740.3
1999	2100.4	168.4	2765.8
2000	2174.9	182.9	2870.9
2001	2431.8	177.1	3137.7
2002	2528.8	162.2	3229.4
2003	2497.1	157.3	3231.9
2004	2437.4	133.7	3185.4
2005	2266.3	132.3	3021.4

Table 3.7 New vehicle registrations Great Britain (thousands)

Source: Annual Abstract of Statistics.

currently licensed each year in the UK. Figures are shown for 'All vehicles' and for two particular categories, 'Private cars' and 'Motor cycles'.

From the table it is evident that different trends are occurring. We see that the All vehicles line and that for Private cars run in parallel, hardly surprising since Private cars is clearly making up most of the All vehicles total. In both cases, new registrations peaked in 1989, followed by a decline for two years but with a steady increase until 2003 followed by a slight decline in 2004 and 2005. It is difficult to see what is happening by comparison with Motor cycles as shown in Figure 3.14. The reason for this is to do with the vertical scale we must use. This must be large enough for All vehicles but, because Motor cycles takes much smaller values, it is impossible to see the detail of this variable. One solution is to use not one vertical axis but two (often referred to as a 2Y time-series graph). This is shown in Figure 3.15, where All vehicles and Private cars are measured on the left-hand axis whilst Motor cycles is shown on the right-hand axis. Note that the right-hand axis has a different numerical scale, from 0 to 200. We now see that Motor cycles follows a similar pattern to the other two variables although the drop in registrations continues for longer – to 1993. After that, registrations begin to climb again although they have declined again since 2000. Although this type of time-series graph is quite common, considerable care needs to be taken over the choice of scales on both axes to avoid misleading the user, and it should always be made clear on the diagram that two different scales are being used. Although we have shown time-series graphs here on an annual basis, they can be used for any time period – quarters, months, days, even hours and minutes, if that is appropriate. All of them are equally relevant for trying to highlight patterns and trends over time.

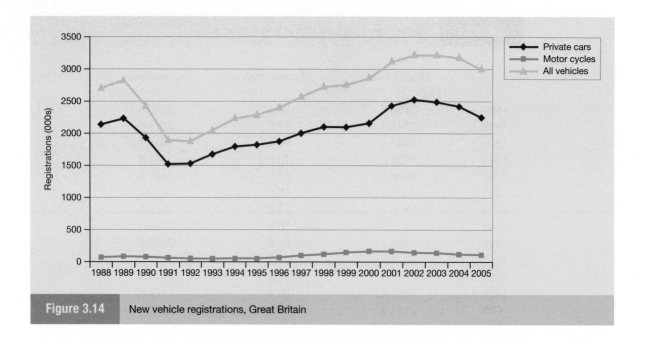

Figure 3.14   New vehicle registrations, Great Britain

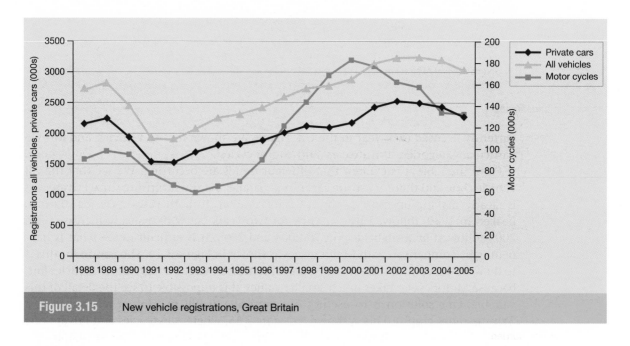

Figure 3.15   New vehicle registrations, Great Britain

Z Charts

The next type of diagram we introduce is the *Z chart*, possibly the most complex in this chapter. The other types of diagram we have introduced are effectively concerned with looking back over time to assess patterns and trends that have occurred. The Z chart is more an operational diagram and concerned with current patterns and trends. Consider the data shown in Table 3.8.

Table 3.8	Number of repairs to council housing completed

	2008
January	150
February	133
March	147
April	126
May	124
June	131
July	140
August	132
September	144
October	153
November	155
December	188
Total	1723

Source: Works Department.

Managers focus on right treatment for faked illness

By Jonathan Moules

Pulling a sickie to nurse a hangover or watch a cricket match used to be the stuff of stand-up routines or pub anecdotes. But the number of workers faking illness is increasingly preoccupying public and private sector managers for a simple reason: its impact on the bottom line.

Although the UK's absenteeism record is not as bad as that of many European countries, including France and the Netherlands, it is a big financial burden, costing business £11.6bn last year alone, according to the CBI, the employers' body.

And the problem is getting worse. The CBI's latest research in May found workplace absence in the private sector increased last year for the first time in five years.

Gordon Brown recognised the scale of the problem in last month's spending review when he pledged to curb uncertified absences in the public sector. Many are genuinely sick due to workplace and personal stresses that could have been alleviated by better management or counselling. But British Airways was so concerned at the numbers it believes may be taking time off unnecessarily that last weekend it refused to agree better pay offers for baggage handling and check-in

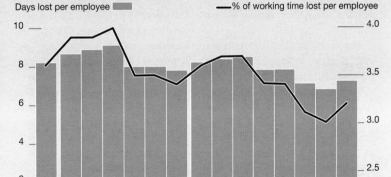

Trends in UK absence levels

Days lost per employee

% of working time lost per employee

staff until it had gained union support for a new absenteeism policy.

The final agreement simplifies the formal procedure for dealing with an absent worker, and dismissing persistent offenders, by cutting the number of disciplinary stages from eight to four.

Ben Willmott, employee relations adviser at the Chartered Institute of Personnel and Development, says the deal shows that concern about absenteeism is not limited to the boardroom. "I am not surprised that the unions are just as anxious to tackle the cost as employers because they see it is a cost to the business."

An average annual absence rate of 12 days will cost companies £600 per employee, Mr Willmott adds. Institute research found that unplanned absence was a particular problem for the transport and services sectors – and generally increased the larger a company grew. BA, whose problem is worse than most companies, hopes its new measures will enable it to trim its absenteeism rate from 17 working days per employee per year to 10.

Tesco is tackling the problem with a pilot scheme that means workers are not paid for the first three days they take off sick. Rival supermarket chain Asda also restricts sick pay while offering rewards for low absenteeism, such as an extra week's leave. Other companies have taken a less aggressive approach, but maintain firm policies to separate the genuinely sick from the lead-swingers. Woolworths, the general retailer,

Source: *Financial Times*, 24 August 2004.

has a dedicated team that works with line managers to deal with absenteeism and other staff-related problems.

This team will support staff who genuinely need time away from work and advise managers on how to minimise unauthorised and unnecessary absenteeism.

Aviva, the insurance group, will consult the employee's GP – with the worker's consent – if a manager is concerned about his or her sickness record. However, the company also provides medical facilities in or near the workplace so staff can have health checks. Sue Winston, Aviva's spokesperson, says: "We are trying to be proactive and understand the reasons why individuals take sick leave."

Incentives to come to work are not necessary, she adds, because Aviva does not feel its absenteeism problem is endemic – a view reflected by various members of the

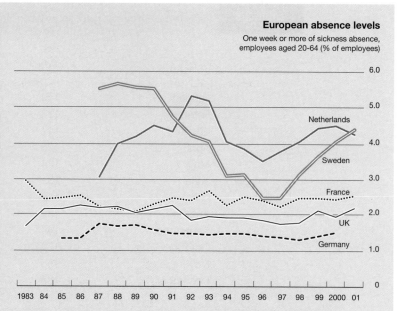

European absence levels

One week or more of sickness absence, employees aged 20-64 (% of employees)

Netherlands
Sweden
France
UK
Germany

1983　84　85　86　87　88　89　90　91　92　93　94　95　96　97　98　99　2000　01

A prescription for employers

- Be fair about absences for all illness but make it clear that you will act if they become a problem
- Ensure that line managers are a key part of solving absence problems among their staff
- Explain to staff that they are taking advantage of colleagues as well as their employer when they fake illness
- Act quickly before an absence problem escalates out of control.

Sources: CBI; ISSA; Chartered Institute of Personnel and Development.

FTSE 250. Companies ranging from LogicaCMG, the computer group, to Marks and Spencer said they did not have a significant problem. However, many companies are simply burying their heads in the sand, according to Anne Payne, executive director at Validium, which provides personnel support for human resource departments. She says: "It is frightening how many companies don't absolutely know their absence figures."

Time series can be used effectively by themselves or in combination with other types of graph, as in this article with a bar chart.

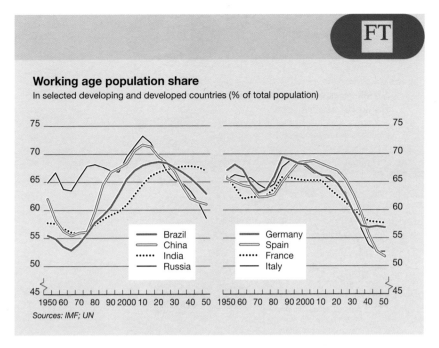

Time series can show differing trends very effectively. Note how the data has been split into two groups to highlight contrasting trends.

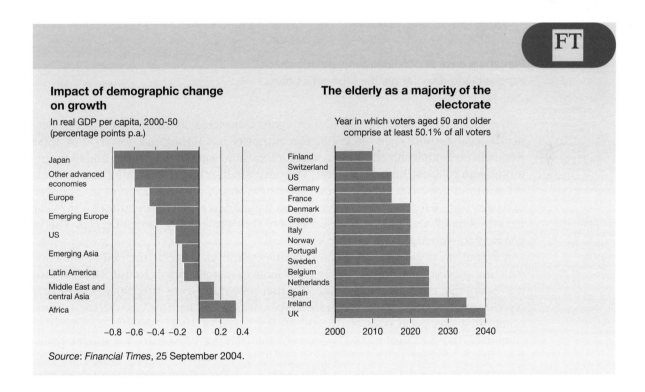

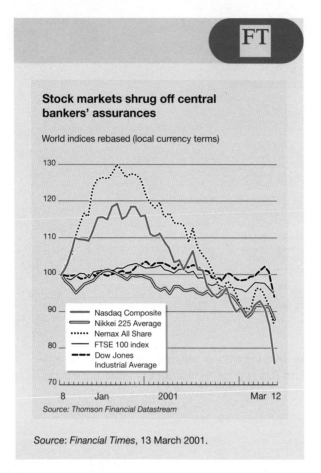

Stock markets shrug off central bankers' assurances

World indices rebased (local currency terms)

Nasdaq Composite
Nikkei 225 Average
Nemax All Share
FTSE 100 index
Dow Jones
Industrial Average

8   Jan   2001   Mar 12

Source: Thomson Financial Datastream

Source: *Financial Times*, 13 March 2001.

Perhaps a case of one line too many! It's almost impossible to disentangle the time series here.

The data relates to the number of roof repairs completed on council housing in a particular local authority area in 2008. The authority has set a target for 2009 of 1800 repairs to be completed, and the manager responsible wants a simple method of monitoring performance through the year. We can visualise that at the end of each month the authority's management information system would provide details of the number of repairs completed during that month and the manager periodically through the year requires a quick and easy way of seeing how this relates to the annual target. This is precisely the function a Z chart serves.

A Z chart to begin with looks and sounds complicated but at the end of the construction process you should be able to see how easy it actually is to use. The first task is to establish a monthly target profile like that shown in Figure 3.16. Note that the line representing the target starts at 0 in December 2008 given that the X axis relates to end-of-month figures, and ends at the end-of-year target of 1800. We have assumed for simplicity that the target of 1800 is split equally over the 12 months. We could equally have drawn a target line which showed differing, non-equal monthly targets to allow for changing work patterns through the year. Consider the situation later in the year when we have the number of repairs completed in the first three months, as shown in Table 3.9.

In the second column marked 2009 total we have the number of repairs completed during each of these first three months. In the next column – 2009 cumulative total – we have the running total to date for 2009, and in the last column – last 12 months – we

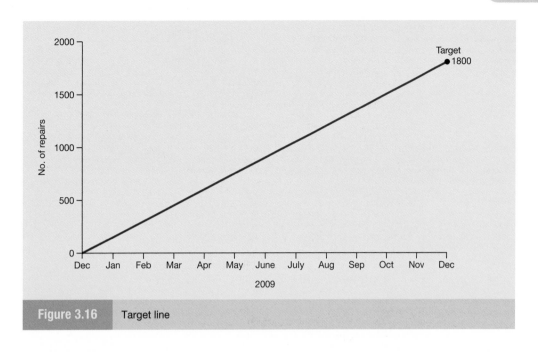

Figure 3.16   Target line

Table 3.9   Number of repairs to council housing completed as at end March 2009

	2008 total	2009 total	2009 cumulative total	Last 12 months
January	150	119	119	1692
February	133	108	227	1688
March	147	127	354	1693
April	126			
May	124			
June	131			
July	140			
August	132			
September	144			
October	153			
November	155			
December	188			
Total	1723			

have the total for the last 12-month period. So, at the end of March the authority had completed 127 repairs during that month, 354 in the year to date (January to March inclusive) and 1693 since the previous April. The last figure is simply the total of the previous 12 months' figures (April 2008 to March 2009). The reason for having each of these series needs comment. The actual number each month is obvious. The cumulative total shows us how close we are to the end-of-year target of 1800. The figure for the last 12 months gives us an idea as to the general long-term trend in the number of repairs being completed, since it indicates performance on an annual rather than a monthly basis. This could be upwards, downwards or constant. Each of these three

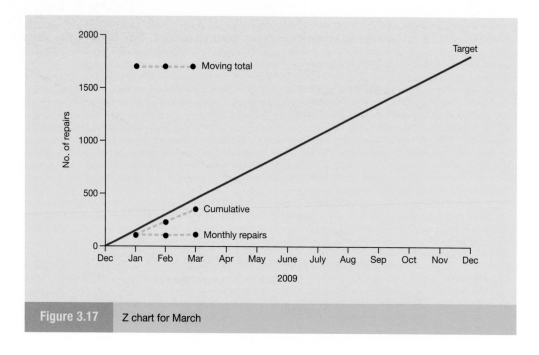

Figure 3.17   Z chart for March

series can now be superimposed on the Z chart, as shown in Figure 3.17. This shows us that our cumulative total is already below the target for the first three months of the year, although the last 12 months shows a reasonably stable trend. Action obviously needs to be taken if we are to achieve the target set. Consider now the use of the Z chart on an ongoing monthly basis. When the next monthly figures are produced, the chart can be updated and a monthly check on progress maintained to see when managerial action is required.

Some of you may have wondered why it's actually called a Z chart. The answer becomes clear if we examine Figure 3.18, which shows the state of play later in the

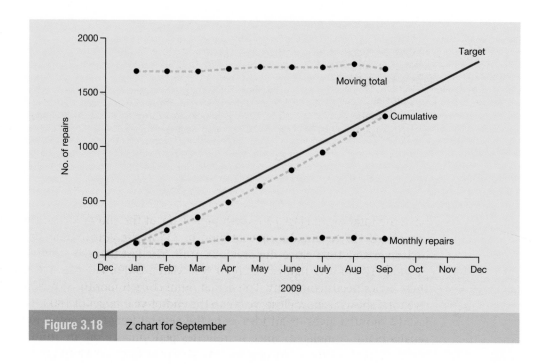

Figure 3.18   Z chart for September

year – at the end of September. It is evident that by the time we get to the end of the year our three series will have combined to form the shape of the letter Z! Z charts are, again, a relatively specialised diagram but extensively used in those situations where it is applicable. Almost every organisation will wish to monitor on a regular basis some variable: housing repairs, number of customers, production of a product, sales of a product, number of patients treated, budget expenditure and so on. It may be appropriate to monitor this on a monthly basis or on a weekly or daily basis, all of which are readily done on this type of diagram.

Scatter Diagrams

The last type of diagram we examine in this chapter is known as a *scatter diagram*. All the situations we have examined so far have been concerned with evaluating one variable at a time – profits, sales, spending, council house repairs. Frequently, however, managers may wish to consider whether some relationship exists between two variables. Examples of this might be:

● the price of a product and the quantity sold
● people's income and their spending patterns
● levels of production and costs.

It is not too difficult to add to the list with pairs of variables which we might think are in some way connected. A scatter diagram is simply a way of showing the data for two variables together. Consider the data in Table 3.10, which returns us to the retail organisation investigating profitability of stores in two regions.

For 20 of the stores in Region A the table shows the annual sales in that store together with profit achieved by that store.

Activity 3.6

In what way do you think these two variables might be connected? What would you expect to happen to one store's profit as its sales increased/decreased?

Clearly there would be reasonable logic in expecting the profits of a store to rise as its sales rose and to decrease as its sales decreased. Whether it would be reasonable to assume this pattern for all the different stores is more problematic. However, it seems reasonable to examine this data graphically and to assess whether there appears to be any evidence of such a relationship. The scatter diagram for this data is shown in Figure 3.19. On the diagram we have, literally, shown the scatter of data for these 20 stores. On the bottom axis we have shown sales and on the vertical, profit. For each store we can then locate its actual sales–profit combination and mark its position with a suitable symbol. Repeating this for all the data points, we begin to build up a picture of the overall relationship between the two variables.

Table 3.10	Sales and profits for 20 stores in Region A

Sales (£s)	Profit (£s)
748 820	42 130
140 776	6 320
702 109	38 470
41 536	−320
96 846	3 650
166 926	7 770
109 048	4 310
263 915	4 530
50 842	−2 690
90 077	3 220
190 590	9 030
91 750	−2 590
141 571	6 390
377 044	24 390
198 690	13 920
62 775	2 130
265 284	17 480
91 802	7 210
231 600	15 620
548 307	33 610

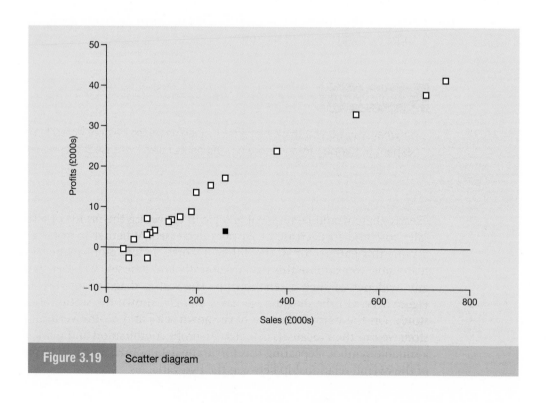

Figure 3.19	Scatter diagram

Activity 3.7

Do you think we have any evidence regarding the relationship between sales and profit that we assumed earlier? Is this relationship exactly the same for all stores? Are there any stores that appear to differ from the norm?

The diagram appears to indicate that, for most of the stores, a relationship between the two variables exists, indicating that as sales increase so do profits. Clearly this relationship is not exactly the same for all the stores; indeed it would be unreasonable to expect this. Profit in any one store will not depend entirely on sales but on other variables also – the location of the store, the number of customers, their income levels and so on. Equally, we are able to identify those stores which are clearly different from the others in the context of this relationship. We see that there is one store which lies away from the general relationship and, given its profit level, appears to have particularly high sales. Consider carefully what this means. It implies that this store has sales which ought to be generating higher profits given the performance of the other stores. In other words, we can regard this store as being 'abnormal' and worthy of management attention. Its performance is clearly at odds with that of the other stores, even after we allow for variability in the sales–profit relationship. A scatter diagram, then, enables us

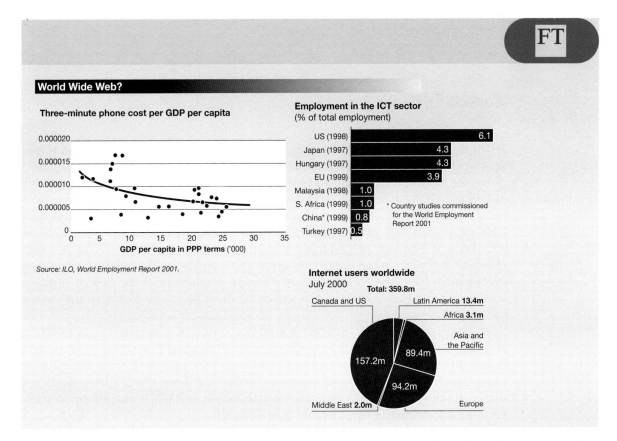

A scatter plot looking at the cost of using the phone system to connect to the internet in a number of countries.

not only to see whether there is any relationship between two variables but also to identify those observations which lie away from such a relationship. Clearly, from a management perspective, we would now wish to quantify the nature of the relationship we have observed, but this will have to wait for a later chapter.

General Principles of Graphical Presentation

It will be worthwhile summarising at this stage the general principles involved in presenting management information in graphical form:

- Diagrams are useful at giving a quick, easy-to-understand overview of general patterns, trends and distributions.
- Diagrams almost inevitably involve some loss of accuracy and detail from the original data.
- Determine at the outset what you are trying to show by using a particular diagram.
- Experiment with different types of diagram to assess which makes the most impact in a reasonably accurate way.
- Do not try to put too much information on to one diagram. Two simpler diagrams are inevitably better than one more complicated diagram. Keep it simple.
- Ensure that the technical details of the diagram – scales, axes, labels and the like – are both appropriate and easy to understand.

Worked Example

To show how we might use these techniques we shall develop a fully worked example. We can visualise a scenario where a national chain of small, high street supermarkets is reviewing its customer service strategy. As part of this review the chain is considering installing cash dispensers (ATMs) in its most popular stores as an added customer facility. It is considering doing this partly in response to its larger competitors, who already have such ATMs, and partly to gain a competitive advantage over other small stores, which do not. The logic behind this is that people may start using such ATMs as a convenience and, while in the store, purchase products on display. The director of business development has asked for a short – and concise – summary of the current situation with regard to ATMs in the UK as a whole. We have been able to obtain the data in Table 3.11.

We see that the number of ATMs around the country has increased from 44 000 in 2003 to 62 000 in 2007. Similarly, the number of transactions taking place (with a transaction being someone using the ATM) has steadily increased, as has the value of those transactions. The amount of money withdrawn from the available ATMs has increased from £74 billion in 2003 to over £108 billion in 2007. Even allowing for inflation this is indicative of considerably increased use.

Since we are required to provide an overview of the situation, a small number of diagrams and supporting statistics is probably most appropriate. Since we are dealing with data over time then line graphs or possibly bar charts will be the most appropriate. Like

Table 3.11	ATM data, UK, 2003–2007		
Year	No. of machines (thousands)	No. of transactions (millions)	Value of transactions (£bn)
2003	44	2228	73.5
2004	52	2455	85.1
2005	56	2481	95.0
2006	59	2614	102.6
2007	62	2746	108.1

Source: www.link.co.uk

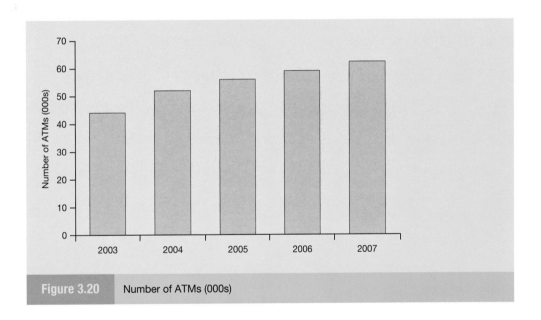

| Figure 3.20 | Number of ATMs (000s) |

much data presentation we shall need to adopt a trial-and-error approach – trying different diagrams to see which looks most useful. Figure 3.20 shows a simple bar chart for the number of ATMs over this period. The graph is moderately useful, showing the steady increase in numbers over the last five years. Clearly, we cannot sensibly use multiple bar charts for the different series since they have radically different numerical scales. We might, however, use a line graph with two Y scales to show trends in both the number of machines and the number of transactions, as in Figure 3.21. Although we must be careful in our interpretation because of the differing Y scales, there appears to be a strong connection between the two series, with both showing a strong upward trend. We can confirm this with a scatter plot, as in Figure 3.22, which shows the strong correlation between the two series.

As the number of ATMs has increased, so has the level of use as shown by the number of transactions. Clearly, levels of use of ATMs are rising almost in proportion to the number there are. We can examine this further through some simple calculations. We

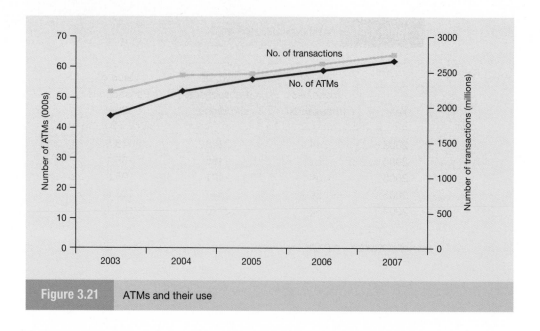

Figure 3.21   ATMs and their use

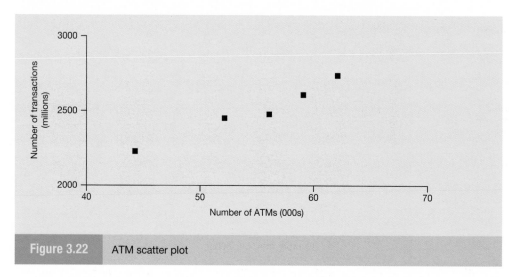

Figure 3.22   ATM scatter plot

can readily work out the average number of transactions per ATM by dividing the number of transactions in a year by the number of ATMs (taking care over the units of measurement). So, in 2003 there were a total of 2228 million transactions on the available 44 000 ATMs. Hence we have 2 228 000 000/44 000 to give 50 636 as the average number of transactions per ATM in that year. That is, on average, each ATM was used just over 50 000 times each year. Comparable calculations for the other years allow us to produce Figure 3.23, which shows that the average number of transactions per ATM has fallen from around 53 000 in 2003 to around 43 000 in the last three years. Clearly, we do not know from this data why this has happened but we might speculate that the ATM network may have reached a plateau in terms of size and customer use.

It may also be worthwhile calculating two further sets of statistics: the average transaction value per ATM and the average value per transaction. The first will provide an indication of how much cash is withdrawn from each machine in a year. The second will indicate how much on average people withdraw each time they use the machine.

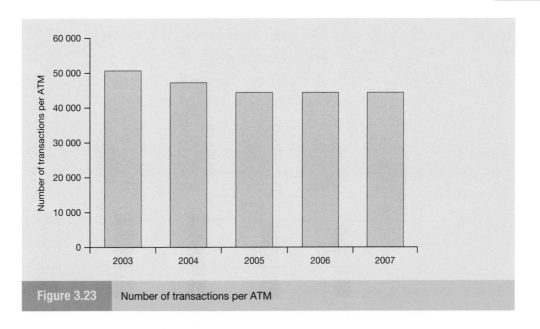

Figure 3.23   Number of transactions per ATM

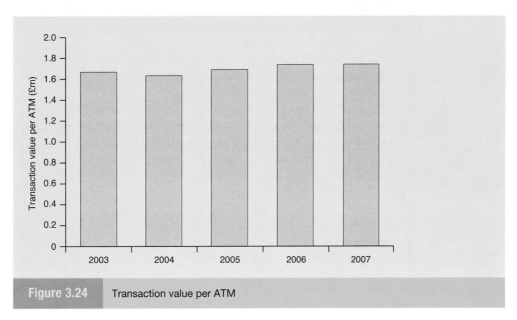

Figure 3.24   Transaction value per ATM

Figures 3.24 and 3.25 show the results. We see from Figure 3.24 that the average amount withdrawn from each ATM in a year rose from about £1.7 million in 2003 to about £1.75 million in 2007. Interestingly, however, from Figure 3.25 (which shows average value per transaction and the total transaction value in each year) the value of the average transaction (the average amount withdrawn each time an ATM is used) has changed relatively little from £33 in 2003 to £40 in 2007, even though the total amount withdrawn from all ATMs has steadily increased. This again implies that there is increasing use of the ATMs, in terms of either more people using each machine or more frequent use of each machine. Either way, potentially this could help the super-market chain because, if people are coming into the store to get cash from the ATMs, there will presumably be an opportunity to encourage them to buy products from the store.

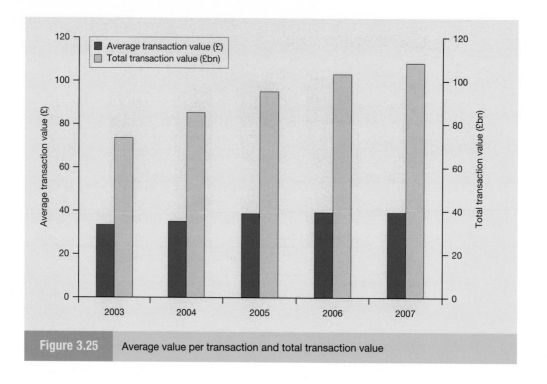

| Figure 3.25 | Average value per transaction and total transaction value |

Naturally, such analysis is relatively superficial and would need to be investigated further, supported by more detailed analysis. However, a few diagrams and some simple calculations allow us to provide a quick overview of the situation. In conclusion, for a report to the director, we might wish to use Figures 3.21 and 3.25, supplemented with a paragraph of text outlining the key findings and their potential implications as we have done here.

 ## Summary

Now we have completed this chapter we hope you are convinced that the production of diagrams and graphs is a useful skill for any manager to develop. Every manager should be spending some time assessing the current situation in the context of their own area of responsibility, keeping an eye on performance, changing circumstances and the like. Diagrams – particularly when supported with computer-based information systems and suitable graphical software – are a quick and easy way to examine data for such patterns and trends. Equally managers are frequently called upon to present information to other managers or to employees. Skills in developing an appropriate presentation are obviously essential.

However, we cannot end this chapter without a reminder of the danger of relying solely on graphical presentations. As you will be aware, graphs can give a misleading picture of the situation – either accidentally or deliberately. This might be because we have chosen the wrong sort of diagram or the wrong numerical scale. We should remember that such diagrams are intended only as the first step in the business analysis approach.

Useful online resources

Detailed below are some internet resources that may be useful. Many have further links to other sites. An updated version is available from the accompanying website (**www.pearsoned.co.uk/wisniewski**). In addition, I would be grateful for details of other websites that have been found to be useful.

> **www.bettycjung.net/Graphing.htm** – Charting and graphing data
>
> **www.windmill.co.uk/xlchart.html** – Excel charting tips
>
> **www.mathleague.com/help/data/data.htm** – Charting data
>
> **http://lilt.ilstu.edu/gmklass/pos138/datadisplay/badchart.htm** – How to produce bad charts and graphs
>
> **www.bized.co.uk/timeweb/buffing/buff_picture_expl.htm** – Different chart types explained
>
> **http://en.wikipedia.org/wiki/Bar_chart** – Wikipedia article on bar charts
>
> **http://openlearn.open.ac.uk/mod/resource/view.php?id=210663** – Working with bar charts and histograms
>
> **http://en.wikipedia.org/wiki/Pie_chart** – Wikipedia article on pie charts
>
> **www.netmba.com/statistics/histogram/** – Article on histograms
>
> **http://cnx.org/content/m10214/latest/** – Article on frequency polygons
>
> **http://syque.com/quality_tools/tools/TOOLS18.htm** – Article on Z charts

QMDM IN ACTION
Cowie Health Centre, Scotland

The National Health Service (NHS) in the UK has been in existence since 1948 and at some time or another provides a service to every person in the country. It has a budget of over £30 billion and directly employs over 1 million people with countless private sector companies dependent on doing business with some part of the NHS – from catering to high-tech medical equipment. Expenditure on the NHS has grown considerably since its creation in 1948 and the range and quality of services provided have expanded beyond the imagination of its creators.

Perhaps not surprisingly, given the size of its annual budget, there has been increasing concern expressed by the government at the services provided in terms of their range, their extent, their quality and their value for money. Since the 1980s, the government has initiated a number of major (and minor) changes in the way parts of the NHS operate, are funded and provide a service to the public. One particular area has been one aspect of service in the primary-care sector. For most people, their first contact point with the NHS when seeking some treatment or diagnosis will be their family doctor: the GP or general practitioner. All citizens are registered with a specific GP, who may provide a service on an individual basis or on a group basis with other GPs. In many cases GPs form the front line in terms of health care, providing treatment or some medical service directly to the patient or referring the patient to another part of the NHS system where appropriate. The financial funding that GPs receive for providing such treatment and medical services arises from a complex system. To oversimplify, GPs receive an annual *per capita* amount for every patient registered (regardless of what that patient requires in terms of treatment through the year) and also payments for specific treatments provided to individual patients.

One area of medical service provided by GPs relates to cervical screening in adult women. The purpose of such screening is to monitor any changes occurring in the cervix. This facilitates the detection of cancers at an early stage when they are most treatable, although it must be remembered that the incidence of such cancers in the general female population is relatively low (around 15 per 100 000) and that the majority of such cancers are treatable. The screening process typically involves a short consultation with the GP and, as part of this, a sample of cells will be taken from the surface of the cervix. These cells are then placed on to a specimen slide, which is sent to a specialist laboratory for examination. The slide is examined by laboratory staff and the results reported back to the GP. Any reported abnormalities require further examination to be undertaken, whereas normal results are reported back to the patient, who is advised to attend for another screening test in three to five years' time. Naturally such a screening process is meant to be carried out on a mass basis to be properly effective and, in the past, concern has been expressed at the take-up rate among women of such screening facilities. Typically, as with this type of health care service, such a screening facility tends to attract those who are least at risk, whereas those who could benefit most from the service tend to have low usage rates. It has been reported, for example, that nine out of every ten women who die from cervical cancer have never had such a smear test conducted, while a study in inner London revealed that around 50 per cent of women were too frightened to come forward to be tested.

To try to encourage a higher take-up of the screening service among women, GPs have been offered incentives to publicise such services and attract more women to them. Such incentives have

taken the form of a 'bonus' payment to GPs when at least 80 per cent of eligible women on the GP's register have been screened in this way. GPs who do not meet this target simply receive a *per capita* fee for each screening test conducted.

Cowie Health Centre in Scotland is a GP practice with four GPs providing a health care service to a population of over 3000 in a large village and the immediate surrounding area. The catchment area for the practice is one with relatively high levels of social deprivation and is affected by the problems that come with this. In such an area the take-up of preventive health care initiatives – such as cervical screening – tends to be lower than average. The staff in the centre had expressed concern about the take-up rate for the cervical screening service provided, and in early 1991 a more rigorous system was put into place to try to improve the take-up rate. The new system took advantage of regular computer printouts supplied by the local health authority responsible for undertaking the examination of the cell samples. These printouts provided details of those patients who had had a test conducted and those who should have had a test conducted (on the basis of the test being repeated every three to five years) but had not. Combined with this, the centre instituted its own monitoring system and began sending reminder letters to patients who should be having a test conducted over the next few months. Figure 3.26 shows the number of screening tests conducted from April 1990 to March 1993 on a monthly basis. (The 'year' begins in April for the centre. It should also be noted that the figures shown have been adjusted by a constant value to maintain confidentiality. This does not affect the overall patterns and trends observed.)

The centre felt that the new approach and systems were gradually having an impact in terms of increasing the number of patients who were attending for their next screening test. With the introduction of financial changes in terms of payments systems, however, it also became important for the centre to monitor the number of tests conducted in relation to the annual target of 80 per cent required to trigger the bonus payments. The use of a Z chart through the year enables their monitoring to be conducted effectively. Figure 3.27 shows the target line

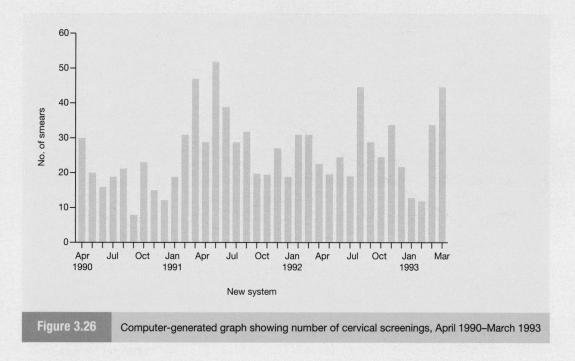

Figure 3.26 Computer-generated graph showing number of cervical screenings, April 1990–March 1993

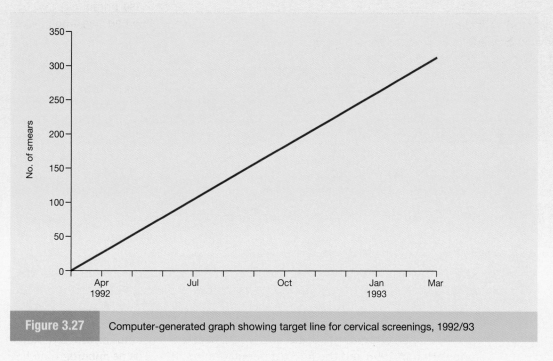

Figure 3.27 Computer-generated graph showing target line for cervical screenings, 1992/93

from the Z chart for 1992/3 and Figure 3.28 shows the Z chart at the end of January. It is clear from the Z chart at this date in the year that the overall target is in danger of not being achieved. In the first few months of the year the number of tests was slightly under target. However, this was followed by several months where performance improved and by October all looked well. However, from the top line of the chart it is evident that October saw the beginning of a downward trend in the monthly number of

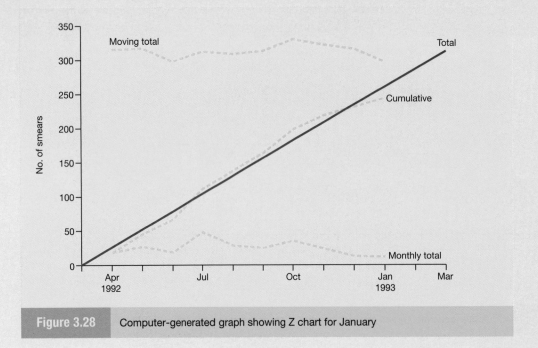

Figure 3.28   Computer-generated graph showing Z chart for January

tests. Clearly, as of January, a concerted effort would have to be made to achieve the annual target required, an aspect of performance clearly high-lighted by use of the Z chart.

The centre did, in fact, meet its target by the end of the year.

I am grateful to the doctors and staff at Cowie Health Centre for the information supplied for this QMDM in action.

 Exercises

1   One of the NHS health boards in Scotland, covering the geographical area of Fife, is currently undertaking a review of its health care services and has asked you to present a short briefing to its senior managers on one aspect of its services. This relates to the anticipated demographic trends over the next few years. Data has been obtained both for the board and for the whole of Scotland on the estimated population in 1998 and the forecast population to 2013. The population data has been broken into different age groups as shown in Table 3.12. Note that the age group 16 to 64 includes females to the age of 60 and males to the age of 64, and the group 65 to 74 includes females from the age of 60 and males from the age of 65.

You are required to prepare a short briefing for senior managers indicating the major changes likely to take place over this period. Use suitable diagrams and additional calculations to help your presentation.

| Table 3.12 | Population by age group |

	Age group (years)					
	Under 5	5 to 14	15 to 64	65 to 74	75 and over	Total
Fife						
1998	21 245	44 325	228 165	30 600	24 565	348 900
2003	19 062	42 507	230 537	30 358	26 304	348 768
2008	18 763	39 484	232 374	31 492	27 057	349 170
2013	18 813	38 252	227 797	36 316	28 423	349 601
Scotland						
1998	316 213	634 411	3 385 235	441 839	342 302	5 120 000
2003	284 776	619 818	3 398 753	439 740	354 230	5 097 317
2008	276 553	578 367	3 406 197	445 857	366 880	5 073 854
2013	271 243	556 070	3 345 275	491 859	383 711	5 048 158

Source: Scottish Health Statistics.
Data available in file 3X1.

2 The board has also obtained supplementary information about the financial costs typically involved in providing health care for people of different ages. On a *per capita* basis the costs are as shown in Table 3.13.

   Although this data relates to England and Wales, the board feels it would be useful to consider the financial implications of expected demographic patterns, given the absence of such financial information for Scotland. You are required to present a second briefing outlining the financial implications of the demographic changes.

| Table 3.13 | *Per capita* costs for health care provision |

Age group	Estimated gross spending per person (£s per head, 1985 prices)
Under 5 years	320
5 to 15	215
16 to 64	180
65 to 74	575
75 and over	1420

Source: Hansard.

3 Table 3.14 shows the UK gross public expenditure on bilateral aid for the financial years 1997/8 to 2005/6 by geographical region of the recipient country.

   Using appropriate diagrams, draft a short report highlighting key patterns and trends.

| Table 3.14 | Total bilateral gross public expenditure on aid by recipient region (£ thousands) |

	1997/8	1998/9	1999/2000	2000/1	2001/2	2002/3	2003/4	2004/5	2005/6
Africa	450 076	574 289	631 475	783 332	879 084	871 018	1 060 942	1 270 918	2 405 795
America	271 336	170 125	239 831	183 828	170 274	216 550	105 875	126 093	85 383
Asia	391 763	349 939	381 890	422 557	545 264	619 917	969 302	1 243 777	1 356 165
Europe	114 537	83 171	191 891	114 155	98 214	384 745	74 871	62 344	90 194
Pacific	26 890	20 251	7 248	5 134	7 042	5 578	4 484	3 272	3 823
Unallocated to a specific region	184 081	181 943	205 694	266 842	303 953	379 074	382 481	405 310	460 378
Total	1 438 683	1 379 718	1 658 029	1 775 848	2 003 831	2 476 882	2 597 955	3 111 714	4 401 738

Source: Annual Abstract of Statistics.

4   Table 3.15 shows the production of passenger cars in the UK by engine size for the period 1980 to 2006.

Using appropriate diagrams comment on the trends in production over this period.

| Table 3.15 | Motor vehicle production: UK, 1980–2006 |

Year	1000 cc and less	1000 cc but less than 1600 cc	1600 cc but less than 2800 cc	2800 cc or more	Total passenger cars
1980	156 735	521 933	209 635	35 441	923 744
1981	229 189	526 498	153 957	45 006	954 650
1982	197 153	547 676	97 536	45 314	887 679
1983	194 064	723 289	77 504	49 740	1 044 597
1984	161 884	637 868	56 587	52 567	908 906
1985	183 383	694 876	109 437	60 277	1 047 973
1986	162 090	665 093	134 802	56 977	1 018 962
1987	153 214	718 046	205 067	66 356	1 142 683
1988	129 446	764 289	260 231	72 869	1 226 835
1989	133 135	716 784	375 309	73 854	1 299 082
1990	93 039	809 219	325 116	68 236	1 295 610
1991	26 621	830 530	338 877	40 872	1 236 900
1992	22 037	793 307	437 951	38 585	1 291 880
1993	98 034	709 615	515 487	52 388	1 375 524
1994	98 178	729 397	573 357	65 891	1 466 823
1995	95 198	814 873	528 444	93 569	1 532 084
1996	108 645	845 084	635 861	96 544	1 686 134
1997	119 894	829 079	653 147	95 881	1 698 001
1998	112 044	814 595	720 556	101 063	1 748 258
1999	113 204	776 111	758 478	138 830	1 786 623
2000	96 043	676 438	723 294	145 677	1 641 452
2001	93 695	632 747	634 573	131 350	1 492 365
2002	79 545	711 553	720 067	118 579	1 629 744
2003	23 985	750 840	740 486	142 247	1 657 558
2004	15 471	796 174	690 759	144 346	1 646 750
2005	6 111	854 687	546 744	188 155	1 595 697
2006	0	792 187	446 143	203 755	1 442 085

Source: Annual Abstract of Statistics.
Data available in file 3X4.

5 Obtain data for the level of passenger car imports and exports and compare these with UK car production over the period 1980–2006.

6 Table 3.16 shows the rates of unemployment by region in the period 1996 to 2006. Compare the patterns of unemployment across the UK.

Table 3.16	Unemployment rates by region, 1993–2006

	1996	1997	1998	1999	2000	2001	2002	2003	2004	2005	2006
England (by region)											
North East	10.8	9.8	8.1	10.1	9.1	7.4	6.9	6.6	5.5	6.8	6.1
North West	8.4	6.8	6.6	6.2	5.3	5.4	5.7	5.1	4.4	4.4	5.3
Yorkshire and											
Humberside	8.1	8.0	7.0	6.5	6.0	5.2	5.5	5.5	4.6	4.8	5.7
East Midlands	7.4	6.3	4.9	5.2	5.1	5.0	4.3	4.3	4.2	4.2	5.4
West Midlands	9.2	6.8	6.3	6.8	6.2	5.2	5.7	5.9	5.5	4.7	5.7
East	6.1	5.8	5.0	4.1	3.6	3.8	3.7	4.2	3.8	3.9	5.0
South East	6.0	5.2	4.3	3.6	3.3	3.2	4.0	3.9	3.7	3.8	4.7
South West	6.3	5.2	4.5	4.7	4.1	3.7	3.7	3.9	3.7	3.2	3.7
Wales	8.3	8.3	6.7	7.0	6.1	6.2	6.2	4.6	4.2	4.6	5.7
Scotland	8.7	8.5	7.4	7.4	7.6	5.9	6.9	5.7	6.0	5.4	5.4
Northern Ireland	9.5	7.5	7.2	7.2	7.0	6.3	5.6	5.4	5.1	4.9	4.2

Source: Monthly Digest of Statistics.
Data available in file 3X8.

7 Table 3.17 shows the distribution of household income in 2003/04 to 2005/06 for two geographical areas in the UK. Using diagrams compare these distributions.

Table 3.17	Distribution of household income

	Under £150	£150 < £250	£250 < £350	£350 < £450	£450 < £600	£600 < £750	£750 < £1000	Over £1000
		Percentage of households in each weekly income group						
London	14	11	8	8	10	10	12	25
Scotland	13	15	13	10	15	10	12	12

Source: Regional Trends.
Data available in file 3X7.

8   Table 3.18 shows data on the distribution of incomes before and after tax in the UK in 2000/01. Using Lorenz curves analyse the data shown.

Table 3.18		Incomes before and after tax in the UK, 2000/01			

Income before tax (£s)			No. of individuals (000s)	Income before tax (£m)	Income after tax (£m)
4 895	<	6 000	1 160	6 310	6 240
6 000	<	7 000	1 120	7 300	7 120
7 000	<	8 000	1 420	10 700	10 300
8 000	<	10 000	2 920	26 200	24 800
10 000	<	12 000	2 810	30 900	28 400
12 000	<	15 000	3 750	50 600	45 200
15 000	<	20 000	5 120	89 000	77 300
20 000	<	30 000	6 200	152 000	128 000
30 000	<	50 000	4 540	170 000	140 000
50 000	<	70 000	1 020	59 100	45 000
70 000	<	100 000	482	39 700	28 700
100 000	<	200 000	366	49 300	34 000
200 000	<	500 000	113	32 700	21 600
500 000	<	1 000 000	22	14 700	9 510
1 000 000 or over			9	18 500	11 900

Source: *Annual Abstract of Statistics.*
Data available in file 3X8.

9   A local authority operates a leisure centre for its citizens, offering a swimming pool, squash courts, badminton and other facilities on a single site. Last year the authority was concerned about the relatively low number of people using the facilities on a daily basis and as a result started to advertise the facilities more widely in the local media. Data was collected before the media campaign on the number of people using the facilities each day over an eight-week period. A similar data collection exercise has taken place after the campaign. The results are shown in Tables 3.19 and 3.20.

Table 3.19		Daily number of users pre media campaign					
213	225	237	262	281	299	173	208
221	229	255	276	295	179	173	179
312	189	204	214	228	189	231	226
248	262	186	302	204	206	221	227
255	276	295	214	173	197	189	204
214	228	174	231	252	237	262	281
278	317	208	221	229	255	276	295

Table 3.20	Daily number of users post media campaign					
299	317	337	363	381	281	262
255	276	295	312	334	359	377
284	272	259	241	228	214	204
208	223	238	249	270	287	301
313	329	262	255	204	208	223
214	276	281	299	295	228	238
249	241	311	316	262	312	214
270	287	301	313	314	300	301

Data available in file 3X9.

Note: the data in both tables are in no meaningful order and have been taken for two eight-week periods which are directly comparable.

You have been asked to draft a short report, highlighting the key changes in users that have occurred, using frequency tables and related diagrams.

10   Table 3.21 shows data for the UK on personal disposable income (PDI) and consumers' expenditure across several categories. Using this data, produce a scatter diagram of PDI and each consumers' expenditure category in turn. Comment on the expected relationship between each pair of variables and that actually observed.

Table 3.21	Household disposable income and consumers' expenditure (£m at 2003 prices)			
		Consumers' expenditure		
	Household disposable income	Food and drink	Alcohol and tobacco	Restaurants and hotels
1986	443 119	32 264	12 174	25 210
1987	459 426	34 482	12 649	27 225
1988	484 677	36 539	13 258	33 422
1989	507 327	39 305	13 755	37 200
1990	524 633	42 285	14 753	40 603
1991	535 207	44 576	16 204	42 077
1992	550 737	45 683	16 996	43 066
1993	565 147	47 171	17 697	46 170
1994	573 521	47 795	18 359	48 098
1995	588 514	49 700	18 776	50 381
1996	602 417	53 025	20 439	55 021
1997	625 184	53 787	21 553	57 164
1998	634 508	55 162	22 459	61 807
1999	652 060	57 040	24 458	64 387
2000	681 249	58 628	24 613	68 557
2001	710 531	59 804	25 158	71 620
2002	722 823	61 310	25 966	76 420
2003	740 389	63 174	27 297	78 902
2004	752 890	65 521	27 713	83 595
2005	768 612	66 979	28 029	88 687

Source: Economic Trends Annual Supplement.
Data available in file 3X10.

4 Management Statistics

Learning objectives

By the end of this chapter you should:

- appreciate the need for management statistics
- be able to calculate the more common types of statistics
- be able to understand and explain the principles of such statistics
- be able to assess the information such statistics provide

In Chapter 3 we saw the usefulness of presenting information visually in the form of tables and a variety of diagrams. Such methods allow the manager to gain a quick impression of the key characteristics of the data under examination. It will be apparent, however, that these presentation methods are not by themselves sufficient for business decision making. Having gained an impression of the overall characteristics of some set of data, we must examine the data in more detail – to develop a more precise, quantitative description of the data. In this chapter we begin this process of closer examination by introducing a number of management statistics.

A Business Example

In the last chapter, we covered a detailed example relating to a sample of profit centres in a retail organisation taken from two different regions. We saw through a variety of diagrams that there are differences in the two sets of data and we began to describe what those differences are. However, our comments have been fairly general and somewhat imprecise. We concluded that with Region B stores there were relatively fewer at the bottom of the profits range and relatively more at the top of the range. For management purposes this is somewhat imprecise, to say the least. Given the management interest in this variable, we clearly need to quantify the differences between the two samples. For this reason we must turn to statistical measures to describe the data rather than diagrammatic measures.

The overall purpose of this chapter is to introduce some of the more common management statistics, not with the intention of turning you into a statistician but to enable you to assess the usefulness – or otherwise – of such statistical information in a decision-making context. After all, if you are presented with statistical information relating to a business problem you need to be able to assess its relevance to the decisions you may have to take. It must be said, however, that the only real way of being able to assess the potential usefulness of statistical information is to have a basic understanding of how such statistics are calculated. Furthermore, today, such statistics are calculated using appropriate computer technology so that, increasingly, a manager does not need to apply some poorly understood statistical formula to obtain a numerical result. However, the computer cannot (as yet) interpret or evaluate such statistical information on your behalf. We shall return later to our continuing example of retail stores' performance. For the time being, however, we shall illustrate the principles of the statistics we need with a different – and smaller – example.

Consider the following. A National Health Service (NHS) hospital in the UK is under increasing pressure to improve its performance. On the one hand the hospital is expected to increase the number of patients receiving treatment in order to reduce waiting lists, and on the other is expected to maintain or improve the quality of health care provided to patients. To make the management task more difficult, it is expected to achieve this with – at best – the same quantity of resources: staff, finance, equipment and so on. The hospital manager has been examining one particular area of medical care provided by the hospital – that is, treatment for one particular illness or complaint. The exact area of care is irrelevant for our purposes but let us assume that it requires patients to be admitted to hospital for an operation, the operation to be carried out, the patient looked after in hospital until they are well enough to be discharged and return home. Last month the hospital's statistician investigated the patients who had been discharged from the hospital and calculated that these patients – 11 in total – had an average length of stay (LOS) in the hospital of 10 days. That is, on average, a patient would spend 10 days from entry into the hospital to discharge back home. This month, after a concerted effort by the hospital to improve performance in this area, the statistician has calculated that for patients discharged this month – again 11 in total – average LOS has fallen to eight days.

Activity 4.1

Why do you think a reduction in LOS would be seen, in management terms, as an improvement in performance, all other things being equal? Based on these statistics would you conclude that, in this area of health care, the hospital has 'improved' its performance?

Why are Statistics Needed?

In general terms you can probably see that – all else being equal – a shorter LOS implies the hospital will require fewer resources to treat an individual patient and, with a shorter LOS, has the possibility of treating more patients with the same resource base. After all, for every day a patient spends in the hospital this implies a hospital bed is being used (that could be used by a newly admitted patient), staff resources are devoted to caring for this patient, catering resources are being used and so on. Equally, it is probably the case for most patients that they would prefer to be in and out of the hospital as quickly as possible, so a shorter LOS would probably be seen as an improvement in 'quality' from their perspective. It is also tempting to conclude that the hospital has improved performance given that LOS has fallen between the two months by two days on average.

However, on reflection, we might wish to be a little more cautious. Exactly what do we mean by an average? Are we implying that last month *every* patient had an LOS of exactly 10 days and that this month *every* patient had an LOS of eight? Clearly these are important questions, given that the statistics may be used by the manager to make important decisions, and it is not an ideal situation for the manager to have to rely on the statistician's evaluation of this information. You will probably realise that the averages by themselves probably make us ask more questions rather than answer existing ones. In particular, one aspect to the average that we need to resolve relates to how well it represents what happened to the typical patient. In fact, in statistical terms, there are usually two aspects to such descriptive statistics we need to consider:

● some measure of an average value
● some measure of variability around this average.

Consider the hospital manager's position. The manager may well be considering using this information for resource allocation purposes. Assume, for example, that the cost of keeping one patient in the hospital for one day is £1000 – the cost of providing medical and nursing care, drugs and medicine, catering provision, laundry and so on. If we anticipate an average LOS of eight days then this implies that we should allocate £8000 per patient to this part of the hospital. However, since we are not (yet) sure whether all patients stay exactly eight days – and this seems unlikely – we would need to make some allowance for possible variation in the LOS. After all, if one patient stays two or three days longer than the average this will increase health care costs. So, an average by itself is of little use. We also need some way of assessing the variability of patients' stay around the average. If we know the average is eight days, can we somehow determine what a typical variation around this average was? Did patients typically have an LOS that varied from this average by only, say, one day or was the variability five days? The difference in management terms is obviously important.

Measures of Average

The arithmetic mean

We shall first examine the concept of an average in the context of our example. Consider the data shown in Table 4.1.

Table 4.1	Duration of stay (days): Month 1									
5	9	6	6	9	8	9	6	38	5	9

This (fictitious) data relates to the NHS hospital for Month 1 and shows how long the 11 patients who were discharged from hospital that month had been in the hospital. We see, for example, that two patients had been in the hospital for five days before discharge, three for six days, one for eight days, four for nine days and one for 38 days.

Activity 4.2

Calculate an average LOS for these 11 patients. How 'good' an average is this?

Most people know how to calculate an average without any knowledge of statistics. What you probably did was simply to add the 11 numbers together and divide by 11 to get an average of 10 days:

Total number of days = 110

Number of patients   = 11

Average LOS $= \dfrac{110}{11} = 10$ days

In fact a statistician would refer to this average as the *arithmetic mean* for, as we shall see soon, there are different averages that can be calculated for the same set of data. In short we can express this calculation as a simple formula. If we denote x as the individual numbers – the items of data – and n as the number of data items, then our calculation becomes:

$$\text{Mean} = \frac{\Sigma x}{n}$$

where Σx refers to the summation (total) of all the x values (go back and read the section on summation in Chapter 2 if you're not sure what this means). However, on reflection, you have probably realised that the mean value of 10 days is not a particularly 'good' measure of average in this case. Ten out of the 11 patients were in fact discharged *before* the mean LOS and it is the one patient who had a (relatively) long LOS who is dragging the average above the majority of values. This is an important point. If the hospital manager simply has a single statistic – the mean LOS (i.e. the number 10) – there is no way of knowing from this whether it is a typical or representative value. We are only able here to comment on its 'reliability' because we have access to the original data and can see the original figures and how they compare to the mean of 10 days. Frequently this will not be the case and we obviously require supplementary statistics to allow us to come to the same conclusion. We shall introduce these shortly. Consider now Table 4.2, which shows comparable data for Month 2.

Table 4.2	Duration of stay (days): Month 2								
1	10	9	10	9	9	10	9	1	10	10

The mean would be:

$$\text{Mean} = \frac{\Sigma x}{n}$$

$$= \frac{88}{11}$$

$$= 8 \text{ days}$$

Once again, however, the mean is not really representative of the data in the set. This time nine out of 11 patients stayed *longer* than the average, although it must be said that most of the actual LOS figures appear closer to the mean for Month 2 than is the case in Month 1. However, consider our original question: has the hospital improved performance as measured by LOS between Month 1 and Month 2? The mean values by themselves imply that it has, although access to the original data indicates that we need to be more cautious about our conclusion.

The median

The arithmetic mean is, therefore, not necessarily a representative indication of an average for a set of data. As we mentioned earlier, there are other measures of average that can be calculated for the same set of data. One of these is the *median*. The median is a measure of average representing the middle value of a set of data which has been ordered (ranked from lowest value through to highest). Frequently the median will differ in value from the mean and this difference may tell us something about the variability within the data. To determine the median for Month 1 we must rank the data. This would give:

5   5   6   6   6   8   9   9   9   9   38

We are seeking the middle value which, since we have 11 items, must correspond to item six in the array. The middle value in this array then corresponds to eight days, which we now call the median. Consider what we can now infer about the set of data – even if we have not seen the original data. Given that the median LOS is eight days, this implies we had an equal number of patients (five in this case) below the median value as above. We know, therefore, that five of the 11 patients were discharged before the median LOS and five of the 11 discharged after (although without the raw data we do not know how much before or after the median). This is something of an improvement over the mean, which gives no indication of how many of the data items fall above or below the mean value. Consider also for this set of data that the median – at eight days – is less than the mean – at 10. What can we infer from this? We know that the mean by definition includes all the data items – including any extreme values. The median,

Investors beware of partisan promises

Truly independent analysis of 3G business models is a rare thing, says Dan Roberts

One sure sign of a bear market is the proliferation of doom and gloom merchants. The once unshakeable mobile phone industry is no exception, particularly since Europe's third-generation licence auctions saddled most operators with mountains of debt.

Unfortunately, independent analysis of 3G business models is rather thin on the ground. To pay off all their debt, operators have employed armies of investment bankers to sell fresh equity and re-finance loans. Nearly every large bank is involved and the quantity of truly independent analysis has nose-dived.

All this has placed a premium on the handful of industry consultants, such as Forrester Research, able to offer a non-partisan view. Its latest conclusions are dramatic.

"A 15 per cent drop in average revenue per user by 2005 will destroy profits, unleashing major business failures and industry consolidation," predicts analyst Lars Godell.

To make matters worse, when mobile operators default on debt payments, European bond markets will implode, forcing the European Central Bank to raise interest rates in response and thus weakening the euro and the 2 per cent of European gross domestic product derived from mobiles.

Even Forrester admits that macro-economic forecasting is not its strong suit, but the analysis that leads up to this scenario is compelling.

Mr Godell's thesis is that the days of steadily rising revenues from voice calls are over, while the promised explosion in internet and

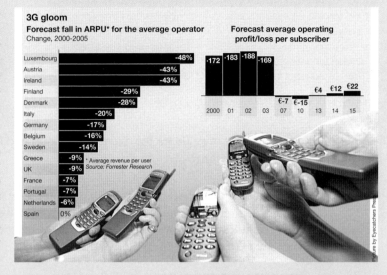

data traffic will not be enough to offset higher 3G operating costs.

It is easy to see why operators should be worried about traditional sources of growth. Yesterday's fourth-quarter subscriber figures from Orange and its new parent, France Telecom, suggest the Christmas sales boom has left two-thirds of the UK population owning a mobile. Penetration rates are even higher in countries such as Sweden and Italy, while Germany and France are catching up fast.

Given that few infants or pensioners use mobiles and that most of us can have only one conversation at once, 80 per cent penetration seems the upper limit.

People use phones for longer as prices continue to fall and average revenue per user (ARPU) has so far continued to grow.

However, 3G auctions have introduced a series of operators and caused others to consider selling wholesale airtime to so-called virtual network operators. Forrester estimates the proliferation

of new suppliers chasing dwindling numbers of phoneless will cause a price war that will devastate ARPU and profit margins.

The trend should be particularly acute in countries where the ratio of networks to adults is higher, but even big markets such as Germany expect fierce price competition with several new entrants.

This will not be news to most operators already coping with tough price competition. What is surprising is how far the analysis suggests ARPU has to fall and how quickly this can hit profits.

After interviewing executives at 26 operators, Forrester concluded revenues per customer from voice and text messaging will fall 36 per cent in five years' time to Euros 313m ($297m).

Meanwhile, growth in access calls and subscription fees from internet-enabled phones will not be enough – up from an average of Euros 1 per user today to Euros 73 by 2005. Revenues from internet content fees, e-commerce, advertising and location-based services will grow steadily from about Euros 0.60 per user today to Euros 33.45 in 2005.

If true, operating profits will disappear in 2007 and take six years to return, forcing all new entrants out of business and leaving just five pan-European groups.

Understandably, this conclusion is fiercely rejected by operators – particularly by new entrants, such as Hutchison in the UK, which point out that it is unfair to judge their business model on the basis of how existing operators are faring.

However, Forrester's report will be interesting next to the positive research expected next week from banks involved in the initial public offering of Orange.

With so much uncertainty over the effect of internet revenues on the overall business model, investors may have to adjust to the fact that 3G will not be the icing on the cake; more the uncertain trial of a whole new recipe.

Source: *Financial Times*, 5 January 2001.

The article discusses 'average revenue for the average operator' and its implications for the industry. Which measure of average, though?

however, simply counts along the ordered data until it gets to the middle. Extreme high values are therefore ignored. Since the mean is above the median and since the mean must include all the data it follows that there must be (at least) one extreme value in the data set to pull the mean above the median.

Activity 4.3

Consider the data item of 38 days. Assume this is a clerical error and should be 48 days. What would you expect to happen to the mean and median values? Determine the median for Month 2. Comparing the two medians as measures of average, what would you now say about the hospital's performance in Months 1 and 2?

Solution is given on p 584.

The median for Month 2 is nine days and we begin to see why, in some ways, statistics has the reputation it does. We could legitimately say that the hospital's performance has improved, since average LOS has fallen by two days (from 10 to eight if we use the mean). We could equally say it has worsened, since average LOS has increased (from eight to nine days if we use the median). Of course, we now know that we should really refer to the statistics as the mean and median rather than the average, and that they show slightly different aspects of the same data.

The catch in using City earnings data

By Chris Giles, Economics Editor

Annual earnings for the average full-time worker in the City of London in the year to April were £46,260, but pay levels were so un-equal that if the total amount paid to full-time staff was distributed evenly, each would earn £85,539.

The Office for National Statistics figures, based on a one in 100 sample of all employees, show average wages in the City are the highest in any local authority and twice the UK average.

The scale of the disparities, however, mean that the growth of average City pay in April 2006 compared with a year earlier depends entirely on whether the median or the mean is used.

Median pay for full-time City staff, including bonuses – the annual earnings of the worker right in the middle of the pay league – was only 2.8 per cent higher than in 2005, less than the 3 per cent increase in UK median pay.

The "arithmetic mean" – dividing the total amount of money paid to City employees by the number of staff – was 15.6 per cent higher, driven by huge bonuses for the richest City employees. The mean pay of full-time City men was 21 per cent higher than a year earlier.

Economists and policy-makers argue over which is the right average to use and there is broad agreement that the answer depends on what the figures will be used for. When the Bank of England, estate agents or retailers want to know the purchasing power of workers in the City or the country as a whole, the mean is generally best since it contains information on the total stock of money available for spending. But for comparisons of pay between different groups in society, the median is preferred as it is not affected by mega-salaries earned by a handful of super-rich.

A variation of an old economists' joke would be that if 10 people were in a City pub and they all earned £20,000, both the mean and the median would be meaningful averages – and the figure would be the same in each case. But if a partner of Goldman Sachs walked in after collecting a £5m bonus on top of his £1m basic pay, while the median would remain £20,000, the mean would rise to £563,636. None of the others would be any better off and might be a bit miffed if the "average" pay in the room was described as "over £500,000", having risen by 2,718 per cent.

Source: Financial Times, 28 October 2006.

Choosing which average to use isn't always easy.

Measures of Variability

We now realise that averages by themselves are potentially misleading and that we really require some measure of variability around the average as well. Consider the hospital manager who knows that the mean LOS is 10 days per patient in Month 1. For planning and management purposes this statistic is inadequate by itself (notwithstanding that the median may well show a different average value). The manager will also want some indication as to how much this LOS is likely to vary from one patient to another. Is a typical variation likely to be one day or two or three or ... ? The importance of knowing likely variability should not be underestimated. Such an average figure may well be used to set staffing levels, number of beds, number of doctors and other trained staff, patient admission rates and so on. We clearly need to consider measures of variability and we shall introduce several.

The range

The first of these measures is the *range*, which is simply the difference between the maximum value and the minimum value in a data set. By simple inspection of Tables 4.1 and 4.2 we see that we have:

Month 1: Maximum = 38
Minimum = 5
Range = 38 – 5 = 33 days
Month 2: Range = 9 days (10 – 1)

We see that for Month 1 the gap between the smallest and largest value was much larger (almost four times) than for Month 2. This implies potentially more variability in the first set of data compared with the second. The range is a fairly crude, but effective, measure of variability. One common use is in the quotation of stock market prices, where the minimum and maximum share price during the year are shown in published data.

The standard deviation

A far more important – and more widely used – measure of variability is the *standard deviation*. Its calculation is relatively straightforward if somewhat tedious when done manually. Consider what we wish to achieve. Just as we have calculated the mean as a statistical measure of average, so we wish to calculate a measure of variability around this average: typically how much do the items in the data set differ from the mean value? Is there a typical variability around the mean of one day, two days, three days ...? A logical first step, therefore, would be simply to determine the individual differences between the actual data and the mean. We show the results for this for Month 1 in Table 4.3.

The final column simply shows the difference – the deviation – of the mean from each actual data value. For the first patient, therefore, the actual LOS was five days less than the mean (hence 05 as the deviation). However, we require a statistic showing variability from the average for *all* the data, not for each item individually. It seems logical, therefore, to consider taking the individual deviations and finding an average deviation for all the 11 patients.

Activity 4.4

Calculate an average (mean) deviation for the whole data set. How do you explain your result?

Table 4.3	Deviations from the mean	
Actual LOS	Mean	Deviation
5	10	−5
5	10	−5
6	10	−4
6	10	−4
6	10	−4
8	10	−2
9	10	−1
9	10	−1
9	10	−1
9	10	−1
38	10	+28

On performing such a calculation we find that the total of all the individual deviations is zero and that if we proceeded to find an average or mean deviation this would be zero also. Clearly this cannot be right as we know that there is considerable variation simply on inspection of the raw data. In fact the sum of the individual deviations will always total to zero for any data set. This must be the case since by trying to calculate an average deviation for the whole data set we are effectively saying: by how much on average do the numbers in the first column deviate from those in the second? The answer must be zero since the numbers in the second column are effectively the same (although they look different) as those in the first (think about how we worked out the mean of 10 days in the first place). So the obvious calculation does not work.

We can still proceed, however, if we reconsider what we require. We are searching for a statistic that indicates the typical difference between all the actual data items and the mean. Since our interest is primarily in this difference – particularly whether it is large or small – then the sign of the individual differences is irrelevant. That is, it does not matter whether an individual deviation is positive or negative but rather whether it is large or small. Since it is the signs of the individual deviations in Table 4.3 that are causing the current difficulty, then we can remove them. The way in which this is done by the standard deviation calculation is to square the individual deviations. This will have the effect of converting all values into positives (remember when multiplying, two minuses make a plus). The calculations are shown in Table 4.4.

This produces a total of 890 (notice also that the squaring has the effect of increasing the importance of the larger deviations in the total). This is a number we can now average over the whole data set. That is, we can now divide by 11 to find an average squared deviation.

Activity 4.5

If we were to perform this calculation, what units of measurement would the resulting number have?

Table 4.4   Squared deviations from the mean

Actual LOS	Deviation	Squared deviation
5	−5	25
5	−5	25
6	−4	16
6	−4	16
6	−4	16
8	−2	4
9	−1	1
9	−1	1
9	−1	1
9	−1	1
38	+28	784
Total	0	890

Since we squared the individual deviations (measured in days) we must also have squared the units of measurement (think about measuring a room for a carpet). We therefore must have a number, 890, whose units of measurement are 'square days' – a meaningless unit of measurement. To revert to something sensible we must therefore reverse the squaring process by taking the square root and thereby reverse the units of measurement also. We therefore have:

$$\sqrt{\frac{890}{11}} = 8.99 \text{ days}$$

That is, the standard deviation for Month 1 is approximately nine days. But how is this interpreted? What does it mean? Remember that we were trying to calculate a statistic which indicates variability around the mean (of 10 days); that is, how much actual lengths of stay vary from the mean LOS. This measure of variability – the standard deviation – is nine days and is an indication of the typical, or standard, difference of the actual data items from the mean we have calculated. Given that the mean is 10, the value for the standard deviation implies (relatively) high variation from the mean within the original set of data. That is, if we are simply told the mean and standard deviation we can infer that the mean is not really a 'typical' value, given the standard deviation is relatively large. Some care must be taken when interpreting the standard deviation but, as we shall see, it is an important statistic in other quantitative areas.

Activity 4.6

What do you think the minimum value for the standard deviation can be for any data set? What does this imply?

Calculate the standard deviation for Month 2 and compare it with that calculated for Month 1.

Solution is given on p 584.

With some thought it becomes evident that the minimum value the standard deviation can ever take for a set of data is zero – implying that all the individual data items take the mean value, hence there is no variability from this average value. At the other end there is, in principle, no upper limit to the value the standard deviation can take: higher values simply imply more variability. But how do we compare two (or more) standard deviations? The answer must be 'carefully'. The reason for this is that in a data set the standard deviation is calculated around the mean value. If, in another data set, the mean value is different, then we could well get a different value for the standard deviation, even though the actual variability is the same. If this sounds unconvincing you should attempt Exercise 1 at the end of this chapter now, to confirm the point. Consider Month 2, where the standard deviation works out at 3.3 days. What can we say about variability of LOS in Month 1 compared with Month 2? We can conclude that, in absolute terms, the variability in Month 2 is less (about 1/3 of that in Month 1). This can be confirmed by recollecting that 9 out of 11 observations in Month 2 were of either 9 or 10 days with a mean of 8. However, the means themselves differ and this might be the cause of (at least some of) the difference in the standard deviations. For this reason it is usually advisable to calculate a related statistic – the coefficient of variation – which we shall examine shortly.

Sarasin banks on its subtle speciality

By Andrew Wood in Hong Kong

Bank Sarasin, the Swiss wealth manager, is well known for its thematic and sustainable funds, which are designed to help investors take advantage of global trends or environmentally appealing opportunities. Now it is promoting a new speciality – nuanced investing. A nuance is "a small change that leads to an enhancement," says Michael Kaimakliotis, who is Sarasin's co-head of nuanced investing. He and José Spescha have been working on nuanced investment products since June 2007, and the bank last week closed subscriptions on its first such funds. Nuanced investing, Mr Kaimakliotis says, draws on insights from behavioural finance to assess clients' attitudes to risk and uses derivatives to help them achieve their returns.

"For a given level of risk, we can get a higher return than with traditional portfolio management techniques," he says. "In particular, the framework allows us to provide greater downside protection without reducing expected returns."

Modern portfolio theory tells investors that choosing the right combination of stocks is as important as choosing individual shares. They should hold well-diversified portfolios to maximise returns for a given level of risk, and borrow money to invest in that portfolio if they want to increase their profits. Risk is defined statistically by how much on average an investment will deviate from its average return – the mean-variance framework – and the unit of measurement is the standard deviation.

But that is not the way ordinary people define risk when they are investing, says Mr Kaimakliotis. "I firmly believe that most clients don't understand standard deviations."

He says he became dissatisfied with the traditional approach to constructing investment portfolios when working for the private banking arm of UBS. "We started getting questions [from clients] as the complexity of the portfolio increased. They didn't understand their portfolio any more." Mr Kaimakliotis turned to behavioural finance. The field was developed by two US psychologists, the late Amos Tversky and his colleague, Daniel Kahneman, who won the Nobel prize for economics in 2002.

Much as the eye can be fooled by optical illusions, people often make irrational decisions about investment because of the way they feel emotionally about losses. Researchers have identified many quirks in the way humans perceive investment that are incompatible with the rational principles of the finance industry.

"The work in this field revolves around the idea that the mean-variance framework is inadequate to capture investors' objectives," Mr Kaimakliotis says.

"For instance, an investor gives me $100 to invest. If the value of the portfolio rises to $101 then he is most likely marginally happier. If the portfolio falls to $99, however, he may be upset that we have lost his hard-earned money."

Consider the example of someone who is investing with a particular goal in mind, such as paying university fees for a child. "If the value of the portfolio falls below a certain limit he may face catastrophic risks. This is inconsistent with a mean-variance approach to managing money but clearly makes sense."

This perspective, Mr Kaimakliotis says, is useful for looking at how investors think about goals. Avoiding catastrophe sets a lower limit on target returns. Many investors have a level of return that they would like to achieve, but may not need.

"In this case outcomes above these levels are like lottery wins – nice to have but not the core objective for your investment portfolio." Between catastrophe and lottery lies range risk.

"We see a stock as a collection of exposures. A long stock can be engineered as a short put, plus a bull call spread, plus a long call."

The short put would be the catastrophic risk, the call spread would be range risk, and the long call would be a lottery-like exposure.

"Since when we buy the stock we are equivalently purchasing each of these option strategies the question becomes: do we want to own all three exposures? By seeing risky assets for their underlying exposures we can take a more nuanced approach to investing and take exposure to only the risks we like."

For example, he says, if an investor thinks a stock will rise from $100 to $120 but no further, then he makes extra gains by selling the exposure to the lottery-like returns above $120.

Source: *Financial Times*, 6 July 2008.

You're not the only one struggling to understand the standard deviation!

Formula for calculating the standard deviation

The calculations we have completed for the standard deviation can be summarised into an appropriate formula:

$$SD = \sqrt{\frac{\Sigma(x - \bar{x})^2}{n}}$$

where x refers to the individual data items, $\bar{x}$ (pronounced 'x bar') is the mean and n the number of data items in the data set. The formula is simply the square root of the sum of the squared deviations divided by the number of items in the data set. All we have done in the formula is express the step-by-step calculations we performed earlier. The formula indicates that we subtract the mean from each data value, square these, sum these for the entire data set, divide by the number of data items and then take the square root. You will sometimes find reference to the term *variance* also. The variance is the square of the standard deviation or

$$\frac{\Sigma(x - \bar{x})^2}{n}$$

Blue chip shares go the way of the white rhino

Investors have exacerbated market volatility, writes Philip Coggan

In theory, a blue chip was the kind of stock that an investor could lock away in a drawer, forget about for 20 years and then use to fund a comfortable retirement.

But it does not seem that easy to find blue chips any more. Old stalwarts such as Procter & Gamble and Xerox in the US and Marks & Spencer and Imperial Chemical Industries in the UK have repeatedly stumbled.

It seems as if the prime quality of blue chips – their reliability – has faded. That anecdotal impression is confirmed by academic research.

A Harvard Economics paper published this year by John Campbell, Mattin Lettau, Burton Malkiel and Yexiao Xu found that there was a significant increase in US company-related share price volatility in the period 1962–97.

The authors suggested several explanations. One is that companies are joining the stock market at an earlier stage of their development, when there is more uncertainty about their prospects. A second is that old-style conglomerates have been broken into their component parts, which tend to be focused on a single industry or product. A third is that the greater use of share options has encouraged company managers to take more risks.

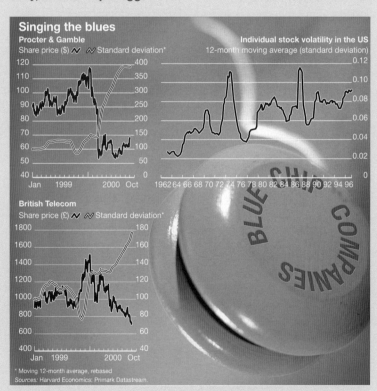

Singing the blues

Procter & Gamble
Share price ($) / Standard deviation*

Individual stock volatility in the US
12-month moving average (standard deviation)

British Telecom
Share price (£) / Standard deviation*

* Moving 12-month average, rebased
Sources: Harvard Economics; Primark Datastream.

More recently, Dresdner Kleinwort Benson's VGER index, which captures the market volatility implied in share option premia, shows there have been three surges in volatility over the last two years – the autumn of 1998, the first two months of 2000 and the last six weeks.

However, one must not get too carried away – the latest surge is much less marked than the previous two. And at the market level, Dresdner's Nigel Croft says volatility in recent years has actually returned to normal, after an unusually quiet period in the early 1990s.

Of course, the fortunes of individual companies have always fluctuated. Only one component of the original Dow Jones Industrial Average – General Electric – still survives; the FTSE 100 index, which was founded in 1984, contains only 39 of its first raft of constituents.

Changes in the market's structure do seem to have accelerated, however, thanks to the rise in the fortunes of technology stocks.

"Things have always come and gone," says Bob Semple, equity strategist at Deutsche Bank, "but technology may have foreshortened the period of change."

The last two years have seen some dramatic sectoral shifts. Already this year, the so-called TMTs (technology, media and telecoms stocks) have powered ahead in January and February, plunged in March, rallied in the summer and stumbled once more in September.

"Old economy" stocks (essentially much of the rest of the market) have tended to move in the opposite direction to the TMTs.

There is a logical explanation as to why TMTs should be more volatile. Much of their value depends on their capacity to grow earnings well into the future. This makes the share prices highly sensitive to small changes in earnings forecasts and the rate at which those future earnings should be discounted.

Momentum investors have exacerbated the trend – they buy stocks which have been performing strongly but sell at the first hint of bad news. As has been seen in recent weeks, companies that fail to meet earnings forecasts can see their share prices savaged.

Technological change may also have made life more difficult for many old economy companies. Media and banking groups, for example, face competition from internet companies that puts downward pressure on prices and forces them to launch heavy investment programmes.

And an era of global competition and low inflation has made it very hard for consumer product companies to raise prices – ensuring that they face an endless struggle to contain costs.

In short, blue chips seem to be going the way of the white rhino.

Source: Financial Times, 4 October 2000.

Standard deviation is routinely used to show the changing volatility of share prices.

Populations and samples

It is worthwhile at this stage making the distinction between sets of data which represent a statistical population and those which represent a sample from a population. A *population* relates to the entire set of data that is of interest to us. A *sample* is a (representative) part of that population. For the example we were using in the last chapter on stores in two regions, we indicated that we had collected data on a sample of stores. This implies that our data is technically incomplete – that we are analysing only a part of the total population, which, in this case, would consist of all stores within each region. The reasons for obtaining and analysing data on only a sample from the population are usually self-evident – particularly in a business context. It may simply not be feasible to collect data for the entire statistical population: it may be too expensive, it may be too time-consuming. For whatever reason, in a business environment we are usually investigating a sample of data rather than the population. Why does this matter?

It matters because, in principle, our data – and thereby our analysis – is incomplete. Potentially, the conclusions we come to, based on our analysis of a sample – of only part of the population – might be different from those we would have reached had we examined the whole population. A considerable area of statistics is devoted to trying to assess how 'accurate' the sample analysis is in the context of the (missing) population data, and this is also an area we will touch on later. For the moment it is sufficient to note the potential problem. We must also begin to distinguish our statistics in terms of whether they relate to the sample or the population, and there is some standard terminology to facilitate this. Typically in statistics, calculations which relate to the population are denoted by a character from the Greek alphabet. Thus:

Population mean = μ (pronounced 'mew')
Population standard deviation = σ (pronounced 'sigma')

The equivalent sample statistics are typically denoted with letters from the standard alphabet:

Sample mean = $\bar{x}$ (pronounced 'x bar')
Sample standard deviation = s

In the context of the sample standard deviation it is also important to note that the formula for its calculation is slightly different from that of the population standard deviation:

$$s = \sqrt{\frac{\Sigma(x - \bar{x})^2}{n - 1}}$$

with the divisor in the equation being n – 1, not n (the reason for this can only properly be explained using some detailed mathematics). This is particularly important when analysing data using a computer package. Spreadsheet programs have in-built statistical functions which allow you to specify a range of data and ask for certain statistics, such as the mean, median or standard deviation, to be calculated automatically without the need for the intermediate calculations (i.e. finding the deviations, squaring them, summing them, dividing by n, etc.). In the case of the standard deviation, however, spreadsheets will usually have two such in-built functions: one to work out the standard deviation assuming it represents the population, and another assuming it represents a sample. You should check carefully which function does which in your own spreadsheet program.

Excel has four different statistical functions for calculating a standard deviation. Make sure you're using the right one!

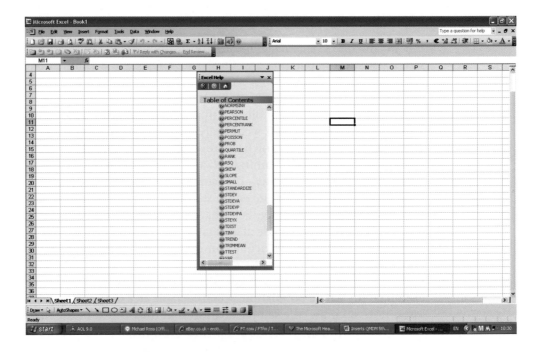

The coefficient of variation

We have seen that it is not always easy to compare and interpret two or more standard deviations. Sometimes when comparing different sets of data it can be helpful to assess their comparative relative variability rather than the absolute variability (as measured by the standard deviations). We can do this through the statistic known as the *coefficient of variation.*

The coefficient of variation is a simple statistic using the mean and standard deviation:

$$CV = \frac{\text{Standard deviation}}{\text{Mean}} \times 100$$

So for Month 1 we have:

$$CV = \frac{8.99}{10} \times 100 = 89.9\%$$

That is, the standard deviation is approximately 90 per cent of the mean value. For Month 2 the CV works out at 41.6 per cent. This implies that, even after allowing for differences in means, relative variation in Month 2 is approximately half that of Month 1. You will probably also realise that potentially the coefficient of variation is a useful statistical measure in those situations where consistency is important (and remember that consistency and variability are effectively the same). We may be producing some product, for example, where we need to ensure (perhaps for trading standards purposes) that the quality of the product is consistent and maintained. Monitoring the variability through the standard deviation may not help if the mean value itself is altering, but using the CV will.

Consider the following scenario. A manufacturing company produces a product in two sizes: a 1000 ml bottle and a 500 ml bottle. The machinery filling the bottles fills an average (mean) of these amounts but, because of mechanical variability, there is a standard deviation of 5 ml and 4 ml respectively. Although the machine filling the smaller bottle has a lower standard deviation – and lower absolute variability – the CVs would indicate that it is the machine filling the larger bottle which is *relatively* more consistent.

Quartiles

The standard deviation is a common measure of variability. However, by definition it measures variability around the mean – only one of the measures of average. As we have seen, the median will occasionally be a more representative measure than the mean and we may wish to calculate an appropriate measure of variability without the mean. We can do this through the use of *quartiles*. We know already that the median is the middle item in an ordered data set. We can describe the median in terms of its percentage position in the data set. The median is the 50th percentile, given that this would be in the middle of the data set. Two other common percentiles are the lower and upper quartiles, often denoted as Q_1 and Q_3 respectively. The lower quartile is the 25th percentile and the upper quartile is the 75th. This implies that a quarter of the items in a data set will have a numerical value up to the lower quartile value, and that a quarter will have a value equal to or higher than the upper quartile value. What this effectively implies is that a distribution can be neatly categorised as shown in Figure 4.1. For any set of data, a quarter of the items will fall below the lower quartile, a quarter between the lower quartile and median, a quarter between the median and upper quartile and a quarter above the upper quartile.

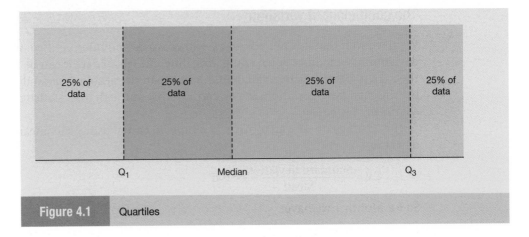

25% of data	25% of data	25% of data	25% of data

Q_1 Median Q_3

Figure 4.1   Quartiles

Note that the two quartiles will not necessarily be equidistant from the median. One of the quartiles may be further away than the other from the median value, typically if the overall shape of the data distribution is not symmetrical. Nevertheless, both will mark the 25 per cent split of the data. We shall illustrate the use of this shortly.

Calculating the quartiles

Calculating the quartiles is, in principle, the same as calculating the median. The data can be sorted and then the item a quarter of the way through and three-quarters of the way through the data can be found. In practice, for any large set of data, a computer package will obtain these values.

The interquartile range

Another measure of variability that can be used in relation to the quartiles is the *interquartile range* (IQR). This is simply the difference between the upper and lower quartiles:

$$IQR = Q_3 - Q_1$$

'Unpalatable choices lie ahead' in quest for more equal society

By Nicholas Timmins, Public Policy Editor, Financial Times

Governments and voters face a set of unpalatable choices, including higher taxes, if the public is to get what it says it wants – a more equal society with good public services – a study by a leading public analyst concludes today.

The study by Professor John Hills, head of the Centre for Analysis of Social Exclusion at the London School of Economics, and a member of the Pensions Commission, highlights the dramatic growth of income inequality over the past quarter of a century.

Since 1979, 40 per cent of the total growth in disposable income has gone to the richest 10th of the population, while the share taken by the poorest 10 per cent has fallen by a third.

Such increases in inequality are not inevitable, he says. Inequality has risen much faster in the UK and US than in most other countries. And government policy can make a difference. Labour's policies since 1997 have reduced child poverty, led to gains for the bottom half of the income distribution, and are set to reduce pensioner poverty.

But reducing inequality, or stopping it getting worse, while sustaining public services such as health and education, "is not going to become any easier", Prof Hills warns.

Income inequality: or how the rich got richer

Inequality rocketed between 1979 and the mid-1990s ...

Change in income, by decile group, 1979 to 1994-95 (%)

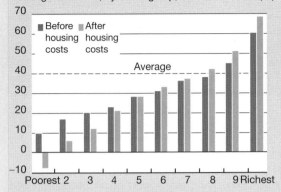

... since then, the growth in incomes has been much more equal ...

Change in income, by decile group, 1994-95 to 2002-03 (%)

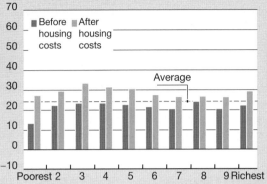

The top tenth saw their disposable income rise by 70 per cent while that of the bottom 10 per cent fell after housing costs

Source: Department for Work and Pensions.

Treasury forecasts, which show that future pressures on public spending are relatively modest, depend crucially on most social security benefits, including pensions and out-of-work support, continuing to be linked to prices rather than earnings (which usually rise faster).

That would imply benefits falling by 60 per cent relative to other incomes over 50 years. "It is hard to see how this could occur without relative poverty rising," Prof Hills says.

It is also something the public does not want, according to in-depth analyses of social attitudes. Eighty per cent of the population believes the gap between rich and poor is too large. Less than a fifth believes large income differences are necessary for prosperity.

Less than a quarter blames the low income of the poor on laziness and there is support for higher social spending – though that is qualified. The public supports higher spending on health and

education. Spending on pensions also looks popular but there is antagonism to the social security budget in general rising, partly because the public thinks far more is spent on unemployment benefit than is the case. And while people say they support tax increases, much of that support appears predicated on the assumption that someone else will be paying.

Given demographic changes, spending would need to rise by 4.5 per cent of gross domestic product by 2051 to keep education, health and social security spending at today's levels – the equivalent of raising all taxes by 12 per cent.

And given that a 50 per cent tax rate on incomes above £100,000 would only raise 0.5 per cent of GDP, higher taxes would have to start lower down the income scale, making it almost inevitable most people would end up paying more.

Reducing social spending would lead to more and deeper relative poverty. Maintaining current levels

of social spending but concentrating it on the poor would produce an increase in means-testing – something that is politically unpopular. It would also imply less for those in the middle of the income distribution.

And higher expenditure, either to keep up with demographic and other pressures, or to go further and meet rising expectations, implies appreciably higher taxes.

A permanent "war on waste" does not offer a way out. Nor does higher economic growth – which would raise affluence but bring higher expectations of what the state should deliver. And nor does a big squeeze on non-welfare state spending, given that other programmes such as transport only take a third of government expenditure.

Prof Hills says the public needs to recognise it must make a choice between higher taxes, a less generous state which would lead to a rise in relative poverty, or more means-testing to focus help on the poorest.

Source: Financial Times, 22 October 2004.

Deciles are another common way of looking at the spread of data. Quartiles divide data into quarters, deciles into tenths and percentiles into one-hundredths.

Index tracking: Information – a double-edged sword

By Jim Pickard

Information is very hard to come by in many property markets. Try buying a building in Dubai, for example, and you will find that working out comparative pricing for recent deals is a tricky task. Investors in the US and the UK – and a growing number of other markets – should consider themselves lucky. In these places transparency has improved over the years thanks to the efforts of researchers.

In the UK, a company called Investment Property Databank (IPD) has long provided the backbone for the entire asset class by collating all the pricing, rental and total returns data from most of the big fund managers and property companies. IPD has also established a presence in 19 other countries including Germany, France and South Africa.

"The IPD has done more for the UK property fund management industry than any other single initiative," says Stuart Beevor, managing director of Grosvenor Fund Management. "Their indices are the best in the world."

This increase in transparency, however, is seen by many as a doubled-edged sword because of its impact on fund management. Rather than go their own way, fund managers are becoming more likely than before to hug the benchmark by buying the same proportional allocations as everyone else. By doing so, they are unlikely to underperform and miss their targets – and therefore bonuses. The same trend has long been established in equity markets, where fund managers do not fear for their jobs even if they

lose money so long as everyone else is in the same boat.

Performance figures for the industry over recent years certainly show a thinning of the gap between best and worst – a fact that many attribute to benchmark-hugging. The spread of returns from "core" fund managers within the IPD universe – termed the "interquartile range" – has narrowed in recent years, says Robin Goodchild, head of European strategy at LaSalle Investment Management.

"If you went back 10 or 15 years it would have been much wider," he says. "Now, fund managers are not going to stray a million miles from the index. So they will all have some industrial, some retail and some offices and within that it's a question of where they take their bets."

Source: Financial Times, 10 July 2006.

Here the interquartile range is used to identify 'core' fund managers – ignoring the best and worst 25 per cent of fund managers.

and, as can be seen from Figure 4.1, always encloses the central 50 per cent of the data. Other things being equal, a lower value for the IQR implies less variability in the central part of the data set. Literally, the lower the IQR value, the closer Q_1, and Q_3 must be to each other. Note, however, that the IQR ignores the data in the bottom and upper quarters of the distribution.

Coefficient of skewness

The final statistical measure that we introduce before putting all of them to use is the *coefficient of skewness*. Such a statistic tries to provide an impression of the general shape of the data distribution in the context of its overall symmetry. Consider Figures 4.2 to 4.4. Figure 4.2 shows a reasonably symmetrical distribution, with the bulk of the data in the middle and two reasonably balanced extremes. However, Figure 4.3 shows a distribution which is decidedly unsymmetrical with the 'hump' towards the lower end of the X axis scale and a long 'tail' of relatively high values to the right. Figure 4.4 shows the reverse pattern to this with the 'hump' now on the right-hand side. Figures 4.3 and 4.4 are said to show 'skewed' distributions. Given the focus of this chapter on statistical – rather than diagrammatic – descriptions of a set of data, we require some quantitative

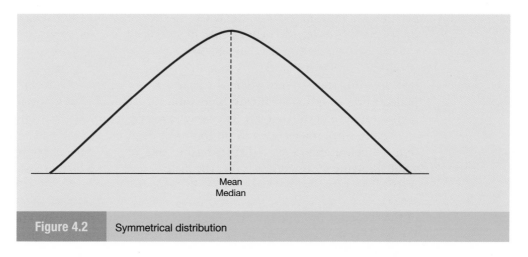

Figure 4.2	Symmetrical distribution

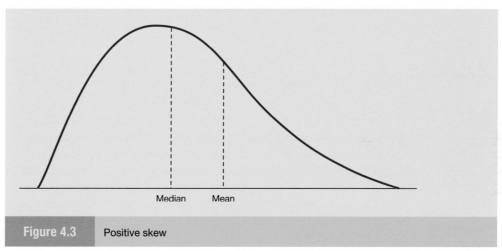

Figure 4.3	Positive skew

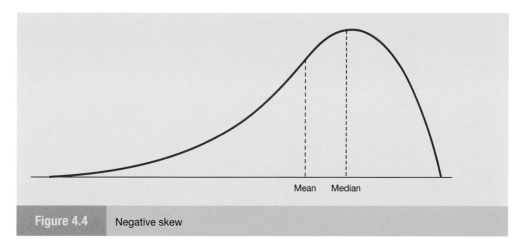

Figure 4.4	Negative skew

method of assessing whether the data we are examining fits into one or other of these patterns. Such a measure is given by the coefficient of skewness (more formally known as *Pearson's coefficient of skewness*), which is calculated as:

$$SK = \frac{3(\text{Mean} - \text{Median})}{\text{Standard deviation}}$$

By reference to Figures 4.2 to 4.4, where the mean and median values are shown, you should be able to see the logic of this. In Figure 4.2 (the symmetrical distribution) the values for the mean and median will be the same, since there are no extreme values on the one side to pull the mean value away from the bulk of the data. The coefficient, therefore, will take a zero value. In Figure 4.3, however, the mean will tend to be pulled upward by the relatively high values in the tail. Thus, the mean will take a higher value then the median. The skewness formula, therefore, will generate a positive result, since the expression on top must be positive, as must the standard deviation (by definition). Such a distribution is said to be positively skewed, with a larger value implying more skewness (i.e. the distribution being further away from the symmetrical distribution in Figure 4.2). By comparison, Figure 4.4 will be negatively skewed with the mean taking a lower value than the median and the expression on top of the skewness formula taking a negative value. Thus, simply by knowing the value for the skewness coefficient, we can infer the general shape of the distribution without resorting to a diagram.

Using the Statistics

We are now in a position to consider the use of all the statistics we have introduced in a management context. To do this, we will return to our earlier example of a sample of stores in Region A and Region B. Remember that we have already examined the data visually. We now wish to compare the two samples statistically and consider the two data sets. If you have access to a suitable computer package you may wish, at this stage, to calculate the statistics we have introduced for both of these data sets. You should duplicate the results shown in Table 4.5, which shows the output from a typical statistical package in terms of a number of the statistics we have developed for profits of stores in Region A and Region B.

Table 4.5	Profits for stores in Region A and in Region B	
	Region A	Region B
Sample size	113	121
Minimum	−13070	−4130
Maximum	93050	98800
Range	106120	102930
Mean	12981.2	17168.8
Median	6840	9580
Standard deviation	17476.3	19688.1
Coefficient of variation	134.6%	114.7%
Lower quartile	3530	3930
Upper quartile	15170	25000
Interquartile range	11640	21070
Skewness	1.0	1.9

Activity 4.7

Take a few minutes to consider the statistics shown in Table 4.5. What conclusions can you make about similarities and differences between the two sets of data? How might such statistics be used in a business context?

The table allows us to develop a considerable number of inferences about the data. Remember the purpose of statistics: to try to provide a reasonably accurate description of a data set in a concise way. We note first that the Region A data has a lower minimum and a lower maximum but a larger range. This implies a wider spread of data, although we must exercise caution since we have no way of knowing, based solely on this information, how many stores in each data set lie close to the extremes. The mean for Region B stores is some £4200 higher. However, in both cases, the median is considerably lower than the mean, implying a (relatively) small number of extreme values at the top end of the distribution. The difference in medians is some £2700. It is noticeable in both cases that the median is almost half that of the mean. The high value for the standard deviation in both data sets indicates considerable variability around the mean value (confirming the range). Absolute variability is lower in the Region A data set but relative variability (as measured by the coefficient of variation) is higher. The lower quartiles are very similar – at £3530 for the Region A and £3930 for the Region B group. Consider the implications of this, particularly in the context of the mean and median values. It implies that although profits in the Region B group are higher overall, both with the mean and the median, for the bottom quarter of stores there is virtually no difference. This is confirmed by the upper quartiles, which exhibit a much larger difference than either the median or the mean. There is a difference in the upper quartiles of almost £10 000, implying that in the Region B group a quarter of stores achieved profits of at least £25 000, whereas for the Region A group the comparable profit level was £15 170. The IQR confirms that the gap between the lower quartile performers and the upper quartile performers is larger in the Region B group. Finally, we note that for both data sets the coefficient of skewness is positive but higher for Region B. Remember that a positive skew implies an overall distribution as seen in Figure 4.4. Although both data sets take this general shape, that for Region B stores is even less symmetrical.

It is worthwhile reiterating what we have achieved after examination of these statistics. We have been able to put together a reasonably accurate management description of both distributions without resorting either to the original data or to diagrams. We have also been able to conclude that, overall, Region B centres have higher profits than their counterparts in Region A, and that the difference is more marked for the high-profit stores with relatively little difference for the lower-profit ones. Management also now know that the mean difference is some £4000 per store.

Clearly, what the statistics do not tell us are the causes of such differences between the two regions. However, having established statistically that such measurable differences do exist, and also having quantified these differences, management may want to take their investigations further to try to establish why some stores are considerably more profitable than others.

Activity 4.8

In Exercise 9 at the end of Chapter 3 data was provided for two samples in respect of users of a sports centre before and after a media campaign. The data is contained in filename 3X9. Using the raw data, calculate appropriate statistics and use these to highlight key changes that have taken place since the media campaign.

Try not to refer back to the diagrams you produced for this data but use only the statistics.

Solution is given on p 585.

Calculating Statistics for Aggregated Data

The methods we have developed for calculating management statistics have all been applied to a set of raw data – where we had access to the individual values in the data set. Frequently this will not be the case; we may only have data which has already been aggregated in some way. This often occurs when we are using secondary data. Consider the frequency distribution we developed in Chapter 3 relating to Region A stores, which we reproduce as Table 4.6.

Assume that this data has simply been presented to us as managers. We do not have access to the raw data but, for obvious reasons, we wish to obtain a statistical description of the distribution. Clearly, the formulae we have developed will not work, since they were based on the availability of the raw data. For the mean, for example, we cannot now add all the individual data items together and divide by 113 as we do not know the individual data values. We must adapt our formula accordingly.

Table 4.6	Frequency tabulation: Region A stores' profits	

	Interval	
Lower class limit (£s)	Upper class limit (£s)	Region A stores frequency
−20 000 <	−10 000	1
−10 000 <	0	13
0 <	10 000	56
10 000 <	20 000	22
20 000 <	30 000	5
30 000 <	40 000	6
40 000 <	50 000	5
50 000 <	70 000	5
Total		113

The mean

Since we do not know the individual values, we must make a simplifying assumption to allow the calculation of this statistic: that the observations in a particular class or interval all take the same value and that that value is the mid-point value in the interval. This sounds unreasonable until you realise that, particularly for intervals with a large frequency, we can logically expect items with a value at the bottom of the interval to be compensated for by those with values at the top. So, for the last interval, for example, the mid-point will be £60 000. Since we are assuming all data items (five) in this interval take this value, the sum of these five items will then be five times £60 000 or £300 000. We can duplicate this arithmetic for the other intervals as shown in Table 4.7.

So our estimated total of all the values in the data set is £1 390 000. Given that we have 113 data items, the mean can then be estimated as:

$$\text{Mean} = \frac{1\,390\,000}{113} = 12\,300.88$$

Notice that this is an estimate of the actual value and that, in this case, there is a difference from the actual mean of £12 981.2 calculated from the raw data. This calculation can be summarised as the formula:

$$\text{Mean} = \frac{\Sigma fm}{\Sigma f}$$

where m is the mid-point for each interval and f the frequency of observations in that interval.

Activity 4.9

Using this formula, calculate the mean for the Region B data shown in Table 3.3.

Solution is given on p 585.

Table 4.7   Calculations for the mean

Interval			Region A		
Lower class limit (£s)		Lower class limit (£s)	Frequency	Mid-point	Mid-point x frequency
−20 000	<	−10 000	1	−15 000	−15 000
−10 000	<	0	13	−5 000	−65 000
0	<	10 000	56	5 000	280 000
10 000	<	20 000	22	15 000	330 000
20 000	<	30 000	5	25 000	125 000
30 000	<	40 000	6	35 000	210 000
40 000	<	50 000	5	45 000	225 000
50 000	<	70 000	5	60 000	300 000
Total			113		1 390 000

The standard deviation

A similar formula can be developed for calculating the standard deviation for aggregated data:

$$\sqrt{\frac{\Sigma fm^2}{\Sigma f} - \left(\frac{\Sigma fm}{\Sigma f}\right)^2}$$

The formula looks complex but simply requires us to square the mid-point (m^2) and multiply by the frequency. Note that the second part of the expression (to be subtracted) is simply the mean value squared.

Activity 4.10

Calculate the standard deviation for both Region A and Region B groups and compare these with those for the raw data.

Solution is given on p 586.

It must be remembered that such statistics based on aggregated data are only estimates of the 'true' figures based on the raw data and should be used with a degree of caution. In this case we have calculated such statistics from the aggregated data even though we have the raw data available. We have done this to emphasise the differences that will occur. In practice, of course, you would not do this. If you have the raw data then you will use it for any statistical calculations. Frequently, however, you may not have the raw data but only the aggregated (perhaps because it has been obtained from published sources, where raw data is not available) and will have to use the frequency table to estimate the statistical measures you are interested in.

The median and quartiles

The median and quartiles can also be estimated from the frequency table. In this case we require the cumulative frequencies as shown in Table 4.8.

   We then require to determine the interval which will contain the middle value. Given that technically we require data item 57 (since this is the middle of 113 numbers) we see from the cumulative frequencies that this will fall in the interval 0 < 10 000. We can then apply a formula to estimate the median value:

$$\text{Median} = \text{LCL} + (\text{MI} - \text{CF})\frac{\text{CW}}{\text{F}}$$

where:

LCL	is the lower class limit of the interval in which the median item occurs;
MI	is the median item;
CF	is the cumulative frequency up to the median item interval;
CW	is the width of the median item interval;
F	is the frequency of observations in the median item interval.

The corresponding numerical values will then be:

$$\text{Median} = 0 + (57 - 14)\frac{10\ 000}{56}$$
$$= 0 + 7679 = 7679$$

Table 4.8	Cumulative frequency		
Interval		Region A	
Lower class limit (£s)	Upper class limit (£s)	Frequency	Cumulative frequency
−20 000 < −10 000		1	1
−10 000 < 0		13	14
0 < 10 000		56	70
10 000 < 20 000		22	92
20 000 < 30 000		5	97
30 000 < 40 000		6	103
40 000 < 50 000		5	108
50 000 < 70 000		5	113
Total		113	

giving a median value of £7679. Once again this is only an estimate of the actual value based on the raw data. If the formula appears to be nothing more than black magic just consider what we are actually doing. We know the median value occurs in this interval, which is of £10 000. We know therefore that the median must be at least equal to the lower value of this interval (£0). But there are 56 data items in this interval. One of them represents the median. Once again, given that we do not know the actual data items, we assume that they are equally spread over the interval (hence 10 000/56). To determine which of these items we require we must take into account the items from earlier intervals (since the median is found in principle by counting along the data from the first item). Hence the (57 − 14).

Activity 4.11

Estimate the median for Region B and compare it against the value for the raw data calculated earlier.

Solution is given on p 587.

The same formula is readily adapted to estimate the lower and upper quartiles for an aggregated data set. Since the lower quartile occurs 25 per cent of the way through an ordered data set we need to locate the lower quartile item rather than the median item. Otherwise the procedure outlined for using the median formula can be used in exactly the same way. Naturally, the upper quartile can also be found by adapting the formula.

Activity 4.12

Use the adapted formula to estimate the lower and upper quartiles for Region A.

Solution is given on p 587.

Index Numbers

Finally in this chapter we return to the idea of an average and look at a special type of average: an *index*. In its simplest form an index is a different form of a percentage. Consider a product that you might be thinking of buying, say, a new car. Last year the showroom price of the car might have been £8756. This year the same car – assuming the same model, features and so on – would cost £9253.

Activity 4.13

By how much has the price of the car changed? What is this change as a percentage?

While you can pull out the calculator and determine both the absolute and percentage change in the price, it would be useful to be able to see this at a glance. Constructing a *simple* index of the price will enable us to do this. Let us take last year's price as our reference point – known in index number terms as the *base period*. We arbitrarily set the price in this year to 100 (not £100 or 100% but simply 100 without units of measurement). The price in the second year can then be expressed as a proportion of the base-period price. We have:

$$\frac{9253}{8756} = 1.057 \text{ (to 3 decimal places)}$$

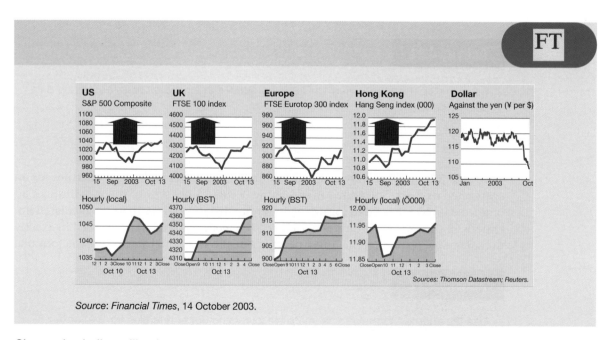

Source: Financial Times, 14 October 2003.

Share price indices, like these, are very common and receive considerable media exposure.

We then multiply this by 100 to provide an index of 105.7. What does this index value mean? It indicates that from an index of 100 last year the car price has increased to an index of 105.7 this year. Effectively the price of the car has increased by 5.7 per cent (hence the reason for choosing 100 as the base index value). A simple index then allows a ready comparison of percentage change in the variable. Clearly we could calculate an index for the price in year 3, year 4 and so on simply by taking the price in that year, dividing by the price in the base period and multiplying by 100. One point to note is that we chose to base our index in the first year. Although this is common practice the choice of base period can be somewhat arbitrary. We could equally have chosen to set the base period in the second year. This would give an index for the base of 100 and an index for the first year of:

$$\frac{8756}{9253} \times 100 = 94.6$$

We would now conclude that the price of the car in the first year is 5.4 per cent below that in the second (you will appreciate of course why the two percentages are different for each choice of base year: if you don't, go back and read the appropriate section in Chapter 2).

It should also be noted that the choice of base period can distort a long time series of index calculations. If the period we chose as base was abnormal or untypical in some way, we might produce a distorted view of the index trends over time.

Deflating using index numbers

One of the common uses of index numbers which measure price changes is to *deflate* a financial time series. You may remember that in Chapter 2 we stressed the importance of the difference between money value and real value. Consider the data shown in Table 4.9, which shows average weekly household income for selected years for the UK for 1995–2005.

Over this period, income appears to have increased markedly from just over £380 in 1995 to over £615 in 2005. However, as we all know, the money value of income is not necessarily the same as the real value of income – what the money income will buy. Because of inflation over this period we may well have a distorted view of what has happened to the real value of weekly income. We wish, therefore, to adjust the money income figures for inflation. Table 4.9 also shows the equivalent data for what is known as the *retail price index*.

Table 4.9	Average weekly household income (UK)	
Year	Income (£s)	Retail price index January 1987 = 100
1995	380.90	149.1
1998	457.00	162.9
2001	540.60	173.3
2005	615.90	192.0

Source: Annual Abstract of Statistics.

This is a composite, or aggregate, index showing the general level of consumer prices. Note that its base period is set to January 1987 (with the index taking a value of 100 in that month). We note that prices have risen between 1995 and 2005. Effectively we wish to calculate the real value of the average income figures (that is to adjust them for inflation over the period). The calculation is:

$$\text{Real value} = \text{Money value} \times \frac{100}{\text{Price index}}$$

If we perform the calculation for 1995 we then have:

$$\text{Real value} = 380.90 \times \frac{100}{149.10} = £255.47$$

Activity 4.14

Provide an interpretation of this result in the context of the problem.

Some care should be taken in terms of interpreting such calculations – they are a frequent source of misunderstanding and confusion. The figure of £255.47 is interpreted as the real value of the money sum of £380.90. That is, the money sum of £380.90 that we had in 1995 was actually 'worth' £255.47 in terms of what it would have bought in January 1987 (the base period we are using). We are saying that the £380.90 in 1995 and the hypothetical sum of £255.47 in January 1987 are effectively the same in terms of their purchasing power.

Activity 4.15

Compare the real value of 1995 income with the income shown for 1998. Was the average household better or worse off in 1998 compared with 1995? Calculate the real value of each of the other years' money income.

We begin to see the use and importance of such deflated data when we examine Table 4.10, which shows both the money income series and the real income series. The money income series shows a generally increasing trend, implying a steadily rising income. From the money income series the average household appears to be some £235 per week better off (since this is the amount by which money income has risen). However, the real income series shows that, at 1987 prices, the average household is actually some £65 a week better off after allowing for general price rises. Without deflating the data we might have developed an incorrect view of what has actually happened.

If we are examining any financial series over time then the only reliable way of examining such data is by deflating using an appropriate price index. What is meant by 'appropriate' we will discuss shortly. We should also note that all the real values are now expressed in terms of 1987 prices (since this was the base year for the price index). A different base period would lead to different real values (although the relationship between them would be unchanged).

Table 4.10	Average weekly household income (UK): Money and real terms	
Year	Money income (£s)	Real income (£s)
1995	380.90	255.47
1998	457.00	280.54
2001	540.60	311.94
2005	615.90	320.78

Aggregate index numbers

We introduced the idea of an index with the simple index that we calculated for two prices. Another type of index is available: the *aggregate* or *composite index*. In fact we have already encountered such an index: the retail price index we used in Table 4.9. This is an index of a group of items – a typical set of goods and services purchased by an average household in this case – rather than a single variable. Such indices are frequently useful in decision making.

Bank study puts underlying inflation at 1.2%

By Alan Beattie, Economics correspondent

New research from the Bank of England argues that underlying inflation could be as low as 1.2 per cent and that disinflationary pressure intensified over the second half of the 1990s.

The research, conducted by Joanne Cutler, a staff economist, and commissioned by DeAnne Julius, a member of the monetary policy committee, suggests that RPIX – the inflation measure targeted by the Bank of England – will remain lower than its 2.5 per cent target for the next 12 months.

It is the third piece of analysis to be produced by the MPC unit – the team of economists set up to provide research support to the independent committee members. The creation of the unit followed a row between the external and internal members over access to Bank research resources.

Ms Cutler develops an inflation measure that takes account of how long movements in prices for components of the overall index persist. She argues that products such as clothing and footwear show persistent deflationary pressure and should be given a bigger weight in the index than, for example, seasonal foods, whose prices fluctuate with the weather. The new measure, RPIXP, shows inflation at 1.2 per cent in February, lower than the official RPIX measure of 1.9 per cent.

The research is the latest attempt to derive a core measure of inflation that excludes the effect of volatile variables and predicts movements in overall inflation. It is likely to be used by Ms Julius – the most doveish member of the committee – as further ammunition for her argument that there is little inflationary pressure in the UK economy and interest rates can safely be cut.

Ms Julius, who has gained increasing respect from independent economists for her views, will soon face a decision on whether to seek reappointment to the committee when her term of office expires on May 31.

Source: Financial Times, 27 March 2001.

The way an aggregate index is calculated can be contentious.

Table 4.11	Hourly rates and hours worked: Part-time staff			
	2005		2009	
	Hourly pay rate (£s)	Total hours worked	Hourly pay rate (£s)	Total hours worked
Cleaning	6.00	4000	7.90	5500
Catering	6.50	2000	8.00	2100
Secretarial	12.50	6000	13.50	7000

Consider the following example. In 2005 an organisation decided to restructure its business by making more use of part-time staff in certain areas: cleaning, catering and secretarial. Over the past few years the finance director has expressed concern about the way the costs associated with these groups of staff appear to have increased. In her view this may have been caused by lack of central management responsibility in negotiating suitable pay scales with part-time staff. You have been asked to investigate and have collected the data shown in Table 4.11 for 2005, when these services were converted to a part-time staff basis, and for 2009, which is the latest year available.

In both cases you have data showing the hourly rate paid to the three types of staff and the number of hours worked by these staff in that year.

Activity 4.16

Is there any evidence that the finance director's suspicions are correct and that costs have escalated?

It is clearly difficult to reach a conclusion based on the data as shown. On the one hand hourly rates have increased, but then so have the number of hours worked. We can readily calculate the total cost in each of the two years:

2005: Total cost = £112 000
2009: Total cost = £154 750

The problem is that, although we conclude part-time wage costs have increased, it is impossible to disentangle the two possible causes: a rise in pay rate and a rise in hours worked. Clearly, from a management perspective, these two possible causes may require different solutions and different control mechanisms. However, if we consider constructing an aggregate index for pay rates this might enable us to determine how important this factor was in the cost escalation. You should be able to see that simply averaging pay rates for 2005 and comparing this average with that for 2009 would not be appropriate, since a simple average would fail to take into account the differing importance of the three types of staff. Accordingly, we need a weighted average. In fact there are two common methods of calculating an aggregate index: the Laspeyres index and the Paasche index.

The Laspeyres index

The first of these is the *Laspeyres index* (pronounced 'Lass-pairs'), which is technically known as a base-date weighted index. Remember that we require an index for pay scales and that we must weight the pay scales by the respective hours worked. The problem is that there are two possible weightings from the table: we could use hours worked in 2005 or hours worked in 2009. The Laspeyres index uses weights from the chosen base period, and here we will choose 2005 as the base. The calculation is then:

$$\frac{\Sigma P_n W_0}{\Sigma P_0 W_0} \times 100$$

where:

P	is the variable for which we require an index (pay scales);
W	is the weight we are using (hours worked);
subscript 0	relates to the chosen base year (2005);
subscript n	relates to the year for which we are calculating the index (here 2009).

You see from the formula that we are using the same set of weights to calculate both the top and bottom part of the expression. Any change in the index over time, therefore, must be caused by a change in P between the two periods, since the weights used in the calculation are constant.

Activity 4.17

Calculate a comparable index value for 2009 using the formula. Comment on the result.

The calculation becomes:

$$\frac{\Sigma P_n W_0}{\Sigma P_0 W_0} \times 100 = \frac{128\,600}{112\,000} \times 100 = 114.8$$

That is, the pay scale index for 2009 is 114.8. Given that by default the index for 2005 is 100 then this implies that – on average – pay scales have risen by 14.8 per cent over this period. We would have paid 14.8 per cent more for the same number of hours. It is important to appreciate exactly what this figure shows – and what it does not. Given its method of calculation, we can interpret this value in the following way: if we had kept the hours worked at the 2005 level then, in 2009, the pay cost would have been 14.8 per cent higher than in 2005. The pay scales have been weighted by the relative importance of the three categories. In management terms, whether we regard this increase as warranting further investigation and action obviously depends on all the other factors pertaining to the investigation.

Updating the Laspeyres index

Naturally, having gone to the trouble of calculating a pay index for 2009, it seems likely that we will wish to use the index to keep track of pay costs over time. Consider that in 2010 pay scales are: cleaning £8.00; catering £8.00; secretarial £14.00.

Activity 4.18

Calculate a Laspeyres index for 2010.

The formula indicates that all we need to do is to calculate a new weighted total for 2010:

$$\frac{\Sigma P_n W_0}{\Sigma P_0 W_0} \times 100 = \frac{132\,000}{112\,000} \times 100 = 117.9$$

and we see that the pay index for 2010 is 117.9 (again based on the assumption that hours worked is at the 2005 level). Updating the Laspeyres index is then relatively straightforward – calculating a new weighted total for the current year. One final point about the Laspeyres index: we chose 2005 as the base year; in practice any year can be chosen as the base – it is not necessary for this choice to be the first year in the series. We could have chosen 2009 as the base: this would then have been the base period which supplied the set of weights we would have used in all the calculations.

The Paasche index

The Laspeyres index used a set of base weights in the calculations. It will be evident that, over time, these base weights will become less and less representative of the situation. It seems sensible, then, to consider using more up-to-date weights for the pay-scale index. Such a calculation is available through the Paasche (pronounced 'Pash') index, which uses *current* rather than base weights. The appropriate formula is:

$$\frac{\Sigma P_n W_n}{\Sigma P_0 W_n} \times 100$$

Notice that once again it is the P variable that is allowed to change in the calculation while the weights remain constant – this time for the current year. The calculation is then:

$$\frac{\Sigma P_n W_n}{\Sigma P_0 W_n} \times 100 = \frac{154\,750}{134\,150} \times 100 = 115.4$$

and we have a pay scale index of 115.4 for 2009. Note that this is a slightly different result from the Laspeyres. The reason is that we are now using the 2009 weights (hours) for the 2005 calculation. The result implies that, based on the 2009 staffing levels, pay costs have risen by 15.4 per cent since 2005. The Paasche index has the advantage of showing the index based on the current (2009) hours worked. However, one of the drawbacks of the Paasche appears if we now move to 2010 and wish to calculate the appropriate index. First of all – given that 2010 is now the current year – we require weights for 2010. Second, to perform the calculation we must now recalculate both the top and bottom part of the equation.

You may well be left with the question: which type of index should I calculate? As ever, the answer will depend on circumstances. However, we can categorise the general features of the two methods:

● The Laspeyres index is easier to calculate for a long series of data. This is because it uses a single set of weights in all the calculations, whereas the Paasche requires the calculation for each period to use that period's weights.

- The Laspeyres tends to be easier in terms of data collection since it requires only one set of weights. The Paasche is relatively 'data-hungry', requiring a set of weights for each period in the series. For more complex series this can be both time-consuming and costly.

- The weights used in the Laspeyres series will gradually become out of date and hence the series will be less and less representative of the current situation. This will affect some variables more than others. Consider a consumer price index. This will need to reflect as accurately as possible actual consumer purchases. Think back only a few years and you will note that a number of items that would appear today in such patterns would not have appeared in the weights used: portable compact disc players, laptop computers and mobile phones would not have appeared in the weights used.

- Linked to the weights, the Laspeyres method will tend to overestimate the effect of price increases. The reason for this is simple. In terms of price increases, consumers (other things being equal) will buy less of a product that experiences such an increase. The relative importance of such an item in their consumption will decrease and hence the lower will be the weight of this item. However, the Laspeyres method uses base period weights, which do not change over time and hence will not reflect this pattern.

Price of a Big Mac shows the Miami–Nairobi gulf

By Frances Williams in Geneva

It takes more than three hours for the average worker in Nairobi to earn enough for a Big Mac. In Los Angeles, Chicago and Miami the global hamburger can be bought for a mere 10 minutes' effort.

UBS, the Swiss bank, uses the Big Mac index in its latest report on prices and earnings around the world.

The survey of living costs and incomes in 70 cities ranks Oslo, Hong Kong, Tokyo, New York and Zurich as the most expensive, followed by Copenhagen and London.

Tokyo, the costliest in 2000 when UBS carried out its previous survey, has become cheaper thanks to deflation and yen depreciation.

Depreciation has also reversed the fortunes of Buenos Aires, which three years ago was the most expensive city in South America.

The Argentine capital is now the cheapest city in the UBS league table with the sole exception of India's Bombay.

The calculations are based on a basket of more than 100 goods and services, excluding rents, reflecting "western European consumer habits".

According to UBS, globetrotters should shop for household appliances in eastern Europe, men's wear in Manila, Bucharest and Sofia, and women's fashion in Manila, Rio de Janeiro or Bombay.

In terms of purchasing power, workers in the four Swiss cities of Zurich, Basle, Geneva and Lugano do best, thanks to high wages and low taxes.

A slew of US cities follows, together with Luxembourg and Toronto.

Zurich workers earn most, with Copenhagen, Basle and Oslo next.

However, workers in Copenhagen pay 43 per cent of their wages in tax and social security contributions.

In Oslo taxes take 31 per cent of earnings, compared with 25 per cent in Zurich and 27 per cent in Basle.

On the other hand, the Swiss work the longest hours in western Europe, putting in about 1,900 hours a year compared with fewer than 1,700 hours in Paris, Copenhagen, Berlin or Frankfurt. More details at www.ubs.com/economicresearch

Source: *Financial Times*, 21 August 2003.

An alternative index!

Overall then the Laspeyres method is easier, quicker and less costly but potentially less accurate, particularly in times of rapid change. Finally, we should also point out that although our examples have been in terms of prices, it is possible – and common – to produce other types of index numbers. One frequent example is an index of quantity rather than price (in a production organisation for example). In such a case the variable to alter in the formulae would be quantity and we would choose some appropriate weight for the problem.

Worked Example

Once again, to show how we might apply some of the techniques introduced in this chapter let us consider Table 4.12. This is taken from the *Financial Times* and shows salaries relating to City of London financial positions. The data is based on over 300 posts in almost 150 banks and finance companies. We work for the corporate finance head in one such institution. She saw the same table while at a business lunch with a colleague, who holds a position as Eurobond trading head. Over the lunch tempers got a little heated, with each of them claiming that people in their particular job were better paid than those in the other job. The boss has now come back to us and asked for confirmation that she was right in claiming corporate finance heads are better paid than Eurobond trading heads. What can we say?

Table 4.12	Salaries in City of London finance			
Position	Lower quartile £s	Median salary £s	Upper quartile £s	Average salary £s
Corporate finance head	100 000	112 500	156 000	127 747
Capital markets head	128 800	142 500	165 500	145 600
Bond sales head	90 000	97 375	105 000	98 343
Fund management director	110 000	133 948	147 000	130 463
Eurobond trading head	105 000	127 500	150 000	127 698
Equity trading head	86 500	100 000	143 750	112 100
Private banking head	74 301	95 286	110 000	94 660
Head of research	70 833	115 000	135 000	105 333
Financial director	66 700	80 715	90 000	86 056
Chief FX dealer	62 502	82 875	95 000	86 053
Legal services head	62 730	70 000	75 000	71 314
Personnel director	60 000	69 000	82 500	76 782
Money markets head	57 385	70 000	79 000	70 556
D-P director	56 135	60 000	73 700	69 974
Credit manager	36 036	46 441	50 800	43 996
Customer services head	26 550	30 150	37 800	31 923

Source: Financial Times, 14 February 1996, p 12.

Clearly, we need to be cautious since we have no details of how the data was collected, how representative it is or how accurate. (For example, if we were to ask someone what salary they earned we might easily get a distorted, higher figure as some might inflate their actual salary.) However, it appears the information is needed only to settle a personal argument, so we can put these issues to one side for the moment.

Examining the table we see we are given data on the average salary for both types of post (presumably the mean) together with the median and quartiles. We have no information on minimum and maximum salaries or on standard deviations. However, there are a few comments we can make. Based on the mean salaries there is no real difference between the two posts, with both showing a mean of almost £128 000. Some differences do occur, however, when we look at the median and quartiles. First, we note that the median Eurobond salary at £127 500 is some £15 000 higher than that for corporate finance. Half of Eurobond heads earn £127 500 or more – higher than the comparable median for corporate finance heads. We also note that the median for Eurobond is almost the same as its mean, whereas for corporate finance the mean is some £15 000 higher than its median. We know that when the mean is higher than the median, the implication is that there are a small number of items in the data set at the top end of the data range, effectively pulling the mean higher. We might conclude that, whereas the mean for Eurobond was relatively typical of the data set (with no extreme values pulling the mean above or below the median), for corporate finance this is not the case, with the implication that there are a few extremely high salary figures pulling the mean up. This appears to be confirmed by the upper quartile, which is higher for corporate finance than for Eurobond. One quarter of corporate jobs earn £156 000 or more compared with £150 000 for Eurobond. We also see from the interquartile range that there is a larger gap between the lower and upper quartiles for corporate (at £56 000) than for Eurobond (at £45 000), again implying relatively more dispersion or variability within the corporate finance data set. In conclusion, then, we cannot really say to our boss that corporate posts are better paid than Eurobond (indeed the median values imply otherwise). Since this response might be career limiting, however, we might (reasonably) point out that there is implied evidence that the top corporate earners are better paid than the top Eurobond earners and we might further report that since our boss is evidently destined for bigger and better things she's bound to end up in this top corporate earners group and hence is likely to be earning more than her Eurobond colleague (well, our staff appraisal is due next month after all!).

 ## Summary

In this chapter we have introduced some of the more common management statistics available. We have tried to develop an understanding of how such statistics can be used in a management context by examining their methods of calculation as well as their direct interpretation. It is once again important to appreciate that such statistics are potentially valuable sources of information about some situation or variable but they do have the capacity to mislead if not evaluated and interpreted in the correct manner. In practice it may be appropriate to calculate a variety of statistics for some problem and then to consider which of these presents a reasonably fair and accurate description.

Useful online resources

Detailed below are some internet resources that may be useful. Many have further links to other sites. An updated version is available from the accompanying website (**www.pearsoned.co.uk/wisniewski**). In addition, I would be grateful for details of other websites that have been found to be useful.

www.bettycjung.net/Graphing.htm – Charting and graphing data

http://en.wikipedia.org/wiki/Arithmetic_mean – Article on the arithmetic mean

http://en.wikipedia.org/wiki/Median – Article on the median

http://en.wikipedia.org/wiki/Mode_(statistics) – Article on the mode

http://en.wikipedia.org/wiki/Quartile – Article on quartiles

http://en.wikipedia.org/wiki/Standard_deviation – Article on the standard deviation

http://en.wikipedia.org/wiki/Coefficient_of_variation – Article on the coefficient of variation

http://en.wikipedia.org/wiki/Price_index – Article on index numbers

QMDM IN ACTION
Halifax plc: house price index

The private sector housing market in the UK is big business in many ways. Construction companies and property developers rely on an active housing market to stimulate demand for new and refurbished houses. A wide range of companies – from carpet manufacturers, to manufacturers of consumer durables, to double-glazing companies to removal companies – rely on an active housing market with people buying, selling and moving house.

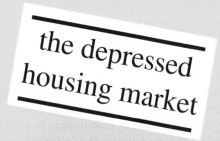

Figure 4.5	The housing market

➔

Halifax House Price Index

Regional House Prices   **Fourth Quarter 2004**

Not for broadcast or publication before 00.01 Hrs Saturday 15th January 2005

UNITED KINGDOM

- The three northern English regions were the only British regions to record house price rises in Britain in 2004 Quarter 4: North West (3.0%), Yorkshire and the Humber (1.2%) and the North (0.7%). All other regions saw a fall in prices during the quarter with the biggest declines in Wales (-6.2%) and the South East (-1.6%). Prices in London fell by 0.5%: the second successive quarterly drop in the capital. **(See Table 1)**

- There was a clear north/south divide in 2004. The biggest annual house price rises in 2004 Quarter 4 were in the North West (27%), the North (26%), Northern Ireland (24%) and Yorkshire and the Humber (22%). The smallest annual price gains were in Greater London (4%) and the South East (7%). **(See Table 1)**

- Scotland is now the only region of the UK where the average price remains below £100,000 (£99,056). London remains the most expensive region with an average price of £241,670. **(See Table 1)**

- 38 out of the total 613 (6%) towns surveyed had an average house price below £100,000 in 2004. This compared with 121 (20%) towns with an average price below £100,000 in 2003. Almost half of the towns where the average price remains below £100,000 are in Scotland (18 out of the 38).

- The number of towns where the average house price is above £300,000 increased from 26 (4% of the 613 towns surveyed) in 2003 to 47 (8%) in 2004. All the towns above this benchmark are in London and the South East with the exceptions of Knutsford in Cheshire and Wimborne in Dorset.

- The differential between the average house price in London and the UK has fallen to its lowest level for almost 7 years in percentage terms. The average price in the capital stood at 1.5 times the national average in 2004 Quarter 4 compared with a peak of 1.9 times in 2001 Quarter 3. The much stronger house price rises in northern Britain during the last three years has seen a significant narrowing in the north/south house price divide with the average price in London now 1.9 times higher than that in the North compared with three times higher in 2002 Quarter 3. The north/south divide remains wider than it was ten years' ago when the average price in London was only 1.25 times the national average.

ABOUT THE HALIFAX HOUSE PRICE INDEX

The Halifax House Price Index is the UK's longest running monthly house price series with data covering the whole country going back to January 1983. Quarterly regional indices are available from 1983 Quarter 1. The Index is based on the lender's mortgage offers. From this data, a "standardised" house price is calculated and property price movements on a like-for-like basis (including seasonal adjustments) are analysed over time. Properties over £1 million are included and the index is seasonally adjusted.

More/....

The latest monthly and quarterly indices are available on the HBOS plc Group internet site at: http://www.HBOSplc.com

Commenting upon the housing market in the UK, Martin Ellis, Chief Economist, said:

"House prices continued to rise in northern England during the final quarter of 2004. Whilst prices in this part of the country increased rapidly during 2004 as a whole, there was significant slowing in house price inflation in the second half of the year as first-time buyers increasingly faced similar difficulties to those in the south in buying a home. This trend is expected to continue in 2005.

The continuation of rapid house price inflation in northern Britain and Wales in 2004 resulted in a sharp drop in the number of towns across the country where the average price is below £100,000. At the other end of the spectrum, there was an almost doubling in the number of towns with an average price above £300,000."

re/....

Table 1: All Houses, All Buyers (Seasonally Adjusted)
4th Quarter 2004

Region	Index 1983=100	Standardised Average Price £	Annual Change %	% of UK Average 2004 Q4
North	518.9	130,933	25.6	81
Yorkshire &The Humber	522.8	120,724	22.2	75
North West	504.9	129,151	27.3	80
East Midlands	557.3	145,671	15.7	90
West Midlands	559.2	157,835	14.5	97
East Anglia	543.2	163,431	12.4	101
Wales	516.9	133,775	15.9	83
South West	558.1	184,532	13.4	114
South East	529.6	214,967	7.2	133
Greater London	606.9	241,670	3.9	149
Northern Ireland	442.2	113,707	24.2	70
Scotland	342.4	99,056	17.4	61
U.K.	524.1	161,940	15.1	100

The Halifax House Price Index is prepared from information that we believe is collated with care, but we do not make any statement as to its accuracy or completeness. We reserve the right to vary our methodology and to edit or discontinue the indices at any time for regulatory or other reasons. Persons seeking to place reliance on the indices for their own or third party commercial purposes do so at their own risk.

Ends.

HBOSplc   HBOS plc
The Mound,
Edinburgh EH1 1YZ

Source: Halifax plc

Confusing measures of house prices fall well short

With residential property valued so highly, economists agree that there is a need for more accurate, timely figures

By Simon Briscoe and Christopher Swann

For those seeking to keep track of the value of their biggest asset, the plethora of measures of house price inflation can cause more than a little confusion.

The Halifax and Nationwide indices last week registered an annual rise in house prices of about 18 per cent in July. The Land Registry figures, by contrast, showed prices rising by just 12 per cent. Newer indices such as Rightmove and Hometrack have also shown more modest rises.

The confusion is not just an issue for curious homeowners. The Bank of England has long bemoaned the lack of clarity in housing market figures. Movements in house prices are central to the performance of the economy, with an impact far outweighing that of the stock market. At the end of last year the total value of residential property was £2,116bn, compared with the £1,370bn of financial assets held directly by households.

City economists agree that there is a need for a more accurate, timely measure of the housing market.

Part of the problem with the housing market figures lies with the inherent difficulty of measuring prices.

Unlike shares or bonds, no two houses are the same. As a result it is not always possible to predict the price of one house based on how much another house has sold for. The fact that houses are sold infrequently also makes it hard to observe price changes. Over the 1990s the number of houses sold per year was about 7 per cent. At this rate, each house was sold on average once every 14 years.

Measure for measure

House buying process	Point at which indices are calculated
Begin search	
	Rightmove
	10 weeks
Verbal offer	Halifax
	4 weeks Nationwide
Mortgage approved	Hometrack
	4 weeks
Exchange of contracts	
	1 week ODPM index
Transaction completed	
	4-6 weeks
Transaction registered	Land Registry

UK house price indices

Index	Sample	Factors included	S/A*
ODPM	5% sample of Council of Mortages Lenders' eligible completion	Adjusted by type, number of bedrooms, gardens etc	No
Halifax	Loans approved for house purchase	More detailed characteristics	Yes
Nationwide	Loans approved for house purchase	More detailed characteristics	Yes
Land Registry	100% of sales registered in England and Wales	Simple price average not adjusted by type	No
Hometrack	Survey of approximately 4,000 estate agents' estimated local average prices	Adjusted by type, number of bedrooms gardens etc.	No
Rightmove	Sellers' asking prices posted on website	Adjusted by type, number of bedrooms gardens etc.	No

*seasonally adjusted   Source: Bank of England and Office of Depty PM.

But there are also significant drawbacks to each of the current gauges of the housing market, with each measuring the market in a slightly different way.

Rightmove, the property website, registers just the asking price for houses. The drawback is that owners may be forced to accept significantly less than the asking price. But the Rightmove index can be a valuable early warning signal of confidence in the market.

The Halifax and Nationwide indices – perhaps the most widely publicised measures – are based on mortgage approvals. The problem with the figures is that they do not reflect the price at which the transaction is finalised. In addition they do not cover all transactions. Official estimates suggest about 25 per cent of house purchases are paid for in cash and these are not captured by the mortgage lender figures.

The measure preferred by the Bank of England is prepared by the Office for the Deputy Prime Minister – a quarterly series based on completions. The sample size is small, with only 5 per cent of transactions captured. In September, the government will start to produce these figures monthly. But the figures will still not be as timely as economists would like.

For economists the most authoritative guide is provided by the Land Registry figures. Halifax captures about 17 per cent of the market while the Land Registry figures contain the final price for all housing transactions in England and Wales.

Here too, however, there are drawbacks. The first is that the figures are released only every three months and even then with a long delay. The second is that they are not adjusted for changes in the type of houses being sold. If, for example, the proportion of large detached houses sold in a given period increases, the average house price will rise even when there has been no real change in the value of either expensive or cheaper properties.

Source: *Financial Times*, 25 August 2003.

Not everyone calculates an index the same way!

Local authorities are affected in a number of ways. New housing developments require the provision of additional infrastructure: roads, public transport, schools, leisure services. The state of the private housing market also affects the demand for public sector housing and, since 1993, part of local authority income has derived directly from property values in their area through the imposition of the council tax. Employers are also affected. The attraction of an area for new employees will, in part, be affected by the quantity, quality and price of the housing stock. For banks and building societies, house purchase provides a large part of their business.

It is hardly surprising then that the state of the housing market – and house prices in particular – is frequently seen as a barometer of economic activity. Headlines such as those in Figure 4.5 are of direct relevance to many business organisations as well as individuals trying to buy or sell their houses.

The construction of such a house-price index follows along the lines of the methods discussed earlier in this chapter, although with considerable technical and computational difficulties to be overcome. It will be evident that an index constructed on the basis of a simple average will not suffice: the mix of housing types in the UK housing market requires some sort of weighted average. At the beginning of 1983 the Halifax Building Society set up a database system to collect data on the house-purchase transactions dealt with by the society. Not only was information about the purchase price of each property recorded but also information on a variety of other

variables relating to each property, including geographical location of the property, type of property, age of the property, number of rooms, type of central heating, whether the property had a garage, and the garden size. The inherent difficulty in constructing a house-price index relates to the reasons why the price at which a property is sold might change over time. Such a property price might change because of what might be described as house-price inflation – a general change in property prices in the economy – or it might change because the property itself has altered over time: perhaps the property has had central heating installed, or has had an extension built, or had the garden landscaped or a garage built. All of these factors might affect the price of an individual property – to make it 'worth' more in the eyes of the purchaser – regardless of what was happening to house prices generally. It is clearly important to be able to distinguish between these two general factors if the house-price index, an important economic barometer, is to reflect house-price inflation. Using the statistical technique of multiple regression (which is explained in Chapter 10) the influence of each of these other variables on the change in property prices over time was calculated statistically for different categories of property (new houses, existing houses, first-time buyers, former owner-occupiers). This then makes it possible to remove from the house-price changes recorded on the database that part caused by changes in the characteristics of houses over time (like central heating). This in turn makes it possible then to assess the general inflationary trend in

The perfect indicator moves closer

New indices from government and the FT provide the best view yet of trends

By Simon Briscoe

The release last week of another house price index – this time from the government – hot on the heels of the launch of the FT's own index, could be seen as a good way of adding to the confusion about the real value of property.

Taken together, though, the FT House Price Index and the new index produced by John Prescott's Office of the Deputy Prime Minister (ODPM) will give most people a sufficiently clear message about house price trends.

Information about the housing market seems confusing because all the indices are measuring different things. But the two latest additions are material steps on the road to the perfect index – one that includes all transactions, is timely and is adjusted both for seasonal variations and changes in the mix of housing transactions (the balance between expensive and cheaper houses).

Although civil servants have been calculating a house price index for 35 years – theirs is the longest running index in the country – it was not widely followed because it was quarterly rather than monthly, and published some time after the period to which it related.

The Treasury and Bank of England asked some years ago for a reliable official index, so that the policymakers would not be subjected to confusion when the figures from Halifax and Nationwide – traditionally the two series most closely watched – gave conflicting messages. Last week, the ODPM, which is responsible for the government's housing policy, obliged with revamped and much improved figures.

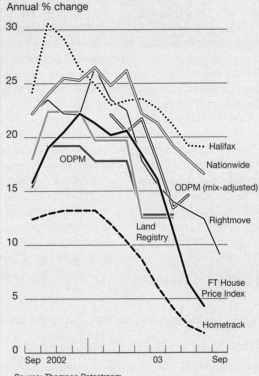

House price rises are slowing
Annual % change

Source: Thomson Datastream.

The ODPM measure shows the inflation rate of house prices falling from 22 per cent in February to $14\frac{1}{2}$ per cent in July. The FT House Price Index shows a larger fall, from 22 per cent at the turn of the year to just under 5 per cent in August. The trend is clear and common, though the FT index falls more sharply, especially in the last two months.

The ODPM index will be monthly and more timely than its predecessor. It will also use an improved methodology in line with the recommendations of experts from the Office for National Statistics, to count only mortgages that lead to completions and exclude remortgages and purchases by sitting tenants (not the case in some other

indices). But it includes only a quarter of all mortgages and excludes cash purchases.

Figures will be published for all sales, new and old dwellings and for first-time buyers and existing homeowners. Regional figures are available.

The coverage and statistical robustness of the index suggests that it will become the benchmark for the trends in the housing market financed by mortgages, superceding to some extent the figures from other sources.

The ODPM had until now been able to publish only a quarterly series because the small sample of transactions from lenders was inadequate for a monthly version. But many of the 49 lenders that supply data are now passing on information about all their transactions rather than a 5 per cent sample.

The increase in sample size from 3,000 a month to 25,000 means a monthly series can be created. The ODPM hopes that an increasing number of lenders will supply full data, but the survey continues to be voluntary.

The index will measure prices at completion, in contrast to most other indices that use figures for mortgage offers or even asking prices. The index uses expenditure weights so that a house in London costing twice the price of a house in the North will have double the contribution to the index. This will lead to the index having a bias in favour of the trends in the south east of the country where prices are higher.

The FT House Price Index, produced by consultants Acadametrics, is more timely. It is published on the same day as the later of the monthly Halifax and Nationwide indices, and will be two months ahead of the ODPM when it is published. Our figure for September will be published in two weeks when the latest data for the government's index will be July.

Our data are seasonally adjusted – although the ODPM is expecting to be able to adjust its data in the next year or two – and includes all domestic property purchases. The FT index is not yet mix adjusted – a weakness that is unlikely to affect the short-term trends, but probably accounts for some of the difference in the rate of inflation shown in the FT and ODPM measures.

None of the existing indices is perfect – each has its faults or omis-

sions. Looking forward, the ODPM says the "ultimate target" of creating a house price index for England and Wales that also reflects cash purchases might be only five years away. The Land Registry's long-term plans for E-conveyancing and the proposed development of a National Property Databank will improve the Land Registry data.

The ODPM's index would then be calculated using Land Registry data instead of the survey of lenders. Such an index could then be extended to cover the whole of the UK pending the commitment of the regional administrations in Scotland and Northern Ireland.

At that stage the nation will be as close to a perfect index as possible. Until that time – and it could be another boom and bust away – the FT and ODPM indices will answer most questions.

Source: *Financial Times*, 20 September 2003.

New indices from government and the FT provide the best view yet of trends.

house prices over time, since once we have removed the effect of these other factors on house-price changes, we must be left with a measure of the general inflation of house prices. However, as with any aggregate index, it is necessary to use some set of weights to calculate an index series. In the case of the Halifax house-price index the weighting method used was the Laspeyres method, with 1983 as the

chosen base period for the weights, a choice in part influenced by the need to update the index on a regular, monthly basis. The various house-price indices produced by the society on a regular basis thus represent the change in average property prices assuming the same overall characteristics as those bought in 1983.

Exercises

In addition to the exercises shown here you should return to the exercises in Chapter 3 and, where appropriate, calculate the statistics introduced in this chapter for each data set. Compare the information obtained from the statistics with that obtained from the diagrams produced for Chapter 3.

1 For the two data sets shown below calculate the mean and standard deviation and comment on the relationship.

Set 1	Set 2
10	100
20	200
30	300
40	400
50	500

2 For the data in Table 4.11, plot the real and money values over time on the same graph. Comment on the potential for misleading the user of money values.

3 In the Laspeyres index in this chapter we used 2005 as the base year. Choose 2009 as the base year instead and recalculate the Laspeyres series for 2005, 2009 and 2010. Comment on these values compared with the index base 2005.

4 Consider the consumer price index which is published by the government (or its statistical agency). Find out:

(a) what weights are used in the calculation of the price index;

(b) how these weights are obtained;

(c) whether the calculations follow the Laspeyres or Paasche method.

How 'reliable' do you think the price index is as a measure of how inflation is affecting the consumer over time?

5 Table 4.13 shows the age distribution of males and females in the UK at the time of their marriage, for 1995, 2001 and 2005.

Table 4.13	Age distribution at marriage: UK					
	Males			Females		
	1995	*2001*	*2005*	*1995*	*2001*	*2005*
Under 21 years	6 302	4 625	3 179	20 643	13 874	8 941
21–24	49 432	25 840	22 105	75 071	45 687	39 067
25–29	105 218	78 687	67 177	100 644	85 647	78 647
30–34	68 245	70 657	67 623	54 819	59 859	60 298
35–44	53 350	65 242	73 559	43 115	52 209	60 401
45–54	24 786	26 122	30 518	19 720	20 459	24 811
55 and over	14 918	14 956	19 580	8 239	8 394	11 566

Source: Annual Abstract of Statistics.

Using the data calculate for each sex:

(a) the mean

(b) the median

(c) the standard deviation

(d) the lower and upper quartiles

(e) the IQR

(f) the coefficients of variation and skewness.

Use these statistics to comment on similarities and differences between the sexes and over time. Consider the potential use of such data for a clothing firm specialising in bridal wear.

6 Table 4.14 shows the size of the fishing fleet in England and Wales by size of vessel in 1995 and 2005 (data at 31 December each year). By calculating and using appropriate statistics comment on the changes that have taken place.

Table 4.14	Fishing fleet by vessel size: England and Wales	
	1995	*2005*
10 m and under	6320	4833
10.01 – 12.19 m	1016	449
12.20 – 17.00 m	622	387
17.01 – 18.29 m	187	112
18.30 – 24.38 m	574	253
24.39 – 30.48 m	212	143
30.49 – 36.58 m	127	55
Over 36.58 m	117	109
Total	9175	6341

Source: Annual Abstract of Statistics.

7 Your organisation has recently started advertising its services on the internet. The marketing manager has indicated that she wants to know how long it takes internet users to access your company's internet screen, since there is concern it is taking too long and deterring interest. You have asked colleagues and friends at a variety of other organisations to access your own company's website and keep a careful record of how long it took them to get into the company's home page. The results for 120 attempts are:

Access time (seconds)	No. of attempts at access
up to 15 seconds	17
15 < 20	24
20 < 25	19
25 < 30	28
30 < 35	19
35 or over	13

(a) Construct an ogive for this data and comment on your result.

(b) Explain which measure(s) of average and dispersion you would suggest using for this data and the reasons for your preference.

(c) Calculate the measure(s) of average and dispersion.

(d) Interpret these, and any other statistics you think might be useful, in the context of the problem.

8   The leisure services committee of a local authority has seen its budget decline over the last few years and is currently having to consider closing a number of its leisure facilities – sports halls, small parks, museums and so on. One closure being considered is that of a small branch library in an outlying village. As a preliminary aspect of the decision some data has been collected on the number of people using the library and its facilities:

No. of people using the library per day	No. of days
less than 10	5
10 < 20	12
20 < 30	28
30 < 40	44
40 < 50	50
50 < 75	30
75 or more	8

Calculate suitable measures of average and dispersion for this data.

9 The data shown in Table 4.15 shows average weekly earnings for all adults, weekly rate of unemployment benefit for adults and the retail price index for the UK for the period 1994–2003.

Using this data comment on any trends in earnings and benefits. Do you think the RPI is the most appropriate index for deflating the unemployment benefit series?

Table 4.15	Earnings, unemployment benefit, retail price index: UK		
	Average weekly earnings £	*Weekly unemployment benefit £*	*RPI 1987 = 100*
1994	325.7	45.45	144.1
1995	336.3	46.45	149.1
1996	351.7	48.25	152.7
1997	367.6	49.15	157.5
1998	384.5	50.35	162.9
1999	400.1	51.40	165.4
2000	416.0	52.20	170.3
2001	441.0	53.05	173.3
2002	461.1	53.95	176.2
2003	472.5	54.65	181.3
2004	498.2	55.65	186.7
2005	516.5	56.20	192.0
2006	537.4	57.45	198.1

Note: Unemployment benefit was replaced in October 1996 by the Jobseeker's allowance.
Source: Annual Abstract of Statistics.

10 A retail organisation has recently been investigating customer spending patterns at two of its stores, Store A and Store B, and has obtained the following data:

	Store A (£s)	*Store B (£s)*
Mean spending per customer	12.25	30.05
Median spending per customer	10.88	29.91
Standard deviation	7.79	7.77
Lower quartile	6.34	25.04
Upper quartile	17.43	35.32

Using these statistics, and any others you can derive, draft a short management report summarising the implications of this data. The Store A figures were based on a representative sample of 500 customers and the Store B figures on 350 customers.

5   Probability and Probability Distributions

Learning objectives

By the end of this chapter you should:

- understand the principles of probability
- understand the terminology of probability
- understand the basic rules of probability
- be able to apply probability to typical business problems
- understand the principles of a probability distribution
- be able to use the Binomial distribution
- be able to use the Normal distribution

This chapter is concerned with introducing the basic principles of probability and discussing how such principles relate to business and to management decision making. Regardless of the organisations with which you are familiar and regardless of the nature and extent of your own management experience, you will appreciate that all business organisations operate in an uncertain environment. Uncertainty exists in a variety of forms: will the company's new product be popular with customers, will we win the new contract, will we gain the export order we have bid for, will our employees take industrial action next week? Doubtless you can add to the list of typical uncertainties yourself. *Probability* is a statistician's way of trying to quantify such uncertainties and we shall begin to see in this chapter how probability can be used as an aid to management decision making. For it is in the area of decision making that such uncertainties cause problems for the manager. If we knew for certain what the outcome(s) of a particular managerial decision would be, then we could rationally choose between the alternative decisions available to us. Consider a firm assessing the price to charge for one of its products. The manager responsible knows that, other things being equal, a price reduction is likely to attract more customers and that, logically, the larger the price reduction the larger the likely number of customers attracted to the product. The difficulty for the manager lies in assessing these likelihoods – they are not guaranteed outcomes. There are too many other factors which might impact on the outcome to offer such guarantees: the effect of advertising, customer attitudes, fashions, competitors' strategy.

Somehow, the manager has to assess such likelihoods and reach an appropriate decision. In many cases the simple principles of probability will help. Equally, probability lies at the heart of market research – an important activity for most organisations today. Private sector organisations frequently commission market research in the context of customer attitudes to price, design, availability, quality and so on. Public sector organisations are increasingly involved in market research: what do patients think of the health services provided, what do local authority 'customers' think of the refuse collection services, the municipal leisure facilities and so on. The principles of such market research are that we collect data on a sample – of customers perhaps – and analyse this using some of the techniques already introduced. So, for example, we might undertake market research on a sample of our customers and determine that, say, 40 per cent of our customers would increase their purchases of our product if we reduced the price by 10 per cent. The difficulty for the manager is that this information relates only to the sample. What the manager is primarily interested in is the population – all customers in this instance. Somehow we have to be able to transfer our conclusions based on the sample analysis to the entire population. This can also be achieved through the application of the probability principles that we shall introduce.

Some ruminations on risk

Even well-educated people find it difficult to reason about matters of probability and fall back on what has been recently publicised or can be expressed in images

By Samuel Brittan

There is little I can usefully add to the millions of words already written about mad cows and the reactions to them of excitable human beings. The interesting aspect of this episode is the exaggerated reaction to very small risks – and indeed the inability or unwillingness of many so-called educated people to reason in terms of probabilities. Quick public judgements are often based not on any kind of risk assessment, but on what psychologists call the "availability error" – that is, whatever first comes to mind. This in turn is determined by what has been recently publicised, sounds dramatic and can be expressed in images rather than abstractions.

Many readers will remember the film *Jaws*, about a man-eating shark. The screening of the film caused a sharp drop in the number of swimmers off the coast of California, where a shark can occasionally be found. Yet the risk of swimmers being snapped up by a shark is very much less than the risk of their being killed in a road accident while on the way to the coast.

The psychologist Stuart Sutherland, in a paperback entitled *Irrationality*, analyses the fears, wishful thinking and prejudices which so often divert people from logical thought.

Most of the book takes for granted the conventional methods of reasoning used by the more numerate of social scientists. However, I became a little more suspicious when he waxed enthusiastic about techniques such as "cost benefit analysis" and "multiple regression analysis". Those who follow economic matters constantly come across references to these techniques and should be aware how often they have been misleading. Multiple regression analysis, for example, has underpinned most of the short-term economic forecasts behind so many recent policy errors.

At this point I thought it only fair to give a hearing to a heretic, John Adams, a reader in geography at University College, London. He is well acquainted with modern methods of risk assessment, but is convinced they often lead us astray. His point is that specialist consultants often do not know the risks themselves and hide this from the public or even themselves.

He has been involved in fierce controversies about safety belts in cars, which serve to illustrate the point. Most of the original arguments in favour of compulsory seatbelts were based on a fall in car accidents in Australia after they were introduced there. So far so good. Indeed Adams rebukes the anti-safety belts lobby for at first relying too much on libertarian arguments against "criminalising self risk".

His main point, however, is that the conventional argument for prohibition ignores the human factor. If drivers know they are protected by safety belts they will be just that little bit more careless. So the saving of lives in accidents will be offset by the greater number of accidents which occur. This is known as the "risk compensation hypothesis": it is like taking fewer precautions to avoid an infectious disease because one has been inoculated.

It is an open question whether the resulting increase in careless driving more than offsets the benefits of safety belts. Such arguments are rarely conclusively settled. It is enough to say that the advocates of compulsion are now a little more cautious in the claims they make. But you have to be numerate in the conventional sense to see the force of Adams' arguments. For he does not need to say that once safety belt laws are enforced people drive around like maniacs. An increase in carelessness so small that most drivers would not be aware of it could be sufficient to more than wipe out the savings in lives from seatbelts.

One common intellectual ploy to defuse arguments on probability is to make a distinction between risk and uncertainty. Risks are calculable and can be insured against – for instance, the chance of a normal single dice throwing a six is one in six. Uncertainty occurs when you do not even know what the risks are – as would be the case if one has no idea what was on the faces of the dice. All or none might be sixes, making it impossible to estimate the likelihood of any particular outcome.

This distinction has never quite convinced me since there are few situations where you can not obtain some vague idea of magnitudes. Suppose that you are considering investing in an oil pipeline in a former Soviet republic. It might be blown up or a new regime might confiscate it; but a little study of history suggests that the chances of this happening are well above zero, but much less than 10 per cent. So already there are some limits.

On the other hand, there can be some doubt about even a conventional risk calculation. The odds against being killed in a road accident on the way to a Californian beach are themselves subject to a considerable margin of error, however specifically you try to pose the problem in terms of distance travelled, weather conditions and so on. It seems to me that there is a spectrum between pure risk – for example, when we are dealing with properly made dice – and utter uncertainty, when we have no idea what is going to happen.

But I would like to move to a rather different example where the odds are said to be poorly understood. That is the addiction of millions to the UK National Lottery. The critics assert that the punters do not realise how heavily the odds are stacked against winning enormous prizes. But this need not be the case. Whether one wishes to pay for a tiny chance of a huge fortune is a matter of personal taste.

There may be a *tendency* for poorer and less educated people to be more inclined to have a flutter on the lottery. But one should look at the opportunities open to people: a successful bet against high odds may be the only possibility available for many to jump to a higher living standard (unlike professional and business people who have other opportunities for advancement in their own careers).

The more sophisticated objection to the lottery is that it is not a fair game. In other words, the takings are not all distributed in prize money, even allowing for administrative costs and the operator's profit. A hefty slice goes to good causes approved by the government.

For this reason it would be illogical to invest in the lottery if such huge prizes were available in alternative forms of betting that returned more of the stake to the punter. But they are not. By selectively legalising its own giant betting shop, the state has got there first. If full liberalisation of betting had been implemented, then either the present prizes would not be available, or one private corporation would have established a monopoly position and taken advantage of the economies of scale obtainable in high-stake betting.

Finally, a confession. I have been avoiding beef – not obsessively but where I have had a clear choice, as in restaurants. I can rationalise my action even if the odds against infection are as high as I would guess them to be. The main reason is that although I like roast beef or a steak occasionally, it is almost no sacrifice to eat poultry, game, fish or even pasta instead. It is not like ice-cream or patisserie, the absence of which would make me feel really deprived. Why suffer from even extremely remote neurotic anxieties when the cost of assuaging them is so small?

Having given a warning that the assessment of risk is often itself controversial and that it is much more difficult to apply impersonal logical principles to uncertainty, I believe it is still better to be numerate than innumerate.

Further reading: *Innumeracy* by the American mathematician J. A. Paulos (Penguin £6.99). Look also at the sequels, *A Mathematician reads the Newspaper* and *Beyond Numeracy* (Penguin). The books demonstrate you do not have to be adept at long computations to follow mathematical ideas. I wish somebody would do the same for econometrics. *Irrationality* by Stuart Sutherland (Penguin) and *Risk* by John Adams (UCL) have been discussed. *The Theory of Choice*, by S. H. Heap and others (Blackwell) is a lively introduction to the controversies in the area.

Source: *Financial Times*, 11 April 1996, p 12.

Probability, risk and uncertainty.

Terminology

A large organisation has realised that as part of its overall strategy it needs to change the organisational culture in the context of customers and service quality. Bluntly, the organisation has realised that many of its staff are not fully committed to providing a quality service to the customer on time and every time. Accordingly, the organisation is considering an organisation-wide training and development programme to raise the awareness of staff in terms of the importance of quality service. However, the organisation is concerned about the reception such a programme might get from staff and has decided to pilot the programme amongst a small number of employees to gauge their reaction before introducing the programme throughout the organisation.

It is important, though, for a cross-section of employees to be exposed to the pilot programme. It is also important that attendance on the pilot programme is not restricted to those who can be spared for a few hours from their normal duties. Accordingly, it has been decided to choose a small number of employees to attend the pilot programme at random from all those employed by the organisation. The words 'at random' imply a selection which is unpredictable and without any particular pattern or guidance. The organisation's employees can be categorised by gender and by age as shown in Table 5.1.

Table 5.1	Employees by gender and by age			
		Age (years)		
	<25	*25 <45*	*45 or over*	*Total*
Male	132	297	206	635
Female	108	152	311	571
Total	240	449	517	1206

Experiments, outcomes, events

We have to start by introducing some of the terminology used in probability. An *experiment* is some activity that takes place. In our example the experiment would relate to the selection of an employee at random from all those employed by the organisation. An *outcome* is one of the possible results of the experiment. In this example there are outcomes representing the possible characteristics of the person chosen – we would identify six different outcomes, the six combinations of gender and age group. Note that the definition of the outcomes may vary even though the experiment does not. We might, for example, define just two outcomes: the gender of the person chosen. Finally, an *event* is the specifically defined outcome(s) that is of particular interest to us. We might define the specific event of interest as selecting an employee under 25 years of age.

Measuring probability

By definition, a probability is the likelihood or chance of a defined event occurring and can take a value between zero and one. The former value indicates literally that the event has no chance of occurring, while the latter that it is certain to occur. In general, there are three ways of obtaining such a probability. The first is theoretical, where, using mathematics and/or logic, we can calculate a probability. The second is empirical, where we directly observe a probability. The third is subjective, where we have an opinion, or hunch, about the chance of something happening. Consider the experiment of rolling a dice which has six sides, with each side showing one number from one to six and with each side showing a different number.

Activity 5.1

If we define an event as the number six showing, what is the probability of this event happening? How do you know? Would you class this as theoretical, empirical or subjective?

Solution is given on p 588.

In its most basic form a probability can be calculated as:

$$P(Event) = \frac{Number\ of\ ways\ the\ event\ could\ occur}{Total\ number\ of\ outcomes}$$

where P(Event) is the standard form of notation indicating that we require the probability of the event defined. In the context of our Activity example we would have:

$$P(6) = \frac{1}{6}$$

That is, there is a probability of 1/6 that when throwing a die we would get a six. Consider carefully the implications of this. It does not mean that if we were to throw such a die six times then on exactly one of those occasions we would throw a six. (If anyone thinks this applies, please contact the author for a game of no-limit poker!) It is, rather, an indication of a theoretical probability – one that in the long run we would expect to observe (and note that we do not define exactly what is meant by 'long run' in this context). In our organisation example, comparable probabilities are also obtained. If we require, for example, the probability of selecting an employee at random who is male we have:

P(Male) = 635/1206 = 0.527 (to 3 decimal places)

Mutually exclusive events

Two events are said to be *mutually exclusive* when they cannot occur simultaneously. For example, we define the experiment of choosing an employee at random. We define three events: Event A the person is male, Event B the person is female, Event C the person is under 25 years. It is clear that Events A and B are mutually exclusive: they cannot happen simultaneously. However, Events A and C are *not* mutually exclusive: they could happen at the same time (as could B and C).

Independent and conditional events

An *independent* event is one where the probability of the event occurring is not affected by other events. A *conditional* event is one whose probability is so affected. It seems reasonable to suppose, for example, that the probability that a person buys this book is independent of the probability of the person being left-handed. That is, the probability of a person buying this book is independent of whether they are left- or right-handed. The probability of a person buying this book, however, may well be conditional on which type of course they are taking at college or university. That is, the probability of a person buying this book is affected by the type of course they are taking. We shall see shortly why it is important to distinguish between conditional and independent events.

Collectively exhaustive events

A group of events are said to be *collectively exhaustive* if they encompass all possible outcomes from the experiment. Consider the experiment of choosing an employee at random. We define two events: the person is male, the person is female. Clearly the two events are collectively exhaustive since one of the two events must occur. This is frequently useful in probability calculations. We know that:

$$P(Male) = 0.527$$

and because they are collectively exhaustive we know that:

$$P(Male) + P(Female) = 1$$

hence

$$P(Female) = 1 - P(Male) = 0.473$$

This is known as the *complement* of the defined event.

Most of us are highly likely to get probability wrong

By John Kay

The Monty Hall problem is named after the host of a 1970s quiz show, *Let's Make a Deal*. The successful contestant chooses from three closed boxes. One contains the keys to a car and the other two a picture of a goat. The choice made, Monty opens one of the other doors to reveal – a goat. He taunts the guest to change the decision. Should the guest switch to the other closed box?

When the solution was published in an American magazine, thousands of readers – including professors of statistics – alleged an error. Paul Erdös, the great mathematician, reputedly died still musing on the Monty Hall problem. But the answer is, indeed, yes: you should change.

This is not the only case where intuition does not correspond to the mathematics of probability. One person in a 1,000 suffers from a rare disease. A friend has just tested positive for this illness and the test gives a correct diagnosis in 99 per cent of cases. How likely is it that your friend has the disease? Not at all likely. In random groups of 1,000 people an average of 10 would display false positives and only one would be correctly diagnosed with the disease. But most people,

including most doctors, think otherwise. "The human mind," said science writer Stephen Jay Gould, "did not evolve to deal with probabilities."

Last month, the General Medical Council struck off Professor Sir Roy Meadow, the paediatrician, from the medical register. He had given misleading evidence in the criminal prosecution of Sally Clarke, whose two infants died in their cots. When Mrs Clarke was charged with their murder, Sir Roy told the jury that the chances of two successive cot deaths in the one family was "one in 73m".

But although the disciplinary committee heard evidence from distinguished statisticians, it does not appear that they understood the application of probability theory to such cases any better than Sir Roy. The committee found that he had underestimated the incidence of cot deaths, and that he had not taken account of genetic and environmental factors that mean a household that experiences one cot death is more likely than average to suffer another. But even if you recognise these effects, his key conclusion remains valid. It is unlikely that such an accident would have happened at all. It is very unlikely indeed that

such an accident could have happened twice in the same family.

Of course it is unlikely. The events that give rise to criminal cases are always unlikely, otherwise the courts would be unable to deal with the backlog. If Osama bin Laden is ever brought to justice, the question will not be "is it likely that two aircraft hit the World Trade Center on September 11?" – to which the answer is no – but "given that two aircraft did hit the World Trade Center on September 11, is it likely that bin Laden was responsible?" Confusion of these two separate issues has become known as "the prosecutor's fallacy".

A cot death in a family increases the probability that there will be another, but a murder in a family may well increase the probability of another murder by even more: wicked parents may continue to be wicked. Sir Roy might have been right to conclude that two cot deaths were more suspicious than one. But the Court of Appeal, releasing Mrs Clarke, was certainly right to have concluded that this statistical evidence could never, on its own, establish guilt beyond reasonable doubt.

You should not trust doctors, or lawyers, with probabilities; and be very hesitant about trusting yourself. Adversarial legal proceedings are a bad forum for unravelling technical issues. And we cannot expunge collective responsibility for mistakes by excoriating selected individuals.

The business and financial system, more than Bernie Ebbers and Henry Blodget, was to blame for the dotcom boom and bust. Failures in legal processes, rather than over-confident professors, led to the unjust conviction of women such as Sally Clarke. But scapegoating has a long history – at least since Leviticus: "Aaron shall lay both his hands upon the head of the live goat, and confess over him all the iniquities of the children of Israel . . . and the goat shall bear upon him all their iniquities unto a land not inhabited".

Source: Financial Times, 16 August 2005.

Understanding probability isn't as easy as it looks.

The Multiplication Rule

We have seen how we can calculate a simple probability. Frequently we require the probability not of one event but of some sequence or combination of events occurring. Consider the experiment of selecting two employees at random. Let us assume that the selection is to be computer-based by using the personnel records of all employees held on the computer network. Let us consider the probability of the first person chosen being male P(M1). This, as we know, is 0.527. Let us now consider the probability that the second person chosen is also male, P(M2).

To determine this we must consider whether the two events, M1 and M2, are independent. This in turn depends on the sample selection process itself. We might consider the scenario where the computer system could select the same person twice (after all, having been selected once their name will still be on the computer file for selection a second time). In this case the two events will be independent and P(M2) will be 0.527 also, since from a total of 1206 employees on file, 635 will be male. Assume we now require P(M1 and M2), that is the probability that both selections are male. The calculation is straightforward, applying what is known as the *multiplication rule*:

$$P(M1 \text{ and } M2) = P(M1) \times P(M2)$$
$$= 635/1206 \times 635/1206 = 0.2772$$

That is, there is a probability of 0.2772 that we choose two males when choosing two employees at random. (Note that when calculating this probability we used the data from the table rather than the rounded probability value we had earlier. This ensures appropriate accuracy in the result.) The rule is readily extended to longer sequences – for example choosing three males or four. However, the rule as currently formulated only applies to events which are independent – as we supposed these two are.

For conditional events the rule must be modified. Consider the following. We now decide to amend the computer program which is selecting names at random from the personnel file. The program is changed so that if a person has been chosen once in any given experiment, they cannot be chosen again. Once more we require the probability P(M1 and M2) – that both people chosen are male. However, this time Event M2 is conditional upon Event M1. Consider P(M1). Given that 635 out of 1206 employees are male this will be 635/1206. Now consider Event M2. Its probability will depend on Event M1 – whether we chose a male the first time or not. Assume that we did (after all the required probability relates to both selections being male). If the first selection was male this implies that of the remaining 1205 employees, 634 are male, hence P(M2) = 634/1205. Technically we should now refer to the probability of Event M2 in a different way, since we have specified that Event M1 must have happened first. The notation for doing this is to denote the probability of Event M2 as:

$$P(M2 \mid M1) = \frac{634}{1205}$$

where P(M2 | M1) is referred to as the probability of M2 *given that* Event M1 has occurred. So technically we now have:

$$P(M1 \text{ and } M2) = P(M1) \times P(M2 \mid M1) = \frac{635}{1206} \times \frac{634}{1205}$$
$$= 0.2770$$

The difference between the two results may seem trivial. It is, however, important to ensure the appropriate calculation is being performed. In practice the resulting difference can be critical.

It is also worth noting that for two independent events, A and B, then P(B | A) = P(B) – if the events are independent then by definition Event A cannot affect the probability of Event B.

Activity 5.2

The training manager is concerned that using this method of selection for the pilot training programme we might just by chance choose four people at random and that all four are aged under 25.

Can we provide any reassurance to the training manager that this is highly unlikely to occur? Assume that if a person is chosen for the programme their name is removed from the personnel file.

We would then have:

$$P(4 \text{ under } 25) = \frac{240}{1206} \times \frac{239}{1205} \times \frac{238}{1204} \times \frac{237}{1203}$$
$$= 0.00154$$

That is, a chance of less than 2 in a 1000 that such a set of events could happen. We can inform the training manager that such a sequence of selections is very unlikely but not zero.

The Addition Rule

The second important rule is the *addition rule*. Whereas the multiplication rule is concerned with situations where we require two or more events to occur, the addition rule is concerned with situations where we require only some of a group of events to occur. Consider the following. We select an employee and define two events: Event A where the person is under 25, Event B where the person is 45 or over. We require the probability of *either* Event A *or* Event B occurring – P(A or B). Simple logic indicates that this would be:

P(A or B) = P(A) + P(B)

$$= \frac{240}{1206} + \frac{517}{1206} = \frac{757}{1206} = 0.628$$

In this case, however, the two events are mutually exclusive. Consider the same Event A but a different Event B: that the person is female. If we now apply our rule we have:

$$P(A \text{ or } B) = \frac{240}{1206} + \frac{571}{1206} = \frac{811}{1206} = 0.672$$

On reflection, however, you may realise that we have effectively double counted: there are some people who are under 25 who are also female. Clearly we have two events which are not mutually exclusive and the rule must be amended:

P(A or B) = P(A) + P(B) – P(A and B)

P(A and B) will be 108/1206 so we will then have:

$$P(A \text{ or } B) = \frac{240}{1206} + \frac{571}{1206} - \frac{108}{1206} = \frac{703}{1206} = 0.583$$

This is the correct probability. As with the multiplication rule you will realise that P(A and B) for mutually exclusive events will be zero.

General form of the two probability rules

Multiplication rule: P(A and B) = P(A) × P(B | A)

Addition rule: P(A or B) = P(A) + P(B) – P(A and B)

QMDM IN ACTION
The National Lottery

Gambling in Britain has been transformed by the National Lottery. The small pink ticket from the newsagent's electronic outlet offers temptation of wealth beyond the dreams of avarice. **John Haigh** *examines a bet that, statistically, not one of our readers will live to win.*

The main game in the UK National Lottery has run since November 1994. Sales figures no longer reach those touched in January 1996, when two separate draws both passed the £100 million mark, but over £50 million worth of tickets are still sold every week. Some 90% of UK adults have played at least once, despite the low rate of return – in most draws, only 45% of proceeds are returned as prizes.

The UK format is to select six numbers from a list of 49, with a prize if you match three or more winning numbers. This is similar to many other lotteries, and teachers worldwide have found them a useful resource for illustrating ideas of probability and statistics. I offer a few here.

Counting tells us that the UK format gives almost 14 000 000 different selections. If they are equally likely, the chance of winning a share of the top prize by matching all six numbers is $p \approx 1/14\,000\,000$. To appreciate how tiny this is, suppose the chance that a particular man has a heart attack within the next year is 1 in 1000: if heart attacks occur at random, then p represents the chance that he has a heart attack within the next 40 minutes. Thus, if he buys his lottery ticket before 7.20 p.m., he is more likely to have a heart attack before the 8.00 p.m. draw than to have selected the winning numbers.

Indeed, if you spend £5 per week, you can expect to wait about

- 10 weeks to win the fixed £10 prize for matching 3 numbers,
- 4 years to win a Match 4 prize (around £62),
- over 200 years to win a Match 5 prize (perhaps £1500) and
- some 9000 years to win a bonus prize (some £100 000).

So forget about winning the jackpot (average £2 million).

The National Lottery Commission (NLC) has published reports about whether the winning numbers pass statistical tests of randomness. So rich are the datasets generated, and so many are the ways in which randomness might apparently be violated, that random chance alone makes it inevitable that some "suspect" events will occur. When Charles Goldie and I reported to the NLC, we noted that number 38 had arisen far more frequently than any other number; indeed, the *a priori* chance that *any* number would be drawn as often as 38 had been was under 1%. We also noted the surprising frequency with which one machine–ball combination selected a very high bonus number, and an unusual "resonance" between draws four steps apart in one of the other games. Our recommendation in each case was identical: check the equipment and carry out a private sequence of dummy draws to see whether this anomalous behaviour repeated.

Nearly 3 years after our (confidential) report was transmitted to the NLC, a Sunday newspaper carried a front-page headline about the excess frequency of number 38, in terms that suggested some scandal. I pointed out to the journalist the inevitability of such freak events from time to time and that, since our report, number 38 had behaved in an impeccable manner. As I write, after 1050 draws, its frequency is some 2.7 standard deviations above average, and 6 ahead of its nearest rival. But, if the lottery continues indefinitely, then the theory of simple symmetric random walks implies that it is certain that all 48 other numbers will overtake number 38 at some stage, but that the mean time for each of them to do so is infinite.

The Advertising Standards Authority has admonished a firm who made false claims about their lottery "wheel". It was marketed as a way to "increase your winning chances" by confining your selections for different tickets to just a dozen (say) of your preferred numbers. But for a given spend, the *mean* number of prizes is the same, however you make your selections. Using a wheel will increase your chance of multiple prizes, but only at the expense of reducing the chance of at least one prize, as compared with making random choices.

Legislation prevents bookmakers from offering bets based on lottery draws. They therefore bought their own machines, identical in format, and make draws twice a day, offering different bets at fixed odds. They have contrasted the £10 that is won by matching three numbers on the National Lottery with the £601 to be won on a bet on three numbers at their odds of 600–1. This is an unfair comparison. First, to win with the bookies, you select three numbers only and all must be correct; in the lottery, you select six numbers and win if any three of them are correct. And, secondly, your bet on the lottery gives you chances of higher prizes for matching more than three numbers.

An open problem is to decide how many tickets one must buy to ensure at least one prize, whatever numbers are drawn. If you can beat the figure of 163 – achieved by careful choice of 86 tickets using only the numbers 1 to 27, along with 77 tickets confined to the numbers 28–49 – then send details to Richard Lloyd at http://lottery.merseyworld.com/. This excellent website also contains a feast of up-to-date lottery information. At the other end of the scale, one can ask how many tickets should be sold so that all $N \approx 14\,000\,000$ choices have been selected. Assuming purchases are made at random, this is an application of the well-known coupon collector's problem, leading to the estimate $N \ln(N)$, around 230 000 000.

The lottery franchisee, Camelot, is coy about releasing figures for the "coverage" data – that is, what proportion of all possible combinations have been purchased at least once in any given draw. It saw this figure as a commercial secret (!), but now the NLC has published a histogram of the data. Obviously, if c is the coverage, then the chance that no ticket matches the winning combination – leading to a "rollover" (the unwon jackpot prize is added to the next draw) – is $r = 1 - c$. If M tickets are bought independently, and each of the N possible combinations is equally likely, the chance of a rollover is $r = (1 - 1/N)^M$; but the actual probabilities of a rollover have been consistently larger than this, as some combinations are chosen far more often than others.

That fact allows a modest amount of skill. Buying the less popular combinations does not affect the winning chances, but it increases the expected amount won. Advice from Henze and Riedwyl[1] is to first select six numbers completely at random (humans find this almost impossible without some outside aid, such as a shuffled deck of cards or the official Lucky Dip option). In that way, you should avoid accidentally using the same thought patterns as other players. Secondly, bias your choice towards the higher numbers by rejecting your selection and choosing again *unless* the numbers total at least 177. Now mark the combination on the ticket, and again reject it unless some numbers, but not all, are on the edge; and unless they fall into exactly two, three or four clusters. Finally, reject them if they form any obvious pattern. All this still leaves over 2 000 000 combinations.

When this strategy was tested against the actual numbers drawn over 2 years, the numbers of Match 5 and Match 4 prizes were close to average, but the prize values were indeed significantly higher. Even so, the overall return is too low for this strategy to be profitable. If UK players act in similar ways to those in other European countries, it is also sound advice to avoid using winning combinations from previous lotteries. This is not because they are less likely to be drawn again: simply that many other players will choose these numbers – perhaps on the naïve grounds that "no one else will think of doing this". Incidentally, another nice problem is to estimate how long it will be before some set of winning numbers is repeated. The same logic that indicates that a group of 23 or more people is more likely than not to have a pair with a common birthday tells us that there is an even chance of a repeat within some 4400 draws (or by the year 2038, at two draws per week).

The NLC (and the RSS) receive statistical queries from members of the public about the lottery. Mr A claimed foul on the grounds that there have been too many draws in which four of the six winning numbers have fallen in a block of six consecutive numbers. A trained statistician will calculate that, if x is the chance that a specific block of six numbers contains four winning numbers – the same as the chance of winning a Match 4 prize or better, around 1 in 1000 – then the mean frequency of this event over K draws is $44Kx$. Note that it happens *twice* if

the winning numbers are, say, 13, 26, 43, 44, 45, 47, as the blocks 42–47 and 43–48 both contain four winning numbers. Even so, the real data show that this event has actually happened a little *less often* than expected. Gut feeling alone is a poor guide.

Gut feeling led Mr B to believe that too many lottery draws were generating a pair of consecutive numbers, or triples of three consecutive numbers. Proper counting shows that almost half of all possible combinations have an adjacent pair and nearly 5% have a triple. And, once again, the lottery data are consistent with these figures.

Mr C and Mr D have claimed that they can use lottery data to forecast future draws and have sent me winning tickets as "proof". But both have been very selective. Mr C would describe how often he kicked himself for not noticing that, say, 14 and 24 had arisen in consecutive draws, making 34 a virtual certainty in the next draw! The data do not support their claims.

Mr E wrote to *The Guardian*, asking what would be the chance that a winning sequence would contain four consecutive numbers. A mathematician responded, noting that there are 41 624 sequences with exactly 4 consecutive numbers and 43 560 with at least 4 consecutive, making the chance about 1 in 336 or 1 in 321, depending on how this "event" is interpreted. But other replies, given equal billing, were complete nonsense, suggesting chances ranging from 1 in 13 841 287 201 to 1 in 22750. An exasperated reader wrote in asking how he was supposed to decide which answer to believe – he has my sympathy.

In their efforts to increase the chances of winning the jackpot, punters have stooped to absurd levels of irrationality. In the USA players have driven great distances to buy their tickets at the "lucky" store that sold the winning ticket on the Powerball game. Just as irrational is the belief that we statisticians should be better than average at forecasting the winning numbers. Your dog would do equally well.

Reference

1. Henze, N. and Riedwyl, H. (1998) *How to Win More: Strategies for Increasing a Lottery Win*. Wellesley: Peters.

Dr John Haigh, Reader in Statistics at Sussex University, is author of *Taking Chances: Winning with Probability* (Oxford University Press).

Source: *Significance* magazine, March 2006, pp. 28–9.

A Business Application

So far our investigation into probability has been somewhat elementary. Let us consider a typical business application at this stage to reinforce what we have covered. A manufacturer of computer hardware buys microprocessor chips to use in the assembly process from two different manufacturers. Concern has been expressed from the assembly department about the reliability of the supplies from the different manufacturers, and a rigorous examination of last month's supplies has recently been completed with the results shown in Table 5.2.

Table 5.2	Reliability of silicon chip supplies		
	Manufacturer A	Manufacturer B	Total
Chips found to be:			
Satisfactory	5828	3752	9580
Defective	119	198	317
Total	5947	3950	9897

On the face of it, it does look as if the assembly department is correct in expressing concern. Manufacturer B is supplying a smaller quantity of chips in total but more are found to be defective in some way compared with Manufacturer A. However, let us consider this in the context of the probability principles we have developed. Let us consider the total of 9897 as a sample. Suppose we had chosen one chip at random from this sample. The following events and their probabilities can then be obtained:

Event A: the chip was supplied by Manufacturer A
Event B: the chip was supplied by Manufacturer B
Event C: the chip was satisfactory
Event D: the chip was defective

and

P(A and C) supplied by A and satisfactory
P(B and C) supplied by B and satisfactory
P(A and D) supplied by A and defective
P(B and D) supplied by B and defective.

Activity 5.3

Calculate the probabilities of the events defined.

We then have:

P(A and C) = 5828/9897 = 0.589
P(B and C) = 3752/9897 = 0.379
P(A and D) = 119/9897 = 0.012
P(B and D) = 198/9897 = 0.020.

Table 5.3	Joint probability table		
	Manufacturer A	*Manufacturer B*	*Total*
Chips found to be:			
Satisfactory	0.589	0.379	0.968
Defective	0.012	0.020	0.032
Total	0.601	0.399	1.000

These probabilities are empirical – they have been observed to occur – and are known as joint probabilities for the obvious reason. In fact we can construct a joint probability table as in Table 5.3.

Note that, as they must, the joint probabilities sum to 1.000 (since all the joint events are collectively exhaustive). But how does this help, given that these probabilities simply express in another form the data we had in Table 5.2? Let us begin to apply the principles of conditional probability that we have developed. Suppose we wanted to know: given that a chip comes from Manufacturer A then what is the probability that it is defective? Using our standard notation this probability would be P(D|A). From Table 5.2 we can derive this probability directly. Some 119 out of the 5947 chips supplied by Manufacturer A were defective hence P(D | A) = 0.02. But as we know, it's more useful to have a general rule to work out such a probability rather than having to resort to direct observation of values in a table. Let's do some simple maths to get this. We have:

$$P(D \mid A) = \frac{119}{5947} = 0.02$$

Let's divide both the numerator (the number at the top) and the denominator (the number at the bottom) by 9897, the total number of chips checked. By dividing both numbers by 9897 we're not actually changing anything. We then get:

$$P(D \mid A) = \frac{119/9897}{5947/9897} = 0.02$$

But 119/9897 is 0.012 which, from Table 5.3, is P(D and A) while 5947/9897 is 0.601 or P(A). So we actually have:

$$P(D \mid A) = \frac{119/9897}{5947/9897} = \frac{P(D \text{ and } A)}{P(A)} = 0.02$$

giving a general rule for any two events X and Y that:

$$P(X \mid Y) = \frac{P(X \text{ and } Y)}{P(Y)}$$

Activity 5.4

Using the general rule calculate the probability that, if the chip was supplied by Manufacturer B, it is defective. Compare the two probabilities.

The same logic can be applied to Manufacturer B:

$$P(D \mid B) = \frac{P(D \text{ and } B)}{P(B)} = \frac{0.020}{0.399} = 0.05$$

Consider what we have determined. If a chip is supplied by Manufacturer A then the probability that it will be defective is 0.02. On the other hand, if the chip comes from Manufacturer B then the probability that it will be defective is two-and-a-half times as high at 0.05. Effectively, we have concluded that the Event D and the source of manufacture are *not* independent events – if they were then conditional probabilities would be the same. Clearly, we cannot conclude, based solely on this evidence, that Manufacturer B has a worse record than Manufacturer A. Many other factors would need to be taken into account: the price charged, design, availability and the fact that we have taken only one month's sample. However, we do have sufficient evidence to warrant a further investigation. We also have a planning tool to quantify the difference in quality between the two manufacturers and to take this into account in the assembly process so that the quality of the finished product is not compromised.

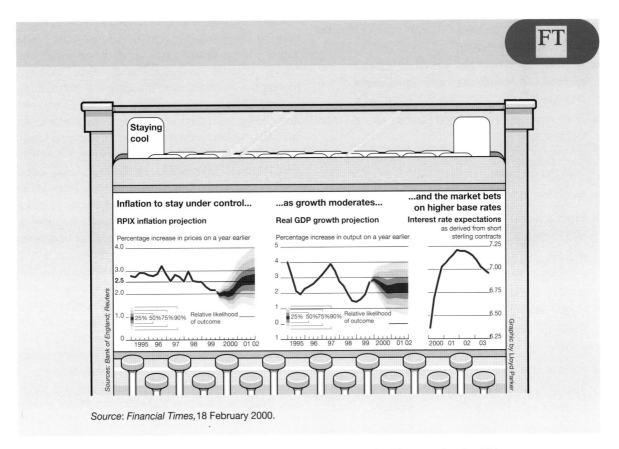

Source: *Financial Times*, 18 February 2000.

Probability distributions are sometimes used in forecasting, as in this case for the UK economy.

QMDM IN ACTION
Microsoft Research

Spam – unsolicited commercial e-mail – is a complex and growing problem, and threatens to derail the internet revolution. **Joshua Goodman** *and* **David Heckerman** *of Microsoft Research describe some statistics-based methods for blocking spam, first by distinguishing it from wanted mail, and then by constructing puzzles they propose to use to challenge suspected spammers.*

Some statistics about spam

Spam is a huge problem. A few statistics can tell us just how huge.

- Brightmail has reported that over 50% of mail on the internet is now spam.

- A recent Infoworld poll identified spam as the number 1 "information technology disaster of the past year".

- From a report by the United States Federal Trade Commission[1]:

  - 66% of spam had false information somewhere in the message;

  - 18% of spam advertises "adult" material.

- From a report by the Pew Internet and American Life Project[2]:

  - 25% of e-mail users say that spam has reduced their use of e-mail;

  - 12% of users spend half an hour or more per day dealing with spam.

Statistics also help to explain why spam is such a problem.

- It costs only about 0.01 ¢ to send spam.

- 7% of e-mail users say they have bought a product advertised in unsolicited e-mail[2].

Given the tiny costs of spamming, even a tiny response rate makes spam economically viable.

Identifying spam – harder than it looks

Around a year ago, MSN's Hotmail service proposed blocking all spam entering their system that was allegedly from Hotmail. Spammers often fake the address that their mail is from, including pretending that such mail is from Hotmail itself. Because there are no standards on the internet to say which IP addresses are allowed to send mail from which domain names, we usually cannot tell when a sender's address has been faked. (Recent proposals such as Microsoft's Caller-ID standard will help to fix this problem in the future.) The one exception today is that Hotmail knows its own valid internet addresses, and knows that mail from outside those addresses that says "From Hotmail" is fake. It sounded reasonable to block all such deceptive mail.

There are, however, a few cases where this faking may be legitimate. For instance, when your friend sends you an on-line birthday card via e-mail, the "From" address has your friend's e-mail address (perhaps at Hotmail), even though the e-mail actually originates on the greeting card company's servers, and comes from their internet address. Fortunately, we had acquired a data set of spam and good mail. We could show that, for every four spams allegedly from Hotmail that would be blocked, one good message would be lost – the exceptions were not as rare as had been thought. A 4-to-1 trade-off is not close to tolerable. This simple analysis was key to preventing an unacceptably large number of deleted good messages, including those birthday cards.

Although there are no hard-and-fast rules for marking mail as spam – even a faked "From" address is only moderately bad – by combining different indicators together, we can often be almost certain that mail is spam, and safely delete it, or very confident that it is spam, and place it in a junk folder. The question is how to combine these indicators.

One of the most popular techniques for stopping spam is the *naïve Bayes method*[3], often mistakenly simply called *Bayesian spam filtering*. In the naïve Bayes method, we try to determine the probability that a given message is spam, or good. We start by using the Bayes rule, which in this case tells us that

$$P(\text{spam} \mid \text{message}) = \frac{P(\text{message} \mid \text{spam}) \times P(\text{spam})}{P(\text{message})}$$

where

$$P(\text{message}) = P(\text{message} \mid \text{spam}) \times P(\text{spam})$$
$$+ P(\text{message} \mid \text{not spam}) \times P(\text{not spam}).$$

$P(\text{spam})$ is simply the prior probability that any given message is spam. For instance, if half the messages you receive are spam, $P(\text{spam}) = 1/2$, and similarly for $P(\text{not spam})$. Also, we need to compute $P(\text{message} \mid \text{spam})$ and $P(\text{message} \mid \text{not spam})$ – these are respectively the probability of receiving any of the billions of possible spam messages and the probability of receiving any particular good piece of e-mail, of the infinite possibilities. Again this is difficult, if not impossible. However, we can make some approximations. In particular, we shall assume that the probability of every word in the message is independent of every other word, conditioned on knowing whether the message is spam. For instance, we assume that the probability of "click" is independent of the probability of "here", given that the message is spam. Clearly, this approximation is not a great one, which is why the technique is called naïve. However, once we have made this assumption, it is easy to compute the message probabilities. In particular,

$$P(\text{message} \mid \text{spam}) = P(\text{first word} \mid \text{spam})$$
$$\times P(\text{second word} \mid \text{spam})$$
$$\times \cdots \times P(\text{last word} \mid \text{spam})$$

$$P(\text{message} \mid \text{not spam}) = P(\text{first word} \mid \text{not spam})$$
$$\times P(\text{second word} \mid \text{not spam})$$
$$\times \cdots \times P(\text{last word} \mid \text{spam}).$$

What is the probability of a particular word given spam? For each word, e.g. "click", we simply count the number of times the word occurred in all spam messages in a "training corpus" (a set of message known to be spam or good) and how many spam messages there were overall. The ratio is an estimate of the probability that any particular spam word is the word "click". We can do the same for words in non-spam messages.

Naïve Bayes is just one of many machine learning techniques, often used because it is the easiest to implement. It can be surprisingly effective, despite the simplicity of the model. If you are willing to label carefully thousands of your messages as spam or good to train the model, it can result in excellent performance for you on your own mail. However, the independence assumption in naïve Bayes limits its effectiveness. A naïve Bayes model will tend to be confused by common spam phrases like "click here

to unsubscribe" that sometimes also occur in good mail, because naïve Bayes does not model the fact that these words occur together. If each word is 10 times as likely in spam as in good mail, a naïve Bayes model will think any such message is 10 000 times more likely to be spam than good ($10 \times 10 \times 10 \times 10$) – a large overestimate of the true ratio. Other model types, such as neural networks, graphical models, logistic regression and support vector machines all make fewer assumptions and can model these kinds of relationships between words implicitly or explicitly, at the expense of more complexity. At Microsoft, we use these more complex model types.

Challenge–response systems

Probabilistic filters can do an excellent job of identifying spam. Nonetheless, like all filtering techniques, they are imperfect: they always occasionally mark some good mail as spam. At Microsoft Research, we have been exploring and adapting an idea due to Cynthia Dwork (now at Microsoft Research, Silicon Valley) and Moni Naor (at the Weizmann Institute of Science in Israel). They proposed using "computational puzzles" to stop spam[4]. We are researching a variation on this idea, in which it is used in combination with a probabilistic filter[5]. If you send me mail, my filter examines it. If it appears good, it goes in my inbox. If it looks like junk, it goes in my junk folder. To make sure that I eventually see any good mail sitting in my junk folder, my e-mail program automatically sends you a "challenge": a request to solve a computational puzzle. Your e-mail program must spend perhaps 15 seconds to solve this puzzle. It solves this puzzle automatically, in the background, without you even noticing, and then sends the puzzle solution back to my program, which verifies the solution, and moves your original message to my inbox.

If you are a legitimate sender, you are willing to spend the time to do this. But, if you are a spammer, you cannot afford to solve these puzzles – you would be able to answer fewer than 6000 puzzles per day per computer, compared with the millions of messages you can normally send.

What do these puzzles look like? One solution is to use a hash function. A hash function takes a string of letters as input and returns a number. The number is a deterministic, but nearly random, function of the input string. Slight changes in the input string result in large and unpredictable changes in the output of the function. The message recipient – the challenger – sends a challenge string based on the actual message to the message sender. The message sender must find some other string that, when put in front of the first string, results in a hash value of, say, 0. If the hash function returns a number between 1 and 15 million, the sender must try about 15 million different strings to find one that results in a zero value. A typical hash function might require 1 microsecond – a millionth of a second. It would thus take, on average, 15 seconds to find a puzzle solution. Meanwhile, the recipient only needs to verify that the solution is correct, meaning running the hash function once, which can be done in just 1 microsecond.

How to get less spam

- Choose an e-mail address that is hard to guess. Many spammers use "dictionary attacks" where they try billions of common words separately and in combination, e.g. Bob, Bob1970, StatisticsNut, etc. Choose a longer name with more words, like BobStatisticsNut1970, and a spammer is much less likely to guess it.

- Do not give your e-mail address to a company you do not trust. Some companies sell the addresses they collect.

- Do not put your e-mail address on web pages. Many spammers "crawl" the web, looking for addresses that they then add to their lists. If you need to put your e-mail address on the web, disguise it, or put it in an image. Spammers do not use image recognition software (yet!).

Designing better puzzles

There is a problem with the simple puzzle described above: it has high variance. On average, the puzzle will require 15 seconds to solve, but sometimes it will require only 1 second, sometimes 30 seconds, sometimes 45 seconds, and even occasionally more than a minute. This can be solved by using a suggestion from Cynthia Dwork and Andrew Goldberg. We can use an easier puzzle, perhaps one that returns a random number between 1 and 1 million, but require the sender to find 15 solutions. This lowers the variance by about a factor of 15. Variance is reduced linearly as the number of puzzles increases (assuming that we keep the total expected time constant). If we used a huge number

of puzzles, say 100, the variance would become negligible. But the size of the solution would also be large, even larger than the original message in some cases.

An alternative solution, also due to Dwork and Goldberg, is to use a hash which returns a number between, say, 0 and 1 billion and then require the sender to find, say, 15 solutions all with the same value, and with that value between 0 and 1000. For instance, the sender could find 15 solutions with a value of 0, or 15 solutions with a value of 1, etc. We can think of this as balls dropping into bins at random, and waiting for one of the bins to collect 15 balls in it. This problem turns out to have much lower variance than simply finding 15 solutions.

Conclusion

Spam is an extremely complex topic, and no single article can hope to describe all the ways to fight it. We have described here those techniques that rely most heavily on statistics, but we are exploring and pursuing many other ideas as well[6]. For example, we are currently exploring new industry standards that can help to stop spam. In particular, our challenge–response systems are expensive for very large legitimate senders. We are exploring standard ways for these senders to become certified as non-spammers.

No single solution will stop spam. New laws will be one part of the solution. Improved filters using better statistical analyses will be another part. Finally, all legitimate senders will be able to bypass any filter mistakes: large senders through certification; smaller senders through low variance computational puzzles. We anticipate a future in which the vast majority of spam is stopped, and all legitimate mail is delivered.

References

1. US Federal Trade Commission (2003) *False Claims in Spam*. Washington DC: US Federal Trade Commission.
2. Fallows, D. (2003) Spam: how it is hurting email and degrading life on the Internet. *Pew Internet and American Life Project*.
3. Sahami, M., Dumais, S., Heckerman, D. and Horvitz, E. (1998) A Bayesian approach to filtering junk e-mail. *American Association for Artificial Intelligence Workshop on Learning for Text Categorization, Madison, July 27th*.
4. Dwork, C. and Naor, M. (1993) Pricing via processing or combatting junk mail. *Lecture Notes in Computer Science*, **740**, 137–147.

5. Goodman, J. and Rounthwaite, R. (2004) SmartProof. Microsoft Research. (Available from http://www.research. microsoft.com/~joshuago/smartproof.pdf.)

6. Goodman, J. (2004) Spam technologies and policies. Microsoft Research. (Available from http://www.research. microsoft.com/~joshuago/spamtech.pdf.)

Joshua Goodman is a Researcher in the Machine Learning and Applied Statistics Group at Microsoft Research. He has been on loan to Microsoft's Anti-Spam product team since its inception. His previous work was on language modelling (predicting word sequences) and fast algorithms for logistic regression.

David Heckerman is founder and manager of the Machine Learning and Applied Statistics Group at Microsoft Research. Since 1992 he has been a Senior Researcher at Microsoft, where he has created applications including junk mail filters, data mining tools, handwriting recognition for the Tablet PC, troubleshooters in Windows and the Answer Wizard in Office. His work includes Bayesian methods for learning probabilistic graphical models from data. David received his doctorate from Stanford University in 1990 and is a Fellow of the American Association for Artificial Intelligence.

Source: Significance magazine, June 2004, pp. 69–72.

Probability Distributions

So far we have been considering the probability of one particular event occurring. We may also be interested in determining the probabilities of all outcomes from some experiment. In such a case we may be interested in evaluating the probability distribution that applies to the problem under investigation. Consider the following. Assume we have two normal dice, each with six sides and each showing the number one through to six. We have an experiment where we throw both dice together and we note the total of the two numbers showing. So, for example, if we threw two sixes then the total (the outcome) would be 12. However, rather than consider one specific event, we are interested in all the possible outcomes and their probabilities.

Activity 5.5

Calculate the probability for each outcome from the experiment.

We can start by determining all the possible outcomes:

Total
2
3
4
5
6
7
8
9
10
11
12

But we note that some of these outcomes can occur in different ways. For example, the outcome of a total of three could occur in two ways: the first die showing one and the second die showing two, or the reverse with the first die showing two and the second die one. It is important to realise that these are two distinct and different ways in which the outcome could occur. If we determine the number of ways each outcome could occur we obtain Table 5.4. There are a total of 36 individual outcomes (6 × 6), which can be grouped into the 11 different categories. Logically, each outcome has the same probability of occurring – 1/36 – so multiplying the number of ways the outcome can occur by this probability will give the probability of that specific outcome occurring. Table 5.5 summarises the results. So, the probability of throwing two dice and that they show a total of nine is 4/36 or 0.111. Technically, what we have produced is the probability distribution for this experiment – the probability associated with each and

Table 5.4	Outcomes

Total	No. of ways outcome can occur
2	1
3	2
4	3
5	4
6	5
7	6
8	5
9	4
10	3
11	2
12	1
Total	36

Table 5.5	Outcome probabilities

Total	No. of ways outcome can occur	Probability of each way occurring	Probability of each outcome	Probability as a decimal
2	1	1/36	1/36	0.028
3	2	1/36	2/36	0.056
4	3	1/36	3/36	0.083
5	4	1/36	4/36	0.111
6	5	1/36	5/36	0.139
7	6	1/36	6/36	0.167
8	5	1/36	5/36	0.139
9	4	1/36	4/36	0.111
10	3	1/36	3/36	0.083
11	2	1/36	2/36	0.056
12	1	1/36	1/36	0.028
Total	36		1/36	1.000

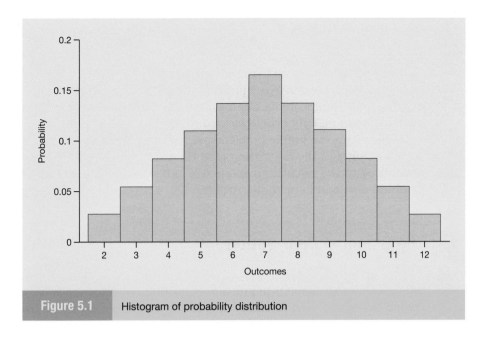

Figure 5.1 Histogram of probability distribution

every outcome. As ever, we can show this visually as in Figure 5.1. The diagram simply shows the probability on the vertical axis and the outcomes on the horizontal.

This is all very well, but what has it to do with management decision making? The answer is that there are a number of theoretical probability distributions which can be of considerable use to managers. We shall be investigating two of these. However, such distributions can be quite difficult to apply when we have to resort to a calculation of the probabilities as we have so far. They are far more useful if we are able to use the features of the distribution as shown in Figure 5.1. This is no more than a histogram for the probability distribution. It is easily converted into a frequency polygon as shown in Figure 5.2.

From Figure 5.2 we can now begin to see the potential of such a probability distribution. So far, in order to obtain a probability, we have had to calculate it using an appropriate formula. We now have the possibility of obtaining a probability from the

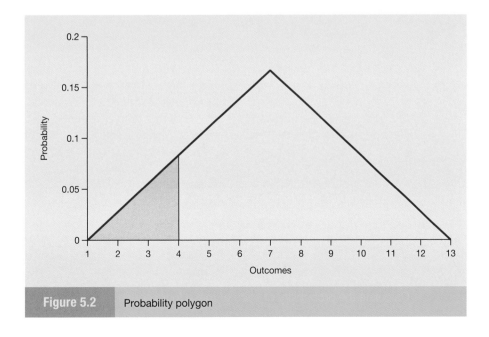

Figure 5.2 Probability polygon

graphical probability distribution. In principle if we wanted, say, the probability of the two dice showing four or less, we could obtain this from Figure 5.2. If we define the total area under the polygon as equal to one (as with probability) then if we were to measure the area under the polygon to the left of four we could express this as a proportion of the total area and hence derive the probability rather than calculate it. It should be evident that the table of probabilities and the probability distribution in Figure 5.2 show the same information. Either could be used to obtain a specific probability.

Naturally, for the simple problems we have examined so far there is no real advantage in doing this: the calculation method is simple enough. However, for some areas of probability the calculation method is not effective and we have to resort to the graphical distribution method instead.

The Binomial Distribution

The first common theoretical probability distribution is the *Binomial*. Consider the following example. On an assembly line, concern has been expressed over the quality of the final item produced. A large-scale investigation has recently been completed to assess the percentage of final output which is defective in some way and must be scrapped. The analysis revealed that on average 5 per cent of output was deemed to be defective in some way. The company – somewhat old-fashioned since it has never heard of total quality management principles – has now set up an inspection system at the end of the production process to monitor the quality of the output produced – specifically to monitor the defect rate of 5 per cent.

Activity 5.6

The inspector chooses one item at random from the production line. What is the probability that it will be defective?

Using the simple probability principles we have developed, the probability will be 5 per cent or 0.05. Similarly, suppose the inspector took two items at random. What is the probability that at least one of them is defective? To calculate this we must first assess independence: are the two events statistically independent? It seems reasonable to assume that as long as the output total is a large one then the two events can be deemed to be independent (if the factory produced only 100 items, for example, this assumption would be questionable). Defining Event A: the first item chosen is defective, and Event B: the second item chosen is defective, we then have the following possible sequences:

- first item defective, second item not defective
- first item not defective, second item not defective
- first item defective, second item defective
- first item not defective, second item defective.

Activity 5.7

Calculate the probability of each of these four sequences.

Calculating the probabilities gives respectively:

$0.05 \times 0.95 = 0.0475$
$0.95 \times 0.95 = 0.9025$
$0.05 \times 0.05 = 0.0025$
$0.95 \times 0.05 = 0.0475$

and this gives a distribution of:

No. of defective items	Probability
0	0.9025
1	0.0950
2	0.0025

We require the probability of at least one defective item from the two chosen and this will consist of the last two probabilities to give 0.0975. That is, with a 5 per cent defect rate overall there is a probability of 9.75 per cent that at least one of the two items chosen will be defective in some way. However, this is a somewhat tedious calculation, even for two items. Consider the situation if the inspector had taken a sample of 100 items and we wished to determine the probability that, say, no more than five were defective. Clearly we need some general method of addressing this type of problem. This is where the Binomial distribution comes in. In fact we can identify the key features of the experiment we have just described (choosing items at random from the assembly line and checking to see if they are defective).

- The experiment consists of a number of trials (choosing two items in our example).
- Two outcomes are possible in each trial (defective, not defective; win, lose; succeed, fail).
- The probabilities of the outcomes in each trial do not change.
- The trials are independent.

If these factors apply then we have what is known as a Binomial experiment. Under such conditions we can use the Binomial formula to calculate directly the probabilities we have determined using (tedious) logic. The formula can be expressed as:

$$^nC_r p^r q^{n-r}$$

where

^nC_r	is the term for determining the number of different ways the event can occur;
p	is the probability of the outcome from the trial under investigation;
q	is $(1 - p)$, the probability of the specified outcome from the trial not occurring;
n	is the number of trials;
r	is the specified number of outcomes we are looking for.

This undoubtedly sounds very complex but is in fact no more than we have done already. In our example we would have:

$p = 0.05$	(the probability of an item being chosen that was defective)
$q = 1 - 0.5 = 0.95$	(the probability of the item chosen not being faulty)
$n = 2$	(the number of trials)
$r = 0, 1$ or 2	(the number of faulty items chosen).

The only term still to explain is the ^nC_r term. This is a shorthand way of referring to the number of ways an event can occur. It is calculated as:

$$^nC_r = \frac{n!}{r!(n-r)!}$$

where ! is a factorial (which we introduced in Chapter 2). If we specify r = 1 (we want the number of ways we can obtain one defective item from a sample of two) then we calculate:

$$^nC_r = \frac{n!}{r!(n-r)!}$$
$$= \frac{2!}{1!(2-1)!} = \frac{2}{1} = 2$$

That is, there are two different ways of choosing one defective item from a sample of two items.

Activity 5.8

How many different ways are there of choosing five items from a sample of 50?

Here we would have n = 50 and r = 5, which would give:

$$^nC_r = \frac{n!}{r!(n-r)!}$$
$$= \frac{50!}{5!(50-5)!} = \frac{50!}{5!45!} = 2\,118\,760$$

That is, there are over 2 million different ways of choosing five items from a sample of 50. You might have a pocket calculator which has a factorial function built into it (often shown as x!). If you don't you might have had a problem with this activity because otherwise the arithmetic is very long. We can short-circuit the arithmetic we need to do. Remember that 50! is actually $(50 \times 49 \times 48 \times 47 \ldots)$ and that 45! is $(45 \times 44 \times 43 \ldots)$. This means that:

$$\frac{50!}{5!45!}$$

is actually the same as

$$\frac{(50 \times 49 \times 48 \times 47 \times 46)}{5!}$$

since the rest of the factorial calculation on the top is actually 45! so the two would cancel (one on top and one underneath). Returning to our probability problem the calculation would then be:

$$P(1 \text{ defective item}) = {}^nC_r\, p^r\, q^{(n-r)}$$
$$= (2)(0.05^1)(0.95^1) = 0.095$$

which is the same as in our earlier calculated distribution. We could equally have set r to 0 or to 2 and used the formula again. But it hardly seems worth it for the current problem. However, for larger problems it may well be.

Consider the following scenario. On another assembly line the inspector has taken a sample of 50 items and checked to see whether or not they are defective. The inspector has been told that the defect rate on this assembly process last week was 6 per cent. The sample results indicate that five items were found to be defective from the sample of 50. Does this mean that the defect rate has got worse?

Consider the logic of our situation. We know that from our sample of 50 items no more than three (6 per cent) should have been defective if the overall defect rate has not worsened since last week. We found five. But we could equally argue that the sample is a fairly small one. Perhaps, just by chance, we happened to pick an extra couple of defective items even though overall the defect rate is still 6 per cent. Perhaps, if we repeated the sample, we might find the next one showed only three items defective. Again, how can probability help? The answer is that we have a Binomial situation and can apply the formula we have introduced. The calculation will not *prove* whether the defect rate is still 6 per cent or not but it will provide additional evidence that might help us reach a decision (bearing in mind that our decision, like any, may turn out to be wrong).

Activity 5.9

Determine the probability of choosing 50 items and finding five of them to be defective. Consider your result in the context of having to make a decision about the actual defect rate.

The calculation is straightforward using the formula. We have:

$$^nC_r\, p^r\, q^{(n-r)} = (2\ 118\ 760)0.06^5 0.94^{45} = 0.102$$

That is, a probability of 0.102 of choosing 50 items at random from the assembly line and finding that five were defective. Let us consider the implications of this in a management context. There is one critical assumption behind this calculation: that the actual defect rate is *still* 6 per cent. Our result implies that *if* this assumption is true then there is approximately a one in 10 chance of having five defective items in the sample (even though on average we would expect only three). To evaluate this position consider a different scenario. Suppose someone passes you a six-sided die and bets £100 that you will throw six sixes. You roll the die six times. Each time it shows a six and you lose the bet. What is your conclusion? Effectively you have two choices: either the die is fixed or tampered with in some way or a highly unlikely sequence of events has actually happened. Given that the probability of rolling six sixes with a fair die is 0.00002 (the multiplication rule, remember?), it is tempting to conclude that the die has been tampered with in some way. However, based on this evidence alone we have no hard proof of this. It is a subjective assessment based on the (very low) probability of the event.

Let us return to our example. We are now in the difficult position of having to assess this result and decide whether the actual defect rate is still 6 per cent or whether it might have worsened. We might argue that a 10 per cent probability is a reasonable one and that we cannot therefore say the defect rate has altered from its level of 6 per cent. On the other hand, we might argue that the probability of 10 per cent is too high to be likely to relate to the original actual 6 per cent defect rate. Like many situations we cannot prove one way or the other what has happened to the defect rate. Our assessment of the sample result must to some extent be subjective. As a compromise we might suggest that if the defect rate is of critical importance to the organisation – perhaps because of its quality policy or its costs – then we should repeat the sample and assess the second sample result. You should be able to see the logic of this. The only reason for rejecting the evidence of the first sample is to say that, by chance, we took more than a proportionate share of defective items from the assembly line. However, if we repeat the sample – particularly if we increase its size – then the chances are we should not repeat this 'bias': we would expect a new result closer to the three defective items we ought to be getting. If, on the other hand, we are still finding a higher number of defective items, this strengthens the case for concluding that the actual defect rate has worsened. A detailed investigation would then be needed to ascertain why this has happened and what corrective action could be taken.

Binomial tables

There is another method of obtaining Binomial probabilities: we can use pre-calculated tables and obtain the required probabilities directly. Then why, you ask, did we bother with the formula we have just introduced? The answer is that the tables typically only show the probabilities for certain combinations of n and p. If the required application falls outside these combinations we will need the formula in any event.

Typical tables are shown in Appendix A and we shall examine their use shortly. To illustrate their use we shall introduce another typical situation. You may be aware that airlines operating passenger flights typically book more passengers onto a flight than there are seats available. They do this because experience has shown that not all passengers booked will actually turn up – they become 'no-shows'. Obviously, if the airline did not take this into account then the flight would typically depart with empty seats (and lost revenue). On the other hand, the airline does not wish to be in the embarrassing position of having too many passengers for a given flight (although this does happen). It is not only airlines who operate on this sort of basis: many organisations providing direct customer services operate on the same principle.

Assume the airline is operating a short-haul flight from Manchester to Edinburgh on a 16-seat aircraft. The typical passenger is an executive going to some business meeting and returning the same day. The airline knows that from past experience 15 per cent of passengers booked on their early morning flight will not appear. They have therefore adopted the practice of taking a maximum of 20 bookings for this flight. The customer service manager, however, is concerned about the likelihood of passengers booked on the flight not having a seat because more passengers than expected turn up for the flight. We have been asked to assess the probability of this happening. As usual we must make assumptions to apply the Binomial principles. We clearly have a sequence of 20 'trials': passengers booked on the flight. The probability of any one passenger not showing is 0.15, and to apply the Binomial we must make the assumption that the trials are independent. This implies that, for example, no two passengers are booked together (and hence will 'not-show' together). We then require the probability that there will be no more than three 'no-shows' (implying that we will have at least 17 passengers for 16 seats). Clearly this requires:

$$P(0 \text{ no shows}) + P(1 \text{ no shows}) + P(2 \text{ no shows}) + P(3 \text{ no shows})$$

That is, we will need several parts of the appropriate probability distribution. Obviously we could use the Binomial formula to work out each of these individual probabilities and the total (and you should do this later to practise the use of the formula approach). However, we can instead use the table in Appendix A, part of which is duplicated here for ease of reference.

Binomial distribution

n	$r \geqslant$	$p = 0.15$
20	0	1.0000
	1	0.9612
	2	0.8244
	3	0.5951
	4	0.3523
	5	0.1702
	6	0.0673
	7	0.0219
	8	0.0059
	9	0.0013
	10	0.0002

The table will require a little explanation. First, take note that the table shows cumulative rather than individual probabilities, hence we show $\geqslant$. We shall explore this in a moment. Second, the table is segmented for various combinations of n, p and r and that we are interested in the combination of n = 20 and p = 0.15 with the values of r relating directly to our problem. The probabilities in the table are straightforward in their application. For example, we have:

$P(r \geqslant 0) = 1.0000$

$P(r \geqslant 1) = 0.9612$

$P(r \geqslant 2) = 0.8244$ and so on.

In the context of our problem – where r effectively equates to a 'no-show' – we have a probability of 0.9612 that there will be at least one no-show, a probability of 0.8244 that there will be at least two and so on.

Activity 5.10

Using the table determine the probability that more passengers arrive for the flight than there are seats available.

Applying some simple logic it is evident that directly from the table we can derive:

$P(r \geqslant 4) = 0.3523$

That is, there is a probability of 0.3523 that there will be at least four no-shows and, therefore, we will have sufficient seats for the remaining passengers. It follows then that we must have:

$$P(r < 4) = P(r = 0) + P(r = 1) + P(r = 2) + P(r = 3)$$
$$= 1 - 0.3523 = 0.6477$$

as the probability that there will not be enough no-shows to avoid an excess of passengers over seats. That is, a probability of 0.65 (approximately) that the airline will have overbooked. If the airline has not yet had complaints from irate passengers who have booked but couldn't get a seat, it soon will have!

Note also that, although the table relates to cumulative probabilities, it can be used to derive individual probabilities. Suppose we had actually wanted the probability of exactly three no-shows: P(r = 3). From the table we have:

$$P(r \geqslant 4) = P(r = 4) + P(r = 5) + \cdots + P(r = 20) = 0.3523$$
$$P(r \geqslant 3) = P(r = 3) + P(r = 4) + \cdots + P(r = 20) = 0.5951$$

Hence we must have:

$$P(r = 3) = P(r \geqslant 3) - P(r \geqslant 4)$$
$$= 0.5951 - 0.3523 = 0.2428$$

Mean and standard deviation of a Binomial distribution

It may have occurred to you that the Binomial distribution (or indeed any other probability distribution) is just a special example of distributions in general, like those we looked at in Chapter 4. For those distributions we were able to calculate a number of summary statistics such as the mean and standard deviation. It seems logical that we should be able to calculate comparable statistics for the Binomial distribution. In our airline example, the mean would indicate the average number of no-shows on each flight, and the standard deviation would show the variability around this mean. We could calculate the mean and standard deviation using the formulae from Chapter 4 with the probabilities as the frequencies and the outcomes as the interval values. However, there is a more direct method. Without proof we state that for a Binomial distribution:

$$\text{Mean} = np$$
$$\text{Standard deviation} = \sqrt{npq}$$

Here we would have:

$$\text{Mean} = 20(0.15) = 3$$
$$\text{Standard deviation} = \sqrt{20(0.15)(0.85)} = 1.597$$

The mean and standard deviation for a Binomial problem can be interpreted and used as with any other set of data. We can expect a mean number of no-shows of 3 per flight with a standard deviation of 1.6 (the mean confirms that with a 16-seat aircraft available and 20 seats sold the airline is heading for trouble). We could also calculate the mean number of no-shows for a range of ticket sales (17, 18, 19, 20, 21, etc.) to assess the likely impact on overbooking.

Activity 5.11

You work for a mail-order retail company which advertises special promotions in the national press. Customers who respond to the promotion asking to buy the product are offered it on a sale-or-return basis. That is, the company sends the product to the customer together with an invoice. If the customer is happy with the product they will pay the invoice. If they are not happy, they can simply return the product to the company and do not have to pay the invoice. Obviously, in the latter case, the company has incurred costs which it cannot recoup (postage, handling, etc.). For past promotions the company has noted that 12 per cent of customers return the product. For the next promotion 50 000 customer orders are expected. Calculate the mean and standard deviation and comment on how this might be used by management.

Solution is given on p 588.

Binomial probabilities in Excel

Excel, and other spreadsheet packages, have built in statistical functions to calculate binomial probabilities directly. The function is:

BINOMDIST(r, n, p, cumulative)

Where:

r is the specified number of outcomes we wish to calculate for
n is the number of trails
p is the probability of the outcome in each trial
cumulative is a logical value that is set to be either TRUE or FALSE. If the logical value is set to TRUE then Excel calculates the cumulative probability up to and including r. If the logical value is set to FALSE then Excel calculates the probability of exactly r outcomes.

So, with the airline example from the previous section we had n = 20 and p = 0.15. Using the function as:

BINOMDIST(4, 20, 0, 15, TRUE)

then Excel would return a value of 0.6477 as the probability of r ⩽ 4. On the other hand using the function as:

BINOMDIST(4, 20, 0, 15, FALSE)

then Excel would return a value of 0.1821 as the probability of r = 4.

The Normal Distribution

We now turn to the second theoretical probability distribution – the *Normal distribution*. The Normal distribution is widely used in business and management decision making and underpins the area of statistical inference that we shall be examining in detail in Chapter 7. It is instantly recognisable graphically, as shown in Figure 5.3. The

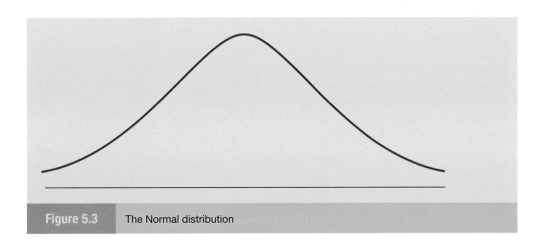

Figure 5.3   The Normal distribution

Normal distribution is symmetrical – often referred to as bell-shaped – and this general shape remains the same no matter what problem we are examining where the Normal distribution applies. This has important consequences as we shall see shortly. What will vary from one application of this distribution to another is not the general shape but two key characteristics of that shape:

● the mean value
● the variability as measured by the standard deviation.

Figure 5.4 illustrates two such distributions where the means vary and Figure 5.5 where the standard deviations vary.

We could build up an entire family of such distributions depending on the specific values of the mean and standard deviation. So how do we determine the appropriate probabilities for such a distribution? For the Binomial we saw that we could either apply a formula or we could use pre-calculated tables. In the case of the Normal distribution the only feasible method is to use tables. The reason for this may become evident if we examine the formula behind the Normal distribution:

$$P(x) = \frac{1}{\sqrt{2\pi}\sigma} e^{-\frac{(x-\mu)^2}{2\sigma^2}}$$

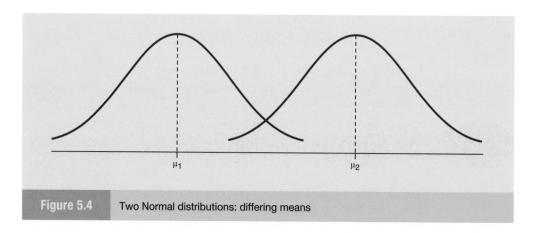

Figure 5.4   Two Normal distributions: differing means

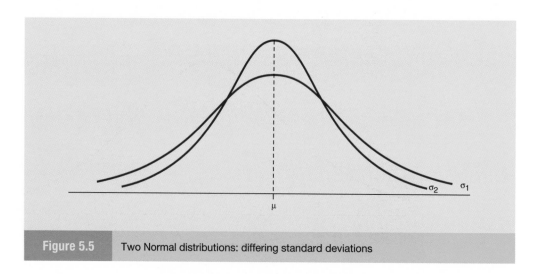

Figure 5.5   Two Normal distributions: differing standard deviations

where:

μ is the mean

σ is the standard deviation

$\pi = 3.14159$

$e = 2.71828$

and x the value for which we require a probability.

Fortunately for all of us, tables of probabilities have been pre-calculated! However, before we can utilise them we must consider the issue of varying means and standard deviations in the family of Normal distributions. Remember for the Binomial distribution certain combinations of n and p gave rise to specific probability values. The number of combinations was fairly limited, partly because the Binomial deals with combinations of n and r which take only discrete values. We could always return to the Binomial formula if a particular combination did not appear in the tables. For the Normal distribution this problem is compounded. The number of possible combinations of mean and standard deviation we might require is much larger, since it is a continuous distribution, and if the particular combination we do require is not available the prospect of returning to the formula is not a happy one. However, we can take advantage of the fact that all Normal distributions follow the same general shape to use what is known as the *Standardised Normal distribution*.

The Standardised Normal distribution

Let us consider the following problem. A large retail organisation has recently been receiving a number of complaints from customers about one of its products: bottles of own-brand hair shampoo. Customers have complained that they think the actual contents of the shampoo bottles are sometimes less than they are meant to be according to the printed contents label on each bottle. The organisation currently sells two bottle sizes: one at 490 ml and one at 740 ml. The shampoo is actually manufactured and bottled by a subsidiary company, and an investigation into the bottling process is currently under way. The process is such that two production lines are in use – one for each bottle size. On each line a computer-controlled machine fills the bottle with shampoo automatically. However, management recognise that the machine is not 100 per cent reliable and some variability inevitably arises in the exact volume of shampoo put into each bottle. Further analysis has revealed that on one line the machine is calibrated to deliver 500 ml of shampoo into each bottle but that the actual process is normally distributed with a standard deviation of 10 ml. This implies – remember Figure 5.3 – that the mean of the distribution is 500 ml but that some bottles will contain less than this and some more. So some might actually contain 495 ml, others 505 ml and so on. Similarly, from the shape of the distribution, it is clear that the further away from the mean we get then the fewer the number of bottles we are considering. On the second line a similar situation applies but with the machine set to deliver a mean amount of 750 ml with a standard deviation of 15 ml, and again the distribution of amount filled is Normally distributed.

Clearly we have two Normal distributions under examination and although both have the characteristic shape, they differ in both their mean and their standard deviation. To determine relevant probabilities it might appear that we need two sets of tables. However, if we examine Machine 1 we can determine a number of possible values for the amount filled as shown in Table 5.6.

Table 5.6	Machine 1						
Amount filled (ml)	470	480	490	500	510	520	530
Difference from mean amount (ml)	−30	−20	−10	0	10	20	30
SDs from mean	−3	−2	−1	0	1	2	3

In the table we show a number of possible amounts filled, varying from 470 ml to 530 ml. However, we can express these amounts in a different way, showing not the absolute amount filled but how much the amount differs from the mean – expressed in ml. This difference in turn can now be shown in a relative way by expressing the difference from the mean in terms of the number of standard deviations (which you will remember was 10 ml). So, an amount of 470 ml is effectively three SDs below the mean, 480 ml is two SDs below and so on for this variable. There appears little benefit from performing such calculations, however, until we do the same for our second distribution.

Activity 5.12

Construct a similar table for Machine 2 showing amounts filled that vary from three SDs below the mean to three SDs above.

Table 5.7 shows results for both machines.

Table 5.7	Machines 1 and 2						
Machine 1 Amount filled (ml)	470	480	490	500	510	520	530
SDs from mean	−3	−2	−1	0	1	2	3
Machine 2 Amount filled (ml)	705	720	735	750	765	770	785

It now becomes evident that although the two Normal distributions vary in terms of their means and standard deviations, we can transform both with a common yardstick – the number of standard deviations away from its mean that a particular value is. But what is the point of all this? Remember that we wanted to be able to use probability tables for the Normal distribution but realised that the number of such tables required – given we need one for every possible combination of mean and standard deviation – would be enormous.

We can now resolve this problem. Instead of analysing each specific Normal distribution – with its own mean and standard deviation – we can effectively standardise all such distributions by converting them to this yardstick measure. This means, for example, that in the case of our two distributions we now recognise that a value of 470 ml for Machine 1 and 705 ml for Machine 2 are effectively at the same point in their own distributions, since both values are three SDs below their own mean. What this means is that rather than use the specific – and often unique – Normal distribution that applies to the problem under investigation we can actually use just one Normal distribution for every problem – once we have transformed the problem values into SDs from the mean.

This particular distribution is known as the Standardised Normal distribution and the process of performing the calculations shown in Table 5.7 is known as calculating a standard score – usually denoted as a Z score. Such a Z score is readily found from the standardising formula:

$$Z = \frac{X - Mean}{SD}$$

where Z is the standard score, X is the specific value we are examining and Mean and SD are the mean and standard deviation respectively of the specific distribution we are looking at. Without justification we state that the Standardised Normal distribution has a mean of 0 and a standard deviation of 1. Pre-calculated tables of probability relating to the Standardised Normal distribution are readily available and one is shown in Appendix B.

Activity 5.13

Calculate the Z score for the following values:

Machine 1	Machine 2
X = 475 ml	X = 745 ml
X = 505 ml	X = 725 ml
X = 518 ml	X = 759 ml

Solutions are given on p 589.

Using Normal probability tables

We can now start to use the Normal probability tables that are available to help us assess our current situation. Remember that for Machine 1 the equipment was calibrated to fill the bottle with an average of 500 ml, SD 10 ml and that the bottles were actually labelled as containing 490 ml. We now wish to assess the probability that any one bottle will actually contain less than 490 ml (and thereby give customers legitimate grounds for complaint). We already have the relevant Z score (Z = –1). Turning to Appendix B (reproduced here for convenience) we see that the table of probabilities is shown by row and by column. Both row and column actually refer to the Z score value. The rows refer to the first two digits of the calculated Z score – ranging from 0.0 through to 3.0. The columns across the top of the table refer to the second decimal digit. So, looking at the first row (0.0) and then moving across the columns, we effectively have Z scores of 0.00, 0.01, 0.02 and so on. Conventionally, Z scores are calculated to two decimal places. Our score is technically Z = –1.00. However, searching for this in the row/column combination we appear to have a difficulty since no negative Z scores are shown.

Areas in the tail of the Normal distribution

Z	.00	.01	.02	.03	.04	.05	.06	.07	.08	.09
0.0	.5000	.4960	.4920	.4880	.4840	.4801	.4761	.4721	.4681	.4641
0.1	.4602	.4562	.4522	.4483	.4443	.4404	.4364	.4325	.4286	.4247
0.2	.4207	.4168	.4129	.4090	.4052	.4013	.3974	.3936	.3897	.3859
0.3	.3821	.3783	.3745	.3707	.3669	.3632	.3594	.3557	.3520	.3483
0.4	.3446	.3409	.3372	.3336	.3300	.3264	.3228	.3192	.3156	.3121
0.5	.3085	.3050	.3015	.2981	.2946	.2912	.2877	.2843	.2810	.2776
0.6	.2743	.2709	.2676	.2643	.2611	.2578	.2546	.2514	.2483	.2451
0.7	.2420	.2389	.2358	.2327	.2296	.2266	.2236	.2206	.2177	.2148
0.8	.2119	.2090	.2061	.2033	.2005	.1977	.1949	.1922	.1894	.1867
0.9	.1841	.1814	.1788	.1762	.1736	.1711	.1685	.1660	.1635	.1611
1.0	.1587	.1562	.1539	.1515	.1492	.1469	.1446	.1423	.1401	.1379
1.1	.1357	.1335	.1314	.1292	.1271	.1251	.1230	.1210	.1190	.1170
1.2	.1151	.1131	.1112	.1093	.1075	.1056	.1038	.1020	.1003	.0985
1.3	.0968	.0951	.0934	.0918	.0901	.0885	.0869	.0853	.0838	.0823
1.4	.0808	.0793	.0778	.0764	.0749	.0735	.0721	.0708	.0694	.0681
1.5	.0668	.0655	.0643	.0630	.0618	.0606	.0594	.0582	.0571	.0559

The reason negative values are not shown is that they are not actually needed. Remember that by definition a Normal distribution is symmetrical around its mean. This implies that the two halves of the distribution are mirror images of each other and effectively the same. So, in probability terms, a Z score of −1.00 and +1.00 are identical. If we now look for Z = 1.00 we read a value from the table of 0.1587. To understand what this shows we consider Figure 5.6. This shows the Standardised Normal distribution together with the Z score of −1.00. The area to the left of the Z score is effectively the area we are seeking (to represent the proportion of all bottles which have contents less than 490 ml). This is also what the figures in the table show – the area under the

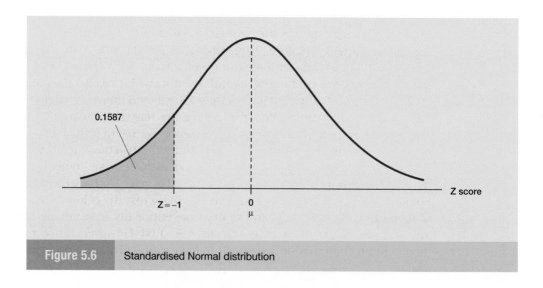

| **Figure 5.6** | Standardised Normal distribution |

curve to the left of the Z score line (or to the right if we had a positive Z score). So, the figure of 0.1587 implies that some 15.9 per cent of all bottles will contain less than 490 ml of shampoo. Used in this way the Normal distribution tables allow us to calculate the proportion of the distribution that falls in any given area. Management would now need to evaluate their position given this new information. Should they carry on regardless and run the risk of customer complaints (and possible violation of consumer protection regulations), should they change the label on which the contents are shown, should they change the setting of the mean amount filled by the machine? All of these are options which would need to be carefully considered based on all the other information pertaining to the problem. You should be able to see by now, however, the importance of applying these probability situations to such a set of circumstances. Such principles do not 'solve' the problem but they do supply the manager with additional information that, arguably, could not have come from any other source. It will be worthwhile at this stage reinforcing the use of the tables with a few worked examples.

Activity 5.14

Determine for Machine 1 the proportion of bottles:
(a) that will contain more than 515 ml
(b) that will contain less than 475 ml
(c) that will contain between 520 and 525 ml
(d) that will contain between 490 and 480 ml.

Until you gain practice it may well be worthwhile sketching the Normal curve and highlighting the area you are trying to determine with the tables, as we did with Figure 5.6. For (a) we require the area to the right of the corresponding Z line. Here we have:

$$Z = \frac{X - \text{Mean}}{\text{SD}} = \frac{515 - 500}{10} = 1.5$$

and from the table this gives a value of 0.0668, i.e. 6.7 per cent of bottles will contain over 515 ml. For (b) we require the area to the left of the Z score:

$$Z = \frac{Z - \text{Mean}}{\text{SD}} = \frac{475 - 500}{10} = -2.5$$

giving a value of 0.0062 from the table or 0.62 per cent of bottles. Parts (c) and (d) are a little different and a sketch is definitely worthwhile to confirm what we require. Figure 5.7 shows the two X values (520 and 525), and the area in between these two lines is the area we require, which corresponds to values between 520 and 525 ml.

The method of calculation is a little more complicated this time. If we find the area to the right of 520 and then subtract the area to the right of 525 this must, logically, give us the area we actually require. The relevant calculation is then:

$$Z_1 = \frac{X - \text{Mean}}{\text{SD}} = \frac{520 - 500}{10} = 2.0$$

$$Z_2 = \frac{X - \text{Mean}}{\text{SD}} = \frac{525 - 500}{10} = 2.5$$

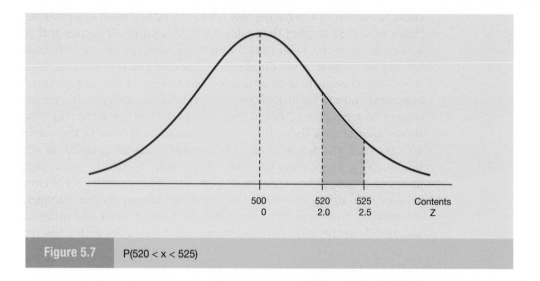

| Figure 5.7 | P(520 < x < 525) |

with the two probabilities from the table being 0.0228 and 0.0062 respectively. This then gives:

$$Z_1 - Z_2 = 0.0228 - 0.0062$$
$$= 0.0166$$

or 1.66 per cent of bottles will contain between 520 and 525 ml. Part (d) follows a similar logic and you should be able to confirm that we obtain a result of 13.6 per cent.

As a final example, let us return to the management problem in hand. Management have now decided that, for a variety of reasons, the situation cannot continue with almost 16 per cent of output below the advertised weight. Accordingly they have decided that Machine 1 will continue as before (delivering a mean content of 500 ml, SD 10 ml) but that a new label will be produced showing the new minimum contents and guaranteeing that no more than 1 per cent of output will fall below this minimum figure. The problem is now to determine what this new minimum figure on the label should be – 480 ml, 470 ml or what?

Activity 5.15

Can you provide any advice to management on what the new minimum contents figure should be?

We need to approach this from a different angle than previously. Up to now we have known the X value in the Z score formula and wanted to determine the Z score and thence the probability. Now we know the required probability – 1 per cent – and require to determine what the X value must be to ensure this. Figure 5.8 illustrates this.

Given that we require a probability of 1 per cent we should be able to search through the table and determine what the associated Z score must be. If we do this we eventually find a value in the table of 0.01 (1 per cent probability) corresponding to a Z score of 2.33. It is important to remember, however, that we are actually examining the left-hand side of the Normal distribution, so technically this Z score is –2.33. If we now re-examine the Z score formula we have:

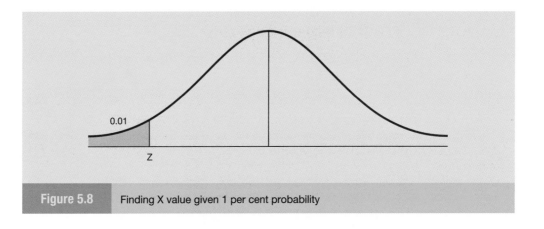

| **Figure 5.8** | Finding X value given 1 per cent probability |

$$Z = -2.33 = \frac{X - \text{Mean}}{\text{SD}}$$

$$-2.33 = \frac{X - \text{Mean}}{\text{SD}} = \frac{X - 500}{10}$$

and rearranging gives:

$$-23.3 = X - 500$$

$$X = 500 - 23.3 = 476.7$$

That is, the new advertised minimum contents to meet the required 1 per cent target must be 476.7 ml. We could always check this is correct by finding the probability of a bottle containing less than this.

Normal probabilities in Excel

Excel, and other spreadsheet packages, have built in statistical functions to calculate Normal probabilities directly. The function is:

NORMDIST(X, mean, sd, cumulative)

Where:

> X is the specified value for which we require a probability
> mean is the mean value for the distribution
> sd is the standard deviation of the distribution
> cumulative is a logical value that is set to be either TRUE or FALSE. If the logical value is set to TRUE then Excel calculates the cumulative probability up to and including X

So, with the shampoo bottle example from the previous section we had one bottle with a mean of 490 ml and a standard deviation of 10 ml. If we wish to determine the probability that $X \leqslant 480$ we have:

NORMDIST(480, 490, 10, TRUE)

And Excel would return a value of 0.1586 as the probability that $X \leqslant 480$.

When it's time to ask for whom the bell curve tolls

By John Authers

"Do you know what a bell curve is? It's a curve, shaped like a bell."

London mayoral candidate Boris Johnson, speaking at the Oxford Union in 1985

As investors we put a lot of weight on the bell curve, perhaps too much weight, and certainly more than we realise. Our investment and risk decisions depend on it. Mr Johnson was describing what statisticians call the "normal distribution," which frequently recurs in nature. As the diagram shows it is, indeed, shaped like a bell.

In nature, all kinds of phenomena – from the height of humans to the number of peas in a pod – follow this distribution. And the assumption that investment returns also follow a bell curve is the building block for a system which is central to the way fund managers approach risk. Known as "Value at Risk" or "VaR", all MBA students learn about it early on at business school.

The diagram shows how it works. Armed with a good sample of past results, statisticians can predict future results with some confidence. Most will be clustered around the mean in the centre. Typically for stocks, this will be a moderate profit. Better returns to this are on the right side of the bell, with outlying strokes of great fortune on the far right. The really nasty losses will all be on the left hand side of the bell, known as the tail.

Using statistical techniques that work in the natural sciences, a risk manager can now work out the risk of such a loss. The line in the diagram shows the level of losses which will happen only 1 per cent of the time. In the jargon, a risk manager can now say that "with 99 per cent confidence" their value at risk is the amount of money that is lost at that point. There is a 99 per cent chance that the investment will do better than that.

If the VaR at this point is too much to swallow, then the risk manager will take steps to move to reduce their risks. It can be a useful common sense tool for thinking about risk.

The problem is that VaR has become ubiquitous. Regulators and ratings agencies allow banks to decide how much capital they should have using VaR models. Since the credit crisis started, VaR has come in for criticism. One problem is that it is backward looking. If the past sample of investment returns was gleaned from a period of low volatility and strong stock returns, as we had from 2003 to 2007, they will not be much use in navigating the current situation. UBS, which has needed to raise more capital, blamed this in part on its VaR model which was "based on five years of data, whereby the data were sourced from a period of relatively positive growth".

VaR also does not take account of what are now known as "black swans" – extreme events that have not happened in the past. These can lead to extreme results, or change the shape of the bell for the future. The unprecedented fall in US national house prices many be such a black swan.

Still another argument is that if everyone moves to the same place on the bell curve – where they expect a good return for little risk – they will change the shape of the curve. If everyone crowds into the same investments, they will create the conditions for sudden reversals and extra volatility. That inflicted bad losses last summer.

The bell curve: how can we measure value at risk?

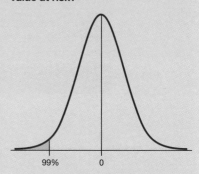

Source: FT research

A new objection which I saw aired last month for the first time is even more profound. Even if we do follow a bell curve, VaR can lead to excessive risk.

David Einhorn, a New York hedge fund manager, offers the following example: you are offered odds of 127 to one on $100 that when you toss a coin, heads will not come up seven times in a row. The chance that you will win is 99.2 per cent. So you can say with 99 per cent confidence that you have no value at risk. Using a VaR model, a bank could hold no capital to guard against a loss on this bet.

But in fact there is a 0.8 per cent chance (not an unimaginable black swan) that they will lose $12,700.

What risk managers need to know, according to Mr Einhorn, is what will happen in the "tail" – the 1 per cent of the time when things go wrong. By ignoring the tails, he says, "it creates an incentive to take excessive but remote risks". It also "creates a false sense of security". Where does this leave us? Risk managers have made horrible mistakes in the past year. But VaR might still have its uses. Academics are working on improvements to VaR, using computers to "stress test" their assumptions for black swan events, or trying to model the effects when many investors make the same decisions. Critics, such as James Montier of Société Générale, lambast VaR as "pseudoscience", "Simply because something can be quantified doesn't mean that it is sensible," he says. "There is no substitute for rigorous critical or sceptical thinking."

He is right about this. But like other tools taught at business school, quantifying risks can be useful, provided they do not take the place of common sense, or imagination. In future, risk managers and investors should use their quantitative tools, and then think much more carefully about what could go wrong.

Source: *Financial Times*, 4 May 2008.

The Normal distribution is used extensively in the financial sector.

Worked Example

At this stage, the material we have introduced on probability and probability distributions can seem very mechanical and of little relevance to management decision making. Let us introduce a scenario where we might apply such principles to assist management. A power company has been examining its long-term strategy in terms of customer loyalty, particularly amongst domestic customers. It is concerned that as the power markets become more competitive, it is in danger of losing some of its customer base to its competitors and hence its revenue and profit stream. It is considering introducing some sort of discount scheme for some of its domestic electricity customers. Senior management are not yet clear as to what such a scheme would entail, or exactly which customers would be targeted. However, they are currently thinking of offering a price discount to relatively large users of electricity (since larger users are by and large more profitable and hence more valuable to the company). We have been asked to undertake some initial analysis and offer what guidance we can to senior management as to how we might target which group of customers to offer such a price discount to. The company currently has around 2.5 million domestic electricity customers and charges domestic customers 6.7p per kilowatt hour (kWh) used, no matter how much they use. We have done some initial data collection from the computerised customer records files and have obtained electricity usage of a representative sample of 1500 customers for the past 12 months. The results are shown in Table 5.8.

You may want to stop reading at this point and see whether you can suggest how we might approach this situation in terms of analysis and recommendations.

Although this is a chapter on probability, we should not forget some of the techniques we introduced earlier. Clearly we have a frequency distribution and we can obtain a histogram from this, as in Figure 5.9.

We gain a visual impression of a symmetrical distribution which, with a little imagination, takes the shape of the Normal curve. In other words, it seems reasonable to say, based on this sample, that electricity consumption is Normally distributed. Given this assumption, we can determine the mean and standard deviation of this distribution. These are calculated from the table as:

Mean = 4996 kWh

SD = 424.4 kWh

Table 5.8	Electricity usage of domestic customers over the last 12-month period (kWh)

Lower limit (kWh)		Upper limit (kWh)	No. of customers
3000	<	4000	11
4000	<	4200	24
4200	<	4400	69
4400	<	4600	141
4600	<	4800	225
4800	<	5000	292
5000	<	5200	281
5200	<	5400	218
5400	<	5600	132
5600	<	5800	71
5800	<	6000	26
6000	<	7000	10
Total			1500

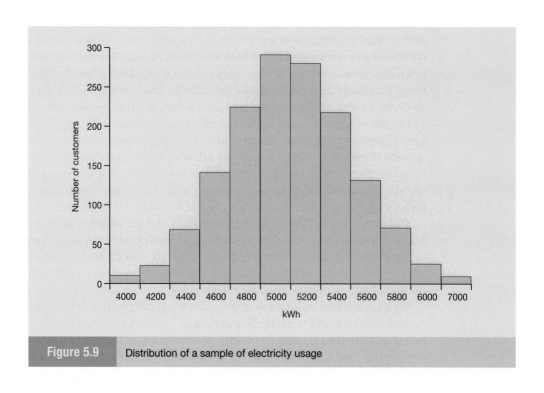

Figure 5.9	Distribution of a sample of electricity usage

and by also calculating the median we can determine that the coefficient of skewness is −0.03, as close to zero as makes no difference, again confirming that we have a symmetrical distribution. Given that we can assume that we have a Normal distribution we can use it to do some 'what-if' analysis to try to help senior management. First of all, we can estimate total annual revenue from domestic electricity sales. Assuming this sample is representative, we know that mean sales are 4996 kWh per customer per 12 months. The company has 2.5 million domestic customers and sells at 6.7p per kWh. This gives annual revenue from sales as:

$$\text{Sales revenue} = 4996 \times 2\,500\,000 \times 0.067 = £836\,830\,000 \text{ or } £836.83 \text{ million}$$

We have little guidance from senior management as to which customers they wish to target but let us, for the moment, assume that it is the top 5 per cent of customers, in terms of their usage – probably a realistic assumption since these will generate most revenue and probably most profit. Using the principles of the Normal distribution we can estimate the annual electricity consumption level that will mark this top 5 per cent. We require the top 5 per cent of the customer distribution. From the Normal distribution table we see that this equates to a Z score of 1.645 (interpolating between 1.64 and 1.65). We know that the mean consumption level is 4996, standard deviation 424.4, so we have:

$$Z = 1.645 = \frac{X - 4996}{424.4}$$

giving X = 5694. That is, to be in the top 5 per cent of electricity users we would need to have an annual electricity consumption of over 5694 kWh. For practical operational purposes we would probably want to round this to 5700 kWh. So, if we wanted to target the top 5 per cent of domestic users, we would have a cut-off of at least 5700 kWh per year as a consumption level. Can we estimate the sales revenue from this customer group? Using the same principles, we know that the top 5 per cent have consumption levels over 5700. The top 4 per cent will have consumption levels over 5740 (check the arithmetic if you want). So, 1 per cent of customers will use between 5700 and 5740 kWh. 1 per cent of customers is 25 000, so we have 25 000 customers using an average of 5720 kwh ((5700 + 5740) ÷ 2) at 6.7p per kWh, giving an estimated revenue from this 1 per cent of customers of £9.581 million. Using the same logic for the next 1 per cent and so on we have the estimates shown in Table 5.9.

Table 5.9	Estimated revenue	
Customer group (kWh)	**No. of customers**	**Estimated revenue (£m)**
5700 < 5740	25 000	9.581000
5740 < 5800	25 000	9.664750
5800 < 5870	25 000	9.773625
5870 < 6000	25 000	9.941125
6000 < 6200	25 000	10.217500

(Note customer group consumption figures have been rounded.)

Probability and distributions

From tossing a coin to opinion polls, probability and distributions are at the heart of statistical analysis, says Ann van Ackere

The concept of probability is used to quantify uncertainty. Something can be uncertain because the true value is unknown (for example, the outcome of a toss of a coin, or the sterling/dollar exchange-rate a year from now) or because it is unknown to you (for example, your competitor's marketing budget for next year).

These uncertain events are generally referred to as "random variables", and are characterised by a "distribution". Consider, for example, tossing a coin. The outcome is a random variable that can take on two values: heads *(H)* or tails *(T)*. Each outcome has a "probability" associated with it. A probability is a number between zero and one, expressing how likely an outcome is. Here, *H* and *T* each have a probability 0.5, which add up to 1. There are no other possible outcomes.

Figure 1 shows this distribution graphically. This is an example of "uniform distribution": all outcomes are equally likely. Note that the total area is equal to 1.

In the coin-toss example, the distribution is derived in an objective way. If the coin is fair, anyone would agree that the probabilities equal 0.5. In other instances, probabilities are subjective. Consider sketching a distribution for the sterling/dollar exchange rate a year from now. You may consider the most likely value to be 1.5 (a "point-estimate"), and be fairly confident that the actual value is somewhere between 1.4 and 1.65.

This would yield a sketch as shown in *Figure 2*. Another person would most likely come up with a different distribution.

Note that in *Figure 2* the distribution is drawn as a smooth curve, rather than as rectangles representing the probability of each possible outcome. This is an example of a "continuous distribution" (the exchange rate could take on any value in the range considered, there is not a specific number of discrete outcomes).

The coin toss example is a "discrete distribution": one can list all possible outcomes and attach a probability to each of them. The outcome of a single toss is referred to as an event. One could be interested in more than one event, for example the number of heads in a sequence of tosses. *Figure 3* shows the distribution of the number of heads in two tosses, and in four tosses. These are examples of the "binomial distribution", which gives the distribution of the number of "successes" (in our example, heads) out of a number of independent "trials" (tosses), where each trial has two possible outcomes (*H* or *T*) with probabilities *p* and (1 – *p*). The binomial distribution occurs commonly in quality testing (how many defective units in a sample of 20?) and opinion polls (how many people out of 1,100 support a specific proposition?).

As mentioned before, some variables have a continuous distribution, i.e., they can take on any value within a given range. Consider, for example, ordering a pint of beer. When pouring your glass, the barman (you hope) intends to pour exactly one pint in your glass. If you were to measure the actual content, you would expect to find a quantity close to one pint. The difference between the actual value, and the target value of one pint, can be thought of as an error.

If one repeated this experiment many times, the data could be used to sketch the distribution of the content of a pint of beer. You would expect that "on average" a pint contains exactly one pint, and that most of the errors are small, with possibly a few larger ones. You might also expect that you are equally likely to get 5 per cent of a pint too much or too little. This would result in a distribution as sketched in *Panel A* of *Figure 4*.

This is the shape of a "normal distribution", also referred to as a "bell-shaped curve". It is characterised by a mean and a standard deviation. *Panel B* of *Figure 4* shows the distribution of the content of a pint of beer, assuming a normal distribution with mean 1 pint and standard deviation .04 pints (and assuming that the glass can contain 1.12 pints!).

Assuming a normal distribution imposes some very specific assumptions on the probabilities of the possible outcomes. Specifically, there is approximately a 66 per cent probability of being within one standard deviation of the mean, a 95 per cent probability of being within two standard deviations of the mean,

Figure 1

Expected number of heads: 1 Toss (%)

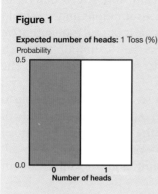

Number of heads

Figure 2

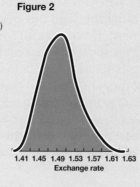

Exchange rate

Figure 3

Expected number of heads:

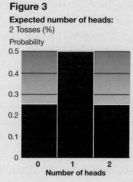

2 Tosses (%)

Number of heads

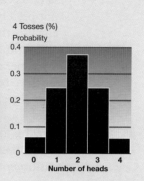

4 Tosses (%)

Number of heads

Figure 4

Panel A. Sketch of the probability distribution of the content of a pint of beer

1 pint

Panel B. Probability density of the content of a pint of beer assuming a normal distribution with mean 1 pint and standard deviation .04 pints

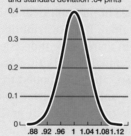

Figure 5

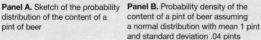

Panel A
Probability

p=0.1   n=30
p=0.7
p=0.5

Number of heads

Panel B
Probability

n=4   p=0.5
n=10
n=30

Number of heads

and a close to 99 per cent probability of being within three standard deviations of the mean. As for discrete distributions, the total area under the curve is equal to 1. A normal distribution with mean 0 and standard deviation 1 is referred to as the standard normal distribution.

The normal distribution is more convenient to work with than the binomial distribution, which becomes cumbersome when the number of trials (n) is large. Fortunately, under some conditions, the binomial distribution is sufficiently similar in shape to the normal that it can be approximated by a normal distribution.

Panel A of *Figure 5* sketches the shape of the binomial distribution for $n = 30$ and $p = 0.1$, 0.5 and 0.7 respectively, while *Panel B* sketches this distribution for $p = 0.5$ and $n = 4$, 10 and 30. Intuitively, when the number of events n is large and the probability p is close to 0.5, the binomial distribution approaches the bell-shape of the normal distribution.

This approximation is especially useful when dealing with opinion polls, where the sample size n typically exceeds 1,000, making the binomial distribution very much untractable.

Summary

Uncertain events, or random variables, are characterised by a distribution. A *uniform distribution* is where all outcomes are equally likely. A "*continuous distribution*" is when variables can take on any value within a given range. A *discrete distribution* allows you to list all possible outcomes and attach a probability to them. The *binomial distribution* gives the distribution of the number of "successes" from a number of independent trials. The *normal distribution* is sometimes referred to as a "bell-shaped curve".

Source: *FT Mastering Management Part 2*, 3 November 1995, p 12.

In total, then, this top 5 per cent of customers will generate almost £50 million in sales revenue. Clearly, this analysis is based on a number of assumptions and we would not pretend that it was 100 per cent reliable (and this is typical of much quantitative analysis that is undertaken by business). However, with some key assumptions (which are not too unrealistic) we can provide some information to senior management. The top 5 per cent of customers are clearly important in terms of company revenue – and we have been able to estimate what they are 'worth' in that sense. We might be able to go one stage further and undertake some market research to estimate the probability of these customers taking their business to a competitor and the probability of them *not* moving to a competitor if we offered a price discount. This would then allow us to calculate the likely loss in revenue if we did not offer a discount, and the impact on our customer base and revenue if we did.

Summary

In this chapter we have examined the idea of probability and introduced two common distributions – the Binomial and the Normal. Both distributions – as well as others we have not considered – find frequent use in management decision making and are based on relatively simple principles. The Binomial distribution requires a number of key characteristics to be satisfied before it can safely be applied to a problem. The Normal distribution, on the other hand, requires only that the variable we are investigating is Normally distributed. A surprising number of variables in practice do follow a Normal distribution – or at least come sufficiently close. However, as we shall see in a subsequent chapter, a far more important use of the Normal distribution lies in its application to the areas of statistical inference.

Some useful numbers to remember for the Normal distribution

For any Normally distributed variable:

- 68.26 per cent of the data (about two-thirds) will be within ±1 standard deviation of the mean
- 95.44 per cent (call it 95 per cent) of the data will be within ±2 standard deviations of the mean
- 99.7 per cent of the data will be within ±3 standard deviations of the mean

Useful online resources

Detailed below are some internet resources that may be useful. Many have further links to other sites. An updated version is available from the accompanying website (**www.pearsoned.co.uk/wisniewski**). In addition, I would be grateful for details of other websites that have been found to be useful.

www.mathforum.org/library/topics/probability/ – Math Forum Probability

www.mathcs.carleton.edu/probweb/probweb.html – The Probability Web

www.andrews.edu/~calkins/math/webtexts/prodtoc.htm – Statistical Probabilities and Distributions

QMDM IN ACTION
ICI Pharmaceuticals

We take for granted these days that drug-based medical treatment will be readily available when we need it. Whether we require an aspirin for a headache, antibiotics to treat some infection, or more advanced and complex drugs for specialist purposes, we have come to expect a wider, and more effective, range of drug-based treatment. The development of new drugs, however, is a complex, lengthy and risky business. A new drug can take up to 20 years to progress from the basic research stage to being widely available for medical treatment. Typically, the process will follow the stages of basic research, initial development, preliminary testing, further development, intensive testing, marketing and product launch. The costs associated can be anything up to 120 million US dollars for a single drug.

During this lengthy period many things can happen that will bring the development to a complete and final halt. The initial research may prove unproductive; the testing stage may reveal harmful side-effects; the production costs may be prohibitive; a competitor may launch a competing product. Increasingly over time the pharmaceutical industry has seen increased rivalry and competition amongst the large international companies, with each trying to maintain its competitive advantage. Naturally the large companies will be involved, at any one time, not in one such research programme but in many. These research programmes will cover a variety of different types of drug, will be following different stages of the product life cycle and will have differing degrees of risk (of failure) attached to them, as well as having different projected financial returns. One important task for management is to manage the research portfolio – the mix of research programmes under way at any one time. Clearly a research programme consisting of, say, ten initiatives all with an expected launch date 20 years hence will not be regarded as desirable. A balanced research portfolio is to be preferred where the balance is achieved across a number of criteria: expected programme duration, expected financial return on the research investment, likelihood of success/failure, amongst others.

ICI Pharmaceuticals (now Zeneca) was at this time part of the worldwide ICI Group and concentrated on the research and production of pharmaceutical products. Over time the company has investigated and used a number of approaches to its research portfolio management: linear programming and cost/benefit analysis to name just two. More recently the company has investigated the application of decision support systems (DSS) to help its portfolio management process. Decision support systems typically involve an interactive computer-based system allowing the manager or decision maker to use available data and supporting techniques while at the same time recognising that the problem under investigation may have a number of 'soft' areas where hard information is not available and where opinions, subjective expertise and 'hunches' also need to be brought to bear. The DSS was developed for use in the cardiovascular pharmacology section of the company to help a group of project managers appraise research projects. Not surprisingly, any given group of managers will typically have differing – and conflicting – views about specific research projects. Figure 5.10 shows part of the attribute structure used to help project managers assess projects.

The four most important attributes are shown – technical feasibility, product champion, competence of staff, competitive position – with sub-attributes for each of these as appropriate. It will be evident that the assessment and evaluation of many of these attributes in the context of a specific project are necessarily subjective and judgemental. One of the aims of a DSS is to try to reconcile the differing judgements managers will have about specific research programmes. For the technical feasibility attribute, two specific sub-attributes were identified: estimates of the likely time required by a project and estimates of the risk involved in the project. This enabled the construction of a probability–time curve for each project, as shown in Figure 5.11.

For four specific projects – labelled as TX, CA, RR and IS – the estimated time to complete the project is shown on the horizontal axis with the probability

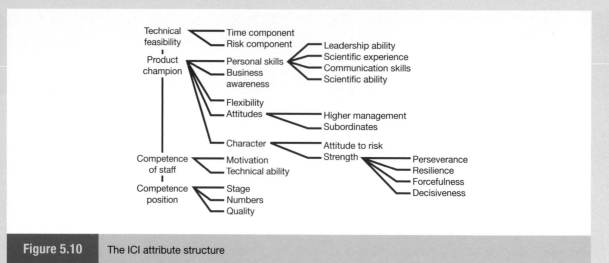

Figure 5.10   The ICI attribute structure

Reprinted by permission of G Islei, G Lockett, B Cox, S Gisbourne and M Stratford. Taken from 'Modeling Strategic Decision Making and Performance Measurements at ICI Pharmaceuticals', *Interfaces*, **21**(6), 1991. Copyright held by the Operations Research Society of America and the Institute of Management Sciences.

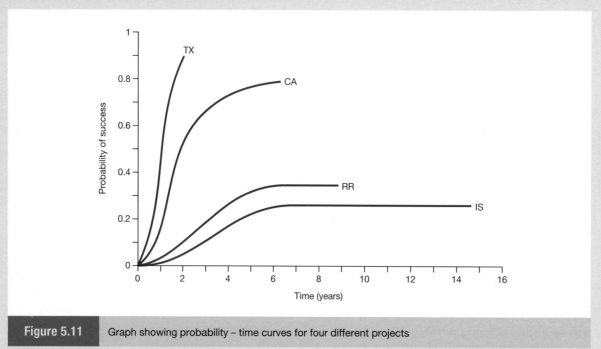

Figure 5.11   Graph showing probability – time curves for four different projects

Reprinted by permission of G Islei, G Lockett, B Cox, S Gisbourne and M Stratford. Taken from 'Modeling Strategic Decision Making and Performance Measurements at ICI Pharmaceuticals', *Interfaces*, **21**(6), 1991. Copyright held by the Operations Research Society of America and the Institute of Management Sciences.

of the project being successful shown on the vertical. Project IS, for example, has been assessed as taking up to 15 years to complete and has a low probability of success of around 0.25. Project TX, by comparison, will be completed in a short timescale – within the next two years – and has a probability of success of around 0.90. The modelling process required by the DSS encouraged managers on a group basis to evaluate their differing and potentially conflicting attitudes to projects under consideration, as well as helping the identification of critical success/failure factors. As part of this process, regular meetings by the group were held to review the research programme portfolio periodically and

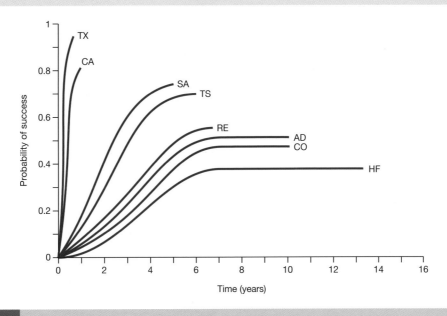

| Figure 5.12 | Graph showing ICI probability – time curves at a later date |

Reprinted by permission of G Islei, G Lockett, B Cox, S Gisbourne and M Stratford. Taken from 'Modeling Strategic Decision Making and Performance Measurements at ICI Pharmaceuticals', *Interfaces*, **21**(6), 1991. Copyright held by the Operations Research Society of America and the Institute of Management Sciences.

to update information relating to the decision-making process. Not surprisingly, over time, new information becomes available, attitudes relating to particular projects change and judgemental data on the relevant sub-attributes changes also. Figure 5.12 shows probability–time curves some two years after those in Figure 5.11. The graph reveals that two projects previously under consideration have now been abandoned (projects IS and RR) with a number of new projects introduced in their place to develop a more balanced research portfolio. The expected duration profile of the portfolio is now more acceptable, with projects reaching completion from one year in the future through to 13/14 years. Similarly, the portfolio encompasses a reasonable range of success probabilities.

It is worth noting in conclusion that this application typifies two important characteristics of many such applications of qualitative techniques to business decision making.

- Real-world applications rarely, if ever, focus on one decision-making technique in isolation. Such applications typically draw upon several areas as appropriate to the problem.

- Many such applications are not meant to be one-off exercises but rather form part of the continuing management decision-making process. As such this implies that the models and approaches developed need to be sufficiently flexible and adaptable to ensure modification with changing business circumstances.

This application is based on the article: 'Modeling Strategic Decision Making and Performance Measurements at ICI Pharmaceuticals', G Islei, G Lockett, B Cox, S Gisbourne and M Stratford, Interfaces, 21(6), 1991, pp 4–22. I am grateful to Interfaces for permission to reproduce the figures shown in this section. Copyright is held by the Operations Research Society of America and the Institute of Management Sciences, 290 Westminster Street, Providence, Rhode Island 02903, USA.

Exercises

1 Return to the example of Machine 2 in the shampoo bottle problem. Assume that management likewise wishes to ensure that the advertised contents satisfy some specific criteria. Determine what the advertised contents should be if management:

(**a**) require no more than 1 per cent of bottles to be under the advertised contents;

(**b**) no more than 5 per cent of bottles to be under the advertised contents.

2 The finance department of a large organisation has responsibility for monitoring costs in other departments of the organisation. A photocopier facility is available for one department's use and data has been collected which reveals that the number of photocopies made on the machine on a daily basis follows the Normal distribution; the mean of the distribution is 380 copies per day with a standard deviation of 35. The cost per copy is estimated at 6p.

(**a**) Determine the probability that daily costs incurred on the photocopier machine will be:
   ● more than £25
   ● less than £22.50
   ● between £24 and £26.

(**b**) Explain the basis of your calculations in a short memo to the finance director.

3 A large retail store buys an item from a supplier in batches of 100. Because of the delicate nature of the item some are inevitably damaged in transit between the supplier and the store and the price the store pays to the supplier reflects this. Over the past few years an average of four items are damaged in each batch of 100. Recently the supplier has used another transport company to deliver supplies. The store has recently checked a total of 25 items and found that three were damaged in transit. As manager of the store, how might you use this information?

4 A small firm has recently purchased a new PC system comprising a colour monitor, a CPU, a laser printer and a keyboard. The supplier of the equipment states that the chance of any one of the components developing a fault in the first year is 1 per cent. What is the probability that the firm will have to have its PC repaired in some way during the first year? What assumptions have you made to work out your result?

5 On average last year a local leisure centre had 230 customers per day, standard deviation 27, and the distribution of customers was found to be Normal. Determine the probability that on any one day the centre has:

(**a**) more than 270 customers

(**b**) less than 210 customers

(**c**) between 225 and 250 customers.

6 An auditor is checking invoices that have been paid to see if they contain any errors. Historically around 7 per cent of all invoices are expected to contain some error. The auditor takes a random batch of ten invoices. Calculate the probability distribution of errors for this batch of ten. What assumptions have you made?

7   An enterprising MBA graduate who has been unable to find gainful employment has taken to visiting an office block in town each lunchtime with an array of freshly made sandwiches for sale. The graduate reckons that he has a 90 per cent chance of selling a sandwich to any of the people working in the office block. He visits one office with 12 employees.

   (a)   Calculate the probability distribution of sandwich sales.

   (b)   Calculate the mean number of sales.

   (c)   How might the graduate use this information to improve the profitability of his activities?

8   A supermarket sells one particular item in its store on a regular basis. It currently has 750 units of this item in stock and no deliveries are expected until next week. The manager knows that average weekly sales of this item are 625, standard deviation of 55, and that sales are Normally distributed. Calculate the probability that the firm will not have enough stock to meet sales.

9   A firm is involved in manufacturing high-quality electrical equipment. Each item produced costs £6000 and total annual output is 500 items. At the end of the production process each item is individually tested for quality and safety. If the item is defective in any way it is scrapped at a complete loss to the firm, since it has been found not cost-effective to repair such items. Historically, one item in 1000 is found to be faulty in some way.

   (a)   Determine the probability that the firm will produce zero faulty items in a year.

   (b)   Determine the probability that the firm will produce no more than three faulty items in a year.

   (c)   The firm is considering employing a quality inspector at an additional cost of £1000 per year. The inspector, however, will be able to prevent any item from being defective. Suggest how the firm might evaluate whether employing the inspector would be cost-effective.

10   Return to the example used in the chapter of two machines filling bottles of shampoo. One machine had a mean of 500 ml, SD 10 ml, the other a mean of 750 ml, SD 15 ml. For each machine calculate the lower and upper amounts (in ml) between which:

   (a)   90 per cent of all output will fall

   (b)   95 per cent of all output will fall

   (c)   99 per cent of all output will fall.

11   Return to the Worked Example in this chapter. After conducting market research we have found that the possibility of a customer in the top 5 per cent group switching to a competitor is 0.85 if we do not offer a price discount and 0.15 if we do. Consider how you could use this information to determine the appropriate level of the price rebate to be offered.

6 Decision Making Under Uncertainty

Learning objectives

By the end of this chapter you should be able to:

- calculate and explain expected value
- construct and use decision trees
- explain the difference between uncertainty and risk
- assess the value of perfect information

As we concluded in the previous chapter much of business decision making takes place under conditions of uncertainty. Frequently we must take decisions with incomplete knowledge or knowing that the outcomes of these decisions are at best uncertain. Although there is no magic solution for the dilemma facing a manager in these uncertain situations, there are ways of examining these decision problems that can help clarify how decisions can be made. This is the area of decision making under uncertainty. In this chapter we shall be exploring the issues involved in making decisions under such conditions and seeing how probability can be used as part of the decision-making process.

The Decision Problem

We shall illustrate the principles of using probability to help reach management decisions with the following example. A small company has established a niche for itself in the personal computer market. It specialises in assembling and selling PC systems for use by family doctor practices throughout the UK – a market which, since the reform initiatives in the National Health Service, has proved particularly lucrative. The company is developing a new PC-based system which it intends to market under its own brand name next year. At present the company is trying to decide on the manufacturing and assembly process to be used. One aspect of this relates to the keyboard that will be used in the system, which will have specially labelled function keys. The company has decided that it faces three alternatives:

- It can manufacture/assemble the keyboard itself.
- It can buy the keyboards from a domestic manufacturer.
- It can buy the keyboards from a manufacturer in the Far East.

The problem is that each of these options has different costs and benefits associated with it. To manufacture/assemble the keyboard itself, the company would require major investment in new production equipment as well as extensive training of the workforce. It is felt that such an investment is only likely to be cost-effective if sales of the new product are particularly good. Buying the keyboard from a domestic supplier will involve the company in less up-front expense and will be safer if large sales do not materialise in the future. Buying from an overseas supplier offers better quality but with the risk of disruptions in supply if there are problems in the supply chain. In other words, there is uncertainty as to which decision to take because there is uncertainty over future sales. To help simplify the situation, the company is planning for one of three possible sales levels in the future: low, medium or high sales.

This problem typifies many situations that organisations have to face in real life. The company is faced with a range of alternative decisions over which it has control (i.e. it can choose between them) and it also faces an uncertain future in terms of sales. This future position is generally referred to as the possible *states of nature*: these states, future sales levels, are outside the direct control of the company but they do include all the possibilities and only one of them can actually occur. So, the basic decision to be made is: which of the three supply options do we go for, given the uncertainty we face as to the state of nature that will actually occur? How do we decide what to do *now* given that we do not know the level of sales we will achieve in the *future*?

Activity 6.1

If you were having to make this decision, what additional information would you like to have?

In order to progress we clearly need additional information to help us assess the alternatives. One of the key pieces of information would relate to the financial consequences of each combination of decision and state of nature. That is, how would the company be affected financially if, for example, it decided to manufacture the keyboard

Game theory helps insurers to judge the risks of terror

Sophisticated analytical tools predict targets and methods of attack, but their accuracy is open to question,

By Jenny Wiggins

The Bush Administration has waged its war against terror on several fronts: it has created a new Department of Homeland Security, established a Terrorist Threat Integration Center and passed the USA Patriot Act.

But despite those measures some companies fear the terrorist will always get through. They have turned to the private sector for help on gauging the potential impact of future attacks.

Shortly after September 11 2001, a small group of companies that specialise in assessing risk for the insurance industry launched US terrorism risk models.

These combine technology and data to predict likely terrorist targets and methods of attack, and possible losses to life and property.

They are aimed at the insurance and reinsurance industry, which already uses similar models to assess potential losses from natural catastrophes such as hurricanes and earthquakes.

"Most major commercial insurers and reinsurers are using terrorism modelling today," says Robert Hartwig, chief economist at the Insurance Information Institute.

Risk Management Solutions, one of the companies that sells the models, says its models identified the Citigroup building in New York and Prudential Financial's building in New Jersey as possible targets ahead of the US government's code-orange threat alert for the financial sector last month.

Andrew Coburn, director of terrorism research at RMS, says the company can pinpoint possible targets because it believes terrorists make rational decisions.

"Their methods and targeting are very systematic," he says.

RMS uses game theory – analytical tools designed to observe interactions among people – in its models. It argues that, as security increases around prime targets, rational terrorists will seek out softer targets.

Industry participants, however, say the predictive abilities of the models are limited, given the difficulty of foreshadowing human behaviour.

"The probability side can't be relied on as it is with natural hazards," says Ryan Ogaard, global practice leader of the modelling unit at Guy Carpenter, a reinsurance specialist.

Still, the information the models contain is considered valuable for assessing the impact of any attack, in part because modelling companies have collated extensive data for their catastrophe risk models.

"We've already built databases of commercial buildings and residences and the people in them for the whole country," says Jack Seaquist, terrorism product manager at AIR Worldwide.

The development of the models has attracted the interest of the US government, which is using some of them in its Department of Homeland Security, according to Dennis Kuzak, senior vice-president at Eqecat.

"We are in fact helping the US government get a better handle on potential risks," he says, adding that this is an "unexpected" use of the model.

How extensively the models will be used in the future remains unclear.

Much depends on the fate of the Terrorism Risk Insurance Act, which was passed in 2002 to provide federal help for any insurance losses sustained as a result of a terrorism attack.

Under the act, the Treasury Department is obliged to cap insurers' liability and reimburse them for some losses.

The act has enabled insurers comfortably to extend coverage to businesses, which are increasingly demanding terrorism insurance.

More than 46 per cent of US businesses bought insurance to cover terrorism risks in the second quarter – nearly double the rate during the same period a year before, according to Marsh, an insurance services group.

The government has not yet decided whether it will extend the act. If it does not, some market participants believe the terrorism risk models could become an increasingly valuable means of underwriting terrorism insurance.

But trade associations for the insurance industry say the inability of the models accurately to assess the frequency of terrorist attacks means they are not a reliable indicator of pricing the risk of catastrophic attacks.

"From a severity standpoint, the total loss from a terrorist event . . . could well exceed the capacity available in the insurance industry," the associations said in a submission to a congressional hearing on the act earlier this year.

Others argue that, if the terror risk act is not extended, interest in the models might diminish because insurance companies could be reluctant to provide terrorism coverage at all.

Meanwhile, the accuracy of the models' predictions remains in doubt.

"But hopefully we'll never see them tested," says the Insurance Information Institute's Mr Hartwig.

Source: *Financial Times*, 8 September 2004.

itself and future sales turned out to be low? What would the financial outcome be if sales were medium or high and so on. We shall assume that such information is available to the company in the form of the profit contribution that would be made to the company's activities in terms of each decision/state of nature combination. This information is presented in Table 6.1.

The table is usually referred to as a *pay-off table* since it shows the financial consequences – or pay-offs – in terms of the alternative decisions that can be made and the alternative states of nature that might result. If we examine the decision option to manufacture the keyboard in-house we see that the pay-off could vary from a loss of £15 000 through to a profit of £55 000. This implies that if this decision is taken and future sales are low, the decision will adversely affect profitability to the tune of £15 000 – presumably because the firm has had to make a major investment, which will not be recouped from low sales levels. On the other hand, if sales turn out to be high the company stands to generate a profit contribution of some £55 000. Equivalent pay-offs are shown for the other two decision alternatives.

Activity 6.2

Considering the information in Table 6.1, which of the three alternative decisions would you recommend?

The answer has to be: it depends. It will depend on a number of factors: how reliable you think the information is, how risky the various options are, how critical the decision is to the company's future and so on. One of the key factors, however, will depend on your own attitude to these future states of nature. In the absence of any other information on the likelihood of each state of nature actually occurring we can consider a number of common attitudes and we shall examine each in turn.

Table 6.1	Pay-off table: profit contribution (£000s)		
	Future sales level		
Decision	*Low*	*Medium*	*High*
Manufacture	−15	10	55
Buy abroad	10	30	25
Buy domestic	5	20	40

The Maximax Criterion

Let us assume for the moment that you have a very optimistic view of the future. If this were the case you would tend to choose the decision which could generate the highest possible pay-off. Such an approach is known as the *maximax* criterion, since we are searching for the *max*imum of the *max*imum pay-offs. In this problem our maximax decision would be to manufacture the keyboard ourselves since this – potentially – generates the highest of all potential pay-offs at £55 000 (compared with the best pay-off of £30 000 for buying abroad and of £40 000 for buying domestically). In general, for this approach, we determine the maximum pay-off for each decision and then choose the largest of these. This approach has the advantage of focusing on the best possible outcome. In summary, such an approach follows two steps.

● For each possible decision, identify the maximum possible pay-off.

● Comparing these pay-offs, select the decision that will give the maximum pay-off.

The Maximin Criterion

However, we are not all optimistic about the future. There is something to be said for examining the worst-case scenario – being pessimistic about future outcomes. In such a situation we can apply the *maximin* criterion, since we search for the *max*imum of the *min*imum pay-offs. For each possible decision we determine the minimum (worst) possible pay-off and then choose the largest of these. In this case this would lead us to choose the option of buying abroad, since this is the largest of each of the minimum pay-offs at £10 000 (the minimum pay-offs being –£15 000, £10 000 and £5 000 respectively). While such an approach has the logic of ensuring that we are in the best possible position if the worst happens, the approach does obviously ignore the potentially larger profit contributions that can be made by the other two decisions. The summary of the approach is:

● For each possible decision, identify the minimum possible pay-off.

● Comparing these pay-offs, select the decision that will give the maximum pay-off.

The Minimax Regret Criterion

A third approach is possible using the concept of opportunity loss or regret. Let us assume we take a decision to buy abroad. Having committed ourselves to this course of action we later observe that sales levels were actually high. Clearly – with hindsight – this was not the best decision given the state of nature that actually occurred. The optimal decision for this state of nature would have been to manufacture ourselves – generating a profit contribution of £55 000 rather than £25 000. Effectively we have

Table 6.2	Pay-off table: regret or opportunity loss (£000s)			

	Future sales level			Maximum regret
Decision	Low	Medium	High	
Manufacture	25	20	0	25
Buy abroad	0	0	30	30
Buy domestic	5	10	15	15

'lost' £30 000 by taking our original decision. This figure is referred to as the opportunity cost – or regret – of the decision for that state of nature. Clearly we can calculate the opportunity loss, or regret, associated with each possible decision and the various states of nature. This is summarised in Table 6.2, which is derived from Table 6.1.

We take each column (state of nature) in Table 6.1 in turn and determine, for that state of nature, what the optimum decision would be if we knew for certain which state would actually occur. So, if sales turn out to be low, the optimum decision would have been to buy abroad. If we had actually taken this decision our 'regret' in financial terms would be zero since it was the best decision. On the other hand, if we had decided to manufacture, the regret would be £25 000 since we could have had a profit contribution of £10 000 but actually incurred a loss of £15 000. Similarly, if we had decided to buy domestically, the regret would be £5000. We can perform similar calculations for the other two state of nature columns.

Activity 6.3

Calculate the maximum regret for each of the other possible decisions. Using this information, which decision would you recommend?

For each of the decision options we can now determine the maximum of these regret values and these are shown in the last column in Table 6.2. The logic we now apply is simple. We consider each decision in turn and the maximum regret value shows the maximum opportunity cost associated with this decision on the assumption that the worst state of nature happens. Effectively we are saying, suppose we take a particular decision, what will it cost us (in opportunity cost terms) if the worst then happens in terms of future sales? Clearly we would then wish to take the decision where this maximum regret was minimised. This would be the decision to buy domestically, since this has the lowest maximum regret at £15 000.

It is worth noting that in this simple example the three different approaches have led us to three different decisions. In itself this is no bad thing since it reinforces the view that – without certain knowledge of the future – there is no one ideal decision. The decision we take will, under these circumstances, depend on the decision maker's view of the future. However, one of the potential benefits of this type of approach is that it forces decision makers to consider and justify explicitly their view of future states of nature. One of the main drawbacks of this approach is that we have treated the three states of nature as being equally likely. In the last approach, for example, the process would lead us to the decision to buy domestically, even though in two out of three states of nature the decision to buy abroad has a zero regret. Clearly it is often more appropriate to view these states of nature as having differing probabilities in terms of their happening. Thus we might feel that medium sales has a higher chance of happening than low sales. We need to be able to incorporate such likelihood information into the decision-making process.

Decision Making Using Probability Information

Let us assume that the company has been able to quantify the likelihood of each of the states of nature occurring by attaching a probability to each. Such probabilities may have been derived from market research, from sales forecasting, or may simply be a 'guesstimate' based on some hard evidence and the experience of the decision maker. The probability of low sales is assessed at 0.2, medium at 0.5 and high at 0.3. Note that, as they must, the probabilities sum to 1 to include all possible outcomes. Clearly we now need to be able to use this additional information to help us reach a decision. The approach we can develop is to calculate the *expected value* for each of the alternative decisions. Let us consider the decision to buy domestically. For this decision there are three possible states of nature, each with a financial outcome, and for each state of nature we now have a probability. It seems reasonable to use these probabilities to calculate a weighted average outcome for this decision. That is:

$$(\pounds5000 \times 0.2) + (\pounds20\,000 \times 0.5) + (\pounds40\,000 \times 0.3)$$

to give a figure of £23 000. This result is known as the expected value (EV) of this decision: the alternative financial outcomes weighted by the respective probabilities. Care needs to be taken in terms of what the EV represents. It is not a guaranteed financial outcome if we were to take this particular decision. Rather it is a measure taking into account both the outcomes and their likelihood – recollecting that probabilities themselves should be seen as long-term averages. The overall purpose of EVs is to facilitate comparison.

Activity 6.4

Calculate the EV for each of the other decision alternatives. Based on this information, which decision would you recommend?

The EVs for all the decisions are then:

Manufacture	£18 500
Buy abroad	£24 500
Buy domestically	£23 000

Based on this information we would logically recommend that we buy the keyboard abroad since it has a higher EV. Once again we must stress that taking such a decision does not guarantee better profitability. The state of nature that actually occurs will generate for this decision a profit of £10 000, £30 000 or £25 000. Overall, however, this decision option is to be favoured since the weighted combination of outcomes and probabilities is higher than that for the other two options.

Risk

Clearly, one aspect of the problem that we have ignored relates explicitly to the decision maker's attitude to risk. Consider the following scenario. Your lecturer or tutor offers you a simple game of chance. A coin will be tossed in the air. On landing, if it shows heads you have lost and must pay the tutor £1. If the coin shows tails you have won and the tutor must pay you £2. The simple question: would you play (assuming your tutor isn't cheating)? The answer must be 'yes', since you have a 50 per cent chance of winning £2 and a 50 per cent chance of losing £1, implying in the long run that you ought to make a profit (the EV would be 50p). However, suppose the rules change slightly. Now if you win the tutor will pay you £2000 but if you lose you will pay the tutor £1000. Would you still play? There is now probably some hesitancy on your part. The odds of your winning are still the same. What has changed is the amount you stand to lose. If you could not afford to lose £1000 on the first throw you would probably decline to take part. Consider if the stakes went up to £10 000, or £100 000. The recommended decision – based on the approaches we have introduced – would not be affected by this. What will be affected is our attitude to the risk that we face.

Returning to our business problem, consider the decision option to manufacture. In principle this could lead to the highest profit contribution – £55 000. But equally it might lead to a loss of £15 000. If the company's cash flow is poor or it already has large debts it might decide – on a risk basis – not even to consider this option but to play safe and take another decision which leads to a surer – if smaller – profit.

Decision Trees

It is also possible – and frequently useful – to represent the type of problem we have been examining in graphical form by constructing what is known as a *decision tree*. The tree diagram shows the logical progression that occurs over time in terms of decisions and outcomes and is particularly useful in sequential decision problems – where a series of decisions need to be made with each, in part, depending on earlier decisions and outcomes. The tree diagram for our keyboard problem is shown in Figure 6.1. The construction starts from the left-hand side and gradually moves across to the right. A box is used to indicate that at this point we must take a decision (the box is technically known as a *decision node*), and the three alternatives branch out from this node: to manufacture (M), to buy abroad (BA) or to buy domestically (BD). Logically we can only move down one of these branches but we do not yet know which one. Each of these branches leads to a *chance* or *outcome node* (indicated by a circle), which represents the possible states of nature: these are outcomes over which the decision maker

QMDM IN ACTION
Cap Gemini Ernst & Young – risk management modelling

Cap Gemini Ernst & Young's client was a major US oil exploration and production company. As part of a major change programme, the client wanted to promote improved decision making amongst its employees through a better understanding of risk management techniques. The client was unsure as to the level of risk the company was exposed to in the different geographical regions in which they operated. Similarly, they were unsure as to the effect that the interrelationships between its different assets had on the overall level of risk. Given the nature of their business, many of their activities were subject to considerable uncertainty. The economic life of an oilfield can be predicted but not with certainty. The economic viability of the field will itself be affected by future world oil prices, which, again, are uncertain. Similarly, changes in technological efficiency and development will be uncertain. All of these factors and more will have a significant impact on key business decisions.

The initial approach was to develop a clear understanding of the client's business and the nature and structure of the risks involved in the different parts of the business. The team then developed a financial model (we shall look at these in Chapter 15) using Microsoft Excel. Uncertainty and risk were built in using a simulation approach (we shall look at simulation modelling in Chapter 14).

A variety of risk models were developed for the business. These simulated financial investment performance by geographical region and provided management information on the risk and return by type of asset, by area and by region. The models helped managers identify and understand the key uncertainties they faced with such decisions. The models also helped identify the potential impact of global risks such as major oil price changes and loss of production due to hurricane activity. A set of training modules based on the risk management modules were developed for use across the company.

The figure below relates to part of the risk management modelling looking at the uncertainty involved in the quantity of oil reserves. The distribution should look familiar!

A number of benefits were realised by the client:

- Improvements in the decision-making process itself.

- An increased understanding of risk by managers in the business.

- Improved information on business assets.

I am grateful to Cap Gemini Ernst & Young for permission to use this case study and to reproduce the figure shown. Further case study applications are available through their website: www.uk.capgemini. com/services/consulting/or/ success_stories
Copyright is held by Cap Gemini Ernst & Young.

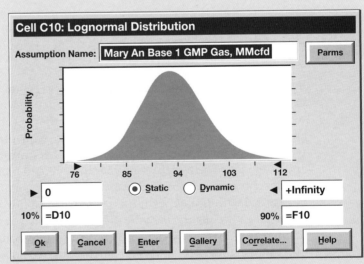

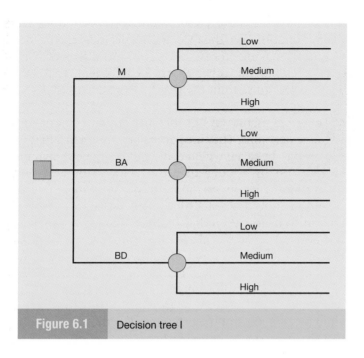

Figure 6.1   Decision tree I

has no control and we will only know in the future which branch we will follow. In our simple example this node along each decision branch is the same: sales could turn out to be low (L), medium (M) or high (H). At the end of each branch originating from a chance node we have a pay-off. We see, therefore, that there are a total of nine possible pay-offs of this problem. The next stage is to add to the tree the relevant information on what the pay-offs are, what the probabilities of the chance branches are and the EVs of each decision branch. This has been done in Figure 6.2. It can be seen that the relevant information has been added: pay-offs, probabilities and expected values.

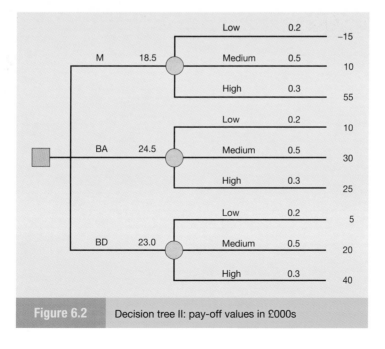

Figure 6.2   Decision tree II: pay-off values in £000s

The decision maker now sees clearly the potential pay-offs from each decision and state of nature combination. Also, the EVs for each decision can be identified and used to assist in the decision-making process, as we have just discussed. Based on this information we would recommend, other things being equal, that we choose the BA branch, although we recognise from the tree that the eventual outcome of this decision is as yet unknown.

Such decision trees are useful ways of showing the outcomes and potential consequences of alternative decisions. They are particularly useful in situations where a series of decisions may need to be taken which could not easily be shown in tabular form.

We can illustrate this by adding an extra factor to our existing problem. The company is still evaluating its options in terms of the keyboard decision. One of the management team has now suggested that if the decision to manufacture is taken and if sales turn out to be low then the company should consider a marketing campaign to try to boost sales. Such a marketing campaign would largely be based on adverts in magazines and trade journals, together with mailshots to family doctors advertising the new PC system. Such a marketing exercise would cost an estimated £10 000. It is felt that such a campaign would have an 85 per cent chance of being successful. If it were successful then the gross pay-off (before subtracting the campaign cost) would be £40 000. On the other hand, if the campaign were not successful, it would still have raised sales sufficiently for the pay-off to be break even, i.e. £0, before the campaign costs have been taken into account. While the company would like to defer the decision on the marketing campaign option, the advertising agency which would handle the campaign wants to know now if their services would be required so that they can ensure they have staff and resources available at the right time.

You can picture the firm's dilemma. The campaign appears to offer an additional option but only *if* the decision is taken to manufacture and *if* sales turn out to be low. But the company cannot delay its decision on the marketing campaign. It needs to decide *now* before sales are known.

Activity 6.5

Amend the decision tree we have for this problem to incorporate the new option.

Referring to Figure 6.2 we see that the only part of the tree that would be affected would be the very top branch relating to a manufacture decision and low sales state of nature. Effectively, if we ever got to this part of the tree we would face another decision (and hence would require another decision node) relating to whether we undertook the marketing campaign (MC) or did not (NMC). If we did launch the campaign, two states of nature might arise: the campaign could be successful (S) or a failure (F). We can now incorporate this information into the decision tree, shown in Figure 6.3.

At the top right of the tree we have added another decision node with two alternatives: launch the marketing campaign or do not. If we launch the campaign then two states of nature are appropriate: the campaign will be successful or it will not. We can then add the new pay-offs, probability information and the new calculations for EV. Starting at the very right-hand side of the tree we see that the pay-off if the campaign is launched and is successful is £30 000 (the gross of £40 000 less the campaign costs).

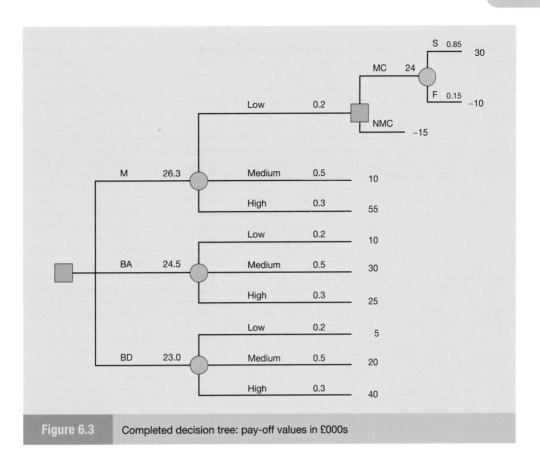

| Figure 6.3 | Completed decision tree: pay-off values in £000s |

If the campaign is launched and is not successful, the pay-off will be –£10 000. The pay-off if we do not have a marketing campaign obviously stays the same as before (–£15 000). The probabilities of 0.85 and 0.15 have been added to the appropriate branches. We can then calculate the EV of the two new alternative decisions. The decision to launch the campaign has an EV of £24 000, while the decision not to launch has an EV of –£15 000 (remember that the pay-off of –£15 000 is 100 per cent certain if we do not have a campaign). Clearly if we found ourselves in the position of having manufactured the keyboard with resulting low sales, our subsequent decision would be to launch the marketing campaign since this has a higher EV than the alternative to do nothing. We can then use the EV of this decision to work backwards to the left and calculate the new EV for the manufacture decision. This figure – originally £18 500 – must change since the pay-off linked to low sales has changed. The new EV is £26 300. Other things being equal, our initial decision would now be to manufacture the keyboard ourselves. However, we now know one of our future decisions. Given that we now decide to manufacture the keyboard we also know that if future sales turn out to be low we will be launching a marketing campaign. We cannot, at this stage, tell the marketing company that their services are definitely needed (after all, low future sales are not a certain outcome) but we can confirm their services will be needed if sales are low. Consider also the timescale for this decision. Once we receive information that sales have indeed been low, we shall not need to spend time considering our options. We have already decided what our future decision would be if we found ourselves in this situation. We would launch the campaign

Decision trees are used here to help organisations decide on the most appropriate type of collaborative agreement.

(always assuming of course that at that time in the future the information relating to probabilities and pay-offs has remained unchanged). The speed of decision making can potentially be improved through this approach, as it allows us to assess in advance our decisions under different scenarios.

The Value of Perfect Information

We shall illustrate one further use of this type of approach. The PC company has been considering extending its activities to the economies of Eastern Europe. With the political and economic changes that have taken place over the last few years the company feels that the time might be ripe for a move into these markets. After some initial analysis and a fact-finding visit to three of the East European economies by the company chief executive, the pay-off table shown in Table 6.3 has been constructed.

Table 6.3	Pay-off table: Eastern Europe (£000s)		
	Market growth		
	Zero	*Low*	*High*
Pilot programme	10	50	150
Major product launch	−300	100	500
Joint venture	−200	200	350

The company is considering three options. The first is to launch the product in one or two key geographical areas as a pilot programme and to postpone a final decision as to whether to market throughout the whole of Eastern Europe until the results of the pilot programme are known. The second option is to go ahead straight away with a major product launch. The third option is to establish a joint venture with key trading partners already operating in these economies. The financial outcomes of these decisions will, in part, depend on the level of market growth achieved over the next three years. For simplicity this has been categorised as zero, low or high. The local chamber of commerce has indicated that, in its opinion, the chance of each of these three growth levels being realised is 0.5, 0.4 and 0.1 respectively. However, the reliability of this opinion is not very high as the chamber readily admits. If we apply the principles of expected value we obtain the following:

Pilot programme	EV = £40 000
Major product launch	EV = –£60 000
Joint venture	EV = £15 000

Based on this information, we would recommend a pilot programme since it has the higher EV. So far this is no different from what we have done previously. However, let us add a twist to the business problem. A market research firm specialising in forecasting in Eastern European economies has approached the company, offering to undertake research into the company's intended markets. The purpose of this research would be to try to provide a firmer view of likely market growth – that is, to try to predict with increased accuracy whether the future growth will be zero, low or high. The key question for the company is: what is this information worth?

Activity 6.6

How much would you be prepared to pay the research company for such information?

From the company's perspective, the whole point of having such additional information is to reduce – and ideally eliminate – the chance of taking a wrong decision based on the limited information currently available. Consider the situation where the research firm *guaranteed* that it could predict with 100 per cent certainty the future market growth. If this were the case the company would, based on this prediction, take the optimum decision. If the prediction were of zero growth, the optimum decision would be to pilot. On the other hand, if the prediction were for low growth, we would decide on a joint venture, and if the prediction were for high growth, we would opt for a major product launch. In short, with perfect information about the future we would make the perfect decision each time. But how does this help? If we now summarise these 'perfect' decisions incorporating both the pay-off and the probability of that state of nature we have:

$$(0.5 \times 10) + (0.4 \times 200) + (0.1 \times 500) = £135(000)$$

as the EV of having perfect information about the future states of nature. Compare this with the EV of £40 000 under the existing conditions. It is then clear that to the company such perfect information has a maximum worth of £95 000 (135 – 40). If the research firm is willing to guarantee its prediction then the PC company would be wise to pay up to this amount for the perfect information. But what if – as is usual – such information is not perfect in terms of predicting the future? Suppose the research firm offers only a 90 per cent chance that it will get the prediction right? In principle it is then possible to evaluate the worth of such imperfect information using a similar approach. The technicalities of doing this, however, take us beyond our remit for this text. It is worth noting that such information can be evaluated and interested readers are referred to the Further Reading section at the end of this book.

Worked Example

A company specialises in establishing local, privately run leisure centres throughout the country. Typically the company will undertake considerable demographic analysis and assess the potential for establishing such a centre in a particular area. Areas targeted are typically those with a high proportion of middle-income families (young age profiles, the parents with professional occupations, car owners) and with poor or non-existent public leisure facilities. The centres offer a range of sporting and related leisure facilities: squash, badminton, swimming, gym, sauna together with a cafe and bar. The centre facilities are offered on an annual membership basis. After some initial analysis the company is considering building one such centre in a particular area. Detailed planning permission has already been obtained and financial support from the company's bank has been approved. On this particular site the company is considering a range of options:

- *Option A*: Build a large centre offering the full range of facilities.
- *Option B*: Build a medium-sized centre now with a selected range of facilities. Over the next two to three years assess whether the centre should be further expanded to the full range of facilities.
- *Option C*: Delay a decision about the size of the centre until more detailed market analysis has been completed (expected to take a further 12 months). At that time a decision would be taken to build either a large centre or a medium-sized centre. This extra market analysis would cost an additional £150 000.

To help in its analysis, the company has commissioned forecasts of the likely levels of use of the centre and undertaken a financial assessment of the various options/outcomes. Preliminary market research indicates that for Option A the chance of demand for the centre's facilities being high is 0.7, and of demand being low is 0.3. With high demand the company stands to make an estimated £950 000 profit. With low demand it would generate a loss of £700 000. For Option B the probabilities of high and low demand remain the same. If demand does turn out to be low then the company has already decided it would not expand the centre any further. Projected profit is £100 000. However, if demand turns out to be high, the company has a further option of expanding the centre, although it has not yet decided if it should do this. Such an expansion might be successful and generate an estimated profit of £650 000 but if it is not successful, the company will lose £100 000. The chance of a further expansion being successful has been put at 0.9.

If more detailed market analysis is undertaken in Option C the probabilities of high and low demand change to 0.8 and 0.2 respectively, since the company will be able to target its marketing and advertising more precisely. However, after such analysis has been completed the company will still have to decide whether to build a large centre (as in Option A) or a medium-sized centre (as in Option B), although in this latter case it would not subsequently be worthwhile expanding the medium-sized centre any further. For a large centre the financial outcomes are a profit of £950 000 if demand is high and a loss of £700 000 if demand is low. If a medium-sized centre is built the company estimates a profit of £700 000 if demand is high but a profit of only £100 000 if demand is low.

What should the company do? Clearly the company faces a range of decisions and possible outcomes so a decision-tree approach seems appropriate. The company faces three initial choices (Options A, B, C) with two of these options having further decisions at a later date. The decision tree for this situation is shown in Figure 6.4. The tree is quite complex and will need careful study. We start on the left with the three basic options available to the company. Option A is the easiest to assess since there are two possible outcomes from the decision. We see the expected value from this decision as +455 (+£455 000). Option B is more complex. If the company builds a medium-sized centre and demand turns out to be low then no further decision is required. However, if demand is high (something we will not know until some time in the future) the company must then decide whether or not to expand the centre. If it does not expand

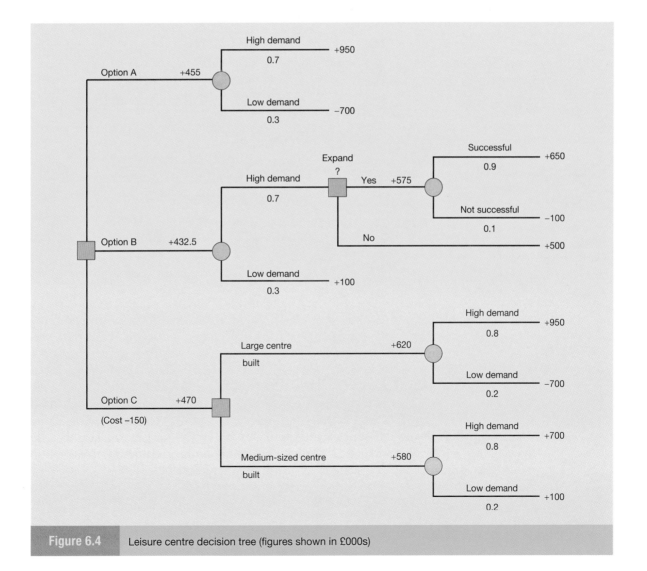

| **Figure 6.4** | Leisure centre decision tree (figures shown in £000s) |

it earns a profit of £500 000. If it does expand, the expansion could be successful (with a probability of 0.9) or it might not be (with a probability of 0.1, or 1 – 0.9). We see that the two expected values are +575 for expansion and +500 for no expansion.

Clearly, based on this information, the logical decision would be to expand the centre if demand turns out to be high. So we already have one benefit from this approach. We know *now* whether we should expand or not in the future if we go ahead with Option B and if demand is high. However, what about Option A versus Option B? Continuing with the Option B branch, although we see that the centre expansion is preferable to no expansion, we also calculate the EV for the whole of Option B as +432.5 – lower than that for Option A.

Option C, however, generates an even higher EV at +470 and would be the preferred option. Effectively, by delaying the decision 12 months and collecting more information we are delaying the decision as to which size of centre to build and also increasing the probability of high demand associated with the decision. We see that the logical decision for Option C would be to build the large centre (since this has the higher EV at +620 compared with +580). From this EV, however, we must subtract the additional cost incurred under Option C of £150 000 for undertaking more analysis. This gives a final EV for Option C of +470.

Clearly, decisions would not be taken based on this information alone. However, the implications of the three options become clear and can be assessed analytically. The company could also use this approach to do some sensitivity analysis. Would the decision change if some of the probabilities changed (since we might influence the probability of high demand, for example, by more extensive advertising and marketing)? Would the decision change if some of the financial data altered? Equally, we can assess the value of additional information. Without Option C, our decision would have been Option A with an EV of 455. Under Option C the EV is 470, an extra £15 000. This is the 'value' of the additional information we have collected over and above the cost we incurred of £150 000. We could advise the company that if the cost of completing additional analysis under Option C is likely to rise its maximum 'worth' to the company would be £165 000 (£150 000 + £15 000).

Summary

In this chapter we have considered the decision-making process in the context of trying to evaluate alternative decisions under alternative states of nature given the ever-present problem of uncertainty. We presented a number of different approaches to trying to reach a suitable decision under such circumstances, both with and without information relating to the probabilities of the different states of nature occurring. We also introduced the decision tree both as a method for summarising this information and for analysing more complex decision scenarios. While we cannot pretend that such approaches solve the uncertainty problems facing the decision maker, they do encourage a logical consideration of such uncertainty and a methodical investigation into the alternative decisions and their possible consequences.

Useful online resources

Detailed below are some internet resources that may be useful. Many have further links to other sites. An updated version is available from the accompanying website (**www.pearsoned.co.uk/wisniewski**). In addition, I would be grateful for details of other websites that have been found to be useful.

> **www.decision-analysis.society.informs.org** – Decision Analysis Society
>
> **www.mindtools.com/dectree.html** – Decision tree analysis
>
> **www.cs.usask.ca/resources/tutorials/csconcepts/1999_6/Tutorial/index.html**– Tutorial on decision making
>
> **http://en.wikipedia.org/wiki/Decision_tree** – Article on decision trees

QMDM IN ACTION
Gulf Oil

The oil exploration and production industry is characterised as one with huge initial investments, often to be taken on very limited information, leading to potentially high returns on that investment or equally high losses and where uncertainty over the outcomes of decisions is particularly high. For an oil company the related decision-making process is a lengthy and difficult one. Typically, a national government will offer areas, or blocks, of the seabed for investigation and development. Such blocks are usually offered for sale through some form of sealed-bid auction process. A company wishing to bid for a particular block, or group of blocks, therefore has to decide:

● whether to bid

● how much to bid if it decides to do so.

The decision problem is compounded by two major factors. The first relates to the information available to an oil company at this stage about the economic and financial prospects for the blocks. Typically this is extremely limited and very uncertain. Usually relatively detailed information will be available on the geological structure itself. A decision must then be taken on the likelihood of such a structure revealing substantial hydrocarbon (gas and oil) deposits. A decision must then be made on the likely nature of the deposits that may be found in terms of the

grades of deposits revealed and their quantity. Next an evaluation of the likely cost of exploiting the deposits is required together with some estimate of production costs once the development is in production. Since such deposits may have an economic life lasting ten to twenty years or more, some judgemental view must also be taken on likely revenue from such production – which requires an assessment of future world oil and gas prices, tax regimes and the like. The uncertainties surrounding each of these areas are, understandably, high.

The second factor compounding the problem for an oil company is that such sealed-bid auction processes are competitive. Competing oil companies are simultaneously assessing the same blocks and will reach their own views on what their own bids should be. On the outer continental shelf (OCS) of the United States the difference between the winning bid for one block and the second highest bid has exceeded 100 million US dollars. As a further complication, any single company will naturally have limited capital resources available for such a bidding process. The question then arises as to the priorities in terms of bidding and, indeed, whether a single company should bid in isolation or should consider some joint venture with another oil company, in terms both of pooling resources and spreading the inherent risk. In the early 1980s Gulf

Oil Corporation developed a lease bidding strategy system (LBSS). This was part of a longer-term effort designed to assist management make the best use of the limited capital resources at their disposal for US offshore oil and gas block sales. Historically, the company undertook an economic evaluation of a block, or blocks, when they were placed at auction. Such an evaluation took into account the geological prospects for the block, the chance of finding recoverable deposits, assumptions about the size and quality of the deposit and estimates of development and production costs. Together with forecasts of future prices and market conditions, this led to estimates of the financial return for the block. However, such estimates were typically point estimates: a single figure produced in terms of expected return rather than a range of figures incorporating different assumptions and different likelihoods of occurrence. It was also felt at the time that a number of managers in the company were unfamiliar with quantitative business techniques in general and with techniques for dealing with uncertainty in particular. An overview of the structure of the LBSS designed to try to improve this decision-making process is shown in Figure 6.5.

The historical database was, as the name suggests, data and information relating to previous auction sales and bids and the information made available at the time for each block. A number of sub-models were then designed. The first of these was the POW (probability of winning) model, which provided an indication of the probability of Gulf winning the bid for a given block based on a bid amount. This model was developed on the basis of the patterns from previous auction sales between the economic evaluation produced by Gulf and competitor behaviour. The model also took into account, when providing a probability estimate, the economic evaluation for the current blocks on offer. The performance model then provides information on the likely performance outcomes arising from any specific bidding decision in the context of sales and revenue performance. Feeding into this model were also the data relating to the economic evaluation for the blocks under consideration as well as management preferences in terms of performance criteria (for example, was the preference for minimising risk, maximising production, maximising revenue, or maximising the number of blocks won). The final part of the system was then an optimisation model

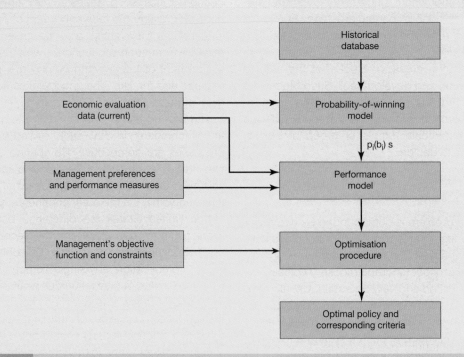

Figure 6.5   Schematic representation of the LBSS

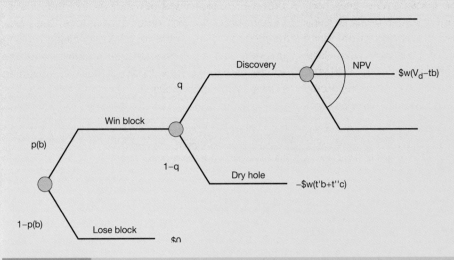

$w(V_d - tb)$

Figure 6.6   Tree diagram showing outcomes from bidding on an isolated single-prospect block

Reprinted with permission from *Operations Research*, **39**(1), 1991. Copyright held by the Operations Research Society of America. No further reproduction permitted without the consent of the copyright owner.

(discussed in detail in Chapter 11), which sought the optimum bidding policy for the blocks currently for auction, subject to a variety of constraints.

Figure 6.6 shows the simplified structure to part of this modelling process in the form of a decision tree. The tree relates to the bidding process for a single block being auctioned. The amount bid for the block by Gulf is denoted as b and the POW model generates a numerical value for p(b), the probability that the amount bid for the block will be successful. By definition, the probability of that bid being unsuccessful is $1 - p(b)$. Naturally, if the bid is unsuccessful the financial outcome is $0. If the bid is successful at auction, Gulf will then have to invest further in the exploration of the block to determine whether hydrocarbon deposits in economically viable quantities are to be found. The probability of such deposits being found is quantified as q. If such deposits are not found then the block is designated as a 'dry hole', with a probability of $(1 - q)$ of occurring. The financial outcome of a dry hole is a combination of b, the amount bid for the block, and c, the exploration costs incurred. In total the financial outcome is shown as:

$$w(t'b + t''c)$$

t' adjusts the amount bid to compensate for the tax regime and t" adjusts for the timing of the exploration costs since, typically, such costs may be incurred over a period of several years (the princi-

ples of such adjustments to cash flows are detailed in Chapter 15). The term w is used to represent Gulf's share in this block, since it may be a joint venture. The larger Gulf's share the closer w will be to 1: the smaller its share the closer to 0. Naturally, for this branch of the tree this financial outcome is negative. The top part of the tree represents an outcome where economically recoverable deposits are located. In such a case the financial outcomes are much less certain (depending on future costs, revenues, oil prices and the like). However, a range of likely outcomes can be developed (an indicative three branches are shown at this point). The financial outcome for any branch is shown as:

$$w(V_d - tb)$$

where V_d represents the net return on the block over its economic lifetime (calculated using the principles of net present value discussed in Chapter 15) and t adjusts the bid cost for taxes and time. The value that V_d takes will vary depending on which branch of the tree is being considered. Also relevant to each branch for this part of the tree is a probability representing the likelihood of that particular outcome over time.

The introduction of such a modelling system and the related techniques into the company was not an easy, or short-term, task. Some parts of management needed considerable evidence that the LBS system would be worthwhile 'under fire', and the development team spent considerable time convincing management of the improvements in decision making that would result. It is also worth noting that a number of spin-off benefits were later realised, notably the need for more detailed and comprehensive information to be fed into the model and the need for a rigorous feedback and analysis procedure following both successful and unsuccessful bids. As with other applications, the introduction of the model into the decision-making process was seen as a long-term activity and one which had to be able to adapt itself to changing business circumstances.

*The above application is based on the article: 'Development and Use of a Modeling System to Aid a Major Oil Company in Allocating Bidding Capital', DL Keeper, F Beckley Smith Jr and HB Back, Operations Research, **39**(1), 1991, pp 28–41. I am grateful to the Operations Research Society of America for permission to reproduce the figures shown in this section.*

Exercises

1 For the pay-off table shown in Table 6.3 construct a decision tree to confirm the decision without perfect information. If the pay-off for pilot/zero growth was now changed to –£10 (000), how would this affect the potential value of perfect information for the company?

2 Consider the pay-off in Table 6.3 *without* the probability information. How could you now evaluate suitable decisions?

3 A manufacturing firm has decided to capitalise on its existing success by building an extension to its production plant to come on stream by 2010. The firm has evaluated the decision and calculated that its profitability will improve by £650 000 if the extension is completed on time. If, however, the extension is delayed then, because of contractual production commitments, the firm stands to lose some £350 000. The firm has invited tenders for the construction work and two contractors have been shortlisted. Contractor A has indicated that they would undertake all the work themselves and that they have a track record such that 75 per cent of previous jobs have been completed on time. Contractor B, on the other hand, has a track record of 95 per cent of jobs being completed on time where Contractor B has done all the work. However, Contractor B occasionally subcontracts work to other companies – some 30 per cent of their jobs have a subcontract element in them. Their completion rate on jobs involving subcontractors is less impressive, with 40 per cent of such jobs not being completed on time.

   Required:

   (a) Draw a decision tree for this situation.

   (b) Using this information, recommend which of the two shortlisted contractors should be given the job.

   (c) In practical terms how useful do you think the technique would be for the firm? What other information might you take into account?

4 A large multinational oil company is considering its strategy in the North Sea. The UK government has announced that a new drilling site in the North Sea will be

offered for sale on a competitive tender basis, the site going to the company making the highest bid. Provisional exploration of the site indicates that, over its life, it can be expected to generate revenue of around £1500 million if the oil reserves turn out to be high, but only £500 million if they turn out to be low. Seismic tests have indicated that the probability of high reserves is 0.60.

If the company is successful in its bid it will also have to decide whether to construct a new oil rig for the site or to move an existing oil rig which is currently operating at an uneconomic site. The costs of the new rig are around £250 million and for moving the existing rig around £100 million. A new rig would be able to boost production by £150 million if reserve levels turned out to be high. The company has decided that if it is to bid for the site, the maximum bid it can afford at present, because of its cash flow situation, is £750 million. In the past, 70 per cent of the company's bids for such sites have been successful.

However, the company is also under pressure to refurbish some of its existing rigs for both efficiency and safety reasons. The £750 million could be used for this purpose instead. If the money is used for refurbishment, there is a 50 per cent chance of increasing efficiency to generate a return on the £750 million of 5 per cent, and a 50 per cent chance of generating a return of 10 per cent. If the decision to refurbish takes place after the bid has been made and failed, only £500 million will be available.

(a) Construct a decision tree for this problem.

(b) Using the decision tree, suggest a suitable decision for management.

(c) Determine the value of perfect information about the size of the reserves on the new site.

5 A small engineering firm is under increasing pressure from foreign competitors and is considering a number of strategic options. One of these relates to changing over from the existing production process to one which is completely automated. The firm has narrowed down its choices regarding this option to two possibilities.

The first, System I, is that the firm could install a production process using computer-controlled production equipment purchased from the Far East. This system is expected to have a marked impact on the firm's operating costs. However, the system would take three years to design and install and would cost some £2.5 million. The projected cost savings are around £1 million a year once the system is operative. The system is expected to have a useful life of 10 years. However, the Far East company which would design and supply the equipment is new to the engineering company and it has been assessed that this course of action has a probability of only 55 per cent of performing satisfactorily.

The second possibility is that the firm could collaborate with the production engineering department at the local university, which is at the leading edge of research in this field. This production system, System II, would be designed to run in parallel with the first, System I, and would cost £1 million to design and develop. However, System II would take three years to implement. The university estimates that it has a 75 per cent chance of coming up with an appropriate system. The problem is that System II is basically for 'insurance' in case System I fails to perform as required. If System I does work satisfactorily, the expenditure on System II will have been for nothing. To complicate the issue the decision to develop System II does not need to be taken now: it can be taken at any time during the 10-year life of System I but bearing in mind that System II takes three years to develop. Ignoring the time consequences of expenditure and cost savings, construct a decision tree for this problem and advise the company on a suitable course of action.

6 A small company finds itself in the position of having to complete a contract for a large customer or pay high financial penalties for failing to deliver. The firm finds itself with a problem. The stocks of one particular component used to assemble the product have been exhausted and the contract cannot be completed. The company has contacted a number of possible local suppliers of this component. The company needs some 10 000 units of the component, which cost £1 each. The quality of the component is very variable, however, and in the past the company has found that 55 per cent of components are acceptable, 30 per cent are of poor quality and the remainder are sub-standard. Poor components can be improved to standard at a cost of 25p per unit while sub-standard components can be rectified at a cost of £1 per unit.

Because of the short timescale for completion of the contract, the company has decided to visit each supplier in turn. A small sample of the component will be inspected and if the components look acceptable, 10 000 will be purchased from that supplier. If the first supplier's sample is not acceptable the company will inspect a sample from the second supplier, and so on. If, however, the company gets to the fourth and final supplier, it will have to purchase all 10 000 items from this supplier regardless of quality.

Construct a decision tree for this problem and evaluate the likely financial consequences for the company of its situation.

7	# Market Research and Statistical Inference

Learning objectives

By the end of this chapter you should be able to:

- understand the difference between a sample and a population
- explain the principles of a sampling distribution
- calculate and explain a confidence interval around a sample mean and a sample percentage
- carry out a variety of common hypothesis tests

We have been exploring some of the principles and applications of probability over the last two chapters. We now introduce one of the key areas to which probability is applied by business – that of market research and statistical inference. Many organisations frequently commission or undertake basic market research into their products, their services, their customers. Production organisations will frequently test-market new products before launching them nationwide. Service organisations seek to assess the public's expectations, perceptions and views on their products and services. Increasingly public sector organisations are trying to assess customers' views on the services provided – whether the customer is a patient in a hospital or a citizen in a local authority district. Such information, from a management perspective, is potentially very valuable. It can provide an insight into areas of uncertainty and may help the manager assess both strategic and operational options for future change. However, such 'research' tends to have one thing in common, no matter which organisation it is for and the purposes for which it is undertaken. The common factor is that such investigations invariably focus on a *sample* rather than on the statistical *population* – that is on part rather than on the whole. We shall explore the reasons for this shortly but the obvious consequence is that the manager must then – somehow – assess the reliability of the results. It is in this area that we can apply the principles of what is known as *statistical inference*.

Pollsters predict a shake-out

Bob Worcester's Mori is up for sale, an example of the need for consolidation as market research goes global

By Tim Burt

Bob Worcester hates Voodoo. The chairman and founder of Market & Opinion Research International, better known as Mori, is worried by the "black art" of self-serving polls favoured by some tabloid newspapers, TV stations and websites. Unlike industry-regulated research, such audience polls invite callers (often at premium rates) to express opinions on the issues of the day – from the death of government scientist David Kelly to Tony Blair's Asian tour – with scant regard to age, background or profile.

"Voodoo polls seem to be becoming more prevalent," says the 69-year-old entrepreneur, dubbed the "high priest of pollsters". But he warns that any survey relying on self-selecting participants – be they voters for Big Brother or Sky News viewers – are often worthless and unrepresentative.

Demand for instant reaction and audience response, nevertheless, continues to sustain the polling industry. It has been a big week for legitimate research organisations, with newspapers rushing to gauge voter sentiment following the David Kelly affair. This government, more than any other, is guided by focus groups and consumer research rather than by conviction.

Worcester – contemplating the industry from his cluttered corner office in the former paper factory that is Mori's London headquarters – says government or public sector research has swept past opinion polls as the mainstay of most companies. "We're known for political opinion polls, which is 1 per cent of our turnover – it's an irony." He says the total revenue of the industry is going up and up, and government is the fastest growing sector.

According to the British Market Research Association, turnover in the UK research industry grew by 2.6 per cent last year to £1.18bn. Globally, the sector enjoys annual sales of £11bn–£12bn – some 70 per cent more than in 1998.

That industry is hugely fragmented, with thousands of research companies offering surveys on everything from a new variety of Coca-Cola to hospital waiting lists. But the demands of government and international companies is forcing polarisation.

When Worcester formed Mori in 1969, the research industry already had 650 players. Since then, the sector has assumed a classic hour-

TOP 10 MARKET RESEARCH COMPANIES BY UK TURNOVER 2002 £M	
Taylor Nelson Sofres	113.2
NOP World	77.2
NFO Worldgroup	47.0
Ipsos	44.0
Mori	35.8
Information Resources	34.7
Maritz/TRBI	25.1
Martin Hamblin	19.3
ISIS	17.2
Synovate	15.6

Source: BMRA
Note: Due to the restrictions of US Sarbannes-Oxley legislation, WWP group members have not been included in this table

glass profile. There are a handful of dominant international market information groups – led by VNU, the US-Dutch group, Britain's WPP and Taylor Nelson Sofres; a small but important group of middle rank companies; and a sprawling base of tiny pollsters.

Mike Kirkham, chief executive of Taylor Nelson Sofres (TNS), is predicting a shake-out. "To serve government or big international companies you have to have international networks and scale," he says. "The smaller companies cannot compete for that kind of work and the middle sector is being squeezed."

Earlier this month, TNS added to its 50-country network by completing the $425m acquisition of NFO World Group from Interpublic, the

US advertising group. The deal bolsters the company's position in the US, where Kirkham expects steady demand from state governments and large companies.

"There will have to be further consolidation to serve those customers and the growing appetite for cross-border research, particularly from bodies such as the World Bank and UN," he says.

The search for scale has prompted more than $7bn of mergers and acquisitions in the past five years as companies including Ipsos of France and Germany's GfK have pursued bolt-on deals.

Mori is poised to join that consolidation wave after last month announcing plans for a trade sale, expected to value the group at more than £75m. Kirkham thinks WPP will look at it, along with Aegis and possibly GfK. But the Mori chairman, who holds 19.5 per cent of the company, is choosy. "If the culture and the price and strategy isn't right we're not going to sell," he says.

The auction follows a decision by 3i, the private equity group, to cash in its 42 per cent holding. The Mori management, holding the remaining shares, would be enriched by a deal.

But Worcester appears to be looking for a partner rather than a dominant parent, or at least a holding company that would grant Mori semi-autonomous status. He argues that Mori's reputation rests on stringent rules and ethical standards. Put simply, the company will not do surveys it doesn't like. Worcester recently rejected an invitation from the BBC World Service to analyse a website poll in which 98 per cent of respondents favoured the BBC against Alastair Campbell, Downing Street's director of communications.

Nevertheless, Mori has only ever sacked two clients – Robert Maxwell and Sir James Goldsmith – for interfering with poll results that they did not agree with. "We have it in our terms and conditions that we vet all copy about our polls. We're the only ones who do that," says Worcester.

Whoever bids for Mori, the company does not expect a big shift in its customer base. In the past 20 years, it has swung from an 80 per cent reliance on corporate clients to 60 per cent government or public sector work.

Worcester attributes the change mainly to Britain's Citizens Charter,

launched by the last Tory government. "It gave people the right to ask people in power why and made governments more aware of the need for accurate survey research." He senses, however, that public sector and corporate clients are growing more alike. "The government is now doing work that Coca-Cola has done for 50 years. It has begun to understand the difference between opinions, attitudes and values in what people want."

In research terms, opinion polls remain the snapshot – quick responses to issues that rarely affect the respondents directly. Attitudes are more deeply held, but are subject to change. Values – reflecting moral, political and religious conviction – are liable only to seismic shifts. Gauging those three sectors has become a lucrative industry for the companies involved, but fewer players may survive.

"We are going to see further consolidation, driven by mergers and globalisation of clients and the increasing costs of technology," says Worcester. "When I started nearly 40 years ago there were very low barriers to entry. Now the barriers are rising."

Source: Financial Times, 29 July 2003.

Market research is big business globally.

Populations and Samples

We made the distinction between samples and populations in Chapter 4. In a statistical sense a population relates to the entire set of items under consideration, whereas a sample is a subset (or part) of that population. The most common example relates to opinion polls which attempt to determine voting patterns at a forthcoming election. Clearly in an ideal world the organisation undertaking the survey would like to contact all voters to determine their intended voting behaviour. From a practical perspective this is unrealistic. The cost of doing this, the resources required, the organising needed, the time required would all make such an approach infeasible. Instead the organisation is likely to choose a subset of the population – a small cross-section of voters from the entire electorate. In the UK, such a sample is likely to consist of around 1000 people – compared with over 20 million voters. Most organisations wishing to collect data to help in their decision making are likely to find themselves in a similar position – forced to consider a sample of data rather than the entire population. An organisation thinking of launching a new product would like to ask all potential customers their opinions but will have to restrict itself to only a sample. A hospital assessing the quality of the health care services delivered would like to ask all patients but will have to satisfy itself with asking only a sample. A production organisation which mass-produces some item would like to be able to check every item for quality but will have to restrict itself to only a sample. The list of examples is endless.

However, from the manager's perspective, although this is understandable, it does cause problems. At the end of the exercise – whether it is an opinion poll, a survey of customers or a quality check – the manager will be presented with data relating to a sample. Based on this sample data, the manager must somehow try to decide how this applies to the whole population – which after all is what the manager is really interested in. In statistical jargon the manager will be trying to infer key characteristics of the population based on sample data.

Consider this example. A specialist music shop has recently opened on a prime retail site in a large city. The shop has deliberately focused on a particular market niche and specialises in CDs of classical music. The manager is interested in trying to determine the profile of customers: their age, gender, socio-economic group, income, preferred composers and so on. The reasons for this should be self-evident: such information will, potentially, assist the manager in matching products/services to customers' needs, in matching advertising to the client base, in matching stocks of CDs with likely demand and so on. As we have already established, the manager is unlikely to be able to carry out a full study of the entire population – all the customers using the shop – but will have to be satisfied with collecting and analysing data on only a sample of customers. However, based on the sample data, the manager will be interested in trying to determine the equivalent characteristics of the (unknown) population. Let us focus on a particular example. The manager has decided to try to obtain information about the income levels of customers. The manager feels that, given the nature of CDs stocked in the shop, customers are more likely to come from middle to higher income groups. The sample data is intended to throw some light on the income profile of customers.

Suppose, for example, the manager has taken a sample of customers and found that the mean income of the sample was £42 000. What does this imply about the mean income of the customer population (on whom we have no actual data)? Would it be appropriate to conclude that the population mean income was also £42 000? Or about £42 000? Clearly some method of transferring our sample findings to the statistical population would be highly desirable. It is this process that is generally referred to as statistical inference – the ability to *infer* the population characteristics based only on sample data.

Before we proceed, however, we must introduce an important note of caution. The whole basis for statistical inference is built on two key assumptions about the sample data:

- the sample is a properly representative subset of the statistical population. In the context of the CD shop, for example, reliable results are unlikely to be obtained if the sample consists predominantly of male customers. The sampling process must ensure that a proper cross-section of customers is obtained. In practice, this is easier said than done and interested students may wish to read the relevant references in the Further Reading section at the end of this book, which provides details of appropriate sampling methodology.

● that the data collected is reliable and accurate. Once again this is a critical assumption, particularly when the statistical sample consists of people. We have to be realistic and accept that people will not always give an 'honest' answer to a question. Consider asking a customer their income level as part of the survey. Although many people might give a reliable response there are likely to be those who 'inflate' their actual income, giving rise to a sample result which is 'inaccurate'. Frequently there is no way of properly assessing the validity of some responses, although careful survey design can help minimise the possibility.

These two assumptions must be remembered when we are applying inferential principles.

Every statistic tells a story

Simon Briscoe looks at how businesses can make best use of the mass of census data.

Cold calling is warming up. Armed with your postcode, a call centre will have a detailed profile of the likely characteristics of families living in your area. They will then be able to ask the questions that are most likely to lead to a sale. Skilful use of such local area data is reducing the speculative nature of call centres' first contact with prospective customers as they carefully select the streets they approach.

This is just one example of the use of census and other small area data that has exploded in the past decade. The government has always used basic census data for allocating resources, but use of the most detailed information in the commercial world has recently grown rapidly. As local area data become more widely and cheaply available in a way that was impossible to imagine just five years ago, the trend looks set to continue.

As computing power is applied to census forms, market research and apparently dull administrative records, useful statistics are created and opportunities open for any person or company interested

in knowing about a locality. The availability of data free on the internet is unprecedented. And when this is linked to data that companies have about their customers, powerful resources can be created.

While the census and its rich core of data largely reflects the needs of the government's policy-makers, it has important ramifications for everyone.

As businesses operate in exactly the same communities, they can use the data to improve their understanding of geographic differentiation, target markets or locate operations.

Companies will be able to decide where outlets should go, which branches should be closed and where advertising campaigns should be focused on the basis of something other than gut instinct. This is of importance. As the sums of money involved are considerable – perhaps £500,000 to refurbish a restaurant or pub and £20m to build a superstore – mistakes are expensive.

The same analysis can be used for the closure of uneconomic bank

branches or the location of a golf course or theme park. It is not only the number of people near an outlet that counts, but the type of people. New types of outlets, such as Tesco Metro or Sainsbury's Local, are in part born from this type of analysis.

The very largest companies have, over the years, been progressively using information from the population census but, as it is held only every decade, the data are often out of date. They have added to it other, non-government, local area data, frequently modelled by commercial data providers that work up local profiles or data sets into user-friendly and more relevant formats.

But most business people have traditionally made only limited use of official data. Numbers that would be of real use are often not available.

While regional data have been around for some time, their quality is variable. They are rarely timely and the regions seem never to dovetail into areas that businesses recognise. It is also clear that averaging over a region can take away much variability in local areas, which is vital to businesses.

Against this background, the new census data – with reliable and truly useful local area data for local authority wards with just several thousand people, and even "output areas" of just a hundred or so households – is to be welcomed.

One driving force for the government's enthusiasm for the use of data is the Neighbourhood Renewal Strategy set up following the Social Exclusion Unit's 1998 report on deprived neighbourhoods. The report explained that "anyone could wander through some of these areas and know that something was badly wrong, but the government has never set out to record or analyse the issues in any comprehensive or systematic way".

Data have been trickling on to the government's neighbourhood sta-

tistics website over the past couple of years, but the addition is the result from the population census that took place in April 2001. The results have mostly been published in the past few months, are readily and freely accessible on the internet and are available free of any complex licensing arrangement.

This is only the start. The Office of National Statistics will be adding extra as yet unspecified information.

The Inland Revenue's tax data, Customs and Excise business data coupled with the ONS's own business and importers' registers, could combine to make a very powerful database. The ONS has promised to make local area income estimates available, given the government's decision not to include an income question in the census. The key point is that the data will reach

critical mass, be of good quality and be generally free for anyone.

Such is the nature of the change that individuals and community groups will also have the opportunity to share the improved "democracy" and better connect with their local communities and service providers.

It will take time for all potential users to learn to make good use of neighbourhood data and effective "data bashing" habits do not develop overnight. But in the same way that the improved availability of good macro data has improved the quality of economic policy debate and decision-making, local area data will have an enormous and more direct impact on businesses. Within a few years, thousands more people will be using local area data as second nature.

Source: Financial Times, 29 September 2003.

Census – or population – data isn't always available but where it is, organisations can make effective use of the data.

Sampling Distributions

Let us return to the sample of customers for the CD store. For simplicity let us assume that the store has a number of regular customers and that a sample of 100 of these has been taken and the results analysed (bearing in mind what we have just said about assumptions). The store found that the mean income of the sample was £42 000 with a standard deviation of £5000. In symbolic form this would be:

$$\bar{x} = 42$$
$$s = 5$$
$$n = 100$$

where n refers to the size of the sample and we have the results in £000s. Note that we use the appropriate symbols for the sample (and not the Greek character symbols, which relate to the population as we discussed in Chapter 4). However, this sample is only one of many that we could have chosen. A second, and different, sample of 100 customers could have been taken (and bear in mind that we would technically only need to change one of the customers in the sample for it to be different).

QMDM IN ACTION
Cap Gemini Ernst & Young – sampling for perfect modelling

Cap Gemini Ernst & Young's client was a major UK utility company. The client had contracted with a third party organisation for receiving and processing over-the-counter payment of bills by its utility customers. The contract between the client and the third party service provider specified standards that had to be achieved in terms of the elapsed time between payment by the utility's customers and the receipt of the transaction data tapes at the client's site. Clearly, the longer it took for the client to actually receive the payment made by its customers to the third party organisation then the worse the effect on its cash flow. Effectively, the client wanted to ensure that the third party's performance met the contractual obligation. However, one of the key difficulties was that there was no electronic capture of the date and time of payment, only a paper record date stamped at payment time. The client wanted a method for monitoring performance that would be cost-effective and would also be acceptable to the third party service provider.

In order to establish a cost-effective monitoring system it was clear that it would have to be based on a sample basis. Statistical sampling principles were used to ensure that robust and representative samples of data were chosen for monitoring purposes. The third party service provider proposed that it should be responsible for operating the monitoring process but that the client would undertake strict audits from time to time to ensure compliance with agreed procedures. Initial audits were conducted by Cap Gemini Ernst & Young to ensure that the sample results were both fair and accurate and that the monitoring operation conformed to recommended procedures.

Rules were developed for regular selection of samples of payment vouchers from all those processed by the third party service provider. The information to be extracted from the sample vouchers was identified. Procedures were then established to determine the elapsed times for processing these vouchers and to convert these into measures of performance. Cap Gemini Ernst & Young pro-

vided initial training to the third party service provider, which, it had been agreed, would be responsible for sampling, data collection and routine monitoring. Cap Gemini Ernst & Young also carried out a series of audits to establish that the sampling system gave a fair picture of the performance of the third party service provider. Monitoring procedures were refined following these initial audits.

Analysis by payment centre is as follows:

% of National	Adjusted % on time
11.5	93.8
14.1	90.8
13.2	90.0
12.1	92.5
13.7	95.0
12.3	100.0
12.8	97.5
10.3	93.3
100	94.1

The benefits are as follows:

- A method for monitoring standards of service was developed that was agreed as fair both by the client and by the third party service provider.

- The provision of robust, cost-effective monitoring information ensures that there is a continuing focus on payment processing performance by both the client and the third party service provider.

- As a by-product of the initial audits conducted by Cap Gemini Ernst & Young, a number of apparent anomalies in the payment process were identified. These were drawn to the attention of the client and the service provider for remedial action.

Activity 7.1

If we took a second, and different, sample would you expect to get a sample mean of £42 000? Why? (Or why not?)

In principle there is no reason why we should obtain a second sample mean of exactly £42 000 since, technically, we have a different sample of customers. However, it does seem reasonable to expect the second sample mean to be similar to the first on the assumption that both are representative of the statistical population. If, for example, the second sample mean had been £18 000 we might have been both surprised and suspicious given the difference between the two sample results. The principle then is that we would expect different samples taken from the same population to generate similar, but not necessarily arithmetically identical, sample means.

Now consider the following scenario. We take repeated, but different, samples from the population and note the mean of each sample. We continue this until all possible samples have been taken from this population. (A word of caution: do not think about actually doing this! There are over six million million million million million million different samples of size 100 that could be taken from a population of just 1000!) So – in principle – we have a large number of sample means. Obviously some of these sample means will take the same value; others will differ. Effectively then we have a data set consisting of sample means and we could analyse this data set in the same way as any other, using principles introduced in earlier chapters. In principle, for example, we could now construct a histogram and frequency polygon for the sample means. What would this histogram look like?

The Central Limit Theorem

To answer this question we must turn to what is known as the Central Limit Theorem. While such a theorem can only be 'proved' using mathematics, the principles can be seen using some simple logic. We have taken all possible samples from the population and for each sample calculated its mean. Logically, there will be one sample – and only one – which contains the 100 customers with the lowest incomes. The mean of this group therefore must be the lowest sample mean. There will be a number of samples, however, which contain 99 of the lowest-income 100 customers. These will have sample means slightly above the lowest. A larger number still will contain 98, yet more with 97 and so on. The majority of samples will, reasonably, contain a cross-section of incomes. It seems reasonable, then, to conclude that the distribution of all these samples means would look like that shown in Figure 7.1. That is, the distribution of all possible sample means will be Normal. The implications of such a distribution are that we have a symmetrical distribution of sample means, with only a few results at each of the extremes and the bulk of results in the middle of the distribution. This distribution is known as sampling distribution. In fact this is what the Central Limit Theorem concludes:

If we take random samples of size n from a population, the distribution of sample means will approach that of the Normal probability distribution. This approximation will become closer, the larger is n.

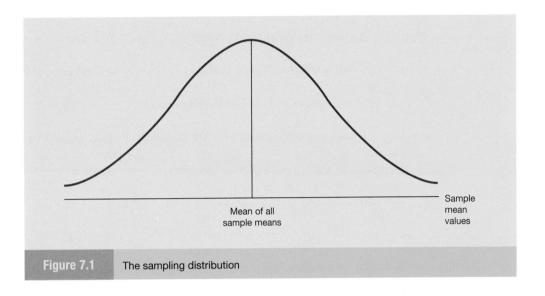

Figure 7.1   The sampling distribution

This is a particularly important conclusion and underpins much of statistical inference. We need to consider its implications. It implies that – no matter what type of
population we are examining – if we take random samples, the distribution of these
sample means will approximate to the Normal distribution. Similarly, the larger the
sample sizes we use, the closer this approximation will become. Consider our example.
We do not know what form our population distribution (of customer incomes) actually takes. It could be Normal or it could be skewed (more likely, given both demographic patterns and the type of shop). However, it really doesn't matter because the
sampling distribution will approximate to the Normal distribution as long as we take
sufficiently large samples. ('Sufficiently large' is generally accepted to be a sample size
of at least 30.)

But so what? How does this help our search for inferences that we can make about
the population based only on a sample? After all, we do not have all these sample
results that make up the Normal sampling distribution. We only have the result from
one sample. To see how we can progress we need to examine further characteristics of
the sampling distribution.

Characteristics of the Sampling Distribution

We have already seen that, under certain conditions relating to sample size, the sampling distribution will approximate to the Normal. Can we say anything else about this
distribution?

Activity 7.2

What are the two statistical characteristics of any Normal distribution that we usually
require?

The sampling distribution – like any other Normal distribution – can be summarised with two statistics: its mean and standard deviation. Let us consider the mean first. Remember that the sampling distribution is made up of all the possible sample means. Suppose we were to take all the individual sample means making up the distribution (in fact to treat them just as any normal data set) and calculate the mean. This is where English gets cumbersome but this effectively requires us to calculate the mean of all the sample means. You should be able to see that if we were to do this then the mean we actually calculate must be the same as the mean of the population (since the sampling distribution by definition covers all the data in the population). So the mean of the sampling distribution is actually μ, the population mean. What about the standard deviation? This is more difficult and we can only state that the standard deviation of the sampling distribution is given by:

$$\frac{\sigma}{\sqrt{n}}$$

where σ is the population standard deviation and n the sample size. In practice, because σ is generally unknown then we can approximate the standard deviation with:

$$\frac{s}{\sqrt{n}}$$

where s is the standard deviation of the sample. So, we are able to describe the sampling distribution in terms of its mean, μ, and its standard deviation $s/\sqrt{n}$. Before seeing how we can use this information, it might be useful to summarise our statistics given that we are starting to talk about different means and different standard deviations. Remember that we are actually talking about three different groups: the sample, the population, and the sampling distribution of sample means. Each of these will have a mean and a standard deviation:

	Mean	*SD*
Sample	$\bar{x}$	s
Population	μ	σ
Sampling distribution	μ	$s/\sqrt{n}$

The standard deviation of the sampling distribution is more frequently referred to as the *standard error* and we shall be using this terminology from now on. To summarise, so far we have established that when we take a sample from a population, the mean of this sample will form part of a (theoretical) distribution which will be approximately Normal with a mean, μ, identical to that of the population and a standard deviation calculated by $s/\sqrt{n}$. But how does this help us evaluate the sample result in the context of the population? To answer this we now introduce the concept of a confidence interval.

Confidence Intervals

We know that our sample mean forms part of a distribution which is Normal: our sample mean of 42 (£000) years lies somewhere in the Normally shaped sampling distribution. However, we have no way of knowing *for certain* whereabouts in this distribution

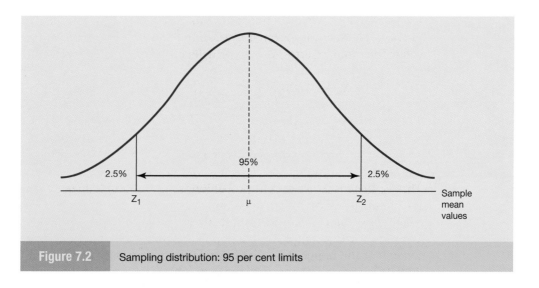

| Figure 7.2 | Sampling distribution: 95 per cent limits |

our mean actually occurs. The sample mean could, for all we know, be identical to the population mean or considerably lower or considerably higher. However, although we cannot know *for certain* where the sample mean lies in relation to the population mean, we can use probability to assess its *likely* position *vis-à-vis* the population mean. The sampling distribution is made up of all possible sample means and, given that the sampling distribution is Normal, we can use the principles we developed in Chapter 5. Let us examine Figure 7.2. The figure shows the sampling distribution and we have set an arbitrary value such that we wish to determine the relevant Z scores to encompass the central 95 per cent of values (which in this case are sample mean values).

Activity 7.3

Determine the relevant Z scores for Figure 7.2.

We require the area in each of the two tails of the distribution to be 2.5 per cent, i.e. a total area of 5 per cent to be outside the denoted central area (this 5 per cent value is generally denoted as α). From the Normal table in Appendix B we note that this equates to a Z score of 1.96. So, a pair of Z scores of +1.96 standard errors and −1.96 standard errors will encompass the central 95 per cent of sample means.

Activity 7.4

What is the probability that a sample mean (chosen from all the others at random) will fall within this central part of the sampling distribution?

Clearly the answer to the question must be 0.95 since, in total, 95 per cent of all sample means must fall in this area. Following from this we can then ask: what is the probability that our sample mean – at 42 (£000) – falls in this area? Again it must be 0.95 or 95 per cent. So, although we do not know for certain how close our sample mean is to the population mean, we now know that there is a 95 per cent chance that it is no further away than ±1.96 standard errors from μ, the population mean. Since we can calculate the standard error, we can actually quantify this distance:

$$\pm 1.96 SE = \pm 1.96 \frac{s}{\sqrt{n}}$$

$$= \pm 1.96 \frac{5}{\sqrt{100}}$$

$$= \pm 1.96(0.5) = \pm 0.98 \; £000$$

That is, there is a 95 per cent probability that the sample mean and population mean are no further apart than 0.98 (£000), or £980.

This is a major conclusion and it will be worthwhile reiterating what we have done. We started with a sample from a population and we were seeking to estimate the mean income of the population. The information we actually had related to the sample of 100 customers, whose mean income was £42 000. But, using the Central Limit Theorem and the principles of probability, we are able to conclude that with a 95 per cent likelihood the population mean income will be within £980 of the sample mean. In other words, the population mean income is likely to be between £41 020 and £42 980.

In fact, what we have calculated is generally referred to as a *confidence interval*. We have taken the sample mean and calculated an interval, ±£980, around this statistic, such that we can state that we are 95 per cent confident that the actual population mean lies within £980 of the estimated mean (which is the sample mean). The confidence interval calculation can be summarised as:

$$95\% \; CI = \pm 1.96 \frac{s}{\sqrt{n}}$$

Based on such an interval there is a 95 per cent probability that this interval contains the (unknown) population mean, μ. This means that, based on sample information, we can infer, for a given level of probability, a likely value for the population mean.

Average weekly earnings and hours of male agricultural workers
England and Wales
At September in each year

	1998	1999	2000	2001	2002	2003
Average weekly earnings (£)	301.24	301.22	298.24	332.66	366.82	352.88
95% confidence interval	(±£12.69)	(±£11.88)	(±£13.84)	(±£15.08)	(±£18.88)	(±£30.30)
Average weekly hours worked	50.7	50.9	49.0	51.9	54.1	51.1
95% confidence interval	(±1.5)	(±1.4)	(±1.4)	(±1.7)	(±2.1)	(±3.0)
Average earnings/hour (£)	5.94	5.92	6.09	6.42	6.78	6.91
95% confidence interval	(±£0.18)	(±£0.15)	(±£0.18)	(±£0.20)	(±£0.19)	(±£0.31)
Number of workers in the sample	274	292	234	251	204	72

Source: *Annual Abstract of Statistics.*

Confidence intervals are used to highlight the fact that the data is based on a sample and to indicate the interval around the figures shown.

Other Confidence Intervals

But why did we choose to use a 95 per cent probability in calculating the interval? The answer is that this was an arbitrary – but common – choice. We could actually have established a confidence interval for any probability figure: 10 per cent, 50 per cent, 90 per cent. Naturally, knowing what we do about the Normal distribution, we realise that changing the probability figure will cause the confidence interval itself to change. In general, our CI formula can be rewritten as:

$$CI = \pm Z_{\alpha/2} \frac{s}{\sqrt{n}}$$

where Z is the Z value from the Normal table associated with the chosen probability value. The term $\alpha/2$ needs clarification. α denotes the area in the two tails of the distribution which delimit the confidence interval (5 per cent in our example). However, given that we require a central CI, this implies that the area in each of the two tails must be $\alpha/2$ (5%/2 or 2.5 per cent) and this provides the value for Z that we seek in the Normal table. In practice, although any level of probability could be chosen to calculate a CI, three tend to be used: 90 per cent, 95 per cent and 99 per cent.

Activity 7.5

Calculate a 90 per cent and a 99 per cent CI for this problem. Provide an explanation as to what these actually are. What do you observe about the size of the CI as the chosen probability increases?

We would obtain:

90% CI = 42 ± 0.82	(Z = 1.64)
95% CI = 42 ± 0.98	(Z = 1.96)
99% CI = 42 ± 0.29	(Z = 2.58)

We see that as we require a higher probability we must accept a wider CI. The logic of this is clear. If we wish the probability of the CI containing the population mean to increase then we must accept a wider interval within the sampling distribution. In practice, the combination of probability and size of CI is a trade-off and we must compromise in our choice.

QMDM IN ACTION
Cap Gemini Ernst & Young – estimating energy consumption through sampling

The client, supplying gas and other energy products throughout the UK, is required to produce auditable financial accounts each month. However, individual customers' gas consumption may only be known when gas meters are read and consumption recorded and for some customers this may occur only – at best – at quarterly intervals. The client must therefore rely on estimates of customer consumption, which need to be as accurate as possible but also to be as cost-effective as possible. In addition, the independent industry regulator requires the estimated monthly accounts for customers to be within 4 per cent of the real bill value.

A panel of customers who read their meters on a weekly basis was established. Cap Gemini Ernst & Young then developed a fully integrated IT system which provided database storage of the panel meter readings, full analysis of the panel data and a process for 'boosting' the panel to replace panel members who withdraw from the scheme. A graphics element to the system allowed users to store and analyse data without accessing the actual database.

Cap Gemini Ernst & Young provided a methodology for collecting information on customer consumption patterns over time. The data could then be used for a range of analyses, forecasts and estimates of gas consumption. Clearly, it was essential that the panel was representative of the population. A stratified sampling procedure was used to select panel members and it was estimated, based on the panel size, that the accuracy of the panel results was within ±2 per cent.

- A cost-effective process for collecting sufficient data was established. The stratified sampling approach that was used meant that a smaller panel size could be used to achieve a given confidence interval than would have been the case with simple random sampling. This in turn meant that the costs of data collection were much reduced.

- An accurate estimate of the volume of gas consumed each month could be produced.

- Accurate data became available that could be used for medium- and long-term planning.

I am grateful to Cap Gemini Ernst & Young for permission to use this case study. Further case study applications are available through their website: www.uk.capgemini.com/services/consulting/or/success_stories

Confidence Intervals for Proportions

So far we have examined CIs in the context of a mean value. There are numerous situations where we may have a sample result expressed not in terms of a mean value (like £42 000) but rather as a proportion or percentage. Consider a company sponsoring market research into a new product and the impact of a TV advertising campaign designed to launch the product. A sample of the public was selected and asked whether they had seen the recent TV adverts for this product. Clearly their response would be either yes or no (we shall discount the don't knows). At the end of the survey we should be able to calculate the proportion – or percentage – of respondents who saw the adverts. But to talk of a mean in this context would make no sense. Let us say we found that 63 per cent of the sample of 250 people saw the adverts. Exactly the same problems arise in trying to evaluate this sample result *vis-à-vis* the statistical population as arise when we had a mean. Can we calculate a comparable CI for this type of problem? The answer is 'yes' but in a slightly different way. The same logic applies. This sample proportion is only one of those which make up the sampling distribution (of all sample proportions) and again this distribution will be approximately Normal. So, if we can calculate the standard error of this distribution, we can then calculate a CI. However, you may appreciate that while we could calculate a standard deviation for a problem with a sample mean, we cannot do this for a sample proportion. Remember that the standard deviation is a measure of variability around the mean (in the last problem we had a mean of 42 and a standard deviation of five). But it clearly doesn't make sense to ask: what's the standard deviation around a 'yes' response? However, we can still calculate the standard error of the sampling distribution using an appropriate formula (which we simply present here as given).

$$\text{SE of a proportion} = \sqrt{\frac{p(1-p)}{n}}$$

where p is the sample proportion. The formula for the CI can then be given as:

$$CI = p \pm Z_{\alpha/2} \sqrt{\frac{p(1-p)}{n}}$$

or as:

$$CI = p \pm Z_{\alpha/2} \sqrt{\frac{p(100-p)}{n}}$$

if we express the sample result as a percentage rather than a proportion. Interpretation and use of such a CI is exactly as before.

Activity 7.6

Calculate a 90 per cent, 95 per cent and 99 per cent CI for the TV advert survey.

We would have for a 90 per cent CI:

$$90\% \; CI = p \pm Z_{\alpha/2} \sqrt{\frac{p(100-p)}{n}}$$

$$= 63 \pm 1.64 \sqrt{\frac{63(100-63)}{250}}$$

$$= 63 \pm 5\%$$

and:

$$95\% \; CI = 63 \pm 5.98\%$$
$$99\% \; CI = 63 \pm 7.88\%$$

The 95 per cent CI, for example, indicates that there is a 95 per cent probability that the sample percentage and the population percentage are no further apart than six percentage points, i.e. a CI of 57 per cent to 69 per cent.

Interpreting Confidence Intervals

Although the calculation of a confidence interval for a given problem may be straight-forward, interpreting and commenting on the result may be less so. Care needs to be taken in terms of how the result is explained. The following two comments are appropriate in the context of our last CI example.

● I am 95 per cent confident that the percentage of people who saw the TV adverts is between 57 per cent and 69 per cent.
● I am 95 per cent confident that my estimate of the population percentage (63 per cent based on a sample of 250 people) is within 6 per cent of the actual population percentage.

The following statement is not appropriate, even though it is commonly made.

● There is a probability of 0.95 that the population percentage is between 57 per cent and 69 per cent.

You can see why this last statement is inappropriate. The population percentage is a fixed, constant value, i.e. it is one number. The population value either will or will not fall into this interval. The probability that it does must, therefore, either be zero (it does not) or one (it does). It cannot be anything in between.

Hypothesis Tests

Our investigation so far into sample data has focused on the calculation of a confidence interval. Although these are useful in quantifying an interval in which the population parameter is expected to occur, there are frequently occasions when we wish to assess whether a *specific* value for the population is likely (rather than a range of values, as in the CI approach).

Consider the following. The company undertaking the TV advertising to support its new product has decided that the cost of such a TV advert campaign can only be justified if more than 55 per cent of people see the adverts. We are now no longer interested simply in calculating a CI for the sample result but wish to assess whether, based on the sample data, this criterion is being met across the statistical population. In such a case we must approach the problem from the perspective of a *hypothesis test*. Fortunately this uses exactly the same principles that we have already established for the CI, although in a slightly different way. We shall examine a number of the more common forms of hypothesis test in the remainder of this chapter. Most of these though follow exactly the same approach as we shall follow. The carrying out of a hypothesis test follows a logical sequence.

● Formulate the null and alternative hypotheses.
● Determine a significance level.
● Identify the rejection area.
● Determine the critical statistical value.

- Calculate the test statistic value.
- Choose between the two hypotheses.

Let us examine these in turn for our TV advert problems. The actual information we have is from the sample:

p = 63%

n = 250

We wish to use this information to assess whether the population percentage was more than 55 per cent. On the face of it, it appears that we have met this target, since the sample result, at 63 per cent, is higher than 55 per cent, but we also know we must allow for what we can call *sampling error* or *sampling variation*: a possible – but legitimate – difference between the sample result and the population result. The term 'sampling error' is a little unfortunate since it implies we have made some sort of mistake. Sampling error indicates that no matter how carefully we have selected and analysed the sample, we must allow for the fact that the sample result may differ from the population result simply because it is a sample – only part of the population data set. Let us denote the population parameter with the symbol π (pi). We wish to assess whether π could take a value of more than 55 per cent, given that the sample result was 63 per cent.

Formulate the null and alternative hypotheses

The first step is to formulate appropriate hypotheses that we can test. We must specify two hypotheses: the null and the alternative. In this example we would have:

H_0: $\pi \leqslant 55\%$

H_1: $\pi > 55\%$

The null hypothesis, H_0, states that π is no greater than 55 per cent (i.e. it does not meet the required target audience) and H_1, the alternative hypothesis, states that π is over 55 per cent. The whole basis of the hypothesis test is that we must, based on the sample evidence, choose between these two hypotheses. We shall make the choice based on what we know about the relationship between samples and populations. Note that, in probability terms, the two hypotheses are collectively exhaustive: they encompass all possible values for π. A common failing in formulating hypotheses is that they do not encompass all possible values. For example, the formulation:

H_0: $\pi < 55\%$

H_1: $\pi > 55\%$

would be technically incorrect since it does not allow for p taking a value of exactly 55 per cent. The order in which we formulate the two hypotheses is also important (and again often the cause of error). The general principle is that H_1 should be formulated in the context of whatever value(s) we wish to test. Our criterion here is whether the adverts were seen by more than 55 per cent of viewers. This minimum figure then becomes the basis for H_1 and H_0 must then be formulated to ensure all other possible values have been included. It is particularly important to remember that H_1 must relate to what we are trying to decide.

The basis for our test is now as follows. We start from the premise that our null hypothesis is the appropriate one for our problem. Only if we can amass sufficient statistical evidence will we accept the alternative hypothesis. In the jargon of hypothesis testing, at the end of the test we will have come to one of two conclusions:

- either we will reject H_0 (and thereby be forced to accept H_1)
- or we will fail to reject H_0.

The terminology may sound odd but it is carefully logical. If we fail to reject H_0 we are not concluding that H_0 is correct but rather that insufficient evidence was available to reject H_0. The analogy that is often used to try to explain this logic relates to criminal law practice in many countries. If you are charged with some criminal act you will be asked how you plead. In many countries the choice is either 'not guilty' or 'guilty' and by presumption you are not guilty until proved otherwise. In other words, the null hypothesis (not guilty) stands unless the prosecution brings sufficient evidence to persuade the judge and/or jury to reject the null hypothesis and accept the alternative (guilty). This is exactly the same as in our test. Unless we can bring sufficient evidence, we have no reason to reject H_0. It is also worth noting that the hypotheses we use will fall into one of three categories:

(a) H_0: $\pi \leq x$
H_1: $\pi > x$

(b) H_0: $\pi \geq x$
H_1: $\pi < x$

(c) H_0: $\pi = x$
H_1: $\pi \neq x$

where x is the appropriate numerical value we wish to test. The first two are technically referred to as *one-tail* tests and the last a *two-tail* test.

Determine a significance level

Having formulated the hypotheses we wish to test we must now choose a level of significance associated with the test. To explain this we need to consider that, whatever our conclusion at the end of the test, we may actually have reached the wrong conclusion about the population based on the sample evidence. Once again, the legal analogy is useful. In your trial, let us assume that you are in fact not guilty (H_0) but that the jury finds you guilty on the evidence presented. Alternatively, let us assume that you are in fact guilty (H_1) and that the jury mistakenly finds you not guilty. In both cases an 'error' has occurred but of two different types. In fact we can distinguish two different possible 'errors' in our test.

Type I error	We reject H_0 when in fact it is correct. In this case what is called a Type I error would occur if we rejected H_0 when in fact the population percentage was no greater than 55 per cent.
Type II error	We should reject H_0 but fail to do so. In our case a Type II error would occur if the population percentage was actually over 55 per cent but we failed to reject H_0 based on the evidence available.

We can summarise the possibilities in tabular form as in Table 7.1.

Table 7.1	Decisions and errors	
	Actual situation	
Decision	H_0 *is true*	H_0 *is false*
Do not reject H_0	Correct	Type II error
Reject H_0	Type I error	Correct

A Type I error is denoted as α and a Type II error as β. Although we would like the chance of making either error to be as low as possible, in practice the two errors are inversely linked. That is, other things being equal, the lower the probability of making a Type I error, the higher the probability of making a Type II and vice versa. In most hypothesis tests we are able to control directly the probability of making a Type I error. We do this by specifying the maximum allowable probability of making a Type I error. Typical values for α are 0.05 and 0.01 and the choice of α will, in part, depend on the consequences of making a Type I error (i.e. incorrectly rejecting the null hypothesis).

Activity 7.7

Consider the analogy of your being tried for murder in a court of law (a crime which in fact you did not commit). Would you want the probability of a Type I error being committed to be low or high?

Naturally you would wish the probability of the jury reaching the wrong decision in the context of H_0 to be as low as possible, hence would choose α at 0.01 rather than 0.05. The less obvious implication of a low choice for H_0 – but particularly important in the context of the test – is that if H_0 were not rejected based on the evidence available there would be a high probability (0.99) of this being the correct decision. However, in other cases we may prefer to see the Type II error probability minimised (with the implication that α will be higher at 0.05).

Consider the situation facing a medical consultant who is examining you for some serious disease. The null hypothesis will be that you do not have the disease (and hence require no treatment). The alternative is that you do have the disease and require treatment. The consultant's decision may, in part, be based on some medical test that has been undertaken. But like any test, the results cannot be guaranteed in terms of their accuracy and reliability. Consider the consultant's position in terms of committing a Type I and II error. A Type I error is committed if the consultant decides incorrectly that you have the disease and provides the appropriate treatment. All this means is that you are subjected to a course of treatment which is actually unnecessary (and hopefully harmless). However, if you do actually have the disease, the consultant would quite naturally wish to minimise the probability of a Type II error – that you do actually have the disease but that the consultant decides you do not and therefore does not provide treatment. In this case the consequences are potentially more severe: i.e. you failed to receive treatment which you actually needed.

All of this may sound unduly complex but actually condenses to a simple choice of either $\alpha = 0.01$ or $\alpha = 0.05$, depending on whether we wish to minimise the chance of a Type I error or a Type II. In many business applications the choice is actually quite arbitrary. The principles are important, however. At the end of the test, whatever conclusion we have come to we must remember there is a possibility that we have made the wrong decision based on the available data.

Activity 7.8

Consider our problem of the TV advertising. Which choice of α would you recommend?

In the case of the TV advert problem it would seem sensible to choose α at 0.01 – to minimise the chance of a Type I error. H_0 by implication means that the TV advert campaign should be halted as it is not reaching what is seen as a sufficient percentage of viewers. We would not wish to go ahead with such an expensive campaign if there was any reasonable doubt that it would not be effective in terms of reaching over 55 per cent of viewers. This implies that we wish to minimise the potentially high cost of a Type I error. On the other hand, it might be the case that the new product's sales success depends on the TV campaign and that the cost of not advertising might be high in terms of lost sales and overall company performance. In this case we might legitimately wish to minimise the cost of a Type II error and choose $\alpha = 0.05$. This simply reaffirms that such a decision cannot be taken as an integral part of the test but rather in the context of the wider decision-making problem. It also reaffirms that such decisions should not necessarily be left to the statistician, who may be unaware of the wider picture. However, let us stick with our first logical position and require $\alpha = 0.01$.

Identify the rejection area

The next stage is to identify the relevant rejection area. Consider Figure 7.3. This shows the sampling distribution for our problem. Note that the population parameter,

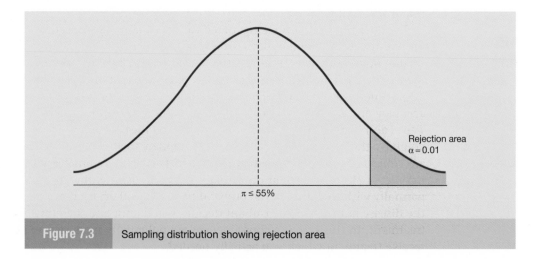

Rejection area
$\alpha = 0.01$

$\pi \leq 55\%$

Figure 7.3   Sampling distribution showing rejection area

$\pi \leqslant 55$ per cent, is based on the assumption that our null hypothesis is true. In other words, this value for π is still not proven. The rejection area is shaded and corresponds to $\alpha = 0.01$: the rejection area equates to 1 per cent of the total area under the Normal curve. The logic of the rejection area is straightforward. We are trying to decide whether to reject H_0 based on the sample evidence. For the sake of argument, let us assume that H_0 is in fact correct and that π is no greater than 55 per cent. We can then apply our knowledge of the sampling distribution in a logical way.

Activity 7.9

Assuming H_0 is correct, what is the probability of taking a sample from this population and finding a sample percentage that falls in the rejection area? What conclusion would you come to if this were actually to happen?

Clearly the probability of any one sample result falling in the rejection area is 0.01 (or 1 per cent) – based on the assumption that H_0 is actually correct. However, consider our position if we did in fact take a sample from this population and found that it fell in the rejection area. We would have to conclude:

● either that a highly improbable event had occurred (actually obtaining a sample result that far away from the population percentage)
● or that our assumption that H_0 was correct is unlikely.

These are the only two possibilities, and the reason for identifying the rejection area now becomes clear. It will allow us to determine whether the sample result we have does fall in the rejection area or not. If it does then we shall be forced to conclude that the assumption that H_0 is correct is unlikely. If it does not fall in the rejection area then we shall have no reason to reject the null hypothesis.

It is worth noting that the rejection area itself will depend on which of the three general types of hypothesis we actually formulate (illustrated in Figure 7.4). For type (a), where H_1 takes the $>$ form, the rejection area will be in the right-hand tail of the distribution (as in our example). For type (b), where H_1 takes the $<$ form, the rejection area will be in the left-hand tail. For the third type (c), where H_1 takes the form not equal to, then we require the two tails each with an area $\alpha/2$ at either end of the distribution. For this reason the first two types of test are known as *one-tail tests* and the last type as a *two-tail test*. With practice you will find it is not necessary to sketch the rejection area each time, although it is advisable to do so to begin with just to confirm which area you are classing as the rejection area.

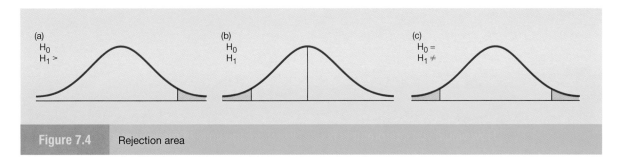

| Figure 7.4 | Rejection area |

Determine the critical statistical value

Using the rejection area and our choice of α we must now obtain a critical statistical value that is associated with this rejection area. In other words, we must find the Z value associated with this area.

Activity 7.10

What is the Z value for the rejection area if we set $\alpha = 0.01$ for a one-tail test?

From the Normal table we see that an area in one tail of 0.01 has a Z value of 2.33. Consider carefully what this implies. It implies that, if H_0 is correct, then 99 per cent of all samples from this population should result in a percentage viewing figure no further away from 55 per cent than 2.33 standard errors. If we put this another way it implies that the probability of any one sample occurring more than 2.33 SEs above 55 per cent is only 0.01, but again on the assumption that H_0 is correct. The critical Z value, in other words, simply marks out the rejection area in terms of standard errors. This value is usually denoted as:

$$Z_\alpha = 2.33$$

Calculate the test statistic value

Having obtained the critical Z value appropriate to our test we must now calculate a Z value for the actual sample result. We do this in exactly the way we developed in Chapter 5, when we were introducing the use of the Normal distribution. Our calculated statistic becomes:

$$Z_{Calc} = \frac{p - \pi}{\sqrt{\dfrac{\pi(100 - \pi)}{n}}}$$

where you will note that the denominator of the equation is just the formula for calculating the standard error for a percentage. The calculation is then:

$$Z_{Calc} = \frac{63 - 55}{\sqrt{\dfrac{55(100 - 55)}{250}}}$$

$$= \frac{8}{3.15} = 2.54$$

Activity 7.11

How would you interpret this figure? What are the units of measurement?

What we have actually done is to calculate how many standard errors the sample result of 63 per cent is away from the (assumed) population value of 55 per cent. We find that the sample result of 63 per cent is 2.54 SEs away from the (hypothesised) population value of 55 per cent. We can now tackle the last step in the test.

Activity 7.12

Would you reject or fail to reject the null hypothesis in our problem?

Choose between the two hypotheses

Logically we would now examine the two hypotheses we initially formulated and try to reach a conclusion. The null hypothesis was formulated on the basis that the target viewing figures had not been reached, based on the sample evidence. However, if this were the case we would not expect a sample result to be more than 2.33 standard errors above the assumed population percentage. In this case the sample result *is* above this critical figure, at 2.54 SEs above the assumed population value. We are forced to reject H_0, therefore, and conclude that the viewing figures for the statistical population exceed the required figure of 55 per cent (but bearing in mind that there is a 0.01 probability of making a Type I error). We have found that the sample result, at 63 per cent, is inconsistent with what we would expect a sample result to be, based on the null hypothesis at the 99 per cent level.

In practice the decision rule for comparing the critical with the calculated Z value is readily summarised. If we take the absolute values for any Z values (that is we ignore any minus signs) then we have a simple decision rule.

- If $Z_{Calc} > Z_\alpha$ then we must reject H_0.
- If $Z_{Calc} < Z_\alpha$ then we cannot reject H_0.

We can summarise the various stages we have followed for this test in a concise manner.

$$H_0 \, \pi \leqslant 55\%$$
$$H_1 \, \pi > 55\%$$
$$\alpha = 0.01$$
$$Z_\alpha = 2.33$$
$$Z_{Calc} = 2.54$$

Reject H_0 (since $Z_{Calc} > Z_\alpha$).

We have deliberately taken a lengthy approach to this hypothesis test to discuss the stages we follow and the rationale behind each stage. With practice, of course, the whole analysis is much quicker and more straightforward and can be completed in a few moments – provided you understand what you are doing. Once again, it is worthwhile summarising what we have been able to do. Through this test we have been able to assess – based on limited sample information – a particular numerical value or values for the statistical population. We have not been able to do this with certainty – indeed the only way to do that would be to collect data on the entire population – but we have been able to quantify the likelihood of our conclusion being the appropriate one. We must also bear in mind the caveats we raised earlier about the reliability, accuracy and representativeness of the sample data.

We must also conclude that no manager in their right mind would base any critical decision solely on a hypothesis test. Such tests – and their conclusions – are but one more piece of information available to the manager. Such information – like that from all other sources – must be assessed in the context of the decision to be taken and not in isolation.

Tests on a Sample Mean

The test we have just completed is technically known as a test on a sample percentage (proportion). There are a considerable variety of other tests that are available (you will find textbooks available with encouraging titles such as '100 Common Statistical Tests') and we shall examine some of the more common. Fortunately, all follow exactly the same process as our first test, with only slight differences occurring. Let us first consider a test on a sample mean. The first difference that occurs is that the two hypotheses must be formulated in terms of the population mean, μ, not the population percentage, π. The second difference is in the formula for calculating the Z statistic. The appropriate formula is now:

$$Z_{Calc} = \frac{\bar{X} - \mu}{\frac{s}{\sqrt{n}}}$$

where the denominator of the expression relates to the standard error of the sampling distribution for the sample mean. Apart from this, the test is conducted in exactly the same way as before.

Let us consider an example. A local authority has one of its administrative centres located out of town and the majority of employees drive to work. As part of the authority's 'green' policy (with the authority wanting more environmentally friendly initiatives and activities) various efforts have been made to encourage employees to car-share: that is for several people to travel to work in one car rather than each use his or her own. The authority is trying to assess the impact of these measures on car-sharing. Last year, in a comprehensive exercise, the authority found that the number of cars parked in the staff car park each day averaged 220. This year based on a sample of 75 days' observations, it has calculated that the mean number of cars parked in the staff car park is 205, with a standard deviation of 32.

Activity 7.13

Based on this data can we comment on the impact of these measures on car-sharing? What assumptions have you made in assessing this data?

We can summarise the test:

H_0: $\mu \geqslant 220$

$$H_1: \mu < 220$$
$$\alpha = 0.05$$
$$Z_\alpha = -1.64$$
$$Z_{Calc} = \frac{205 - 220}{32/\sqrt{75}} = -4.06$$

Reject H_0.

The null hypothesis is formulated on the assumption that there has been no change in car-sharing as measured by the mean number of cars in the car park – that the mean number of cars is still 220 or more. The alternative hypothesis is that the mean number of cars has fallen. The choice of α is arbitrary in this example but we have chosen 0.05. From the Normal table this gives a critical Z value of –1.64 (since our rejection area will lie in the left-hand tail of the sampling distribution). Calculating the Z value for the data gives a result of –4.06, hence using the decision rule we must reject the null hypothesis, which states that there has been no reduction in cars parked. We are forced to conclude, based on the sample evidence, that the mean number of cars has reduced.

Once again it will be worthwhile reinforcing the logic of what we have done. We start with the hypothesis that the mean number of cars has not decreased since last year. Based on this assumption we can calculate the maximum expected variation of a sample mean from this (assumed) population mean. This is expressed in SEs as the Z_α. We then calculate how far the observed sample mean actually is from the population mean. In this case it is further away than we would expect on the basis of the assumed population mean. It seems more likely, therefore, that the population mean has changed, based on the sample evidence, and we are forced to accept H_0.

Apart from the usual assumptions relating to the statistical logic underpinning the test, it is also important to be aware of other assumptions – often implicit – that we are making. The key assumption is that all other factors that might impact on the number of cars parked have remained unchanged since last year: the number of people working at the centre, the type of staff employed, working patterns, income patterns and so on. We should also remember that we have not 'proved' that the measures introduced by the authority have increased car-sharing. Other factors may well have affected behaviour: petrol prices, public transport prices/availability and the like. Nevertheless, we should not underestimate the usefulness of such statistical inference in management decision making.

Tests on the Difference Between Two Means

Our next two tests are concerned with assessing the difference between two samples rather than comparing a sample result with an assumed population value. First, we shall examine the difference between two sample means. For this we shall return to the situation we were examining in Chapters 3 and 4. Remember that a retail organisation had collected and analysed data on a sample of its stores in two regions, A and B. The variable measured was the profit achieved by profit centres in each of the two regions. The information we have available is shown in Table 7.2.

That is, mean profit of the sample of stores was £12 981.2 in Region A and £17 168.8 in Region B. We wish to determine, based on this data, whether there is a statistically significant difference in mean profit between the two samples of profit centres. Once again, the logic of the test process can be applied. In this case, however, we are testing

Table 7.2	Profit achieved in Regions A and B	
	Region A sample	Region B sample
$\bar{x}$	£12 981.2	£17 168.8
s	£17 476.3	£19 688.1
n	113	121

not one mean but two, and we need briefly to discuss the principles of the test we are about to undertake. We can treat each sample as if, in principle, it came from a separate and distinct population. That is, our Region A sample represents one statistical population while the Region B sample represents a second and potentially different population. The difference between the two populations relates to their mean values. Given that we have in principle two populations then we also have in principle two population means, μ_1 and μ_2. Effectively what we wish to test is whether there is any difference between these two populations' means. Our two hypotheses then can be formulated in terms of $(\mu_1 - \mu_2)$. As you might expect, the rest of the test procedure is as before, with the exception of the calculation for the Z statistic. This then becomes:

$$Z_{Calc} = \frac{(\bar{x} - \bar{x}_2) - (\mu_1 - \mu_2)}{\sqrt{\dfrac{s_1^2}{n_1} + \dfrac{s_2^2}{n_2}}}$$

The formula looks horrendous but is actually straightforward to calculate. The denominator is once again the standard error of the relevant sampling distribution and you may be able to see that it is effectively an average of the standard errors of the two individual populations; that is, we use the standard deviations of the two samples, s_1 and s_2.

Activity 7.14

Complete the appropriate test to determine whether there is a significant difference in mean profit between the two regions. How do you explain your conclusion given that the difference between the means of the two samples is over £4000?

We are required to test to see if there is a difference between the two groups (not whether one is larger than the other), hence a two-tail test is appropriate:

$$H_0 (\mu_1 - \mu_2) = 0$$
$$H_1 (\mu_1 - \mu_2) \neq 0$$
$$\alpha = 0.01$$
$$Z_\alpha = 2.58$$
$$Z_{Calc} = \frac{(12\ 981.2 - 17\ 168.8) - 0}{\sqrt{\dfrac{17\ 476.3^2}{113} + \dfrac{19\ 688.1^2}{121}}} = -1.72$$

Do not reject H_0.

A two-tail test requires α/2 to determine the critical Z value. Note also that we have chosen α = 0.01 given the potential importance of the conclusion. The test does not provide us with sufficient evidence to reject H_0 so we cannot conclude that there is a significant difference between the two groups. We would conclude, based on this sample data, that there was no evidence of a significant difference in the mean profit of stores in Region A compared with stores in Region B. If we had been thinking, for example, of offering some financial bonus to managers in Region B to reward their 'better' performance then this test indicates we have no evidence to conclude that mean profits in Region B are any different from those in Region A. To people unfamiliar with hypothesis testing such a conclusion may seem odd given that numerically there is a difference of over £4000 between the two sample means. Noting that, in the case of both samples, the sample standard deviation is relatively very large, we might comment that although there is a large numerical difference between the two sample means, once we allow for the variation we might expect in the sampling process, this difference cannot be said to be statistically significant.

Two final points can be made about this test. The first is that the formulation of the hypotheses can test for any numerical difference between the two means not just, as in our case, zero. Thus, if we had wanted to see if there was a difference of at least £4000 between the two groups, we could have formulated H_0 as $(\mu_2 - \mu_1) > £4000$. This would be rewritten as:

$$H_0(\mu_2 - \mu_1) - £4000 > 0$$

for the purposes of carrying out the test. The second point to note about the test is that for the test to be valid, the two samples must be obtained independently. This is the case in our example: sample 1 and sample 2 are not connected (apart from the fact that all the profit centres are part of the same organisation). However, consider a different scenario. Suppose we had collected data on only one region's stores for last year and for this year with a view to assessing where profits had changed. In such a case, the two samples would not be independent (since each sample would contain exactly the same profit centres). The test we have just conducted would not be appropriate for testing to see whether there was a difference in profit. If we did want to conduct such a test, the easiest way would be to calculate the difference in profit for each profit centre and then to find this mean difference. This mean could then be tested (against zero) using the one-sample test we completed in the last section.

Tests on Two Proportions or Percentages

Given that we can conduct a test on two means it seems logical to consider an equivalent test on two proportions or percentages. Let us illustrate with the following example. An organisation operates on two different sites and both sites have support services available – personnel, training, finance and so on. On Site A the Finance Department still operates on a largely manual basis, whereas in Site B they have invested in computerised accounts and invoicing systems. Management concern has recently been expressed in terms of the number of invoices the organisation receives which are not properly checked against goods and services received. For example, if someone in the organisation orders a computer, a copy of the order is sent to Finance. When the computer supplier has delivered and installed the computer, then an invoice for the appropriate amount should be passed to Finance for payment authorisation.

There are concerns, however, that the Finance Department receives – and pays – invoices which do not exactly match the goods supplied. For example, the original order may have specified a PC with a CD-ROM but a PC without CD-ROM was actually supplied and the invoice still detailed the original order and payment. Accordingly, a detailed investigation has been carried out at each of the two sites into a sample of recently paid invoices to determine the percentage of these where an overpayment occurred, i.e. where the organisation paid the supplier more than it should (management are less concerned about underpayment). At Site A, 250 invoices were checked and it was found that 13 per cent represented overpayments. At Site B, 200 invoices were checked and only 8 per cent were overpaid. Is there any evidence of a difference in overpayments at the two sites? Once again, we can assume two independent samples, each, in principle, representing a different statistical population. Our hypotheses this time are formulated in terms of $(\pi_1 - \pi_2)$.

$$H_0 (\pi_1 - \pi_2) = 0$$
$$H_1 (\pi_1 - \pi_2) \neq 0$$
$$\alpha = 0.05$$
$$Z_\alpha = 1.96$$

The calculated value for the Z statistic can once again be obtained, but for this test we need to explain as we progress. According to our null hypothesis there is no difference between the two population percentages. If this is the case then $\pi_1 = \pi_2$ and we can average the two sample results to provide one estimate of the population percentage.

$$p = \frac{n_1 p_1 + n_2 p_2}{n_1 + n_2}$$

$$= \frac{250(13) + 200(8)}{250 + 200} = 10.78\%$$

You will see that this is effectively a weighted average of the two sample results. We can now use this value of 10.78 per cent to calculate the standard error for the relevant sampling distribution and obtain a figure of 2.94.

$$SE = \sqrt{p(100 - p)\left(\frac{1}{n_1} + \frac{1}{n_2}\right)}$$

$$= \sqrt{10.78(89.22)\left(\frac{1}{250} + \frac{1}{200}\right)}$$

$$= \sqrt{8.66} = 2.94$$

Our calculated Z value then becomes:

$$Z_{Calc} = \frac{(p_1 - p_2) - (\pi_1 - \pi_2)}{2.94} = \frac{(13 - 8) - 0}{2.94}$$

$$= 1.70$$

We would have no reason to reject the null hypothesis based on this data. That is, we have no evidence that there is a significant difference in the percentage of invoices overpaid. Once we allow for sampling variation, then we cannot conclude that the two samples come from statistically different populations.

You may also remember that for the two-sample test on means it is possible to formulate the two hypotheses so that we do not assume the populations are equal but rather that one is greater than the other or that the difference between them exceeds some numerical value. The same applies to this test. In such a case it would not be appropriate to use the two sample results to find an average estimate of the population percentage (since we are now not assuming they are the same). The SE formula would then be:

$$SE = \sqrt{\frac{p_1(100 - p_1)}{n_1} + \frac{p_2(100 - p_2)}{n_2}}$$

Tests on Small Samples

The next test we introduce is that relating to small samples. You will recollect the basis of our being able to use the Normal distribution in the test process: the Central Limit Theorem indicates that as long as we take sufficiently large samples then the sampling distribution will approximate to the Normal. For our purposes we defined a sufficiently large sample size as over 30. But what if the sample size is not sufficiently large? Suppose our sample has only a few observations? Can we carry out a hypothesis test on small samples? The answer is a qualified 'yes'. The qualification is needed because we cannot carry out the tests we have looked at so far, since they are based on the Normal distribution. Instead we must base our test for a small sample on something known as the t distribution. The t distribution is similar in appearance to the Normal distribution – that is, it is symmetrical and bell-shaped. However, its exact shape will depend on the sample size. The larger is n, then the closer the t distribution becomes to the Normal. The smaller is n, then the worse the approximation to the Normal distribution. The general relationship is shown in Figure 7.5, where the Normal distribution and two t distributions are shown. Notice that the t distributions follow the general shape of the Normal but tend to be flatter and have wider tails. This feature is further exaggerated as the sample size for the distribution decreases. In Figure 7.5 distribution t_1 has a smaller sample size than t_2 and is 'flatter'. The implications of this are that if the sample size is sufficiently large then for our purposes there are no practical differences between the Z and t distributions. Once the sample size gets smaller, however, then we must be careful to use the t distribution in our tests. In effect there is such a t distribution for each possible sample size. That is, the t distribution for a sample size 10 will be slightly different from that of sample size 11, 12 and so on. Once again, such tables have been pre-calculated and are shown in Appendix C. The table contains much the same information as the

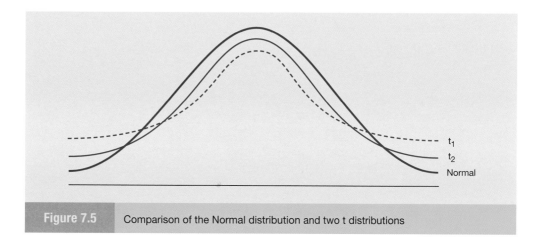

| Figure 7.5 | Comparison of the Normal distribution and two t distributions |

Normal but is presented in a slightly different way. The rows of the table relate to what is known as degrees of freedom. This is defined as (n – 1), one less than the size of the sample. Across the top of the table we distinguish columns in terms of the appropriate level for a (the significance level) that we are using for the test in question. These range from 0.10 to 0.005.

Activity 7.15

Assume a sample size of infinity (∞). For $\alpha = 0.05$, 0.025 and 0.005 determine the t value from the table. Compare this with the equivalent Z values from the Normal table. What conclusion do you come to about the t and Z tables?

From the table we see that for an infinite sample size the t values are identical to those we would obtain from the Normal table, implying that for large samples there is no difference between the two distributions. If we follow the $\alpha = 0.05$ column upwards we see that as the degrees of freedom decrease, the area in the tail gradually gets larger (which is what we showed in Figure 7.5). Apart from this we can conduct a t test on a sample mean in exactly the same way. Consider the following problem. A manufacturing company has recently completed a retraining programme for some of its assembly-line staff to try to improve quality, productivity and performance. Fifteen employees performing the same task on the assembly line went through the training programme and the time it took them to perform an assembly operation was noted before the training and again afterwards. The result was that on average these 15 employees were able to complete their tasks 1.6 minutes faster after the training (with a standard deviation of 0.34 minutes around this mean). Can we conclude that the training has been effective?

Activity 7.16

Carry out the appropriate test for this situation.

Our test follows the usual procedure. We have:

$\bar{x} = 1.6$ (where $\bar{x}$ is the mean time saved)

$s = 0.34$

$n = 15$

and the test is then:

$H_0: \mu \leq 0$

$H_1: \mu > 0$

$\alpha = 0.01$ d.f. = 14

$t_{\alpha,14} = 2.624$

$$t_{Calc} = \frac{\bar{x} - \mu}{\frac{s}{\sqrt{n}}} = \frac{1.6 - 0}{\sqrt{\frac{0.34}{15}}} = 10.63$$

Reject H_0.

The null hypothesis is formulated such that we assume that the mean time saved has not increased; therefore μ is no greater than zero. The degrees of freedom is 14 (n – 1) and for the one-tail test the critical t value from the tables is found to be 2.624 (compared with 2.33 if this had been a large-sample Z test). Calculating the t value gives a value which forces us to reject the null hypothesis and conclude that there has been a significant reduction in time taken to complete the task after the training programme. It is important to realise that a t test automatically makes allowances for the fact that any conclusion we come to about the hypotheses is based on only a small sample. You will frequently encounter the criticism from other managers along the lines 'but it's based on only 15 employees!' The allowance for the fact that we have only a small sample is built into the critical t statistic that we use in such a test by default. Effectively, the critical t statistic will be larger than its Z counterpart. This implies that we must have 'stronger' evidence from a small sample before rejecting the null hypothesis we have formulated.

One large caveat must be made, however, for a t test. With the Central Limit Theorem we were able to say that as long as sample sizes were sufficiently large then the sampling distribution will approximate to the Normal no matter what the original population distribution. For the t distribution, however, this is not the case. For the t test to be valid we must make the assumption that the population from which the sample was taken is Normal. In practice this is often an assumption impossible to assess and we must carry out the t test anyway. We must remember though that the test conclusion is suspect unless we are confident that the population is Normally distributed.

Although the t test demonstrated here relates to a test on a mean, the t test can also be applied to percentages/proportions and to tests on two means (t tests on two percentages or proportions are not usually undertaken, since the standard error is often too large to make the test worthwhile). Be warned, however, that in the case of a t test on two means the calculations for the standard error become complex and there are further critical assumptions that apply. Use the more advanced tests only with considerable caution and, preferably, supported by a friendly and comprehensible statistician. Figures 7.6 and 7.7 summarise the key tests on both large and small samples, together with the relevant standard errors and calculated Z or t statistics.

Inferential Statistics Using a Computer Package

Increasingly, inferential analysis is based around the output from some suitable computer package: EXCEL, MINITAB, STATGRAPHICS, SPSS, SAS. Although the structure and format of such packages varies, they all typically provide many of the statistics we have introduced in this chapter (as well as others that we have not introduced). Table 7.3 shows the output produced when analysing the mean profit levels of stores in Region A and Region B (remember the test on two means that we carried out). The raw data was analysed by the package and the one-tail test on two sample means conducted. Summary details of the two samples are provided (n, the mean, the sample standard deviation) and the difference between the two means shown (–4187.61). At the bottom of the table the results of the test are shown.

In this example, we have set up the null hypothesis for a one-tail test (that Region A ≥ Region B) and for α = 0.01. We see from the output that H_0 is set up as diff = 0 with the alternative hypothesis (ALT) that Region A is less than (LT) Region B. The calculated

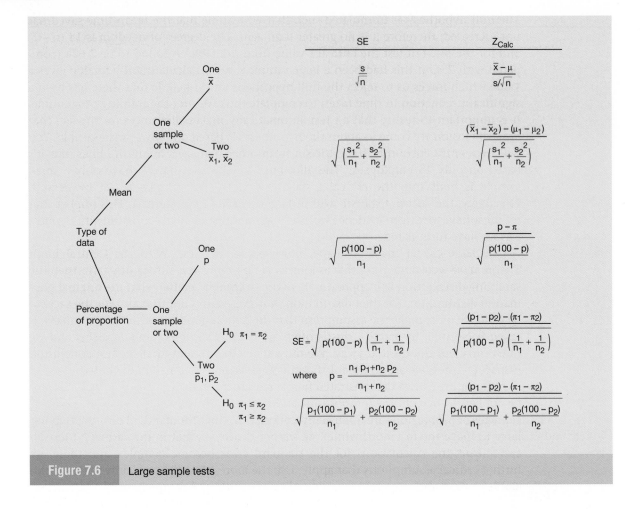

Figure 7.6   Large sample tests

Z statistic is shown at −1.71609 (we worked it out earlier as −1.72) and the package conveniently interprets the result for us telling us, with this sample data, that we do not reject H_0.

p Values in Hypothesis Tests

It will be evident that in any hypothesis test the choice of α is to some extent arbitrary. In the previous illustration we set α at 0.01. We could just as easily have set it at 0.05 or indeed 0.001 or 0.005. With some thought you should realise that different choices of α may lead us to different conclusions about whether or not to reject the null hypothesis, H_0. At one level of α we might – correctly – reject H_0, whereas at another level of α we do not reject. It is partly for this reason that, with tests typically being generated through some computer package rather than a manual calculation, common use is made of something known as the *p value*. The p value in a test is the smallest value for α for which the sample results become statistically significant. In the case of the test in Table 7.3 this is reported close to the bottom right of the table as:

```
Sig. Level = 0.0437404
```

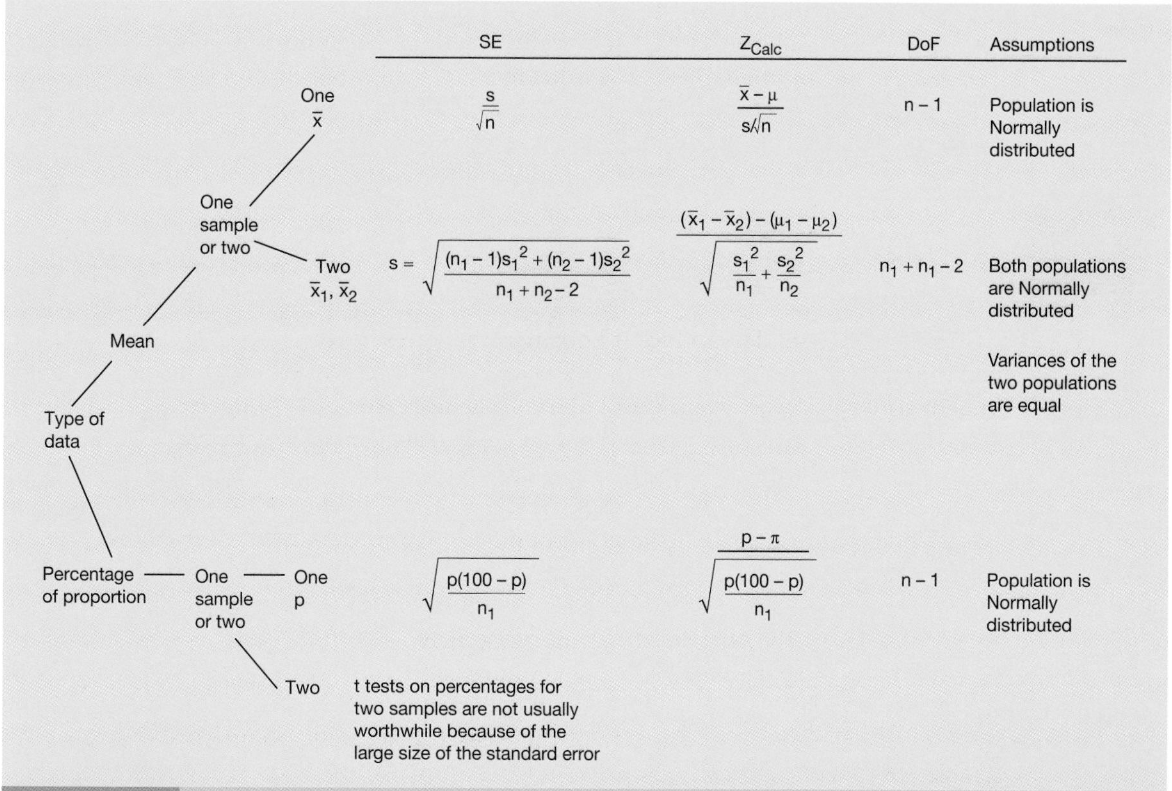

	SE	Z_{Calc}	DoF	Assumptions
One $\bar{x}$	$\dfrac{s}{\sqrt{n}}$	$\dfrac{\bar{x} - \mu}{s/\sqrt{n}}$	$n - 1$	Population is Normally distributed
Two $\bar{x}_1, \bar{x}_2$	$s = \sqrt{\dfrac{(n_1 - 1)s_1^2 + (n_2 - 1)s_2^2}{n_1 + n_2 - 2}}$	$\dfrac{(\bar{x}_1 - \bar{x}_2) - (\mu_1 - \mu_2)}{\sqrt{\dfrac{s_1^2}{n_1} + \dfrac{s_2^2}{n_2}}}$	$n_1 + n_1 - 2$	Both populations are Normally distributed
				Variances of the two populations are equal
One p	$\sqrt{\dfrac{p(100 - p)}{n_1}}$	$\dfrac{p - \pi}{\sqrt{\dfrac{p(100 - p)}{n_1}}}$	$n - 1$	Population is Normally distributed

Mean — One sample or two

Type of data

Percentage of proportion — One sample or two — One p

Two — t tests on percentages for two samples are not usually worthwhile because of the large size of the standard error

Figure 7.7   Small sample tests

Table 7.3   Computer output

```
                    Two-sample analysis results


                                Region A      Region B      Pooled
Sample statistics:   Number of obs.   113          121 234
                     Mean             12981.2      17168.8       15146.5
                     Variance         3.0542E8     3.8762E8      3.47937E8
                     Std. deviation   17476.3      19688.1       18653.1
                     Median           6840         9580          8025

Difference between means = -4187.61
Conf. interval for diff. in means:      95 per cent
  (Equal vars.)    Sample 1 - Sample 2  -8996.47      621.252       232DF
  (Unequal vars.)  Sample 1 - Sample 2  -8976.99      601.772       231.4DF

Ratio of variances = 0.787937
Conf. interval for ratio of variances:  0 per cent
                 Sample 1 Sample 2

Hypothesis test for  H₀: diff=0         Computed t statistic=-1.71609
                     vs ALt: LT  Sig.   LeveL=0.0437404
                     at Alpha=0.01      so do not reject H₀
```

That is, for any α value up to this value of 0.043 740 4 we would decide not to reject H_0. For any α value above 0.043 740 4 we would reject H_0 and accept H_1. The p value removes the need to establish an α value first and, importantly, allows others using our results to see precisely at what significance level a null hypothesis would be rejected.

χ^2 Tests

The last test we shall introduce is known as the χ^2 test (pronounced 'ki square'). This is an example of something known as a *non-parametric test* (of which there are many different sorts, just as we have Z and t tests). The tests we have conducted so far have, in fact, been on key parameters of the data set we have examined – on the mean or the percentage. Effectively we have been conducting various *parametric tests* up to now. There are frequently times, however, when we are interested not in a specific parameter of a data set – such as the mean – but on the whole set of data. Consider the following scenario. The Education Department of a large local authority has been concerned for some time about traffic accidents to children that occur immediately outside schools. Frequently such locations are very busy and often quite chaotic as parents arrive in cars to deliver or collect their children and as other traffic becomes congested. Over the last few months data has been collected in terms of the number of accidents that occurred and noting the day of the week the accident occurred. This is given in Table 7.4.

Clearly we have a distribution and could work out the mean number of accidents, but to what point? Our interest in this data is in the entire distribution, not simply in one of its parameters, the mean. In this case it appears there is some sort of variation in the number of accidents occurring on a daily basis: the numbers on a Monday and Friday appear higher than those on the other days. However, since we are dealing with a sample set of data we must somehow try to take sampling variation into account. In other words, our question must be: is there a statistically significant difference in the number of accidents on a daily basis? It is in this type of situation, where we are interested in the distribution of the data, that we can apply the χ^2 test.

Let us apply some simple logic to the situation in Table 7.4. If there were no particular pattern in the distribution of accidents on a day-by-day basis then it would be

Table 7.4	Traffic accidents involving school children
Day of week	*No. of accidents*
Monday	20
Tuesday	13
Wednesday	12
Thursday	12
Friday	18
Total	75

logical to expect the same number of accidents each day. This then becomes our null hypothesis, H_0. Since we have observed the total number of accidents at 75 over this sample period then we would expect, given H_0, that there would be 15 accidents each day (75/5). Clearly, from Table 7.4, there are not exactly this number each day. However, given that we are dealing with a sample set of data we must make allowances for the sampling variation that exists between the number of accidents each day actually observed and those expected.

Let us show the observed frequencies as O and the expected as E. If the null hypothesis, H_0, is correct then we would expect there to be no significant difference between O and E. If, however, there were a significant difference we would be forced to reject H_0 and conclude that there was some difference in the number of accidents on a daily basis. To perform such a test we use something known as the χ^2 distribution, where:

$$\chi^2 = \sum \frac{(O - E)^2}{E}$$

We will look at the calculations involved in a moment. Like the Binomial, Normal and t distributions this is a probability distribution and like our other tests we can obtain two χ^2 values: one we calculate (from the formula above) and one from tables (shown in Appendix D). As with the t distribution, there are many different χ^2 distributions – each one varying with the degrees of freedom. As with the other tests, we have a simple decision rule. If the calculated χ^2 (obtained from the sample data using the above formula) is greater than the critical χ^2 (obtained from the table) we must reject the null hypothesis. One good thing about a χ^2 test is that the null hypothesis is always the same: that there is no significant difference between the observed frequencies and the expected.

Let us perform the test on this data. The relevant calculations are shown in Table 7.5.

This calculation gives a calculated χ^2 at 3.74. The calculation itself deserves a little explanation. We are interested in whether the differences between the observed frequencies and the expected are significantly different from zero (if they were zero it would imply the distribution was exactly as expected). However, there is little point summing the (O – E) figures, as they will always sum to zero (remember the standard deviation calculation?) So, as with the standard deviation, we square them. However,

Table 7.5	χ^2 test calculations				
	Observed	Expected	(O – E)	(O – E)²	$\frac{(O - E)^2}{E}$
	20	15	5	25	1.67
	13	15	−2	4	0.27
	12	15	−3	9	0.60
	12	15	−3	9	0.60
	18	15	3	9	0.60
Total	75	75	0		3.74

we must also divide each by its respective E value and then total. The division by its respective E is necessary since, in some applications, the E values themselves may differ within the distribution. Consider for example if we had had a simple situation where:

O	E	(O – E)	$(O - E)^2$	$(O - E)^2/E$
50	75	–25	625	8.33
50	25	25	625	25.00

The (O – E) deviation is the same in both cases (so the $(O - E)^2$ figure must be also). However, it is evident that this deviation is proportionally more important for the second category (with E at 25) than for the first (with E at 75). In fact, the second category's deviation is effectively three times that of the first (with the two E's at 75 and 25 respectively). Dividing the $(O - E)^2$ values through by E keeps this relative relationship (25 to 8.33).

Following the standard test methodology we now have:

● Formulate the hypotheses:

H_0 is that there are the same number of accidents each day of the week (O = E). H_1 is that the number of accidents varies between the days of the week (O ≠ E). (Note in H_1 we are not saying which days are higher.)

● Determine a significance level:

Let us set this at $\alpha = 0.01$.

● Determine the critical statistical value:

For a χ^2 test we must determine the relevant degrees of freedom. For this type of test it is defined as:

d.o.f. = (no. of classes or categories in the distribution) – 1

Here we have five classes or categories (days of the week) so we have four degrees of freedom. From Appendix D, with $\alpha = 0.01$ and four degrees of freedom, the critical χ^2 is 13.3 and we have the situation illustrated in Figure 7.8.

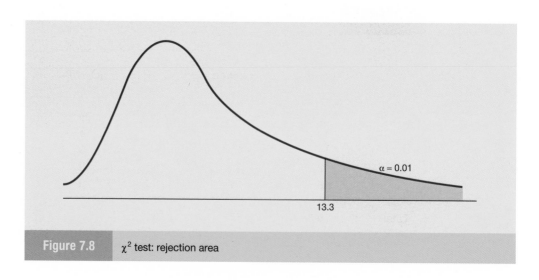

Figure 7.8 χ^2 test: rejection area

The critical value at 13.3 relates to the null hypothesis and the calculated statistic from the sample. Although we would expect some difference between a sample and some hypothesised population in this case (with four degrees of freedom and α at 0.01) we would expect the sample result to generate a calculated statistic of no more than 13.3 *if* the null hypothesis is not to be rejected. If we found that our sample generated a statistic of more than 13.3, we would have to reject H_0.

- Calculate the test statistic value:

  We have already done this at 3.74.

- Choose between the two hypotheses:

  We apply the same decision rule as before: if the calculated statistic exceeds the critical, we reject H_0. In this case it does not, so we cannot reject the null hypothesis. Effectively we conclude that the number of accidents is the same each day. Any variation on a particular day is purely random, arising from the sampling process.

Activity 7.17

The local chamber of commerce has commissioned some market research into the spending habits of the local adult population. A random sample of 500 adults has been selected as follows:

Age group (years)	Number in sample
18 < 21	54
21 < 30	63
30 < 45	167
45 < 60	85
60 and over	131
Total	500

From government census statistics it is known that the local adult population has the following distribution:

Age group (years)	% of population
18 < 21	13
21 < 30	12
30 < 45	38
45 < 60	15
60 and over	22
Total	100

What comment can you make about the age profile of the selected sample compared to that of the population?

Solution is given on p 589.

This type of test involving χ^2 is known as a *goodness of fit test* because we are testing whether an observed distribution fits some expected distribution (as defined in the null hypothesis). It is worth noting that the test can also be applied to determining whether an observed set of data fits some theoretical distribution like the Binomial or the Normal. If we were wanting to see whether a set of data fitted a Binomial or Normal distribution then the process is as before but now calculating an appropriate Binomial or Normal distribution for the expected values. The degrees of freedom associated with a test on the Binomial or Normal are then:

> *Binomial*
> d.o.f. = (no. of classes/categories in the distribution) – 2
> *Normal*
> d.o.f. = (no. of classes/categories in the distribution) – 3

Tests of association using χ^2

There is a second application of the χ^2 tests known as the test of association, sometimes known as a contingency table test. To illustrate, consider the following scenario. A local health clinic currently operates a no-appointments system if a patient wishes to see a doctor. That is, a patient wishing to see a doctor turns up at the clinic and waits until the doctor is free. This may take a few minutes or an hour or more depending on how many other patients are waiting. Some patients have indicated that they would prefer to have an appointment at a specific time rather than simply turn up, and the clinic has recently completed some basic market research. A representative sample of patients were asked whether they would prefer the clinic to move to an appointments system or not. The results are shown in Table 7.6.

So, for example, out of 153 male patients 106 were in favour of an appointments system, 27 were against and 20 had no preference either way. Simple observation of the survey results appears to indicate that there is a divergence of opinion by gender. Males appear to be in favour, whereas females appear to be against. However, this is only a sample and again we must allow for sampling variation. Clearly our interest lies in trying to answer the question: do men and women have different views about an appointments system? The reason Table 7.6 is referred to as a contingency table is that we are effectively asking the question: is opinion about the appointments system contingent (or dependent) upon gender?

Table 7.6	Patient responses			
	Patient view on appointments systems			
Patient gender	*For*	*Against*	*No preference*	*Total*
Male	106	27	20	153
Female	97	166	34	297
Total	203	193	54	450

To undertake a χ^2 test we need a set of expected frequencies as well as the observed. What is less clear is where these expected frequencies are to come from. The answer begins to appear if we consider the last question posed: is opinion about the appointments system dependent upon gender? The word 'dependent' has a clear meaning in a probability context (as we discussed in Chapter 5). Let us for the moment assume that the two characteristics – gender and response to the question – are independent. *If* they are independent then we can use basic probability to calculate the expected frequencies.

Activity 7.18

How could we use probability to determine the expected number of males who were *for* the new system?

We see that there was a total of 153 males in the sample (out of 450 people). The probability of someone in the sample being male is then:

P (Male) = 153/450 = 0.34

Similarly, the probability of someone in the sample being for the new system, regardless of gender is:

P (For) = 203/450 = 0.451

So *if* gender and response to the new system are independent we have:

P (Male and For) = 0.34 × 0.451 = 0.15334

and hence we would expect 69 males (0.15334 × 450) to have responded 'For' *if* the two characteristics are independent. The calculation can be summarised as:

$$\frac{153}{450} \times \frac{203}{450} \times 450$$

which simplifies to:

$$\frac{153 \times 203}{450}$$

or in general:

$$\frac{\text{Row total} \times \text{Column total}}{\text{Sample total}}$$

Clearly we can calculate the expected frequencies for the other cells in the table in exactly the same way.

Activity 7.19

Calculate the rest of the expected frequencies for Table 7.6.

The calculations are summarised in Table 7.7.

Table 7.7	Expected frequencies			
Table cell	O	E	(O – E)	(O – E)²/E
M–F	106	69.02	36.98	19.81
M–A	27	65.62	−38.62	22.73
M–NP	20	18.36	1.64	0.15
F–F	97	133.98	−36.98	10.21
F–A	166	127.38	38.62	11.71
F–NP	34	35.64	−1.64	0.08
Total	450	450		64.69

For each cell in the table (Male–For, for example, or M–F) the expected frequency is shown, and these total, as they must, to 450. We can now complete the test in the usual way.

The null hypothesis is that the two characteristics – gender and response – are independent (which is how we worked out the E frequencies). *If* they are independent, we can determine from Appendix D the maximum χ^2 we would expect from the sample results. If we set $\alpha = 0.01$ we can determine the critical χ^2 if we have the relevant degrees of freedom. For a contingency table test this is calculated as:

d.o.f. = (No. of rows − 1) × (No. of columns − 1)

where the number of rows and columns in the table *excludes* the totals. Here we have:

d.o.f. = (2 − 1) × (3 − 1) = 2

From Appendix D we see a critical χ^2 of 5.99. The calculated χ^2 at 64.69 is greater than the critical, so we must reject H_0 – effectively rejecting the hypothesis that the view of a patient on the new system is independent of gender. We conclude therefore that the patient's view *is* dependent on gender.

As with other tests, computer-based statistics packages will perform the various calculations for you. Typical output for the problem we have examined would look like this:

Chi-Square	D.F.	Significance	Min E.F.	Cells with E.F.<5
64.69	2	.0000	18.36	None

We see the calculated χ^2 at 64.69 with the degrees of freedom (D.F.) at 2. The Significance figure shows the p value indicating that we should reject H_0 – there is a significant difference between the observed and expected frequencies.

In summary, the χ^2 test is particularly useful where we require a non-parametric test either in terms of goodness of fit or as a contingency table. There are three other points about the use of the test to note:

- The test can only be used on frequencies/counts. It cannot be used where the observed data shows percentages or proportions.

- Technically, the test should be applied only where all E frequencies are at least five in value. As a rule of thumb, the test can still be applied as long as no more than 20 per cent of E values are less than five. If there are more E values than this it might be possible to combine classes/categories together. When using computer output like that shown earlier, you are often told what the minimum calculated expected frequency for the problem was (18.36 for the computer output shown earlier) and told how many expected values were less than five (none in our example).

- In the event of a test which has only one degree of freedom (for example on a 2 × 2 contingency table) then something known as Yates' correction must be applied to the calculated statistic, which becomes:

$$\chi^2 = \sum \frac{(\mid O{-}E \mid - 0.5)^2}{E}$$

Again, a statistics package will normally perform this adjustment for you.

Worked Example

In Great Britain, in addition to paying income tax, households also have to pay a council tax, which is effectively a local tax levied on a residential property. The amount of tax to be paid is, in part, dependent on the value of the residential property and all properties in England are classified into one of eight value groups, Band A to Band H, with Band A corresponding to the lowest value category and Band H to the highest. A household in a Band A house, for example, would pay less council tax than a household living in a Band B house. One local authority has recently completed a survey of 2500 residential properties in its area in terms of which band they fall into, and has been investigating how this compared with the England average. The results of the survey are shown in Table 7.8, together with the percentage distribution in England for the 1994/95 financial year.

So, for example, we see that the local authority found 734 out of a sample of 2500 residential properties fell into the lowest band, A. For England as a whole just over 25 per cent of residential properties fall into this band. The local authority has asked us to assess whether the local distribution of residential properties between the bands is different from that for England as a whole since, if it is, this might have implications for the amount of council tax the authority is able to collect. If, for example, lower bands are over-represented in the local authority's area compared with England then the local authority may be able to collect less tax because these properties pay less than higher-band properties. Can we help in determining whether there is a significant difference?

Clearly we have an observed distribution from the survey carried out by the local authority, and if we can obtain an expected set of frequencies, we can conduct a χ^2 test. We can readily obtain an expected set of frequencies. We know the England percentage distribution and if we use these percentages multiplied by 2500 (the sample size) this will give us the distribution we would expect based on the England averages.

Table 7.8	Council tax bands of residential properties	
Band	England percentage	District number
A	25.3	734
B	19.3	505
C	21.6	490
D	15.2	413
E	9.5	187
F	5.0	98
G	3.6	45
H	0.5	28
		2500

England percentages are taken from Office for National Statistics.

We can then compute a χ^2 test in the usual way. The relevant calculations are shown in Table 7.9.

The E column shows the expected number of properties in each band based on the hypothesis that they follow the England percentages (632 is obtained from 0.253×2500). None of the expected frequencies is less than 5, so we can proceed to perform the necessary calculations as shown in the final column. This gives a calculated χ^2 value of 81.63. To conduct the test we need a critical value for χ^2 from tables in Appendix D. Setting $\alpha = 0.01$ we have seven degrees of freedom (8 bands − 1). From Appendix D we obtain a critical χ^2 of 18.48. The null hypothesis is that there is no significant difference between the observed and expected frequencies. However, since the calculated statistic at 81.63 exceeds the critical at 18.48, we are forced to reject the null hypothesis and conclude that there is a statistically significant difference between the

Table 7.9	χ^2 test calculations			
Band	England (%)	District O	E	$(O - E)^2/E$
A	25.3	734	632	16.46
B	19.3	505	482	1.10
C	21.6	490	540	4.63
D	15.2	413	380	2.87
E	9.5	187	238	10.93
F	5.0	98	125	5.83
G	3.6	45	90	22.50
H	0.5	28	13	17.31
Total	100.0	2500	2500	81.63

observed and expected frequencies. We conclude, therefore, that based on this sample the local distribution of residential properties among council tax bands in this local authority area is significantly different from the England average. The test does not, however, tell us what the difference is. By simple inspection of the data though we realise that the O values for the first four bands (A–D) are higher than the E values, while the reverse is true for the four higher bands (E–H). It seems reasonable to conclude, then, that for this local authority it has more properties in the lower tax bands than England as a whole and fewer in the higher tax bands.

Taking samples

Sampling is at the heart of applied statistics – we only have to look at the opinion polls. But behind the simple idea lies some complex mathematics.

By Ann van Ackere

This section focuses on the use of samples of data to infer information about the population from which they are taken. The most commonly encountered form of sample data in the press is opinion-polling: interviewers poll a sample of about a thousand people and make inferences about what the target population thinks about a specific issue.

This article addresses four issues: (i) why sample; (ii) how to take a sample; (iii) how to make inferences from a sample without prior knowledge about the population (confidence intervals); and (iv) how to use a sample to support or reject a hypothesis about the population (hypothesis testing).

The first question is: why sample? Why not use the whole population? When thinking about opinion polls the answer is obvious: time and cost. This also applies to manufacturing environments: testing every unit that comes off the production line is a lengthy and expensive process. In some cases, using the whole population is simply not an option because of destructive testing. On the other hand, sampling can be very accurate. In many instances there is no need to consider the whole population,

as an appropriately selected and analysed sample can provide us with the desired degree of accuracy.

The term target population refers to the group of people or objects from which the sample should be taken. The sample is actually taken from what is known as the sampling frame; i.e. the list of people or objects assumed to match the population. For example, consider sampling the workforce of a multinational company. The target population consists of the actual workforce. The sampling frame (for example, the list of names you receive from head-office) may differ from this, as people who recently left many still appear on the list, while new ones have not yet been added. This is one source of bias in sampling: if the sampling frame is very different from the target population, the sample is unlikely to be representative of the population. Of course some names could have been intentionally omitted, but that is another story ...

An accurate sampling-frame is no guarantee of a representative sample. Two main causes of bias are non-response (in opinion-polls and surveys) and inappropriate

sampling methods. Non-response is a problem to the extent that people who elect to respond to a survey may differ from those who do not. For example, a survey on customer satisfaction may yield a higher response rate from dissatisfied customers, causing a bias in the reported results. The resulting distortions can be quite dramatic, especially as response rates of 20 per cent or lower are not uncommon for such surveys.

To enable statistical analysis, a sample should be taken randomly; i.e. each element of the sampling frame must have the same probability of being selected or, if for some reason the probabilities do differ, this must be taken into account in the analysis.

The simplest sampling method is random sampling. With this method, each element of the sampling frame is assigned a number. Then a series of random numbers is generated, using either a computer or a table of random numbers. The sample consists of those elements whose number appears on the list of random numbers.

Table 1 shows an example of a random numbers table. Each digit is equally likely to be followed by any

Figure 1

Confidence intervals

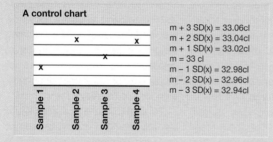

Hypothesis testing

Figure 2

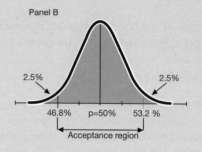

Figure 3

A control chart

$m + 3\ SD(x) = 33.06cl$
$m + 2\ SD(x) = 33.04cl$
$m + 1\ SD(x) = 33.02cl$
$m = 33\ cl$
$m - 1\ SD(x) = 32.98cl$
$m - 2\ SD(x) = 32.96cl$
$m - 3\ SD(x) = 32.94cl$

Figure 4

Example of control charts

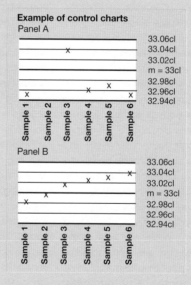

Table 2: Quota sampling

Gender:	Male		Female	
Commute by:	Car	Public transport	Car	Public transport
Age: 18–25	5	15	5	15
26–40	10	20	10	20
41–65	20	30	20	30

Table 3: Hypothesis testing

	Do not reject the null-hypothesis	Reject the null-hypothesis
Null-hypothesis true	(a) OK	(b) Type I error
Null-hypothesis false	(c) Type II error	(d) OK

Table 1: Random numbers

91	01	78	50	50
70	37	55	94	53
11	06	17	48	24
60	37	89	98	61
37	41	11	09	04

one digit. Consider having to select a random sample of five people out of 60 individuals. First, assign a two-digit number to each individual, for example, number them from 00 to 59. Then randomly pick a starting point in the table, for example the seventh digit of the second row, a 9. Next, look at the first pair of numbers: 94. (If there were 200 elements numbered 000 to 199, we would consider the first triplet of digits, 945.) There is no element in our population with this number, so skip it. The next pair is 53. The first element of our sample is the individual who was assigned number 53. The second element of the sample will be the individual numbered 11, and so on.

When information about different subgroups of the population is available, the use of stratified sampling can improve the quality of the sample. Intuitively, one wants to sample more from the larger subgroups and from those subgroups that exhibit more variation among the elements of the subgroup.

Consider polling customers of a supermarket chain. The population in the catchment area of a store located near a medium-sized village may be quite similar in terms of socioeconomic background. Therefore a small sample may be sufficient to get a reasonably accurate picture of this population. On the other hand, a store located in a city centre may face a mix of local people, commuters and tourists, resulting in a much more varied population. A larger sample will be required to insure that these different customer types are represented.

Stratified sampling will insure that (i) the sample includes customers from all types of stores (the different strata) and (ii) the more heterogeneous populations are sampled more extensively. The analysis will take into account that

these groups are over-represented in the sample by applying appropriate correction factors.

Cluster sampling is used to reduce costs when the population is spread over a large geographical area. Consider again the supermarket chain. If this chain has 500 stores across the UK and requires a sample of 2,000 customers, sending interviewers to each store to interview four people is not efficient. It may be more appropriate to randomly select, say 20 stores (possibly using stratified sampling to insure that all types of stores are represented) and interview 100 customers at each of these stores.

In this example, each store represents a cluster of the population. The company randomly selects a number of clusters and then interviews customers from these selected clusters.

There are circumstances where random sampling is inappropriate, either because it is too expensive, or simply impossible (for example, because of confidential or unobtainable data). For opinion polls, quota sampling is the most commonly used method. Interviewers are given specific instructions on the composition of the sample they must select. For example, Table 2 shows how an interviewer could be asked to select 200 people for a poll on traffic congestion. The aim is to avoid interviewer bias (an interviewer might be inclined to mainly select people from the same age-group) and location bias (picking people near a tube station might result in an over-representation of people commuting by public transport). Setting up a sampling frame of the UK population and selecting a random sample would be vastly more expensive.

Convenience sampling describes the situation where one uses whatever sample happens to be available, either to cut costs or

because no other data can be collected. The large number of behavioural studies using undergraduate students as sample is a classical example. This does raise the issue of generalisability of the results.

Once a sample has been selected, we can move on to the analysis stage. As mentioned in the introduction, two cases occur: (i) no prior information about the population is available and the sample is used to provide estimates about the population and (ii) the sample is used to test a hypothesis about the population. *Figure 1* sketches these two scenarios.

Consider an opinion-poll aimed at estimating what percentage of people would favour travelling to the continent by Eurostar rather than by plane if both offered the same price. Assume that out of the 1,000 people interviewed, 650 express a preference for Eurostar. Based on this data, our best guess (or point-estimate) of the percentage of people who prefer Eurostar is $\hat{p} = 650/1,000 = 65$ per cent. The $\hat{p}$ above the p indicates that this number is an estimate of the true (but unknown) proportion p.

How accurate is this estimate; i.e. how confident are we that the true value is close to the estimate $\hat{p} =$ per cent? As $\hat{p}$ follows approximately a normal distribution when the sample is sufficiently large, it is possible to write down a 95 per cent confidence interval [62 per cent, 68 per cent]. This means that if we were to take many such samples, we would expect the observed proportion $\hat{p}$ to lie between 62 per cent and 68 per cent for 95 per cent of these samples.

Obtaining a higher confidence level, say 99 per cent, comes at the expense of a larger confidence interval. In this example, we would expect 99 per cent of observed sample proportions $\hat{p}$ to lie between

61 per cent and 69 per cent. On the other hand, increasing the sample size results in a smaller confidence interval, i.e. a more accurate estimate. If 2,600 people out of 4,000 favour Eurostar, the point estimate $\hat{p} = 2,600/4,000 = 65$ per cent is unchanged, but the 95 per cent confidence interval equals [63.5 per cent, 66.5 per cent]. Note that multiplying the sample size by four only results in halving the confidence interval.

Next, let us consider hypothesis testing. The Eurostar management may be convinced that, at equal price, half the travellers prefer Eurostar while the other half prefer flying. Denoting the proportion of travellers who favour Eurostar by $\hat{p}$ this results in the following null-hypothesis: $p = 50$ per cent, the alternative hypothesis being $p \neq 50$ per cent.

Assume we take a sample of 1,000 people. If the null-hypothesis is true, the observed proportion of people who prefer Eurostar, $\hat{p}$, should be close to 50 per cent. If $\hat{p}$ is very different from 50 per cent we would reject the null-hypothesis in favour of the alternative $p \neq 50$ per cent. Thus, we need to define what we mean by "very different". Relying once more on the normal approximation, we obtain a picture as shown in *Panel A* of *Figure 2*. Whatever the limits we choose, there is always some probability that we observe a value of $\hat{p}$ outside these limits, although the null-hypothesis is true. This probability is known as the significance level or type I error. It is the probability of rejecting the null-hypothesis when the null-hypothesis is true.

Consider a 5 per cent significance level, as illustrated in *Panel B* of *Figure 2*. This implies that whenever we observe a value $\hat{p}$ outside the interval [46.8 per cent, 53.2 per cent], we reject the null-hypothesis.

In other words, if we observe a value of $\hat{p}$ so far away from the hypothesised value of $p = 50$ per cent that the probability of this happening is less than 5 per cent, we reject the null-hypothesis.

The type I error (i.e. the probability of rejecting the null-hypothesis when it is true) can be reduced by decreasing the significance level (i.e. increasing the acceptance region, see *Panel A* of *Figure 2*). The drawback is that a decrease of the type I error results in an increase of the type II error: the probability of not rejecting the null hypothesis when we should.

Consider an example of warranty claims, with null-hypothesis that the product satisfies the quality requirements versus the alternative hypothesis that the product does not satisfy the quality requirements. *Table 3* shows the four possible cases. There are no problems with cases (a) (the null-hypothesis is true and we do not reject it) and (d) (the null-hypothesis is false and we do reject it). In case (b) we commit a type I error: the null-hypothesis is true but we reject it. In this example, this amounts to accepting a warranty claim, or scrapping a batch of goods, when the product satisfies the quality requirements. In case (c) we commit a type II error: the null-hypothesis is false, but we fail to reject it. This amounts to refusing a warranty claim when the product is defective.

The trade-off between type I and type II errors is therefore a trade-off between accepting unjustified warranty claims and rejecting justified claims. The choice of an appropriate significance level then rests on trading off the costs to the company of the two types of error: paying out unnecessary warranties versus unhappy customers. The only way to reduce both types of error simultaneously is to increase the sample

size. But this is expensive in its own right.

Hypothesis testing plays a crucial role in quality control, and lies at the basis of the 6-sigma-chart. Consider a production process that consists of pouring an amount of liquid m in each can. If the process is under control, the actual amounts poured will be clustered closely around the target value of m. The null-hypothesis is thus that the average content per can equals m. If we take a sample of cans and observe an average content $\bar{x}$ very different from m we should conclude that the process is out of control and intervene. In this context, a type I error means intervening when the process is in control, i.e. an unnecessary interruption of production, while a type II error means not intervening when the process is out of control.

Consider filling cans of soft drink, with a target level of 33cl per can, i.e, the null hypothesis is that $m = 33$. Assume that the filling process has a standard deviation of 1.2cl, and that we consider samples of 36 cans. In this case, the standard deviation of the sample mean equals 0.02cl. The 6-sigma-chart would look as shown in *Figure 3*. The bold horizontal line in the middle indicates the target $m = 33$. The four dotted lines are respectively 1 and 2 standard deviations above or below the mean.

The bold lines at the top and bottom are 3 standard deviations away from the mean. As production goes on, samples are taken at regular intervals and the observed sample means are indicated on the chart (the crosses). This provides an easy visual way of spotting if something is wrong. For example, the chart in *Panel A* of *Figure 4* indicates the process is out of control: several means are more than 2 standard deviations away from the mean. This is a very unlikely occurrence if the process is under control. The chart in *Panel B* also shows something is wrong. Although the sample means are within 2 standard deviations of the mean, there is a clear trend showing the production process is gradually getting out of control.

Source: FT Mastering Management Part 3.

Summary

In this chapter we have explored the ideas behind statistical inference and introduced a number of formal tests to allow us to assess the characteristics of some statistical population based on sample information. The potential behind such tests is apparent. Most managers and decision makers find themselves in situations where decisions must be taken on limited and often incomplete information. In those situations where sample data can be collected and analysed, the tests we have covered offer a valuable aid to the manager in evaluating options and alternatives. All the tests we have introduced are based on similar principles even though the exact calculations may vary slightly. Such tests do not offer a guaranteed solution to a manager's problems but they do offer a cost-effective method of supplementing the information available. Such information, however, needs to be carefully evaluated alongside that from other sources. This can only be done properly with an adequate understanding of the basic principles behind inferential techniques. It should also be remembered that we have only touched upon some of the more common tests available. A whole barrage of additional tests exists and details can be found in the relevant references.

Useful online resources

Detailed below are some internet resources that may be useful. Many have further links to other sites. An updated version is available from the accompanying website (**www.pearsoned.co.uk/wisniewski**). In addition, I would be grateful for details of other websites that have been found to be useful.

www.researchinfo.com/docs/library/index.cfm – Market research case studies

www.nao.org.uk/publications/Samplingguide.pdf – National Audit Office Sampling Guide

www.mrs.org.uk/mrindustry/downloads/newcomers.pdf – A Newcomers' Guide to Market and Social Research

www.ipsos-mori.com – Ipsos Mori market research website

www.ifigure.com/math/stat/testing.htm – Statistical testing calculator

www.stats.gla.ac.uk/steps/glossary/confidence_intervals.html – Statistics glossary on confidence intervals

www.measuringusability.com/stats/ci/ci_instr1.php – Article on confidence intervals and estimation

QMDM IN ACTION
Queen's College, Taunton

Market research has long been recognised as important for private sector organisations at both the operational and strategic levels. At the strategic levels such research can help a company focus on potentially profitable new products or services, to identify emerging consumer demands and so on. At the operational level market research can establish customer preferences in terms of different product lines and can help establish perceptions of service quality. In many parts of the public sector such market research has often evoked images of 'marketing' (a dirty word for many public sector managers) and commercialism. However, many such organisations are beginning to realise that the information generated by such research can play a constructive role in both improving operational performance – with increased 'customer' satisfaction – and the long-term development of the organisation. This is particularly the case when such public sector organisations face an increasingly uncertain

| Figure 7.9 | Queen's College, Taunton |

and complex future. Hospitals are carrying out surveys to assess the quality of care provided and patients' perceptions of the services provided and those expected. Local authorities are conducting surveys into public attitudes to the changing roles of the organisation and changing priorities. Schools are beginning to conduct surveys into the attitudes and expectations of parents.

Queen's College was founded in Taunton, Somerset, United Kingdom, in 1843 by a group of Methodists. It stands today on a site of around 30 acres on the southern outskirts of Taunton and is a fee-paying, co-educational boarding and day school with around 700 pupils from four years of age up to 18/19 years of age. It is structured into a pre-preparatory department for pupils from four to eight years, a junior school from eight to twelve years and a senior school from twelve years upwards. In the senior school around 40 per cent of pupils are female and approximately the same proportion of all senior pupils are boarders. The school also attracts a number of overseas pupils and pupils from parents who are in the Armed Services. Although a fee-paying school, Queen's does not focus primarily on academic ability and exam performance. As is reflected in the school motto – *Non Scholae Sed Vitae Discimus* – the school believes it is providing a preparation for life which involves more than just academic attainment in the classroom. The school sees itself very much as a small Christian community with a tradition of encouraging personal fulfilment, regardless of the level of individual talent and ability.

On a day-to-day basis the management of the school is the responsibility of the headmaster. For longer-term planning and development, the headmaster and the board of governors of the school take responsibility. As part of the Methodist Foundation, it is also one of a group of schools for which the Board of Methodist Colleges and Schools is ultimately responsible. In 1991 a new headmaster was appointed to the school and together with the chairman of the school's board of governors undertook a fundamental review of the school's position and possible future. The college was in a particularly strong and sound position. Highly committed and professional staff, outstanding exam results, excellent buildings and infrastructure, excellent support staff and facilities and a close rapport between pupils,

parents and staff as well as with the wider local community. Nevertheless, it was felt appropriate to undertake such an evaluation in order to ensure continuing, future success on the basis that consideration of change and the future is best done from a position of strength and solidarity rather than one of weakness and crisis. The aim of this review was to contribute to the process of drawing up a development plan for Queen's for the next decade. It was intended that the plan would adopt a structure of:

- assessing the current position
- establishing the preferred future position
- the development of a detailed strategic plan
- identifying methods of achieving the plan.

One of the factors stimulating this approach was that the overall environment in which the college was operating (and indeed in which all schools are operating) was facing considerable change and uncertainty. Some of the factors that needed to be assessed included:

- the effect of the demographic downturn in the school-age population;
- the decline experienced in the independent schools' sector in general in demand for boys' boarding places;
- an unexpected decline in numbers at sixth-form level;
- the impact on demand for places in the independent schools sector following a decade where increases in school fees had outstripped inflation;
- the impact of the Armed Services review under way at the time by the government and which was expected to result in a sizeable decrease in the Armed Services;
- the imminent change of status for Hong Kong (approximately 25 per cent of overseas pupils attending independent schools in the UK were from Hong Kong at the time).

At the time, a general election was imminent, giving rise to further uncertainty regarding:

- the potential withdrawal of charity status from independent schools;
- the potential withdrawal of the Assisted Places scheme, whereby the government funds a

number of places at independent schools for pupils whose parents are on low incomes;

● the potential of increased direct competition from the state sector with an increase in the number of grant-maintained schools – state schools able to opt-out of local authority control.

In 1992, as part of the review process, the college commissioned an image research exercise. The purpose of the research was to collect information about parents' perception of the college and the quality of the services and resources provided. This information could then be consolidated with that available from other sources to help the college review its long-term strategic position. It was decided to conduct the research through a questionnaire that would be distributed to a randomly selected sample of parents. The questionnaire consisted of some 30 questions in total, ranging from questions about how parents initially found out about the school, through to perceptions of the quality of teaching and related support, to a consideration of future changes in services and facilities. The questionnaire was initially distributed to over 150 parents and generated a response rate of 67 per cent. To illustrate the type of findings produced and their contribution to decision making, two areas will be discussed. The first relates to the source of initial contact with the college: how parents first came into contact with the college when considering sending their child to an independent school. Table 7.10 shows the summary results.

From the sample it can be seen that 77 per cent of parents indicate that the source of initial contact was either that they knew of the school personally or that it had been recommended by a friend, col-

Table 7.10	Queen's College: source of initial contact

Source of initial contact

Personal knowledge	45%
Personal recommendation	32%
ISIS*	14%
Newspapers/magazines	5%

* ISIS is the Independent Schools' Information Service.
Source: author's research.

Table 7.11	Queen's College: preference for foreign language at A level

Preference for foreign language at A level. Percentage of parents indicating a preference who gave that language first or second priority at A level

	First	Second
French	60	6
German	12	38
Spanish	1	17
Italian	0	3

Source: author's research.

league or relative. Since the result relates only to a sample, a confidence interval is potentially worthwhile calculating. For the result of 77 per cent, the 95 per cent confidence interval is calculated at ±7 per cent, implying that at least 70 per cent of parents make initial contact with the school in this way. Clearly such a finding is of considerable interest to the school in a climate of change and uncertainty since it implies the college has developed a strong and very positive reputation. As any private sector business knows, word of mouth is a very cost-effective way of attracting new customers. The results also have implications for the college's future marketing strategy and priorities.

The other area relates to the provision of services, notably foreign language teaching to pupils. Parents were asked to indicate their preference as to which foreign languages should be available at the college and their order of preference. Focusing on the provision of languages at A level the findings shown in Table 7.11 were produced.

The findings indicate that for French, for example, some 60 per cent of parents would wish French to be available as first priority language and 6 per cent as second priority. In terms of overall preferences there is clearly a demand for French followed by German, Spanish, then Italian. This may seem both unsurprising and unremarkable. However, the image research was conducted at a time when German was not available at Queen's while Spanish was. Clearly the research provided evidence of strong potential demand, currently unfulfilled, for offering

German to pupils. An appropriate hypothesis test confirms, at the 99 per cent level, that German is given higher priority by parents than Spanish.

Overall, many of the findings produced as a result of the research came as little surprise to the college. This, in itself, was reassuring that the research was adequately reflecting views and opinions of parents and also that the college had a currently strong position in the marketplace. Equally it implied that staff at the school were, by and large, accurately in touch with parents' views and expectations. However, a number of findings were revealed that the college could use both to improve its operational performance and as part of the longer-term development planning. The research also highlighted some infor-

mation needs of the school. It had been intended to conduct comparable research among parents who had contacted the school regarding a place for their child but who had then subsequently not chosen Queen's. Clearly such research would have been potentially beneficial in terms of providing information as to why some parents chose a 'competitor' instead. However, details of such parents were not currently retained – not really surprising since such data was not up to now seen as important – and this aspect of the research was not attainable. One of the recommendations arising from the image research was that the college should retain such data in the future to help it assess why it might be losing potential 'customers' to the competition.

I am grateful to Mr C T Bradnock, formerly headmaster at Queen's College, for permission to reproduce Figure 7.9 and the data discussed in this section.

Exercises

1   Return to Exercise 8 in Chapter 4. Calculate the mean and standard deviation if you have not already done so. Given that this data is a sample, calculate the 90 per cent, 95 per cent and 99 per cent confidence intervals around the mean. Provide a management interpretation of these in the context of the problem and explain why the interval gets larger.

2   Return to Exercise 9 in Chapter 4. The Finance Department in the local authority has estimated that at least 45 people per day on average need to use the local library to justify the cost of keeping it open – costs relate to staff wages, heating, lighting, cost of periodicals and so on. You have been asked to evaluate the data collected on the mean number of people using the library in the context of this minimum figure.

Draft a report to the committee (most of whom have low levels of numeracy) evaluating the information available. If you had been given the task of collecting data on the number of users how would you have done this and how would you try to ensure you had a representative sample?

3   Several years ago a new chief executive was appointed to a group of firms. On appointment the CE expressed concern about the quality of the senior management in one of the major companies in the group. He felt that this group of managers was by and large out of touch with new technology, new market opportunities and so on and, in spite of boardroom opposition, the CE has tried over the past few years to encourage a younger age structure among these senior managers via an active promotion and recruitment policy. Data has been provided on the age structure of these senior managers in 1990. The group had a mean age of 53 years. A sample of 20 senior managers this year finds an average age of 46, standard deviation 4.6 years. Can the CE conclude that his policies have had an effect in terms of reducing the mean age of senior managers?

4 In the Worked Example in Chapter 5 we had a distribution of a sample of customers' electricity consumption. Test whether this distribution is Normal.

5 A small engineering firm manufactures high-precision components for the aeronautical industry. In order to ensure quality, the production equipment has to be regularly maintained. One particular component in the production equipment must be replaced regularly. At present the component is supplied by a Japanese company and has a mean life of six months. A French company has approached the firm claiming to supply a comparable component at lower cost. The French company has supplied six of the components for testing and the life of the components has been found to be, in months:

6.2; 7.6; 6.5; 7.4; 6.3; 6.3

Recommend whether you think the engineering firm should switch suppliers based on this information.

6 A local authority has a pool of cars available for staff to use on official business. One particular make and model of car, of which the authority has a considerable number, claims to give a miles per gallon (mpg) performance of 52 mpg for simulated out-of-town driving. For a sample of 20 cars the transport manager has calculated that the actual mpg for such driving has been 47 mpg, standard deviation of 7 mpg.

Based on this information would you conclude that the car manufacturer's claimed mpg is unrealistic? What assumptions have you had to make to reach a conclusion?

7 A local hospital is trying to assess its performance *vis-à-vis* national performance. The Department of Health has recently indicated that, nationally, for a particular hospital-based treatment the mean length of stay of patients in hospital was 8.6 days. The local hospital has checked the records of 150 of its patients who have recently been discharged from hospital having received this treatment and found the mean LOS was 7.5 days, standard deviation 1.1 days. The hospital manager is keen to contact the local media to publicise that the hospital is performing better than the national average in this treatment area. Would you recommend her to do this?

8 A local training agency is trying to get government support for its activities – which relate to the provision of industrial and commercial training for the local labour force – on the basis that unemployed workers who are better skilled have a better chance of finding new employment than unskilled workers. A group of people who have recently been unemployed but now found work has been investigated. One group, the skilled, comprised 120 people who had been unemployed for a mean of 16.2 weeks, standard deviation 1.3 weeks, before finding employment. The second group, 150 unskilled workers, had been unemployed for an average of 24.9 weeks, standard deviation 2.1 weeks. Is there any evidence that the training agency argument is valid?

9 An organisation is trying to evaluate which of two PC computer systems to standardise on within the organisation. In terms of price, specification and performance there is little to choose between the two models being considered, Model A and Model B. However, the computer services manager is concerned about the possible maintenance and repair costs of the two models. Based on a sample of 40 of each type, the annual maintenance costs have been estimated at £45.60 for Model A, standard deviation £4.20, and at £39.65 for Model B, standard deviation £6.52. Would this information help the organisation choose between the two models?

10 Historically it has taken a local council an average of 18 weeks to reach a decision about planning applications for building development work submitted by construction companies. The companies have complained that decisions are taking too long and delays are costing them money. The chief executive of the local council has initiated a streamlined system for such applications with the intent of reducing the time taken to reach a decision. After a few months' operation, a sample of 250 planning applications has been analysed and a mean time of 15 weeks found with a standard deviation of 5.2 weeks. Has the streamlined system led to a reduction in mean time taken?

11 The Inland Revenue has introduced a self-assessment system for tax payments whereby citizens themselves calculate the amount of tax to be paid on income each year. Naturally, the Inland Revenue checks such self-assessments, although it does not have the resources to check them all each year. At the start of the new system, it was felt that at least 90 per cent of such self-assessed tax returns would be correctly completed by the citizen (with the remainder containing errors which are either accidental through miscalculation or deliberate as the result of an attempt to defraud). Some months after the start of the new system a sample of 1750 self-assessments has been rigorously checked. 11.8 per cent were found to be incorrect in some way. Comment on the initial view that at least 90 per cent would be correctly completed.

12 A company employs largely part-time staff, and in the past has found staff turnover to be 23 per cent each year (that is 23 per cent of staff in any one year leave the company). This is felt to be too high, with implications for morale, motivation and costs (since new staff have to be recruited and trained). The company has recently put into place a performance management system intended to improve productivity, morale and staff retention. The latest figures based on a sample of 20 teams of staff in the company indicate staff turnover is 18.6 per cent, standard deviation 1.7. Is there any evidence that staff turnover has fallen?

13 An international company routinely rotates its senior managers every five to six years around its activities worldwide. Staff are financially compensated for such moves but with many staff buying a house in their new location, there are concerns about relative house prices. The company has recently surveyed house prices in two cities where it is based:

	Mean price (£)	Standard deviation	Sample size
City A	235 000	12 750	132
City B	261 000	15 680	161

Prices are for comparable houses and have been adjusted for exchange rates. Is there any evidence of a difference in mean house prices between the two cities?

14 Recent legislation requires adherence to detailed and complex food-labelling requirements on products sold to consumers. A recent survey examined whether the food labelling on supermarket own-brand products met these requirements. The results were categorised as:

● Complete compliance with legislation.

● Satisfactory compliance, indicating that some minor irregularities occurred.

● Unsatisfactory compliance, implying that major breaches of the legislation had occurred, with the supermarket liable to a fine as a result.

The results of the survey were as shown in Table 7.12.

Table 7.12	Number of items complying with legislation			
		Compliance		
Supermarket	Complete	Satisfactory	Unsatisfactory	Total
A	80	23	9	112
B	121	32	17	170
C	105	27	12	144
D	172	58	12	242
Total	478	140	50	668

Do the supermarkets have the same performance in the sense of compliance with this legislation?

15 An airline operating between London and Aberdeen knows that a large part of its customer base represents business executives. The airline is considering offering a limousine service to/from the airport to be included in the airline ticket price, which would have to increase as a result. A survey has recently been completed on a number of flights of 10 executive passengers asking if they (or their company) would be willing to pay 10 per cent extra for their flight if this service was included. The responses were:

No. responding Yes from 10 surveyed	No. of flights
0	6
1	12
2	15
3	13
4	9
5	3
6	2
Total	60

Estimate p as the total number responding yes/total number surveyed.

Determine whether these responses follow the Binomial distribution.

Why do you think the airline might be interested in whether responses follow the Binomial distribution?

16 The author has been involved in research into the use of something known as compensation orders in Scottish courts (*The Use of the Compensation Order in Scotland*, J Hamilton and M Wisniewski, Scottish Office Central Research Unit, 1996). Convicted offenders can be ordered to pay compensation to those suffering loss or injury from the crime which led to conviction. For example, if someone is convicted of breaking all the windows in my house, the court can order them to pay me compensation to get the windows replaced.

The research investigated the use of such orders by Scottish courts. As part of the research, a sample of convictions and compensation orders was taken from four individual courts and records checked several months afterwards to see whether in fact the offender had paid the compensation to the victim. It was found that the payment outcome might fall into one of three categories:

- Paid in full: the full amount of the compensation ordered by the court had been paid by the offender.
- Part paid: only part of the amount had been paid.
- Nothing paid: none of the compensation had been paid.

The results for the four courts are shown in Table 7.13.

Table 7.13	Payment of compensation orders by court (figures relate to no. of compensation orders)			
	Payment outcome			
Court	*Paid in full*	*Part paid*	*Nothing paid*	*Total*
A	274	25	15	314
B	250	24	24	298
C	136	9	7	152
D	252	11	21	284
Total	912	69	67	1048

The payment outcome was also assessed by the gender of the offender, as shown in Table 7.14.

Table 7.14	Payment of compensation orders by gender			
	Payment outcome			
Gender	*Paid in full*	*Part paid*	*Nothing paid*	*Total*
Male	754	62	61	877
Female	157	7	6	170
Total	911	69	67	1047

(a) Determine whether the payment outcome shows any difference between the four courts.

(b) Determine whether the payment outcome shows any difference between offender gender.

17 In Chapter 1 reference was made to a survey undertaken by the author into the use of quantitative techniques by businesses. One of the questions in the survey asked whether businesses were using such techniques, with responses as either yes or no. The survey was undertaken across three countries independently: Denmark, UK and Scotland. Part of the survey also determined the size of the companies, measured by number of employees. The data has been analysed and the relevant computer output is as follows:

```
                        Are Techniques Used?
              Count    YES       NO
Q4->                                       Row
                        1         2        Total
Employees  ─────────────────────────────
              1       171       125        296
<200                                       68.2
              2        66        15         81
200-499                                    18.7
              3        25         5         30
500-999                                     6.9
              4        24         3         27
1000-4999                                   6.2
           Column     286       148        434
           Total     65.9      34.1       100.0

Chi-Square    D.F.      Significance    Min E.F.    Cells with
                                                    E.F.<5

_____  ____    _____  _____   _____
27.86341       3         .0000          9.207       None
```

```
                       Are Techniques Used?
              Count  │  YES      NO
Q4->                 │                        Row
                     │    1        2        Total
Country        ──────┤
                 1   │  123       94          217
DENMARK              │                        50.0
                 2   │   84       20          104
UK                   │                        24.0
                20   │   79       34          113
SCOTLAND             │                        26.0
              Column │  286      148          434
              Total     65.9     34.1       100.0


Chi-Square    D.F.      Significance    Min E.F.    Cells with
                                                    E.F.<5
_____   ____      _____    _____     _____
19.24628       2           .0001         35.465       None
```

Comment on the use of techniques in relation to the size of the company and its country location.

18 Return to Exercise 10 in Chapter 4. Test to see whether there is a significant difference between mean customer spend in the two stores. Draft a short report explaining your conclusion in non-technical terms for the store managers.

8 Quality Control and Quality Management

Learning objectives

By the end of this chapter you should be able to:

- understand the importance of quality management for all business organisations
- be able to apply statistical process control
- be able to apply Pareto charts to quality issues
- be able to construct and use an Ishikawa diagram

In the major Western economies today significant efforts are being made to catch up with Japanese and Asian companies in the areas of product and service quality and reliability. Over the past 30 to 40 years quality of product and quality of service have not been seen by most Western businesses as a key part of their overall business strategy. Rather their focus historically has been on cost reduction, improving efficiency, increasing sales, maintaining and increasing profit margins. Importantly this focus has often been short-term. Today this focus has changed dramatically. Most major business organisations now accept that, literally, their long-term business survival may be at stake if they do not improve the quality of the goods and services they provide to compare favourably with Japanese and other Far Eastern economies. Manufacturing companies in the late 1970s gradually began to realise that quality products were essential if they were to survive in a global market. Gradually this focus on quality has extended to the service sector and increasingly into the public sector, where the ideas of quality, standards and customer satisfaction are becoming more widespread. In the UK many areas of the public sector economy are engaged in major programmes to improve the service provided to their customers through quality initiatives. In fact, in the UK, central government is now requiring many public sector organisations to take the issue of quality of customer service very seriously and to publish their criteria for 'good' or quality service.

Historically, this relatively new emphasis on 'quality' took root in the manufacturing sector – largely thanks to the ever-increasing success of Japanese companies in the world market. In this chapter we shall explore some of the issues relating to quality management and some of the techniques available to the manager to help monitor and improve quality of product and service.

The Importance of Quality

What makes quality important to any organisation is that, if the organisation provides goods or services which more than satisfy the customer, then that business is likely to be successful, other things being equal. Organisations which do not provide quality goods and services are likely to fail. Obviously this is a gross oversimplification: many other factors will contribute to an organisation's success or failure. Increasingly, however, quality is seen as a critical factor in the success/failure position of a business organisation. Any business organisation is constantly searching for what a business strategist would call the source of its competitive advantage: what allows one organisation to compete successfully against other organisations. What distinguishes this organisation – particularly from the perspective of the customer – from others?

Organisations which identify and then exploit their competitive advantage are well on the way to success and continued survival. One popular way of examining the principles of business strategy is to consider different possible sources of such a competitive advantage: how an organisation can establish and maintain such an advantage. As a generalisation, such competitive advantage can be exploited through one of two broad strategies: cost or differentiation. Quality has a potential impact on both of these.

Through a cost focus, an organisation tries to ensure its advantage lies through ensuring the cost of producing the good or supplying the service is lower than that of its competitors. All its strategic focus is on ensuring that this cost advantage is maintained. In the UK, for example, it is estimated that between 30 per cent and 40 per cent of effort in business may be spent detecting errors, problems and poor quality and in taking the necessary corrective action. Consider the cost savings if an organisation gets quality right first time. Consider translating these costs into a competitive advantage *vis-à-vis* competing organisations.

On the other hand, a differentiation focus implies that an organisation is trying to ensure that its product/service is seen by customers as different in some meaningful way from that of its competitors. Differentiation can be achieved in a variety of ways: through the range of products or services offered; through the availability of the product/service; through the standard of product/service offered; through quality.

In both cases – cost and differentiation – a quality focus can help establish and maintain the organisation's competitive advantage. On the cost side, quality procedures and processes can ensure that quality of output is kept high and therefore the costs associated with faulty output are kept low. Equally, on the differentiation side, high quality can differentiate a product/service from that of competitors.

Techniques in Quality Management

Naturally, quality management is more than just the application of techniques to the quality problem in an organisation. Quality management is also concerned with organisational structure, organisational culture, interpersonal relationships, links between

Bad service 'costing companies millions'

By Patrick Harverson

Bad customer service is costing companies hundreds of millions of pounds a year in lost revenue, according to a study published today by the Henley Centre, the research institute.

The study on the financial impact of poor customer service, the first of its kind, suggests that over a five-year period a business with annual turnover of £500m could lose more than £1.8bn in revenue and £267m in profits because of such poor service.

The data are based on an analytic model of a "typical" consumer-oriented company constructed for the study, which was commissioned by Ventura, the customer service management group. The research suggests that bad service results in a customer spending on average £234 less with a company over five years.

It also finds that a reduction in customer service problems of only 1 per cent could increase profits by £16m over five years, and that companies could double their profits over the same period if they eliminated all customer service problems.

Mr Bob Tyrell, chairman of the Henley Centre, said that while previous research established that bad service could be expensive for com-

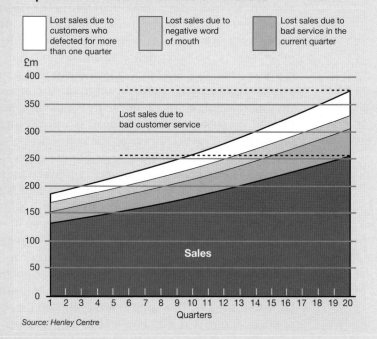

Impact of bad customer service on revenues

Source: Henley Centre

panies, the new study "traces systematically the cost of bad service" through an analytical model.

The centre devised a business with sales of £500m a year and a consumer base of 5m adults spending an average of £25 with the company each quarter.

It estimated that 17 per cent of the company's customers were affected each quarter by a range of

service problems, such as poor product information, out-of-stock goods, poor telephone service, rude staff and general inefficiency.

Of customers affected, the study calculated that 14 per cent would miss one quarterly transaction with the company as a result of the bad service, 2 per cent would take their business elsewhere for 12 months, and 1 per cent would defect for three years. The centre said these assumptions are based on conservative interpretations of existing research into customer behaviour.

This research included recent work it carried out for financial service retailers, which found that 15 per cent of customers who switched banks had done so because of bad service. Another earlier study found only 5 per cent of customers who were unable to buy a product because it was out of stock later returned to make the purchase at the same store.

The centre said its calculations were also based on the findings of research group TARP Europe, which said that, depending on the magnitude of the problem encountered, unhappy customers told up to nine others about their bad service experience.

Source: *Financial Times*, 29 November 1996, p 14.

The costs of poor quality service are often hidden – but always high.

customers and suppliers, motivation, team building and the like. However, it is widely acknowledged that a number of common 'tools' have an important part to play in any organisation's search for improved quality. These tools can be applied at different stages of the quality process, which can be simplified, according to Juran, as:

- planning for quality
- controlling for quality
- improving for quality.

Given that a central part of the modern quality philosophy relates to the prevention of quality-related problems rather than their detection and correction, the planning and improving phases of the process take on an increased importance. We shall introduce three techniques commonly used in quality management: control charts, Pareto charts and Ishikawa diagrams. Other techniques are available for use in the quality area and references can be found in the Further Reading section at the end of the book.

Statistical Process Control

We shall illustrate the first of these quality-related techniques with reference to a production environment. An organisation produces and packages a range of soft drinks. One of the product lines has recently been launched on the market and consists of a tropical fruit fizzy drink sold in cans. The production line operates in such a way that several hundred thousand cans are processed each day. The automated machinery is set to fill each can with an average (mean) content of 400 ml. Naturally, we expect some variation in this mean amount and this has been quantified as a standard deviation of 10 ml. It is also known that the distribution of filled contents is Normal. Clearly, from a quality management perspective, we would wish to establish some quality inspection process to check that the mean quantity filled does meet these specifications. Over time we would expect to have to maintain, adjust and repair the automated machinery delivering this mean amount. Naturally, we would not want large quantities of the product which were underfilled to be distributed and sold. Equally, we do not want large numbers of cans to be overfilled, as this will add to our costs. We would require some quality control procedure to monitor the quality of output on a regular basis so that substandard quality can be detected at an early stage and the production process adjusted or repaired as necessary to bring the production process back to the required quality level.

Given the volume of production each day, management will require some easy and cost-effective method of quality control. Clearly we cannot afford to check the entire production batch each day; nor can we afford to halt production while we check output quality. It is evident that in this type of situation we shall require some sort of sampling process to be undertaken: to select a random sample of output to check for quality. However, this sampling process will bring its own difficulties. If we take too large a sample then the physical task of checking quality will be both time-consuming and expensive. On the other hand, too small a sample and our conclusions based on the sample evidence might be suspect. Consider also the dilemma of the manager if the sample evidence appears to reveal that quality problems are occurring in production. Knowing what we do about statistical inference, we know that such a conclusion based on sample evidence cannot be guaranteed: it will be based on some stated significance level. If such sample evidence appears to reveal production problems, the manager is faced with a major dilemma:

- to accept the sample evidence and stop production to rectify the problem and suffer the consequences of this lost production; or
- to hope that the sample evidence is wrong and continue production.

The other side of this picture is equally worrying. Suppose that the sample leads us to conclude that production quality is acceptable when in fact it is not? That is, that the sample fails to reveal a production problem. The dilemma faced by the manager in this context can be summarised as shown in Table 8.1.

The manager is faced with two alternative decisions based on the sample evidence: to continue production or to stop production. There are also two alternative states of nature (and remember that the manager has no control over which state of nature occurs): the quality level of production is acceptable or the quality level is unacceptable. Clearly there are two situations where the correct decision will have been taken and two where it will not.

Table 8.1	Decisions and outcomes	
	State of nature	
Decision	Quality level acceptable	Quality level not acceptable
Continue production	Correct decision	Type II error
Stop production	Type I error	Correct decision

Activity 8.1

What is meant in this context by a Type I error and a Type II error?

Using the terminology we introduced in Chapter 7 we can refer to these as Type I and Type II errors respectively. If we base our logic around the null hypothesis that the quality level is acceptable, then a Type I error occurs when we decide to stop production based on the sample evidence and the quality level is actually acceptable. A Type II error occurs when we should have taken the decision to stop production but did not do so. In the terminology of quality management, the situation of the quality level being acceptable is referred to as *the process being in control* and that of the quality level being unacceptable as *the process being out of control*. So, a Type I error occurs when we decide to adjust a process which is actually still in control and a Type II error occurs when we allow an out-of-control process to continue. We can use the statistical principles we have developed in earlier chapters to help in the quality management area.

Control Charts

We clearly need some technique to allow us to assess whether a situation is in control or not. Such a technique is available through the use of *control charts*. These are a graphical method of monitoring such a process on a regular and frequent basis and helping to evaluate whether it is in control or not. The principles of control charts were actually developed in the 1920s but saw a resurgence of interest in the 1980s. It is important to stress that such charts can be applied to any situation where we are 'measuring' quality and not just to production situations, as in our example.

The logic behind such charts is straightforward and based on the principles of the sampling distribution that we introduced in Chapter 7. We know that in some particular process – like that of our production line example – there will be some inherent variation around the quality target. In our example, we know the production line is meant to put 400 ml into each can (our quality target) but we also know that there is some inherent variability around this target; after all, this is what the standard deviation of 10 ml indicates. However, it is also possible over time that additional variability will occur, perhaps because of incorrect machine settings, the need for equipment maintenance and repair or because of inappropriate employee behaviour. In other words, there may be more variability in the production process than we expect. We can denote the one type of variation as *process variation*: the variation we would normally expect in such a process (as measured by the standard deviation); and we can denote the other type of variation as *assignable variation*: variation which is not normally expected and which, once we know about it, we would try to assign to particular factors which can be controlled or corrected (like the need for machine maintenance or repair).

It should also be clear that in many such situations we would want to be checking our quality target – and trying to determine whether the process was in control or not – on a frequent and regular basis. In other words, we would be taking frequent samples from the production line and checking the sample to make inferences about the population variability. This, obviously, is where we return to the sampling distribution concept. Suppose we take a sample of size n from the production line. We know from our understanding of the sampling distribution concept that we would expect 95 per cent of all sample means to lie within 1.96 standard errors of the population mean. That is:

$$\mu \pm 1.96 \frac{\sigma}{\sqrt{n}}$$

This is obviously no more than a 95 per cent confidence interval that we have examined and used elsewhere. For use in control charts we also calculate a second interval, this time relating to 99.8 per cent of sample means. From Normal probability tables this will be:

$$\mu \pm 3.09 \frac{\sigma}{\sqrt{n}}$$

We now have the basis for a simple and straightforward sampling approach to check periodically whether the production process is still in control: i.e. the observed variation is within predicted limits. The logic is straightforward. The 95 per cent interval is used to establish what are referred to as *warning limits* for the process. On the assumption – the null hypothesis – that the process is properly in control, then 95 out of every 100 sample means should lie within these calculated limits. If a sample mean falls outside these limits, we take it literally as a warning that the production process *may* be out of control – exhibiting more variation than the process itself contributes. However, such evidence is not seen as definitive but as a warning only. The 99.8 per cent interval is used to establish what are known as *action limits*. We would expect 998 out of every 1000 sample means to fall within these limits. If a particular sample mean does not, then the probability that the process is still in control is no more than 0.2 per cent and we would be justified in taking action – perhaps even to the extent of stopping the production process until the source of the assignable variation has been traced and corrected.

All this means, of course, that we are simply applying the principles and concepts of sampling and confidence intervals from the previous chapter. In diagram form we have the situation as shown in Figure 8.1, with the sampling distribution Normal as predicted by the Central Limit Theorem and the two confidence intervals we are now referring to as the warning and action limits.

Let us stop and reflect on what we have here. Effectively, the warning and action limits that we can calculate give us a decision tool. We want to know, based on sample evidence, whether we have a quality 'problem' with some process, in this case our

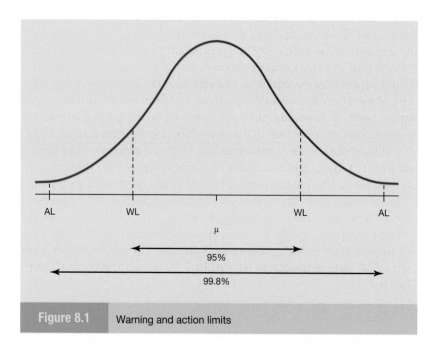

Figure 8.1   Warning and action limits

production line. Fundamentally, from time to time, management will ask the question: is the production line still in control in the sense that production is in line with the target set? If we take a sample of production, measure the mean contents of the sample items and then plot the sample mean on Figure 8.1 (after we have substituted precise numerical values for the action and warning limits), we can decide at a given probability level whether the production process is in control or not. If the sample result is inside the warning limits, we need do nothing. If the sample mean is outside the action limits we should take immediate action to stop production, as we have evidence that something is wrong – the process is exhibiting more variation than we would expect. If the sample mean is in between the warning and action limits, we investigate to see whether this is some sort of fluke event even though the process is still in control or whether the process genuinely is going out of control.

On a practical note, given that we will want to take samples repeatedly over time and not just once, it is more helpful to turn Figure 8.1 on its side, as in Figure 8.2. If we then remove the Normal curve, since we used this simply to show the derivation of the limits, we have the control chart in Figure 8.3. Anyone in the organisation, from managing director through to shop floor, can then use this control chart to check whether a particular process is in control and whether action needs to be taken. They do not even need to understand the principles of statistical inference to use the chart.

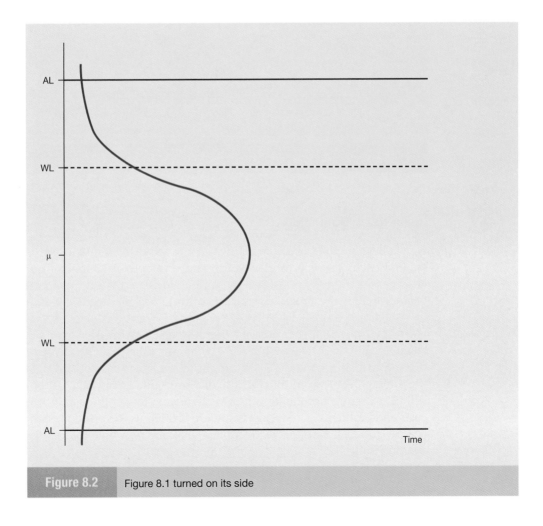

Figure 8.2   Figure 8.1 turned on its side

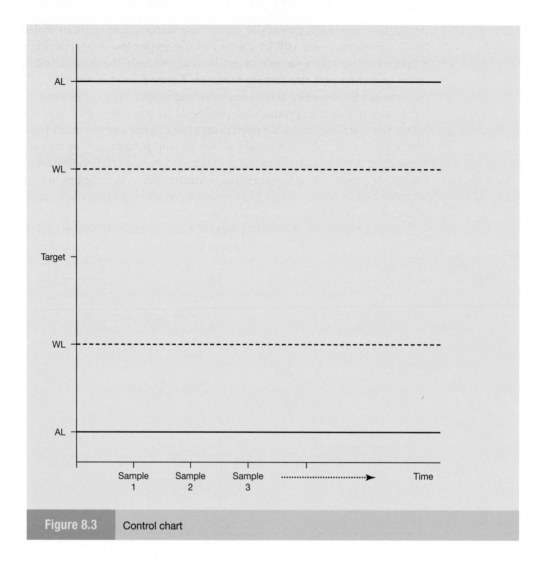

Figure 8.3	Control chart

Using the control chart

Let us illustrate the use of the chart with the following scenario. Returning to the production example, we have decided to take a sample of 10 items from the production
line every 15 minutes and for each sample calculate the sample mean to enable us to
check whether the process is still in control. You may consider that the number of
items sampled is small. The purpose of control charts, however, is to allow a quick and
cost-effective sampling process to be undertaken frequently over a short period. We
could, in principle, take samples of 100 items rather than 10 each time. The potential
problem is that such sample sizes might take some time to assess in terms of calculating the sample mean. While this calculation is under way then, in principle, we could
still be operating a production process that is no longer in control, with all the related
costs and problems. 'Do it quickly and do it often' is the principle behind such control
charts. However, with a given sample size we are now able to quantify the action and
warning limits.

Activity 8.2

Calculate the action and warning limits for this problem.

With n at 10 and σ at 10 ml we have:

Warning limits:
+1.96(10/√10) = +6.2 ml
−1.96(10/√10) = −6.2 ml

and with the mean μ, at 400 we have:

Upper WL = 406.2
Lower WL = 393.8

Action limits:

+3.09(10/√10) = +9.8 ml
−3.09(10/√10) = −9.8 ml

giving:

Upper AL = 409.8
Lower AL = 390.2

The control chart is shown in Figure 8.4.

Over a period of time we would take samples of 10 items from the production line, calculate the mean of each sample and plot this mean on the control chart. Gradually over time we would build up a picture of successive sample means taken from production. If the process is in control then we would expect a series of sample means like that shown in Figure 8.5. The series of sample means taken 15 minutes apart are all within

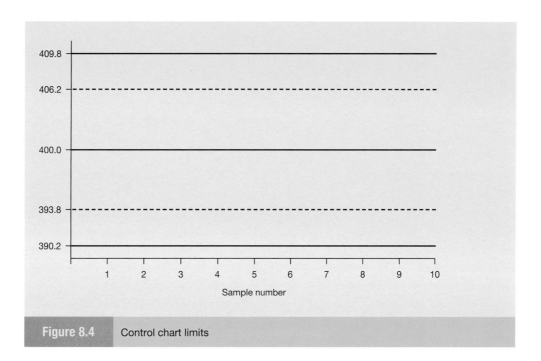

Figure 8.4   Control chart limits

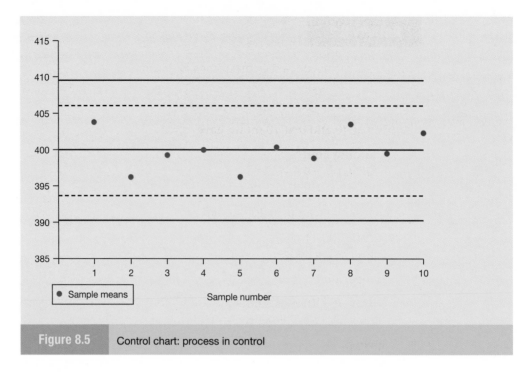

Figure 8.5   Control chart: process in control

the limits of process variation that we have calculated – within the warning limits. Although there is variability in production, this is within the predicted limits and no action is required. It is important to realise that a chart such as this would not be seen solely after sample 10 had been calculated but would rather be in continuous use over this entire period so that any trends or patterns can be identified.

The chart can also be used to track potential problems, as shown in Figure 8.6. We see here that from sample 3 onwards a trend in variability is clearly developing. By the

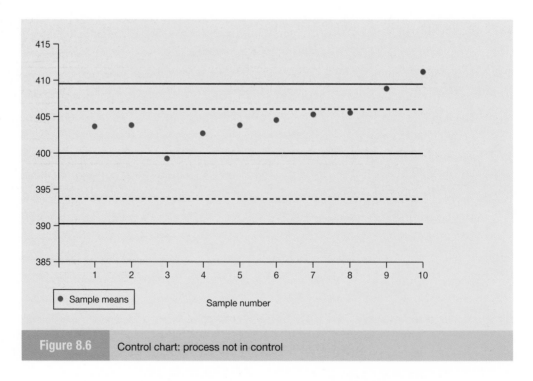

Figure 8.6   Control chart: process not in control

time we take sample 9 we breach the UWL and this should indicate cause for concern about the assignable variation. Sample 10 clearly confirms the process is out of control and that the cause of the increase in assignable variation needs to be identified and corrective action needs to be taken. In practice, after sample 9 when the UWL has been breached, another sample should be taken immediately, rather than waiting for the appropriate time. The reason for this is based on the logic of the chart: such a sample mean should not have occurred if the process is still in control but we do not have sufficient evidence to stop the process. Rather than wait for the next sample to be taken at its allotted time – and run the risk of continuing an out-of-control process in the meantime – it is advisable to take another sample immediately to check the sample 9 result. Control charts can be used to monitor the process, and investigations or actions should take place when we observe:

- any result outside the action limits
- a series of means in one particular direction
- a series of means on one side of the population mean
- more than 5 per cent of sample means lying above the WLs but below the ALs
- any other apparent non-random pattern.

Control charts are easy to construct and easy for any employee in an organisation to use and understand – even if the principles of statistical inference are unheard of. Although a production example has been used to illustrate the principles, their applicability to a wide range of service areas goes a long way to explaining the recent resurgence of interest in them as part of a wider quality management policy. Such charts can be used in almost any management situation where some quality target is appropriate – telephone answering times, customer complaints, absenteeism, financial performance, the list of applications is extensive.

QMDM IN ACTION
Cap Gemini Ernst & Young

Over the last decade or so, call centres have sprung up everywhere. A key issue in operational terms is measuring the performance of staff working in such a centre. Cap Gemini Ernst & Young were involved in establishing a suitable performance measurement system for a call centre operating in the travel and transport sector. The client required a performance measurement system that was based on measures that were relevant to call centre staff's jobs, were easily understood, helped identify areas for improvement, were flexible enough to cope with changing business circumstances and which would recognise sustained performance improvement.

Cap Gemini Ernst & Young identified core business processes within the call centre and discussed these with all staff involved to determine a complete set of measures.

Given the nature of the client's business, the fundamental purpose of the call centre was to increase sales. Staff in the call centre were accordingly measured on revenue generated per hour from their activities. In addition, a number of contributory drivers (or factors) that helped explain the revenue per hour achieved were established. These drivers included measures such as average call duration and the conversion rate (effectively the proportion of calls resulting in a sale). Using methodology developed in-house from a proprietary system called iChart, Cap Gemini Ernst & Young were able to introduce statistical process control charts as the method for recording and monitoring performance at all levels through the call centre.

Statistical process control charts were used to track performance at different levels in the call centre: for the call centre as a whole, for families of teams, for teams, for individual members of staff. The charts were found to be simple to understand and staff were able to visualise changes in performance easily. Charts were produced for revenue per hour and for five key contributory drivers, allowing changes in the main performance indicators to be monitored and understood.

The benefits are as follows:

- Call centre staff were motivated to improve their performance as their improvement is highly visible through the use of SPC.

- Staff morale improved as there was an agreed and fair measurement system in place.

- Overall improvement in performance as attention was focused on prioritised areas for improvement.

- Performance improvement initiatives could be evaluated on a sound, rigorous basis in terms of their impact over time on the key performance indicators.

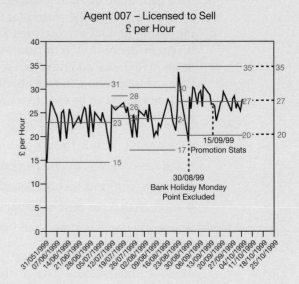

Agent 007 – Licensed to Sell
£ per Hour

I am grateful to Cap Gemini Ernst & Young for permission to use this case study and to reproduce the figure shown. Further case study applications are available through their website: www.uk.capgemini.com/services/consulting/or/success_stories

Control Charts for Attribute Variables

In some instances we may monitor product or service quality in terms of percentages rather than means. Consider the following example. A large organisation has recently expressed concern over the number of incorrect invoices it receives for goods/services and over the fact that many of these invoices are paid without proper checking. Such invoices cause problems because the firm finds it is consistently paying more than it should: goods invoiced but not yet delivered, an invoice for goods delivered to a different specification and so on. As part of a quality drive the Finance Department has calculated that last year 5 per cent of invoices were overpaid, and a determined effort is being made this year to reduce this percentage. On a weekly basis a sample of 100 invoices paid is taken and the percentage which were overpaid calculated. A control chart can be used in such a situation even though we have no mean and standard deviation. Remember that in Chapter 7 we gave the standard error of such a percentage as:

$$\text{SE} = \sqrt{\frac{\pi(100 - \pi)}{n}}$$

and we can again calculate warning and action limits:

$$\text{WL} = 5 \pm 1.96 \sqrt{\frac{\pi(100 - \pi)}{n}}$$

$$= 5 \pm 1.96 \sqrt{\frac{5(100 - 5)}{100}}$$

$$= 5 \pm 4.3$$

and

$$AL = 5 \pm 3.09 \sqrt{\frac{\pi(100 - \pi)}{n}}$$

$$= 5 \pm 3.09 \sqrt{\frac{5(100 - 5)}{100}}$$

$$= 5 \pm 6.7$$

Note that in this case the lower WL and AL would probably be omitted from the control chart. The reason for this is that a reduction in the percentage of invoices overpaid would be seen very much as an improvement and not as a problem.

Activity 8.3

A local supermarket knows that, on average, it receives 12 customer complaints a day about poor quality service, damaged goods and so on. The standard deviation around this average is five. The supermarket manager wants to set up a control chart to monitor this aspect of performance, with results compiled for each two-week period (the store is open seven days a week).

Calculate warning and action limits for this situation.

The first seven sets of results are:

13.4, 11.3, 14.2, 12.5, 11.1, 10.7, 9.5

Comment on the store's performance in this context.

Solution is given on p 590.

Pareto Charts

We introduced Pareto charts in Chapter 3 as a general method of data presentation. They have a particularly useful role to play in quality management. Let us develop the scenario we had in the last section. Let us assume that the large firm checking its invoice payment performance has found that performance had worsened: the percentage of overpaid invoices has increased. Clearly the use of control charts will help the firm identify that the problem exists at an early stage. What the control chart will not do, however, is identify the causes of the problem or possible solutions. In practice a 'quality' problem is likely to have a number of contributory factors. What management must do is identify these causes and prioritise them, since it is unlikely that all the problem's causes can be resolved simultaneously. Assume that an investigation into factors contributing to the worsening performance in the context of overpaid invoices has been completed, with the results as shown in Table 8.2.

A variety of factors are contributing to the problem: some internal, such as clerical errors, and some external, such as those originating with the supplier. A Pareto diagram like that in Figure 8.7 of these factors will help management prioritise in terms of which of these should be investigated first. Clearly the first two factors – delivery not as per invoice and wrong price charged by supplier – account for over half of the errors in the overpaid invoices and, other things being equal, should be investigated first in detail. Pareto charts can help put into context the management priorities in terms of the factors contributing to the quality problem.

Table 8.2	Causes of overpayment of invoices

Factor	Percentage frequency
1 Wrong price charged by supplier	20
2 Incorrect price discount calculated	6
3 Incorrect quantity delivered	10
4 Initial order changed	8
5 Delivery not as per invoice	36
6 Goods returned to supplier	2
7 Clerical error by Finance Dept.	18
Total	100

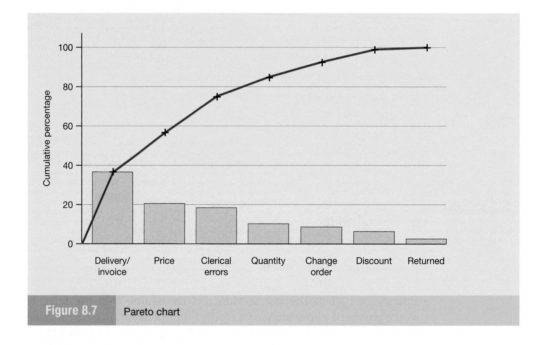

Figure 8.7	Pareto chart

Ishikawa Diagrams

The final topic we examine in this chapter is the Ishikawa diagram – alternatively known as the cause–effect diagram or the fishbone diagram. Such diagrams can help management focus on the specific problem faced in a quality management context and identify the factors contributing to that problem. The general format of the diagram is shown in Figure 8.8. We start with the observed effect. This is the characteristic or factor that we are focusing on in a quality context. Typically this might be the particular problem that needs to be resolved. The major causes, or contributory factors, to this effect are then identified and used to label the ends of each major branch as shown. Factors which in turn contribute to these major causes can then be determined in turn and used to label each branch coming from a main cause branch. In effect, the Ishikawa diagram is a method of focusing on the major factors causing a particular quality effect.

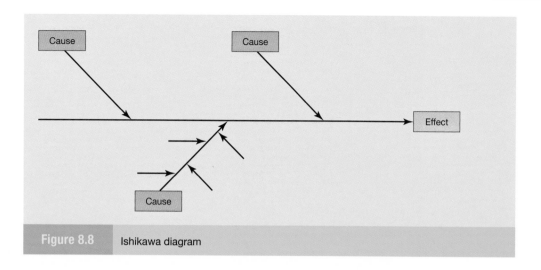

Figure 8.8   Ishikawa diagram

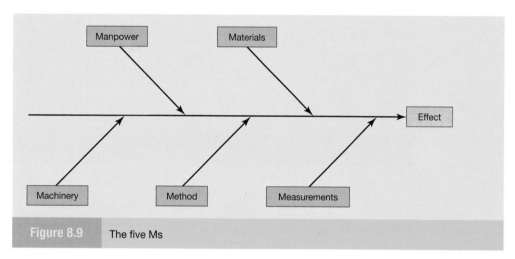

Figure 8.9   The five Ms

It seems very simple and straightforward but is deceptively powerful when used in the right way. Clearly a team approach is likely to be needed to develop a complete diagram for some designated effect, since most processes and activities will involve a group of people rather than one individual.

It should be noted that the exact format of the diagram depends entirely on the nature of the application. How many main cause branches there are and how many sub-branches for cause branches depends entirely on the context of the problem. The main principle is that the diagram should include all suspected causes. In a manufacturing or production context, the major causes may well be categorised as the five Ms: Manpower, Materials, Machinery, Methods and Measurements (or Information) as shown in Figure 8.9. This can provide a very useful and focused structure to the investigation. In a service context, as one might expect, the structure will be far more variable. To illustrate, let us return to the example in the section on Pareto diagrams. Let us assume that management have decided to investigate in detail one of the factors contributing to the over-payment of invoices: clerical errors. Although this does not have the highest priority in the Pareto diagram, we may assume management have decided to investigate this factor because it is internal to the organisation and may, therefore, be more amenable to a prompt solution than factors contributing to the problem from outside the organisation. Figure 8.10 illustrates the diagram we might produce. In this case the effect is the clerical errors and four major causes have been identified: Suppliers, Staff, Methods and Systems.

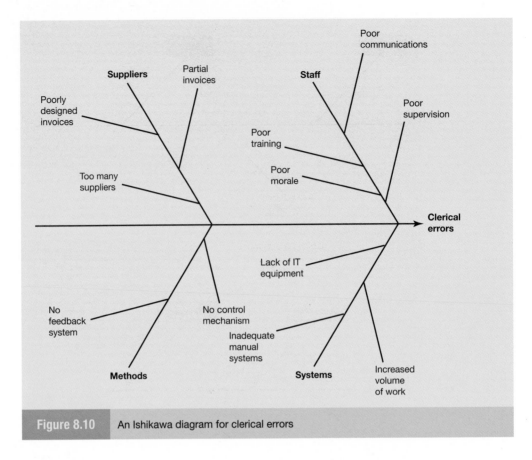

Figure 8.10 An Ishikawa diagram for clerical errors

Under Suppliers, factors contributing to this major cause are: poorly designed invoices used by suppliers, which cause problems for the clerical staff; partial invoices submitted by suppliers; and too many different suppliers, making it difficult to keep track of different goods. On the Staff cause, we have: poor training of clerical staff; poor supervision of clerical staff, poor communications with clerical staff, who are unsure who to contact in the event of queries or problems; and poor morale of staff. On the Methods cause, we have: no feedback system to allow clerical staff to monitor the quality of their own work; and no control mechanism to monitor the quality of performance in this area on an on-going basis. Finally, on the Systems cause, we have: lack of IT equipment for staff to use; manual systems in use are inadequate; and staff have seen a marked increase in the volume of work recently. Although the diagram is illustrative, it clearly demonstrates the potential. Having identified causes, management can now consider solutions to some, or all, of these factors. For example, we could consider requiring all our suppliers to use a common invoice form that has been designed in-house; we could introduce a focused training programme for clerical staff; we could invest in additional equipment. Whatever the possible solutions, the diagram allows management to assess the impact each solution could be expected to have on the effect. This by itself can be a valuable conclusion to reach. Improving staff training, for example, we now realise will not solve the entire problem, given that there are other factors contributing to the problem that will not be solved by this initiative.

Equally, although the diagram is readily applied to quality problems, it can also be applied to quality 'success'. If one feature of a product or service is seen as particularly successful this method can be a useful mechanism for identifying the key factors that have contributed to this success, with a view to replicating these factors for other products/services.

Worked Example

A health clinic has a no-appointments system for patients wishing to see one of the doctors. This means that if a patient wishes to see a doctor they attend one of the available clinics and wait their turn until the doctor is free to see them. In the past there has been considerable criticism from patients about the length of time they have had to wait. Some months ago a number of initiatives were put into place to try to improve the situation. The clinic has found that under the new arrangements the average (mean) waiting time is 12 minutes with a standard deviation of 7 minutes. The doctors at the clinic are keen to ensure that these initiatives have a long-term effect on reducing waiting time and want to monitor the situation to ensure that the problem does not reoccur.

We have been asked to draft a report to the doctors explaining how, with samples of 25 patients, you could set up an effective monitoring system to assess whether waiting time complies with this level of performance in the future.

Your report might run as follows:

The clinic has established a performance level of 12 minutes for average patient waiting time. Clearly this does not mean that every patient will wait exactly 12 minutes before seeing the doctor. Some will wait more, some will wait less. However, it is an indication of the average time a patient might expect to wait. Naturally, on a day-by-day or week-by-week basis there will be some variation around this average due to the inherent variability of the clinic's activities (since we cannot guarantee that every patient will require exactly the same time with the doctors). If, in one week, the average time is found to be 13 minutes, this does not necessarily mean we are failing to meet the 12-minute target in the long term. However, it is important that we monitor our performance in this context to ensure the waiting time of 12 minutes does not worsen. Everyone in the clinic is clearly very busy, so we need an easy-to-use monitoring system to enable us to check waiting time performance. We are proposing that this is done cost-effectively based on a sample of 25 patients each week. The clinic reception staff should then take a random sample of 25 patients each week as they enter the clinic (spread over the days the clinic is open and also spread during each day to give as representative a sample as possible). Each of these patients should be given a small card noting their arrival time as they enter the clinic and asked to leave the card with the doctor. The doctor can then note the time they actually saw the patient on the card. At the end of the week the reception staff can work out the average waiting time for the sample of patients and plot it on the attached chart.

The idea behind the chart is a simple one (although supported by some complex statistical theory). Using some statistical principles, we know that our weekly monitoring is based only on a sample of 25 patients (out of several hundred we might see each week), so we must make allowance for this. Using these same statistical principles we can calculate how much variation, in minutes, from the target of 12 minutes we might normally get for each sample of 25 patients. These allow us to construct what are known as warning limits and action limits, shown on the chart (Figure 8.11).

If that week's result is above the upper line marked Action Limit it is highly likely the average waiting time in the clinic as a whole is higher than the target of 12 minutes (even though our result is based on only 25 patients). In fact we would be over 99 per cent sure if this were to happen that we were no longer meeting the overall target of 12 minutes. Action will then need to be taken to find out what has happened that week to cause substandard performance. If the week's result is above

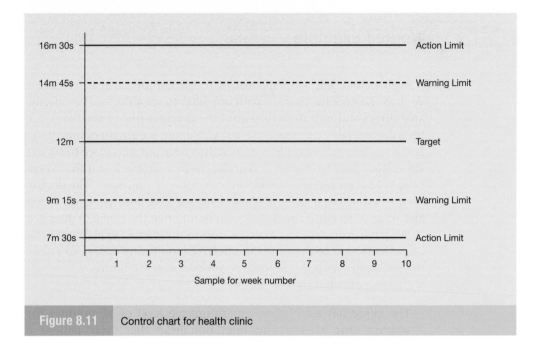

	Sample for week number

Figure 8.11   Control chart for health clinic

the upper line marked Warning Limit but below that marked Action Limit, this should be taken as an indication that average waiting time might be higher than the target of 12 minutes. It is recommended if this happens that another sample be organised as soon as possible to confirm, one way or another, whether the target is still being met. There are also action and warning limits shown below the target time. Although sample results falling below these lines are not a problem in the sense of patients waiting longer than the average of 12 minutes they do indicate a fundamental change in the average waiting time. The situation should be investigated to see what has occurred to enable waiting times to fall.

The task for the reception staff each week is a fairly easy one of handing time cards to 25 patients, collecting the cards back in, and at the end of the week working out a simple average from the 25 times recorded. They then need to plot this time on the chart. If the time for that week is within the two warning limits, no further action is needed. If it is outside the warning or action limits then the reception staff need to bring this immediately to the attention of the clinic manager.

 # Summary

In this chapter we have introduced a number of techniques that can readily be applied to the area of quality management in both production and service organisations. The track record of these techniques, in terms of the range of organisations who have found them of considerable benefit, is considerable and none of the techniques requires any great quantitative knowledge as such, which is one of their considerable strengths. In the quality area more than any other, though, it must also be stressed that quality management is about more than the application of these types of technique to problems and issues. This is illustrated with the Six Sigma approach adopted by many organisations.

Adventures in Six Sigma: how the problem-solving technique helped Xerox

Like many other US companies, Xerox was introduced to Six Sigma through its interactions with General Electric. The financial services to biotechnology conglomerate adopted the metrics-mad process improvement technique in the mid-1990s. Thanks to its size and influence, it has served as an effective missionary.

Anne Mulcahy's conversion came as she was negotiating the outsourcing of Xerox's troubled billing and collections operation to GE Capital. She recalls: "I remember sitting there and watching the discipline with which [the GE team] defined the problem, scoped the problem and attacked it from a Six Sigma perspective. I remember feeling for the first time that the problem would be fixed."

The precise definition of Six Sigma quality is an error rate of 3.4 per million. More important than the exact number, however, is an approach to problem solving that emphasizes small teams, measurement and economic return.

Quality improvement techniques were by no means new to Xerox. In the 1980s, it was one of the first US companies to adopt Total Quality Management (TQM) as it fought to turn back the tide of Japanese competition.

As an up-and-coming manager, Ms Mulcahy experienced TQM first hand. "The financial metrics were not as precise with TQM," she recalls. "Six Sigma is very rigid and very disciplined by comparison. Every project is managed with economic profit metrics. There is none of the squishy stuff."

The "squishy stuff" is the emphasis in TQM on consensus building that, while part of an earnest desire to replicate the best of Japanese management, did not always play well at US companies.

Ms Mulcahy is also at pains to point out that Xerox practises Lean Six Sigma, a variation that asks managers to think not only how processes can be improved but also how waste can be reduced: "Lean is an important nuance. The leaning process begins with taking out waste, working out where value gets added and where it does not. For big companies, this is very important."

While companies generally adopt Six Sigma to improve efficiency, converts insist that there are other benefits. The introduction of a company-wide approach to project management is reckoned to break down barriers between departments, and make it easier to work with suppliers and customers. Ms Mulcahy says: "The reality of our business is that in order to compete you have to find ways to deliver 8, 9, 10 per cent productivity improvements every single year. You only get there if you have a systemic approach."

Source: *Financial Times*, 23 September 2005.

The 'sigma' in Six Sigma refers to the standard deviation which is used to measure the variability around the mean of the process. The error rate of 3.4 defects per million comes from Normal probability calculations.

Useful online resources

Detailed below are some internet resources that may be useful. Many have further links to other sites. An updated version is available from the accompanying website (**www.pearsoned.co.uk/wisniewski**). In addition, I would be grateful for details of other websites that have been found to be useful.

www.asq.org – American Society for Quality

www.csom.umn.edu/Page1293.aspx – Juran Centre for Leadership in Quality

www.isixsigma.com/tt/ – Six Sigma quality tools and templates

www.qualityamerica.com – Quality America website

www.businessballs.com/sixsigma.htm – Six Sigma summary

QMDM IN ACTION
Hewlett-Packard

Hewlett-Packard is an internationally known company manufacturing and selling under its own name a variety of computers, computer peripherals and related equipment and instruments. The company recognised a number of years ago that a key element of its corporate strategy had to be quality. To a large extent such a focus was driven by two external factors:

● changing customer expectations, whereby what customers expected the company to provide was changing in terms of rising standards and expectation;

● competition, where the external environment in which the company operated generated increased worldwide competition in the electronics industry.

Variants of quality management have been around in the company for almost 20 years. A Japanese subsidiary, Yokagawa Hewlett-Packard, has been focusing on total quality control (TQC) since 1977 largely in order to be able to compete in its home market of Japan. In addition to winning the coveted Deming Prize in 1982, a number of specific achievements were identified:

● a reduction in assembly defects from 0.4 per cent to 0.04 per cent;

● a reduction in the lead time associated with product manufacture from eight weeks to two weeks;

● reduction in product warranty costs from 6.5 per cent to around 1 per cent per 1000 US dollars of value produced.

The company concluded that such a focus on TQC would not only bring quality benefits but also contribute to company performance in terms of profitability and growth. From 1985 considerable effort was focused on introducing basic TQC techniques and tools to all levels of employees. The UK operations of Hewlett-Packard have been in existence over 30 years, with a headquarters in Berkshire and

manufacturing operations near Bristol and Edinburgh. Approximately 4000 people are employed directly and the company has a UK sales turnover of around £600 million. A comprehensive training, development and awareness programme was instituted. The importance of quality and customer satisfaction was incorporated into employee-induction programmes, a three-day quality skills course was developed for key staff, and all other employees were able to attend a quality-awareness course. On the quality skills course various techniques were introduced: the use of histograms, line and scatter diagrams, Pareto charts, control charts and cause–effect diagrams. Figure 8.12 shows such a diagram from the UK Customer Support Group when assessing reported customer problems. Virtually all employees attending the TQC skills course found little difficulty understanding the techniques introduced and, even though the focus was on a service environment rather than a manufacturing one, 87 per cent of those attending the course had used Pareto charts and 80 per cent had used control charts when the programme was evaluated at a later date. Overall, employees developed considerable motivation to practise the quality principles and quality techniques to which they were introduced. This motivation was partly related to the contribution this made to overall business performance but also to the benefits brought to the individual's own work environment.

The above application is based on the articles:

'The Role of Training in Total Quality Implementation', P Walley and E Kowalski, Journal of European Industrial Training **16** (3), 1992, pp 25–31.

'The Quality Focus at Hewlett-Packard', JA Young, Journal of Business Strategy, **5** (3), 1985, pp 6–9.

'Employee Receptivity to Total Quality', E Kowalski and P Walley, International Journal of Quality and Reliability Management, **10** (1), 1993, pp 23–37.

I am grateful to MCB University Press for permission to reproduce Figure 8.12.

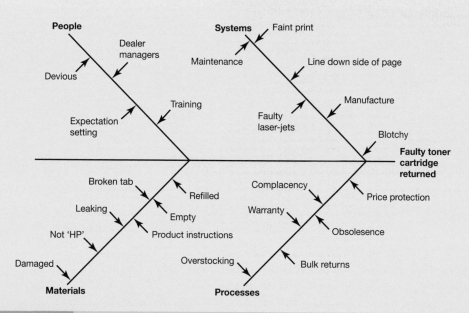

People
Dealer managers
Devious
Expectation setting
Training

Systems   Faint print
Maintenance
Line down side of page
Manufacture
Faulty laser-jets
Blotchy

Faulty toner cartridge returned

Broken tab
Refilled
Leaking
Empty
Not 'HP'
Product instructions
Damaged
Overstocking
Materials

Complacency
Price protection
Warranty
Obsolesence
Bulk returns
Processes

 Figure 8.12   A sample cause-and-effect or Ishikawa diagram from the Hewlett-Packard UK sales region

Copyright held by MCB University Press. Taken from Employee Receptivity to Total Quality', E Kowalski and P Walley, *International Journal of Quality and Reliability Management*, **10**(1), 1993.

? Exercises

1 To try to illustrate how effective the Ishikawa diagram can be, focus on one particular problem that you are having in your studies. The problem might be a general one, it might relate to one subject or it might relate to one topic in a subject area. Apply the fishbone principles to try to determine the factors contributing to that problem. Such factors might include lack of study time, poor teaching, a poor textbook and domestic pressures. When you have constructed the diagram, use it to try to identify how the problems might be resolved.

2 A large manufacturing firm is concerned about lost production: that is, production capability that was not utilised for a variety of reasons. One of the causes of such lost production has been identified as employees taking time off work because of illness. Last year the firm estimated that around 53 000 units of production were lost each week due to this cause, with a standard deviation of 4800. The Personnel Department has decided to monitor, on a weekly basis, a small sample of 15 employees on the production line in terms of their attendance at work and to translate this into a weekly production loss figure for the company. For the first eight weeks the results are as follows:

Estimated lost production (000 units)

Week 1	50.3
Week 2	53.9
Week 3	55.6
Week 4	51.2
Week 5	51.0
Week 6	50.9
Week 7	48.7
Week 8	49.3

(a) Using this information construct a control chart for Personnel to use.

(b) Draft a short report outlining the potential for using control charts on a regular basis in this context.

(c) Explain what is meant by Type I and Type II errors in this context.

3 A hospital laboratory has the task of screening blood samples of patients and producing a summary report for clinicians. Because of the limitations of equipment, staff training and time, the laboratory manager knows that there is an error rate involved in the production of such reports. It is estimated that 4 per cent of such reports produced are incorrect in terms of their results. Over the past few months the lab has been under increased pressure from clinicians to reduce the turn-around time in the production of the test reports. The manager is concerned that this improvement has been at the expense of an increase in the error rate. Accordingly, using the principles of statistical process control, it has been decided on an experimental basis to take samples of 50 reports a day and double-check them to monitor the error rate. The results for the first two weeks are as follows:

Error rate	Percentage
Day 1	6.9
Day 2	4.3
Day 3	6.6
Day 4	5.2
Day 5	6.8
Day 6	8.5
Day 7	8.9
Day 8	9.5
Day 9	9.8
Day 10	11.5

(a) Construct a suitable control chart for use by the lab.

(b) Do you think that control charts would be useful and reliable in this context?

4 A public transport organisation has had a reputation for many years of caring little for its customers – the passengers it carries. In particular, the enquiry office has had a particularly poor reputation. New management have decided to try to improve the office's performance and image, and staff have recently been sent on a series of training programmes to help develop a customer focus. The organisation has a formal complaints procedure and, before the training programme, the enquiry office typically received around 15 complaints a week, about its service, staff attitudes and the accuracy of information given to passengers. The office manager has asked for advice on how the office's performance can be monitored on a regular basis. Draft a short report outlining some of the options that are available in terms of monitoring this aspect of performance.

9 Forecasting I: Moving Averages and Time Series

Learning objectives

By the end of this chapter you should be able to:

- understand the different approaches to forecasting that can be applied in business
- calculate a trend using moving averages
- calculate and interpret seasonal components
- calculate and interpret seasonally adjusted data

Business organisations put a high value on reliable information about the future: future sales, future costs, future patterns of consumer demand, future prices of supplies. As we have seen in earlier chapters, many management problems arise simply because the future is unknown or has a high degree of uncertainty about it. Not surprisingly, considerable attention has been focused on methods of trying to predict future values of some key business variable. In this chapter we will look at the general principles of forecasting and introduce a number of common techniques. In the next chapter we shall extend the coverage of forecasting to include the technique of regression. As we shall see in this chapter many important business variables follow some regular, and potentially predictable, pattern over the period of a year. From a management perspective it is important to be able to quantify such a pattern to help efficiency, performance and forward planning.

The Need for Forecasting

To some extent the question as to why business organisations need to forecast should be largely rhetorical at this stage in the text. The increasing complexity of the environment in which organisations have to function and survive, together with changing demands and expectations, implies that every organisation needs to establish some view as to future values of key variables, even though these key variables are different for each organisation. As with other techniques, forecasting is primarily concerned with trying to reduce the uncertainty that exists about some part of the future. Managers in an organisation hope that by applying forecasting techniques they can generate additional information about the future that may help them assess the future consequences of existing decisions and to evaluate the consequences of alternatives. What is likely to happen to sales if we maintain our current pricing policy? What is likely to happen if we increase the price by 5 per cent, or 10 per cent? Will a hospital be able to provide an effective and efficient health care system with existing staff levels given future demographic changes? How will altering the staffing mix affect the level of service that we can provide?

It is important to appreciate the role of forecasting in the wider decision-making process. Figure 9.1 illustrates this. At the centre of this process lie the decisions that the manager must make. These will be strongly influenced by the organisation's chosen strategy with regard to its future direction, priorities and activities. Such decisions logically lead to the establishment of a planned performance – what the organisation is expected to achieve in the way of products/services provided, together with all the concomitant results. However, influencing such decisions will also be the information generated from the forecasting methods adopted by the organisation. Given that, in principle, these are designed to tell us something about the future then we would expect management decisions to take such forecasts into account along with all other

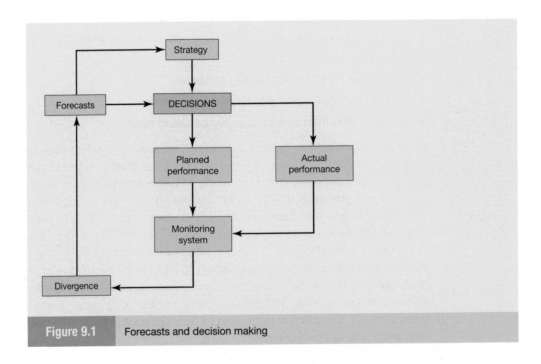

Figure 9.1   Forecasts and decision making

factors influencing such decisions. Depending on the variables being forecast, the methods adopted for forecasting and the perceived accuracy of the forecasts, such information may also affect the strategy formulation process itself. The organisation will clearly need to establish some monitoring system to compare planned performance with actual. Where, inevitably, some divergence between the two occurs then this should be fed back into the forecasting process. Given that predicted performance was

Narrow-bodied jets to take 70% of market

FT

By Michael Skapinker, Aerospace Correspondent

Almost 70 per cent of new aircraft ordered over the next 20 years will be narrow-bodied jets carrying fewer than 230 passengers, Boeing of the US said yesterday.

The forecast, carried in Boeing's annual survey of the aircraft market, comes as the US company and Airbus Industrie, its European rival, study plans for the introduction of "super-jumbo" jets with 550 seats or more.

Boeing said it expected airlines to spend $1,100bn on 15,900 aircraft between now and 2015, of which only 10 per cent would be of the size of a Boeing 747 or larger. A 747 carries about 400 passengers. Even measured by value, larger aircraft would account for only 23 per cent of airline spending on aircraft over the next decades.

Boeing plans to build an extended version of the 747 – the 747-600X – capable of carrying over 500 passengers. Airbus is studying the development of the A3XX, which could carry 550 or more.

Boeing said the demand for large aircraft would become more apparent after 2015 than it is today. The Boeing 747 accounts at present for three-quarters of capacity on flights across the Pacific and between Asia and Europe.

Air travel: the future fleet

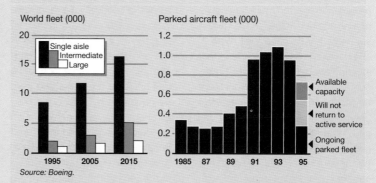

Source: Boeing.

Across the North Atlantic, however, the 747 accounts for only one-third of seats.

Boeing said the demand for an aircraft larger than the 747 would come largely from the Asia-Pacific region where airports were congested and flight frequencies were limited by international agreements. By 2015, these problems would become more acute, Boeing said.

Smaller single-aisle aircraft would account for 68 per cent of deliveries by 2015, Boeing said. In value terms, smaller aircraft would make up 41 per cent of airline spending.

China is expected to be one of the biggest markets for single-aisle aircraft, for use on domestic routes and shorter regional flights.

This follows the pattern of the US, whose airlines are among the biggest buyers of small aircraft. The aircraft are used on "hub and spoke" systems, where passengers are flown from smaller towns and cities to large airports where they catch connecting flights. Smaller aircraft are also used by low-cost carriers providing budget flights between cities.

Boeing said Europe would become a bigger market for single-aisle aircraft as the aviation market was liberalised, although some passengers would be lost to high-speed train services.

The fast-growing segment of the market, however, will be intermediate-sized aircraft, such as the Boeing 777. These will account for 22 per cent of deliveries and 36 per cent of spending by 2015.

Source: *Financial Times*, 7 March 1996, p 5.

Every organisation has to think about the future and, somehow, forecast key variables.

not achieved – no matter whether the divergence was large or small and no matter the causes of such divergence – new forecasts will need to be produced which begin the whole cycle again. As we shall see, there is no one ideal approach to forecasting for any organisation. Alternative methods and approaches exist and a manager needs to be aware of what is possible as well as what is feasible in this context.

Fixing a forecasting model that ain't broke

FT

By Alec Chrystal

It would be hard to question the proposition that the monetary policy regime in place in the UK for the last six years has worked well. Who in 1997 would have predicted that inflation would stay within 1 percentage point of the 2.5 per cent target for the next six years, that unemployment would steadily fall and that output growth would remain close to its potential throughout? Yet this is what has happened. Inflation targeting with an independent monetary policy committee has enabled the Bank of England to deliver low inflation and a stable economy. Can it last?

There has been some comment on the fact that the composition of the MPC will change this year. But these changes are unlikely to lead on their own to worse policy decisions. After all, the entire committee was new in 1997 and yet it established its credibility very quickly. The core of the MPC will remain in place. It has accumulated considerable experience, as has the Bank team that advises it.

Of greater concern, perhaps, is the Bank's plan to start using a new forecasting model in the near future. One cannot help but wonder why the model is to be changed when the whole process has been working so well.

A forecasting model is a set of equations that predicts the movement over time of the key variables in the economy, such as consumer spending, gross domestic product and inflation. The coefficients on these equations are estimated on the available economic data. Forecasts are generated from these equations by adding assumptions about external variables, such as the oil price and world trade, and then running the equations forward. Changing the model will inevitably alter the forecast. If it did not there would be no point in changing it.

The forecast round preceding the MPC's May interest rate decision will use the old and new models in parallel, but after that the new model is on its own. The committee has repeatedly denied that there is any mechanical link between the forecast and the interest rate decisions. However, a glance at the fan charts in past quarterly Inflation Reports would suggest that the forecast is an important influence on monetary policy decisions. The central projection at two years out is always remarkably close to 2.5 per cent. Were it not so the interest rate would almost certainly have been changed prior to publication.

One criticism of the MPC's previous forecasting record has been that it over-estimated inflation for several quarters in a row in 2000 and 2001. How much of this was due to a bias in the model is debatable. The explanation given at the time was persistent under-estimation of the value of sterling, an external variable. This could have been due to mistaken judgments or unexpected events, rather than a faulty model.

Nonetheless, the Bank has been working for some time on a new forecasting model. The motive is to keep up with economic theory rather than to correct for forecast failures of the old model. With intellectual coherence the objective, the changes are expected to be substantial.

Keeping up with latest developments in the economics profession is a good idea in itself. But applying a new model to inform policy decisions may be dangerous unless the changes have been fully analysed, are widely understood and accepted as valid. The new model has not yet been fully tested. Yet by the summer it is supposed to provide the main vehicle for British monetary policy.

This may all work out fine. But what if the new model turns out to provide worse forecasts than the old one? To avoid this possibility, and in the interest of maintaining transparency and credibility, it would be desirable for the Bank to publish the new model and a run of forecast comparisons well ahead of the old model being ditched. Also it might be sensible (although expensive) to run the two models in parallel for rather longer than currently planned until it becomes clear, not just to the MPC but also to the public at large, that the new model is at least as reliable as the old.

The dangers of a hasty switch of forecasting models are heightened by modifications to the national accounts from this summer. The Office for National Statistics plans to re-base the volume measures of national activity. This could change the interpretation of the recent performance of the economy in unpre-

dictable ways. The Bank will be sailing on an unusually choppy sea and perhaps in a thick fog in the months ahead. Worries about the first mate taking over from the old skipper may be misplaced, but changing the pilot, the navigation device and the local landmarks all at once seems a bit rash.

Source: *Financial Times*, 20 February 2003, p 17

Accuracy of analysts' profits forecasts hits record low

By Dan Roberts in New York

Analysts are getting it wrong. The accuracy of Wall Street earnings forecasts has fallen to a record low as tighter disclosure rules make it harder for over-cautious research analysts to gauge the strength of the recovery.

Consensus forecasts under-estimated the rapid growth in quarterly earnings by an average of six percentage points in 2003 – the highest margin of error since Thomson First Call began detailed tracking in 1994 and nearly double the normal discrepancy.

Another study to be published this week by Parson Consulting shows many individual estimates even wider of the mark. One-third of big companies missed forecasts by more than 10 per cent in the third quarter, again mostly due to under-estimates.

Analysts defend their record by pointing to the fact that this was the

first sustained period of growth since new disclosure regulations stopped companies privately guiding analysts before earnings releases.

"This shows our independence," said the head of equity research at one top-tier bank. "The most important thing is that we get the long-term direction right, not that we are spoon-fed precise numbers."

But the severe criticism of past links between analysts and investment bankers may have encouraged a degree of caution about earnings growth and price targets.

"There is no doubt people have tended to be a lot more cautious about their price targets since the days when Henry Blodget said Amazon would hit $400 and this could be correlated with the accuracy of earnings forecasts," added the research chief.

It is also clear that "beating the street" still moves markets.

Ericsson shares, for example, jumped 12 per cent on Friday after the company reported earnings twice as high as analysts were expecting. Cisco shares fell 9 per cent on Wednesday after its strong results beat consensus forecasts by just 6 per cent. Both companies gave cautious guidance for 2004 orders, yet markets focused on the Ericsson "surprise" and Cisco's "caution".

But accuracy of forecasts is increasingly in question. Thomson First Call analysis shows that the number of consensus estimates that prove to be spot on has fallen to just one in five, the lowest level since widespread analyst conference calls became common in the mid-1990s.

Source: *Financial Times*, 9 February 2004.

And getting it wrong is high-risk!

Approaches to Forecasting

It will be useful at this stage to provide an overview of the general approaches that can be adopted to forecasting. Figure 9.2 summarises some of the more common. One of the most basic distinctions is between forecasting approaches which are primarily *qualitative* as opposed to those which are primarily *quantitative*. The distinction is sometimes misleading since some of the qualitative approaches will generate numerical results and some of the quantitative approaches will be based on subjective, qualitative assumptions.

Qualitative approaches

A number of different approaches fall under this heading and, because they typically involve a considerable element of subjective assessment, they are often categorised as judgemental methods.

Personal assessment

This is probably the most widely used method in practice although this is not necessarily an argument supporting its reliability. Based on his or her own judgement, an individual produces some forecast of the future situation. In some circumstances, such an assessment can be relatively reliable and accurate. It is particularly appropriate in an operational environment when asking the 'front-line' staff their view of the immediate future: whether a particular machine will need repair or maintenance in the next month; whether stock levels are likely to last until the next delivery takes place; whether the appointments system in a health clinic will be adequate for the number of patients next month.

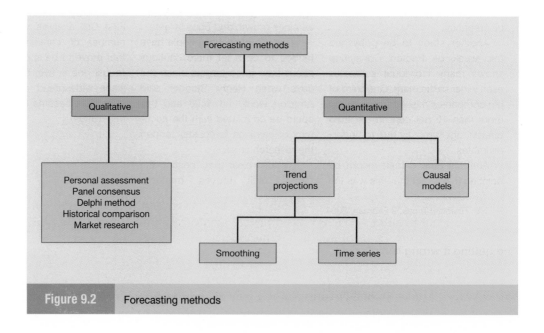

Figure 9.2   Forecasting methods

Activity 9.1

What difficulties do you see arising from such a forecasting approach?

The problem with such personal assessments, however, is that as well as relying on an individual's experiences and knowledge (which can be very variable) they are also affected by that person's prejudices and ignorance. The machine operator may not be aware of problems that have arisen with other machines of the same type and age; the stock control assistant may be unaware of a planned increase in production which will deplete stock levels rapidly next week; the health clinic receptionist may be unaware of a health education campaign about to be launched. Nevertheless, such personal assessments should not be arbitrarily discounted. They have their place, particularly in short-term, operational areas. They can also serve a useful function in cross-checking forecasts produced by other methods. Having developed some extensive and expensive computer-based forecasting model, it is frequently worthwhile checking the results produced by such a model against such personal assessments to help validate the more sophisticated approach.

Panel consensus

To try to take advantage of personal experience in the forecasting process and, at the same time, reduce the prejudices and ignorance that may exist in one person's view of the future, it may be possible to develop a panel consensus view of the future value of some variable. Such an approach collects together a group of individuals and in a structured format tries to develop a shared idea of the view among the group, encouraging them to share information, opinions and assumptions. Such an approach can be particularly productive in areas where the organisation has little comparable historical data: for example where an organisation is launching a radically different product, or service, or moving into an untested part of the market. The difficulty with such an approach, however, is that it is very dependent on group dynamics and frequently requires a skilled facilitator to 'manage' the process of developing a consensus.

Delphi method

The Delphi method adopts a similar approach to the panel consensus by once again attempting to use the collective experience and judgement of a group of experts. The difference, however, lies in how the group consensus is reached. In the Delphi method the experts never actually meet and, typically, do not know who the other panel members are. Each expert is given an initial questionnaire to complete relating to the area under investigation. A summary is then produced from all the questionnaires and this summary distributed to each expert, who is given the opportunity of revising the responses to the questionnaire in the light of this summary of the group's views. This process is repeated until either an adequate consensus is reached or an agreed number of iterations have been completed. Typically, the Delphi method is used to produce a narrow range of forecasts rather than a single view of the future.

Historical comparison

Under limited circumstances it may be possible to produce forecasts based on observed patterns of some similar variable in the past. Many products and services, for example,

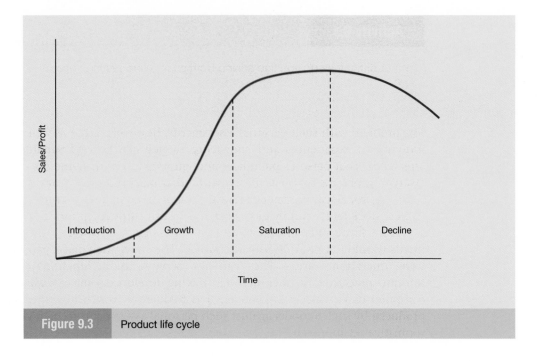

| Figure 9.3 | Product life cycle |

will tend to follow the life-cycle process illustrated in Figure 9.3. A new product, for example, follows a well-defined series of phases: the introduction phase, where customers and the market are becoming familiar with the product/service; the growth phase, where, if the product is successful, rapid growth will be experienced in terms of demand for the product/service; a saturation phase, where demand stabilises as the market reaches saturation point; and a decline phase as demand enters a period of relatively rapid decline.

Consider an organisation which has launched a new product and is trying to predict future sales. If product sales have reached the saturation phase of the life cycle then it would be foolhardy to predict that future sales will continue at this plateau level: they are likely to decline at some stage in the future. The trick, of course, is to try to predict accurately when this downturn will occur. It may be possible to do this by turning to a similar product which has already reached the decline phase and, using this historical data, assess the likely pattern of demand for the existing product. To illustrate, consider the problem facing a local authority. The manager of leisure services has noticed a recent explosion in the number of young people in the area with rollerblade roller skates. Because of pressures from parents, elected representatives and the police about the dangers of youngsters rollerblading on the roads and highways, the manager is under pressure to provide off-road facilities for these youngsters. The difficulty the manager faces is trying to assess, given a declining budget, whether this is just another fad that will pass with time or whether it is likely to be a continuing feature of young people's leisure patterns in the future. What the manager may be able to do is to assess the future with reference to some comparable historical analogy, for example the skateboard 'boom' in the 1980s or that of BMX bikes in the 1990s. These leisure products followed a typical life-cycle pattern and the manager was under comparable pressure then to provide off-road skateboard and BMX facilities. Assuming that adequate data was kept, it might be possible to track the skateboard and BMX phenomena over their life-cycle timings and assess the current rollerblade position.

Market research

The final qualitative approach is that based around market research. We have discussed the potential for such an approach in general terms already in Chapter 7. It is evident, however, that for the examples used so far in this chapter, market research could have provided information to help assess the future situation.

Quantitative approaches

Quantitative approaches tend to fall into two general categories: *trend projections* and *causal models*. The rest of this chapter will focus on common methods of trend projections, while causal models will be the focus of Chapter 10. Suffice it to say for the present that trend projections are concerned with taking some observed historical pattern for some variable and projecting this pattern into the future using a quantitative approach. Simply, we take the trend in the variable we have observed in the past and project it into the future. Such an approach does not attempt to suggest why the variable in question will take some future value. This is left to the application of a causal model, which tries to identify factors which influence the variable in some way or cause it to behave in some predictable manner.

Trend Projections

Trend projections methods themselves fall into two broad categories: smoothing, or moving average, methods and time-series decomposition. We shall begin by looking at moving average methods.

Moving averages

Given that we are concerned with observing the movement of some variable over time and trying to project this movement into the future, it seems logical to try to smooth out any irregular pattern in the historical values of the variable and use this as the basis of a future projection. The simplest way of doing this is to calculate a series of moving averages. Consider the data in Table 9.1 and the corresponding graph of the data in Figure 9.4.

The data relates to the weekly sales of some product. It can be seen from the graph that over this 15-week period sales have been relatively stable (showing no marked upward or downward pattern) but have fluctuated erratically on a week-by-week basis. The method of simple moving averages attempts to smooth out these irregularities to calculate the underlying trend and uses this smoothed value as the forecast. For example, suppose we are currently at the beginning of Week 3 and are trying to provide some numerical estimate of that week's sales.

Activity 9.2

How would you suggest we estimate sales in Week 3, given we have actual data only for Weeks 1 and 2?

Table 9.1	Weekly sales

Week	Sales units
1	246
2	256
3	255
4	248
5	263
6	254
7	256
8	258
9	249
10	257
11	259
12	243
13	255
14	251
15	253

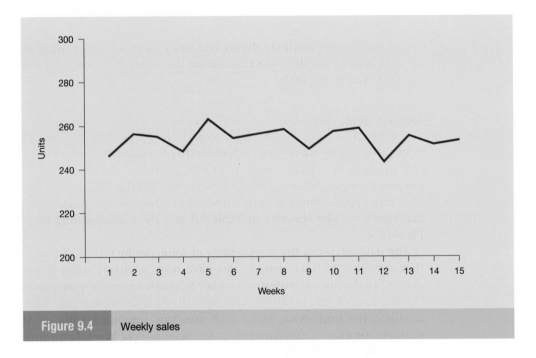

Figure 9.4	Weekly sales

The logical thing to do would be to average the data we have on actual sales for Weeks 1 and 2 and use this as our forecast for Week 3. This would give:

$$\text{Forecast} = \frac{246 + 256}{2} = 251$$

which, when compared with the actual for Week 3 of 255, is reasonably accurate. Clearly we could proceed in this way on a week-by-week basis. That is, for Week 4 we could produce a forecast which was an average of the first three weeks' sales, for Week 5 an average of the first four weeks' sales and so on. The problem with this approach is that over time it uses a lot of data (all the previous weeks' sales figures that are available) and it is not particularly responsive to recent changes in demand. For example, assume an 11-week period where, for the first 10 weeks, sales were all 250 units per week. In Week 11 sales jump to 5000. The forecast for Week 12 would be heavily weighted by the 10 weeks where sales were much lower than the last week's. For this reason it makes more sense to calculate a moving average rather than a simple average: that is, an average where we use a given number of the most recent weeks. For example, suppose we decided that each forecast would be an average of the two previous weeks' sales. The forecast series would then be that shown in Table 9.2. The forecast for Week 3 is the average of Weeks 1 and 2. The forecast for Week 4 is the average for Weeks 2 and 3 and so on through the series. You will also appreciate from the calculation why we refer to this as a *moving* average. In mathematical form the calculation is given as:

$$F_{t+1} = \frac{\Sigma(D_t + D_{t-1})}{n}$$

where F refers to the forecast and D to the actual data (sales). It will be worthwhile explaining the subscript notation we are using, as this is a common way of representing a moving-average calculation. We denote the time periods using the variable t, which in our example could take a value from 1 to 15. We require a forecast for the *next* time period, denoted as t + 1. The current period is then denoted as t and the previous period as t − 1. So, in our first calculation we would have:

t + 1	Week 3
t	Week 2
t − 1	Week 1

Table 9.2	Weekly sales and a two-week moving average	
Week	Sales	Two-week average forecast
1	246	–
2	256	–
3	255	251
4	248	255.5
5	263	251.5
6	254	255.5
7	256	258.5
8	258	255
9	249	257
10	257	253.5
11	259	253
12	243	258
13	255	251
14	251	249
15	253	253
16		252

and the first moving average would be found by the actual sales for Weeks 1 and 2 and dividing by n = 2. Clearly as we progress through the series t changes its numerical value. In this example we have n = 2. In other cases we might wish to average the series over a different number of periods: 3, 4, 5 … In other words n could take any numerical value. The expression for the moving average would then become, in general:

$$F_{t+1} = \frac{\Sigma(D_t + D_{t-1} + D_{t-2} + \cdots + D_{t-n+1})}{n}$$

The results of the forecasts are shown in Figure 9.5, together with the actual values. The forecasting method appears to perform reasonably well on a period-by-period basis, although there are one or two periods where our forecasts are relatively inaccurate. It will also be evident that in this example we used a moving average of n = 2 with no real justification as to why this particular average should be used. In practice this is quite a common situation: the choice of n is to some extent arbitrary. A larger value for n will base the forecast on a larger number of actual values but will also make the forecast relatively unresponsive to recent changes. On the other hand, a smaller value for n will make the forecast more responsive but may be oversensitive to random fluctuations in the variable from one period to the next.

Forecast errors

It will also be evident that we will need some method of assessing the overall accuracy of the forecasting method. The 'error', e, involved in the forecast can be defined as:

$$e_{t+1} = D_{t+1} - F_{t+1}$$

where the error is simply the difference between the actual value of the variable (once it can be observed) and the forecast. The error of the forecast for Week 3 is +4 (255 − 251) and that for Week 4 is −7.5 (248 − 255.5). Typically we wish to assess the

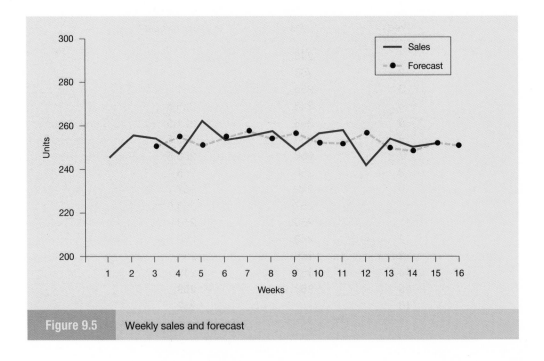

Figure 9.5   Weekly sales and forecast

Baby store's boom might just have got ahead of itself

By Alison Smith

A baby's progress rarely goes unremarked; and, in the past few months, the advances made by baby goods retailer Mothercare have been noticed as well. The shares have pretty well doubled since they slipped to 84½p in February – the lowest closing price in its three years as a separate entity. Yesterday, they ended the day close to the 12-month high of 169½p achieved this week. The rise owes something to a three-year recovery plan by Ben Gordon, chief executive. Alongside a still-chunky pre-tax loss revealed in May, he delivered some encouraging news: UK underlying sales were up in current trading and the gross margin was improving. Some analysts think Mothercare will creep

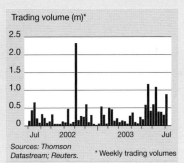

into profit again this year but the most bearish also has a small pre-tax loss pencilled in for next year. That forecast looks severe, as there should be some easy wins on the

margin. Yet it feels as though the share price rise has got ahead of itself – especially since Icelandic retailer Baugur reduced its stake and so lowered any hopes that it might bid for the group. Improved trading may come to justify this price level, or even a higher one, but current trading does not.

Source: Financial Times, 12 July 2003.

Moving averages can give an idea of the long-term trend. This one shows 200 consecutive trading days.

accuracy of the forecasting method over the entire period and there are two common methods of calculation: the *mean absolute deviation* or the *mean squared error.*

Mean absolute deviation

This method takes the absolute value of each individual error and averages these absolute errors over the entire period. The absolute value of a number is simply that number without a positive or negative sign. An absolute value is usually denoted with the symbol $|X|$ (known as a modulus) and would be pronounced 'the absolute value of X'. So, for example:

$$|-10| = |+10| = 10$$

that is, the absolute value of -10 and $+10$ is the same at 10. The calculations for our example are shown in Table 9.3.

The total of the absolute deviations is 68.5, giving a mean absolute deviation (MAD) of 5.27 (68.5/13). On average, then, the forecast is 5.27 units away from the actual value. The MAD calculations can be summarised as:

$$MAD = \frac{\Sigma|e|}{t}$$ where t is the total number of forecast errors.

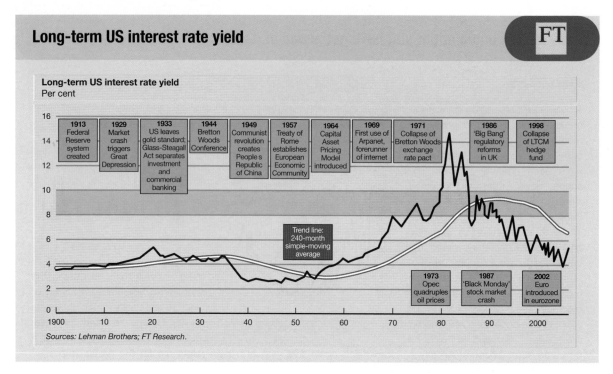

Long-term US interest rate yield

Long-term US interest rate yield
Per cent

Sources: Lehman Brothers; FT Research.

A trend line shows the long-term movement in a variable. This one uses 240 months – 20 years!

	Table 9.3	Mean absolute deviation		
Week	Sales	Forecast	Error	Absolute deviation
1	246	–	–	–
2	256	–	–	–
3	255	251	4	4
4	248	255.5	−7.5	7.5
5	263	251.5	11.5	11.5
6	254	255.5	−1.5	1.5
7	256	258.5	−2.5	2.5
8	258	255	3	3
9	249	257	−8	8
10	257	253.5	3.5	3.5
11	259	253	6	6
12	243	258	−15	15
13	255	251	4	4
14	251	249	2	2
15	253	253	0	0
16	–	252	–	–
Total				68.5

Activity 9.3

For this data series calculate a four-week moving average. Calculate the MAD of these forecasts and compare it with that of the two-week moving average.

Table 9.4 shows the forecasts produced by a four-week moving average and the corresponding error.

The MAD in this case is 4.70 (51.75/11), a marginal improvement over the two-week forecast. A four-period total seems to give slightly more accurate forecasts than a two-period model over the entire forecasting period.

Mean squared error

The MAD method produces a forecast error that is relatively straightforward to understand but it attaches no particular importance to large forecast errors. From Table 9.4 we see that there are large errors in Weeks 5 and 12. It may well be, from a management perspective, that we want to 'punish' a forecasting model that produces relatively large errors like these. As far as management is concerned, one such large error might be far more costly to the organisation than a series of smaller errors. Consider a scenario where one method produces a weekly absolute error of two units over, say, 10 weeks. Another method produces a weekly absolute error of zero units for nine weeks and 20 units for one week. Which is the better forecasting method? Clearly the MAD will be the same in both cases. Depending on circumstances, we might prefer a method

Table 9.4		Four-week moving averages		
Week	Sales	Four-week average forecast	Error	Absolute deviation
1	246	–	–	–
2	256	–	–	–
3	255	–	–	–
4	248	–	–	–
5	263	251.25	11.75	11.75
6	254	255.5	–1.5	1.5
7	256	255	1	1
8	258	255.25	2.75	2.75
9	249	257.75	–8.75	8.75
10	257	254.25	2.75	2.75
11	259	255	4	4
12	243	255.75	–12.75	12.75
13	255	252	3	3
14	251	253.5	–2.5	2.5
15	253	252	1	1
16	–	250.5	–	–
Total				51.75

Table 9.5		Mean squared error					

Week	Sales	Two-week average forecast	Error	Squared error	Four-week average forecast	Error	Squared error
1	246	–	–	–	–	–	–
2	256	–	–	–	–	–	–
3	255	251	4	16	–	–	–
4	248	255.5	–7.5	56.25	–	–	–
5	263	251.5	11.5	132.25	251.25	11.75	138.0625
6	254	255.5	–1.5	2.25	255.5	–1.5	2.25
7	256	258.5	–2.5	6.25	255	1	1
8	258	255	3	9	255.25	2.75	7.5625
9	249	257	–8	64	257.75	–8.75	76.5625
10	257	253.5	3.5	12.25	254.25	2.75	7.5625
11	259	253	6	36	255	4	16
12	243	258	–15	225	255.75	–12.75	162.5625
13	255	251	4	16	252	3	9
14	251	249	2	4	253.5	–2.5	6.25
15	253	253	0	0	252	1	1
16		252			250.5		
Total				579.25			427.8125

which has smaller individual errors. This is why, under some circumstances, we might prefer a different method of assessing forecasting accuracy: the *mean squared error*. Rather than taking the absolute value of each error, the errors are squared before summing and averaging. Table 9.5 shows the calculations for both moving-average models.

We then have:

MSE two-week model: 44.56 (579.25/13)
MSE four-week model: 38.89 (427.8125/11)

Note that the larger errors in both models have become more 'important' in the calculation. Effectively this error calculation penalises larger errors. Once again, the four-week model appears to perform better than the two-week. Note also that we cannot compare the MAD with the MSE for one particular model.

It is important to realise that moving-average models are unlikely to generate highly accurate forecasts by their very nature. However, this is relatively unimportant as long as such models are applied to problems where high accuracy is not the sole criterion. Consider the scenario of a supermarket with an in-store bakery. Each day the bakery supervisor must decide on that day's production, since unsold bakery items must be disposed of at a loss at the end of each day. Clearly in such a situation a number of criteria would apply to the use of a suitable forecasting model. It would need to be:

● simple to use

● quick to use

- easy to understand
- low cost
- reasonably accurate.

Given that such a model will be in use each day – and will be used to support decisions that must be made quickly – forecast accuracy is only one feature of a suitable model. The managerial consequences of forecast error in such a scenario are relatively minor. If the model produces a 'large' forecast error at the end of one day, the supermarket will not go out of business. On a daily basis accuracy should be reasonable. On the other hand, on a long-term basis we could not afford to use a model which repeatedly produced large errors as this would affect profitability.

QMDM IN ACTION
Cap Gemini Ernst & Young – improving forecasting accuracy

Cap Gemini Ernst & Young's client was a major UK mail order retailer. The client launches two mail-order catalogues each year with the majority of products shown in the catalogue being new each season. As a result, little previous sales history is available to develop sales forecasting and to support purchasing decisions (i.e. how many items of a particular product should the client contract to purchase from its suppliers). To compound the problem, there are relatively long lead times involved in the business and consequently contracts for large volumes of stock have to be negotiated well in advance of each season. The client already used a number of statistical forecasting models to predict sales demand. However, the client also knew that even small percentage improvements in the accuracy of these models could lead to large savings both by reducing lost sales (because a customer wanted to buy an item that was now sold out) and by reducing excess stock holdings.

By applying a combination of additional forecasting and quantitative techniques Cap Gemini Ernst & Young were able to segment the client's catalogue. Essentially, this enabled Cap Gemini Ernst & Young to identify groups of similarly behaving products. This in turn enabled the development of more accurate forecasting models for each of the different product groups.

Cap Gemini Ernst & Young worked closely with the client's own modelling group. They developed a

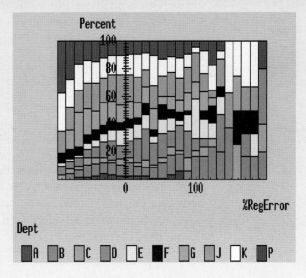

number of models to forecast demand at an individual product level for different parts of the catalogue. The models were developed using data from one previous season's sales and then used to forecast the following season so that actual demand could be compared with the statistical forecasts and the forecast errors identified. A business case was also made for integrating the new forecasting methods into the existing purchasing and stock management systems.

The initial models indicated a 3–5 per cent improvement in forecasting accuracy, which translated to between £8m and £15m in profit. A second phase of development indicated further improvements in accuracy of 2–3 per cent (worth c. £6m) from using new input variables.

The graph shows forecasting errors by product type. Such errors helped to identify groups of products which could be modelled separately to improve forecasting accuracy.

The benefits are as follows:

- Improved forecasting accuracy leading to a reduction in lost sales and in excess stock.
- Knowledge transfer to the client's own modelling team.

I am grateful to Cap Gemini Ernst & Young for permission to use this case study and to reproduce the figure shown. Further case study applications are available through their website: www.uk.capgemini.com/services/consulting/or/success_stories
Copyright is held by Cap Gemini Ernst & Young.

Exponential smoothing

The moving-average model developed in the previous section poses the manager two questions regarding its use and development.

- How many periods should be used in calculating the average?
- Is it logical in the context of the problem for each item used to have an equal weight in the calculation?

Answers to both these questions must be largely subjective. Daily data might use a seven-period average, weekly data a four-period average and so on. The second question may need some explanation. If we consider, say, a four-period moving average the formula:

$$F_{t+1} = \frac{\Sigma(D_t + D_{t-1} + D_{t-2} + D_{t-3})}{4}$$

can be rewritten as:

$$F_{t+1} = 1/4D_t + 1/4D_{t-1} + 1/4D_{t-2} + 1/4D_{t-3}$$

Each item in the average is given the same weight. In some circumstances it may seem more reasonable to allocate larger weights to more recent items, since the 'older' an item gets the less it reflects the current situation. Such a method is provided using *exponential smoothing*, a widely used moving-average method. The forecast formula for this method is given by:

$$F_{t+1} = \alpha D_t + (1 - \alpha)F_t$$

where α is a weight taking a value between 0 and 1. The method looks deceptively simple: the forecast for period $t + 1$ is some proportion (α) of the latest data item, D_t plus some proportion $(1 - \alpha)$ of the forecast produced for the previous period, F_t. To appreciate the formula fully it will be worthwhile exploring the mathematics which develop it. Consider what we require: a moving average where more recent items are given larger weights. This can be represented as:

$$F_{t+1} = w_1 D_t + w_2 D_{t-1} + w_3 D_{t-2} + \cdots + w_n D_{t-(n+1)}$$

where w represents the weights to be used. We impose two restrictions:

$$\Sigma w = 1$$
$$w_1 > w_2 > w_3 > \cdots$$

That is, the sum of the weights must total to 1, and each weight is larger than the weight immediately preceding it (to give more importance to later data items). From a management perspective we clearly have one important difficulty: how do we establish

Table 9.6	Exponential pattern: $\alpha = 0.2$			

Period			Weight	Cumulative
t	α	0.2	0.2	0.2
t − 1	$\alpha(1 - \alpha)$	0.2(0.8)	0.16	0.36
t − 2	$\alpha(1 - \alpha)^2$	$0.2(0.8)^2$	0.128	0.488
t − 3	$\alpha(1 - \alpha)^3$	$0.2(0.8)^3$	0.1024	0.5904
t − 4	$\alpha(1 - \alpha)^4$	.	0.08192	0.67232
t − 5	$\alpha(1 - \alpha)^5$	.	0.065536	0.737856
t − 6	$\alpha(1 - \alpha)^6$	.	0.052428	0.790284
t − 7	$\alpha(1 - \alpha)^7$	.	0.041943	0.832227
t − 8	$\alpha(1 - \alpha)^8$	.	0.033554	0.865782
t − 9	$\alpha(1 - \alpha)^9$	.	0.026843	0.892625
t − 10	$\alpha(1 - \alpha)^{10}$	.	0.021474	0.914100
t − 11	$\alpha(1 - \alpha)^{11}$	.	0.017179	0.931280
t − 12	$\alpha(1 - \alpha)^{12}$	.	0.013743	0.945024
t − 13	$\alpha(1 - \alpha)^{13}$	.	0.010995	0.956019
t − 14	$\alpha(1 - \alpha)^{14}$	.	0.008796	0.964815
t − 15	$\alpha(1 - \alpha)^{15}$	.	0.007036	0.971852
t − 16	$\alpha(1 - \alpha)^{16}$	.	0.005629	0.977482
t − 17	$\alpha(1 - \alpha)^{17}$	.	0.004503	0.981985
t − 18	$\alpha(1 - \alpha)^{18}$	.	0.003602	0.985588
t − 19	$\alpha(1 - \alpha)^{19}$	.	0.002882	0.988470
t − 20	$\alpha(1 - \alpha)^{20}$	$0.2(0.8)^{20}$	0.002305	0.990776

what the weights should be? The method used by this model is to use weights which follow what is known as an exponential pattern. Such exponential weights are denoted as α with α taking a value between 0 and 1. The exponential pattern is illustrated with $\alpha = 0.2$ in Table 9.6, which shows the weights for the first 20 periods.

In the first period the weight used is equal to α at 0.2. In the second period the weight is a proportion of the first. Given that $\alpha = 0.2$ then $(1 - \alpha) = 0.8$, with a resulting weight of 0.16. This second weight is less than the first (as required by the exponential-smoothing model). The third weight is then a proportion of the second and so on through the series. It can be seen that the individual weights gradually decrease over time, whereas the total of all the weights to that period, the cumulative, gradually increases and approaches to 1.0, again as required by the model. Figure 9.6 shows the graph of the individual weights over time with the decreasing pattern clearly visible. It is apparent that, had we continued our calculations past t − 20, further weights would have become smaller and smaller and the cumulative weight gradually closer to 1.0. But how does this help? Let us return to the general formula we had earlier and express it in terms of the exponential weights:

Equation 1

$$F_{t+1} = \alpha D_t + \alpha(1 - \alpha)D_{t-1} + \alpha(1 - \alpha)^2 D_{t-2} + \alpha(1 - \alpha)^3 D_{t-3}$$

$$+ \cdots + \alpha(1 - \alpha)^{n-1} D_{t-(n+1)}$$

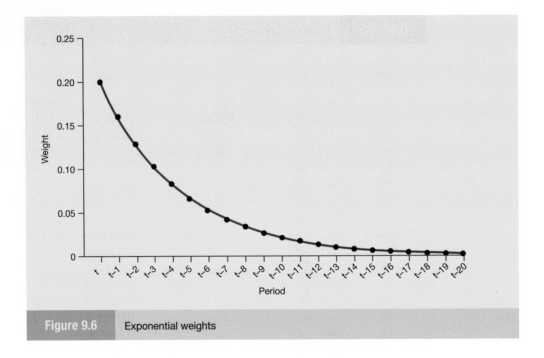

Figure 9.6   Exponential weights

However, this hardly seems to fit the criteria we established for the application of a moving-average model: simple, easy to use, etc. Let us consider some simple rearrangement of this formula. The term $(1 - \alpha)$ is common to all parts of the RHS of the equation except for the first term. This means that we can rewrite Equation 1 as:

Equation 2

$$F_{t+1} = \alpha D_t + (1 - \alpha)[\alpha D_{t-1} + \alpha(1 - \alpha)D_{t-2} + \alpha(1 - \alpha)^2 D_{t-3}$$
$$+ \cdots + \alpha(1 - \alpha)^{n-2}D_{t-(n+1)}]$$

Study Equation 2 carefully. It is exactly the same as the previous one except that we have taken the common term, $(1 - \alpha)$, out of the expression and reduced each subsequent weight accordingly.

Activity 9.4

Obtain a formula for producing a forecast for period t comparable to Equation 1.

The formula for the forecast for period t would be:

Equation 3

$$F_t = \alpha D_{t-1} + \alpha(1 - \alpha)D_{t-2} + \alpha(1 - \alpha)^2 D_{t-3} + \alpha(1 - \alpha)^3 D_{t-4}$$
$$+ \cdots + \alpha(1 - \alpha)^{n-2}D_{t-(n+1)}$$

Consider what this formula represents. F_{t+1} is the forecast for the next period: what we can regard as the new forecast. F_t is then the old forecast: what we forecast in the previous period for the current period. However, on inspection we can see that Equation 3 is identical to that part of Equation 2 that was in the square brackets [ ]. So, the formula for F_t in Equation 3 can be substituted into that for F_{t+1} in Equation 1 to give:

$$F_{t+1} = \alpha D_t + (1 - \alpha)F_t$$

which was what we stated the exponential-smoothing model to be in the first place. This diversion into the mathematics underpinning the model is important. On the face of it the model we have derived looks too simple. After all, it represents a forecast which is made up of a proportion of the latest item of data and a proportion of the previous forecast. However, by returning to the derivation of this formula we see that implicit in the calculation is the use of *all* historical data: every single D value is actually incorporated into the forecast calculation and each of them has a decreasing weight. So we have derived a moving-average model that actually uses all the available data even though it does not require this data for the calculation. We can make the model even easier to use, however. We have:

$$F_{t+1} = \alpha D_t + (1 - \alpha)F_t$$

Let us expand the term involving F_t to give:

$$F_{t+1} = \alpha D_t - \alpha F_t + F_t$$

and rearranging gives:

$$F_{t+1} = F_t + \alpha(D_t - F_t)$$

Activity 9.5

In non-mathematical terms what do the term F_t and the term $(D_t - F_t)$ represent?

F_t is clearly our 'old' forecast: the forecast we produced in the previous period for the current period. The term $(D_t - F_t)$ is the difference between the actual value of the variable in the current period and what we forecast it would be: the forecast error in other words. So, our sophisticated exponential-smoothing model, underpinned by some complex mathematics, actually simplifies to a method which says that:

New forecast = Old forecast + α(last forecast error)

So we have developed a model which is deceptively simple to use and understand, has considerable managerial logic and yet is underpinned by the appropriate mathematics. To illustrate the calculations let us return to the unit sales data we had for the earlier moving-average model. We shall use $\alpha = 0.2$ and to begin the process we shall assume that the forecast for Week 1 was the same as the actual at 246. The forecast error for this period will then be zero. The forecast for Week 2 will then be:

$$F_2 = F_1 + \alpha(D_1 - F_1) = 246 + 0.2(0) = 246$$

Clearly with no forecast error from Week 1 there is no reason to alter the forecast since it was 100 per cent accurate. We note that in Week 2 the actual sales were 256. The forecast for Week 3 then becomes:

$$F_3 = F_2 + \alpha(D_2 - F_2)$$

$$= 246 + 0.2(256 - 246)$$

$$= 246 + 2 = 248$$

The logic is clear. The forecast for Week 2 was an underestimate of what actually occurred. Accordingly, the forecast for the next week is increased by a proportion (0.2) of the underestimate. The forecasting model can proceed in this way on a period-by-period basis. In the event of an underestimate the next period forecast is increased and likewise in the event of an overestimate the next forecast is adjusted downward. Similarly, the larger the error, the larger the adjustment. But what of the choice of α at 0.2? α must take a value between 0 and 1 to satisfy the logic of the model. Other things being equal, the smaller the value of α then the less responsive the model becomes to forecast errors. In practice, values of α are typically between 0.15 and 0.35. Too high a value for α and we may be over-responding to a forecast error in one period. In practice we may also be able to gain an insight into an appropriate choice for α by applying varying values to historical data and assessing which gives a 'better' set of forecasts using either the MAD or the MSE that we introduced earlier.

Extensions to the exponential-smoothing model

To illustrate the principles of the model, we have examined a simple, and stable, variable which fluctuates over time but shows no other pattern in terms of either trend or seasonality. In practice many variables do exhibit such patterns. The exponential model can readily be adapted, however, to take such factors into account and the interested reader will find references in the Further Reading section at the end of the book.

Technical analysis: How to identify your friend the trend

FT

By Vince Heaney, FT.com site

The Chartists were a 19th century working-class movement seeking political reform, but in recent years the name has been applied to those who use technical analysis of price graphs to forecast stock price movements.

While the Chartist political movement ended in failure in 1848, three consecutive years of declining equity markets have bestowed credibility on technical analysis. In a market where the disgraced cheerleaders for the equity bubble have incurred fines from financial regulators and face reforms to curb their conflicts of interest, chartists have emerged as more dispassionate observers. Above all, they have been largely right in their bearish forecasts for equities.

Part of the appeal of technical analysis lies in its lack of bias; unlike long-only fund managers, chartists are not encumbered by the requirement always to be bullish or at worst neutral. The same chart data is available to both retail and professional investors – a far more level playing field than applies to company research.

Technical analysis works on the premise that, in an efficient market, prices will discount all the relevant information about the stock or index in question. History may not repeat itself exactly, but patterns of price development are repeated. Studying these patterns over time can offer insight into their future development.

Technical analysis attracts its fair share of purists – chartists who feel no need to consider fundamental economic factors, because their impact is fully discounted in the price. However, at the risk of causing apoplexy among the purists, I believe technical analysis can be used in conjunction with fundamental analysis. There is a place for macroeconomics and a study of corporate balance sheets. But the charts are useful in establishing the direction of the prevailing market trend and help investors to time entry and exit points through studies of market momentum.

Accepting that markets are not entirely random is one of the basic tenets of charting; in the "A" to "Z" of charting "T" is for trend and identifying the prevailing trend is one of the cornerstones of the approach. Markets do not travel in a smooth linear fashion. An uptrend is characterised by successively higher highs, while the periodic pullbacks form successively higher lows.

The reverse is true of a down-trend. The market reaches successively lower lows while the bear market rallies within the trend form a series of lower highs.

It is important to remember that there is a third possibility when looking for the prevailing trend. Markets spend a lot of time moving sideways in trading ranges. Many of the tools used by chartists are trend-following in nature, and do not perform as well in markets that are stuck in a range. The important lesson is not to try to invent a trend when one is not apparent.

Having established the direction of the prevailing trend the chartist can construct a trendline. In a rising market a line can be constructed underneath the successive lows formed by the pullbacks within the bull move. A valid trendline needs to have at least three points of contact. The larger the number of contact points and the longer it has been in existence, the more significant the line becomes. In a bear market the trendline will be a downward sloping line connecting the tops of the bear market rallies.

Some chartists believe that the closing price should be used when constructing trendlines, but I believe it is more valid to include the whole range of the day's activity.

The trendline is a very basic tool, but a powerful one. Pullbacks to an upward sloping trendline in a bull market can be used as buying opportunities by those who have missed out on the initial move. When a trendline is violated, it is an important early signal of a change in the direction of the trend. If the market closes below a trendline – one that has supported the market on repeated occasions over several months of a bull market – it is a signal that the technical trader ignores at his peril.

A further important tool of trend analysis is found under "M" for moving average, one of the most widely used technical indicators. A simple arithmetic mean of a previous run of closing prices is one of the most popular moving averages. The number of closing prices used is at the trader's discretion, but 10, 20 and 50-day averages are frequently used. A moving average

smoothes the trend, producing a line on the chart that lags behind the price data, but makes the trend more easily identifiable. Linearly and exponentially weighted averages can also be used to give more relevance to the most recent price data.

As well as a visual guide to the prevailing trend, moving averages are used to generate buy and sell signals. In a bull market, when the current price drops below the chosen moving average, a sell signal is generated. A shorter-term average follows the price data more closely, but will generate more false signals. To smooth out some of the false signals, two moving averages can be used, such as the 10-day and the 50-day. In the bull market example, the sell signal is generated when the shorter-term average crosses below the longer-term one.

A brief article can provide only a glimpse into technical analysis, but hopefully can provide the spark for further research into a powerful trading tool. If the "trend is your friend", you have to identify it first.

A variety of moving averages are used to try to predict stock price movement.

Time-Series Models

The issues of trend and seasonality take us logically to the next group of models, which are expressly concerned with forecasting under such conditions. Consider the data shown in Table 9.7 and the corresponding graph in Figure 9.7. The data refers to the number of inward passengers to the UK travelling by air on scheduled services during the period from the first quarter of 1995 to the fourth quarter of 2007. The graph illustrates a clear pattern in the data. Within each year there are peaks and troughs in terms of the numbers of passengers, with the third quarter each year showing the highest number and the first quarter the lowest. Such a pattern is not difficult to explain. We would expect a large proportion of such passengers to be travelling to the UK for a holiday or returning to the UK from a holiday abroad and would expect such holidays to be more frequent in the summer months – the third quarter of the year. In fact a time series such as this can be analysed in terms of a number of components.

Table 9.7		UK passenger movement by air: Inwards 1995 I to 2004 III (000s)			

Year	Quarter	Passengers	Year	Quarter	Passengers
1995	I	9 337		III	22 987
	II	13 335		IV	14 684
	III	16 545	2002	I	14 269
	IV	11 287		II	18 858
1996	I	10 262		III	23 347
	II	13 572		IV	16 702
	III	16 583	2003	I	15 150
	IV	12 075		II	19 430
1997	I	11 003		III	24 521
	II	14 926		IV	17 818
	III	18 147	2004	I	16 447
	IV	13 066		II	21 602
1998	I	11 929		III	26 213
	II	16 323		IV	19 006
	III	19 949	2005	I	18 030
	IV	14 251		II	23 299
1999	I	13 083		III	27 679
	II	17 249		IV	19 943
	III	21 137	2006	I	18 731
	IV	15 110		II	24 655
2000	I	13 665		III	28 642
	II	18 636		IV	20 554
	III	22 743	2007	I	19 409
	IV	16 034		II	25 064
2001	I	14 302		III	29 921
	II	17 782		IV	21 425

Source: *Monthly Digest of Statistics*.
Data available in file 9T7.

Components of a time series

In general we can distinguish three components of a time series:

- the trend
- the seasonal components
- the random element.

The trend in a time series is the long-term, underlying movement in the variable. The trend may be upward as is the case in Figure 9.8, downward or relatively flat. The trend is an indication of the long-term direction of the variable. The seasonal components refer to the variability that occurs in the series within the year and that typically repeats itself each year. It is worth mentioning that some variables may exhibit

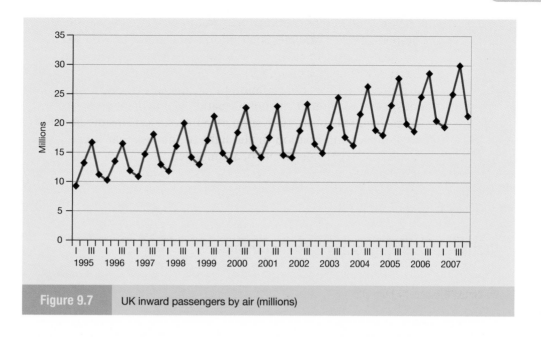

Figure 9.7 UK inward passengers by air (millions)

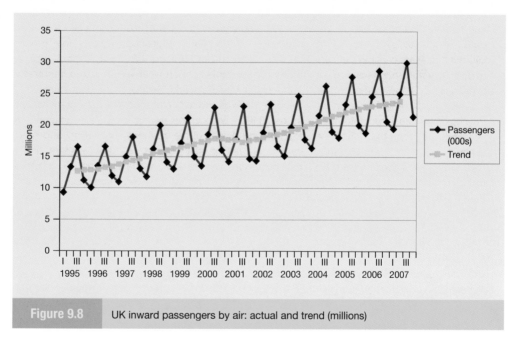

Figure 9.8 UK inward passengers by air: actual and trend (millions)

'seasonal' patterns in a shorter timescale than one year. Demand for electricity for example follows a predictable pattern within each 24-hour period as well as a seasonal pattern through the year as a whole. Finally, the random element refers to the difference between the actual series and what we would have expected the series to be, based on the trend and the seasonal component. It relates to random, unpredictable events which will cause the actual series to deviate from what would normally be expected. Given that by definition such an element is unpredictable, its future impact on the variable cannot be determined. Random elements may relate to features such as unexpected weather patterns (severe storms for example); to labour disputes; to outbreaks of hostilities; or to any 'shock' event.

The overall purpose of time-series analysis is to try to quantify the trend and seasonal components of a variable. Such information can then be used both to assess current performance and to predict the future. Consider the passenger data we have introduced. The manager of a UK airport such as Heathrow is likely to want to know – in quantifiable terms – the variation in passenger throughput that can be expected from one quarter to another. Such information will help in terms of planning resources that will be required: meals, staff, support vehicles, etc. Consider not having planned on the basis of such information in the light of the fact that it can cost around £1000 per *minute* to delay the departure of a jumbo jet.

Statistics: Learning to live with distortions

By Simon Briscoe, FT.com site

It seems as if there is often something wrong with newly-released data, some distortion which means that the latest twist or turn in the trend is to be taken with a pinch of salt. Such caveats can leave uncertainty in investors' minds and make it difficult to know whether the economy is entering recession or growing. The latest monthly retail sales release from the Office for National Statistics, for example, says: "There are always problems in adjusting for the effects of spending around Christmas. An additional uncertainty this year is the timing of the December trading period."

Much of the data being released at this time of year refers to the Christmas period, perhaps the time of greatest distortion each year. But distortions can occur at any time of year – the extra May bank holiday and jubilee celebrations last year distorted many series too.

The weekly, monthly or annual time series that the statisticians produce can be seen as comprising several different types of trend: the long-term or secular trend; cyclical fluctuations; seasonal variations; short to medium-term movements; and irregular (random, non-recurring or residual) fluctuations.

Time series analysis deploys a number of statistical techniques designed to separate out the various elements of the trend but just being aware of the influences on the recent run of numbers can throw considerable light on what is happening in the real world. Secular trends – such as the fall in inflation in the 1990s – and cyclical trends – the ups and downs of the business cycle – are not of daily concern to investors who want to look at the latest few months of data to know what is happening now and divine what it means for the future.

The majority of economic figures show a seasonal pattern that repeats itself each year. For example, retail sales rise in December as people prepare for Christmas and spend in the sales. The data show that the value of retail sales – the amount that people actually spend – can be up to 50 per cent higher in December than the average month. Similarly, factory output falls in the peak of the summer when many factories are closed.

To help the short-term analysis, a process called seasonal adjustment is used to adjust the raw or unadjusted data for the seasonal pattern. The seasonal adjustment process would analyse the monthly or quarterly patterns over a number of years so as to isolate the seasonal factor. In the vast majority of cases, the process of seasonal adjustment vastly improves the ability to interpret the series and is the best version of the data to look at. The statistical procedure of seasonal adjustment is complex, however, and has a large subjective element and means different things to different producers of statistics.

It is ideal, therefore, to be aware of the manner in which the adjustment has been made. A seasonally adjusted series will sometimes include other adjustments designed to smooth the series, for example, allowing for the number of working days and the timing of bank holidays. Some continental European series are presented in "calendar adjusted" form. There will be times when it is desirable to look at the unadjusted version of the data. Unadjusted retail sales data help to explain, for example, why our high streets are so much busier and why retailers employ temporary staff in December. It is clear, however, that economic trends will be easier to see in the adjusted version.

The seasonally adjusted version is normally preferable for analysis since it shows a less erratic trend from month to month. But seasonal adjustment never delivers a perfectly smooth series. There are short-term non-seasonal trends – such as rising fresh food prices during a winter cold snap – which will not be taken out. Normal month-to-month volatility which can either be random or semi-predictable – such as lower corporation tax payments from struggling companies – will still remain. One-off special factors such as the death of Diana, Princess of Wales, which suppressed sales in September 1997, strikes or a big sporting event, such as the football World Cup, can leave their imprint on the data.

Being aware of such factors makes it a little easier to understand what is happening in the economy and it makes it far less likely that any third party analysis will end up misleading the investor by focusing on just one figure, which might be the wrong one. The Bank of England's quarterly inflation report, last published on Wednesday, February 12, shows how data can be deconstructed to yield the maximum information.

www.statistics.gov.uk
www.bankofengland.co.uk

Source: Adapted from *Financial Times*, FT.com site, 22 February 2003.

Understanding why a variable is changing over time is critical as is being able to quantify the different components making up the time series.

Time-series decomposition

The process of quantifying the components of a time series is often referred to as *time-series decomposition*. In general we can identify a model such that:

$$D = T + S + R$$

where:

D refers to the data series
T to the trend
S to the seasonal components
R to the random element.

We wish to quantify the T and S elements of the model. To do so we must first use moving averages to estimate the trend and then use the trend to estimate the seasonal factors.

Estimating the trend

By definition the trend is the underlying, long-term movement in the variable. It seems logical then to consider estimating the trend using the principles of simple moving averages. Further, since the seasonal components fluctuate during the year, it seems logical to calculate a four-quarter moving average for the trend, since this average will cover a 12-month period and must, by definition, include all the seasonal components. Consider the data in the first four quarters of Table 9.7. If we total these and average we get 12 626 – the average number of passengers per quarter for the period from 1995 I–IV inclusive. Later in the calculation we shall wish to compare this average with the actual value to begin to estimate seasonality. At the moment, however, we have difficulty in doing so. Which quarter does the figure of 12 626 correspond to? The logical answer would seem to be the middle of the year to which it corresponds. But the middle of the year does not correspond to one particular quarter: rather it falls 'between' two quarters – 1995 II and 1995 III in this case. So, to align these moving averages with specific quarters we must adopt a process known as *centring the trend*.

Activity 9.6

Calculate the second moving average for the period 1995 II to 1996 I.

The corresponding moving average for this second period of four quarters is 12 857.25. We have the same problem of assigning this to any particular quarter. The centring process resolves the problem by taking the two moving averages and averaging them in turn, as shown in Table 9.8.

The average of the two moving averages – at 12 741.63 – can then be centred on the third quarter of 1995. This figure still contains an equal number of the four quarters of the year to include the different seasonal components. This average then becomes the estimate of the trend value. The calculations for the entire series are shown in Table 9.9 and the graph of the actual series, together with the trend, is shown in Figure 9.8.

The graph clearly shows the trend in this variable over this period – a pattern that was not particularly evident from the original data. We see that there has been a consistent upward trend in inward passenger numbers over this period. Clearly, as with the other models in this chapter, we do not know the causes of this trend; we simply observe and quantify its pattern. However, it is noticeable that the trend line takes a noticeable dip downwards in 2001 with the lowest part of the dip coinciding with 2001 III – a period which included the 9/11 attacks in the USA. We are not yet in a position to forecast this trend into the future: this must wait until later, although even cursory visual inspection of the trend provides valuable management information that is not evident from the original series. The estimation of the trend provides a useful piece of information to the manager, allowing us to quantify the trend changes on a quarter-by-quarter basis.

Table 9.8   Centring the trend

Year	Quarter	Actual	Moving average	Trend
1995	I	9 337		
1995	II	13 335		
			12 626.00	
1995	III ...	16 545	...	12 741.63
			12 857.25	
1995	IV	11 287		
1996	I	10 262		

Table 9.9		Trend calculations (000s)							
Year	Quarter	Actual	Moving average	Trend	Year	Quarter	Actual	Moving average	Trend
1995	I	9 337				III	22 987		17 434.63
								17 430.50	
	II	13 335				IV	14 684		17 565.00
			12 626.00					17 699.50	
	III	16 545		12 741.63	2002	I	14 269		17 744.50
			12 857.25					17 789.50	
	IV	11 287		12 886.88		II	18 858		18 041.75
			12 916.50					18 294.00	
1996	I	10 262		12 921.25		III	23 347		18 404.13
			12 926.00					18 514.25	
	II	13 572		13 024.50		IV	16 702		18 585.75
			13 123.00					18 657.25	
	III	16 583		13 215.63	2003	I	15 150		18 804.00
			13 308.25					18 950.75	
	IV	12 075		13 477.50		II	19 430		19 090.25
			13 646.75					19 229.75	
1997	I	11 003		13 842.25		III	24 521		19 391.88
			14 037.75					19 554.00	
	II	14 926		14 161.63		IV	17 818		19 825.50
			14 285.50					20 097.00	
	III	18 147		14 401.25	2004	I	16 447		20 308.50
			14 517.00					20 520.00	
	IV	13 066		14 691.63		II	21 602		20 668.50
			14 866.25					20 817.00	
1998	I	11 929		15 091.50		III	26 213		21 014.88
			15 316.75					21 212.75	
	II	16 323		15 464.88		IV	19 006		21 424.88
			15 613.00					21 637.00	
	III	19 949		15 757.25	2005	I	18 030		21 820.25
			15 901.50					22 003.50	
	IV	14 251		16 017.25		II	23 299		22 120.63
			16 133.00					22 237.75	
1999	I	13 083		16 281.50		III	27 679		22 325.38
			16 430.00					22 413.00	
	II	17 249		16 537.38		IV	19 943		22 582.50
			16 644.75					22 752.00	
	III	21 137		16 717.50	2006	I	18 731		22 872.38
			16 790.25					22 992.75	
	IV	15 110		16 963.63		II	24 655		23 069.13
			17 137.00					23 145.50	
2000	I	13 665		17 337.75		III	28 642		23 230.25
			17 538.50					23 315.00	
	II	18 636		17 654.00		IV	20 554		23 366.13
			17 769.50					23 417.25	
	III	22 743		17 849.00	2007	I	19 409		23 577.13
			17928.75					23 737.00	
	IV	16 034		17 822.00		II	25 064		23 845.88
			17715.25					23 954.75	
2001	I	14 302		17 745.75		III	29 921		
			17 776.25						
	II	17 782		17 607.50		IV	21 425		
			17 438.75						

Table 9.10			Deviations from the trend (000s)						

Year	Quarter	Actual	Trend	Deviation	Year	Quarter	Actual	Trend	Deviation
1995	I	9 337			2002	I	14 269	17 744.50	−3475.50
	II	13 335				II	18 858	18 041.75	816.25
	III	16 545	12 741.63	3803.38		III	23 347	18 404.13	4942.88
	IV	11 287	12 886.88	−1599.88		IV	16 702	18 585.75	−1883.75
1996	I	10 262	12 921.25	−2659.25	2003	I	15 150	18 804.00	−3654.00
	II	13 572	13 024.50	547.50		II	19 430	19 090.25	339.75
	III	16 583	13 215.63	3367.38		III	24 521	19 391.88	5129.13
	IV	12 075	13 477.50	−1402.50		IV	17 818	19 825.50	−2007.50
1997	I	11 003	13 842.25	−2839.25	2004	I	16 447	20 308.50	−3861.50
	II	14 926	14 161.63	764.38		II	21 602	20 668.50	933.50
	III	18 147	14 401.25	3745.75		III	26 213	21 014.88	5198.13
	IV	13 066	14 691.63	−1625.63		IV	19 006	21 424.88	−2418.88
1998	I	11 929	15 091.50	−3162.50	2005	I	18 030	21 820.25	−3790.25
	II	16 323	15 464.88	858.13		II	23 299	22 120.63	1178.38
	III	19 949	15 757.25	4191.75		III	27 679	22 325.38	5353.63
	IV	14 251	16 017.25	−1766.25		IV	19 943	22 582.50	−2639.50
1999	I	13 083	16 281.50	−3198.50	2006	I	18 731	22 872.38	−4141.38
	II	17 249	16 537.38	711.63		II	24 655	23 069.13	1585.88
	III	21 137	16 717.50	4419.50		III	28 642	23 230.25	5411.75
	IV	15 110	16 963.63	−1853.63		IV	20 554	23 366.13	−2812.13
2000	I	13 665	17 337.75	−3672.75	2007	I	19 409	23 577.13	−4168.13
	II	18 636	17 654.00	982.00		II	25 064	23 845.88	1218.13
	III	22 743	17 849.13	4893.88		III	29 921		
	IV	16 034	17 822.00	−1788.00		IV	21 425		
2001	I	14 302	17 745.75	−3443.75					
	II	17 782	17 607.50	174.50					
	III	22 987	17 434.63	5552.38					
	IV	14 684	17 565.00	−2881.00					

The seasonal components

Using the trend values we can now estimate the seasonal components for each quarter. Remember the basic model:

$$D = T + S + R$$

If we ignore R, since by definition it cannot be predicted, and rearrange we have:

$$S = D − T$$

That is, the seasonal components are the differences between the actual series and the trend. Table 9.10 shows these deviations.

So, for example, we see that in the fourth quarter of 1995 the actual number of passengers was around 1600 below the long-term trend.

Activity 9.7

Why are the deviations in the same quarters of the different years not the same?

Table 9.11	Average deviations per quarter (000s)			

	Quarter			
Year	I	II	III	IV
1995			3803.38	−1599.88
1996	−2659.25	547.50	3367.38	−1402.50
1997	−2839.25	764.38	3745.75	−1625.63
1998	−3162.50	858.13	4191.75	−1766.25
1999	−3198.50	711.63	4419.50	−1853.63
2000	−3672.75	982.00	4893.88	−1788.00
2001	−3443.75	174.50	5552.38	−2881.00
2002	−3475.50	816.25	4942.88	−1883.75
2003	−3654.00	339.75	5129.13	−2007.50
2004	−3861.50	933.50	5198.13	−2418.88
2005	−3790.25	1178.38	5353.63	−2639.50
2006	−4141.38	1585.88	5411.75	−2812.13
2007	−4168.13	1218.13		
Mean	−3505.56	842.50	4667.46	−2056.55

To calculate the seasonal component for each quarter of the year we can average these individual deviations, as shown in Table 9.11, by summing the deviations for a particular quarter and dividing by the number of deviations that were summed.

This averaging is necessary because the quarterly deviations include not only a seasonal component but also a random component, which will vary from one year to the next. Such random factors in this case might include industrial action, the outbreak of hostilities in other countries, or a special promotional campaign by other airlines. By definition such random factors will not occur every year. We see from Table 9.11 that there is considerable consistency in the variation within each quarter. All the deviations in Quarter IV, for example, are negative and around the same value. If this had not been the case we might wish to check first our calculations for any arithmetical error and then the stability of the seasonal pattern of the data over time. It might be we had a data series without a consistent seasonal pattern.

If we now take the mean deviation for each quarter we obtain the results shown in the final row of Table 9.11. However, these deviations typically require a final adjustment before we can refer to them as seasonal components. The sum of these deviations should total to zero, since the sum of the four quarterly seasonal components should cancel over a year. They rarely do, however, and must be adjusted accordingly. If we total the four mean deviations we find they equal −52.16 rather than zero. The deviations are in total 52.16 less than they should be. Accordingly we need to adjust them upwards by this amount. We do this by arbitrarily increasing each quarter's mean deviation by one quarter of 52.16 to give the seasonal components:

	I	II	III	IV
Seasonal component	−3492.52	855.54	4680.50	−2043.51

Thorntons' chief hopes to taste seasonal success

Alison Smith examines the changes wrought by new boss at chocolates group following two profit warnings and an embarrassing Easter

When Peter Burdon says he does not want "a repeat of seasonal excesses", he does not mean too much turkey and alcohol.

The chief executive of Thorntons is making it clear that it will not indulge in the sort of overstocking that left it with £1.4m of unsold Easter eggs, which had to be sold off at half-price.

Indeed, if current rates are maintained, Mr Burdon expects to sell out of special Christmas lines such as chocolate polar bears, reindeer sets and Chicken Run figures.

The eggs debacle is memorable because it led to a profits warning in June – Thorntons' second this year – just a few weeks after Mr Burdon's arrival from Boots, where he had been a trading director. The first profits warning had triggered the departure of his predecessor, Roger Paffard. Mr Burdon's first Christmas is an important opportunity to show how Thorntons has changed under his leadership. More than half the group's £154m turnover comes from a handful of occasions: Christmas is the most important of these and makes up "a good proportion" of that total.

Even before he was appointed, the former McKinsey management consultant put together his own ideas on what needed to be done at the company. After seeing that Mr Paffard had left, he wrote to John Thornton, chairman, setting out his views.

At that point, he says, he saw three issues: the company was overexpanding; was doing too many things at once; and did not

have in place a scheme giving retail staff real incentives to sell.

He has already cut back on plans to extend the store network from 400-plus to 500, and on the expansion of the e-commerce offering.

The appearance of the shops is lighter and more modern, and there is now a sales-driven incentive scheme for stores that exceed their internal targets.

Other changes are also in train. The brand's advertising no longer dwells on its heritage, and focuses more clearly on the customer.

The Thorntons' slogan of "Chocolate heaven since 1911" has been replaced by the less distinctive but – Mr Burdon hopes – more effective "There's lots in store for you". The advertising also has a sharper edge. This year the television campaign for Christmas started in the advertising break during Cadbury-sponsored Coronation Street.

In two other areas – promotions and products – Mr Burdon has clearly been influenced by his experience at Boots. "One of the things I learnt at Boots is that promotions have to be new or provide good value, such as a 'three for two' offer. Previously at Thorntons the promotions were focused on discounts, but you shouldn't discount your premium lines."

He highlights Boots' success in using new products to get people to trade up and sees scope for that at Thorntons. He must also make room for new products in key parts of the £2.7bn chocolate confectionery market, such as packets for

families to share, where Thorntons has yet to make much impact.

But Mr Burdon also wants to avoid cluttering the shelves with too many novelties. One of his first acts was to discard some of the fringe innovations, such as chocolate-scented T-shirts, brought in by Mr Paffard.

"I stopped a lot of product development, and turned the development process from a chute into a funnel," he says. "We will reduce the range by about 10 per cent over the year, and we have a new rule on products – one in, one out."

If Mr Burdon achieves the "solid" Christmas he is seeking, it will provide the first festive cheer Thorntons shareholders have experienced for some time. They are more used to the disappointments of profits warnings. In its most recent results, pre-tax profit for the year to June almost halved from £10.5m to £5.5m.

Since January the shares have lost 60 per cent of their value, closing yesterday at 70p. Last year (1999) they reached a peak of $250\frac{1}{2}$p in the spring before falling back to 177p in December.

Even a positive trading statement would leave Mr Burdon to resolve the deeper issue facing Thorntons: how to reach the mass market without over-expanding its own network of shops or diluting the brand.

Finding the answer will be even harder than striking the right balance of innovation and restraint over the festive season.

Source: *Financial Times*, 14 December 2000.

The cost of seasonality.

The interpretation of these results is straightforward. They represent the typical impact of each quarter on the number of passengers travelling by air. In the first quarter of each year we would expect the number of passengers to be some 3.5 million below the trend or long-term average. Similarly, in the third quarter, we anticipate an increase above trend of around 4.7 million passengers. These 'forecasts' of seasonality do not, of course, take random effects into account but potentially are of considerable benefit to the manager in operational planning. Consider their use in terms of manpower planning, for example. Airports will employ staff to unload baggage from aircraft as they arrive. Fewer passengers in the first quarter of a year implies fewer aircraft arriving and a need for fewer staff. Given we can quantify how many fewer passengers to expect, we can translate that into a manpower requirement for staff.

The seasonally adjusted series

The final part of the decomposition process is to produce what is known as the seasonally adjusted series. Effectively this is the original series but with the seasonal component removed, thus showing the underlying trend together with random fluctuations. As before, the original model can be rearranged to give:

$$D - S = T + R$$

with (D – S) being the seasonally adjusted series. Table 9.12 shows the calculations and Figure 9.9 the corresponding graph.

Note how the seasonally adjusted series is slightly more irregular than the trend, since it incorporates random changes in the series as well as the trend.

Forecasting with a time series

Forecasting a time-series variable such as ours requires two separate elements to be forecast:

● the trend
● the seasonal components.

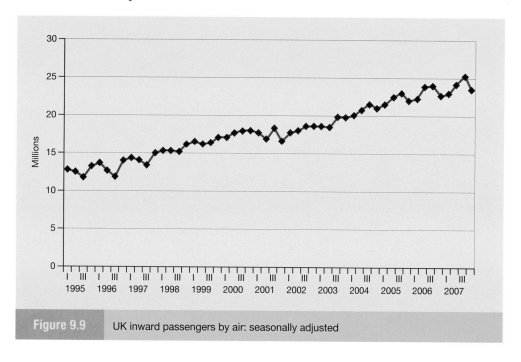

Figure 9.9   UK inward passengers by air: seasonally adjusted

Table 9.12   Seasonally adjusted series (000s)

Year	Quarter	Passengers (000s)	Seasonal component	Seasonally adjusted data
1995	I	9 337	−3492.52	12 829.52
1995	II	13 335	855.54	12 479.46
1995	III	16 545	4680.498	11 864.50
1995	IV	11 287	−2043.51	13 330.51
1996	I	10 262	−3492.52	13 754.52
1996	II	13 572	855.54	12 716.46
1996	III	16 583	4680.498	11 902.50
1996	IV	12 075	−2043.51	14 118.51
1997	I	11 003	−3492.52	14 495.52
1997	II	14 926	855.54	14 070.46
1997	III	18 147	4680.498	13 466.50
1997	IV	13 066	−2043.51	15 109.51
1998	I	11 929	−3492.52	15 421.52
1998	II	16 323	855.54	15 467.46
1998	III	19 949	4680.498	15 268.50
1998	IV	14 251	−2043.51	16 294.51
1999	I	13 083	−3492.52	16 575.52
1999	II	17 249	855.54	16 393.46
1999	III	21 137	4680.498	16 456.50
1999	IV	15 110	−2043.51	17 153.51
2000	I	13 665	−3492.52	17 157.52
2000	II	18 636	855.54	17 780.46
2000	III	22 743	4680.498	18 062.50
2000	IV	16 034	−2043.51	18 077.51
2001	I	14 302	−3492.52	17 794.52
2001	II	17 782	855.54	16 926.46
2001	III	22 987	4680.498	18 306.50
2001	IV	14 684	−2043.51	16 727.51
2002	I	14 269	−3492.52	17 761.52
2002	II	18 858	855.54	18 002.46
2002	III	23 347	4680.498	18 666.50
2002	IV	16 702	−2043.51	18 745.51
2003	I	15 150	−3492.52	18 642.52
2003	II	19 430	855.54	18 574.46
2003	III	24 521	4680.498	19 840.50
2003	IV	17 818	−2043.51	19 861.51
2004	I	16 447	−3492.52	19 939.52
2004	II	21 602	855.54	20 746.46
2004	III	26 213	4680.498	21 532.50
2004	IV	19 006	−2043.51	21 049.51
2005	I	18 030	−3492.52	21 522.52
2005	II	23 299	855.54	22 443.46
2005	III	27 679	4680.498	22 998.50
2005	IV	19 943	−2043.51	21 986.51
2006	I	18 731	−3492.52	22 223.52
2006	II	24 655	855.54	23 799.46
2006	III	28 642	4680.498	23 961.50
2006	IV	20 554	−2043.51	22 597.51
2007	I	19 409	−3492.52	22 901.52
2007	II	25 064	855.54	24 208.46
2007	III	29 921	4680.498	25 240.50
2007	IV	21 425	−2043.51	23 468.51

Sharp down turn in German job creation

By Bertrand Benoit in Berlin

Germany's three-year-old job recovery was showing signs of losing steam on Tuesday when the country's statistical office published employment figures for last month that showed a sharp slowdown in job creation. According to the seasonally-adjusted statistics, only 3,000 jobs were created in May, leaving the total number of Germans in work at 40.2m, virtually unchanged from April. This contrasted with a 54,000 increase in job creations in April.

The Federal Statistical Office said it was too early to tell whether the slowdown signalled the end of the extended period of robust job creation the German economy has enjoyed since the start of the economic recovery about three years ago. The mild winter at the begin-

ning of the year, it said, could have distorted the statistics because the seasonal adjustment formula could not account for the lower-than-usual job losses during the winter months.

Yet most economists expect Germany's labour market to mark a pause as the pace of economic growth slows down in Europe's largest economy this year and next.

Although sentiment surveys show a persistent willingness of companies to hire, several large companies heavily exposed to slowing international markets, including Siemens, the engineering group, are planning job cuts due to growing economic uncertainty.

A downward turn in the labour market could spell trouble for the government's plans to deliver a

balanced federal budget by 2011 since the plan depends more on fast-rising tax revenues than on spending cuts.

Unemployment figures for June published by the Federal Labour Office showed a rosier picture, with a seasonally-adjusted fall in the number of jobseekers by 38,000 following a small rise in May. That pushed the total number of unemployed below the 3.2m mark.

The fall, however, was below an average monthly decrease in unemployment of 46,000 in the months since December. Internationally comparable figures using the methodology of the International Labour Office showed an unemployment rate of 7.2 per cent in May.

Source: Financial Times, 1 July 2008.

It's only by looking at the seasonally adjusted data that you can assess whether any real change has occurred in some variable. But the calculations themselves can be problematic.

It is usual to assume that the seasonal components will remain unchanged, so we are only required to forecast the trend. The actual mechanics of forecasting the trend must wait until the next chapter, when we have introduced regression as a forecasting technique. However, to illustrate the process of developing a forecast for the time series we will take the forecast for the trend as given. In fact, this situation illustrates the potential of such forecasting methods as an aid to decision making.

Assume we are trying to forecast for the last quarter of 2008 to help with our operational planning. Looking at the trend in Figure 9.8 and the seasonally adjusted data in Figure 9.9 we might develop two scenarios. The first (Scenario A) is to use the trend over the entire period from 1995 to 2007 to produce a forecast for the future trend. An alternative scenario is to say that the trend post September 11 seen in Figure 9.9 may be slightly different from that before. Accordingly we might wish to use the trend data only from 2002 I onwards (Scenario B). Naturally, bearing in mind the qualitative approaches we discussed earlier in the chapter, a number of other alternative scenarios could easily be developed and quantified. However, in the context of the two we have put forward, denoted as Scenario A and Scenario B, we can quantify the trend projection for 2004 IV as:

	Trend forecast for 2008 IV
Scenario A	25 008.5
Scenario B	26 069.1

(Explanation as to how we arrived at these numbers will have to wait until Chapter 10.) To obtain a forecast of the actual number of passengers, we must add in the seasonal factor for Quarter IV of −2043.5 to give:

	Series forecast for 2008 IV
Scenario A	22 965.0
Scenario B	24 025.6

Although the mechanics of producing a time-series forecast are straightforward, the two scenarios illustrate the role of such forecasts in the decision-making process. The two forecasts are different: over 1 million passengers. However, this information provides a starting point for managers to consider and assess the future.

Models which are not quarterly

There is no reason why we should not wish to apply these principles to variables which show data in a format other than quarterly. Variables which are monthly can readily be analysed in the same way. The only differences would relate to the periods covered by the moving-average calculations (which would need to be averaged over twelve months rather than four quarters) and to the fact that we will derive twelve seasonal factors rather than four. Indeed, a variable relating to any period within a year can in principle have such a model developed. Data which is daily would be just as suitable although the calculations become somewhat tedious unless using a specialist package and the quantity of data required becomes cumbersome.

Additive and multiplicative models

The time-series model we have developed is technically known as an additive model since the components of the time series are added together: $T + S + R$. The alternative model is known as the multiplicative since it denotes the time series as:

$$D = T \times S \times R$$

In practice the multiplicative model is the one more commonly used. The reason for this lies in the trend movement of the variable. The additive model is adequate as long as the trend in the variable is relatively stable. For technical reasons, if the trend shows a marked change over time, either positive or negative, then the multiplicative model will generally be more appropriate. In our example of passengers we should use the multiplicative model as the trend has a strong upward movement. Fortunately, the calculations involved in the multiplicative model are similar to those we have already developed:

● Estimate the trend using moving averages as in the additive model.

- Estimate the quarterly deviation by dividing D by T. Whereas in the additive model we subtracted T from D to find the quarterly differences, for the multiplicative model we calculate a ratio instead. As ratios they will vary about the value 1.0.

- The seasonal factors will then be estimated by ensuring that the four quarterly ratios total to 4.0 and adjusting the average deviations accordingly. A seasonal factor of, say, 1.05 for a data series using this type of model indicates that the data is typically 5 per cent above the trend in this quarter.

To illustrate, assume that we had applied the multiplicative model to our earlier problem. The trend estimate would remain the same but we would now have the quarterly seasonal deviation as shown in Table 9.13, where each deviation is D/T. We see, for example, that the actual value in 1999 III is 26.4 per cent above the trend and 1999 IV is about 11 per cent below the trend. These individual deviations then must be averaged for each quarter and adjusted to ensure they total to 4.0. The results are shown in Table 9.14.

Table 9.13 Multiplicative model

Year	Quarter	Actual	Trend	Deviation	Year	Quarter	Actual	Trend	Deviation
1995	I	9 337			2002	I	14 269	17 744.50	0.8041
	II	13 335				II	18 858	18 041.75	1.0452
	III	16 545	12 741.63	1.2985		III	23 347	18 404.13	1.2686
	IV	11 287	12 886.88	0.8759		IV	16 702	18 585.75	0.8986
1996	I	10 262	12 921.25	0.7942	2003	I	15 150	18 804.00	0.8057
	II	13 572	13 024.50	1.0420		II	19 430	19 090.25	1.0178
	III	16 583	13 215.63	1.2548		III	24 521	19 391.88	1.2645
	IV	12 075	13 477.50	0.8959		IV	17 818	19 825.50	0.8987
1997	I	11 003	13 842.25	0.7949	2004	I	16 447	20 308.50	0.8099
	II	14 926	14 161.63	1.0540		II	21 602	20 668.50	1.0452
	III	18 147	14 401.25	1.2601		III	26 213	21 014.88	1.2474
	IV	13 066	14 691.63	0.8894		IV	19 006	21 424.88	0.8871
1998	I	11 929	15 091.50	0.7904	2005	I	18 030	21 820.25	0.8263
	II	16 323	15 464.88	1.0555		II	23 299	22 120.63	1.0533
	III	19 949	15 757.25	1.2660		III	27 679	22 325.38	1.2398
	IV	14 251	16 017.25	0.8897		IV	19 943	22 582.50	0.8831
1999	I	13 083	16 281.50	0.8036	2006	I	18 731	22 872.38	0.8189
	II	17 249	16 537.38	1.0430		II	24 655	23 069.13	1.0687
	III	21 137	16 717.50	1.2644		III	28 642	23 230.25	1.2330
	IV	15 110	16 963.63	0.8907		IV	20 554	23 366.13	0.8796
2000	I	13 665	17 337.75	0.7882	2007	I	19 409	23 577.13	0.8232
	II	18 636	17 654.00	1.0556		II	25 064	23 845.88	1.0511
	III	22 743	17 849.13	1.2742		III	29 921		
	IV	16 034	17 822.00	0.8997		IV	21 425		
2001	I	14 302	17 745.75	0.8059					
	II	17 782	17 607.50	1.0099					
	III	22 987	17 434.63	1.3185					
	IV	14 684	17 565.00	0.8360					

Table 9.14	Seasonal components: multiplicative model			

Year	I	II	III	IV	
1995			1.2985	0.8759	
1996	0.7942	1.0420	1.2548	0.8959	
1997	0.7949	1.0540	1.2601	0.8894	
1998	0.7904	1.0555	1.2660	0.8897	
1999	0.8036	1.0430	1.2644	0.8907	
2000	0.7882	1.0556	1.2742	0.8997	
2001	0.8059	1.0099	1.3185	0.8360	
2002	0.8041	1.0452	1.2686	0.8986	
2003	0.8057	1.0178	1.2645	0.8987	
2004	0.8099	1.0452	1.2474	0.8871	
2005	0.8263	1.0533	1.2398	0.8831	
2006	0.8189	1.0687	1.2330	0.8796	
2007	0.8232	1.0511			
Mean	0.8054	1.0451	1.2658	0.8854	Total = 4.0017
Adjusted	0.8051	1.0447	1.2653	0.8850	

The seasonal factors can be used in exactly the same way as in the additive model, both for analysis and for forecasting.

Time-series decomposition with specialist packages

Normally, we would use spreadsheet facilities for performing the calculations required for time-series decomposition. An increasing number of such spreadsheets have in-built functions for calculating moving averages, which can help with this task, although you should check carefully on the exact method your spreadsheet uses (perhaps with a set of data where you already know the results). There are also specialist computer packages available which will perform the time-series decomposition calculations automatically. Such packages usually have sophisticated algorithms for smoothing out the random terms.

Worked Example

Concern has been expressed by a national road safety group about the increasing volume of road traffic and the number of road casualties in Great Britain, particularly amongst children. We have been asked to provide a background report summarising key trends over the last few years. We have collected the data shown in Table 9.15. The data shows road casualties in Great Britain from 1994 to 2007 on a quarterly basis. Two categories are shown: total casualties and casualties aged under 16 years.

The first step is to produce a time-series graph of the two series, using both Y axes because of the differing scales. This is shown in Figure 9.10. We see from this quite interesting differences. Both series show clear signs of seasonality, but for the total the

Table 9.15		Road casualties in Great Britain: quarterly, 1994–2002						

Year	Quarter	Total	Under 16 years	Year	Quarter	Total	Under 16 years
1994	I	73 496	9 627	2001	I	74 816	8 116
	II	74 942	12 421		II	75 214	10 548
	III	79 313	12 608		III	78 474	10 412
	IV	87 438	10 495		IV	84 805	9 193
1995	I	73 428	9 078	2002	I	70 837	7 714
	II	72 380	11 781		II	72 403	9 185
	III	81 417	13 083		III	75 578	9 617
	IV	83 281	9 846		IV	83 787	8 173
1996	I	72 139	8 853	2003	I	67 794	7 056
	II	76 423	12 107		II	71 244	8 745
	III	81 531	13 233		III	74 681	8 888
	IV	90 209	10 642		IV	76 888	7 299
1997	I	75 344	9 338	2004	I	65 814	6 853
	II	81 287	12 138		II	69 430	8 616
	III	81 551	12 527		III	70 743	8 400
	IV	89 621	10 543		IV	74 853	7 131
1998	I	74 061	9 121	2005	I	62 037	6 066
	II	80 602	12 019		II	67 547	7 787
	III	81 880	12 109		III	68 616	7 646
	IV	88 669	10 196		IV	72 817	6 627
1999	I	74 119	8 971	2006	I	59 358	5 283
	II	77 056	11 344		II	62 594	6 848
	III	82 004	12 053		III	67 333	7 157
	IV	87 131	9 683		IV	69 119	6 235
2000	I	75 059	8 738	2007	I	58 983	5 242
	II	78 575	10 902		II	62 188	6 557
	III	79 386	10 671		III	63 562	6 516
	IV	87 263	9 404		IV	63 047	5 492

Source: Annual Abstract of Statistics.
Data available in file WECH9.

'peak' quarter is Quarter IV each year (October–December), whereas for the under 16s the peak quarter is Quarter III (July–September). On reflection this is not really surprising. Although we cannot be complacent about road accidents to children occurring in the two winter quarters (IV and I), it is the summer months when most road accidents tend to occur in this group. This can be confirmed through calculations of the seasonal factors for each series. Using a specialist package and the multiplicative method we derive the following:

Seasonal indices

Quarter	I	II	III	IV
Total	0.92	0.97	1.02	1.09
Under 16s	0.84	1.09	1.12	0.95

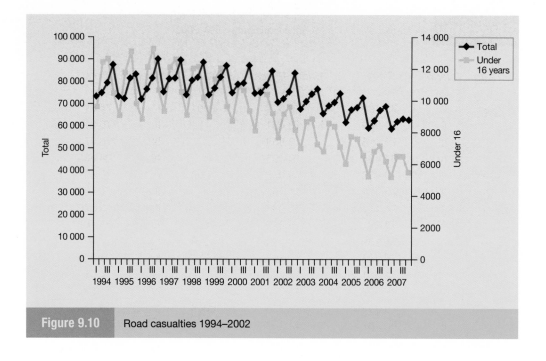

Figure 9.10   Road casualties 1994–2002

This confirms the two differing seasonal patterns and highlights that the middle two quarters of the year are the danger quarters as far as road accidents involving children are concerned. Clearly this has implications for the timing of road safety campaigns aimed at this age group.

We can also calculate the trends for the two series, which are shown in Figure 9.11. The two trends are evidently very similar over this entire period, implying that whatever factors are causing the trends to change are affecting both the total and the under

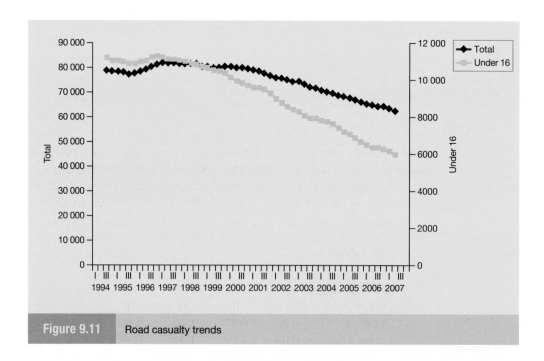

Figure 9.11   Road casualty trends

16s equally. We see that from 1994 until the end of 1995 both trends were falling. From then until the beginning of 1997 both trends increased. Since then both have shown a consistent fall. Naturally, if this were to be more than a background report we would need to investigate further, perhaps by obtaining and analysing monthly rather than quarterly data, perhaps by breaking the total into a number of categories to assess trends amongst these different groups, perhaps by trying to determine which other factors (e.g. government road safety campaigns) might be influencing the trends we have observed.

 ## Summary

In this chapter we have considered some of the issues involved in business forecasting. We have seen that generally two approaches can be adopted: to develop qualitative forecasts or to develop quantitative forecasts. Qualitative methods use opinions, judgements and expertise to develop some numerical forecast about a variable. Quantitative methods that we have introduced in this chapter are built around the principles of moving averages. Such averages can help smooth out random fluctuations in a variable and allow us to produce reasonably accurate forecasts in situations where forecast accuracy is not the sole criterion used to assess a forecasting model's suitability. Such moving averages are also at the heart of time-series decomposition. This is a particularly important technique for analysing, and then projecting into the future, some variable which exhibits a seasonal pattern. Given that many business variables will exhibit such patterns, it is important for a manager to be able to quantify such seasonal variability and to take this into account when trying to assess the underlying movement in some variable.

 ## Useful online resources

Detailed below are some internet resources that may be useful. Many have further links to other sites. An updated version is available from the accompanying website (**www.pearsoned.co.uk/wisniewski**). In addition, I would be grateful for details of other websites that have been found to be useful.

www.forecastingprinciples.com – Forecasting Principles website

www.itl.nist.gov/div898/handbook/pmc/section4/pmc4.htm – Introduction to time series analysis

www.lbma.org.uk/publications/alchemist/alch33_averages.pdf – Moving averages

www.businessintelligence.com/ex/asp/code.9/xe/article.htm – Stop Looking Back: An Introduction to Forecasting for Business Intelligence

home.ubalt.edu/ntsbarsh/Business-stat/stat-data/Forecast.htm – Time series analysis for business forecasting

www.statsoft.com/textbook/sttimser.html – Time series analysis

www.stats.gla.ac.uk/steps/glossary/time_series.html – Time series glossary

QMDM IN ACTION
Retail supermarket, UK

For reasons of commercial confidentiality the organisation used for this application cannot be named. Similarly the data used to illustrate this application have been adjusted by a constant.

A large retail organisation operates a number of retail supermarkets in the UK. These range in size, location and profitability. Some of the stores are relatively small, operating in the high street. Others are located at out-of-town sites, typically as part of a larger retail complex. One supermarket in the group had approximately 15 000 square feet of floor space and formed part of a small retail park that had been established on the fringes of a large market town some 20 years ago. The supermarket had not been purpose-built at the time but had been converted from an existing industrial building. In the late 1980s a larger retail complex had been built on the opposite side of the town. This comprised a number of well-known retail organisations offering furnishings, electrical goods and DIY. On that site one of the company's direct competitors had opened a purpose-built supermarket with almost twice the floor space. This competition had directly affected trading performance of the company's supermarket.

After a major assessment of the situation, the company decided to undertake a programme of varied promotional activities to try to win back customers and improve trading performance. The promotional period lasted approximately 15 months in total. During that time a variety of activities were introduced for short periods: local media promotions, bonus products when a customer spent more than a stated amount, free local bus services to and from the supermarket. At the time, management of the supermarket felt that these initiatives had had a positive impact on trading performance. Towards the end of this promotional period, however, senior management in the company felt that the long run of promotions had probably had all the effect they were likely to have and the promotional programme was halted. Some two years after the end of the promotional campaign a more detailed analysis of the supermarket's performance over this period was undertaken using the principles of time-series analysis.

Figure 9.12 shows the supermarket's turnover over the relevant five-year period. The supermarket operates a reporting system such that the financial

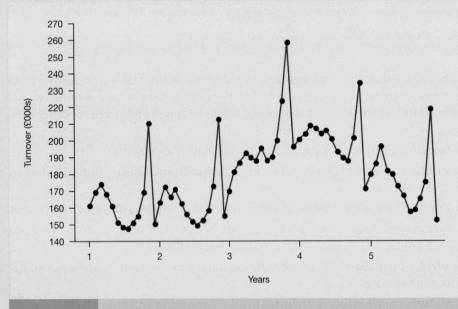

Figure 9.12   Supermarket turnover over five-year period

year begins in February each year and turnover figures are reported on a four-weekly basis. This means that over the year there are 13 four-week reporting periods. From Figure 9.12 a number of points are evident:

- For the first two years of this period turnover was relatively stable but low. The competing supermarket had opened some 18 months prior to Year 1.
- From Year 3 a positive change in turnover begins to appear.
- During Year 4 turnover began to decline.
- The Christmas effect is very marked each year.

A centred moving-average trend was calculated for the data and superimposed on the actual turnover. This is shown in Figure 9.13. The change in trend is evident from the end of Year 2 with strong growth through Year 3. From the beginning of Year 4, however, the trend reverses into a continuing decline. The duration of the promotional activities is also shown on the diagram. These commenced at the start of year 3 and continued, at varying rates, until the first quarter of Year 4.

Although cause and effect cannot be established, it is evident from the time-series analysis that the strong upward movement in the trend coincides with the period of active promotion and that when these promotional activities cease the trend moves into decline. The supermarket's manager was convinced that the commencement/cessation of the promotional campaign was a major contributory factor to the trend changes and that, with hindsight, the decision to stop the promotional campaign had been inappropriate.

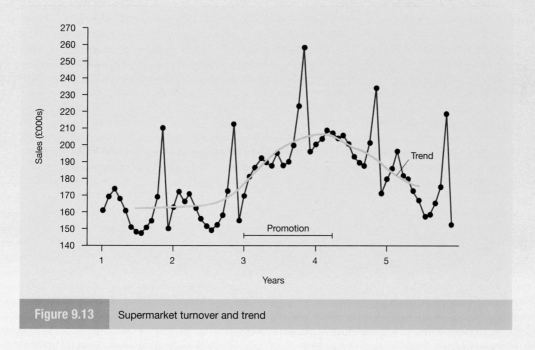

Figure 9.13 Supermarket turnover and trend

Exercises

1 Return to the unit sales data used in this chapter. Apply the exponential-smoothing model to this data using values for α of 0.15, 0.2, 0.25 and 0.3. Assess the accuracy of each choice of α and decide which you would use to forecast future values.

2 Consider the two sets of sales data in Table 9.16.

Table 9.16		Weekly sales

Week	Sales units	Sales Units
1	246	246
2	256	256
3	255	255
4	248	248
5	263	263
6	254	254
7	306	306
8	308	338
9	304	372
10	307	412
11	306	459
12	308	514
13	305	570
14	301	628
15	303	693

Data available in file 9T16.

Apply the exponential-smoothing model to this data with a variety of values. What do you observe about the accuracy of the model over time in the two series?

3 The following exercises all relate to the development of a suitable time-series decomposition model for the data shown. In each case you should adopt the following procedure:

(a) Plot the original data as a time-series graph.

(b) Determine whether an additive or multiplicative model would be appropriate.

(c) For the model chosen determine the trend.

(d) Determine the seasonal components.

(e) Determine the seasonally adjusted series.

(f) Plot the seasonally adjusted series on the same graph as (a).

(g) From the seasonal components try to determine what factors might be causing the seasonal pattern you have estimated and whether the seasonal pattern is likely to remain stable in the immediate future.

You may also want to update the information shown in the tables and see whether the seasonal pattern calculated shows any signs of change over time.

(i) Table 9.17 shows sales of gas and electricity to domestic customers in the UK for the period 1994 to 2007. The two variables shown are:

- domestic gas sales, gigawatt hours
- domestic electricity sales, terawatt hours.

Assess the seasonal patterns and trends for the two variables and their management implications for the two industries.

Table 9.17		Sales of gas and electricity to domestic customers, UK					
Year	Quarter	Gas	Electricity	Year	Quarter	Gas	Electricity
1994	I	131 225	31.31	2001	I	154 586	35.05
	II	62 963	22.11		II	69 547	25.66
	III	32 518	19.69		III	35 197	23.11
	IV	103 004	28.30		IV	120 097	31.53
1995	I	134 293	31.90	2002	I	145 289	33.59
	II	54 841	21.86		II	67 539	25.08
	III	30 818	19.17		III	38 340	23.28
	IV	106 058	29.27		IV	125 205	32.57
1996	I	160 624	33.90	2003	I	154 439	34.48
	II	71 981	22.94		II	63 191	25.00
	III	36 844	20.12		III	35 253	22.81
	IV	106 392	30.56		IV	133 101	33.47
1997	I	135 798	31.41	2004	I	159 333	35.27
	II	60 899	22.24		II	69 159	24.66
	III	34 728	20.21		III	37 870	23.68
	IV	110 928	30.17		IV	132 540	34.11
1998	I	134 260	32.46	2005	I	155 265	33.80
	II	68 490	24.28		II	68 004	25.87
	III	34 005	21.09		III	32 854	23.87
	IV	119 140	31.98		IV	125 756	33.27
1999	I	138 776	33.51	2006	I	157 496	34.99
	II	65 981	23.70		II	65 969	25.66
	III	31 805	21.55		III	28 750	23.34
	IV	119 505	31.21		IV	112 340	32.46
2000	I	145 896	34.40	2007	I	135 388	33.04
	II	68 795	23.64		II	57 298	25.29
	III	35 382	23.37		III	34 826	23.65
	IV	124 075	32.20		IV	123 327	33.90

Source: Monthly Digest of Statistics.
Data available in file 9T17.

(ii) Table 9.18 shows the number of marriages and number of registered deaths in England and Wales for the period 1994 to 2006.

Consider this information if you were the manager of a chauffeur-driven hire car company.

Table 9.18		Marriages and registered deaths in England and Wales (000s)					
Year	Quarter	Marriages	Deaths	Year	Quarter	Marriages	Deaths
1994	I	36.8	149.8		III	116.7	118.6
	II	83.9	133.0		IV	45.6	132.4
	III	118.4	127.1	2001	I	28.8	147.7
	IV	52.1	143.2		II	70.9	129.0
1995	I	34.0	154.1		III	105.5	121.0
	II	81.4	135.3		IV	44.2	134.8
	III	119.8	126.1	2002	I	31.9	144.9
	IV	47.8	150.3		II	70.9	128.8
1996	I	36.5	159.6		III	105.6	124.0
	II	80.7	131.8		IV	46.9	137.7
	III	114.0	126.8	2003	I	33.9	143.1
	IV	47.8	144.8		II	74.8	129.2
1997	I	34.9	160.0		III	111	124.3
	II	76.7	133.2		IV	48	142.6
	III	113.2	124.7	2004	I	35	142
	IV	47.7	139.8		II	75	122.5
1998	I	33.4	146.9		III	113.2	119
	II	75.0	134.0		IV	49.9	130.6
	III	110.2	125.8	2005	I	30.4	145.3
	IV	48.7	146.6		II	68.2	125.9
1999	I	32.5	161.7		III	105.3	115.4
	II	73.2	126.1		IV	44	126.2
	III	109.5	122.4	2006	I	25.8	141
	IV	48.4	143.3		II	65.8	123.9
2000	I	30.8	161.4		III	105	114.6
	II	74.1	125.5		IV	40.4	123.1

Source: Monthly Digest of Statistics.
Data available in file 9T18.

(iii) Table 9.19 shows consumers' expenditure in the UK on different categories. How do you explain the difference in seasonal patterns and trends between the series?

Table 9.19		UK household final consumption expenditure, £m at constant prices									
Year	Quarter	Food and Drink	Alcohol and Tobacco	Clothing and Footwear	Restaurants and Hotels	Year	Quarter	Food and Drink	Alcohol and Tobacco	Clothing and Footwear	Restaurants and Hotels
2000	III	14 451	5991	8 780	18 327	2004	II	15 913	6485	11 232	19 339
2000	IV	15 088	6677	11 224	17 803	2004	III	15 499	6415	11 664	20 839
2001	I	14 291	5686	7 716	15 275	2004	IV	16 673	7331	14 396	17 394
2001	II	14 150	6055	8 675	17 020	2005	I	16 106	6412	9 821	18 710
2001	III	14 506	6181	9 106	19 242	2005	II	16 636	6698	10 914	21 294
2001	IV	15 940	6872	12 016	18 524	2005	III	15 956	6766	11 167	22 434
2002	I	14 551	5925	8 559	16 188	2005	IV	17 533	7449	14 508	21 455
2002	II	14 988	6286	9 497	18 203	2006	I	16 375	6230	10 115	18 528
2002	III	14 825	6243	10 097	20 001	2006	II	17 020	6605	11 501	21 139
2002	IV	16 360	7063	13 163	19 264	2006	III	16 514	6655	11 889	22 591
2003	I	15 248	6028	9 110	16 522	2006	IV	18 061	7410	15 565	21 390
2003	II	15 589	6358	10 196	18 552	2007	I	17 278	6346	10 842	18 847
2003	III	15 130	6366	10 747	20 673	2007	II	17 495	6727	12 160	21 571
2003	IV	16 211	7213	13 994	20 026	2007	III	17 141	6744	12 537	22 775
2004	I	15 563	6153	9 967	17 209	2007	IV	18 541	7530	16 126	21 347

Source: Monthly Digest of Statistics.
Data available in file 9T19.

4 Table 9.20 shows the official seasonally adjusted series for the consumer expenditure categories shown in Table 9.19. Compare these with your own calculations. Comment on any differences.

Table 9.20	UK household final consumption expenditure, £m at constant prices, seasonally adjusted			
Year	Quarter	Food and Drink	Alcohol and Tobacco	Clothing and Footwear	Restaurants and Hotels
2000	III	14 717	6131	9 064	17 095
2000	IV	14 602	6111	8 985	17 200
2001	I	14 612	6059	9 119	17 162
2001	II	14 146	6137	9 379	17 003
2001	III	14 856	6325	9 444	17 906
2001	IV	15 317	6268	9 648	17 800
2002	I	14 908	6322	10 051	18 167
2002	II	14 899	6380	10 241	18 331
2002	III	15 202	6385	10 430	18 563
2002	IV	15 715	6430	10 594	18 595
2003	I	15 561	6435	10 704	18 538
2003	II	15 575	6463	10 925	18 624
2003	III	15 473	6529	11 127	19 251
2003	IV	15 589	6538	11 291	19 360
2004	I	15 842	6575	11 710	19 320
2004	II	15 879	6597	11 992	19 391
2004	III	15 858	6501	12 105	19 415
2004	IV	15 975	6631	11 815	19 665
2005	I	16 402	6853	11 445	21 168
2005	II	16 550	6808	11 538	21 037
2005	III	16 514	6898	11 620	20 876
2005	IV	16 765	6766	11 807	20 812
2006	I	16 593	6652	11 852	20 838
2006	II	16 993	6715	12 175	20 866
2006	III	17 024	6766	12 404	20 988
2006	IV	17 360	6767	12 639	20 956
2007	I	17 513	6794	12 656	21 187
2007	II	17 461	6841	12 845	21 269
2007	III	17 695	6849	13 027	21 101
2007	IV	17 786	6863	13 137	20 983

Source: *Monthly Digest of Statistics*.
Data available in file 9T20.

5 A large retail organisation is currently investigating a number of areas of its operations with a view to improving performance in terms of efficiency, sales and profits. The organisation has been monitoring the monthly sales of one of its more profitable products for the last few years with a view to trying to forecast future demand. Someone in the organisation has applied time-series analysis to the monthly sales figures and calculated both the trend and the seasonally adjusted sales figures for the first five months of the current year (the latest available). These are shown in Table 9.21.

Table 9.21	Seasonally adjusted sales figures (£000s)		
	Actual sales	Trend	Seasonally-adjusted sales
Jan	63	78.50	76.3
Feb	85	80.88	80.7
Mar	100	83.88	84.5
Apr	81	85.88	87.5
May	89	86.47	88.6

Unfortunately, the person who completed the analysis has left the company and none of the senior managers understands the information provided. You have been asked to provide a short briefing report to management.

(a) Explain in the context of the application what is meant by time-series analysis and why it is important.

(b) Explain why the actual sales figures are of little value by themselves for forecasting purposes.

(c) Explain what is meant by seasonally adjusted sales and how this information could be used.

6 Working with a small group of colleagues, develop a consensus view of private car sales in Western Europe in five years' time. In order to do this you will need to:

● collect historical data on car sales

● collect data on related variables: population trends, income levels, public transport, etc.

● collect published market research data

● apply quantitative techniques for trend projection

● integrate these projections with likely scenarios.

7 Investigate sources of published statistics that show a seasonal pattern in publications such as *Monthly Digest of Statistics, Economic Trends*. For a variable which is published in both unadjusted and seasonally adjusted format, find out the seasonal adjustment method used.

10 Forecasting II: Regression

Learning objectives

At the end of this chapter you should to able to:

- understand the principles of simple linear regression
- be able to interpret the key statistics from a regression equation
- be able to explain the limitations of regression in business forecasting
- be aware of the extensions to the basic regression model

In the last chapter we introduced a number of ways of trying to forecast some variable in which we were interested. As we saw, a variety of non-causal models exist for attempting this – models which simply try to predict future changes in the variable without attempting to provide an explanation as to what is causing such change. In this chapter we introduce another method of forecasting, which is to develop a causal model – where we do try to analyse the causes of change in the variable we are trying to forecast. This method is known as regression and we shall be examining the basic form of the model, known as simple linear regression.

The Principles of Simple Linear Regression

To illustrate the principles of simple linear regression we shall return to an example we introduced in Chapter 3, where we were looking at the use of scatter diagrams. The data related to a sample of profit centres in a large company and for each profit centre we had data relating to the centre's profit last year and its sales or turnover figure. Consider a situation where the company is opening a new store with an anticipated initial sales level of £78,000. The Finance Director has asked for a forecast of this store's profit. The data for the existing stores is duplicated in Table 10.1 and the scatter diagram in Figure 10.1. As we saw in Chapter 3, and as is confirmed by the scatter of points on the diagram, for the existing stores there appears to be some definite connection between the two variables in that as one variable takes higher values so does the other. In the context of the business problem this is unsurprising, as we would anticipate that a store with higher turnover would, by and large, generate higher profits. What we seek to establish is the exact numerical relationship between the two variables so that, for any given profit centre, we can try to forecast profit based on some turnover level. This would then allow us to forecast profit for the new store. We begin by clarifying what we believe – or hypothesise – the relationship between the two variables to be:

$$\text{Profit} = f(\text{Sales})$$

Table 10.1	Sales and profits for 20 stores in Region A
Sales (£000s)	Profit (£000s)
748.82	42.13
140.78	6.32
702.11	38.47
41.54	−0.32
96.85	3.65
166.93	7.77
109.05	4.31
263.92	4.53
50.84	−2.69
90.08	3.22
190.59	9.03
91.75	−2.59
141.57	6.39
377.04	24.39
198.69	13.92
62.78	2.13
265.28	17.48
91.80	7.21
231.60	15.62
548.31	33.61

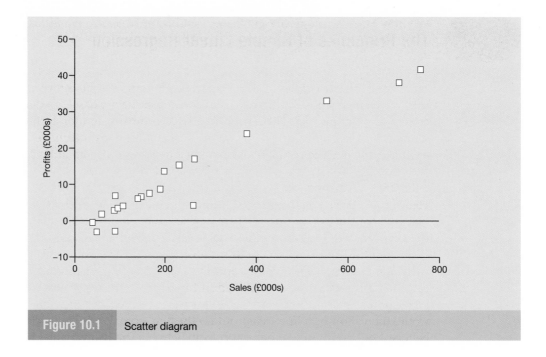

Scatter diagram

Mathematically this indicates that profit is a function of sales (the term $f(\ )$ indicates 'a function of'). We should be clear about the implications of this specification. We are implying in this formulation that profit 'depends' on sales. That is, in some, as yet unspecified, way sales influences or 'causes' profits. Clearly in a business context such a causal relationship makes considerable sense. In general we would specify the relationship between any two variables as:

$$Y = f(X)$$

where Y is known as the *dependent* variable and X as the *independent* or explanatory variable. We will also go one stage further and assume that the relationship between the two variables is a linear one: it will result in a straight line if plotted on a graph. This seems reasonable on visual inspection of the scatter diagram. We should note that such an assumption is not always appropriate and will depend much on the context of the problem. This means the general form of our relationship can be specified as:

$$Y = a + bX$$

where a and b are known as the parameters of the linear equation: the numerical values which give the equation its form. a is generally referred to as the intercept of the function and b as the slope. Before we consider the implications of this for forecasting we need to ensure that the principles of intercept and slope are clear.

The intercept of a linear function

The intercept of a linear function indicates where that function would cross – or intercept – the vertical, Y, axis. Another way of considering this is to say that the intercept term indicates the value that Y takes when X = 0. Consider the linear equation:

$$Y = 10 + 5X$$

We now know without any graphs or calculations that this equation will cross the Y axis where Y = 10. Equally we can see that if we set X = 0 then Y must take the intercept value of 10. We also realise that a second linear equation:

$$Y = -10 + 5X$$

differs from the first only in its intercept value. In the second instance the intercept equals –10, so this equation will cross the vertical axis at Y = –10.

Activity 10.1

Assume a third linear equation such that:

$$Y = 5X$$

Where would this cross the vertical axis?

The third example has a zero intercept: it could be rewritten as:

$$Y = 0 + 5X$$

implying that it will pass through the origin, where Y = 0. The effect on an equation of a change only in the intercept is illustrated in Figure 10.2.

The slope of a linear function

The slope of a linear function is given by the *b* term in the equation and shows the relationship between a change in the X variable and a change in the Y variable. The *b* term is sometimes referred to as the gradient. It literally indicates the steepness of the straight line representing the function. Let us return to the first function:

$$Y = 10 + 5X$$

Its slope is 5. This indicates that a change in X will bring about a five times change in Y. Let X = 2 and we calculate that Y = 20. If X now changes to 3 (a change of 1) then Y will change to 25: a change of 5 – the *b* value. Note that the same logic applies to a

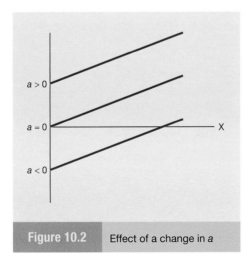

Figure 10.2   Effect of a change in *a*

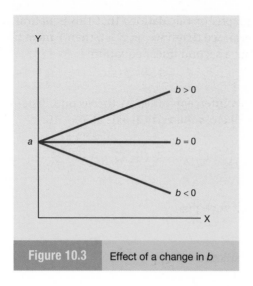

Figure 10.3	Effect of a change in *b*

negative change in X. If X reduces from 3 to 2 (a change of −1) then the change in Y must be −5. The *b* term, in other words, provides an indication of the change relationship between the two variables. As with the *a* term, different *b* values are readily compared. A function:

$$Y = 10 + 10X$$

would be twice as steep as the first function: its slope is twice as great. This time a change in X will bring about a tenfold change in Y. As with the *a* term, the *b* value can be negative as well as positive. Consider an equation:

$$Y = 10 - 5X$$

In the first example we saw that with a positive slope a change in X brought about some (multiplied) change in Y: an increase in X was followed by an increase in Y, a decrease by a decrease. With a negative value for *b* the reverse occurs. An increase in X now brings about a decrease in Y. Graphically a function with a negative value for *b* would slope downwards as we look at it from left to right. The effect on an equation of a change in *b* is illustrated in Figure 10.3.

It is important to be able to visualise the implications of different values for *a* and *b* without resorting to a graph or to calculations.

Activity 10.2

For the following equations sketch each group of functions on the same diagram. The diagram should be drawn without performing any calculations.

(a) 1. $Y = 100 + 5X$
     2. $Y = 100 + 10X$
     3. $Y = 100 - 5X$

(b) 1. $Y = 100 + 5X$
     2. $Y = -100 + 5X$
     3. $Y = 5X$

Solutions are given on p 591.

One final aspect relating to the slope of a linear function needs to be considered. We saw that *a* could take a zero value. What of *b*? If the slope is zero then it implies that as X changes Y remains unchanged. Graphically we would have a line parallel to the X axis: Y would always take the same value regardless of X. More importantly in terms of the functional expression, this would imply that X and Y were *not* functionally related: Y did not depend on X for its value – it was independent of X. This is an important point, to which we shall return later.

Activity 10.3

In the case of the profit/sales relationship we had earlier:

Profit = *a* + *b*Sales

What general numerical values would we expect *a* and *b* to take in this business context: negative, zero or positive?

It is important in this type of analysis to consider carefully the contextual – as opposed to the mathematical – interpretation of the *a* and *b* terms. The exact business interpretation of the parameters will depend on the business context. The *b* term is the slope or gradient of the straight line and, in general, indicates the change in Y that occurs for a given change in X. In our context this would be the change in profit for a change in sales. The *b* term, therefore, will be an indication of the profit margin on sales and we would normally expect this to be positive: as sales increase so do profits. The *a* term is the intercept and indicates, graphically, where the line intercepts the Y axis. It can also be interpreted as the value that Y takes when X = 0. Here, *a* will indicate the profit when sales are zero. Of course, we would never expect to encounter such a situation, but there is an obvious implication. It is unrealistic to expect profit to be positive when sales = 0. At best we would expect profit to be zero also or, more realistically, negative (i.e. representing a loss, since some overhead expenses are likely to have been incurred even when sales are zero). So we might expect a relationship between our two variables such that:

Profit = *a* + *b*X

where $a \leq 0$ and $b > 0$. Clearly from a business perspective it would be extremely useful to have such an equation which quantified the relationship between two such variables. Such a linear equation can be estimated using the principles of simple linear regression – so called because we are trying to quantify the parameters of a *linear* equation and because we are dealing with the *simplest* equation, which has only one explanatory variable. We shall see later how the approach can be adapted both to non-linear situations and to situations where we have multiple explanatory variables.

The Correlation Coefficient

Before we consider the process of estimating such an equation, it will be worthwhile seeing first whether we can measure statistically the strength of the relationship that might exist between the two variables. We might, in general, encounter a situation where there is, literally, no connection between the two variables. Equally, we might encounter a situation where the connection is a particularly strong one. Although the scatter diagram is useful in providing a graphical, but subjective, assessment about the strength of the relationship between two variables, we clearly need a statistical measure. Statistically such a connection is referred to as *correlation* and we can calculate what is known as the coefficient of correlation between the X and Y variables. Such a coefficient will take a value between 0 and 1: zero implies literally no correlation between the two variables, while one implies perfect correlation. Anyone in their right mind these days will use a spreadsheet or a statistical package to calculate such a statistic. While we encourage you to do this, we shall introduce and use the appropriate calculation formula, which, because of the mathematics, we simply present as:

$$r = \frac{\Sigma(x - \bar{x})(y - \bar{y})}{\sqrt{\Sigma(x - \bar{x})^2}\ \sqrt{\Sigma(y - \bar{y})^2}}$$

where r is used to denote the correlation coefficient and the calculations are effectively measuring the difference of x and y values from their respective means. For calculation purposes this is usually rewritten as:

$$r = \frac{\Sigma xy - (\Sigma x \Sigma y)/n}{\sqrt{\Sigma x^2 - (\Sigma x)^2/n}\ \sqrt{\Sigma y^2 - (\Sigma y)^2/n}}$$

where n is the number of pairs of data items. Although both formulae might look equally horrendous, the second is actually much easier to use for calculation purposes, since all we actually require from the data are the terms:

$$\Sigma x,\ \Sigma y,\ \Sigma x^2,\ \Sigma y^2,\ \Sigma xy$$

Activity 10.4

Using profit as Y and sales as X calculate the totals shown in the last equation and calculate the value for r for this data.

Table 10.2 shows the results of these calculations for our data, with the values of interest being the column totals.

These can be readily substituted into the r formula:

$$r = \frac{\Sigma xy - (\Sigma x \Sigma y)/n}{\sqrt{\Sigma x^2 - (\Sigma x)^2/n}\ \sqrt{\Sigma y^2 - (\Sigma y)^2/n}}$$

$$= \frac{(104\ 732.59) - (4610.33)(234.58)/20}{\sqrt{1\ 888\ 170.77 - (4610.33)^2/20}\ \sqrt{6078.73 - (234.58)^2/20}}$$

$$= \frac{50\ 658.03}{\sqrt{825\ 413.63}\ \sqrt{3327.34}} = \frac{50\ 658.03}{(908.52)(57.68)}$$

$$= 0.97$$

giving a correlation coefficient of 0.97. Interpretation is as follows. First of all we note that the correlation coefficient is positive (it can be negative). This implies a positive relationship between the two variables: as one increases so does the other, and this is exactly what we would expect in a business context for these two variables. A negative coefficient would imply an inverse relationship: as one variable increases the other decreases. Second, we note that on the scale from 0 to 1, the coefficient is very close to one (perfect correlation). This implies that there is a very strong relationship between the two variables. It seems reasonable to conclude that there is a strong positive relationship between profit and sales (although we do not yet know numerically what the relationship is).

Table 10.2	Calculations for r			

x	y	x^2	y^2	xy
748.82	42.13	560 731.39	1 774.94	31 547.79
140.78	6.32	19 819.01	39.94	889.73
702.11	38.47	492 958.45	1 479.94	27 010.17
41.54	−0.32	1 725.57	0.10	−13.29
96.85	3.65	9 379.92	13.32	353.50
166.93	7.77	27 865.62	60.37	1 297.05
109.05	4.31	11 891.90	18.58	470.01
263.92	4.53	69 653.77	20.52	1 195.56
50.84	−2.69	2 584.71	7.24	−136.76
90.08	3.22	8 114.41	10.37	290.06
190.59	9.03	36 324.55	81.54	1 721.03
91.75	−2.59	8 418.06	6.71	−237.63
141.57	6.39	20 042.06	40.83	904.63
377.04	24.39	142 159.16	594.87	9 196.01
198.69	13.92	39 477.72	193.77	2 765.76
62.78	2.13	3 941.33	4.54	133.72
265.28	17.48	70 373.48	305.55	4 637.09
91.80	7.21	8 427.24	51.98	661.88
231.60	15.62	53 638.56	243.98	3 617.59
548.31	33.61	300 643.86	1 129.63	18 428.70
Total 4 610.33	234.58	1 888 170.77	6 078.73	104 732.59

However, a few words of caution are necessary about the use of this coefficient. First, the coefficient measures the strength of the relationship between two variables. It does not measure cause and effect. Our choice of which variable to label x and which y was based on logic and the context of the problem, not on statistics. You may be able to see, on inspection of the coefficient formula, that if we now called profit x and sales y and recalculated the coefficient we would come up with exactly the same numerical value. (If you can't see this then do the recalculation now.) This makes perfect sense, since the strength of the relationship must be the same no matter which variable we label x and y. The second point is that technically the coefficient measures the strength of the *linear* relationship between the two variables. Here we have evidence of a strong linear relationship between profit and sales. In some cases there may be a strong relationship between two variables which is not linear. We need to consider the implications of this for the coefficient.

Consider the scatter diagram shown in Figure 10.4. It is evident that there is a strong relationship between the two variables and equally that this relationship is not a linear one. The correlation coefficient in such a situation would show a value of 0, or there-abouts. We must be cautious then in interpreting the correlation coefficient. It actually indicates the strength of the *linear* relationship between the two variables. A low value for the coefficient implies little evidence of a linear relationship but tells us nothing about other possible relationship forms. However, the calculation for our problem at 0.97 indicates evidence of strong linear relationship and we now need to progress to see how we can quantify this relationship.

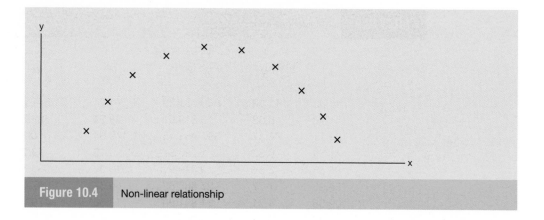

Figure 10.4   Non-linear relationship

Why states must grow

By Stephanie Flanders

Do countries sustain economic growth by limiting the size of government, or do they limit the size of government by sustaining growth? Three years as the Governor of Hong Kong have left Chris Patten believing in the first proposition.

In his view, lean government helped east Asia grow rich, and it could do the same for the lethargic economies of western Europe – if only our over-burdened political systems would allow it. Yet, even if we assume with Mr Patten that east Asia's success was grounded more in universal economic principles than in cultural norms, the lessons for Europe would be less obvious than he suggests.

There is no getting around the fact that government outlays take up a far smaller share of GDP than in most western European countries. Government spending in the "tiger" economies of Hong Kong, Singapore, South Korea and Taiwan averaged 20 per cent of GDP between 1980 and 1993, compared to an average share of 48 per cent for the European industrial countries.

Those who argue that small government is the result – rather than

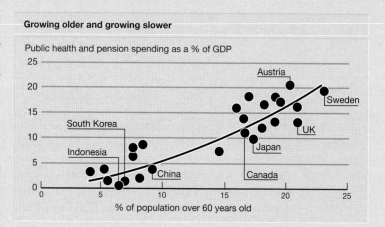

Growing older and growing slower

Public health and pension spending as a % of GDP

% of population over 60 years old

the cause – of east Asia's success can point out that it is far easier to keep government expenditure rising in line with GDP when the denominator is going through the roof. The tigers' real GDP per capita grew by roughly $6\frac{1}{2}$ per cent a year, on average, between 1980 and 1993.

In the long run, though, it is one of the best-established relationships in economics – Wagner's law, named after Adolph Heinrich Wagner, a nineteenth century German economist – that the ratio of government spending to GDP will rise as a country grows richer. This is because publicly-provided services, such as education and

health, are "superior goods": a 1 per cent increase in income triggers a more than 1 per cent rise in demand.

Over the years, every industrialised country has tended to confirm Wagner's prediction. The tiger economies do seem so far to have avoided it, even though real GDP per capita, at least in Singapore and Hong Kong, is now close to European levels. But the fact that they have managed to achieve western standards of living without western-style expenditure growth may have very little to do with their approach to government, and everything to do with demography.

Alongside the region's rapid development was an equally dramatic move towards rich country rates of population growth. This rapidly declining birth rate had two highly favourable consequences for government spending. First, because there were fewer young people, governments could meet the demand for higher levels of education without actually having to spend more on education as a share of GDP. The second bonus was higher national saving, because a rising share of the population was going through the "high-saving" years of the life cycle. This formed part of a virtuous cycle by which high saving made for continued high rates of growth, leading to a further rise in overall saving, because saving by richer, middle-aged workers exceeded the dis-saving of their retired parents.

Sooner or later, the logic of declining population growth will start to work the other way round, leading to higher levels of government spending on health and pensions. In Singapore, for example, the Asian Development Bank calculates that nearly 30 per cent of the population will be over 60 in 2025, compared to less than 9 per cent in 1990. Traditional, informal systems of providing for the elderly have so far been surprisingly resilient against the effects of rapid economic and social change. But the World Bank and others firmly expect the region to move towards more formal, public methods of support in future.

This does not necessarily mean the government share of GDP will reach European levels. It all depends on whether east Asia can avoid the two problems which have done most to speed the workings of Wagner's law in Europe. First, and most important, was a rapid decline in average rates of economic growth since the early 1970s, which put further upward pressure on public spending just as the effects of an ageing population were beginning to kick in.

Europe's second problem was its reliance on "pay as you go" pensions systems, which fund public pensions using current workers' contributions. This may have produced a vicious circle which is an exact reversal of east Asia's youthful, virtuous one.

Middle-aged people, expecting to receive a public pension, may save less than they would otherwise. At any event, their contributions have not added to national saving – as they would under a funded scheme. Indeed, public dis-saving has risen, as governments struggle to meet pension demands in a low investment, low growth environment.

As many of Mr Patten's critics have pointed out, east Asian governments have not generally been known for their *laissez faire* approach – particularly with regard to the mandatory pension schemes and state provident funds employed to increase national saving. Ironically enough, the most relevant lesson for Europe of east Asia's growth miracle may in fact be the need for more rather than less state involvement in the functioning of certain parts of the economy. Adopting an Asian approach to ensuring that baby boomers save for their old age would not, in itself, free Europe from the trap of low savings and growth rates. But it might stop us moving ever further in the wrong direction.

Source: *Financial Times*, 6 November 1995, p 25.

Use of scatter diagram and line of best fit to show the link between two variables.

The Line of Best Fit

We wish to obtain precise numerical values for the *a* and *b* values of the linear equation linking profit to sales. The mathematics underpinning regression is quite formidable and we shall make no attempt to justify it here. However, the general approach can be understood using a little logic and will be worth developing. If we return to Figure 10.1, the scatter diagram, we are looking for an equation that quantifies the linear relationship between the two variables. Such an equation graphically would give us a straight line. However, it is also clear from the diagram that the 20 points we have do not all lie on one straight line (if they did the correlation coefficient would have been 1). It seems sensible though to try to obtain the straight line that comes as close as possible to as many of the points as possible. You can picture that we could try to do this ourselves by drawing on the graph a straight line that we felt came as close to the points as possible. However, such an approach would clearly be quite subjective with different people drawing (slightly) different straight lines. Mathematically, however, we can do the same thing. The mathematics we shall shortly use calculates the parameters of the straight line that comes closest to these points by minimising the sum of the squared deviations of the pairs of observations from the line. This sounds complex but is in fact based on calculations very similar to those we had for the standard deviation of a set of data. The method often goes under the name of *least squares* for this reason. Remember that we require an equation such that:

$$Y = a + bX$$

where a and b are calculated by:

$$b = \frac{\Sigma xy - (\Sigma x \Sigma y)/n}{\Sigma x^2 - (\Sigma x)^2/n}$$

$$a = \frac{\Sigma y}{n} - b\frac{\Sigma x}{n}$$

The numerical values for a and b can be calculated from the formulae shown. We first calculate the b value and then use this b value to calculate a. You may realise at this stage that we have already calculated all the component parts of the formulae in our correlation coefficient calculations in Table 10.2. The calculations are then:

$$b = \frac{\Sigma xy - (\Sigma x \Sigma y)/n}{\Sigma x^2 - (\Sigma x)^2/n}$$

$$= \frac{104\,732.59 - (4\,610.33)(234.58)/20}{1\,888\,170.77 - 4\,610.33^2/20}$$

$$= \frac{50\,658.03}{825\,413.64} = 0.0614$$

$$a = \frac{\Sigma y}{n} - b\frac{\Sigma x}{n}$$

$$= \frac{234.58}{20} - 0.0614\left(\frac{4\,610.33}{20}\right)$$

$$= 11.729 - 14.15 = -2.421$$

giving an equation:

$$Y = -2.421 + 0.0614X$$

or

$$\text{Profit} = -2.421 + 0.0614\text{Sales}$$

This equation is the line of best fit, or the regression equation for our data. We have estimated the numerical relationship between the two variables based on the data available.

Activity 10.5

What meaning or interpretation can you give to the a and b values we have estimated in the context of this problem?

As we indicated earlier, the *a* term is the intercept of the equation while the *b* term is the gradient or slope. The gradient indicates the change in Y (profit) as X (sales) changes. Consider a change in sales of one unit. Y would then change by 0.0614 units. Effectively, an extra £1 sales will lead to an increase in profit of 6.14p, hence for these 20 centres there is an average profit margin of 6.14 per cent. The *a* term indicates where the line intercepts the vertical axis. Here it intercepts on the negative part of the axis. This means that for low values of X (sales), Y (profit) will be negative. We can actually calculate when the change from negative to positive profit will occur. Let us set Profit = 0. We then have:

$$\text{Profit} = -2.421 + 0.0614\text{Sales} = 0$$

and rearranging gives:

$$0.0614\text{Sales} = 2.421$$
$$\text{Sales} = \frac{2.421}{0.0614} = 39.43$$

So, if sales are below 39.43 (£000), profit will be negative, whereas if sales are above this value, profit will be positive. Effectively we have found the break-even position for this group of stores. A store, on average, needs a sales level of around £39 000 before it starts showing a profit. Note also that the numerical values for *a* and *b* are in line with what we initially thought they should be ($b > 0$, $a \leq 0$). In fact we can superimpose this line of best fit onto the scatter diagram, as in Figure 10.5. This can often help us visualise both the relationship between the variables and the closeness of the various points to the line. We see that a number of points lie on, or close to, the line we have estimated. Although some individual points occur away from the line of best fit, the line does appear to come reasonably close to most of the points shown.

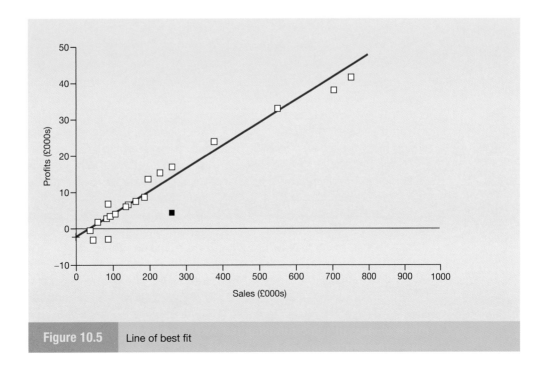

Figure 10.5   Line of best fit

Using the Regression Equation

In fact the diagram with the line of best fit superimposed helps us see how we can now use the regression equation we have estimated. There are two broad uses. The first is to use the equation directly for forecasting; the second is in terms of performance evaluation.

Forecasting

Forecasting with the regression equation is arithmetically straightforward. We were told earlier that the organisation is thinking of opening another store with anticipated sales of £78 000. Can we predict or forecast likely profit for this store? Using the regression equation all we have to do is to substitute the sales value into the equation to obtain:

$$\text{Profit} = -2.421 + 0.0614(78) = 2.3682 \text{ (in £000)}$$

That is, on this sales figure, profit would be forecast to be around £2400. Although the derivation of such a forecast is straightforward, we must exercise considerable caution in its evaluation and use. First of all we must note that such a forecast is not a guaranteed outcome. Effectively, what we have done in the regression procedure is to find an average, and historical, relationship between the two variables for the 20 stores in the data set. Like any average – even though the regression calculations make this relatively sophisticated – it is subject to variation within a data set. The forecast clearly is our best 'guess' based on past performance. Also we need to ensure that the other characteristics of this profit centre – its size, its location, its staffing levels, etc. – are reasonably comparable with those of the sample of 20 centres from which we derived the equation. Second, given that the equation is a measure of the past relationship between the two variables, there is no guarantee that this relationship will continue unchanged in the future (which is where we are forecasting). Naturally, we would hope that the past relationship will continue, but once again there are no guarantees and in evaluating the reliability of the forecast we would need to take into account any supplementary information about possible changing circumstances (for example, a major competitor opening up a short distance away from our store). Third, the forecast we have produced is technically known as an *interpolation* – the X value used to produce the forecast is within the observed limits of other X values. That is, the value of 78 is within the range of previously observed X values. Consider, however, if we had used an X value of 900 – for a store with sales of £900 000. This would be outside the previously observed range of X values for this sample of 20 centres. Although we could produce a forecast in exactly the same way – and this would be 52.839 – this would represent an *extrapolation*: a move into unknown territory. Technically, our regression equation was derived by observing behaviour between the two variables when sales was in the range 41.54 to 748.82. We have no way of knowing from this data what happens to the relationship between sales and profit – which is what the regression equation shows – once sales exceeds the maximum observed figure. By using the profit forecast of 52.839 we are extrapolating the historical relationship beyond its observed range and this increases the risk of the forecast being incorrect, since the relationship between the two variables might change in some fundamental way. Stores with larger sales, for example, might have larger profit margins than smaller stores.

However, despite these caveats we have succeeded in producing a forecast which we might regard as reasonably reliable, particularly given r = 0.97, indicating a strong linear correlation between the two variables under consideration.

Performance evaluation

The second use of the regression equation is in the context of performance evaluation of the existing stores. Effectively what the regression line shows us is the profit a particular store *should* have made given its sales level. Stores which have an actual profit figure above the line are 'over'-performing: turning in a profit which exceeds what we would have expected based simply on sales. Similarly stores which have an actual profit below the line are 'under'-performing. Clearly we would not evaluate performance simply on the basis of this analysis but the estimated equation does provide an insight into relative performance of individual stores. We note from Figure 10.5, for example, that one store, shown as a solid square, with sales of around £264 000, is considerably below the line. In terms of priority and focus we might use the regression equation as a means of assisting management. This store should perhaps be one of the first to be investigated in terms of its profit performance: it appears to be under-performing since its profit is considerably below average given its sales level. Naturally there will be other factors that might emerge from the investigation: the store might recently have been closed for major refurbishment; a large local employer may have closed down, decreasing local income levels; a new competitor might have opened up nearby. Nevertheless, the use of the regression equation to highlight performance at variance with what we would have normally expected should not be underestimated.

A better burger thanks to data crunching

FT

By Robert Matthews

HG Wells foresaw a time when what he called "statistical thinking" would play a key role in the running of society. Those who think of statistics as a way of keeping tabs on Albanian coal output will see this as one of his less inspirational predictions. But for anyone who believes in the power of data to create a better world where evidence reigns supreme, the good news is that the future is already here.

Or at least the foundations are, in the form of data mining: the extraction of insight from data gathered during the operation of everything from airlines and bookstores to supermarkets and schools.

This was all-but impossible before machine-readable records and computing power to crunch the stuff. But now we have both, and it is starting to transform our lives, as Yale Law School econometrician Ian Ayres shows in Super Crunchers, this entertaining, enlightening tour of our data-driven world.

Two statistical techniques lie at the heart of the revolution: regression and randomisation. The former uncovers connections between, say, the chances of people defaulting on their mortgage and factors influencing that risk, such as age, income and type of work.

Airlines, supermarkets, car hire companies and even dating agencies all run computerised "regression analysis" on their raw data to identify the key factors behind everything from sales of dog food to success in love.

The effects can be felt by consumers, says Ayres, in subtle changes in the way they are treated. For example, when airlines cancel flights, some no longer woo faithful frequent fliers, but focus instead on the customers that regression analysis reveals are most likely never to fly with the airline again. Similarly, credit card users wanting to close accounts are assessed using regression methods – only those predicted to be profitable get the sweet-talk.

To reveal the influence of a single factor – say, some new education policy - in the presence of lots of extraneous effects, data miners turn to randomisation.

People are randomly allocated to two groups: those who will and those who won't be exposed to the new policy. Differences between the two groups can then be put down to the effect of the policy change, as all the other factors have been evenly distributed between them.

Medical scientists have used the technique for decades to identify life-saving new therapies, via patients recruited into randomised controlled trials (RCTs). Now its power is being seized on by business. Ads, mail-shot campaigns, even book titles, are tested before launch in colossal RCTs involving hundreds of thousands of people.

National policy programmes are starting to be based on RCT results. Ayres cites Mexico's Progresa programme, which targets grants and nutritional supplements on families whose kids stay at school.

Ayres balances his infectious enthusiasm with tales of where data mining can and has gone wrong. Correlation is not causation, and "garbage in" still means "garbage out" – as demonstrated by the salutary story of how honest mistakes led to a spurious correlation between wider gun ownership and lower crime rates – and to several US states changing their laws in line with the "evidence".

As Ayres points out, some people have a visceral loathing of the suggestion that the quality of a wine, a movie script or a relationship can be reduced to mere numbers. Yet those seeking a better world, or just a better burger, may have to get used to the idea that, to paraphrase Churchill on democracy, data mining is the worst possible basis for big decisions – apart from all the others.

The reviewer is visiting reader in science at Aston University, UK

Source: Financial Times, 6 September 2007. © Robert Matthews

Regression is in more widespread use than you might at first think.

Further Statistical Evaluation of the Regression Equation

We can develop the statistical evaluation of the regression equation further. We shall explore this by introducing the coefficient of determination and statistical tests on the equation parameters. To explain the coefficient of determination we need to return to the idea of the regression equation as that of the method of least squares. One way of looking at regression is to say: we have observed some variation within the y values and we can measure this (as we might the standard deviation). We also have observed variation in the x data. Regression is effectively trying to link the variation in the y variable with the variation in the x variable (seeing if the two variations happen at the same time, if you like). We might find that all the variation in y can be associated with the variation in x, or, at the other extreme, that none of the variation in y can be so associated. In fact we can distinguish three types of variation:

- the total variation in y
- the variation in y associated with variation in x
- the variation in y not associated with x.

Activity 10.6

In terms of the regression equation, given the total variation, would you prefer the variation in y associated with variation in x to be as high or as low as possible?

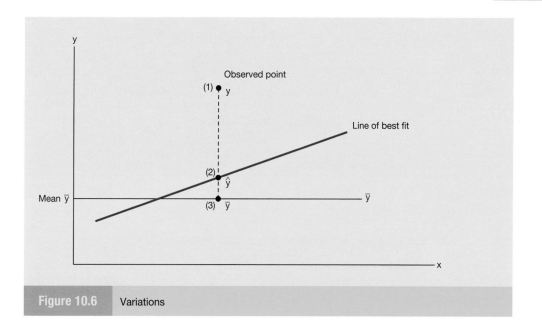

Figure 10.6   Variations

Clearly the whole purpose of regression is to try to allocate as much of the total variation in y to the variation in our chosen x variable. We would want, therefore, this variation to be as high as possible. In regression terminology these three types of variation are referred to as total variation, explained variation and unexplained variation respectively. Let us examine Figure 10.6. This shows our line of best fit together with a horizontal line representing the mean of the y values in the data set and one (fictitious) observed point. To help distinguish between the various parts of the diagram we will use the following notation:

y   the observed, actual, y value
$\bar{y}$ the mean of all the y values (pronounced 'y bar')
$\hat{y}$ the value of y predicted by the regression equation (pronounced 'y hat').

You will remember that we said earlier that the regression equation is estimated using the principle of least squares. We can view the difference between y and $\bar{y}$ (between point 1 and point 3 on the graph) as a measure of the total variation: the difference between an individual y value and the mean of all the y values. Of this total variation $\hat{y} - \bar{y}$ (point 2–3) is the variation 'explained' by the regression line, whereas $y - \hat{y}$ (point 1–2) is that part of total variation which is 'unexplained'. Given that we measure variation in terms of squared differences (as with the standard deviations) then for this single observation we have:

Total variation: $(y - \bar{y})^2$
Explained variation: $(\hat{y} - \bar{y})^2$
Unexplained variation: $(y - \hat{y})^2$

Note that we require the explained variation to be as large as possible in relation to the total variation and that the explained variation will be larger the closer the observed y value is to the estimated (given the line of best fit). In other words, the closer the estimated regression line is to the observed y value, the higher the explained variation will be in relation to the total variation. This applies to our single y value but clearly also applies to all the y values taken together. For all the data set we then have:

Total variation:	$\Sigma(y - \bar{y})^2$
Explained variation:	$\Sigma(\hat{y} - \bar{y})^2$
Unexplained variation:	$\Sigma(y - \hat{y})^2$

If we take a ratio of the explained variation to the total variation:

$$\frac{\Sigma(\hat{y} - \bar{y})^2}{\Sigma(y - \bar{y})^2}$$

we have what is known as the coefficient of determination. This is denoted as R^2 (R squared).

Activity 10.7

What are the maximum and minimum values that R^2 could take for any set of data? How would you interpret these?

On reflection you should be able to see that the maximum value R^2 could take would be one, implying that all the variation was explained, or accounted for, by the regression equation. At the other extreme the minimum value would be zero. Typically we would expect the value to be between the two and, preferably, closer to one than zero. As such, the statistic will indicate the percentage of the total variation in y accounted for by the x variable. In practice, such a statistic would normally be computed by the regression software program you were using. In the case of our problem, the R^2 works out at $R^2 = 0.93$. Ninety-three per cent of the total variation in profit (y) can be accounted for by variation in sales (x). We should also note that r, the correlation coefficient, is the square root of R^2, so either value can be calculated if we know the value of the other. Clearly we have statistical evidence of a strong relationship – as measured by our estimated equation – between the two variables. In fact we can test the estimated equation using the principles of hypothesis testing that we developed in Chapter 7.

Statistical tests on the equation parameters

You will remember from Chapter 7 that it was possible to test a sample statistic, such as the mean, against some hypothesised value for the population. In a variety of ways we can view our estimated regression equation as being a sample: we have used data for only a sample of 20 stores; we have used data for only a sample of years; we might have included data on other explanatory variables and so on. So, we can hypothesise about the population linear relationship and generalise this as:

$$Y = \alpha + \beta X$$

where α (alpha) and β (beta) are the population parameters of the equation (we continue using Greek characters to show population values). Clearly what we now have in our estimated equation $Y = -2.421 + 0.0614X$ is a sample result, and we might wish to test the statistical significance of this result. There are a variety of ways of doing this but we shall consider only one: a test on the *b* parameter in the estimated equation. Remember that the *b* term in the equation measures the slope of the line of best fit.

Activity 10.8

Suppose we set the H_0: $\beta = 0$. What would this imply for the relationship between X and Y?

The b term quantifies the relationship between X and Y in terms of how Y changes as X changes. If b were actually zero this would imply that Y did not change with X, i.e. there was no connection between the two. Suppose, then, we set up a hypothesis test to determine whether the b term in the equation (which is after all only a sample result) could actually have come from a statistical population where the slope, β, was actually zero. If we conclude that this has happened then it would imply that there was actually no statistically significant relationship between the two variables. If we rejected this hypothesis then we would be forced to conclude – based on the sample data – that b was not zero and that there was a significant relationship between X and Y (which is best estimated using the calculated regression line). The principles of such a test are basically as detailed in Chapter 7.

$$H_0: \beta = 0$$
$$H_1: \beta \neq 0$$
$$\alpha = 0.05$$
$$\text{d.f.} = n - 2 = 18$$
$$t_{\alpha,18} = 2.101$$
$$t_{Calc} = \frac{b - \beta}{SE_b}$$

The null hypothesis is formulated such that we assume there is no relationship between X and Y: that $\beta = 0$. This requires us to provide sufficient evidence that there is such a relationship if we want to use the regression equation. The significance level is set at 0.05 and we must use the t distribution for the test, given we technically have a small sample. For a simple linear regression the number of degrees of freedom is given by $(n - 2)$, here 18. From the t table this gives a critical value of 2.101. The calculated t value is then found by taking the difference between the sample value and the hypothesised population value and dividing by the standard error of b. Although the standard error can be manually calculated from the formula:

$$SE_b = \sqrt{\frac{\Sigma(y - \hat{y})^2/(n - 2)}{\Sigma x^2 - \left(\frac{\Sigma x}{n}\right)^2}}$$

it is more realistic to assume it will be produced by an appropriate software package. Such a package for our data would produce a result such that $SE_b = 0.003833$ and $t_{Calc} = 16.03$. Given that the calculated t statistic is greater than the critical, we would be forced to accept H_1 at the 95 per cent level and conclude that there is a significant relationship between the two variables (that is, that the slope of the population equation is not zero).

Consider again the logic of the test. We have estimated the slope of the regression line with sample data. We hypothesise that, notwithstanding the numerical result, the 'true' value of the equation for the population is $\beta = 0$: effectively that there is no statistically significant relationship between the X and Y variables. If this is the case we can measure the maximum distance, expressed in SEs, between β and *b* we would expect at the 95 per cent level. This distance is 2.101SEs: if H₀ is correct then β and *b* should be no further apart than this. We actually find that *b* is 16.03 SEs away from the hypothesised value for β. This is more than we would have expected on the basis of the null hypothesis and we are forced to reject the null hypothesis and accept the alternative instead. We have statistical evidence that there is a significant relationship between the two variables, profit and sales, based on this data, although remembering as we always must with statistical inference the possibilities of a Type I or II error.

It is important to understand that such a test is essential before considering the use of a regression equation in business forecasting. When performing regression we always get the line of best fit for the data being analysed. However, the term 'best fit' can be misleading. Best fit does not necessarily mean 'good fit' in the sense that we have a statistically significant relationship between the X and Y variables being analysed. The only reliable way to assess whether a regression equation is statistically sound is to perform a formal hypothesis test as we have just done. Even then, this is no guarantee that the regression equation will be reliable in a forecasting sense.

Using computer output

These days, regression models are produced via the result of some computer software, whether this is a simple spreadsheet system or a more sophisticated statistical modelling package. The output from such software varies but the general principles are relatively common. We show the results from one such package in the context of our problem in Table 10.3. The *Summary Output* shows the key statistical information. The *Regression Statistics* show the *Multiple R* at 0.96663826. This is our correlation coefficient value (note that there are slight differences between the computer output and our manual calculations as we kept the latter simple by rounding values down). Under this we have the *R Square* at 0.934389526. At the bottom of the summary output we have the regression equation results. We see an *Intercept coefficient* of –2.418465725 and a *Sales coefficient* result of 0.061372898, confirming our own calculated regression equation. For each of the equation parameters we also see a *Standard error*, a *t Stat*, a *P-value* and a *Lower 95%* and *Upper 95%* statistic. We saw earlier that we could undertake a statistical hypothesis test on the *b* value. The output gives us the calculated t value (at 16.01) and also the associated p-value. We looked at p values in Chapter 7. Recollect that the p value is a quick way of seeing how likely the null hypothesis is, based on the sample data. The lower the p value then the less likely the null hypothesis and if the p value is less than the significance level of the test (where we usually choose to do the test at either the 5 per cent or 1 per cent level) then we reject the null hypothesis. Recollect also, that when testing the *b* coefficient in the regression equation the null hypothesis is the *b* = 0. The p value from the output is 4.30781E–12, which seems a very odd number if you're not used to seeing them in this format. This is a standard way in many computer packages of showing very small numerical values. The E term actually represents the number 10 so we actually have:

$$4.30781E - 12 = 4.30781 \times 10^{-12}$$

which is 0.000 000 000 004 307 81.

In other words a very small p value! In this case the p value confirms that the null hypothesis (that *b* = 0) is highly unlikely implying that we have a highly significant result. The *Lower 95%* and *Upper 95%* statistics give us a calculated 95% confidence interval around the *b* value. Note that the same analysis can be done on the other parameter of the regression equation, the *a* term or intercept. Although less common, it

Table 10.3	Computer output for regression model

SUMMARY OUTPUT

Regression Statistics	
Multiple R	0.96663826
R Square	0.934389526
Adjusted R Square	0.930744499
Standard Error	3.482561605
Observations	20

ANOVA

	df	SS	MS	F	Significance F
Regression	1	3109.029944	3109.029944	256.3464394	4.30781E-12
Residual	18	218.308236	12.12823534		
Total	19	3327.33818			

	Coefficients	Standard Error	t Stat	P-value	Lower 95%	Upper 95%
Intercept	-2.418465725	1.17779207	-2.053389377	0.05485855	-4.892916958	0.055985509
Sales	0.061372898	0.003833213	16.01082257	4.30781E-12	0.05331961	0.069426187

RESIDUAL OUTPUT

Observation	Predicted Y	Residuals
1	43.53878802	-1.408788025
2	6.221610906	0.098389094
3	40.67205994	-2.202059942
4	0.130964473	-0.450964473
5	3.525499482	0.124500518
6	7.826512199	-0.056512199
7	4.274248842	0.035751158
8	13.77906961	-9.24906961
9	0.701732428	-3.391732428
10	3.11000496	0.10999504
11	9.278594974	-0.248594974
12	3.2124977	-5.8024977
13	6.270095496	0.119904504
14	20.72157187	3.668428127
15	9.77571545	4.14428455
16	1.434524834	0.695475166
17	13.86253675	3.617463248
18	3.215566345	3.994433655
19	11.79549754	3.824502465
20	31.23290817	2.377091825

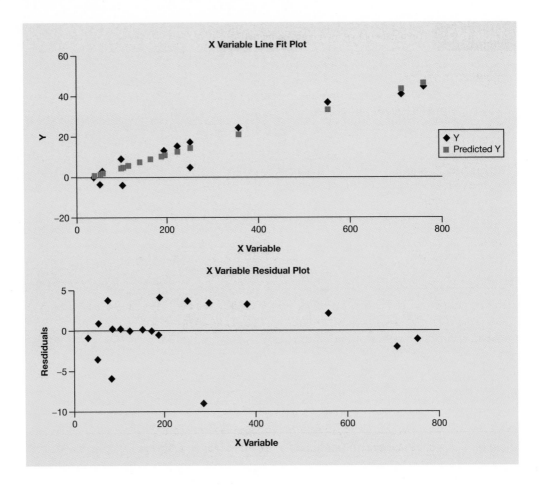

follows exactly the same principles. This test focuses on whether the *a* term is zero which implies that we think the line of best fit should actually go through the origin on a graph, which may better represent some business situations. Such packages also typically produce additional output as a standard option, here including what is known as Residual Output, and can also automatically generate charts of the key results. Note also that additional statistics appear that we have not mentioned. This is an important point for regression modelling. Although in principle regression appears a straightforward technique, the assumptions underpinning the validity of the approach are quite complex. Regression is, arguably, one of the most widely used techniques while simultaneously being the worst understood. These additional statistics – and a veritable array of others – simply underpin the complexity of the technique in terms of its valid application in the business world.

Prediction intervals for forecasts

It may have occurred to you that we have already applied a number of statistical inference principles to the regression analysis. One obvious area of application that we have so far not considered is that of a confidence interval around a forecast produced from the regression equation. Such an interval can be calculated and is known as a *prediction interval*. For the simple linear regression situation a prediction interval around some predicted value of Y, $\hat{Y}$, can be calculated from:

$$\hat{Y} \pm t_{\alpha/2,n-2}s \sqrt{1 + \frac{1}{n} + \frac{(X_F - \overline{X})^2}{SSx}}$$

where X_F is the numeric X value used to produce the forecast for Y from the regression equation and

$$S = \sqrt{\frac{\Sigma(Y - \hat{Y})^2}{n - 2}}$$

and

$$SS_X = \Sigma X^2 - \frac{(\Sigma X)^2}{n}$$

Suppose we want a 95 per cent prediction interval around forecasted profit for a store with sales of £400 000. From the regression equation the forecast would be:

$$\text{Profit} = -2.421 + 0.0614X = -2.421 + 0.0614(400) = 22.14$$

We then have:

$$\hat{Y} = 22.14 \text{ and } X_F = 400$$

To calculate S we require $\Sigma(Y - \hat{Y})^2$. Table 10.4 shows the relevant calculations.

Thus, from the table, $\Sigma(Y - \hat{Y})^2 = 218.3091$. This then gives:

$$S = \sqrt{\frac{\Sigma(Y - \hat{Y})^2}{n - 2}} = \sqrt{\frac{218.3091}{18}} = 3.482565$$

(in fact this S value is found in the Summary Output table we looked at earlier and is shown as Standard Error) and from Table 10.2:

$$SS_X = \Sigma X^2 - \frac{(\Sigma X)^2}{n} = 1\ 888\ 170.77 - \frac{4610.33^2}{20} = 825\ 413.63$$

and $\overline{X} = 230.5165$

Table 10.4	Calculations for $\Sigma(Y - \hat{Y})^2$				
Sales X	Profit Y	$\Sigma(Y - \hat{Y})^2$	Sales X	Profit Y	$\Sigma(Y - \hat{Y})^2$
748.82	42.13	2.0350	91.75	−2.59	33.6684
140.78	6.32	0.0094	141.57	6.39	0.0141
702.11	38.47	4.9220	377.04	24.39	13.4010
41.54	−0.32	0.2021	198.69	13.92	17.1515
96.85	3.65	0.0155	62.78	2.13	0.4848
166.93	7.77	0.0034	265.28	17.48	13.0524
109.05	4.31	0.0012	91.8	7.21	15.9559
263.92	4.53	85.6307	231.6	15.62	14.5982
50.84	−2.69	11.4960	548.31	33.61	5.5921
90.08	3.22	0.0121			
190.59	9.03	0.0631	Total		218.3091

Table 10.5		Prediction intervals			
X_F	$\hat{Y}$	Interval	X_F	$\hat{Y}$	Interval
50	0.65	7.6372	400	22.14	7.6208
100	3.72	7.5709	450	25.21	7.7031
150	6.79	7.5255	500	28.28	7.8054
200	9.86	7.5016	550	31.35	7.9268
250	12.93	7.4992	600	34.42	8.0665
300	16.00	7.5184	650	37.49	8.2235
350	19.07	7.5591	700	40.56	8.3970

Substituting we have:

$$S\sqrt{1+\frac{1}{n}+\frac{(X_F-\overline{X})^2}{SS_X}} = 3.482565\sqrt{1+\frac{1}{20}+\frac{(400-230.5165)^2}{825\,413.63}} = 3.6272$$

To calculate the prediction interval we require the relevant t value from Appendix C. With 18 degrees of freedom and $\alpha/2 = 0.025$ we see a t value of 2.101. The prediction interval is then:

$22.14 \pm 2.101(3.6272)$
or 22.14 ± 7.62
or 14.52 to 29.76

We should note that the sample size (here n = 20) has a large effect on the size of this interval. Realistically, we should be using a larger sample of data for our analysis, which would have the effect of reducing the size of the prediction interval. We should also note that the size of the interval will change as we forecast Y using different values for X. In fact, the size of the interval is smallest as X approaches the value $\overline{X}$ and increases the further away X gets from $\overline{X}$. To illustrate this we have calculated the interval for varying X values as shown in Table 10.5.

The general effect is illustrated in Figure 10.7, confirming again the inherent difficulties of extrapolated forecasts.

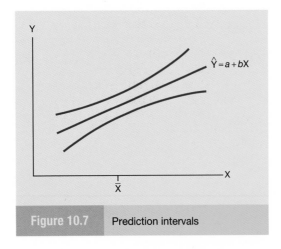

Figure 10.7　Prediction intervals

Bank lifts hopes on inflation target

By Robert Chote, Economics Editor

The Bank of England said yesterday that the government was back on course to hit its inflation target, reinforcing expectations among City economists of another early cut in interest rates.

The Bank's comments, in its quarterly Inflation Report, came alongside official figures showing the biggest monthly drop in unemployment in January since the end of 1994 and the largest quarterly rise in factory employment for at least 17 years. These eased fears that the economy had weakened significantly at the turn of the year.

The Bank cut sharply its forecasts for price increases over much of the next two years. The report said it was clear economic growth had been weaker last year than initial estimates suggested, improving the outlook for inflation.

It was now "a little more likely than not that inflation will be somewhat below 2.5 per cent in two years' time", the Bank predicted.

The government's target is to achieve underlying inflation – excluding mortgage interest payments – of 2.5 per cent or less from the spring of 1997 onwards.

The report put the chances of hitting this target in two years' time at a little under 55 per cent.

"We think the chancellor will be delighted with the Bank's report," said Mr Andrew Cates, at Swiss investment bank UBS.

"He will take comfort from the Bank's lower inflation forecast and will probably press for another quarter point base rate reduction at

next month's monetary meeting," he said.

The report predicted that any further slowdown in the economy was likely to be temporary as companies cleared shelves of unsold goods. Stronger consumer spending would then lend the economy momentum later in the year.

However, the Bank cautioned that growth might turn out to be depressed for a more protracted period in 1996 if spending remained weak in UK export markets, especially France and Germany. On the other hand, the subsequent rebound in growth could also be stronger than expected.

Yesterday's figures, meanwhile, showed that, after adjusting for seasonal patterns, the number of people without work and claiming social security benefits fell by 29,300 in January to 2,205,800. This took the proportion of the workforce unemployed below 8 per cent for the first time in almost five years.

Economists also took cheer from figures showing that average

earnings growth was stable at 3.25 per cent in the year to December, posing little inflationary threat.

Mr Mervyn King, the Bank's chief economist, said the new forecast showed that the quarter-point cuts in base rates in December and January had been justified. But he warned that the report should not be seen as a "green light" for further significant rate cuts.

The Bank also argued that the recent cuts had made a further dent in the credibility of policy, increasing market expectations of inflation in the very long term. Independent economists give the government only a one-in-three chance of meeting its inflation target at the end of next year.

The Bank expects inflation to drop steadily this year, before picking up gradually through 1997. It remains worried that rapid growth in the amount of money circulating in the economy might pose inflationary dangers if it persists.

Underlying inflation projection

Increase in prices on a year earlier (%), excluding mortgage interest payments

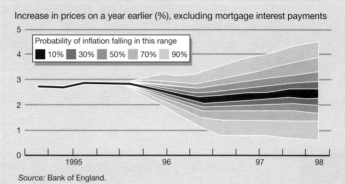

Source: Bank of England.

Source: *Financial Times*, 15 February 1996, p 1.

Use of confidence intervals around forecasts.

Estimating a trend using regression

You will remember that in the previous chapter when we were examining time-series models we identified a trend for a time-series variable using moving averages and we produced a forecast of the trend to allow us to forecast the data series we were examining. Regression can be applied to such a trend variable to predict the trend at some future period. Table 10.6 shows the data we were analysing in Chapter 9, the number of inward air passengers to the UK, together with the trend which we calculated using moving averages.

As far as the trend is concerned, we can view this as a variable which alters over time, that is:

$$\text{Trend} = f(\text{Time})$$

Table 10.6		UK inward passengers by air: actual and trend							

Year	Quarter	Actual	Trend	T	Year	Quarter	Actual	Trend	T
1995	I	9 337			2002	I	14 269	17 744.50	27
	II	13 335				II	18 858	18 041.75	28
	III	16 545	12 741.63	1		III	23 347	18 404.13	29
	IV	11 287	12 886.88	2		IV	16 702	18 585.75	30
1996	I	10 262	12 921.25	3	2003	I	15 150	18 804.00	31
	II	13 572	13 024.50	4		II	19 430	19 090.25	32
	III	16 583	13 215.63	5		III	24 521	19 391.88	33
	IV	12 075	13 477.50	6		IV	17 818	19 825.50	34
1997	I	11 003	13 842.25	7	2004	I	16 447	20 308.50	35
	II	14 926	14 161.63	8		II	21 602	20 668.5	36
	III	18 147	14 401.25	9		III	26 213	210 14.88	37
	IV	13 066	14 691.63	10		IV	19 006	214 24.88	38
1998	I	11 929	15 091.50	11	2005	I	18 030	218 20.25	39
	II	16 323	15 464.88	12		II	23 299	221 20.63	40
	III	19 949	15 757.25	13		III	27 679	223 25.38	41
	IV	14 251	16 017.25	14		IV	19 943	22 582.5	42
1999	I	13 083	16 281.50	15	2006	I	18 731	228 72.38	43
	II	17 249	16 537.38	16		II	24 655	230 69.13	44
	III	21 137	16 717.50	17		III	28 642	232 30.25	45
	IV	15 110	16 963.63	18		IV	20 554	233 66.13	46
2000	I	13 665	17 337.75	19	2007	I	19 409	235 77.13	47
	II	18 636	17 654.00	20		II	25 064	238 45.88	48
	III	22 743	17 849.13	21		III	29 921		49
	IV	16 034	17 822.00	22		IV	21 425		50
2001	I	14 302	17 745.75	23					
	II	17 782	17 607.50	24					
	III	22 987	17 434.63	25					
	IV	14 684	17 565.00	26					

We can, in one sense therefore, regard time as an explanatory variable of the trend. If we denote the time variable as T we can then specify a model:

Trend = $a + b$T

and this model clearly fits into the regression structure we have developed. To obtain a regression line in such a situation we already have numerical values for the trend variable. For T, the time variable, we arbitrarily allocate numerical values of 1 for the first period, 2 for the second, 3 for the third and so on through to n for the last period, as shown in Table 10.6. Note that T = 1 for the first period for which we have a trend, not for the first period of the entire series. Using these numerical values we can then apply the regression model and obtain the line of best fit, together with the other supporting statistics.

The appropriate regression results can then be produced, using T = 1 to 48 as shown in Table 10.7.

Table 10.7	Regression results

```
SUMMARY OUTPUT
```

```
          Regression Statistics
```

Multiple R	0.990312199
R Square	0.980718252
Adjusted R Square	0.980299083
Standard Error	466.6308307
Observations	48

```
ANOVA
```

	df	SS	MS	F	Significance F
Regression	1	509451142.8	509451142.8	2339.675792	4.27188E-41
Residual	46	10016239.28	217744.3321		
Total	47	519467382.1			

	Coefficients	Standard Error	t Stat	P-value	Lower 95%	Upper 95%
Intercept	12307.70423	136.837379	89.94402208	2.36292E-53	12032.26488	12583.14359
X Variable 1	235.1658774	4.861793011	48.37019529	4.27188E-41	225.3795958	244.952159

From the computer output we obtain an equation:

Trend = 12 307.7 + 235.17T

We see that the R^2 is high (at 0.99) and that both parameters in the equation (intercept and slope) are statistically significant (both p values are extremely small) indicating a statistically strong result. Interpretation of the results is straightforward. Over this period, the underlying growth in trend passenger numbers has been 235.17 (000) per quarter. Now by substituting specific numerical values for T into the equation we can forecast future trend values.

Assume we want a trend forecast for the quarter 2007 IV. According to our arbitrary allocation of numerical values for T this period would take a value T = 50. Substituting T = 50 into the regression equation gives a trend forecast of 24 066.2 (000) passengers.

Clearly we would not necessarily attach a high degree of reliability to such a forecast. After all, it is based on the critical assumption that the growth pattern in the trend evidenced over the period will continue. However, it is easy to see how alternative scenario forecasts could easily be produced and the range of scenario forecasts can then be assessed by management.

Activity 10.9

In Chapter 9 we developed a second scenario around the trend forecast for this data. This was to assume that the trend had fundamentally altered from the beginning of 2002. Using the trend from 2002 I onwards, determine the relevant regression equation and associated statistics. Use the regression equation to obtain a trend forecast for 2007 IV.

Statistically, do you think the regression equation for Scenario B is better than that for Scenario A?

Solution is given on p 592.

Non-linear Regression

It is also worth noting that regression is readily adapted to situations where we have some non-linear relationship between two variables. Effectively, we can take the actual X and Y data and perform an appropriate mathematical transformation so that a corresponding linear expression can be obtained. The mathematics of this takes us beyond the limits we have set for this subject matter but it is worth being aware that this possibility exists. Clearly if, from the scatter diagram, there is evidence of a non-linear relationship between two variables, this does not necessarily mean that regression must be abandoned as a forecasting approach. It may be possible to adapt the model to a non-linear format, but this will depend on the exact circumstances of the problem and the non-linear relationship between the two variables. Such non-linear transformations are usually available in specialist computer software. An example is shown in Figure 10.8. This relates to work undertaken by British Gas in terms of trying to model and forecast the demand for gas in the UK from industrial customers. From the diagram it can be seen that the actual demand over the period 1967/68 to 1978/79 was clearly non-linear and any attempt at modelling and then forecasting such demand based on a linear regression model would clearly be worthless. A non-linear model was developed (based on logarithms) and using a number of explanatory variables through multiple regression (which we examine in detail in the next section) and it can be seen from Figure 10.8 that this non-linear model was able to produce highly accurate predictions of industrial gas demand over this period.

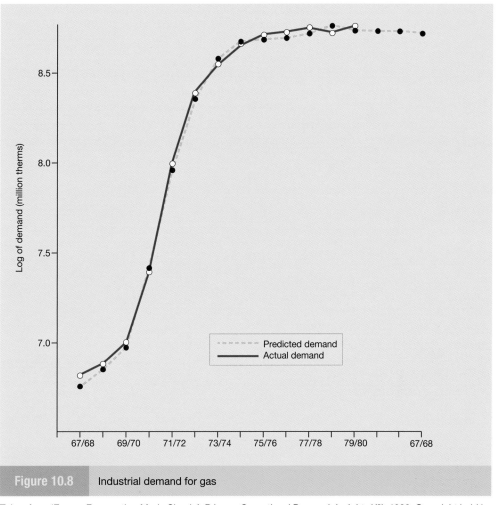

Figure 10.8   Industrial demand for gas

Taken from 'Energy Forecasting Made Simple', P Lang, *Operational Research Insight*, **1**(3), 1988. Copyright held by the Operational Research Society.

QMDM IN ACTION
Cap Gemini Ernst & Young – controlling staff costs through regression analysis

Cap Gemini Ernst & Young's client was a major public house operator. The main expense for any of the client's outlets is staff costs. Historically, these had been a predictable percentage of turnover. However, over the last two years staff costs had been increasing whilst, at the same time, the client was moving into a new market by expanding the amount and variety of food that was available across its chain of pubs. The client wanted an analysis of

the factors causing staff costs to increase together with possible ways of improving the profitability of its outlets.

The client already had considerable data on factors which influence staff operating costs. It was decided to use a statistical approach to determining categories of variables that influenced staff costs most. Multiple regression was then used using these categories as explanatory variables.

Because of problems with the quality of the data available, *ad hoc* analysis also took place to identify outlets which were outliers in the data set.

The client's existing database was used to collect data on an outlet-by-outlet basis. Because both the type of outlet and the size of outlet are likely to influence staff costs it was important that outlets were categorised accordingly. This was achieved with a combination of questionnaires to a sample of pub managers and by direct data collection on site.

A statistical technique known as factor analysis was used to determine categories of variables that could be interpreted as the main drivers of staff cost. These were then used by a multiple regression analysis that helped identify which of these categories influenced cost. Finally, to prove that the identified cost drivers could actually be influenced or controlled by pub management, an outlet was chosen to modify the operating procedure.

An example of one of the scatter diagrams used during the project is shown below. Outliers are clearly visible from this approach and can be investigated further.

The benefits are as follows:

● A clear picture of the factors that affect staff operating costs can be obtained.

● The ability to drive down staff operating costs.

● Better management information for pub managers about how they could control staff costs.

● Recommendations about data collection and storage.

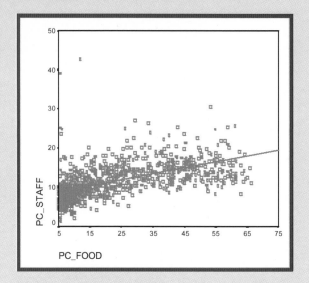

I am grateful to Cap Gemini Ernst & Young for permission to use this figure shown. Further case study applications are available through their website: www.uk.capgemini.com/consulting/or/success_stories
Copyright is held by Cap Gemini Ernst & Young.

Multiple Regression

So far we have examined regression in the context of a single explanatory variable. It is unlikely in practice that a business variable, Y, will be influenced by only one other variable, X. We might more reasonably expect a number of explanatory variables to affect the Y variable we are investigating. It is for this reason that *multiple regression* has been developed, where we try to explain some Y variable with several explanatory variables and not just one. An increasing number of regression models in business are based on this approach. In this section we shall introduce the ideas behind multiple regression although, again, we must comment that in practice the development of such models for business forecasting should be left to those with a detailed statistical understanding of the approach. Multiple regression models are particularly complex in both their structure and the statistical assumptions which underpin them. On the surface, such a model may appear appropriate for forecasting in some business situation, whereas in reality it has some fundamental statistical flaw apparent only to the statistical expert. Hasty use of such models may lead to serious forecasting errors with major – and adverse – business consequences.

However, in this section it is our intention to develop a conceptual understanding of the general approach so that the principles, if not the statistical detail, can be properly understood. In general, then, we can develop a multiple regression model of the form:

$$Y = a + b_1X_1 + b_2X_2 + b_3X_3 + \cdots + b_mX_m$$

with some number, m, of explanatory variables. Clearly this is an extension of the simple regression model. The calculations involved in multiple regression are both complex and tedious and any real application will rely on a suitable specialist computer package. The principles behind the method, however, remain as before. The method of least squares will estimate a relationship which 'best' fits the data across all the X variables and the results can be evaluated in much the same way as before. Consider the simple regression analysis we have just completed, linking profits to sales in a sample of 20 stores. Let us picture a scenario where the company is considering expanding its operations by opening another store. It currently has two alternative sites for the store under examination and is trying to assess the likely profitability of opening a store on the two sites. It might be more realistic to develop a model where we considered additional explanatory variables we felt might logically affect profit. These might include:

- The size of each store measured in thousands of square feet. The larger the store, other things being equal, the more customers and the more profit we might reasonably expect.

- The number of different product lines carried by the store. Again, the more product lines carried, the more 'popular' the store is likely to be with customers.

- The distance from the nearest major competitor measured in kilometres.

Table 10.8 shows the data we shall be analysing collected from 20 existing stores. We can then formulate a model where:

$$\text{Profit} = a + b_1 \text{ Sales} + b_2 \text{ Size} + b_3 \text{ Lines} + b_4 \text{ Distance}$$

Table 10.8	Data for 20 stores			
Profit (£000s)	Sales (£000s)	Size (000s sq ft)	Lines	Distance (km)
42.13	748.82	6.0	150	0.1
6.32	140.78	1.4	75	0.1
38.47	702.11	5.0	170	0.5
−0.32	41.54	1.0	75	0
3.65	96.85	1.2	75	0.2
7.77	166.93	1.5	75	0.5
4.31	109.05	1.3	75	0.3
4.53	263.92	1.1	80	0.4
−2.69	50.84	1.1	75	0
3.22	90.08	1.2	75	0.6
9.03	190.59	1.4	80	0.5
−2.59	91.75	1.2	75	0
6.39	141.57	1.4	80	0.3
24.39	377.04	3.5	160	1.2
13.92	198.69	1.5	100	0.7
2.13	62.78	1.3	75	0.1
17.48	265.28	2.1	110	0.9
7.21	91.80	1.3	85	0.3
15.62	231.60	2.5	120	0.9
33.61	548.31	4.5	200	0.5

that is, where profit in a particular store is determined not just by sales but by a combination of the explanatory variables. Multiple regression then provides the numerical estimates for the *b* parameters in the equation. However, there is more to multiple regression than simply feeding numbers into a computer package (and most spreadsheets will perform multiple regression) and getting the numerical results. A common approach is to break the analysis into a number of key stages:

- Determine the expected *b* values.
- Produce individual scatter plots.
- Produce the multiple regression results.
- Assess the overall fit of the model.
- Assess the individual *b* parameters.
- Check the multiple regression assumptions.
- Where necessary amend the model and go through another iteration.

It is frequently the case that multiple regression requires an iterative approach. It is unusual to produce the 'best' multiple regression model at the first attempt. Normally, some aspect of the current model will be deemed to be inappropriate and the model adjusted and then reassessed. We shall illustrate with our example.

Determine the expected *b* values

The first stage is to consider the numerical values for the *b* parameters that you would expect, given the business context of the problem. It is important before you start looking at any results that you have a clear view as to the likely results so that you can apply 'common sense' to them before more rigorous statistical analysis.

Activity 10.10

What numerical values would you expect for $b_1 \ldots b_4$: positive, negative or zero?

It seems logical in this case to expect all the *b* parameters to take positive values: that is, an increase in any of them would be expected to lead to an increase in profit. Once we produce results, we can check the logical consistency of our results against these expectations.

Produce individual scatter plots

You should understand why it is not possible to produce a scatter plot of the Y variable, profit, against all the X variables on a single diagram: we have only two axes after all and five variables. It is often worthwhile producing a scatter plot of the Y variables against each of the X variables in turn. This then allows us to see the relationship between Y and each X and, importantly, to check visually whether each relationship appears linear. Such a visual check is not particularly rigorous but does help our overall assessment of the model. Figure 10.9 shows the four scatter plots.

All four plots appear reasonably linear, although to differing degrees. However, we are not looking for perfect correlations between profit and each X but rather no obvious sign of any non-linear relationships.

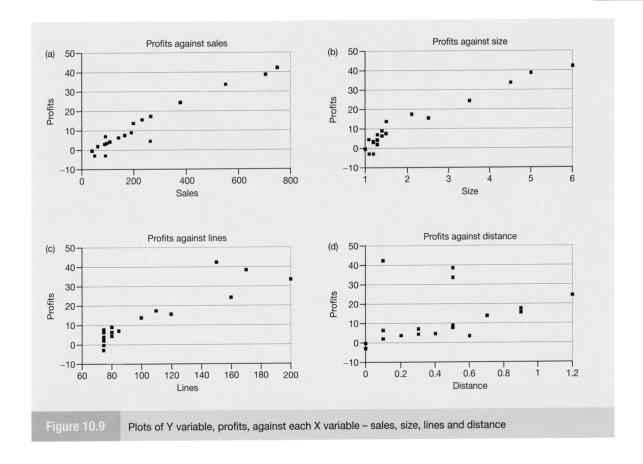

Figure 10.9   Plots of Y variable, profits, against each X variable – sales, size, lines and distance

Produce the multiple regression results

We have the results from a regression computer package as shown in Table 10.9.

Table 10.9 is typical of such computer output, showing the equation results and something known as an Analysis of Variance table, often referred to as an ANOVA table.

Assess the overall fit of the model

The next stage is to assess the results produced. We do this in several ways, the first of which is to assess the overall fit of the model: overall, how good is the equation we have obtained? The first thing to check is the actual numerical values of the b terms compared with what we expected. It is not uncommon for some of the calculated b values to be different from those expected. If this occurs it should make us reconsider the model itself. It may be that under such circumstances our understanding of the relationships between the variables is incorrect or incomplete; we may have suspect data; there may be a fundamental flaw in our approach. Whatever the reason, we should investigate to try to assess the cause of such an inconsistency.

From Table 10.9 we see each of the explanatory variables listed and next to these (labelled 'Coefficients') the estimated numerical coefficient. We also see that the constant term is shown. The estimated equation is then:

$$\text{Profit} = -7.24086 + 5.84462\text{Distance} + 4.54926\text{Size} + 0.01193\text{Lines} + 0.02587\text{Sales}$$

However, in our example all appears well. Each of the b terms in the estimated equation is positive – consistent with what we initially expected to find. Similarly, although we

Table 10.9	Regression results

SUMMARY OUTPUT

Regression Statistics

Multiple R	0.986949961
R Square	0.974070225
Adjusted R Square	0.967155618
Standard Error	2.398292891
Observations	20

ANOVA

	df	SS	MS	F	Significance F
Regression	4	3241.061048	810.265262	140.8713835	1.05404E-11
Residual	15	86.27713186	5.751808791		
Total	19	3327.33818			

	Coefficients	Standard Error	t Stat	P-value	Lower 95%	Upper 95%
Intercept	-7.240858922	2.092137285	-3.460986511	0.003492213	-11.70014673	-2.781571115
Sales	0.025873382	0.010332636	2.504044708	0.024310908	0.003849877	0.047896888
Size	4.549262843	1.773743489	2.564780574	0.021556558	0.768615766	8.32990992
Lines	0.011928598	0.040904073	0.291623731	0.774568575	-0.075256423	0.09911362
Distance	5.844624421	2.085939851	2.801914167	0.013407842	1.398546139	10.2907027

did not say this earlier, the *a* term, or constant, which is negative also, takes a logical value given the business context. If all the X variables were set to zero, profit would be negative, implying a store has some break-even position in terms of distance, size, lines and sales.

We can also evaluate the overall fit of the model statistically by examining the R^2 value. However, on inspection we see that the table actually has two R^2 values:

R Square at 0.97407 and Adjusted R Square at 0.96716

We shall look at the R Square value at 0.97407 first. You will remember that we also obtained an R^2 value for a simple regression equation. When we regressed profit only on sales we obtained an R^2 value of 0.93, which was seen as a particularly high value, given that the R^2 for any situation must take a value between 0 and 1. We interpreted this as implying that 93 per cent of the variation in Y (profit) was accounted for by the X variable (sales). For a multiple regression equation we can interpret R^2 in exactly the same way: 97.4 per cent of the variation in Y is accounted for by the variation in the X variables we have used in the equation. Our overall model, then, appears to provide a good fit, with only a small amount of the variation in Y unexplained by the X variables we have chosen. If the R^2 had been lower, say 0.61, we would have been concerned that the X variables were not 'explaining' enough of the variation in the Y variable and that, perhaps, there was some important X variable that we had overlooked and omitted from the analysis.

R^2 can also be confirmed from the ANOVA shown in Table 10.8. Earlier in the chapter we saw that R^2 was the ratio of the explained variation to the total variation. The total variation, logically, is the sum of the explained variation and the unexplained variation. The explained variation is shown in the ANOVA as the *Regression Sum of Squares* at 3241.061048, and the unexplained variation as *Residual Sum of Squares* at 86.27713. The total variation is then 3327.33818 (3241.06105 + 86.27713). This gives R^2 as 3241.06105/3327.33818 or 0.97407, confirming the R^2 shown in the table. However, we can go one stage further. It will be evident that we do not have any rigorous method for assessing whether R^2 is sufficiently high or not. Clearly in this example 0.97 is a high value. Would we have had confidence in the regression equation if R^2 had been 0.87, or 0.77 or 0.67? The method for statistically assessing the overall goodness of fit of the equation is through the application of what is known as an *F test*, effectively a hypothesis test on R^2. With such a test we formulate the same H_0 every time: that the *b* terms in the equation are not statistically different from zero. That is:

$$H_0 \ \beta_1 = \beta_2 = \beta_3 = \beta_4 = 0$$

If at the end of the test we reject H_0, it implies that at least one of the X variables is statistically significant. If we fail to reject H_0 it implies that none of the X variables is significant: Y is statistically independent of the X variables and the estimated equation is not reliable. All the details we require for the test are contained in the ANOVA part of the table. The F statistic itself is calculated as:

$$F = \frac{\text{Mean square for regression}}{\text{Mean square for error}} \ \text{or} \ \frac{\text{MSR}}{\text{MSE}}$$

MSR is given as:

$$MSR = \frac{\text{Sum of squares for regression}}{v_1}$$

where $v_1 = m$, that is the number of explanatory variables included in the equation. Here we have:

$$MSR = \frac{3241.06105}{4} = 810.26526$$

We see from Table 10.9 that all the relevant calculation is in fact given. The mean square is shown at 810.26526 with v_1 at 4, shown as df (or degrees of freedom). MSE in turn is given by:

$$MSE = \frac{\text{Sum of squares for error (or residual)}}{v_2}$$

where $v_2 = n - m - 1$. Here we have:

$$MSE = \frac{86.27713}{15} = 5.75181$$

and again we see this figure in the ANOVA. The calculated F ratio is then:

$$F = \frac{MSR}{MSE} = \frac{810.26526}{5.75181} = 140.8713$$

and again, this is shown in Table 10.9 for us. Like any hypothesis test, this calculated F ratio is to be compared against a critical F that we obtain from appropriate tables. If the calculated F is greater than the critical we are forced to reject H_0, which in this case means that we would conclude there was a statistically significant relationship between Y and the X variables used. Appendix E shows the relevant table for the F statistic for $\alpha = 0.05$. Note that, unlike the other tests we have conducted, the F statistic has two sets of degrees of freedom associated with it, v_1 and v_2. We have $v_1 = 4$ and $v_2 = 15$. The columns of the table relate to v_1 and we locate the column where $v_1 = 4$. The rows relate to v_2 and we locate the row corresponding to $v_2 = 15$. We read a figure of 3.06. This is the critical F value. If the calculated F is greater than the critical then (like every other test we have done) we reject H_0. If the calculated F is less than the critical then we cannot reject H_0. In this case the calculated F at 140.87 is greater than the critical at 3.05 so we are forced to reject H_0 and conclude that there is a significant relationship between Y and the X variables. As is often the case with computer output, this test has actually been done for us. The term *Significance F* shown in the table is in fact the p value associated with the test. That is, it is the probability that we should *not* reject H_0. Given that this is zero, we are being told to reject H_0. The F test is a critical part of the evaluation of a multiple regression model. No matter what the R^2 value, we should conduct such a test to assess the overall goodness of fit of the estimated equation. If we fail to reject H_0 at this stage, there is no point going further in our evaluation. Effectively, the estimated equation is worthless and we would need to reconsider the model we are trying to develop.

Assess the individual *b* parameters

However, in our case, the equation has, literally, passed the test and we move on to the next stage of the evaluation. This is to examine the individual *b* parameters. It is important to realise that the F test we have just conducted assesses the overall equation. It may well be that even though the equation overall is statistically significant there are parts of it that are not. In other words, we have four explanatory variables in the model. How do we know whether each of these by itself is making a significant contribution to the overall equation? For example, if we took out, say, the Size variable, would it really make much of a difference to the R^2? We can answer this by assessing the statistical significance of each *b* term in turn through an individual t test. We have already applied this test on a simple regression equation and the principle is no different. For parameter β_1, for example, associated with the distance variable, we set up the hypothesis test as:

$$H_0 \quad \beta_1 = 0$$
$$H_1 \quad \beta_1 \neq 0$$

That is, could we set β_1 to zero and not affect the overall fit of the model? Note that we have a two-tail test here. In some cases a one-tail test might be appropriate but the principles do not alter. As with simple regression, the calculated t is found by:

$$t_{Calc} = \frac{b_1}{SE_{b_1}}$$

that is, the estimated coefficient, b_1, divided by its standard error. The standard error is shown in Table 10.8 as SE B at 2.08594 and we obtain the calculated t as:

$$t_{Calc} = \frac{b_1}{SE_{b_1}} = \frac{5.84462}{2.08594} = 2.802$$

which again is shown in the computer output as *t Stat*. As before, we must compare this with a critical statistic from the t table. The relevant degrees of freedom is given by:

$$v = n - m - 1$$
$$\text{or } v = 20 - 4 - 1 = 15$$

From Appendix C with $\alpha = 0.05$ we have a critical t of 2.131 (remember it's a two-tail test). As ever, with the calculated t greater than the critical t we reject H_0 and are forced to conclude that β_1 is significantly different from zero. That is, this Distance variable is making a statistically significant contribution to the estimated equation (and hence to the overall R^2). However, once again, the test is implicitly done for us by the computer package. The *p-value* figures shown in Table 10.9 are again the p values associated with each test. For β_1 we see a figure of .0134, implying that the associated probability of not rejecting H_0 is only just over 1 per cent. With $\alpha = 0.05$ for the test we would decide not to reject H_0 only if the p value was greater than 0.05.

Activity 10.11

Carry out the tests for each of the other explanatory variables in the estimated equation.

The comparable tests for the other variables lead us to conclude at the 95 per cent level that Size and Sales also are statistically significant (that is, they make a significant contribution to the equation and to the R^2). However, for Lines the test would lead us not to reject H_0. We could not reject the hypothesis for this variable that β_3 equals zero. There is no evidence to conclude that Lines is making a significant contribution to the overall equation. In other words, based on these results, the Lines variable should *not* be included in the equation. This is an important conclusion and one sometimes leading to confusion. The F test we conducted earlier showed that the equation overall was significant. These *b* tests indicate that some of the X variables make a significant contribution to the equation but that the Lines variable does not. So what should we do? The answer is that we go into the next iteration of the regression process. We must drop the Lines variable from the model and recalculate the entire equation and the associated statistics and then re-evaluate the new results.

It is important to realise that by deciding to drop the Lines variable we cannot simply erase it from the existing estimated equation and use the rest of the equation for forecasting. The estimated equation coefficients will be affected by the removal of one variable and the entire equation must be re-estimated before we can proceed. Once it is re-estimated we must evaluate it again – we cannot assume the new equation is statistically sound just because we have dropped one variable at this stage. We must treat the new estimated equation in exactly the same way. The computer output is shown in Table 10.10.

Activity 10.12

Evaluate the results of this model.

Table 10.10	Regression results: second model

SUMMARY OUTPUT

Regression Statistics

Multiple R	0.98687548
R Square	0.973923212
Adjusted R Square	0.969033815
Standard Error	2.328710628
Observations	20

ANOVA

	df	SS	MS	F	Significance F
Regression	3	3240.571889	1080.19063	199.1908364	7.05484E-13
Residual	16	86.76629099	5.422893187		
Total	19	3327.33818			

	Coefficients	Standard Error	t Stat	P-value	Lower 95%	Upper 95%
Intercept	-6.746895165	1.192356946	-5.65845252	3.55986E-05	-9.274578402	-4.219211928
Sales	0.02562451	0.009998574	2.562816441	0.020855446	0.004428485	0.046820535
Size	4.84848802	1.404865382	3.451211825	0.003285156	1.870307124	7.826668916
Distance	6.193605355	1.658966238	3.733412538	0.001810049	2.676754829	9.710455881

We follow much the same process as before, although clearly we do not need to repeat the stage where we determine the expected values for the *b* terms or produce the scatter diagrams, since these will be unchanged. First we must assess the equation:

Profit = −6.7469 + 6.19361Distance + 4.84849Size + .02562Sales

Once again, the *b* terms are all positive as we anticipated. Note also that there are slight changes in all the coefficients as a result of removing the lines variable. We see that R^2 at 0.97392 is again high and is, in fact, little changed from our first model at 0.97407. This confirms that we were right to remove the Lines variable – it was adding little to the overall fit of the model. Without the Lines variable we are 'explaining' 97.392 per cent of the variation in profit. With the lines variable we are explaining only another 0.015 per cent! To test the overall fit of the equation we conduct an F test. We see from the ANOVA that the calculated F is 199.19 and the Signif F at .0000 indicates that we reject the null hypothesis and conclude that overall there is a good fit to the model. (You should confirm that the total sum of squares has not altered and also ensure you understand why the degrees of freedom values have altered since Equation 1.)

As before, the F test indicates the equation overall is a good fit, but this does not necessarily imply that each variable is making a significant contribution. However, by looking at the *t Stat* values we do in fact confirm that each of the three explanatory variables is statistically significant at the 95 per cent level, since all the t Stat values are less than 0.05. We conclude, therefore, that this equation is statistically significant, not just in overall terms through the F test but also in each of its component parts. Having decided that the equation looks satisfactory so far we move on to the last stage in the analysis.

Check the regression assumptions

There are four key assumptions behind this type of regression model and we need to check as best we can that our results are consistent with these assumptions. Assumptions 1–3 apply equally to simple regression models.

Assumption 1: There is a linear relationship between Y and the X variables.

It is easy to forget in the complexity of some of the analysis that this is a fundamental part of the model. This is one of the reasons we produced the scatter plots at an early stage. There, we saw no evidence of non-linear relationships and relatively strong evidence of linear ones. This assumption appears to hold for our data. To add to the complexity of multiple regression non-linear models can also be developed as we did for simple regression.

Assumption 2: The regression errors have a constant variance.

The 'errors', e, are simply the difference between each actual Y value and the Y value predicted by the regression equation. You will remember that the variance is simply the square of the standard deviation for a set of data. The implication of this assumption is less clear, but critical. This assumption effectively means that the errors, e, remain relatively constant over the entire range of data. Consider Figure 10.10 for some hypothetical situation where we plot the errors, e, against $\hat{Y}$, the Y values predicted from the regression equation. The variation in the errors remains relatively constant over the $\hat{Y}$ range. Now consider some other situation in Figure 10.11, where we see the errors, e, showing more variation at high levels of $\hat{Y}$ and less variation at lower levels of $\hat{Y}$. In this case we would conclude that the assumption of constant variance of the errors was not being met in the data set we were analysing. Not having constant error variance is often an indication that some important explanatory variable has been omitted from the equation (no matter how high the R^2 of the existing equation might be). Such visual

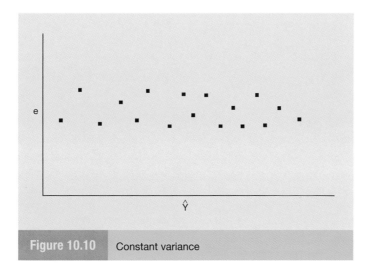

Figure 10.10   Constant variance

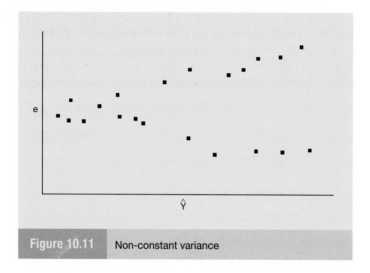

Figure 10.11   Non-constant variance

inspection of the errors is often referred to as *residual analysis*, as the errors are frequently referred to as the residuals.

Figure 10.12 shows plots of the residuals from Model 2 of our analysis, with the residuals plotted against $\hat{Y}$, the predicted Y value. There is no real evidence of any problem with this assumption, although there is a slight hint in the diagram that there might be more variation in the residuals for lower $\hat{Y}$ values than for large (i.e. for stores with lower profits). However, it is difficult to be sure, because the impression may be given from one or two stores with relatively high residuals and the fact that we have only a few stores in the high profit levels. We shall proceed assuming this assumption is not being violated.

Assumption 3: The regression errors are independent of each other.

This assumption implies that each error, or residual, is independent of the errors before it and the errors after it. If this assumption is not met then it is often said that *autocorrelation* exists: errors are strongly correlated with each other. There is a statistical test that can be conducted on the residuals to check for autocorrelation but it is beyond the scope of this textbook (although for those interested it is referred to as the *Durbin–Watson test* and you will often find a Durbin–Watson statistic on computer output from

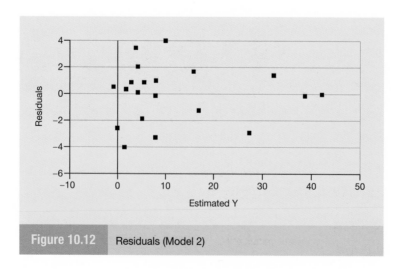

Figure 10.12   Residuals (Model 2)

a regression package). For our purposes, visual inspection of the residuals will often reveal whether any obvious pattern in the e's exists. If it does, the regression equation should not be used for forecasting purposes. Evidence of autocorrelation often indicates that, again, we have omitted some important variable or that the form of the model is inappropriate for the data (perhaps where we should be using a non-linear model rather than a linear one). Autocorrelation is particularly prevalent where we are using time-series data in the equation: that is, where the Y and X variables have some sort of time sequence to them.

Assumption 4: The X variables are independent of each other.

The final key assumption behind multiple regression is that the X variables we have included are each strongly correlated with Y but are independent of each other. If the X variables are not independent then we have a problem of *multicollinearity*. In such a situation the regression equation we have estimated is unreliable. One worthwhile check of the data being analysed is to calculate what is known as a correlation matrix: the correlation coefficients between all the variables being used in the equation (although this will not always reveal the presence of multicollinearity). Table 10.11 shows the matrix for our data. We note the following. The diagonal elements of the matrix (from top left corner to bottom right) are all 1.0000. This is because this coefficient shows each variable correlated with itself. Second, the two halves of the matrix (that below the diagonal and that above) are identical since each shows the correlation between each pair of variables. Third, the package we used to produce this matrix also performs a hypothesis test on each correlation coefficient to assess whether it is significantly different from zero, here at the 99 per cent level.

So, what do we make of this? First, we see that our Y variable, Profit, is significantly correlated with Sales and Size (at 0.9666 and 0.9673 respectively) but less so with distance at 0.3937. However, more interesting in the context of this assumption is the correlation between the three X variables. We see that Sales and Size are significantly correlated at 0.9660, whereas other pairwise correlations (between Sales and Distance and Size and Distance) are not. On reflection it is no real surprise to see a correlation between Sales of a store and its Size as we might expect, other things being equal, a larger store to have higher sales. We would conclude here that two of our X variables are correlated and, therefore, our regression equation is suspect.

Multicollinearity is a common problem in business regression modelling since, not unreasonably, many business variables will be correlated with each other. In principle, the solution is straightforward. We can omit one of the two correlated X variables and

| Table 10.11 | Correlation matrix |

Correlations:	PROFIT	SALES	SIZE	DISTANCE
PROFIT	1.0000	.9666*	.9673*	.3937
SALES	.9666*	1.0000	.9660*	.2658
SIZE	.9673*	.9660*	1.0000	.2404
DISTANCE	.3937	.2658	.2404	1.0000
N of cases:	20	1-tailed Signif: * - .01		

Table 10.12	Model 3

SUMMARY OUTPUT

Regression Statistics

Multiple R	0.981437031
R Square	0.963218645
Adjusted R Square	0.958891427
Standard Error	2.683106254
Observations	20

ANOVA

	df	SS	MS	F	Significance F
Regression	2	3204.954174	1602.477087	222.5953488	6.42445E-13
Residual	17	122.3840059	7.19905917		
Total	19	3327.33818			

	Coefficients	Standard Error	t Stat	P-value	Lower 95%	Upper 95%
Intercept	-8.272705437	1.190300612	-6.950097611	2.34374E-06	-10.78402372	-5.761387157
Size	8.319263423	0.430442355	19.32724168	5.23118E-13	7.411108169	9.227418677
Distance	6.763540333	1.894184772	3.570686679	0.002353989	2.767154213	10.75992645

recompute the regression equation. Statistically, we would probably drop the variable least correlated with Y – here Sales, which has a lower correlation at 0.9666. From a business perspective this seems a logical choice also. Recollect that we are wanting to try to forecast the likely profit from two new stores we are thinking of opening. In such a situation we would certainly know the intended size of each store but not the actual sales levels. So back to the drawing board with our analysis!

Table 10.12 shows the new model. A quick scan of the results (you should be getting used to this by now!) indicates that we have *b* values for the two explanatory variables which are as expected (both positive) and both statistically significant. The ANOVA indicates the overall equation is significant and we see that R^2 is still high at 0.96. Clearly we do not need to check for multicollinearity again as the correlation matrix will not have altered.

Figure 10.13 shows the plots of the residuals and again there appears to be little evidence that Assumptions 2 and 3 are being violated. Finally, we produce Figure 10.14, which shows a plot of the observed Y variable against that predicted by the regression equation. We note again that the model appears to be producing quite reasonable forecasts of each store's profits using these two explanatory variables. We conclude, then, that this final model appears to be a reasonably reliable basis for forecasting profit based on the two explanatory variables chosen. Let us return to the scenario where the

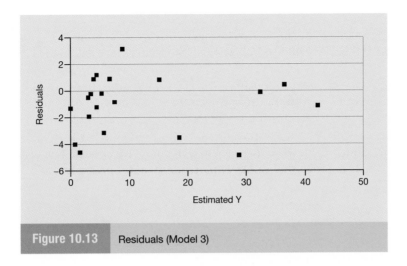

Figure 10.13   Residuals (Model 3)

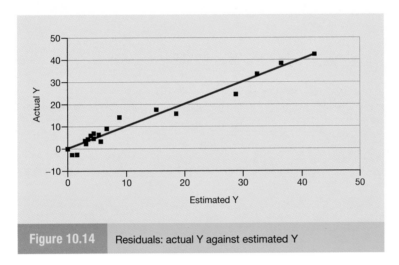

Figure 10.14   Residuals: actual Y against estimated Y

company was considering on which of two sites to open a store. Assume we have the following:

> *Option A*
> Floorspace 5.2 (000) sq ft
> Distance from nearest competitor 0.5 km

> *Option B*
> Floorspace 4.8 (000) sq ft
> Distance from nearest competitor 0.3 km

Using Model 3 we would obtain the following profit forecasts:

> *Option A*
> Profit forecast: £38.37 (000)

> *Option B*
> Profit forecast: £33.69 (000)

Option A has the higher forecast profit. Clearly we would not base such a strategic management decision solely on the regression analysis. Additional information on site acquisition and construction costs, planning permission, demographic forecasts and market research would all need to be taken into account. However, we are able to quantify expected profitability to help the decision maker in this situation.

We do not want you to go away with the impression that multiple regression is more trouble than it is worth for business forecasting. Used properly it is a particularly powerful statistical model for business forecasting and analysis. Although we have stressed the problems in developing an appropriate model, these problems are not insurmountable in practice and can, in most cases, be overcome. What is required, however, is a complete understanding of the principles behind this model. The saying that 'a little knowledge is a dangerous thing' is particularly appropriate to multiple regression in business.

The Forecasting Process

Over the last two chapters we have introduced a variety of methods that can be applied to the area of business forecasting. Through the application of such methods information about a possible future can be produced. It is important, however, to realise that the generation of such information is only part of a wider forecasting process which it is frequently advisable to apply to a forecasting activity. This can be summarised in a series of stages.

- Identify at the outset the intended purpose of the forecast.
- Determine the time period we wish to forecast for and how frequently we wish to forecast.
- Select an appropriate forecasting technique.
- Collect appropriate data.
- Produce the forecasts.
- Evaluate the reliability and suitability of the forecasts.
- Monitor the accuracy of the forecasts.

Identify the intended purpose of the forecast

It is important for a manager who is either producing forecasts directly or asking for forecasts to be produced to be clear as to what such forecasts are for and how such forecast information will be used. At one extreme the forecasts may be simply to provide general background information – comfort information – to the decision maker. At the other extreme the forecast information may be used as direct input into the organisation's business plan, with implications for pricing, resource allocation, profitability and the like. Part of the consideration at this stage will be the desired reliability of the forecast information, with the obvious implication that the more important the use of the forecasts then the higher the required degree of reliability.

Determine the time period

This is a two-stage process. First we must decide how far into the future we wish to forecast. Depending on circumstances, the answer might be that we require a short-term forecast, possibly only a few hours ahead, through to medium-term, say one or two years, to longer-term. The second issue relating to time period is that of the frequency of the forecasts to be produced. We may require such forecasts on a regular basis: daily or weekly for example. Alternatively such forecasts may be required only once a year as part of the business planning cycle.

Select an appropriate forecasting technique

Part of the consideration of what will be an appropriate forecasting technique to apply to the variable in question will be influenced by our views on the first two issues. As we have discussed, some of the techniques introduced are more appropriate to some circumstances than others. For example, if for stock control purposes a large organisation wanted to produce daily forecasts of demand for a range of several hundred items and these forecasts were to be produced each and every day, then regression models would almost certainly be inappropriate, given the technical complexity and data requirements of such models. On the other hand, if the same organisation is trying to predict demand for some of its key products over the next two to three years for planning and investment purposes then an exponentially weighted moving-average model would certainly be inappropriate. As a crude generalisation, non-causal models tend to be applied to situations which are either very short-term or very long-term, and causal models are applied largely in the medium term (see Figure 10.15).

The choice of technique will once again be heavily influenced by the foregoing evaluation. The choice of technique will also be influenced by the capabilities of the organisation itself. If no one in the organisation is technically capable of developing, say, a multiple regression model then the choice of technique must match organisational capabilities. This may still apply even if the organisation 'buys in' appropriate expertise to develop and produce technically complex forecasts. Such forecasts may not be capable of being evaluated properly by the organisation's management and may prove more 'dangerous' than simpler, subjective assessments of the future.

Collect appropriate data

Once again, at this stage we cannot determine what data we require in order to produce forecasts of our chosen variable until we have ascertained a suitable technique. The choice of technique will largely determine the data we require. A moving-average model

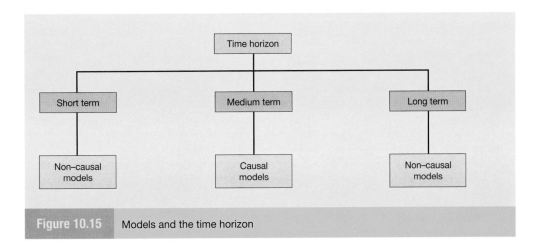

Figure 10.15   Models and the time horizon

Strategy by computer

Victoria Griffith on enthusiasm for Performance Focus Management

When the Bank of Montreal reviewed its Quebec operations two years ago, it experimented with a technique called Performance Focus Management.

Armed with vast amounts of data and a tailored computer program to analyse it, the group decided its resources were misallocated. "We increased the number of personal lenders at some branches and cut down at others," says Andrew White, executive vice president of planning for the bank. The result, according to White, was a 5 to 10 per cent improvement on initial performance projections. Today, the bank considers the program an important tool.

The Bank of Montreal is just one of a number of companies relying on the new information technology system. It has also been adopted by US West, Exxon, Barnett Bank and Florida Power.

Performance Focus Management is management by computer. It processes large amounts of data through regression analysis to help managers make decisions about where to direct resources.

Performance Focus Management focuses on the impact of forthcoming events. "We always projected a little into the future," says Allen Lastinger, president of Florida-based Barnett Bank. "For example, we would decide whether we thought interest rates were going up or down and build that into our business plan. But this is far more specific."

In one case, the bank took into account the negative impact the closure of a military base would have on a nearby branch. In another instance, the bank decided the relocation of an important company to another neighbourhood would substantially improve the business potential of the branch there.

Managers say detail is key in Performance Focus Management. In the Bank of Montreal's case 10 people worked to set up the program, which has been in place company-wide for less than a year, and five employees continue to run it.

The program considers the impact of small events as well as bigger concerns such as interest rates. Subtle shifts in disposable income and demographics in specific neighbourhoods, the plans of competitors, and the expected effect of technological improvements in certain branches, for example, are taken into account.

Because the management tool focuses on detail, the program must be tailored specifically to the company. Managers say Performance Focus Management is as much a philosophy as a technique, but most of the companies that have adopted the model rely on customised programs put in place by the consultancy Booz, Allen & Hamilton.

"We told Booz Allen that they needed to transfer the technology to us completely," says White. "They helped us set it up, but now we run it with no help from them. We couldn't be left depending on them, because if you can't manage your business without a consultant, you're dead."

One of the main challenges of Performance Focus Management is the quality of information that goes into the computer program. The Bank of Montreal, for example, collects income and tax data from the federal agency Statistics Canada, information on competitors from newspaper clippings, and interest rate forecasts from economists. If the necessary information is not easily available, the bank generates it, conducting surveys in specific marketplaces to bolster its data.

To provide the necessary precision, users of Performance Focus Management are forced to dissect their businesses. At Barnett Bank, for instance, the company is first divided into 32 geographical areas, then split into more specific business areas such as mortgage lending and consumer credit.

"We have hundreds of categories," says Lastinger. "The beauty of this is that we have a prediction for how things like small-business lending in a specific part of town can be expected to perform. It gives us something against which to measure actual performance."

Proponents of the new tool say it has weaned them from a number of bad management habits. One problem with traditional management, they explain, is that it placed too much emphasis on the salesmanship of second-tier executives. "In the past, it has been management by negotiation," says John Shank, a professor at Dartmouth's Amos Tuck School of Management in New Hampshire.

Because the process is less subjective under Performance Focus Management, managers say they feel more confident about allocating resources. The program dictates everything from personnel levels to technological investment, and allows managers to react swiftly to market changes. A mortgage lender in one branch, for instance, may be switched to the consumer credit section of another branch overnight, if the computer decides that area has more growth potential.

The constant review of resources means companies using Performance Focus Management must have a flexible workforce. Proponents believe they can meet that challenge through improved hiring and training methods. "There is nothing novel about that," says consultant Joel Kurtzman. "A company without flexible employees in the 1990s is doomed to failure."

Managers say one important advantage of the computer program is that employees are evaluated on potential as well as actual performance. Traditional management models may fail to consider events beyond executives' control. Workers at a fast-food restaurant, for instance, may be praised by the chain's management for boosting burger sales even if they had nothing to do with the improvement.

"How do we know if they sold more burgers because they were working more efficiently, or if they sold more burgers because a new shopping mall is attracting more people to the area," asks Shank. Performance Focus Management, say supporters, prevents employees from being rewarded or punished erroneously by taking outside influences into account.

The technique has potential weaknesses, however. Inaccurate data, for instance, could distort vital business decisions. A computer may also fail to consider the human side of management. Switching employees from one branch to another may make sense from the program's viewpoint, but could wreak havoc on employees.

"The system assumes a lot," says Kurtzman. "You have to have good information going into the computer to get valuable information coming out. And you have to assume that employees can adapt to the computer's recommendations."

Source: Financial Times, 17 April 1996, p 24.

Automated management decision making?

requires data simply on the variable itself. A causal model requires data on explanatory variables as well. It also has to be said that in many organisations the choice of technique may well be affected by availability of data. We might prefer to develop a suitable causal model but if, as is all too common, the organisation historically has not collected data on the model's key variables then we may have to resort to a less preferred technique for which data is available. The non-availability of suitable data is a major problem in the application of forecasting techniques in the real world.

Produce forecasts

This is the easy stage! The technical production of a set of forecasts is relatively straightforward, given computer technology and given our decisions about the earlier stages of the process.

Evaluate the reliability and suitability of the forecasts

Having produced a set of forecasts it will be necessary to evaluate both their potential reliability/accuracy and their suitability for the situation at hand. The evaluation of reliability/accuracy will, of necessity, be a combination of both technical and subjective assessment. We can evaluate a model in terms of its statistical reliability, using MAE, MSE, R^2, as appropriate. But a subjective assessment by the decision maker is still important. The example of forecasting the trend in air passengers illustrates this point particularly well.

Monitor the accuracy of the forecasts

The final stage in the process is to ensure that, at some time in the future, we assess how accurate the forecasts actually were compared with what eventually happened to the variable. It is all too easy in an organisation to use forecasts to assist decision making and then discard the forecasts once used. As part of the evaluation process it is important to monitor their accuracy. The one thing we can almost guarantee about any set of forecasts is that they will turn out to be wrong. From the forecaster's viewpoint, what is of critical importance is to what extent they were wrong – the size of the forecast error – and why they were wrong: were they wrong because of the wrong choice of model, explanatory variables or data used, or because of critical subjective assumptions on which we based the scenario of the future? Only by monitoring in this way can we hope to produce improved forecasts in the future.

Worked Example

We have been asked by a leading retailer to provide a short report on spending patterns over the past few years in the UK to help them try to assess which parts of the market they should consider from a strategic perspective. We have collected the data in Table 10.13.

Table 10.13	Household disposable income and consumers' expenditure on selected categories (£million at 2003 prices)			
	Income	*Food and Drink*	*Alcohol and Tobacco*	*Clothing and Footwear*
1985	425 528	47 417	28 080	15 837
1986	443 119	49 058	27 742	17 031
1987	459 426	50 323	27 977	17 795
1988	484 677	51 377	28 401	18 211
1989	507 327	52 392	28 520	18 035
1990	524 633	52 244	28 514	18 216
1991	535 207	52 342	27 713	18 716
1992	550 737	52 923	26 869	19 741
1993	565 147	53 972	26 451	20 799
1994	573 521	54 435	26 342	22 273
1995	588 514	54 483	25 666	23 355
1996	602 417	56 292	26 798	24 777
1997	625 184	57 261	27 125	25 696
1998	634 508	58 058	26 829	26 736
1999	652 060	59 904	27 623	28 689
2000	681 249	61 944	26 704	31 744
2001	710 531	61 048	26 497	34 485
2002	722 823	62 143	26 884	38 499
2003	740 389	63 174	27 297	41 155
2004	752 890	65 181	27 444	44 087
2005	768 612	65 690	27 279	46 107

Source: Economic Trends.
Data available in filename T1012.

We have data on the following series:

- household disposable income
- consumers' expenditure on Food and Drink
- consumers' expenditure on Clothing and Footwear
- consumers' expenditure on Alcohol and Tobacco.

We note that all variables are expressed in constant prices so that inflation is removed and will not distort our analysis. It seems reasonable to start by assuming that each of the three expenditure variables can be linked to income through a simple linear regression. However, let us first examine the individual scatter plots. These are shown in Figures 10.16–10.18. The relationship between Income and expenditure on Food and Drink seems reasonably linear (Figure 10.16) and we seem justified in using linear regression to estimate the relationship. Figure 10.17, for Clothing and Footwear, seems reasonably linear although the relationship at the bottom left of the diagram looks slightly different from the rest of the data set. Figure 10.18 for Alcohol and Tobacco shows no evidence of any real relationship at all. Clearly in this case there seems little value in undertaking regression at all so we will continue just by modelling the other variables.

Table 10.14 shows the computer output for both regression models. Note that the analysis of variance has been omitted as it is redundant for a simple regression.

Let us look at the results for Food and Drink first of all. We have an estimated equation:

$$\text{Food} = 25\,933.2 + 0.051\,\text{Income}$$

with an R^2 of 0.99. R^2 is comfortingly high and the b parameter is sensible in the context of the question, as is the a parameter. In the case of the a term it is sensible that, even if income were zero, food will still take a positive value (people have to eat after all) with food purchases perhaps funded through past savings or through credit. The b term indicates that with an increase in income of £1, 5.1p of this would be spent on Food and Drink. A check on the p values in the output indicates both a and b are

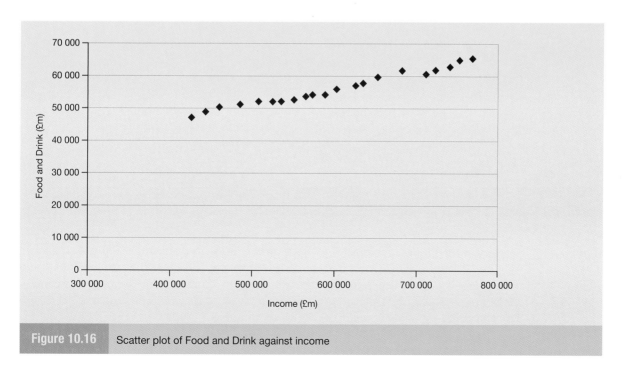

Figure 10.16   Scatter plot of Food and Drink against income

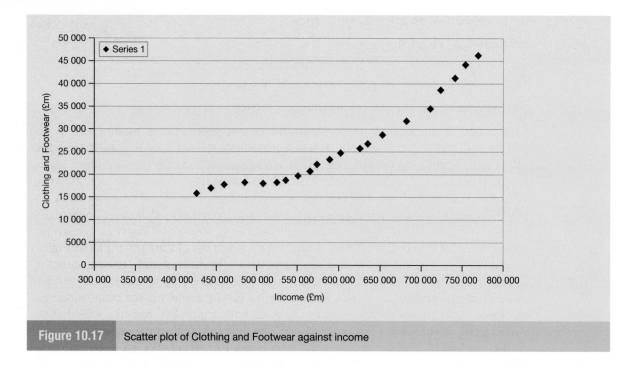

Figure 10.17   Scatter plot of Clothing and Footwear against income

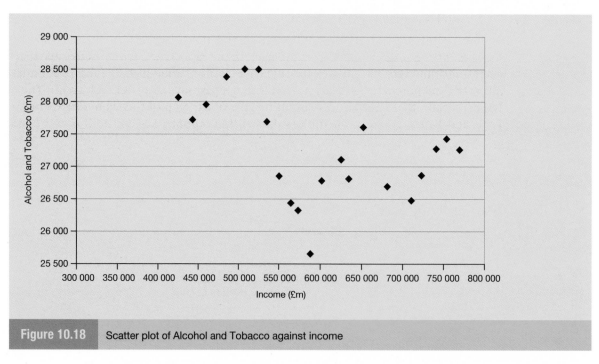

Figure 10.18   Scatter plot of Alcohol and Tobacco against income

significantly different from zero. A check on the residuals from this equation (shown in Figure 10.19), however, indicates we have a problem. It is clear from the residual plot that there is a cyclical pattern to these residuals: in some periods the model is consistently over-forecasting, in others it is under-forecasting. It would be unwise of us to use this equation for analysis and forecasting. Although the regression statistics themselves (R^2, t values) look appropriate, there is something fundamentally wrong with the simple linear model. Given the cyclical nature of the residuals it would appear that there is some other explanatory variable that we need to include in our analysis to help

Table 10.14   Regression results

```
SUMMARY OUTPUT      Food & Drink

        Regression Statistics

Multiple R              0.988934608
R Square                0.977991659
Adjusted R Square       0.976833325
Standard Error          821.1554289
Observations                     21
```

ANOVA

	df	SS	MS	F	Significance F
Regression	1	569314420.6	569314420.6	844.3090561	3.27943E-17
Residual	19	12811628.53	674296.2385		
Total	20	582126049.1			

	Coefficients	Standard Error	t Stat	P-value	Lower 95%	Upper 95%
Intercept	25933.21302	1059.295381	24.48156906	7.84199E-16	23716.08231	28150.34373
Food & Drink	0.050768106	0.00174719	29.05699668	3.27943E-17	0.047111194	0.054425017

```
SUMMARY OUTPUT      Clothing & Footwear

        Regression Statistics

Multiple R              0.953296779
R Square                0.908774748
Adjusted R Square       0.903973419
Standard Error          2944.604465
Observations                     21
```

ANOVA

	df	SS	MS	F	Significance F
Regression	1	1641151647	1641151647	189.2756648	2.49266E-11
Residual	19	164743213.7	8670695.458		
Total	20	1805894861			

	Coefficients	Standard Error	t Stat	P-value	Lower 95%	Upper 95%
Intercept	-25221.50865	3798.557251	-6.639760042	2.37084E-06	-33171.98033	-17271.03697
Clothing & Footwear	0.086196419	0.006265299	13.75774926	2.49266E-11	0.073082997	0.099309842

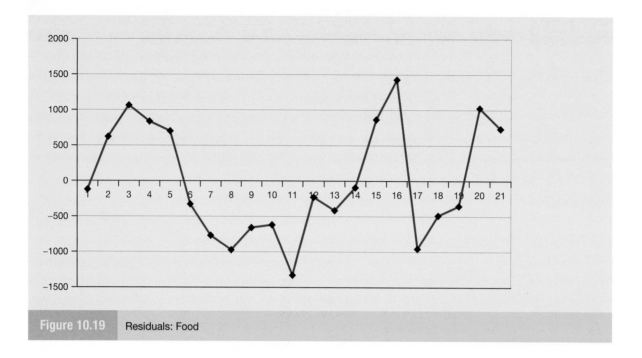

Figure 10.19   Residuals: Food

improve the model. Obviously the residuals themselves give no indication as to what this should be. It might be unemployment, it might be wage increases, it might be expectations about future inflation, or it might be some level of confidence in the economy. If we were taking this analysis further we would need to incorporate variables we felt were logical, given the economic and business context, and then evaluate the resulting model as before. In fact, the absence of some key explanatory variable is further highlighted if we also examine the residual plots of the other equation, for Clothing and Footwear (Figure 10.20). Here, the residuals evidence a different problem.

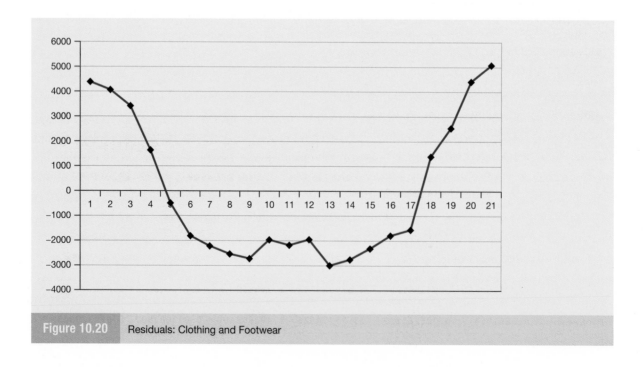

Figure 10.20   Residuals: Clothing and Footwear

The simple model is over-forecasting at the beginning and end of the period and under-forecasting during the middle. We must conclude, therefore, that with the data currently available, no useful analysis can be provided. We would need to collect further data on potential explanatory variables and develop multiple regression models to see if they perform better. No one ever said these techniques work every time!

Summary

In this chapter we have introduced the basic regression model as a method of forecasting. The prime use of regression is as a causal model and such models are of critical importance to any business organisation. The principles of simple linear regression are straightforward although underpinned by rigorous mathematical assumptions. Although such a model can be developed and used for relatively simple applications, its development into more complex models is a matter more appropriate for the expert rather than the typical manager. The manager, however, still needs to be aware of the underlying principles applied in order to be able to evaluate the potential use and reliability of the forecasts generated.

Useful online resources

Detailed below are some internet resources that may be useful. Many have further links to other sites. An updated version is available from the accompanying website (www.pearsoned.co.uk/wisniewski). In addition, I would be grateful for details of other websites that have been found to be useful.

www-marketing.wharton.upenn.edu/forecast/ – Forecasting Principles

www.itl.nist.gov/div898/handbook/pmc/section4/pmc4.htm – Introduction to time series analysis

www.number-10.gov.uk/su/survivalguide/skills/eb_forecasting.htm – Looking forward: forecasting

www.lbma.org.uk/publications/alchemist/alch33_averages.pdf – Moving averages

www.businessintelligence.com/ex/asp/code.9/xe/article.htm – Stop Looking Back: An Introduction to Forecasting for Business Intelligence

home.ubalt.edu/ntsbarsh/Business-stat/stat-data/Forecast.htm – Time series analysis for business forecasting

www.statsoft.com/textbook/sttimser.html – Time series analysis

www.stats.gla.ac.uk/steps/glossary/time_series.html – Time series glossary

QMDM IN ACTION
RAC

The RAC (Royal Automobile Club) is a motoring organisation primarily providing a service to its member motorists whose vehicles have broken down. Members of the RAC who experience a vehicle breakdown will typically telephone a central hotline number, details will be taken by the RAC, and one of its fleet of vehicles will be despatched to provide assistance. The RAC prides itself on reaching members within 60 minutes of receiving a request for assistance. With around five million members the management of this service is a particularly complex task. Predictably, the roadside rescue side of its activities is supported by a considerable IT system, with the roadside operations being managed through CARS (computer-aided rescue service). CARS provides a number of performance measures for the roadside operations, including measures of overall level of service, the rescue patrol attendance rate and the vehicle fix rate. Figure 10.21 shows the key performance measures as well as a number of key terms used.

Although the RAC has a fleet of over 1300 vehicles available to respond to assistance requests, these are distributed throughout the whole of the UK. However, if available resources are already at full capacity when an assistance request is received, the RAC can call on a supplementary fleet operated by contractors. In addition, as one might expect, management of these operations is further complicated by considerable areas of uncertainty and unpredictability: weather patterns, local traffic conditions, the very randomness of vehicle breakdowns. However, to try to help management, a project was initiated to help develop an understanding of the links and interrelationships between the various performance measures and to assess whether the impact of changes in these influence measures on key performance measures could be reliably predicted. One of the first stages in the project was to develop what is known as an 'influence map', showing the relationships that exist between various parts of the organisation and its key systems. This was felt to be particularly important because the interrelationships between many

aspects of performance were complex and not necessarily understood in terms of their detail and logic. Figure 10.22 shows the influence map produced, which gave management a clear, overall view of the complexity of the factors affecting roadside performance. To illustrate the logic and importance of this approach we shall follow through part of the map in detail. At the top of the map we have the number of members, a key parameter if the RAC is to survive and be successful. In part, the number of members is 'influenced' by the proportion of existing members who decide each year to renew membership. In turn, this will be influenced by the level of customer satisfaction a particular member has (since logically the more satisfied a customer is with an organisation, the more likely they are to remain a customer). Although, as can be seen from the map, a large number of factors influence customer satisfaction, one of the key influences is felt to come from OLOS (the overall level of service, defined as the percentage of breakdowns which received roadside assistance within 60 minutes).

Importantly, as the authors of this article point out, the influence map was effectively created by managers and key personnel themselves (and not by the quantitative expert). This provided a sense of ownership among management of the overall approach being developed, and was felt to improve the chances of successful implementation of any performance improvements that might emerge from later analysis. This is a particularly important point, relating to more complex quantitative techniques, which has been mentioned a number of times in this text so far. It may be relatively easy for a quantitative specialist to model and analyse some business situation and then produce a set of performance improvement recommendations based on that analysis. The managers who are then left with the task of deciding whether, and how, to implement those recommendations may well respond with, at best, a degree of inertia and, at worst, downright disbelief in the validity of the recommendations. Such a response can arise because managers have not been involved in the model development and

AGNT (Agent (Contractor) Go-Not-Tow)	The percentage of contractor rescue jobs that are completed with the vehicle being remobilised.
CARS (Computer-Aided Rescue Service)	The RAC s computer service, used to gather and store breakdown details and report on the various quality and efficiency measures.
Contractor	A complementary resource to the RAC patrols, which are appointed garages approved to act on behalf of the RAC.
Despatcher	A member of staff who allocates an appropriate patrol resource to each service job.
HAT Job (Hire Accommodation Travel Job)	A service job that results in the member receiving a hire car, hotel or accommodation or some form of onward travel.
OLOS (Overall Level of Service)	The percentage of service breakdowns with a resource at the breakdown scene within 60 minutes.
Opportunity	$\text{Opportunity} = \dfrac{\text{Number of Attended Service Breakdowns}}{\text{Number of Patrols}}$
PGNT (Patrol Go-Not-Tow)	The percentage of patrol rescue jobs that are completed with the vehicle being remobilised.
Productivity	$\text{Productivity} = \text{Opportunity} \times \dfrac{\text{Rescue PAR}}{100}$
Recovery Job	A service job which is completed with the vehicle being towed more than 20 miles.
ROLOS (Recovery Overall Level of Service)	The percentage of recovery jobs with a resource at the breakdown scene within 120 minutes.
Recovery PAR (Recovery Patrol Attendance Rate)	The percentage of the recovery jobs completed by patrols.
Rescue Job	A service job which is either completed without a tow or is completed with a tow that is under 20 miles.
Rescue PAR (Rescue Patrol Attendance Rate)	The percentage of rescue jobs completed by patrols. $\text{Rescue Par} = \dfrac{\text{Productivity}}{\text{Opportunity}}$
Service Breakdown	A breakdown where some form of rescue and/or recovery service is provided.
VFR (Vehicle Fix Rate)	The percentage of attended service breakdowns which are fixed.

Figure 10.21   Key terms and performance measures

may feel it has simply been imposed on them and their business by some outside 'expert'.

The next stage was to try to quantify some of these key relationships and then try to develop predictions of key performance variables based on assumed changes in key influences. It was decided to adopt a regression-modelling approach to this analysis. At an operational level the RAC divides the UK into six regions, with each region further split into zones (denoted by a letter). One particular region, Central England, was used to assess whether the modelling approach was feasible and data collected on the 17 zones of this region (denoted as zones A to Q). As is usual with this approach, the data collection process itself was no easy task. Because of previous organisational changes a few years earlier, it was felt appropriate to collect data only for the period after this change (limiting the amount of data that could be used for modelling). The geographical boundaries of some zones

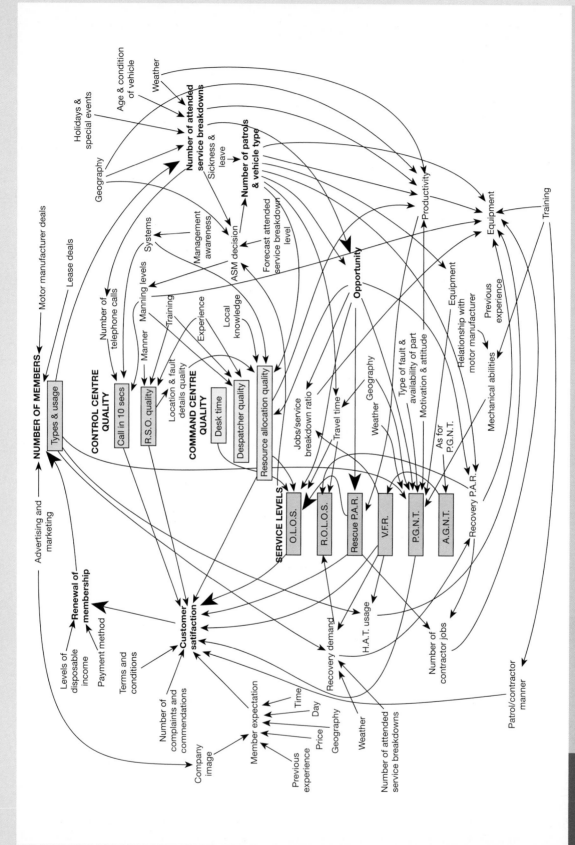

Figure 10.22   RAC roadside operation influence map

Dependent Variable	Explanatory Equation
Central Region Costs	$= a_1$ $+ x_1$ Productivity $+ x_2$ Number of Contractor Jobs $+ x_3$ Number of Hire. Accommodation. Travel (HAT) Jobs $+ x_4$ Jobs/Service Breakdown
Customer Satisfaction Index (CSI)	$= a_2$ $+ x_5$ OLOS $+ x_6$ POLOS $+ x_7$ VFR $+ x_8$ Jobs/Service Breakdown $+ x_9$ Rescue PAR
Jobs/Service Breakdown	$= a_3$ $+ x_{10}$ VFR $+ x_{11}$ Opportunity
Number of Attended Service Breakdowns	$= a_4$ $+ x_{12}$ Weather Index $+ x_{13}$ Number of Individual Members $+ x_{14}$ Number of Motorman Members $+ x_{15}$ Number of Fleet Members
Number of Contractor Jobs	$= a_5$ $+ x_{16}$ Number of Panel Van Patrol Vehicles $+ x_{17}$ Number of Lift and Tow Truck Patrol Vehicles $+ x_{18}$ Number of Attended Service Breakdowns $+ x_{19}$ Recovery Demand $+ x_{20}$ Rescue PAR
Number of Patrols	$= a_6$ $+ x_{21}$ Number of Attended Service Breakdowns $+ x_{22}$ Geography Index
Overall Level of Service (OLOS)	$= a_7$ $+ x_{23}$ Desk Time $+ x_{24}$ Geography Index $+ x_{25}$ Weather Index $+ x_{21}$ (Number of Patrols)^2 $+ x_{20}$ Rescue PAR
Patrol Go-Not-Tow (PGNT)	$= a_8$ $+ x_{28}$ Weather Index $+ x_{8_9}$ Number of Individual Members $+ x_{30}$ Number of Fleet Members $+ x_{31}$ Number of Motor Cycle Patrols $+ x_{32}$ Number of Small Van Patrol Vehicles
Productivity	$= a_9$ $+ x_{33}$ Geography Index $+ X_{34}$ Weather Index $+ x_{35}$ Jobs/Service Breakdown $+ x_{36} \dfrac{\text{Number of Attended Service Breakdowns}}{\text{Number of Patrols}}$ $+ x_{37}$ (Number of Patrols)^2
$\log_a$ (Recovery Demand)	$= a_{10}$ $+ x_{38}$ Number of Attended Service Breakdowns $+ x_{39}$ VFR $+ x_{40}$ Geography Index $+ x_{41}$ Number of Motorman Members $+ x_{42}$ Weather Index
Recovery Overall Level of Service (ROLOS)	$= a_{11}$ $+ x_{43}$ OLOS $+ x_{45}$ Recovery PAR
Vehicle Fix Rate (VFR)	$= a_{12}$ $+ x_{45}$ PGNT $+ x_{46}$ Agent (Contractor) Go-Not-Tow (AGNT) $+ x_{47}$ Rescue PAR

Figure 10.23 Multiple regression equations

had also altered. Some data was available internally from the CARS system, while other data had to be collected externally (weather information, pollution statistics). The influence map was used to identify the key dependent variables of interest and then the potential independent variables influencing each dependent variable. The multiple regression approach that has been described in this chapter was adopted to try to develop appropriate multiple regression models. Scatter plots were used to assess initial linearity (or non-linearity in some cases). R^2 values were assessed, as were residuals, which were examined to test the basic multiple regression assumptions. An iterative approach was adopted until acceptable regression equations had been obtained. A total of 12 equations were developed in this way, with the format of each illustrated in Figure 10.23 (note that for reasons of commercial

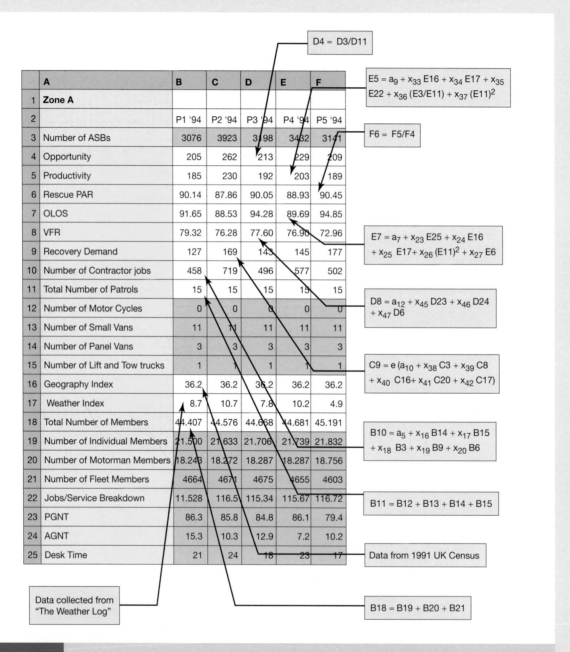

Figure 10.24   Model output and logical relationships for periods 1 (P1) to 5 (P5) of 1994 (shaded cells indicate user inputs)

confidentiality the numerical parameters of the equations are not reported). So, for example, the Customer Satisfaction Index was found to be dependent on five key variables: OLOS (the overall level of service), ROLOS (the recovery overall level of service), VFR (the vehicle fix rate), Jobs/Service breakdown and Rescue PAR.

Further analysis of these equations led to five of the estimated equations being used for what-if mod-

elling purposes, with output from the model equations shown for one zone in Figure 10.24. The authors of the article comment that 'this modelling methodology ... [stimulated a] new understanding of the business environment', with management now intending to develop a national model using the same fundamental approach.

This application is based on the article 'Corporate Modelling at RAC Motoring Services', S Clarke, A Hopper, A Tobias and D Tomlin, Operational Research Insight 9(3), 1996, pp 6–12.

The figures in this section are reproduced with permission of the Operational Research Society.

Exercises

1 For the following data calculate the correlation coefficient and plot the data on a scatter diagram. Do you think it measures the strength of the relationship accurately?

x	1	2	3	4	5	6	7
y	8.25	7	6.25	6	6.25	7	8.25

2 Return to the variables used in Chapter 9, Exercise 3. In that exercise you were required to obtain a trend for each variable using moving averages. For each trend that you obtained, forecast the trend one year into the future using regression. Evaluate the result both statistically and in the context of the variable. Assess how reliable you think such a forecast would be for each variable.

3 Table 10.15 shows data on two variables for the UK from the Central Statistical Office for the period 1970 to 2005, the latest available.

    Cars   New registrations of cars shown in thousands as a monthly average.

    Income   Real household disposable income, per head at 2003 prices.

(a) What type of causal relationship might you expect between these two variables?

(b) Draw a scatter diagram for this data and comment on any relationship observed.

(c) For the period 1970–89 estimate a regression model for this data. Estimate a second equation for the entire period. Estimate a third for the period 1991 to 2005.

(d) Evaluate the regression models statistically.

(e) Evaluate the regression equations in terms of their likely reliability for forecasting.

(f) Using the equations, forecast Cars for 2009. Assess the reliability of your forecasts. Comment on the likely factors causing inaccuracies in your forecasts.

Table 10.15	New registration of cars and *per capita* income: UK

	Income	Cars		Income	Cars
1970	5 352	91.4	1988	8 516	184.2
1971	5 390	108.5	1989	8 888	192.1
1972	5 819	138.6	1990	9 166	167.1
1973	6 171	137.3	1991	9 318	133.3
1974	6 120	102.8	1992	9 564	133.3
1975	6 183	98.6	1993	9 793	148
1976	6 160	106.5	1994	9 911	158.9
1977	6 037	109.4	1995	10 142	161.5
1978	6 480	131.6	1996	10 358	168.2
1979	6 856	142.1	1997	10 721	179.7
1980	6 958	126.6	1998	10 850	188.4
1981	6 922	124.5	1999	11 111	186.8
1982	6 907	132.1	2000	11 570	194.8
1983	7 044	150.5	2001	12 021	214.8
1984	7 295	146.6	2002	12 184	223.5
1985	7 525	153.5	2003	12 433	220.5
1986	7 817	156.9	2004	12 583	216.6
1987	8 088	168	2005	12 764	203.6

Data available in file T1015.

4 A small engineering company has been monitoring its total costs over the last few years on a quarterly basis together with the number of employees and production level. In order to assist the company to evaluate alternative strategic and operational options, the data has been put through a computer package to develop a multiple regression model of the form

$$\text{Costs} = a + b_1 \text{Employees} + b_2 \text{Production}$$

The results of the regression are shown in Table 10.16.

Table 10.16	Regression output

```
                    Model fitting results for: Costs


Independent variable      Coefficient      Std. error      t-value


CONSTANT                       63.75          13.7861        4.6242
Employees                    4.02926           0.8587        4.6923
Production                   0.04714           0.0057        8.2702
```

R-SQ. = 0.9633
24 observations fitted, forecast(s) computed for 0 missing val. of dep. var.

You have been asked to provide a short report to the company chairman explaining both the principles of regression in this context and an evaluation of the results in terms of their potential usefulness in decision making.

5 The corporate planning department in a large brewing company has been trying to develop a medium-term forecasting model relating to the demand for one of their products: a low-alcohol lager. The method used has been based around multiple regression. The department has collected and analysed data on a monthly basis for the last two years. All data has been seasonally adjusted and is based on constant prices. The variables currently under examination are:

C1 Lager sales, thousands of pints
C2 Number of pubs supplied
C3 Number of supermarkets and off-licences supplied
C4 Price of lager, pence per pint
C5 Price of beer, pence per pint
C6 A time trend increasing by 1 per month.

The results of the latest model are shown in Table 10.17.

Table 10.17	Regression output		
Variable	Coefficient	Std. Error	t-value
Constant	24.52	4.609	5.32
C2	1.02	0.357	2.86
C3	2.39	0.699	3.42
C4	-0.59	0.401	1.47
C5	0.082	0.126	0.65
C6	0.98	0.394	2.49

R-SQ. = 0.843

23 observations.

You have been asked to summarise the current model for a report to be shown to the managing director, to interpret and evaluate the current model and to suggest possible improvements to the model or alternative methods of trying to forecast this variable.

6 As manager of a local leisure centre you are investigating the frequency of use of the centre by its members. You hope that by understanding some of the key factors that influence how often members use the centre's facilities you will be better able to market the centre and attract more members. Over the last few weeks you have collected data on a representative sample of members. The relevant data is shown in Table 10.18.

The variables relate to:

Attend   The number of times the member made use of the centre's facilities during a week
Travel   The distance between the member's home and the centre (miles)
Children The number of children in the member's family (family use of the centre is encouraged)
Income   The annual income of the member (in £000s).

Using the principles of multiple regression, develop a suitable model for forecasting *Attend*.

Table 10.18	Sample of 20 members						
Attend	Travel	Children	Income	Attend	Travel	Children	Income
5	3	2	23	1	8	0	19
4	2	1	34	2	2	0	21
2	3	0	51	2	3	2	45
6	3	3	37	1	9	3	38
7	1	3	29	0	5	0	36
4	3	2	17	2	3	0	19
3	3	1	23	2	4	0	23
4	3	1	28	2	5	0	21
8	2	3	40	1	6	2	46
0	8	1	38	1	7	1	28

Data available in file T1018.

7 A large retail organisation has a number of home-furnishing outlets in a particular region, selling products such as carpets, curtains, domestic furniture and fittings. The organisation has been affected badly by the downturn in domestic property sales in the region over the last few years, as it has found that much of its business comes from customers redecorating or refurnishing a home they have just purchased. The company has collected and analysed data over the past two years to try to assess the impact that regional property sales have on its business. Two variables in particular have been specified:

- the number of house sales in the region on a monthly basis (000s)
- gross monthly sales in the organisation's outlets in the region (£000,000s).

Data has been obtained for the last 24 months on these two variables and the data analysed using a spreadsheet package applying simple linear regression with the number of house sales as the X variable. The results are:

```
Regression Output:
Constant                              -0.532
Std Err of Y Est                       3.2577
R Squared                              0.83584
No. of Observations              24
Degrees of Freedom               22
X Coefficient(s)        0.476
Std Err of Coef.        0.380121
```

Explain the principles of simple linear regression in the context of this problem. Assess and comment on the reliability of this analysis for forecasting purposes.

8 A training agency is currently reviewing part of its operations. It runs one particular scheme whereby young people who are unemployed are put through a training course which provides them with a variety of IT skills including word-processing, spreadsheets, database systems, e-mail and the Internet. On completion of the training course, participants take a standard test and receive an ability score (from 0 to 40, with 40 being the highest). The training agency then finds them a suitable job with a local company. The agency is trying to assess the wages its trainees receive from the companies they go to work for in relation to the ability test score they received and the number of years of prior, relevant job experience the trainees had. Data has been collected as given in Table 10.19.

Table 10.19	Trainees' wages, ability scores and job experience		
Wage	**Score**	**Years**	
271	37	0	
233	29	1	
213	24	2	
242	32	1	
261	36	1	
198	27	0	
228	31	0	
205	22	2	
323	38	3	
181	21	1	
225	30	3	
298	34	5	
209	28	0	
200	25	1	
278	33	2	
270	35	1	
223	29	2	
231	34	2	
242	32	1	
216	26	1	
189	25	1	
228	31	0	
205	22	2	
343	38	5	
191	21	1	
225	30	3	
318	34	5	
209	28	0	
203	24	1	
287	34	3	

Data available in file T1019.

Wage   Represents the gross weekly wage (£s) of trainees once they have found employment

Score Represents the ability score they received in the test

Years Represents the number of years of relevant job experience.

Analyse the data to assess whether *Wage* could be reliably predicted based on score and years of experience.

9 A senior police manager is reviewing manpower allocation of police officers to a number of geographical districts which fall under her responsibility. Data has been collected on a number of variables, as shown in Table 10.20.

Table 10.20   Policing variables

Crimes	Officers	Support	Unemployment	Retired
860	26	5	6	18.3
890	27	2	7	10.2
852	20	3	5.2	14.7
889	28	3	4.3	13.1
1037	25	4	13.5	7.6
1257	21	6	13.2	8.4
1136	20	3	14.1	8.2
1038	25	4	13.9	8.3
1240	19	4	13.6	7.8
1439	15	5	17.1	4
1126	17	5	8.4	7.1
724	27	3	6.7	18.5
1023	19	6	6.3	7.3
960	22	4	12.3	15.7
890	25	3	8.7	10.2
952	21	4	6.7	9.7
989	26	3	5.3	14.1
1037	25	4	14.5	11.2
1321	20	6	12.3	4.4
1402	16	3	14.1	4.2
1038	25	4	13.9	8.3
941	19	4	8.6	9.8
767	26	5	7.1	17
826	24	5	7.4	16.1
724	27	3	6.7	16.5
823	23	6	6.3	16.3

Data available in file T1020.

Crimes	The number of reported crimes
Officers	The number of full-time equivalent police officers
Support	The number of civilian support staff
Unemployed	The unemployment rate for that area
Retired	The percentage of the local population who are retired.

(a) Find the most appropriate statistical model for predicting *Crimes* in any given area.

(b) Do you think regression could be used to predict the number of police officers that should be deployed in a given area?

11 Linear Programming

Learning objectives

By the end of this chapter you should be able to:

- understand the principles of constrained optimisation
- be able to explain the relevance of optimisation to business decision making
- be able to formulate a linear programme
- be able to solve a two-variable linear-programming problem
- be able to complete simple sensitivity analysis on the optimal solution

So far in the text we have developed a variety of different quantitative models. Such models generate information that may be used by the decision maker to help resolve some problem that is faced. Typically, for many of the problems facing a manager, certain restrictions or constraints will exist in terms of what can, and cannot, be done. A manager may see a possible solution to a problem in terms of recruiting extra staff but knows that approval for this will not be given by senior management. A solution to some problem may exist if only the organisation could raise extra capital to replace existing production machinery but the manager knows that this is unlikely in the current economic climate. In short, a manager will be restricted in terms of solutions that can be adopted and yet at the same time that manager is expected not only to solve the problem but, ideally, also come up with the 'best' solution. Not surprisingly, given that so many business problems have these characteristics, a number of quantitative models have been developed to help managers reach such 'best' decisions under the constraints they face. We shall introduce and examine one of these models: linear programming (LP). This is a model that lies at the heart of this type of problem and is typical of optimisation models, often referred to as mathematical programming models.

The Business Problem

We shall develop a detailed example to illustrate the principles of LP. Assume an organisation manufactures a liquid detergent. The detergent is manufactured from two basic ingredients, which are both a mixture of appropriate chemicals: Mix A and Mix B. The detergent is packaged and sold to two separate markets: the household market aimed at individual consumers and the industrial/commercial market aimed at large organisations such as hospitals, hotels and local authorities. The exact composition of the detergent sold varies between the two markets and Table 11.1 shows the composition. The two products are sold in five-litre bottles. For the household detergent (H) each five-litre bottle requires four litres of Mix A and one litre of Mix B, whereas the corresponding composition of industrial/commercial detergent (C) is three litres of Mix A and two litres of Mix B. On a weekly basis the company has supplies of no more than 20 000 litres of Mix A available and 15 000 litres of Mix B. In addition, the plastic containers in which the detergents are sold are limited in supply. The company buys these containers from a specialist supplier, who can supply no more than 4000 containers a week for H and 4500 a week for C. The company's accountant has been able to quantify the profit contribution of each product: H contributes 30p to profit per five-litre bottle produced and C contributes 25p. The manager's problem is a simple one: on a weekly basis, what combination of the two products should be produced?

On the face of it, product H appears more profitable than C – 30p as opposed to 25p – and we might be tempted to suggest that production be concentrated on this product. However, it is also evident that there are resource implications of concentrating production on H. For example, this product is relatively costly in terms of Mix A, requiring twice as much per five-litre bottle as product C. Additionally, there is a limit of 4000 to the number of units of H that the company can produce. Clearly we require some rigorous method of trying to resolve this problem. In fact this problem is an example of what is referred to as *constrained optimisation*. The manager will be searching for an optimum solution – in this case in the sense of maximising profits. At the same time solutions to the problem are constrained by the other characteristics of the problem: limited resource availability and so on. As we shall see, linear programming provides a general-purpose solution method for such constrained optimisation problems.

Table 11.1	Chemical composition of detergents per five-litre bottle	
	Household detergent (H)	*Industrial/Commercial detergent (C)*
Ingredient		
Mix A	4 litres	2 litres
Mix B	1 litre	3 litres

Private users: How shops use the information

By Simon Briscoe, FT.com site

Census data can be used as a basis for mathematical models that predict the level of customer trips between residential zones and retail outlets or centres.

Retail location models, more accurately described as gravity or spatial interaction modelling, are used by the UK's leading supermarket and high street retail chains for planning store networks and predicting expected revenues for new sites.

The growing popularity of gravity modelling, which tries to simulate the trip-making behaviour of consumers within the market, owes much to the advantages it has over traditional statistically based models, such as multiple regression. Whereas multiple regression models and their variants provide the answer to one question – what is the expected revenue at each outlet, gravity models provide additional information about market performance, such as the impact that a new site or a closure has on existing outlets, including those belonging to competitors, and the shape and size of each outlet's expected catchment area and the degree of overlap between catchments.

As Steven Halsall of GeoBusiness says, companies will want to avoid opening a profitable outlet which, due to impacts on existing outlets, results in a net loss to the company. Similarly, in a franchise situation, gravity models can be used to estimate the impact of planned outlets on existing franchisees. So successful have the modelling techniques been that more recently they have been extended to retail financial services and to the leisure and health market sectors.

Retailer location – WHSmith

When WHSmith needed to understand how current stores interacted with each other and how to fill holes in their network coverage, they commissioned a bespoke sales prediction model, built by CACI, to help understand the likely turnovers of new stores and the impact these stores will have on their existing portfolio. This capability was all the more relevant given their stated aim of expanding the high street store network and the potential move into factory outlet centres and edge-of-town locations.

"What if?" scenarios were run and the results mapped using CACI's Geographical Information System – InSite – to view the likely catchment of a new store. Demographic reports were generated comparing the new store catchment with the national average and with WHSmith average customers. In addition the model identified likely cannibalisation of the existing portfolio from new store openings, giving a clear view of the real value of a new store.

The process also provides performance measures for the existing store network. A key output from the model is a prediction of "expected" sales from each WHSmith store based on its current size. This measure reflects the potential for WHSmith in that location, given the current size of store, based on the catchment and retail profile. A benchmark based on external factors is invaluable in measuring store performance. Dina Dawes, Estates Manager at WHSmith said that sales predictions have been borne out by recent store openings.

Cinema site planning – Odeon Cinemas

The UK cinema market has never been so competitive, with many of the key operators fighting for a decreasing number of prime sites. Location decisions have to consider a range of complex factors in order to arrive at some estimate of trading level. According to Steven Halsall of GeoBusiness Solutions, these factors relate to the proposed site in question (quality, accessibility, size, and mix), the competitive offer in the local market, and the satisfied and unsatisfied levels of demand – especially the number of 25–34 year olds – in the market. The use of GIS software, data and modelling techniques, can help to make sense of such intricate local markets.

Mr Halsall says the basic system itself comprises the GIS software usually coupled with drive time functionality and a demographic reporting tool and any externally available data. The external data usually consists of: background context mapping (roads, rail, urban sprawl, locations); census or demographic information by small area (census counts, geodemographic or lifestyle profiles); administrative geography (postcodes, postal sector boundaries, TV regions); and competitor locations (quality and location of competitive outlets, open or planned), and if possible, trading levels.

The main source of competitive advantage in such a system is that of internal data – the information held by an organisation that is not generally available to competitors. One significant source of internal data is that about the company's own customers. Odeon Cinemas generate a large amount of local market knowledge from the collection of customer information through their call centre or by box office surveys. For example, gathering postcode information allows Odeon to quantify the "distance decay effect" – the decreasing propensity to attend as one lives further away from a venue. This effect differs by geographic location and is governed by the transport infrastructure as well as the location of competing offers.

For Odeon gravity models are useful in predicting sales or admissions, the likely impact on own or competitor outlets, and market share by small area. It is not only about opening or closing outlets, says Mr Halsall, it is also about performance versus potential, location planning, repositioning or even marketing and media planning. Odeon have applied the use of GIS to help in site openings, campaign analysis at the local, regional or national level, and in customer acquisition and retention. Luke Vetere, Marketing Manager at Odeon Cinemas, says that the GeoBusiness work based on Mapinfo technology plays a "vital role in the company's decision support process".

Market research
The census underpins most mainstream market research conducted in Britain. According to Corinne Moy, Director of Statistics at NOP, it provides the bedrock of information about the dispersion of populations and households, which is essential for planning, controlling and executing all types of consumer research. Some populations – such as ethnic minorities or very affluent people – are almost absent from many areas of the country, and targeting can ensure that survey resources are used to maximum effect. The new questions on religion and caring and

the more detailed information on ethnic groups will improve the value of the data.

Market researchers use the census to ensure that they achieve representative samples of particular populations. These may be used to plan interviews of predetermined quotas of people in particular age and sex categories. In other instances, the census is used with the Postcode Address File to draw up sample frames of addresses. In both cases a scientific approach achieves more accurate results at a lower cost.

The market research business also makes use of the Samples of Anonymised Records. These samples – around 2 per cent – of individuals and households allow the investigation of relationships and variables for distinct groups of the population in a flexible way. They were introduced for the first time after the 1991 census and are supported by the Centre for Census and Social Research in Manchester. These would allow, for example, analysis of the family structure of mothers under 25 with certain qualifications.

Lottery terminals – Camelot
One of the largest network optimisation projects ever carried out was for Camelot Group to optimise the location of the National Lottery Network of terminals. In 1999, Camelot commissioned the development of an integrated model and map-based GIS (Geographical Information System) known as "Optimum". The aim of Optimum was to provide a decision support tool to ensure that 35,000 National Lottery Terminals were in the ideal locations to maximise lottery sales.

The project by Business Geographics and GeoBusiness Solutions was described as a "milestone in spatial interaction model-

ling" in a review carried out by the Oxford Institute of Retail Management. Camelot used the model results and methodology in their successful bid to retain the National Lottery Franchise. Chris Green, Director, Player and Retailer Services at Camelot said that the system "maps out the detailed geographic performance of the network and provides key decision support on the future location of terminals".

RNLI
The Royal National Lifeboat Institution is a registered charity that saves lives at sea. It provides, on call, the 24-hour service necessary to cover search and rescue requirements to 50 miles out from the coast of the United Kingdom and the Republic of Ireland. The RNLI depends on voluntary contributions for its income and volunteer crew to operate the lifeboats and the census plays a role in determining policy in both these areas.

As Ginette Tessier, research manager at the RNLI, says, "Knowing where to place a lifeboat station is a combination of local knowledge, experience and detailed risk assessment." Once an assessment has been made of the type of rescues likely to be required in an area – and therefore the type of boat that will best perform the job – the RNLI needs to work with the local community to assess the best place for a station.

It is that immediate community that provides the lifeboat crew, so it is vital that it has a good supply of men and women who meet the rigorous fitness levels, are readily available for a call out 24 hours a day, 365 days a year and are likely to volunteer. The improved availability of the small area census data will, say the RNLI, increasingly allow the organisation to monitor population demographics and migration for a particular area, to gauge the likely success in recruiting volunteer crew.

The RNLI raises money in many ways but legacies are a big source of income. The census information on mortality and life expectancy plays a part in income forecasting – it is only by studying the data that a reasonable estimate can be made of when pledged monies will arrive.

Pub redevelopment – matching customers with outlets – Inn Partnership

Following a change of ownership in 1999, the Inn Partnership decided to develop the way it evaluated a site for redevelopment and targeting new opportunities. Previously ideas had been developed through operational teams at the front line in conjunction with the Licensees. Inn Partnership developed this process through their marketing team by analysing the estate and looking at successful pubs by pub type (for example, community local, town bar, rural characters, young venues) and by their consumer profiles, finding areas to replicate the success by either developing existing sites or taking over new ones.

CACI produced reports for each business development manager so that they could further understand the profiles of people in their areas. This allowed the managers to look at data at an individual pub level. The information could be combined with data from other sources to show what sort of products are being drunk and where, and an idea of how Inn Partnership is comparing to the competition. The resulting reports gave the company a clearer view as to the type of customer they are targeting, providing vital facts and figures to support acquisitions, refurbishments and disposals.

Source: *Financial Times*, 7 October 2003, FT.com site.

Optimisation models are used successfully across very different organizations.

Formulating the Problem

The first stage in the solution process is to translate the problem faced into a mathematical formulation. We require this both for the constraints we face and for the objective, profit, we are seeking to maximise.

Constraints

In this problem we face four constraints, or restrictions, in terms of what we can, and cannot, do to resolve the problem. The four constraints relate to:

- availability of Mix A at 20 000 litres
- availability of Mix B at 15 000 litres
- availability of containers for product H at 4000
- availability of containers for product C at 4500.

For each constraint we can express the restriction mathematically. Consider the first constraint, relating to availability of Mix A. We have a maximum of 20 000 litres available. This supply will be used to produce units of H and/or C. Each unit of H produced requires four litres and each unit of C requires two litres. If we denote the number of units of the two products produced as H and C respectively then the amount of Mix A required for any combination of H and C will be given by:

$$4H + 2C$$

For example, if we decided to produce 1000 H and 500 C then the quantity of Mix A required would be:

$$4H + 2C = 4000 + 1000 = 5000 \text{ litres}$$

So, for any given combination of production we can quantify the requirement using this expression. The supply of Mix A is restricted to a maximum of 20 000 litres. If we incorporate this into the expression we then have:

$$4H + 2C \leqslant 20\,000$$

which indicates that the quantity required ($4H + 2C$) must always be less than or equal to ($\leqslant$) that available (20 000). This is the first mathematical constraint for the problem.

Activity 11.1

Formulate an equivalent expression for each of the remaining constraints in the problem.

The constraints would be:

$$4H + 2C \leqslant 20\,000 \qquad \text{(Mix A)}$$
$$1H + 3C \leqslant 15\,000 \qquad \text{(Mix B)}$$

The demand for Mix B arising from producing units if H and C cannot exceed the available supply at 15 000.

$$1H \leqslant 4\,000 \qquad \text{(Containers for H)}$$
$$1C \leqslant 4\,500 \qquad \text{(Containers for C)}$$

Note that the last two constraints are formulated in terms of only one variable rather than two since the limitation imposed is only on one variable. We can produce no more than 4000 units of H and no more than 4500 units of C.

Other types of constraint

In this problem all the constraints are expressed in terms of a less than or equal to formulation ($\leqslant$). It is common to encounter other types of constraint which may be formulated in terms of $\geqslant$ or $=$. The $\geqslant$ term implies that some *minimum* value must be satisfied. For example, the company may have a contract with a national hotel chain to supply *at least* 2500 units of C each week. This would then give rise to a constraint:

$$1C \geqslant 2500$$

indicating a minimum value for this variable. Similarly, a constraint involving $=$ implies that the left-hand side (LHS) and right-hand side (RHS) of the constraint must be exactly the same. For example, suppose the company's marketing department has redesigned the label that is used on the front of each bottle. However, the company is keen to use up existing stocks of the old labels before using the new ones. If stock of the old labels is 4000 and the label can be used on either product then a constraint:

$$1H + 1C = 4000$$

would be appropriate, forcing the company to produce appropriate quantities regardless of profitability.

The objective function

Just as we have formulated a mathematical expression for the constraints, so we can do the same for the objective of the problem: profit in this case. The profit achieved from any combination of production would be given by:

$$Profit = 0.30H + 0.25C$$

where profit would be measured in £s. Each unit of H produced contributes 30p to profit and each unit of C 25p. This expression is known as the *objective function*. Note that, unlike the constraints, the objective function has no numerical value attached to it (like 20 000 for the first constraint). We do not yet know what profit we will make, since we have not yet determined the optimum combination of H and C to produce.

The complete formulation

We can bring these expressions together into a full LP formulation:

$$Maximise\ 0.30H + 0.25C$$

subject to:

$$4H + 2C \leqslant 20\ 000$$
$$1H + 3C \leqslant 15\ 000$$
$$1H \qquad \leqslant 4\ 000$$
$$1C \leqslant 4\ 500$$
$$H,\ C \geqslant 0$$

This indicates that we are seeking to maximise the value of the objective function subject to the restrictions imposed by the four constraints. Note that we have added an extra 'constraint' known as the *non-negativity condition*, H, C ≤ 0. This is an expression which simply indicates that negative values for the two variables are not permitted: they clearly would make no sense in a business context. We should note two further points about the formulation of an LP problem.

● The number, and type, of constraints will be determined by the problem.
● Some problems may require a minimum value for an objective function. For example, we might require to minimise production costs rather than maximise profit. Such an objective function would then be shown as a minimisation rather than maximisation.

Activity 11.2

Return to the chemical mix problem in the chapter. The company now decides that instead of maximising profits it wishes to minimise the total costs of producing the two products. The cost per unit of C is £1.10 and of H £0.85. In addition to the existing constraints, the firm has also decided that minimum acceptable production of H is 2000 units and of C is 2500.

Formulate the new problem.

Solution is given on p 592.

Graphical Solution to the LP Formulation

Having formulated the problem we now seek some general method of solution. In fact the problem as formulated involves expressions which are all linear in format: they would give straight lines on a graph. We can use this feature to develop a graphical solution method which follows a logical sequence of stages.

- Graph the constraints.
- Graph the objective function.
- Determine the solution visually.
- Check the solution algebraically.

Graph the constraints

The first stage in the solution process is to graph all the constraints to the problem. Given that all the expressions are linear, this implies that to draw each one we require two sets of coordinates for the graph. The line representing each expression in the formulation can then be obtained by joining the two coordinate points together. Consider the first constraint:

$$4H + 2C \leqslant 20\,000$$

The two sets of coordinates are typically obtained by setting each variable in turn to zero and solving for the other. Let us set H to zero. Logically this then implies that all 20 000 litres of Mix A are available to produce C, which requires two litres of Mix A per five-litre bottle. Maximum production of C will then be given by:

$$20\,000/2 = 10\,000$$

One set of coordinates is then:

$$H = 0, C = 10\,000$$

Repeating the logic but this time setting C to zero we have:

$$H = 5000, C = 0$$

These are then the two coordinate sets for this first constraint, which can now be plotted on a graph.

Activity 11.3

Obtain similar coordinate sets for the remaining constraints.

We obtain the following coordinate sets:

> For constraint 2: H = 0, C = 5000; H = 15 000, C = 0
> For constraint 3: H = 4000 for any value of C
> For constraint 4: C = 4500 for any value of H

Figure 11.1 shows the graph for the first constraint. The two points are marked at C = 10 000 and H = 5000 and the line representing this constraint then joins these two

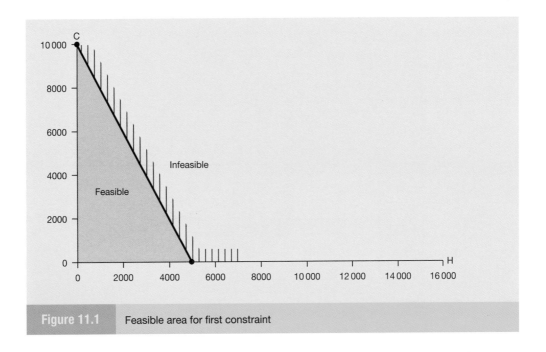

Figure 11.1   Feasible area for first constraint

points. We need to consider carefully the information implicit in the diagram. The line itself actually represents all combinations of H and C which require *exactly* 20 000 litres of Mix A (in other words where the constraint takes the form =). The area below the line represents all combinations of H and C which require *less than* 20 000 litres (where the constraint takes the form <). Together this area and the line itself represent what is known as the *feasible* area: those combinations of H and C which are feasible for this constraint. It follows that the area above the line represents the *infeasible* area: combinations which cannot be achieved given the restriction of 20 000 litres. Typically the infeasible side of the line is marked as shown on the diagram. What this effectively means is that we have now limited where the optimal solution to this problem must be: it can only be in the feasible area. Clearly this feasible area relates only to the first constraint. As we add further constraints to the graph, however, the feasible area will alter and will show the feasible area for *all* constraints.

Activity 11.4

Add the other three constraints to the graph and mark the area which is feasible for all four constraints.

Figure 11.2 shows all four constraints for the problem. Take a few moments to study the diagram. All four constraints are shown and marked (1) to (4). The infeasible side of each constraint line has been marked. The area which is feasible to all four constraints simultaneously is marked. Its boundary is marked by the origin, by 4500 on the C axis, the intersection of constraints (2) and (4), the intersection of constraints (1) and (2), the intersection of constraints (1) and (3), 4000 on the H axis and back to the origin. This area, by definition, must contain the solution to the problem since it shows all possible solutions which are feasible. Clearly, in order to determine which of the many feasible solutions is optimal, we require the objective function.

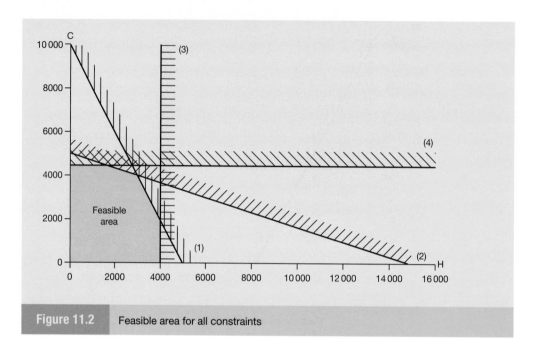

Figure 11.2   Feasible area for all constraints

Graph the objective function

To graph the objective function we must adopt a slightly different approach to that for the constraints. The reason for this is that we currently have no numerical value for the objective function (indeed that is what we are actually seeking to calculate). To graph the objective function line, however, we can give the function some arbitrary numerical value. One convenient arbitrary value can always be found from a multiple of the two coefficients in the function. If we multiply 0.30 and 0.25 we obtain 0.075. If we scale this result upwards to 750 we can use this to ascertain the graphical characteristics of the objective function.

Activity 11.5

Using a profit of 750 determine the two sets of coordinates of the objective function for the graph.

Setting profit to £750 we would then obtain coordinates:

$$H = 0, C = 3000$$
$$H = 2500, C = 0$$

However, these coordinates and the corresponding line are associated with a level of profit that was entirely arbitrary. A different profit value would clearly have given different coordinates. Figure 11.3 shows a series of such profit lines from £750 to £1500. It is evident that the different profit lines are all parallel (mathematically they must be because they have the same slope, which is given by the ratio of the two profit coefficients). Equally, the higher the profit value then the further away the line is from the origin.

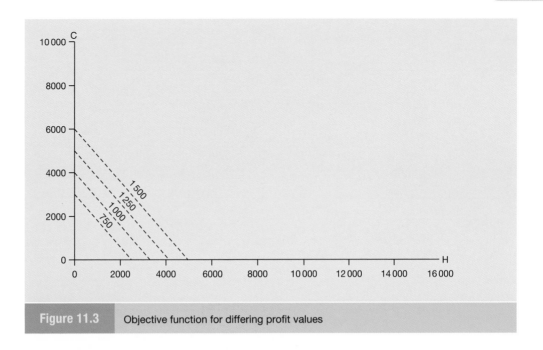

Figure 11.3   Objective function for differing profit values

Activity 11.6

From the manager's perspective, which of these four profit lines would you prefer given a free choice?

Clearly, given the objective of maximisation, we would prefer to be on a profit line which was as far above the origin as possible. £1500 would be preferable to any of the others shown. A related aspect to this is that we would be indifferent as to *where* on a particular profit line we were since all points on the same line generate the same profit. That is, as long as we were on the £1500 profit line it would not matter where on that line we were: i.e. what combination of H and C we were producing as long as it generated this much profit. Returning to the feasible area in Figure 11.2, however, it becomes apparent that some profit lines may well lie outside the feasible area: they represent a value for the objective function which cannot be achieved given the constraints we face.

Obtaining a solution

What we require is to combine the graphical information about the feasible area with that for the objective function to help us determine the optimal solution. The general principles are evident. We seek a profit line as far above the origin as possible yet still within the feasible area. The principles involved are shown in Figure 11.4. To help understand the process involved the diagram shows only the feasible area rather than the full graph of the constraints, and the scale has been enlarged. Also shown on the diagram are two profit lines for £750 and £1500. Let us consider the profit line of £750. All combinations of H and C which generate this particular level of profit fall within the feasible area, hence all of these are solutions to the problem. However, we see that it is possible for the profit line to move further away from the origin and still remain in the feasible area. The profit line for £1500, for example, is preferred to that of £750

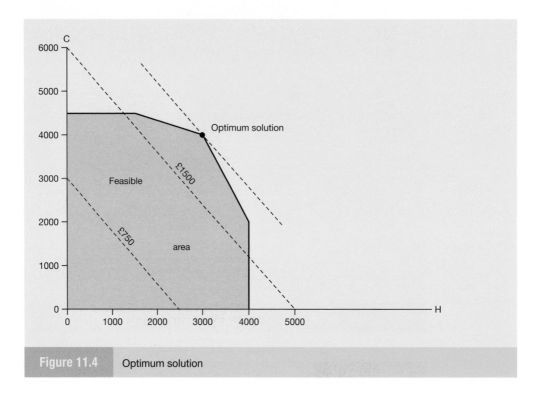

Figure 11.4   Optimum solution

(given the maximisation objective). Although some parts of this profit line fall outside the feasible area (representing infeasible solutions) part of the line is still within the area. Hence we conclude that it is possible to generate a profit of £1500 and still satisfy all four constraints. However, it is clear that there are further profit lines above £1500.

Consider the principles, however. It is apparent that as the profit line moves away from the origin, less and less of the line remains in the feasible area. Clearly there will come a time when a particular profit line has part of it just within the feasible area and the rest outside: literally one point on the line will be feasible and the rest will not. Consider the next possible – and higher – profit line. Given that the last one had only one point in common with the feasible area then the next higher line will have left the feasible area entirely. None of the solutions on this line will be feasible. So, we are searching for a profit line which just passes through a single point of the feasible area. This point will represent the combination of the two products which represents the optimal solution: this point will generate the highest possible profit that is feasible. Such a point is marked on Figure 11.4 and can be seen to represent H = 3000 and C = 4000. Obviously this profit line – like all others – will be parallel to the two we have already drawn. It is also important to note that the solution to such a problem will invariably occur at one of the corner points of the feasible area. The reason for this is to do with the mathematics underpinning the approach, but we can take advantage of this fact for any LP problem. Effectively what we must do to determine the solution is identify all the corner points for the feasible area and decide, in the context of the objective function line, which of them represents the optimum solution.

So, the solution is:

H = 3000

C = 4000

Profit = £1900 = (0.3(3000) + 0.25(4000))

To summarise the graphical solution process:

● Graph the constraints to the problem.
● Mark the feasible area.
● Graph the objective function by assigning it an arbitrary numerical value.
● Visually locate the point of the feasible area that the objective function line would encounter *last* as it is pushed outwards from the origin.

This last point needs some comment. With practice we do not actually need to draw a separate graph for the objective function or a series of objective function lines. If we simply draw *one* such line on the same graph as the constraints we know that all other lines will be parallel to this. By visual inspection of the graph we can then determine which corner point of the feasible area the line would encounter *last* as it is pushed outwards.

Minimisation problems

The solution process for minimisation problems is identical except for the direction we would push the objective function line. A minimisation line is seeking to get as close as possible to the origin (rather than as far away as possible). Typically, the feasible area will prevent a minimisation line from actually reaching the origin but the point the line intersects last as it approaches the origin will be the minimisation solution.

Binding and non-binding constraints

So the solution to the maximisation problem is to produce 3000 units of H and 4000 units of C. From the objective function we determine that this will generate a weekly profit of 1900. From each constraint we note that:

(1) $4H + 2C \leqslant 20\,000$

   $12\,000 + 8000 = 20\,000$

That is the optimal solution, using all available supply of Mix A;

(2) $1H + 3C \leqslant 15\,000$

   $3000 + 12\,000 = 15\,000$

and all the available supply of Mix B;

(3) $1H \leqslant 4000$

   $3000 < 4000$

but there are 1000 unused containers for product H; and

(4) $1C \leqslant 4500$

   $4000 < 4500$

there are 500 unused containers for product C.

The first two constraints, for Mix A and B, are technically known as *binding* constraints: at the optimal solution they limit (or bind) the objective function from taking an improved value. From Figure 11.2 we note that the optimal combination of H and C actually occurs on the line of both these constraints (and remember that for any point on the constraint line the RHS of the constraint expression equals the LHS). The other two constraints are *non-binding*: at the current optimal solution they do not prevent the objective function from taking an improved value. We could produce more of H and C as far as these two constraints are concerned. From the graph we note that the optimal combination lies below these two constraint lines: there are surplus resources available for these two constraints. In fact we can use the binding constraints to confirm the graphical solution using mathematics.

Confirming the solution with simultaneous equations

The two binding constraints at the optimal solution can be rewritten as:

(1) $4H + 2C = 20\ 000$

(2) $1H + 3C = 15\ 000$

We also note from the graph that the solution occurs where these two constraint lines intersect: where the equations are equal. Using the method of *simultaneous equations* we then confirm the solution. This is a simple method for finding the values of two variables (here H and C) when we have two equations. From Equation 1 we take the the numerical coefficient associated with the first variable: here the coefficient is 4 (associated with H). We then multiply each term in Equation 2 by this coefficient, 4, and subtract the result from Equation 1 to get:

$$(1) \quad \begin{array}{r} 4H + 2C = 20\ 000 \\ -4H - 12C = -60\ 000 \\ \hline -10C = -40\ 000 \end{array}$$

giving C = 4000. Substituting this value for C back into either Equation 1 or 2 we obtain H = 3000 to confirm the graphical solution. It is always worthwhile using simultaneous equations in this way to confirm the graphical solution. However, such an approach can also generate useful management information through what is known as sensitivity analysis.

Sensitivity Analysis

Clearly LP is useful as a means of determining the optimal solution to a given problem. Management are likely to be interested in more than this, however. Typical questions are likely to be: what would happen to the solution if we could obtain an extra 5000 litres of Mix A? What would happen if H's profitability per unit increased? What would happen if the supplier of containers decreased their availability? One approach to providing an answer to such what-if questions would be to recalculate the entire problem and determine the solution to the amended formulation. Even for small problems, however, this can be time-consuming and tedious. A different approach is to examine the sensitivity of the current solution to marginal changes in the problem formulation. This allows us to assess readily a change in one part of the problem without the need for an entire recalculation. Typically such sensitivity can be undertaken on the constraints and on the objective function.

Constraints

Let us return to the optimal solution, where we found that the two binding constraints were the availability of the two chemical mixes. Consider Mix A. We have a weekly supply of some 20 000 litres, all of which is used at the optimum. If we pose the question: would it be worthwhile obtaining extra supplies of Mix A then the answer clearly has to be 'yes'. Additional supplies of this mix will allow additional production and hence more profit, other things being equal.

Activity 11.7

Consider the related question. How much would extra supplies of Mix A be worth to the company?

This is more difficult. In principle the answer would relate to profit. Given that extra supplies of Mix A will lead to increased profit via increased production then the 'worth' or value of this extra supply will clearly be linked to extra profit. What we obviously require is some method for calculating this effect. Let us consider the following scenario. The company decides it is possible to obtain one extra litre of Mix A for use in the production process.

Activity 11.8

Examine Figure 11.2. What would happen to the constraint line for Mix A? What would then happen to the optimum production of C and H?

Figure 11.5 shows the principles of the situation. We see that constraint line (1) would be pushed outwards by a small amount as one extra litre became available. The feasible area would change marginally also, although it would be impossible to show such a small change on the solution graph. The corner point of the feasible area representing the optimal solution would also change: it would move down the constraint (2) line. This would represent a slight (or marginal) reduction in C and a marginal increase in H. Using simultaneous equations we can quantify this effect. We now have:

$$(1) \quad 4H + 2C = 20\,001$$
$$(2) \quad 1H + 3C = 15\,000$$

and we obtain:

$$(1) \quad 4H + 2C = 20\,001$$
$$\underline{\qquad -4H - 12C = -60\,000}$$
$$-10C = -39\,999$$

giving a new solution for C = 3999.9 and therefore H = 3000.3. That is, a reduction of 0.1 units of C and an increase of 0.3 units of H. The new profit will be:

$$0.3(3000.3) + 0.25(3999.9) = £1900.065$$

– an increase of £0.065 in profit achieved. What we now have is a means of assigning a monetary value to the extra supply of Mix A. An extra litre of Mix A adds 6.5p to profit

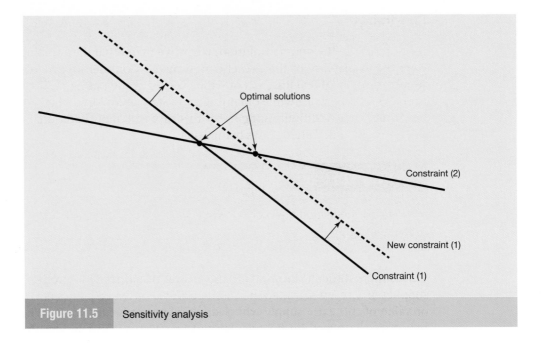

| Figure 11.5 | Sensitivity analysis |

and this is its *marginal value*: the value to the company over and above what it would normally pay for a litre of Mix A. This marginal value in LP is often referred to as *opportunity cost* or *shadow price*. It shows the change in the objective function for a marginal, one-unit, change in the right-hand side of a binding constraint.

If one extra litre of Mix A is worth 6.5p, does it then follow that two litres are worth 13p, 3 litres 19.5p and so on? The answer is a qualified 'yes'. Further marginal increases in the supply of Mix A will lead to further marginal increases in profit at a rate of 6.5p per litre of Mix A. However, this cannot continue indefinitely. The only reason that Mix A has a positive opportunity cost is because it is in scarce supply. As we increase the supply of this resource we gradually change the feasible area. There will come a point where some additional constraint becomes binding and the current binding constraint for Mix A becomes non-binding. In fact we can usually identify this from the graph. In Figure 11.2 we see that as constraint line (1) moves outwards as we increase supply of Mix A, it will eventually reach the point where constraint lines (2) and (3) intersect. This will be a new corner point of the feasible area and, given the slope of the profit line, which remains unchanged, will be the new solution. The new solution will now be:

$$H = 4000$$

and from constraint (2) when H = 4000, C = 3666.67. This combination of C and H will require from constraint (1) a total of 23 333.33 litres of Mix A. The maximum worthwhile increase in supply of Mix A is then 3333.33 litres. Increasing the supply of Mix A past this amount will not lead to any further increase in profit, since we will have run out of containers for product H: all 4000 will now be in use. Such a sensitivity analysis, therefore, allows us not only to put a value, or opportunity cost, on scarce resources but also to quantify the maximum worthwhile change in resource availability.

Activity 11.9

Undertake a similar sensitivity calculation for constraint (2).

For constraint (2) we would have:

$$(1)\ 4H + 2C = 20\ 000$$
$$(2)\ 1H + 3C = 15\ 001$$

and we obtain:

$$(1)\ 4H + 2C = 20\ 000$$
$$-4H - 12C = -60\ 004$$
$$-10C = -40\ 004$$

giving C = 4000.4 and H = 2999.8 with a profit of £1900.04 – an increase in profitability of 4p per extra litre of Mix B. Using the same approach as before we note from Figure 11.2 that the new maximum solution point will occur at the intersection of constraints (1) and (4), where by default C = 4500. This gives H = 2750. This combination of C and H would require a total of 16 250 litres of Mix B, which represents the maximum worthwhile amount before constraint (4) becomes binding. An extra 1250 litres would be worthwhile obtaining. Such sensitivity analysis also allows us to prioritise in the context of scarce resources. The opportunity cost of Mix A is 6.5p per litre and that of Mix B 4p per litre. Other things being equal, it will be more profitable to increase supplies of Mix A before those of Mix B.

Activity 11.10

Consider increasing the supply of resources in a non-binding constraint. What would be the associated opportunity cost?

It is important to realise that a positive opportunity cost is associated only with constraints that are binding at the current optimal solution. Non-binding constraints, by definition, must have a zero opportunity cost. Since a non-binding constraint already has unused resources then increasing the total supply of this resource will not allow an increase in production and hence in profit. Opportunity cost is often referred to in an LP context as the dual value or shadow price of a binding constraint.

The objective function

Just as we can undertake sensitivity analysis on constraints, so we can do the same for the objective function. In this case we are considering changes in the coefficients for the two variables in the objective function: in this example the profit contributions made by each product. In principle, a change in either profit contribution will affect the slope of the objective function line. If the slope of the objective function line changes sufficiently then it will move the optimal solution to a new corner point of the feasible area. The mathematics of calculating when this will occur are too complex for our consideration of the topic here but it is worthwhile noting that this information can be produced for a specialist LP computer program.

Computer Solutions

In practice, of course, LP problems are solved using an appropriate computer package. This might be available as part of a spreadsheet program, for example SOLVER in Microsoft Excel. It might also be a specialist LP program such as LINDO or XPRESS-MP.

The reason for this is that such problems will typically involve more than two variables – and hence cannot be solved on a two-dimensional graph – and a considerable number of constraints. However, the information such solutions typically generate is no different in principle from that we have produced. Table 11.2 shows typical computer output that was obtained for this problem. The optimal solution is shown first with the objective function (shown as zmax) taking a value of 1900 and the values for H and C as calculated. This is then followed by two variables labelled S3 and S4. LP programs typically refer to the *slack* for each constraint at the optimal point: the difference between the LHS of the constraint expression and the RHS. For constraints 3 and 4 these are, respectively, 1000 and 500 and represent the two types of unused container. Slack for constraints 1 and 2 is zero since these are binding. Sensitivity analysis results are then shown for the constraints. The opportunity cost for each binding constraint is shown, together with the range of variation. This shows the range within which the RHS of that constraint can vary and still remain a binding constraint. Although we only calculated one side of this range manually – at 23 333.3 – a reduction in the RHS value can also be calculated. Finally, sensitivity analysis for the objective function is shown. This

Table 11.2	Computer output

basis	value
H	3000.00
C	4000.000
S3	1000.000
S4	500.000

zmax	1900.00

Sensitivity on constraint

con	opp. cost	constr constant	permitted range of variation* from	to
1	0.06500	20000.0	15000	23333.3
2	0.04000	15000.0	10000	16250
3	0.00000	4000.00	0	+∞
4	0.00000	4500.00	0	+∞

Sensitivity on objective

var	optimal value	obj fun coeft	permitted range of variation* from	to
H	3000.00	0.30000	0.083	0.50
C	4000.00	0.25000	0.15	0.90

*The current basis remains optimal in this range.

indicates that for the H variable, for example, the profit coefficient could vary between £0.083 and £0.50 without altering the corner point of the feasible area at which the optimal solution occurred.

Assumptions of the Basic Model

Like all the quantitative models we introduce it is important to be aware of the implicit assumptions behind the model. If these are not appropriate to the business problem to which the model is being applied then the output from that model must be suspect.

Linearity

The model assumes that all relationships are linear in form. One of the implicit aspects behind such an assumption is that of proportionality. In this example, this assumes that if we produce twice as much C then we require twice as much of all the resources that C requires. Clearly in the real world this may not always be appropriate. Economies of scale may come into play after some output level is reached, for example, meaning that we may not require twice as much labour for twice the output.

Divisibility

The second assumption is one of divisibility: that all variables are continuous rather than discrete. In our context this implies that we can have fractions of products or resources. Again, for some problems this is not a difficulty, for others it might be. Clearly if our solution had shown that we had to produce, say, 3000.2 bottles of C, this is a physical impossibility.

Certainty

The third assumption relates to certainty: that we know for certain the numerical values of the linear relationships specified. In practice this can be a major difficulty in applying LP to real problems.

Single objective

The last assumption relates to the fact that we specify a single objective which we seek. Again, in practice a manager may be searching for a solution which satisfies several objectives simultaneously and not just a single one.

Dealing with More than Two Variables

Extensions to the basic LP model are not difficult to incorporate with ready access to computer solution packages. Additional variables are easily incorporated into programs, as are larger numbers of constraints. Naturally, once additional variables are added to the problem, the graphical method can no longer be used (since the graph has only two axes for two variables). Such larger problems are solved through the use of a suitable computer program, which typically will use what is known as the *simplex* method of solution. Briefly, this is a set of mathematical and arithmetic rules for checking the corner points of the feasible area for the problem to see which represents the optimum solution. To illustrate the solution output we would typically obtain, let us amend our basic problem. Let us assume that the company is now considering a third type of detergent for the export market (E). This would contribute 35p to profit per five-litre bottle and would consist of 3 litres of mix A and 2 litres of mix B. The problem formulation would then be:

Maximise $0.30H + 0.25C + 0.35X$

subject to:

$$4H + 2C + 3X \leqslant 20\ 000$$
$$1H + 3C + 2X \leqslant 15\ 000$$
$$1H \qquad\qquad \leqslant 4\ 000$$
$$\qquad 1C \qquad \leqslant 4\ 500$$
$$H,\ C,\ X \geqslant 0$$

Table 11.3 shows the computer output for this problem. The first part of the table, labelled tableau, shows details of the optimal solution. The objective function (labelled zmax) takes a value of 2350. From the last column of the tableau we see that X takes a value of 6000, C a value of 1000, S3 a value of 4000 and S4 a value of 3500. Any variable that does not appear in this column takes a value of zero. The solution, in other words, is to produce:

0 units of H

1000 units of C

6000 units of X

which will generate a profit of £2350. Such a combination of production will use all of chemical Mix A (S1 = 0 by default), all of chemical Mix B (S2 = 0 by default). The slack associated with constraint 3 will be 4000 (since H is zero at the optimal solution) and the slack associated with constraint 4 will be 3500. The optimal solution may seem surprising since, per unit, H is more profitable than C and yet we are producing zero H. The answer, of course, lies not in the unit contribution as such but the contribution in relation to the use of the limited resources available. We see from the solution that it is preferable to produce C instead of H. Sensitivity analysis is shown in the rest of the table: on the constraints first, then on the objective function. For the constraints we see confirmation that constraints 1 and 2 are binding whereas 3 and 4 are not. The opportunity cost for each of the binding constraints is shown as 0.11 (11p) for constraint 1 and 0.01 (1p) for constraint 2. Interpretation is as before. Increasing the available supply of Mix A would allow an increase in profit of 11p per extra litre obtained. This extra profit would occur for increases in the supply up to 22 500 litres (shown in the last column).

For the objective function, the sensitivity analysis is particularly revealing given that we are only producing two of the three products in the product range. For C and X the range of variation can be interpreted as before: for X, for example, the unit profit contribution can vary between 27.5p and 37.5p without affecting the profit-maximising combination of production. Let us examine H, however. This is a product not currently being produced (since it is not profitable to do so given the limited resources). The value of 45p shown actually indicates the minimum profit contribution this product would have to make in order for it to take a non-zero value in the solution. That is, the

Table 11.3	Computer solution

Tableau

basis	X1	X2	X3	S1	S2	S3	S4	rel value
zmax	-0.15	0.000	0.000	-0.11	-0.01	0.000	0.000	= 2350.000
X	2.000	0.000	1.000	0.600	-0.40	0.000	0.000	= 6000.000
C	-1.00	1.000	0.000	-0.40	0.600	0.000	0.000	= 1000.000
S3	1.000	0.000	0.000	0.000	0.000	1.000	0.000	= 4000.000
S4	1.000	0.000	0.000	0.400	-0.60	0.000	1.000	= 3500.000

Sensitivity on constraint

			permitted range of variation*	
con	opp. cost	constr constant	from	to
1	0.11000	20000.0	11250.0	22500.0
2	0.01000	15000.0	13333.3	20833.3
3	0.00000	4000.00	0.00000	$+\infty$
4	0.00000	4500.00	1000.00	$+\infty$

Sensitivity on objective

		obj fun	permitted range of variation*	
var	optimal value	coeft	from	to
H	0	0.30000	$-\infty$	0.45000
C	1000.00	0.25000	0.23333	0.40000
X	6000.00	0.35000	0.27500	0.37500

*The current basis remains optimal in this range.

per-unit profit contribution of H would have to be at least 40p in order for the company to find it worthwhile (in terms of increased profit) to produce this product. Clearly this now provides management with the opportunity of assessing where such a profit contribution could be realised: either by increasing the selling price and/or by reducing the production costs of this product.

QMDM IN ACTION
Cap Gemini Ernst & Young – optimising the supply chain

Cap Gemini Ernst & Young's client was a global manufacturer in the consumer packaged goods sector. The client was undertaking a complete review of their operations across Europe. One of the major elements of the review focused on improving the performance of the supply chain. The client was considering several options for the future supply chain infrastructure and they need a technique to explore these options against a number of possible future demand scenarios.

It was decided to adopt an optimisation model approach to the problem. A supply chain model was developed incorporating costs, product demands and supply chain resources. The model was then used to demonstrate how costs could be minimised for each given supply chain configuration that was being considered by management.

The model was designed from the outset as a decision support tool for senior management. This allowed them to assess the impact of potential changes through the modelling environment. An LP model was formulated for a supply chain which consisted of 15 factories; 14 distribution centres; 2500 products; 7500 components; 1000 component suppliers; 25 000 customers.

Data on procurement, manufacturing, warehousing and distribution was collected for the entire European supply chain. Data analysis allowed activity costs to be obtained. A specialist optimisation package, XPRESS-MP, was used together with a Windows graphical user interface to make it easy for senior management to understand and explore the results of the optimisation model.

The figure illustrates the complexity of the supply chain that had to be modelled.

The benefits are as follows:

● As a result of restructuring its supply chain the business achieved savings of around 10 per cent per annum (c. £10m).

● For the first time the client was able to view the complexity in the supply chain and the associated costs.

● For the first time the client was able to develop a European-wide view of the supply chain.

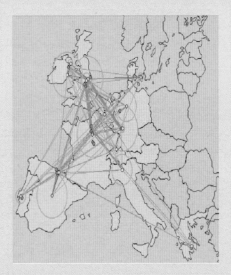

I am grateful to Cap Gemini Ernst & Young for permission to use this case study and to reproduce the figure shown. Further case study applications are available through their website: www.uk. capgemini.com/consulting/or/success_stories
Copyright is held by Cap Gemini Ernst & Young.

Extensions to the Basic LP Model

Because of some of the assumptions underpinning the model, a variety of additional programming models have been developed. *Integer* programming is concerned with those problems where some or all of the variables can take only integer values. *Non-linear* programming has been developed for use in situations where some, or all, relationships are non-linear. *Goal* programming allows the relaxation of the assumption of a single objective. In addition, a number of models have been developed for specialist use in more restricted applications, a common example being the *transportation* model, which is concerned with 'transporting' items from a variety of origins to a variety of destinations. All of these are developments that are worth exploring.

Worked Example

A local health board is producing a healthy-living guide for sale primarily to schools, voluntary agencies, hospitals and clinics. The guide provides advice on health education, healthy lifestyles and the like. The board intends to produce the guide in two formats: one will be in the form of a loose-leaf printed binder, the other as a short video. The board is currently trying to decide how many of each type to produce for sale. The video will sell for £5 and the binder for £3. Given the effort that has gone into the guide, the board is keen to maximise the revenue it gets from sales. It has estimated that it is likely to sell no more than 10 000 copies of both items together. However, it thinks that it will be able to sell at least 4000 copies of the video and at least 2000 copies of the binder, although sales of the binder are not expected to exceed 4000 copies. The company manufacturing the video on the board's behalf has also indicated that it takes 24 minutes to make each video and that for the fixed price it has quoted it can allocate only 5000 hours to the video production.

Getting the combination right

How can managers make sure they are making the right mix of products to gain maximum profits? One answer is "optimising" – a mathematical modelling system that is now a simple spreadsheet application.

By Kiriakos Vlahos

Management often faces situations in which a limited amount of resources of various types, such as capital, labour, machine time and raw materials, need to be allocated to a number of different uses or activities (production, R&D, training, marketing and so on) so as to promote the company's objectives (profit, market share, employee satisfaction).

Most managers try to tackle these problems with what-if? types of analysis in which the impact of alternative courses of action is investigated. But in decisions

involving allocation of scarce resources, it is often desirable to ask normative "what's best?" questions, for example what is the best production mix? or how much should I be spending on marketing?

The term optimisation describes a set of techniques that allow us to ask this type of question. More specifically, mathematical programming helps us to solve optimisation problems when the relationships between the different factors can be expressed as mathematical equations.

When the mathematical relationships are linear the solution tech-

nique is known as linear programming. It should be pointed out that in this context, programming does not refer to computer programming but rather to scheduling, i.e. what activities will be performed and at what level.

Here are some examples of business problems that can be addressed using optimisation techniques:

● a manufacturing company, with a range of products and limited production facilities, making decisions about the product mix.
● a company operating an oil refinery deciding which type of crude

oil to purchase and which oil products to produce.

- a fund manager allocating a certain amount of capital to different investment opportunities.
- a retailer that wishes to supply outlets from central depots to minimise costs.
- an airline company allocating crews to flights.

All these problems have the same structure: how to allocate scarce resources to various activities in order to optimise a specific objective. A simple product mix example that demonstrates the main concepts follows:

A small company manufactures TVs, stereos and speakers using a common parts inventory of power supplies, speaker cones and so on. The contribution of each product is $75, $50 and $35 respectively. It is the company's policy to produce at least 50 units of each product. The company would like to determine the most profitable mix of products

to build for the next month given that parts are in limited supply.

It is fairly easy to set up a spreadsheet that models the above problem and calculates total profit as a function of the production levels for the three products. The layout of

such a model is given in *Table 1*. You can see that for production levels of 100 for all products the total contribution to profit is $16,000. You can improve this contribution by trying different combinations of production levels but it is quite difficult to find

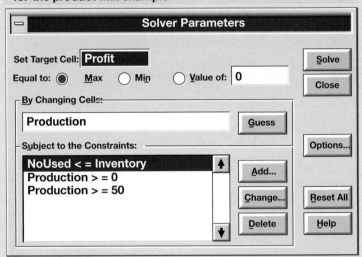

Figure 1: The Excel Solver Parameters dialogue box for the product mix example

Figure 2: The efficient frontier for the portfolio problem of table 3

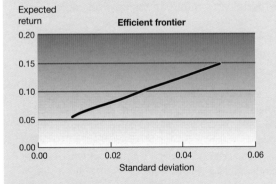

Table 1: A product mix example

			TV set	Stereo	Speaker
		Number to build->	100	100	100
Part name	Inventory	no. used			
Chassis	450	200	1	1	0
Picture	250	100	1	0	0
Speaker cone	800	500	2	2	1
Power supply	450	200	1	1	0
Electronics	600	400	2	1	1
Profit contribution:			75	50	35
Profit:	By product		$7,500	$5,000	$3,500
		Total	**$16,000**		

Table 2: Slack and dual prices

Name	Final value	Shadow price	Constraint limit	Slack
Chassis no. used	375	0	450	75
Picture tube no. used	175	0	250	75
Speaker cone no. used	800	12	800	0
Power supply no. used	375	0	450	75
Electronics no. used	600	25	600	0

Table 3: A simple portfolio optimisation problem

Assets	A	B	C		Correlation	
Return	8%	15%	5%		A,B	0.5
Standard deviations	0.04	0.05	0.01		A,C	0.2
					B,C	-0.1

the most profitable production mix while making sure that the various constraints are satisfied. Fortunately, modern spreadsheets have built-in optimisation capabilities. The methodology for solving such a problem is as follows:

● **Step 1. Specify the objective function.** You need to decide what you are aiming to achieve in a given business situation. In this case you are trying to maximise the total contribution to profit. One thing you need to remember when you specify the objective function is that costs you have already paid for or you cannot avoid are *sunk* costs and irrelevant in the context of this decision.

● **Step 2. Specify the decision variables.** The decision variables are the levers under the control of management that can influence profit by changing the production levels for TVs, stereos and speakers.

● **Step 3. Specify the constraints.** In most business situations there are a number of internal or external factors that limit our choice of action. In this example you need to make sure that you use no more parts than you have available and that production quantities are greater than 50 units. In addition, you need to specify that the production quantities are positive, i.e. greater than zero. These last constraints are called non-negativity constraints.

● **Step 4. Solve the optimisation problem and find the optimal solution.** For this step you can rely on one of the many optimisation packages that are available. In most cases standard spreadsheet solvers will be sufficient. In *Figure 1* you can see how steps 1–3 are carried out using the Excel spreadsheet solver. "Profit", "NoUsed", "Inventory" and "Production" are named cell ranges. Instead of typing these names you can just point to the appropriate parts of the

spreadsheet using the mouse. Solving the optimisation problem is just a matter of pressing the "Solve" button. The optimal solution to this problem is to produce 175 TVs, 200 stereos and 50 speakers, resulting in a total contribution to profit of $24,875.

The same problem can be expressed algebraically as follows:

Decision variables:
    TVs   : no of TVs produced
    Stereos : no of stereos
                produced
    Speakers: no of speakers
                produced
Objective function:
Maximise contribution to profit (in $) = 75 *TVs + 50 *stereos + 35 *speakers

Constraints:
a) Chassis inventory:
$$TVs + stereos \leq 450$$
b) Picture tube inventory:
$$TVs \leq 250$$
c) Speaker cone inventory:
$$2* TVs + 2* stereos + speakers \leq 800$$
d) Power supply inventory:
$$TVs + stereos \leq 450$$
e) Electronics inventory:
$$2* TVs + stereos + speakers \leq 600$$
f) Non-negativity constraints:
$$TVs \geq 0, stereos \geq 0, speakers \geq 0$$

As you can see, all of the mathematical expressions used to define the objective function and the constraints are linear functions of the decision variables, so this is an example of a linear programming problem.

When we deal with complex real-world problems a single numerical answer is of limited value. We usually aim to develop a better understanding of the problem and the relationships between the problem parameters – often approx-

imately known – our decisions and the outcomes. The sensitivity of the outcomes to parameter changes is of paramount importance. Often in this process, we discover unknown relationships and hidden links that lead to the creation of new decision alternatives.

Fortunately, the solution of an optimisation problem is accompanied by useful information that helps us understand the problem better and grasp the sensitivities in an efficient way. Two concepts that are useful in analysing the results of an optimisation problem are the "slack" of the constraints and the "shadow prices".

Slack

Slack is the surplus amount of a limited resource (or the amount by which we exceed a minimum requirement) at the optimum. It is reported in the output of an optimisation problem (*see Table 2*). Constraints with zero slack are said to be *binding*. These are the important constraints that influence the optimal solution. Removing non-binding constraints from the problem formulation would not change the solution.

Shadow prices

At the optimum, associated with each constraint is a quantity known as shadow price (also called dual price). This is *the amount by which the objective value will improve if we relax the constraint by one unit*, i.e. if we had an additional unit of a limited resource available. In economic terms, *it is the most we would be willing to pay to obtain an additional unit of that resource*.

If a constraint is not binding at the optimum (i.e., there is some slack), then the shadow price is always zero. This is logical because if not all of the available quantity of a resource is used, there is no incentive to obtain more of it. Conversely, we can deduce that if the dual price is non-zero, there is no slack in the constraint.

In *Table 2*, for example, we can see that the binding constraints (zero slack) are the speaker cones and the electronics inventory constraints. The shadow prices for these constraints show us that we could increase the profit contribution if we had an additional speaker cone or electronics unit by $12 and $25 respectively.

This is very useful information. For example, if we could purchase additional speaker cones for less than $12 we should certainly investigate that possibility further.

There is still a question about how many additional speaker cones we should buy if the price is less than $12; the optimisation results can provide us with an answer, but this is beyond the scope of this article. It should be noted, though, how the first iteration of solving this problem has already helped us to identify new courses of action that may have escaped us initially, namely the possibility of purchasing additional quantities of the different parts. This could lead to a new formulation of the profit contribution.

There are many applications of optimisation to financial problems. One of the best known problems is that of portfolio optimisation.

Given a set of assets with specified returns, standard deviations and correlations of returns, find the portfolio that minimises risk (i.e. variance or returns) for a certain level of return.

This is the well-known Markowitz Mean/Variance portfolio model. A simple example with three assets, A, B and C, is in *Table 3*. The problem of minimising risk for a given level of return is a non-linear optimisation problem because the variance of the total returns is a quadratic function of the variables denoting the fraction of the investment that goes into each of the assets. In our simple example the optimal portfolio that gives at least 13 per cent return consists of 80 per cent asset B and 20 per cent asset C. By repetitively solving this problem for different levels of return we can construct the *efficient frontier*.

Figure 2 gives you the efficient frontier for the example problem, calculated using Excel. Fund managers often solve portfolio optimisation problems with hundreds of assets.

Many industries have a strong tradition in using optimisation techniques with great success. Airline companies use large-scale optimisation to schedule flights and crews and manage ground operations. Oil companies use optimisation to control the blending of input in refineries and reduce the distribution costs of oil products. Electricity companies rely on optimisation-based decision-support systems for short-term operational and long-term investment planning.

In the past optimisation was a tool for specialists with access to vast amounts of computing power. Now it is accessible to any manager with a PC and a spreadsheet. In many situations involving allocation of scarce resources, the power of optimisation can improve results dramatically. So, it is worth developing the habit of asking "what's best?" questions in addition to "what if?" ones.

Summary

Many business problems involve the allocation of scarce resources to activities in order to optimise an objective. These can be addressed using optimisation techniques – "what's best" rather than "what if?".

Modern spreadsheets have built in optimisation capabilities typically requiring the user to specify the objective, any decision variables and constraints.

Two concepts are useful in analysing the results of an optimisation exercise. The "slack" is the surplus amount of a limited resource at the optimum (constraints with zero slack are said to be "binding"). The "shadow price", also known as the dual price, is the most one would be willing to pay to obtain an additional unit of a limited resource. It opens up the possibility of purchasing additional quantities of parts to improve the profit contributions. Airlines (for flights and crew schedules), oil companies (to control the blending of inputs into refineries) and electricity companies (for operational and investment planning) have an optimisation tradition. But the technique is available to any manager with a PC and a spreadsheet.

Source: FT Mastering Management Part 8, 15 December 1995, p 25.

We are seeking to maximise the revenue earned from sales of these two products. Denoting the video as V and the binder as B we can obtain the following problem formulation:

Maximise $5V + 3B$

subject to:

$$1V + 1B \leq 10\,000$$
$$1V \qquad \geq 4\,000$$
$$1B \geq 2\,000$$
$$1B \leq 4\,000$$
$$0.4V \qquad \leq 5\,000$$
$$V, B \geq 0$$

The fifth constraint shows that the time required to make each video (24 minutes or 0.4 hours) multiplied by the number of videos made cannot exceed the time available, 5000 hours. Using a computer package we obtain the information in Table 11.4 regarding the optimal solution. (You may wish to produce your own graphical solution.)

Table 11.4	Computer solution

```
basis       value

V           8000.00        zmax    46000.00
B           2000.00
S2          4000.00
S4          2000.00
S5          1800.00


Sensitivity on constraint

                                permitted
                                range of
            opp.     constr     variation*
con         cost     constant   from        to

1           5.0      10000.0    6000.0      14500.0
2           0.0      4000.0     0           8000.0
3           2.0      2000.0     0           4000.0
4           0.0      4000.0     2000.0      +∞
5           0.0      5000.0     3200.0      +∞


Sensitivity on objective

                      obj       permitted
                                range of
            optimal   fun       variation*
var         value     coeft     from        to

V           8000.0    5         3           +∞
B           2000.0    3         −∞          5>


*The current basis remains optimal in this range.
```

First of all we see that the optimal solution is to produce 8000 videos and 2000 binders and that this will generate a revenue of £46 000. As usual with optimisation problems, the solution is rarely our sole interest and in this case we might wish to assess some of the implications surrounding the optimal solution. We see that constraints 2, 4 and 5 are non-binding. Constraint 2 relates to the minimum production of videos, which, at 4000, is being exceeded at the optimal solution by another 4000. Constraint 4 relates to the maximum production of binders and our optimal solution is some 2000 binders below this. Constraint 5 is the constraint imposed by the video manufacturer. We can see that the 5000 hours currently budgeted for will not all be required, with some 1800 hours not needed (and we may wish to go back to the video manufacturer to renegotiate the production contract). We see that by default constraints 1 and 3 are binding. The sensitivity analysis provides information about the extent to which the optimal solution remains stable if we change the right-hand side values of constraints.

We see first of all that only constraints 1 and 3 have non-zero opportunity costs (since they are the two binding constraints). For constraint 1 we see an opportunity cost of 5. This implies that if we were able to find a market for more than 10 000 of these guides (perhaps by getting health boards in other areas interested in them) the sales revenue would go up by £5 for each extra guide, implying that we would produce extra units of the video. Equally, of course, if this 10 000 figure proved optimistic and we realised we could sell fewer, the sales revenue would decrease by £5 each time. We see that this constraint will remain binding in the range from 6000 to 14 500. The opportunity cost of £2 for constraint 3 needs more thought, since it does not appear to be the revenue either from videos (at £5) or from binders (at £3). This constraint relates to the minimum sales of binders, estimated at 2000. Effectively, if we reduced this constraint by one (to 1999) we would produce one less binder. Given that constraint 1 would still be binding, one less binder means we could produce one more video (since we still have unused video production hours). The net change in sales revenue then would be a loss of £3 and a gain of £5, a net gain of £2. In summary, then, we might suggest to the board that, as well as determining the optimal combination as 8000 videos and 2000 binders, it should:

● attempt to renegotiate the contract with the video manufacturer, since this appears to be based on a need for 5000 production hours, 1800 more than will be needed;

● attempt to find other markets for the guide, since each extra guide sold above the 10 000 limit will generate an extra £2. Up to 4500 additional guides could be produced with the currently unused production time (and of course if we were able to increase sales in this way, we would not want to renegotiate the contract with the video manufacturer);

● reconsider whether a minimum of 2000 binders should be available. Given the anticipated fixed demand for the guide of 10 000, the board should consider producing only video versions (unless it has other information that some purchasers would not buy a video version but only a binder version).

Summary

In this chapter we have introduced and developed the linear programming model as an example of a model applied to constrained optimisation problems. The LP model, in its many different forms, is a widely used technique and, as the Further Reading at the end of the book indicates, has been applied to a considerable variety of problems in both public and private sector organisations. The principles of the model are relatively simple, requiring a problem formulation, a solution, and an evaluation of the solution. Often the first part of this process, the formulation of a business problem into a linear programme, can be particularly difficult and may call for considerable skill on the part of the practitioner. The solution process is typically computer-based, although the graphical method is useful for illustrating general principles in a form a manager can understand.

Useful online resources

Detailed below are some internet resources that may be useful. Many have further links to other sites. An updated version is available from the accompanying website (**www.pearsoned.co.uk/wisniewski**). In addition, I would be grateful for details of other websites that have been found to be useful.

www-unix.mcs.anl.gov/otc/Guide/faq/linear-programming-faq.html – Linear Programming: frequently asked questions

carbon.cudenver.edu/~hgreenbe/glossary/index.php – Mathematical Programming Glossary

www.economicsnetwork.ac.uk/cheer/ch9_3/ch9_3p07.htm – Teaching Linear Programming using Microsoft Excel Solver

www.me.utexas.edu/~jensen/ORMM/models/unit/linear/index.html – Tutorial on LP

QMDM IN ACTION
Blue Bell Inc.

Blue Bell Inc. is a US-based company that few people outside the USA have heard of. Yet, in the 1980s at the date of this application, the company achieved annual sales of over $1.2 billion, generated an annual net income of almost $50 million and employed almost 30 000 people worldwide. While the company itself may not be well known, its product ranges certainly are. The largest part of its business consists of the Wrangler Group, producing and selling denim jeans and related clothing. In the early 1980s senior management in the company became increasingly concerned about one aspect of the Group's operations: that relating to stock control and the amount of capital tied up in stock. The business itself was classed as one which was very intensive in terms of working capital. The number of product lines, styles of product and markets served

had increased markedly. Figure 11.6 illustrates the product complexity for one particular product, jeans. Given that annual output of jeans at the time was around 35 million pairs scattered across 37 production facilities the stock control problem was a severe one. At a time when short-term interest rates were particularly high, the company as a whole found that its interest charges had increased from just over $1 million in 1979 to almost $22 million by 1982, with the obvious consequences on operating costs and corporate performance. A company task force was established with the aims of:

● assessing the opportunity for reducing stock levels

● developing a suitable programme for achieving such stock reduction

● implementing such a programme.

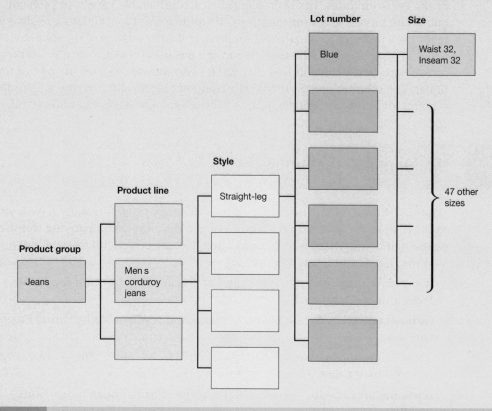

| Figure 11.6 | The product hierarchy for jeans |

Reprinted by permission of JR Edwards, HM Wagner and WP Wood. Taken from 'Blue Bell Trims its Inventory', *Interfaces*, **15**(1), 1985. Copyright held by the Operations Research Society of America and the Institute of Management Sciences.

The task force investigated this complex problem from a number of different perspectives – forecasting sales, assessing required stock levels, planning the production process – which were all an interrelated part of the overall problem. One aspect in particular that was investigated related to what is known as marker planning and selection. A simplified overview of the production process is that, on a weekly basis, sufficient fabric must be cut to shape to form the components for manufacturing into a pair of jeans. Typically, layers of the appropriate fabric are placed on a cutting table and a marker – a pre-prepared pattern showing the parts to be cut – placed on top of the fabric to be used as a cutting guide. An example of a marker is shown in Figure 11.7.

Given the complexity of possible production plans – with the variety of jeans in terms of sizes, designs and fabrics – a library of such markers is available. The design and use of appropriate markers in the cutting process is of critical impor-

tance. Fabric may form over 50 per cent of the production cost of an item and any increase in fabric waste will have an obvious consequence for profitability. The design of the marker itself will contribute to fabric waste, which may be anything up to 15 per cent of the fabric used. The problem for the company in this context was to try to minimise fabric waste while at the same time ensuring that the utilisation of cutting room capacity was in line with production requirements. A linear programming model to assist in this part of the task was formulated. The model took into account a number of critical factors:

● the number of different stock parts (which could vary from 75 to 125)

● the production lead time required

● the estimated production requirements over the planning period for each stock part

● the fabric waste on markers

● the frequency of use of the different markers.

Blue Bell

| Figure 11.7 | Example of marker |

The LP formulation was a particularly complex one, given the production set-up in the company, and the model actually used had to be adapted to ensure it was cost-effective to run the model on the required weekly basis. Understandably, given the complexity of the new approaches and the consequences should they fail to work satisfactorily, the new systems were pilot-tested in a single profit centre. The testing consisted of utilising the new approach in parallel with the planning systems currently in use. The first stage was to use the new approach as part of the planning process. Later this was extended to use the new approach for scheduled production, again on a test-site basis first of all. The reported results were impressive. Within a two-year period, stock levels had been reduced by some $115 million without affecting sales volumes or requiring a reduction in the size of the product line. Raw material costs – through reduced fabric waste – were also substantially reduced with annual cost savings estimated at $1 million.

Exercises

1 A manufacturer is trying to determine the combination of two products, A and B, that should be produced. Each product passes through a three-stage production process: Stages I, II and III. For product A Stage I takes three hours of labour, Stage II four hours and Stage III one hour. For product B the comparable data is four hours, two hours and two hours. Labour hours currently cost £4.50 per hour. Product A sells for £38 a unit and B for £40. At present 11 people are employed on Stage I, 12 on Stage II and 10 on Stage III, with all employees working 40 hours each week.

   (a) Formulate this problem in terms of determining the profit-maximising combination of the two products on a weekly basis.

(b) Solve the problem graphically.

(c) Confirm the solution using simultaneous equations.

(d) Identify the binding and non-binding constraints.

(e) Undertake sensitivity analysis on each of the binding constraints and evaluate the management information that this generates.

(f) What rate of overtime should the firm be willing to pay its employees?

2 For the problem in Exercise 1 assume the firm now wishes to maximise revenue rather than profit.

(a) Formulate this problem in terms of determining the revenue-maximising combination of the two products on a weekly basis.

(b) Solve the problem graphically.

(c) Confirm the solution using simultaneous equations.

(d) Identify the binding and non-binding constraints.

(e) Undertake sensitivity analysis on each of the binding constraints and evaluate the management information that this generates.

(f) What rate of overtime should the firm be willing to pay its employees?

3 A small engineering company makes two products for export, A and B. Both products go through a four-stage process: turning, grinding, polishing, finishing. The two products are produced in batches of 100 items and the time taken, in hours, for each batch to go through each stage is shown in Table 11.5.

Profit contribution per batch of product A is £4 and for product B is £5.

Table 11.5	Time taken for production processes		
	Hours per batch		Hours
Stage	Product A	Product B	available
Turning	12	18	240
Grinding	30	45	450
Polishing	20	60	480
Finishing	40	30	480

(a) Formulate this problem in terms of determining the profit-maximising combination of the two products on a weekly basis.

(b) Solve the problem graphically.

(c) Confirm the solution using simultaneous equations.

(d) Identify the binding and non-binding constraints.

(e) Undertake sensitivity analysis on each of the binding constraints and evaluate the management information that this generates.

(f) What is it worth to the company to have extra hours available in turning?

4 A small electrical repair shop finds it has two main types of work. Customers bring items in for repair: TVs, videos, etc. require major repair; other repairs are classed as minor. At present the shop has more business than it can handle and is trying to prioritise the work it should do. The firm charges £25 per hour for effecting a major repair and £10 per hour for a minor one. The shop currently has two trained repair engineers, who each work a 40-hour week. The shop will not allow overtime. The manager of the store has the following requirements:

- Repair work must generate at least £800 per week income.
- Major repairs should form at least 60 per cent of the weekly work.
- Minor repairs should form at least 30 per cent of weekly work.

(a) Formulate this problem in terms of determining the revenue-maximising combination of the two types of work on a weekly basis.

(b) Solve the problem graphically.

(c) Confirm the solution using simultaneous equations.

(d) Identify the binding and non-binding constraints.

(e) Undertake sensitivity analysis on each of the binding constraints and evalute the management information that this generates.

(f) What is it worth to the company to allow the engineers to work overtime?

12 Stock Control

Learning objectives

By the end of this chapter you should be able to:

- understand the stock-control problem
- be able to identify the major stock costs
- understand the simple EOQ model
- be aware of the MRP and JIT approaches to stock control

In this chapter we examine a specialised – but important – area of management decision making. Every organisation faces what are known as stock-control problems – the difficulty of maintaining adequate stocks of certain goods to ensure that customers' requirements are met or services can continue to be provided. The dilemma facing a manager with responsibility in this area is that, on the one hand, stocks should be kept as high as possible to ensure supplies are always available when needed. On the other hand, such high stock levels incur a variety of costs for the organisation. The dilemma therefore is balancing high stock levels required to meet likely demand against the costs incurred in keeping stocks high. In this chapter we shall examine some of the basic problems of stock control and some of the approaches that can be taken to help resolve the problem.

The Stock-Control Problem

Assume that we have been asked to assist the manager of a company with a stock-control problem. The company specialises in the maintenance and repair of business PC systems and much of its market consists of local small- and medium-sized businesses which have taken out an annual contract with the repair company. Under this contract the repair company guarantees to repair a customer's PC within 24 hours or to provide an equivalent replacement until the repair is effected. The company prides itself on customer service, so it is keen to ensure that its 24-hour target is met wherever possible. No other local company offers this type of guarantee and the company sees this as a major part of its competitive advantage in the marketplace. However, in order to meet this target, the company has to have an efficient and effective stock system so that adequate supplies of spare parts are readily available. Clearly if the service engineer finds that a PC requiring repair needs a specific replacement part – say a new graphics card – then the company cannot afford to be in the position of having to order this from the supplier and wait for delivery if it is to meet its guaranteed repair time. In fact, to help us focus on the key features of the stock-control problem, let us examine in detail just one of the key parts the company has to have in stock: a Super VGA card. The company can purchase these from the supplier at £100 each and anticipates that over the coming 12 months 250 cards will be needed. The supplier will supply any quantity we require and, because the supplier is local, delivery of the order is immediate. The company, however, also realises that placing an order incurs certain costs: someone has to find the time to get the order sent off, when the order is received it has to be checked to ensure that what was ordered has been supplied, payment then has to be authorised and so on. The best guess of the company is that all of this 'costs' the company £50 each time an order is sent. The basic problem the company currently faces is: how many of these cards should be ordered now from the supplier?

Activity 12.1

Can you advise the company on a suitable decision?

One approach we might take is to say: order the quantity of cards now that we require over the next 12 months. This way we can effectively guarantee we will have the card in stock when required (at least for virtually all of the year). However, the problem with this is that the company will have to spend £25 000 (250 × £100) on the stock now and this capital will be tied up in the stock for most of the year. The company also has the problem of looking after the stock over this period – costs relating to security, insurance, obsolescence, etc. The alternative appears to be that of placing several orders throughout the year. For example, the company might place an order now for 50 cards and then a further order, say, every two months. This has the advantage of keeping the capital invested in stock lower but obviously the firm may then be increasing the chance of not having a card in stock when needed. In fact this is the classic dilemma of the manager with stock-control responsibility: on the one hand trying to minimise the costs incurred and on the other trying to ensure that a 'stockout' (running out of stock) does not occur. Let us clarify the various costs involved in the problem.

Costs Involved in Stock Control

We can distinguish between a variety of key costs:

- order costs
- purchase costs
- holding costs
- stockout costs.

Order costs

Order costs are the costs incurred whenever a stock order is generated. These relate to the costs involved with all the stages from the time an order is placed through to when the order is paid for. These might involve the costs relating to clerical, administrative and managerial activities linked to the order process; costs of transportation; costs of receiving and inspecting orders; costs of finance and accounting support. Order costs are often assumed to be fixed, regardless of the size of the order, in stock-control models. In our problem the order cost is assumed to be £50. In real life this cost may be difficult to quantify and the full cost often remains hidden.

Purchase cost

Purchase cost is the actual cost of purchasing the stock item from the supplier. In the simpler stock-control models this cost is usually assumed to be constant. In more sophisticated models, however, it is possible to build in discount systems, i.e. lower unit purchase cost with larger orders. We shall assume a fixed cost of £100 per item.

Holding costs

Holding costs are those associated with the company holding a fixed quantity of stock over a given period of time. Such costs can include the cost of capital tied up in the value of the stock, storage costs (heating, lighting, security), depreciation, insurance and obsolescence. Typically the holding cost is calculated as a cost per unit held in stock per year. We shall assume that for this company the holding cost is £15 per item per year. That is, if the company held one graphics card in stock for one year it would cost £15 (made up of the opportunity cost of the £100 purchase cost, security costs and the like).

Stockout costs

The final cost we consider is that incurred when stock is not available. This is typically made up of two elements. The first is the cost that may be incurred in obtaining supplies of the item at short notice. It may be possible, for example, for the firm to obtain supplies of the card at short notice by going to another supplier who charges a higher price, or by sending someone to the supplier's premises to collect directly. The second element is more difficult to quantify but represents a 'goodwill' cost: the customer may in future take their business elsewhere or complain to other customers' ultimately leading to a loss of business. Such costs are understandably difficult to quantify and for the purposes of the basic stock-control model we shall ignore shortage costs.

Retailers hope tighter stock control will stem theft and fraud losses

By Sophy Buckley

UK retailers preparing for a tough Christmas sales season are gearing up to tackle poor stock control, which could be responsible for €100bn (£68.4bn) slipping through retailers' fingers worldwide.

Khuram Kirmani, chief executive of IntelliQ, a data mining consultancy, suggests billions of pounds could be lost in the UK from stock losses through causes as diverse as shrinkage – shoplifting and theft by staff – fraudulent returns and simple process errors. The loss comes straight off the bottom line. Mr Kirmani says it is the last area of easy wins for retailers, who are desperate to offset the effects of consumer slowdown combined with rising rents, rates, payroll costs and utility bills.

"This is the last area of free money on the table," he says. "They've already done everything else – squeeze suppliers, automate systems, cut costs. This is free money because they've already earned it."

Mr Kirmani is keen to stress that the loss does not just come from stealing – big losses also come from areas such as process errors. He says: "It's also about fraudulent

returns, credit card fraud, failure to implement a company policy or even just human error. Loss is distinct from shrinkage. "Although no one knows exactly how much it's worth, we know it is many millions and it's a board-level issue. If shrinkage is estimated at about €25bn a year in Europe, add these other elements and I think you can multiply that by four."

Mr Kirmani claims that data mining tools such as RetailKey Loss can quickly identify problems and generate a report, speed being the essence of prevention. IntelliQ, set up three years ago, has about a dozen retail clients, including B&Q, the DIY group owned by Kingfisher; BHS, owned by Philip Green; and Argos, part of the GUS group. This month New Look, the UK's third biggest women's fashion retailer, signed up. Mr Kirmani says an IntelliQ solution costs from six figures, but insists clients have achieved pay-back within a year.

Laurence King, director of profit protection at B&Q, says: "We identified £250,000 of fraud within only six months." But the gains do not stop there. "As a rule of thumb, for every hard £1 saved through

identified fraud another is gained through deterrence," he adds. At Woolworths, the general retailer, Steve Lewis, director of retail and distribution, admits the problem is huge and says the pressures on retailers to combat it are growing. "Every penny of loss is a penny off the bottom line," he says. "The market is becoming increasingly competitive and people are more and more sophisticated in the way they buck the system, so if you don't use technology those losses are only going to grow."

Although Woolworths looked at an IntelliQ products, it decided to develop a solution in-house, which has just started trials. Its system is only tracking internal fraud, which Mr Lewis estimates as costing the company "several million pounds a year". He says: "We are looking for a 10 per cent reduction in loss through fraud and the plan is to roll this out across the company next year, assuming it pays dividends, which I'm sure it will." But he admits that after that, Woolworths will probably have to look outside the company for a system that goes beyond seeking out fraud.

Source: *Financial Times*, 21 November 2005.

Stock control is big business – and for good reason.

QMDM IN ACTION
Cap Gemini Ernst & Young – improving stock management

Cap Gemini Ernst & Young's client was a global manufacturer of packaged consumer goods. As part of their review of European operations, the client was reviewing its supply chain (see also the Cap Gemini Ernst & Young QMDM in Action on p 430). Cap Gemini Ernst & Young were called in to examine ways of improving supply chain performance in terms of stock levels currently maintained, raw material and packaging costs and sales forecasting. Inadequate forecasting of sales or inadequate reporting of existing stock levels can both lead to inefficiency and higher cost in terms of stock control. Similarly, better use of the existing supplier base can generate significant cost savings. Equally, given that product sales forecasts drive the entire supply chain the accuracy of such forecasts is critical to the cost efficiency of the supply chain operations.

Data was collected for around 2500 product lines across the client's European operations on weekly production, sales and forecasts for a 12-month period. Purchase ledgers were used for component and supplier information. The data collected was stored in a central database for detailed analysis.

A comprehensive analysis of the data was undertaken across the areas of stock levels, raw material and packaging costs and sales forecasting. Some of the findings from the analysis include:

- Average stock levels were excessive when compared with weekly demand.

- In principle stock levels could be reduced by 50 per cent together with an improvement in average service levels of 98 per cent.

- Similar components were purchased from numerous different suppliers (with potential for rationalisation of purchasing).

- A large percentage of suppliers provided only one component to the client.

- Sales forecasts on average were 30 per cent above actual sales figures and in some cases 100 per cent higher.

- Further analysis indicated that the forecasting methods used across the various European markets had wide differences in approach.

The graph below is taken from part of the analysis and shows the percentage of stock items against the number of weeks of stock cover.

The analysis:

- provided the client with information and motivation to develop new stock control processes;

- demonstrated the opportunity for restructuring purchasing and procurement and was the first step towards supplier partnering;

- provided the evidence and motivation to develop new approaches to forecasting.

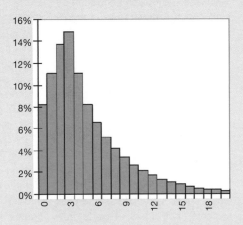

I am grateful to Cap Gemini Ernst & Young for permission to use this case study and to reproduce the figure shown. Further case study applications are available through their website: www.uk.capgemini.com/services/consulting/or/success_stories
Copyright is held by Cap Gemini Ernst & Young.

The Stock-Control Decision

Clearly the major decision the manager must face in terms of the stock-control problem is what quantity of stock to order at any one time. Following from this decision a subsequent decision needs to be taken on how frequently to order stock. As we have already seen, the manager faces an inherent conflict between the order costs involved and the holding costs involved in the decision, since these will vary depending on the quantity ordered each time. To add to the problem, these two costs are affected in different ways by the order-quantity decision. The larger the quantity ordered at any one time then the lower the total order costs over a year (since fewer orders will be made to meet annual demand). Holding costs, however, will increase with the order size, since larger quantities of stock will be held at any one time. It seems sensible, therefore, for the manager to consider trying to minimise the total costs involved – the sum of both the order costs and the holding costs.

Let us consider the effect of different decisions. We first define the notation we shall be using:

D = the annual demand for the item, here 250
C_0 = the cost of placing each order, £50
C_h = the cost of holding an item for one year, £15
Q = the size of the order to be placed (currently unknown).

Activity 12.2

Determine the total order costs if the manager decides:

(a) to place orders for 10 units at a time
(b) to place orders for 250 units at a time.

Consider setting $Q = 10$: that is the manager decides to place a stock order for 10 items. This will necessitate 25 (250/10) orders through the year at a cost of £50 each order and will lead to a total order cost, OC, of £1250. Conversely, if we decide to set $Q = 250$ we will require only one order each year and total order costs will be £50. But what of holding costs for these two options? This is slightly more complicated since we need to consider the average number of items held in stock at any one time and then multiply this by C_h. Consider the manager's position. He or she knows that, in our first scenario, a stock order will consist of 10 items. On some given day, then, 10 items will arrive from the supplier. Gradually over time these will be used up. Ideally, what the manager would like to see is that on the day that the last of these 10 items is used the next order for 10 items arrives from the supplier so that no stockout ever occurs, while at the same time ensuring we are not carrying too many stock items. From this it follows that, at any one time, the average number of items held in stock will be $Q/2$ (since at the beginning we will have Q items; at the end we will have 0 items). The holding cost will then be given by:

$$Q/2 \times C_h = 10/2 \times £15 = £75$$

So, with an order size of 10 units, OC will be £1250 and HC £75. But what of our other option – ordering 250 items?

Activity 12.3

Calculate holding costs when Q = 250.

Holding costs are just as readily calculated:

$$HC = 250/2 \times £15 = £1875$$

and this compares with OC = £50 for this value of Q. We see, numerically, that the two cost elements move in opposite directions as we alter Q, the size of our stock order. Order costs will decrease as Q increases but holding costs increase. Clearly we require some compromise position between the two. Table 12.1 shows the order costs, holding costs and total costs for a variety of order sizes, Q.

It can be seen that as we increase the order size, Q, the order costs, OC, decline. At the same time, however, holding costs, HC, increase. Total costs exhibit a different pattern altogether. At first as Q increases TC decreases. After some point, however, TC begins to rise again with Q. Consider Figure 12.1, which shows a graph of the two cost elements, OC and HC, up to Q = 250. We see that order costs are especially high when Q takes low values but gradually decrease as Q increases. Holding costs, on the other hand, steadily increase with Q (in fact you may recognise this as a linear relationship). You can also see from the graph that OC and HC take equal values (they intersect) when Q is around 40 units. Consider the implications of this. The manager is trying to balance the conflicting cost pressures. For Q less than 40, OC will be higher than HC. For Q greater than 40, the position is reversed, with OC greater than HC. At Q = 40 (or thereabouts) the two cost elements are the same. This is reinforced if we consider Figure 12.2, where the total cost (that is OC + HC) is shown on the same diagram. We see clearly that total cost will be minimised where OC = HC. In other words, this value for Q will minimise the total costs involved in stock.

Table 12.1	Order costs and holding costs			
Q	Orders	OC	HC	TC
10	25	1250.00	75.00	1325.00
25	10	500.00	187.50	687.50
50	5	250.00	375.00	625.00
75	3.3	166.70	562.50	729.17
100	2.5	125.00	750.00	875.00
125	2	100.00	937.50	1037.50
150	1.7	83.30	1125.00	1208.33
175	1.4	71.40	1312.50	1383.93
200	1.25	62.50	1500.00	1562.50
225	1.1	55.60	1687.50	1743.06
250	1	50.00	1875.00	1925.00

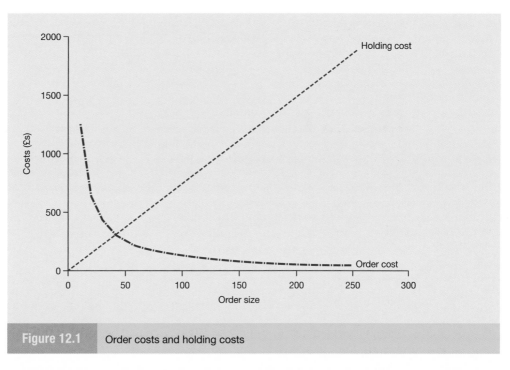

Figure 12.1   Order costs and holding costs

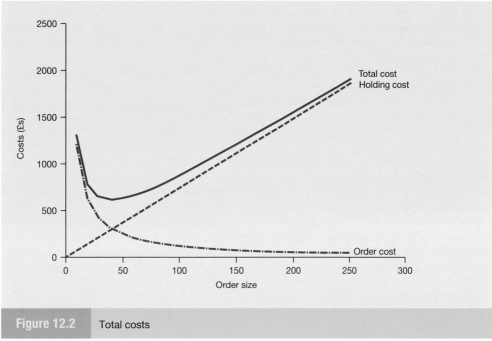

Figure 12.2   Total costs

The Economic Order Quantity Model

In fact what we have developed here is technically known as the *economic order quantity model*: establishing the value for Q that minimises total cost. This value for Q is referred to as the economic order quantity (EOQ). Clearly, the graphical solution method is a clumsy and tedious one and we require a more direct and accurate method for deriving Q. Using some fairly complex algebra we can derive a suitable formula for locating the value of Q where OC = HC. This formula is presented as:

$$Q = \sqrt{\frac{2\,C_0\,D}{C_h}}$$

Activity 12.4

Using the appropriate values for the variables shown, calculate the EOQ for this problem.

The calculation simply requires direct substitutions of our problem values:

$$Q = \sqrt{\frac{2\,(50)\,(250)}{15}}$$
$$= 40.82$$

where the EOQ is found to be 40.82 units. This is the order size, Q, that will minimise the total costs involved and balance the conflict between order costs and holding costs. We can readily determine that these two costs will be equal at this value of Q, allowing for rounding errors.

Order cost: $\frac{250}{40.82} \times £50 = £306.22$

Holding cost: $\frac{40.82}{2} \times £15 = £306.15$

Clearly, in a practical sense, the manager will need to order either 40 or 41 units with each order, rather than 40.82 units. In fact we can calculate that 41 units offers a very marginal cost saving over 40 units, although the manager may prefer keeping the number more straightforward at 40. Thus the manager has a ready means of determining the size of the stock order that will keep costs to a minimum.

The Reorder Cycle

From the EOQ calculation we can also determine what is known as the *reorder cycle* – the frequency or timing of orders through the year. This offers potential advantages to the manager in terms of administration and management involved in the stock process. Warehouse staff can be notified in advance as to the next expected delivery date; the finance department will know the expected delivery dates and hence invoice and payment requirements and so on. Equally, if a larger organisation is considering its policy on several hundred – or thousand – different stock items, it is unlikely to want all of these items to be delivered on the same day of the week. Calculating the cycle is straightforward. Let us assume the manager has opted for 40 units as the preferred number. The number of orders each 12-month period will then be:

250/40 = 6.25 orders

and the number of (calendar) days between each order will be:

365/6.25 = 58.4 days

or approximately every two months.

Assumptions of the EOQ Model

It will be worthwhile at this point reviewing the implicit assumptions behind the EOQ model. Although we have not articulated them, the key assumptions underpinning our calculations have been:

● demand is known for certain;
● demand is constant over time;
● orders are received as soon as they are made;
● a stock order is made when existing stock levels reach zero;
● the order quantity remains constant over time;
● all costs are constant.

Clearly, a number of these assumptions are unrealistic for many organisations. It is worth stressing, however, that the basic EOQ model is readily adapted to allow some of these assumptions to be relaxed. Our concern, however, is to illustrate the basic principles rather than the more complex solution methods. However, we will consider one extension to the basic model.

Incorporating Lead Time

Let us consider a variation on our basic problem. We shall assume that over a year there are 50 working weeks. This implies that with D = 250 the company will use five items each week. Let us further assume that the supplier of the items can no longer guarantee immediate delivery but indicates that delivery of a stock order may take up to two working weeks from the time the order is placed.

Activity 12.5

Consider how the manager might change the stock policy from the previous problem.

The problem is now slightly different in that one of our key assumptions of the basic EOQ model – that orders are received as soon as they are made – no longer applies. We were assuming before that we could allow stock levels to fall to zero on any given day since the next order would arrive the same day and we would thereby avoid running out of stock. We can no longer afford to do this. If we allow stock to fall to zero before placing our next stock order we may have to wait up to two weeks for delivery. During this time we will have no stock items left to meet demand. Clearly we must now ensure that we place the order at a time which ensures that we have sufficient stock to meet demand while we are waiting for the next delivery. Given that we might have to wait up to two weeks for delivery, we must ensure that when we place an order we still have two weeks' stock still left. This implies that we know we will have sufficient items in stock to meet daily demand, even if the order takes the maximum time to arrive. Given that we require five items to meet demand each week, this implies that we need to

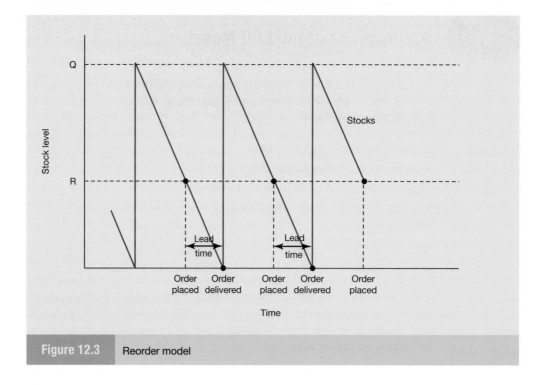

| Figure 12.3 | Reorder model |

reorder stock when our stock levels reach 10 items. The two weeks we may have to wait for delivery is known as the *lead time*. We can generalise the required calculation as:

$$R = d \times L$$

where R is the reorder level, d is the demand per time period and L the number of periods of lead time. In our problem we would have d = 5 and L = 2, giving R = 10. The situation is shown in Figure 12.3. This shows R and the stocks available over time. As stocks are gradually depleted there will come a time when they hit the reorder level, R. An order is placed for Q items and, allowing for the lead time, the order is delivered replenishing stock levels. The cycle continues.

The management implications of this also need to be considered. We now need some system in the organisation for regularly keeping track of stock levels. Under the simple model we could predict how many weeks would elapse before another order needed to be placed. With more complex, and uncertain, models someone must have the responsibility for monitoring stock levels and ensuring that the next stock order is issued when stock levels fall to R.

Classification of Stock Items

So far we have assumed that the manager simply has to establish a suitable policy for stock ordering for one single item. Clearly this is unrealistic, since the organisation will use or require a large number of items in its production or service provision. One of the difficulties the manager faces is that of prioritisation: deciding which stock items are worthy of his or her detailed attention in terms of decision making and which are not. It would not be a productive use of the manager's time to try to determine a suitable

EOQ policy for the reordering of paper clips used in the office. Such a trivial item – trivial in the sense of both its unit cost and the cost to the organisation of running out of stock – would not warrant serious management attention. Other items, however, clearly will justify management attention.

One approach that has been developed tries to classify stock items into different categories, with the different categories requiring different approaches to stock control. The system is known as the *ABC system* or the *Pareto system*. The method is simple in principle. All stock items are categorised into one of three groups – A, B and C – in terms of their relative importance to the organisation. Category A items are the most important and C the least important. Importance may be defined in different ways. It may relate to the financial contribution that each item makes to the organisation's activities, to the costs of the organisation, to the overall business strategy, to frequency of use, to opportunity cost and so on. For example, in a retail organisation, a tin of soup could be categorised as C, whereas a high-price DVD system would be category A since the contribution to the company's sales and profitability will be much larger for the DVD system than for the tin of soup. Similarly, the opportunity cost of a lost sale due to stock not being available will be much higher. The notion of importance will not, however, necessarily relate directly to monetary value. In a production organisation low-cost component parts may have serious knock-on effects in terms of production if they are not available. Running out of stock for car headlight bulbs may well halt the whole production process in a car assembly plant. Figure 12.4 illustrates a typical stock classification. Category A items are few in number but important in terms of value, while category C items are many in number but low in terms of value. Category B items fall in the middle.

In practice, for most organisations the number of items falling into the A classification will be relatively small – often around 20 per cent of all stock items. But these items have a disproportionate effect in terms of importance, often accounting for around

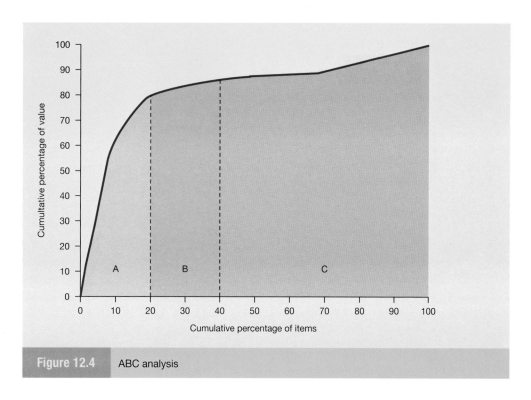

Figure 12.4   ABC analysis

80 per cent of whatever measure of importance the company is using. Thus 20 per cent of items may contribute 80 per cent to, say, profit. Category B items typically comprise the next 10 to 20 per cent of all items and contribute about 10 to 20 per cent (i.e. a relatively proportionate impact) to importance, while category C items make up the bulk of stock (around 70 per cent) but contribute only 10 per cent to importance. From a management perspective, therefore, it clearly makes sense to focus attention on category A items first, followed by B and C. The implications are that category A items are worthy of a detailed investigation in terms of a suitable stock policy – determining order costs, holding costs, usage patterns, lead times and the like – and variations of the basic EOQ model will be potentially worthwhile developing. Equally, regular management monitoring of the situation should be ensured. For category B items some formal stock process – like the EOQ model – is probably appropriate, with less need for ongoing monitoring. For category C items the effort and cost of applying stock control methods is probably not justified and simpler stock systems are needed – possibly as simple as just ordering another box of paper clips when the last box has been used.

To illustrate, consider the following situation. A company is investigating its stock policy on 10 different items. Table 12.2 shows the 10 items, coded A1 to A10, together with the level of annual demand for each item and the cost per unit of each item. So, for example, item A1 has an annual level of use of 250 units and costs £10 per unit. To categorise these items under the ABC system involves a series of simple calculations. First of all we calculate the total number of items required over the year by the company, 2590, and show each stock item as a percentage of this total. We then calculate the total cost for each stock item (annual level of use × unit cost) and again express this as a percentage of the total costs for the year. The resulting calculations are shown in Table 12.3.

We see, for example, that stock item A1 accounts for 9.7 per cent of all stock items by volume and 6.8 per cent by value. We now take these percentage volume and value figures and rank them in ascending order by volume. That is, we show the lowest

Table 12.2	ABC classification: Use and value	
Code	Annual level of use (units)	Cost per unit (£)
A1	250	10
A2	80	75
A3	320	10
A4	40	115
A5	90	95
A6	500	1
A7	830	5
A8	120	30
A9	150	18
A10	210	5
Total	2590	

Table 12.3	Percentage use and costs				
Code	Annual use	% of total	Cost per unit (£)	Value	% of total
A1	250	9.7	10	2 500	6.8
A2	80	3.1	75	6 000	16.3
A3	320	12.4	10	3 200	8.7
A4	40	1.5	115	4 600	12.5
A5	90	3.5	95	8 550	23.2
A6	500	19.3	1	500	1.4
A7	830	32.0	5	4 150	11.3
A8	120	4.6	30	3 600	9.8
A9	150	5.8	18	2 700	7.3
A10	210	8.1	5	1 050	2.8
Total	2590	100.0		36 850	100.0

Table 12.4	Ranked cumulative percentages			
Code	% Use	Cumulative % use	% Value	Cumulative % value
A4	1.5	1.5	12.5	12.5
A2	3.1	4.6	16.3	28.8
A5	3.5	8.1	23.2	52.0
A8	4.6	12.7	9.8	61.7
A9	5.8	18.5	7.3	69.1
A10	8.1	26.6	2.8	71.9
A1	9.7	36.3	6.8	78.7
A3	12.4	48.6	8.7	87.4
A6	19.3	68.0	1.4	88.7
A7	32.0	100.0	11.3	100.0

volume item first, the second lowest next and so on. For this ranked data we then calculate cumulative percentage volume and value figures as shown in Table 12.4. This indicates stock item A4 accounts for only 1.5 per cent of stock items by volume but 12.5 per cent by value, whereas at the other extreme stock item A7 accounts for only 11.3 per cent by value but 32 per cent by volume. Figure 12.5 shows the Pareto diagram produced for this example and using this we might identify items A4, A2 and A5 as category A; A8, A9, A10 and A1 as category B; and items A3, A6 and A7 as Category C. It should be noted that the exact classification is somewhat subjective and will depend on what the manager regards as a suitable measure of importance for that stock item.

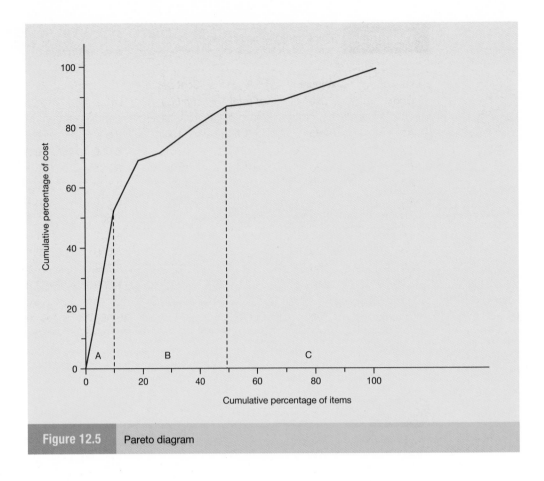

Figure 12.5   Pareto diagram

MRP and JIT

Unsurprisingly, given the large amount of capital tied up in stock levels in any modern organisation, considerable attention has been given to adapting and developing the basic stock-control models. We shall briefly describe just two of the recent developments in this field: *material requirements planning* (MRP) and *just-in-time* (JIT) *management*.

MRP is, as the name suggests, primarily an approach for manufacturing, although it can be adapted for service situations also. Consider the following scenario. An organisation manufactures, among other things, large-screen colour TVs. For simplicity, assume that the production process takes five days – that is on day 1 parts of the TV are assembled and tested, further parts are added on day 2 and so on until day 5, when the production and testing are complete. Let us further assume that the last production task – late on a Friday afternoon – is to fit a moulded plastic plug to the TV so that the customer does not have to fit such a plug themselves before the product can be used. If we expect production that week to be, say, 1000 TVs, then clearly we require 1000 plugs to be available at the appropriate time on a Friday afternoon. Stock levels of this item at any other time in the week can be zero. Clearly our basic EOQ model would be inappropriate since it assumes a continuous demand for an item over time with a gradual depletion of stock levels. Assuming an average daily demand of 200 items and gearing our stock policy to this would clearly be inappropriate. An MRP system, however, can

The challenge of changing everything at once

By Stephen Pritchard

For Kolok, a South African distributor of printer consumables, such as ink cartridges and toner, meeting demand meant making changes. It moved premises, more than doubling warehouse space, added additional shifts, and installed new warehouse and enterprise resource planning systems – all at the same time. In southern Africa – Kolok's main market is South Africa but it also exports to neighbouring countries including Namibia and Botswana – customers expect quick delivery.

Kolok, part of the Bidvest group, sells to retailers and directly to larger businesses. Neither set of customers wants to hold large stocks of supplies and many simply cannot afford to.

"The South African market is not like the US or Europe," says Allan Thompson, Kolok's managing director. "We have persuaded our customers not to tie up their resources in stock, but to use our resources. And corporate customers expect delivery within a couple of hours."

The weakness of the rand and other southern African currencies against the dollar and euro adds to this pressure, but also puts pressure on margins at both Kolok and its customers.

"Inflation here is 14 per cent and that affects customers' spending ability, even though IT markets are growing at 19 per cent," says Mr Thompson. He adds that currency swings can quickly wipe out any margins. On the day Mr Thompson spoke to Digital Business, the rand fell 6 per cent against the dollar. As a result, much of Kolok's recent investment has been aimed at improving stock control.

Within South Africa, Kolok's Johannesburg warehouse covers a territory that stretches 1,200km north and 1,400km south, to the Cape. The company handles 4,500 product lines from a 7,000m² warehouse with 8,000 storage locations, some of which are 12 metres high. It also has to manage a mix of long and short-term products. Some stock turns over 16 times a year but other lines turn just twice a year. The existing infrastructure could not cope.

"In the past, we would take deliveries and it would take four to five days to unload the containers," admits Mr Thompson. "Once we had put the stock away, we didn't know where it was. We had spreadsheets we were trying to update, which was impossible with the volumes we handle. We now have stock management on a 24-hour basis, instead of a nine hours a day basis, and our 'pick and pack' operations run for 16 hours rather than eight. We are getting much better utilisation of our assets."

For the systems update, which took place alongside the relocation of the company's main Johannesburg warehouse, spending on software and IT infrastructure came to $3.5m. This excluded costs such as training, and management time. However, the changeover was as smooth as Kolok had hoped. The scale of the upgrade – bringing warehouse storage locations onstream; updating the warehouse system with software from Manhattan Associates; and installing a new ERP platform in the shape of Microsoft Dynamics AX – put the company under real strain. Some staff, used to the previous Dos-based systems, had never operated a computer with a mouse before. Integrating the ERP and warehouse systems proved harder than the company, and its suppliers, had expected. Service standards fell and Mr Thompson says these are only now returning to a level he considers acceptable.

"I would not update both the ERP and warehouse management systems at the same time again, but we had no option," he explains. "For a year, we could not find stock, and we had to find stock to sell it. We had a short period from inception to the go-live date to have all the software tested, so we could not do the ERP today and the warehouse tomorrow. We would have been totally in the dark."

Integration was further hampered by the difficulty of taking staff away from the job for training. And the security situation and poor public transport in South Africa do not allow staff to stay late for training courses. But the systems have now been integrated, at least for larger customers. "The big customers are now seeing the benefit, but for me, it's as important to serve the small and mid-sized companies who might grow into large ones," Mr Thompson says.

The results for the business overall have justified the investment. Volumes handled by Kolok are up 27 per cent on February 2007, and capacity in the warehouse operations has doubled.

"We are more efficient, and have more control of our assets, both mechanical equipment and human resources. Now, we can see where the pressure points are and where resources are needed. Previously, we had to go on gut feeling." An order can now be ready for customer collection or delivery 15 minutes after it reaches the warehouse.

Once the integration problems have been resolved, Mr Thompson expects to realise a full return on investment in the IT side of the project

within 18 months, primarily through better visibility of stock levels.

"We need to move stock as quickly as possible," he says. "If it is

a Monday, and we get 14 containers, we want to have none left by Friday."

Source: *Financial Times*, 2 April 2008.

Because stock control is big business it often needs a big investment.

Systems are never good enough

There are always improvements to be made in the planning and control of manufacturing systems. Any company that is content with what it has needs to ask itself questions

says Thomas E Vollmann

Manufacturing planning and control systems (MPCS) have always been an area for improvement in manufacturing companies. Organisations seem perpetually to wish they had better forecasts, more achievable scheduling systems, enhanced flexibility in responding to unforeseen customer requests, reduced inventory levels, higher customer order fill rates, shorter delivery times, greater capacity utilisation, and a host of other desirables.

Moreover, there is no end to it. The appropriate answer to a question of a desired inventory turnover rate is always the same: twice what it is at the present time.

A key conclusion for this quest is the need never to be content with the present manufacturing planning and control system in a company. In fact, we often advise companies that if they have not had a hard look at these systems (as well as the related logistics systems) for several years, there is an excellent chance that significant payoffs can be achieved if they do.

But there is a natural progression in manufacturing planning and control systems that managers should think about in evaluating

their own progress. Our experience indicates that one can find examples at almost any point along this progression.

Step 1: Informal systems

Informal systems for manufacturing planning and control are most obviously seen where there is a lack of computers, the throughput times for products are high, inventory accuracy is low, and the order of the day is expediting and panic. The same problems and conditions, it has to be said, are sometimes seen where there are indeed formal systems.

The key lesson is that one should never believe that "what is purported to be the case is in reality the case." No, it is always necessary for MPCS to pass the reality test of a visit to the factory to see that systems are in fact being used precisely as they are purported to be.

Informal systems are not prevalent today in larger manufacturing companies. Most of these firms have been so handicapped by such approaches that they are now out of business. An example is a large fork-lift truck company we examined several years ago. It had a good product, a great brand name,

but all the classic problems of informal systems – the company no longer exists.

Step 2: Basic material requirements planning (MRP) systems

The first progression toward a modern MPCS environment is to implement a basic MRP system. This bases the need for all components on exploded information from bills of material. That is, for example, the exact number of rear left-hand green door panels in any particular time period is calculated directly from the schedule for how many four-door green cars are to be assembled in that time period. The need is not estimated, forecast or guessed: it is calculated exactly.

In order for this approach to work, several things are required. First, the bills of material must be accurate. Next, the assembly schedule must be met. Also, the detailed schedules for all the components must also be met – in order to meet the assembly schedule. This is not as easy as it sounds, but the results are impressive.

The shift from informal systems to a working MRP system usually results in major benefits, such as inventory reductions of 40 per cent and similar improvements in lead times, meeting customer promises, and productivity improvements. Moreover, a working MRP system allows the company to know – not just guess – whether it can achieve particular objectives. For example, at a major producer of hospital beds, a very large unexpected order for their most expensive bed came in from Saudi Arabia. The MRP system allowed the company to see where it would run into problems with enough time to find solutions to them – and to fulfil the order.

Step 3: Enhanced MRP systems

The first MRP system is rarely the last – and if a company has had the same one for many years it needs to take a long hard look. MRP systems have been widely used for about 25 years. The early ones used home-grown software, but no one in their right mind would write their own software today – unless it was a very special situation. One example would be an integrated circuits manufacturer that ended up with several quality grades of product coming from one batch; a customer order for a particular grade could be satisfied by substituting a superior grade.

In fact, many companies are now actively implementing new MRP-based systems based on packaged software. The intent is to use these systems to perform the basic manufacturing planning and control and to devote any special system design activities to practices that are unique to their particular company situation. This focus of resources is quite prevalent in attaining the benefits discussed under *Steps 5* and *6* below.

More importantly, first MRP systems tend to use large periods – or "buckets" – such as months. This leads to inherent extra costs and other problems. For example, a large food manufacturer traditionally gave its factories the schedule for month X on the 15th of month $X - 1$. Meeting this schedule required the factories to carry extra inventories of almost everything, since it was not possible to get all their components from ground zero and still meet the monthly schedule.

Moreover, the schedule was "met" if the products were finished on day 1 or day 31 of month X. This meant that sales needed to order one month ahead to be sure the goods would be available, which incurred the costs of both an extra month's worth of inventory and the larger forecast errors associated with an extended time horizon (and related panic costs of trying to meet unforecasted demands).

A related problem with monthly periods is what manufacturing people call the "hockey stick" effect. A plot of output over the month starts low and increases sharply toward the end of the month rather than being constant. The end of the month panic conditions usually require overtime and other inefficiencies in order to meet the schedule. In addition, the panic conditions often also result in the organisation falling back into the informal systems phase – as heroic efforts are made to meet the schedule.

This problem is greatly magnified when the true monthly schedule is concerned with meeting shipments measured in financial terms. Then, a common practice is "cherry picking" the next month's schedule in order to move large currency orders into the present month. Unfortunately moving the cherries from month $X + 1$ into month X leaves month $X + 1$ with the "pits" – i.e. this process guarantees that it will need to be continued. And almost always cherry picking is done outside the formal systems – demolishing their credibility.

All of this means that a fundamental enhancement to basic MRP systems is to work with smaller time periods. Many companies have moved first from monthly time buckets to weekly, then to daily and finally to essentially real-time or "bucketless" systems. The move involves much more than running a computer more often. Work schedules and activities have to be synchronised with the new approach.

For example, in moving to weekly timing, companies typically run the system over the weekend, analyse the data on Monday/Tuesday, issue new orders on Wednesday, update data on Thursday/Friday, and re-run the system again over the weekend. Similar transformations in working approaches accompany daily and real-time systems.

There are other fundamental improvements that can and are being implemented in manufacturing companies. For example, one major food company is now exploring a new packaged MRP system that will give it a better integration between its various factories.

Step 4: Manufacturing resource planning

Basic MRP systems and their descendants are primarily focused on the middle part or "engine" of *Figure 1*. The emphasis is on lining up the schedules of component parts with those of the assembly of finished goods. But *Figure 1* also shows a "front end" that results in a master production schedule (MPS) and a "back end" concerned with the detailed execution necessary on the shop floor in order to achieve the MPS. It is the entire MPCS shown in *Figure 1* that truly determines the efficacy of a company's detailed planning. Enhancements thus come in all three areas of the figure, and companies need to work in all of them. Detailed improvements in all three areas are beyond our present scope, but a few examples of major improvement approaches should provide a check-list for examining the performance of a company.

Figure 1

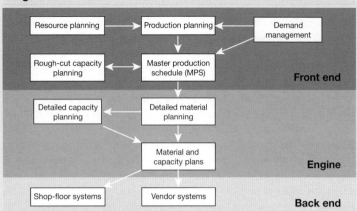

In the front end, demand management is an important area for improvement. Fundamentally, demand management recognises that the forecast is only one input to the MPS and that order entry is a process by which forecasts are consumed. That means that order entry and the order backlog are very important in managing MPCS systems effectively.

Production planning is often a key area for enhancing MPCS performance. For many companies, it is only after achieving a good MPS system that they duly learn to understand the necessity of a monthly production planning cycle that drives the monthly financial meeting. That is, in well run companies the production plan becomes the driver and the financial results are the passengers.

Rough-cut capacity planning is an approach to test continually the MPS for feasibility – that is, can the plan be executed? Detailed capacity planning is performed at a much lower level of aggregation; it focuses on the same question but now using the entire data base of shop schedules and detailed MRP records.

Shop-floor scheduling systems are at a base level concerned with continually lining up the priorities of orders to match the assembly schedules. Improvements are aimed at better utilisation of capacity,

attention devoted to bottlenecks, faster throughput times and closer coupling of schedules with customer priorities.

Step 5: Continuous improvement

All of the classic MPCS approaches tend to follow the "mass production" model where centralised controls are implemented, tight procedures are followed and management is essentially of the "command and control" variety. But at some point this approach is often rejected. Empowerment, self-directed work teams, no distinction between "direct labour" and other workers, and a culture where everyone searches for ways to improve the processes by which work is accomplished leads to a very different approach to manufacturing planning and control.

Just-in-time systems focus on speed as a key objective. They also are a part of reducing the "hidden factory" of paper work and transactions. JIT systems try to minimise the number of discrete shop orders – instead basing manufacturing on simplified fast flows that are controlled only by the shop-floor people.

An example is a car company that can be fairly sure that every car shipped will have one and only one radiator. If the supplier of radiators delivers several times each day there will be so few radiators in

inventory that no one really cares, any bad ones can be sent back or tossed out, and the supplier can be paid on a daily basis by counting the cars completed, multiplying by the price per radiator and electronically transferring that amount into the supplier's bank account. All this is done with no paper: no invoices, no shipping papers, no bills of lading, no receiving papers, nothing.

JIT is supported by on-going process improvements, such as set-up time reduction, statistical process control, total preventive maintenance and a host of other activities that lead to "lean manufacturing". The focus is on execution: routine foolproof execution with no problems and no need for systems constantly to check up on people.

One firm in the electronics industry coined the term "coping mechanism" to describe any activity that was done to "cope" with problems that should not exist in an ideal world. Thus inspection is there to cope with the fact that products may not be made right. The implication? Spend the money on making it right rather than on checking to be sure that it is right. There are many such coping mechanisms.

All cost money and they need to be rooted out. Further examples include cycle counting and locked storerooms to be sure that procedures are followed, most transactions associated with shop-floor control (the work should either not be started or completed so fast that there is no point keeping track of it) and most other control documents.

The "M" in MBP has never stood for "miracle". Yet many times we have been asked to examine an MBP system because it does not seem to work. But in fact, the system is working quite well. It is the execution of the system commands that are at fault. When scrap is made instead of good product, there will almost always be a scheduling problem. Someone will have to scramble to make the schedule.

Thus we see that MPCS is not a stand-alone approach to improving manufacturing operations. But it is the backbone of improvement. If one cannot make schedules and hit them, then there will be little ability to achieve other objectives.

Supporting all of these initiatives is the fundamental shift in approach from command/control to teamwork and an empowered workforce. Indeed, the objective in such companies is to "maximise the idle time" of all workers – so that other work currently done by middle managers can be made a part of the basic manufacturing infrastructure and these people in turn made free to work more closely with customers to maximise customer perceived values.

A natural consequence of this form of thinking is a need for a change in performance measurements. But this is the source of another section in this series.

Step 6: Supply chain integration

As stated at the outset, there is no real end to improvements that can be made to manufacturing, planning and control systems. At some point one does run into definition problems, such as those noted above when the focus turns to techniques that allow for better execution of the MPCS. But that is not the issue. The goal is always to improve manufacturing; to make the routine things routinely; to reduce costs and improve customer perceived values – at the same time.

Supply chain management is another separate section in this series, but at this time, it is still instructive to understand how better relationships with customers and suppliers is a logical extension of MPCS, and why it makes sense for companies to look here for further benefits.

Everything we know about MPCS suggests that there are always two avenues to pursue for improvement. The first is to improve a particular situation in terms of its present problem definition. Thus one can do a better job of MRP, one can put in a new programme, one can enhance the MPS, one can improve the shop-floor scheduling and so on. But another avenue is to redefine the problem in a broader context. The move from MRP to MRPII is a classic move in this direction, where a fundamentally larger problem is defined and solved – in an integrative fashion.

The boundaries depicted in *Figure 1* certainly do not need to limit the search for operational excellence. Many firms have implemented logistics improvements where connections are built between well-functioning MPCS systems and the similar systems of their customers and suppliers. As noted above, this work is now often based on using packaged software to support the basic manufacturing activities. Doing so is largely a matter of redrawing the boundaries for the analysis. It is also a matter of overall optimisation, based on some overall cost-objective function – and the elimination of the "zero-sum thinking" that pervades the thought process of far too many business people.

Conclusions

Manufacturing planning and control systems have a long history of improvement in manufacturing companies. This history has been continuous and it shows no signs of letting up. The managerial implications are that every manufacturing company should ask itself whether it has had a fundamental look at its MPCS approaches in recent times, what are the latest features of the best software packages – and what might these do for the company, where is the company in terms of the continuum defined here for MPCS improvement, where should it benchmark its MPCS approaches, and how fast are improvements being implemented? Fundamentally, every manager owes this investigation to his company.

Summary

Companies should never be content with their manufacturing planning and control systems (MPCS). "Informal" ones – typified by a lack of computers, high throughput times and low inventory accuracy – are no longer prevalent in large companies. Those that had them have mostly gone out of business.

The first step towards acquiring a modern MPCS is a basic material requirements planning (MRP) system. This allows a company to know whether it can achieve particular objectives. Early ones used home-grown software but many companies are now actively implementing them with packaged software. A fundamental enhancement to basic MRP systems is to work with smaller time periods – weekly, daily, or even real-time. The efficacy of a company's detailed planning, however, goes beyond lining up the schedules of component parts with those of the assembly of finished goods. Enhancements can also be made to the master production schedule at the "front end" – in areas like demand management and production planning – and to detailed shop-floor execution at the "back end".

Source: FT Mastering Management Part 3, 10 November 1995.

be designed to cope with such circumstances. MRP requires us to predict the final level of production (1000 TVs) and to develop a master production schedule. This schedule can then be exploded into its component parts, or broken into key elements, by detailing the exact production process that is used to produce the item. This results in a list of all the items or materials that are required to meet the end production target. This produces a list of the gross requirements – listing each item and the quantity required. An MRP system then compares these gross requirements with current stock levels to determine the net requirements – the extra stock that will be required. Combining this with details of exactly when in the production process each item will be required enables us to match availability with demand. This all sounds very simple in principle but is, understandably, very complex in practice, typically necessitating the development of specialist computer-based systems. However, the results of an appropriate MRP system can be impressive in terms both of reducing stock-related costs and of improved production in the absence of stock shortages.

JIT is a more ambitious system, with a prime goal of achieving zero stock levels not just within a single part of the production or service process but throughout the whole supply chain, and is typically seen as part of a wider movement towards total quality management (TQM) within an organisation. The implications of JIT are that the organisation needs to involve itself in a planning system which ensures that materials and supplies are available in terms of both quantity and quality at the appropriate time and place. JIT proponents argue that many of the reasons for holding stock (and thereby incurring costs) are due to inadequate management attention and control over both quality and the supply chain. For example, one reason for holding stock is the uncertainty as to when the supplier will actually deliver the next order. If this uncertainty can be reduced through other quality management initiatives then so can the need for holding stock. This, potentially, can be achieved using a number of the quality management approaches: involving the supplier more in the company's systems, sharing information, developing better working practices between the two organisations and so on. JIT, therefore, is much more than a stock-control system.

Worked Example

A local education authority has responsibility for purchasing supplies for all the schools in its area. One of the items it buys in and then supplies to schools is packs of pens to supply to teachers and support staff. Over the past couple of years annual demand for these packs has been around 75 000 with each pack costing the authority 50p and bought directly from the manufacturer. The supplies manager has estimated that each order that is placed with the manufacturer costs the authority about £5. For financial purposes it is assumed that holding costs for any item are 20 per cent of the purchase cost of that item. The manager currently orders 2750 packs at a time (the EOQ is actually 2738.6 but the manager has rounded this for convenience). However, the supplying manufacturer has recently sent round a letter indicating that it is willing to offer volume discounts on the purchase price: that is, customers who order in quantity will be sold the packs at a lower unit price. The details of the scheme are as shown in Table 12.5.

So, if the manager decides to order between 3000 and 4000 packs each time, a discount of 5 per cent of the pack price of 50p will be offered, effectively bringing the unit price per pack down to 47.5p. Naturally the supplies manager has expressed interest in this since her annual budget is constantly under pressure and any potential cost savings have to be considered. However, it is clear that the current EOQ of 2750 packs falls

Table 12.5	Purchase price discounts on pens		
Order band		Discount (%)	New unit price (pence)
A	up to 3000 packs	0	50
B	3000 < 4000	5	47.5
C	4000 < 5000	10	45
D	5000 < 20 000	17.5	41.25
E	20 000 or more	18	41

short of the minimum of 3000 required to earn a discount. The question for the supplies manager is then how the various costs (purchase, order, holding) will be affected by the discount scheme. The approach she has decided to take is to perform the required calculations on a spreadsheet. Her first step is to calculate the EOQ for each order band. This is necessary but C_h – the holding cost per item – is linked to the purchase cost and since this will change depending on the order size, so might the EOQ. The calculations are shown in Table 12.6.

For each band the holding cost per item per year is shown (at 20 per cent of the unit price) together with the EOQ for that band. The apparent bad news for the manager is that in each order band the calculated EOQ is below that required to trigger the price discount. In band C, for example, the EOQ is calculated as 2887, with a minimum order of 4000 needed to obtain the unit price discount. However, the manager also knows that one of the key assumptions of the EOQ approach is that costs remain constant. This is clearly not the case here, with C_h varying and the unit price varying. She then decides to recalculate all the various costs for each order band assuming that the minimum order size has been placed. That is, for example, calculating the order costs, the holding costs and the purchase costs for band C assuming the minimum order of 4000 packs has been placed. The total costs associated with each order band can then be evaluated. The relevant calculations (with figures rounded to the nearest £) are shown in Table 12.7.

So, for example, with the EOQ of 2750, 28 orders will need to be placed each year at a cost of £140 (28 × 5). Holding costs will be £138 and purchases costs £37 500 (75 000 × £0.50) giving a total cost of £37 778. If the manager decides to place orders of 20 000, however, to gain the maximum benefit from the price discount, the total cost drops to

Table 12.6	EOQ calculations			
Band	Discount	Unit price	C_h	EOQ
A	0	50	10.00	2738.6
B	5	47.5	9.50	2809.8
C	10	45	9.00	2886.8
D	17.5	41.25	8.25	3015.1
E	18	41	8.20	3024.3

Table 12.7	Total order costs				
Minimum order size	Orders per year	Order costs (£s)	Holding costs (£s)	Purchase costs (£s)	Total costs (£s)
(2750)	28	140	138	37 500	37 778
3 000	25	125	143	35 625	35 893
4 000	19	94	180	33 750	34 024
5 000	15	75	206	30 938	31 219
20 000	4	19	820	30 750	31 589

£31 589 (with purchase cost and order cost both decreasing but holding cost increasing). From the calculations we see that, based on this information, placing orders of 5000 packs each time will lead to the lowest total cost of £31 219. Although the maximum price discount is not earned, the balance between the three costs is maximised. The manager knows that an annual saving of £6559 (37 778 – 31 219) can be achieved, although clearly additional storage space will need to be found for the extra order size (with the order size effectively doubling from the EOQ level).

Summary

In this chapter we have introduced the basic dilemma facing a manager with stock-control responsibility and considered how the differing cost pressures can be reconciled to try to determine a suitable stock-control policy. Although the model we developed is essentially a simple one based on rigid assumptions, the principles involved are readily transferable to more complex situations and the interested reader is referred to the Further Reading section at the end of the book.

Useful online resources

Detailed below are some internet resources that may be useful. Many have further links to other sites. An updated version is available from the accompanying website (**www.pearsoned.co.uk/wisniewski**). In addition, I would be grateful for details of other websites that have been found to be useful.

> **www.bpic.co.uk/erp.htm** – Enterprise Resource Planning
>
> **www.inventoryops.com/economic_order_quantity.htm** – EOQ
>
> **www.cris.com/~kthill/sites.htm** – Inventory control sites
>
> **webiet.ipfw.edu/105/2.html** – MRP
>
> **www.inventoryops.com/safety_stock.htm** – Optimising safety stock
>
> **www.businesslink.gov.uk/bdotg/action/layer?topicId=1074039371** – Stock control and inventory

QMDM IN ACTION
Unipart

The Unipart Group of Companies (UGC) was created in 1987 as part of a management buy-out from BL (British Leyland). Initially the organisation focused on the supply (primarily to wholesalers) of parts and supplies for BL, Rover and Jaguar cars. Since its creation, however, it has widened its activities to include a chain of motor-factory outlets, retail outlets for motor parts and related product lines. In the late 1980s the company established a strategic project in the area of demand chain management which became known as the 'responsive delivery project'. In short, the project team was responsible for identifying ways of improving customer service, primarily in the area of parts delivery. The demand chain of which the company formed a part is illustrated in Figure 12.6. Unipart clearly forms part of a longer chain linking the original supplier of parts and equipment to the final retail customer (a fundamental principle in the area of quality management). The company's immediate customers are the national network of parts wholesalers who in turn service both franchised dealers and independent traders. At the time the project was initiated, the delivery service provided to this network was thought, overall, to be good and, indeed, better than the competition in some cases. Nevertheless, fundamental improvements were thought both possible and desirable as part of a long-term corporate strategy. A typical situation can be described as follows. A parts wholesaler might issue an order to the company for a variety of parts and products. Because of the geographical distribution in Unipart of product location and stock location, this might mean the customer receiving the order in a fragmented and uncoordinated manner. Some parts ordered might be delivered directly from the original supplier. Other parts would arrive at different dates from different Unipart warehouses and distribution centres. From the customer's perspective, this lack of coordination on the part of Unipart meant that the customer was faced with the problem of coordinating the various deliveries, checking *ad hoc* deliveries against the order issued and not being able to plan when specific orders might arrive. Coupled with this was the service that Unipart offered of deliveries of

emergency orders (known as VOR, or vehicle-off-road, orders) that might need a much quicker response. To try to provide a more responsive service to wholesalers – and allow them to maintain their own competitive advantage – the company instituted a number of major changes in the distribution system. Among these were:

- providing a single daily delivery to every customer rather than a set of fragmented deliveries;
- the reorganisation of existing distribution centres into shipment centres which themselves did not hold stock but which facilitated the rapid throughput of orders from source to the customer;
- the replacement of the existing delivery fleet to provide roll-on, roll-off vehicles more suitable for rapid loading and unloading;

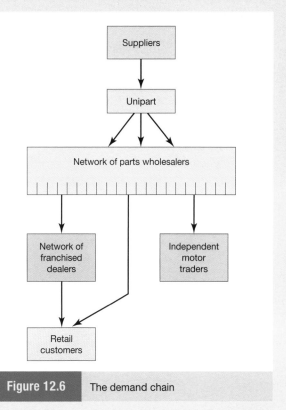

Figure 12.6   The demand chain

Taken from 'Responsive Delivery!', T Taylor, *Operational Research Insight*, **4**(2), 1991. Copyright held by the Operational Research Society.

- fundamental changes in the working practices in warehouses to allow processing of stock orders overnight;

- the introduction of a bar code system, alone costing almost £1 million, for despatch and receipt;

- capitalising on an existing initiative to provide all wholesalers with a direct computer link to the company's mainframe system to facilitate electronic ordering by the customer.

Given the nature and extent of the proposed changes, the company felt it appropriate to test the new systems and procedures with a pilot exercise prior to full launch throughout the organisation. Table 12.8 illustrates some of the reported effects of the responsive delivery initiative.

The company now provides a service such that emergency orders received prior to 6.00 p.m. will be delivered by the start of the next working day. Turnaround time between receiving a customer's order to delivery of that order has been reduced from five days to one (remember that the customer is now able to place an order electronically, reducing the lead time still further). As well as providing a more responsive service, Unipart has also found direct benefits to some of its customers' business performance with stock investment reduced by up to 30 per cent compared with the previous systems. It is once again interesting to note that the drive to alter stock and delivery systems was motivated by a desire to improve service quality. Naturally such changes did not happen overnight or without considerable organisational 'pain'. It is also interesting to note that the company decided to appoint a main-board director as chairman of the project group given the responsibility of driving this just-in-time approach.

Table 12.8	Effects of responsive delivery initiative		
		Before changes	*After changes*
Latest receipt of VOR orders for same-day processing		10.45 a.m.	6.00 p.m.
Delivery of VOR orders		35% by 9.30 a.m. next day, 30% after 9.30 a.m. next day, 35% day after next	100% by 8.00 a.m. next day
Period between customer stock reviews		5 days	1 day
Turnaround time from receipt of order to delivery		5 days	1 day
Time to check stock bin, update computer		2–5 days	1 day

Taken from 'Responsive Delivery!' by T Taylor, *Operational Research Insight*, **4** (2), 1991. Copyright held by the Operational Research Society.

*This application is based on the article: 'Responsive Delivery!', T Taylor, Operational Research Insight, **4** (2), 1991, pp 14–18.*

The table and figure in this section are reproduced with permission from the Operational Research Society.

Exercises

1 What are the basic decisions that a manager with stock-control responsibility faces and what are the likely objectives of such a manager in this context?

2 Describe the quantitative techniques that are available to assist a manager with stock-control responsibilities in an organisation.

3 A company requires a particular item from an outside supplier for its production process. Annual demand for the item is 3000 units. Order costs are estimated at £15 and holding costs at 20 per cent of the purchase price of the item, which is £5.50 per unit.

(**a**) Determine the optimum order quantity.

(**b**) What are the critical assumptions behind this calculation?

4 A local authority operates over a large geographical area. The Education Department is responsible for ensuring that stocks of a certain item are kept for distribution to schools through the area on request. In order to try to ensure supplies reach the schools promptly, the department currently operates two store warehouses, which operate independently of each other. The department is trying to assess the pros and cons of merging the two store warehouses and offering a centralised facility. For one item under consideration demand is 250 items per annum via Store A and 100 items per annum via Store B. Order costs are £10 at Store A and £11 at Store B, with holding costs 20 per cent of stock value. The item costs £4 per unit.

(**a**) Calculate the impact on costs if the two stores merge and place combined orders for this item.

(**b**) What other factors would you want to take into account before making a decision as to whether or not to merge the two stores?

5 Following internal reorganisation in a large brewing company, a comprehensive review of stock-control procedures is currently being undertaken. You have been asked to investigate stock control in the context of one of the firm's products: low-alcohol lager. The company operates a sophisticated forecasting and production planning system to forecast demand for this product from its own pubs and from other customers (off-licences, supermarkets, hotels) on a four-weekly cycle. That is, the company tries to forecast four weeks ahead and updates these forecasts each week. Over this four-week period, production of lager takes place and the output is stored until delivery to customers takes place at the end of the four-week cycle. Customers are able to place and receive orders outside this cycle but only at additional cost. Additionally, the company is thinking of installing a new computer network which will link all the company's pubs so that the stock-control manager will be able to monitor stock levels and sales.

Draft a management report outlining the importance of an efficient and effective stock-control policy for the company. You should include in your report a suggested stock-control policy that you feel is appropriate for the company and this should include reference to:

- the links between the forecasting role and stock control;
- the potential benefits of the new computer system;
- the data requirements of your suggested stock-control policy;
- the problems and difficulties that you think might arise if your policy is implemented.

6　A domestic appliance manufacturer is evaluating its delivery system from the production plant to showrooms around the country. One item used in the transportation of large appliances is a prefabricated polystyrene-foam packing case. These are supplied by an outside contractor and have to be ordered well in advance. Over the last few years, annual output of large appliances at the production plant has been 4000 units a year. The cost of placing an order is estimated at £25. Traditionally, the company has charged 15 per cent of the purchase cost of any item as the stock holding cost. The supplier charges £7.50 for each packing case.

(a)　Determine the optimum order quantity and the time between placing orders for the company.

(b)　Describe the key assumptions that you have made to determine (a).

(c)　Realistically what effect do these assumptions have on the method adopted in (a) to solve this problem?

(d)　If the supply of packing cases had a variable lead time how would this affect your suggested solution?

7　A large construction company has recently won the contract for routine inspection and maintenance of the Channel Tunnel linking the UK to France. Obviously, routine maintenance and repair work, unless carefully planned, will have adverse consequences on traffic flows through the tunnel and on operating revenue. You have been asked to investigate alternative policies that might be appropriate for stock control in terms of the building and construction materials that will be required to support these routine maintenance and repair operations. Effectively you have been asked to investigate appropriate policies for such items as cement, steel girders, rail track, electrical wiring and the like.

Draft a management report discussing in detail the alternative stock-control approaches that might be appropriate under such circumstances and recommend the type of policy that you think should be investigated in more detail with regard to feasibility. Your report should include a discussion of the data that would be required, the practical difficulties of implementing and operating stock-control policies and the potential contributions of the MRP and JIT approaches to stock control.

13 Project Management

Learning objectives

By the end of this chapter you should be able to:

- explain why complex projects require planning and managing
- develop a network diagram for a project
- incorporate time information into a network diagram and identify the critical path for a project
- construct a Gantt chart for a project
- incorporate uncertainty into network models
- be able to use information on crash times and costs

Most managers will, from time to time, be involved in the management of a project. The project might be large – such as the construction of the Channel Tunnel – or it might be small – such as the purchase of some new item of office technology. The manager's involvement might be central to the project – the manager may have full responsibility for managing the project – or it might be as part of a larger team. Given both the frequency with which managers become involved in projects and the degree of importance of such projects for the organisation, it is not surprising that models have been developed to assist the manager in the task of managing some project. In this chapter we shall be developing and using the basic project planning model that is available.

Characteristics of a Project

Given the focus of this chapter on project management, we should begin by ensuring we understand what is meant by a project. Although there is no hard-and-fast definition, projects have a number of key characteristics.

Activity 13.1

Think of a project that you have personally been involved in. It might be a personal project, such as planning the next holiday, or a work-based project. List the key features that make this a 'project' and that distinguish this from routine day-to-day activities.

Projects are typically self-contained and involve a set of related activities. They usually:

- have clearly defined aims and objectives;
- have a set completion date;
- are often unique, one-off events or at least different from routine activities;
- involve a set of related activities which comprise the project;
- have resources allocated specifically to them, often in the form of a project budget;
- involve a team of people.

A project almost always has a clearly defined set of aims, objectives or goals. Very often these may be 'imposed' on the project manager from above and may often be both varied and in conflict with each other. A construction company, for example, may have to complete a new building for a client to the agreed specification. Such a project will also have some specified completion date, very often with financial penalties for late completion if the project is a major one, and involve a number of related activities, all of which have to be completed to 'finish' the project. Projects typically have some sort of budget allocated. This may be a financial budget or it may be expressed in terms of other key resources: skilled staff, essential equipment, computer time. Large projects almost invariably involve a team of people and can rarely be completed by one individual working in isolation.

Network Rail fined £2.4m for late delivery

By Tom Griggs

The rail regulator has imposed a £2.4m fine on Network Rail – the group's largest financial penalty unrelated to a crash – for the late delivery of a signalling scheme in Portsmouth. ...

Source: Financial Times, 31 July 2007.

Project delays can be very expensive.

Project Management

The manager responsible for the project typically faces a dilemma in project management terms. The project manager is expected to deliver the project:

- on time
- within budget
- on target (in terms of key aims, objectives or quality standards).

Although each of these individually presents no major difficulties, the problem is that these requirements will frequently clash with each other during the life of the project. If the project falls behind schedule in terms of the timescale and completion date, this can often be rectified, and the project brought back to schedule, by increasing costs (paying overtime rates to the workforce, for example) or by reducing the targets, perhaps lowering the quality standards specified. Similarly, if the project looks as if it is going over budget or if it looks as if the project will not be to target, we can bring it back under control by altering the other two requirements: putting back the completion date to ensure we are still within budget, for example. Problems with any one of the requirements can usually be resolved by altering the others. However, this is usually unacceptable since the project manager is usually required to meet all three features simultaneously. The project management problem then becomes one of simultaneous achievement of these requirements rather than a trade-off between the three. From the project manager's perspective, therefore, there will be a number of tasks involved in managing the project:

- ensuring that individual activities are completed on time so that later activities – and the project completion – are not delayed;
- being able to identify potential problems before they occur so that appropriate corrective action can be taken to head off a potential problem;
- having an effective monitoring system for the project so that progress can be assessed easily and effectively at any time;
- being able to react quickly to planned or accidental deviations from the project in terms of both identifying the likely knock-on effects and assessing options for re-establishing control;
- being able to plan resource requirements to fit into the project timescale to ensure that critical and scarce resources are in the right place at the right time;
- being able to prioritise between different activities and their resource requirements.

As we shall see, the model we shall be developing in this chapter will meet these requirements and help considerably in the simultaneous achievement of the three features of projects.

European centre proves invaluable for project planning and liaising with customers

By Maija Palmer

Satyam Computer Services, India's fourth largest software company, outsources IT work to India for companies such as Reuters and Johnson & Johnson, writes Maija Palmer.

But although much of the work can be done more cheaply by Indian programmers, not everything can be moved there. The company has operated a European software development centre in Basingstoke, Hampshire, since 2001, and may add to the number of technology experts it employs there. Keshab Panda, head of Satyam's European operations, says the Basingstoke centre is invaluable for liaising with customers.

Project planning often takes place in the Basingstoke office with IT consultants who have deep knowledge of a particular vertical market such as banking or telecoms. Often, when a company is moving its IT work offshore for the first time, it wants to do this in stages, running a small pilot scheme at the Basingstoke centre first, before finally committing to going abroad.

There are between 20 and 50 IT staff in Basingstoke, depending on the number of projects ongoing at any one time. While this is only a small fraction of the company's more than 20,000 employees the numbers are growing gradually.

Source: *Financial Times*, 15 September 2005.

Good project management is critical for business success.

Spiralling costs of big road schemes criticised

By Christopher Adams, Political Correspondent

Spiralling costs on big road-building projects have brought the government agency responsible for England's motorways and trunk roads under fire from MPs.

In a damning report published yesterday, the Commons transport committee estimated the total bill for more than 80 road improvement schemes could rise by a further £1bn if the agency failed to get a grip on costs. The MPs said that the Highways Agency had "lost budgetary control" of the schemes. If cost overruns continued at their current rate, some yet to be completed projects approved more than three years ago would be 50 per cent more expensive than estimated.

"Such an increase would be an irresponsible and unacceptable waste of public money," the committee said. Gwyneth Dunwoody, chairman, said the agency was risking millions of pounds in taxpayers' money by failing to contain the "appalling high" roadbuilding costs. She criticised its project planning and staff management and voiced scepticism that the leadership was "pulling its weight".

According to government figures submitted to the committee, the cost of more than 40 of the most ambitious road projects is forecast to be £3.2bn, £1.5bn more than originally envisaged. One of the most controversial, to build a tunnel under Stonehenge, will cost £345m more than anticipated.

The Department for Transport said it would consider carefully the issues and recommendations in the report. An independent review of the Highway Agency's approach to cost estimating and project management was due to report in the autumn.

Source: *Financial Times*, 28 July 2006.

And getting it wrong brings its own problems.

Business Example

We shall illustrate the development and use of the model with the following example. As part of its new overall corporate strategy, a local authority is keen to ensure that the services it provides to local citizens match the needs and aspirations of the local community. As part of this matching process it has been decided to undertake a survey of citizens' current attitudes to the services provided. This will enable managers in the local authority to develop a view of customers' perceptions of current services as well as trying to identify needs not currently being met. You have been put in charge of the survey and are under pressure from both senior managers and elected officials to get this 'project' completed as soon as possible. Naturally, the 'quality' of the information collected must not be compromised and, understandably, the resource costs of this project will need to be carefully monitored and controlled.

Clearly, in this context, we have a typical project that has all the characteristics we discussed earlier. To develop the model to help us in project management we will need to follow a sequence of tasks.

Fines could help fill holes in the road

Cathy Newman and Juliette Jowit report on new powers to impose daily fines of £500 on companies failing to finish works on time

Utility companies that clog up the nation's roads by failing to complete works on time will be fined about £500 a day under new powers announced by the government last night.

Lord Sainsbury, the trade and industry minister, told the House of Lords that "repeated and prolonged streetworks by telecoms operators have . . . caused extensive disruption."

Daily charges of £500 or more are expected to be levied for works on main roads, although the new mayor of London will be free to set his or her own fines. Although the move was greeted with relief by pressure groups in congested cities such as London, concern remained about the chaos caused by the absence of a central authority to co-ordinate roadworks.

London First, the business lobby group, said: "The ownership of digging holes is really all over the place – spread between myriad agencies. Any system of charging would have to go hand in hand with a method of centrally co-ordinating streetworks."

Evidence that more roads are being dug up by utilities is not available nationally – because nine years after a national register was announced it has not been set up.

The transport department blames technical problems and

points instead to an internet database launched last year. But the database is still not fully functioning.

Drivers, however, are in little doubt that there are more works. Highways authorities cite examples of digging works on the same roads up to 233 times.

Others suffer bad co-ordination, such as simultaneous roadworks in Parliament Square and the Strand, which caused mayhem in central London earlier this year.

There is the annual problem of roadworks in March, when local authorities spend the last of their budgets before year end.

But the greatest single factor is the almost untrammelled powers granted to utilities by parliament in 1847 and extended to telecommunications companies in the 1991 New Roads and Street Works Act. Eighty-six gas, electricity, water and telecoms companies have Department of Trade and Industry licences to dig almost at will.

The main condition is that they give local authorities an average 28 days' notice – except in emergencies. But it is the utilities that decide if it is an emergency.

The Transport Research Laboratory found that nine out of 10 roads and pavements were reinstated badly after works were carried out.

Lord Sainsbury's announcement came in a Lords debate initiated by Lord Peyton of Yeovil, the former Tory transport minister.

Citing the old proverb that "the axle that squeaks the loudest gets the most grease", Lord Peyton said it was time "his very tiresome nuisance" was raised "with insistence, and if necessary with a degree of anger as well."

The number of companies licensed to tear up the highway has grown substantially since the privatisation of the water, electricity and telecoms companies.

Lord Peyton described the "formidable" task faced by "the average highway authority", which, he said, received 20,000 applications a year to dig up roads.

The Department of Trade and Industry, which grants the utility companies powers to dig up the roads, said a total of 138 gas, electricity, water and telecoms groups currently hold such licences.

Increased competition in the telecommunications market is partially responsible for the increase. Some new operators have been allowed to lay cable in the streets without obtaining separate licences from local highway authorities. The idea was to allow the fledgling companies to get on with the work as quickly as possible.

Source: Financial Times, 6 April 2000.

What price good project management?

- Identify the key activities that will make up the project.
- Determine the estimated time each individual activity will take to complete.
- Identify the sequencing of activities in terms of their interdependencies.

With this information we will then be able to develop a suitable model which will not only allow us to determine the expected completion date of the project but will also fulfil the other requirements of a project-planning system that we identified earlier. In practice, of course, these three tasks can prove problematic and time-consuming in their own right. For our purposes we will take the relevant information as given but the time and effort to obtain this in practice should not be underestimated. We will assume that the key activities that will make up the project have been identified and are as shown in Table 13.1.

A list of key activities is shown together with a description of what that activity involves. Take a few moments to study the information carefully. It is evident that the list of activities is an abbreviated one (to help us develop a manageable model in the text). In practice the list of activities will typically be much longer. It is easy to see how, for example, Activity K could be broken into its set of individual sub-activities. Each major activity could be treated as a sub-project in its own right, perhaps with another manager having delegated responsibility for it.

However, the requirements of the model now become clear, as do the difficulties faced by the project manager. All these activities have to be managed, and as project manager you are being asked now how long the project will take. To answer this, of course, we need additional information, which brings us to the second task: estimating the time taken by each activity. For our purposes we will develop a model based on the time information shown in Table 13.2.

For each activity, its duration, shown in days, is given. Activity A, for example, is expected to take three days; Activity B six days and so on. Once again this can in practice be a difficult task. At best such activity durations should be seen as estimates of the time to be taken to complete each activity. We shall see later in this chapter how we can incorporate uncertainty about these times into the model, but for now we will take them as given and assume they are definite and certain.

Activity 13.2

Using the information in Table 13.2 can you suggest how long, in days, it might take to complete the project?

At first sight, it might appear that the information we have in Table 13.2 is sufficient to allow us to determine the duration of the entire project. It looks as if we can simply add together all the individual activity durations to give the project duration. However, on reflection this will be inaccurate. Such a calculation assumes that all the activities are sequential – that they take place one after the other. Clearly in any project this will not be the case. Some activities will be strictly sequential: Activity B cannot take place until Activity A is complete, for example. However, other activities will not be sequential: they can take place simultaneously with other activities. Consider Activities B and C. There appears to be no reason why these two activities cannot take place simultaneously (although both of them would have to wait for Activity A to be completed first). So, before we can answer the question relating to the completion time of the project, we need to consider the third task: determining the dependencies or interrelationships between the various activities. Again, in practice this can be a complex task and

Table 13.1	Key activities

Activity	Description	Activity	Description
A	**Agree survey objectives** The key objectives of the survey will need to be agreed with senior managers and key elected officials to ensure there is consensus over what the survey is trying to achieve, what information is being collected and why it is being collected.	H	**Print questionnaire** The questionnaire to be used in the main survey will need to be printed and got ready for use.
B	**Design questionnaire** It has already been decided that data will be collected through the use of a face-to-face interview conducted with a sample of local citizens. Each interview will follow the structure specified in a specially designed questionnaire.	I	**Select sample** The sample of local citizens who will be surveyed will need to be chosen according to the agreed methods.
		J	**Conduct survey** The main survey will be conducted and completed.
C	**Agree method of sample selection** Since the survey will collect information from only a sample of local citizens, there must be agreement on the method to be used to identify the sample. It is expected that this will require an input from specialist advisers both in and outside the organisation.	K	**Enter data** The results from the completed questionnaires will be entered into the organisation's computer system ready for analysis.
D	**Conduct pilot survey** Because of the importance of the survey and its likely use in the strategy-planning process it has been decided that a pilot survey is essential. This pilot will test both the questionnaire design and the sample selection procedure before the full survey is conducted.	L	**Debrief interviewers** A formal debriefing of interviewers will take place to help assess qualitatively the information that has been collected. Interviewers may well be able to provide feedback on whether they felt those being interviewed were providing honest and reliable answers to questions, for example.
E	**Amend questionnaire and sample selection** Depending on the results from the pilot survey, it may be necessary to amend the questionnaire design and/or the methods used to select the sample. However, this will be entirely dependent on the results of the pilot survey and cannot be predicted at this stage.	M	**Analyse data** The analysis of the quantitative data collected can take place. This will be done by the project manager together with a small team of specialist staff.
F	**Recruit interviewers** Following the pilot survey, those people who will do the interviewing in the main survey will need to be recruited.	N	**Produce report** The project manager is responsible for producing a final report on the project to include its quantitative and qualitative findings as well as information on completion dates, quality and resource costs. This report will go to senior managers and to elected officials. Because of the committee structure in the local authority, the chair of the appropriate committee that will receive the final report needs to know now when the report will be available so as to ensure it appears in the appropriate agenda. This particular committee meets only once every three months.
G	**Brief interviewers** Before the main survey actually gets under way it will be necessary to provide a briefing session for all interviewers to ensure they fully understand what is expected of them and their role in the survey and to ensure consistency between different interviewers.		

Table 13.2	Time required	
Activity	*Description*	*Time taken*
A	Agree survey objectives	3 days
B	Design questionnaire	6 days
C	Agree method of sample selection	4 days
D	Conduct pilot survey	10 days
E	Amend questionnaire and sample selection	5 days
F	Recruit interviewers	10 days
G	Brief interviewers	1 day
H	Print questionnaire	5 days
I	Select sample	8 days
J	Conduct survey	15 days
K	Enter data	5 days
L	Debrief interviewers	2 days
M	Analyse data	10 days
N	Produce report	2 days

frequently requires a team approach: getting those staff with first-hand experience of each activity to evaluate what must be done first before this activity can start. For our purposes we shall assume that the dependencies are as shown in Table 13.3.

For each activity we show the immediately preceding activities that must be completed first. We see, for example, that Activity A has no dependencies – none of the other activities have to be completed before this one. Activities B and C, however, both have A shown as a dependency. This indicates that, before either of these activities can

Table 13.3	Dependencies	
Activity	*Description*	*Dependencies*
A	Agree survey objectives	None
B	Design questionnaire	A
C	Agree method of sample selection	A
D	Conduct pilot survey	B, C
E	Amend questionnaire and sample selection	D
F	Recruit interviewers	D
G	Brief interviewers	E, F
H	Print questionnaire	E
I	Select sample	E
J	Conduct survey	G, H, I
K	Enter data	J
L	Debrief interviewers	J
M	Analyse data	K
N	Produce report	L, M

start, A must have been completed. The interpretation of the rest of the table is similar. Note that some activities have several dependencies shown, indicating that several activities must be completed first. Note also that only the immediately preceding dependencies are shown. For example, Activity E shows only D as a dependency. D in turn, however, is dependent on B and C, and B and C in turn are dependent on A. Activity E, therefore, is implicitly dependent on A, B and C, although this is not explicitly shown. We are now in a position to develop the model we can use to help us manage the project.

Network Diagrams

Project-planning models are built around the concept of a network diagram. As we shall see, such diagrams are particularly helpful at providing the information about the project we indicated earlier that a manager would require. Network diagrams will be familiar to most readers – although not necessarily by that name. When looking at a map, for example, you are actually using a road network showing the road connections between various towns or cities. Using an Underground or subway map you are using a network diagram to show how you can travel between various parts of a city. In project management we develop such a diagram along very simple lines but using a standard format. Figure 13.1 shows a typical component of a network diagram that we shall be constructing. The diagram shows two events – denoted with a circle and known as a node – joined together with a line. The line itself represents some activity – here labelled activity X – and the two events indicate the start of that activity and its completion respectively. We can think of events as specific moments in time when activities start/end. Dates can be allocated to events.

The network diagram for a project such as ours is made up of a series of components like that shown in the diagram. Drawing a network diagram is relatively straightforward, although there are one or two aspects which do require practice. Such diagrams follow a series of 'rules' or conventions. Most are obvious, but some take getting used to in terms of their implications.

- All diagrams must have one start node and one end node.
- Each event must have at least one preceding activity.
- Each event must have at least one subsequent activity.
- Any two events can be joined by only one activity.

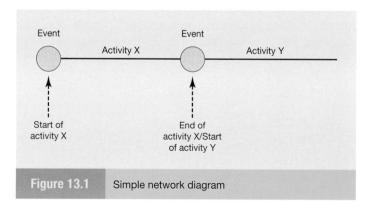

| **Figure 13.1** | Simple network diagram |

Table 13.4	Illustrative project
Activity	**Dependency**
A	None
B	A
C	A
D	A
E	B,D
F	C

In addition we should note that it is conventional to label each event to help identification, and that the completed structure of the diagram will show the logical sequencing of all activities making up the project. One aspect of these diagrams that can take some getting used to is the fact that the actual length of the activity lines does not relate to the time taken to complete each activity. The length of these lines is determined by whatever is appropriate to produce a diagram that accurately describes the relationship and linkages between the activities in the project. We should also note that, when drawing such diagrams manually, several attempts may be needed before a correct diagram is produced. It is worth getting into the habit of drawing one or two rough attempts at such a network diagram before producing the final and correct version. In practice, of course, for complex projects, project planning software is readily available.

To illustrate all of this, let us develop a smaller and simpler example before applying these principles to our problem. Table 13.4 shows a small illustrative project consisting of six activities.

We show the dependencies but not the durations, as we do not require these at present because we wish simply to illustrate the principles of diagram construction. Figure 13.2 shows the beginning of the diagram we would construct. This shows the start of the project (both start and end are usually drawn using the diamond shape shown) and the first activity and event. Event 1 marks the completion of Activity A, which has no dependencies so can commence at the start of the project.

We now proceed to add to the diagram the other activities and their dependencies. We see that activities B, C and D can all start on completion of activity A. This means that Event 1 not only marks the end of activity A but is also the start of these three activities. The next part of the diagram might then look like that shown in Figure 13.3 with three activities leading to three separate event nodes. Note that event node 1 satisfies the general rules: it has at least one preceding activity and at least one subsequent.

To continue the diagram, incorporating activity F is straightforward: it starts when C is finished, at Event 3. But what of E, which requires both B and D to be complete? It will help if we redraw the diagram slightly (as you frequently have to do in practice).

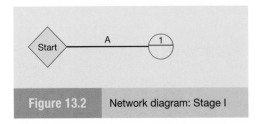

Figure 13.2   Network diagram: Stage I

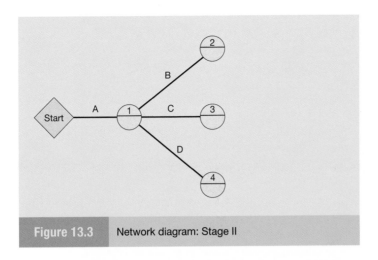

Figure 13.3   Network diagram: Stage II

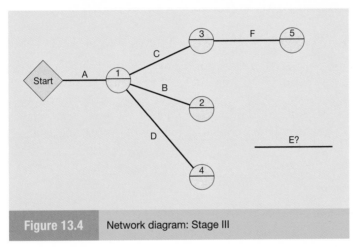

Figure 13.4   Network diagram: Stage III

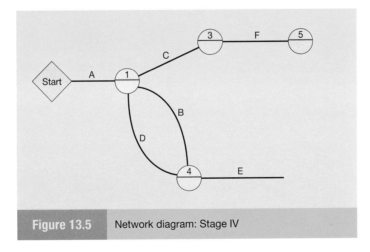

Figure 13.5   Network diagram: Stage IV

Figure 13.4 shows the current position. We have rearranged the layout of B, C and D and added F as appropriate. The problem we have is with E. This can start only when both B and D are finished, but how do we show this?

We might try drawing the diagram as shown in Figure 13.5 with E now starting as soon as both B and D are complete (Event 4). The problem is that this breaks one of the

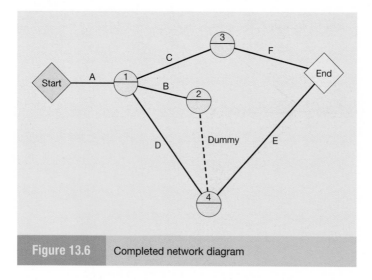

Figure 13.6 Completed network diagram

'rules': that any two events can be joined by only one activity. Events 1 and 4 are now joined by two activities. The way round this problem – because after all we cannot alter the actual dependencies shown in the project table – is to introduce what is known as a *dummy* activity. A dummy activity is not a real activity which forms part of the project but is an artificial activity designed to get us out of this particular difficulty when trying to draw a diagram that conforms to the 'rules'. As such, a dummy activity takes no time and requires no resources: it does not actually exist except on paper on the diagram. Such a dummy activity – and in fact the completed network diagram – is shown in Figure 13.6. The dummy activity – usually shown with a dotted line – allows us to keep the required dependencies without violating the rules. From Event 1 both B and D can start. At Event 4 both B and D have been completed and hence E can start. Note that we have completed the project when we reach the end event, which both E and F feed into. The dummy activity could equally well have been drawn so that D related to the dummy and not B. It would make no difference to the problem.

The diagram keeps all the required rules while showing the sequencing and dependencies specified in the project. Note also that the length of the activity lines does not relate to duration. Simply because the line for activity B is shorter than activity E does not imply that E takes longer than A. The length of the lines relates only to the construction of a logical and understandable diagram. We shall see later how we incorporate duration information into the diagram. No matter how complex the project, we can, in principle, construct such a diagram and this diagram is at the heart of the model we wish to develop to assist the project manager.

Activity 13.3

For the survey project draw a comparable diagram. This may take you more than one attempt and you should check your completed diagram carefully to ensure it follows the rules yet at the same time shows the dependencies specified in the project. In particular check your diagram to ensure it has dummy activities in the appropriate places.

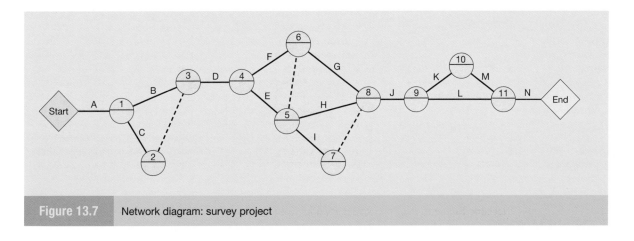

Figure 13.7   Network diagram: survey project

The completed network diagram for the survey problem is shown in Figure 13.7. Take a few moments to study it and compare it with your own. The diagram may look different from your own version but this is unimportant, as long as it shows the sequencing correctly. Note that we require three dummy activities in this case and that once again some of the dummies could be shown slightly differently. We require a dummy for Event 3, since D is dependent on both B and C. We need a second dummy at Event 6, as G is dependent on E and F (but not on H and I). J is dependent on G, H and I.

Developing the Network Diagram

We are now in a position to start to use the network diagram to help us produce information that we can use in managing the project. To do this we need to do the following:

● incorporate time information into the network;
● calculate earliest finish times for each activity;
● calculate latest finish times for each activity;
● identify the critical path through the network.

What is known as the critical path through the network will actually identify the time taken to complete the entire project. We shall follow this sequence.

Incorporate time information into the network

This is a straightforward task and we simply add the estimated duration of each activity onto the diagram as shown in Figure 13.8. Note again that longer lines in the diagram are not necessarily those that take a longer time to complete.

Calculate earliest finish times for each activity

The next stage is to calculate what is known as the *earliest finish time* (EFT) for each activity. To do this we commence at the start of the project and conventionally assign a time period 0 to the start point. This time is written in the node itself. We then work our way forward through the network identifying for each event in turn the earliest possible time we could reach that event. For Event 1, for example, the calculation is straightforward. If we start at day 0 and A takes three days to complete then the EFT for

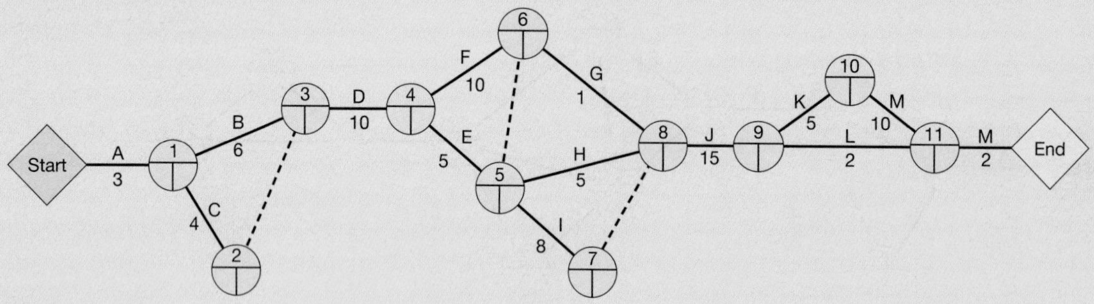

Figure 13.8   Network diagram: survey project activity durations

Event 1 is Day 3 (technically the end of Day 3). This EFT would be written into the node for Event 1. Similarly, for Event 2 its EFT would be seven, with the logic that C cannot start until Event 1 is complete. Notice that by definition the EFT for Event 1 indicates the earliest start time (EST) for the next activity.

Activity 13.4

What is the EFT for Event 3?

Event 3 is a little more difficult since we must reach this event in two different ways: via B and via C. Going via C would get us to Event 3 by Day 7 (since by definition the dummy activity takes zero time). Going via B would take us to Day 9 since B takes six days and the earliest it can start is Day 3. So we have a choice for Event 3 of an EFT of seven or nine days. Logically we must choose the larger of the two EFTs at Day 9 since both B and C must be completed for Event 3 to be reached.

Activity 13.5

Complete the rest of the EFT calculations for the network.

Figure 13.9 shows the network with EFTs added. Most of the calculations are straightforward. Only where we have multiple activities branching from a particular event do we need to be careful to ensure that the EFT incorporates the longest durations. Event 8, for example, has an EFT of 32 arrived at via Event 4 at 19 and via activities E and I since these represent the longest of all available routes (in time) from Event 4 to Event 8. It may also have occurred to you that we now have one critical piece of information: how long the project will take to complete. The answer is given as 64 days – the EFT at the end event. Literally, the earliest we can reach this part of the project is at the end of Day 64, based on the information we currently have about the project. This is obviously useful to the project manager and answers one critical question about the project. However, this was not the sole information requirement of the project manager and it will be worthwhile completing the rest of the calculations we said we required to see what other information we can generate.

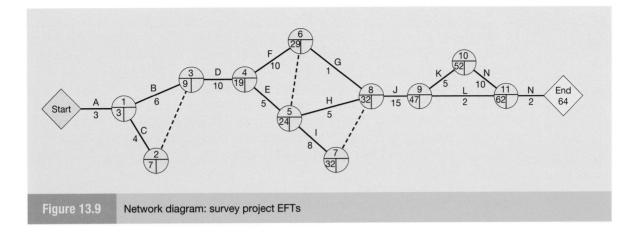

Figure 13.9   Network diagram: survey project EFTs

Calculate latest finish times for each activity

Just as we have calculated the EFTs for each event, we now require the *latest finish times –* LFTs. This is the time by which each event must be reached if the project is to be completed by the end of Day 64. To obtain these, we work backwards through the diagram from the end event. The end event has a time of 64. To obtain the LFT for Event 11 we know that Activity N takes two days, so if we are to reach the end event by Day 64 we must reach Event 11 by Day 62 (64 – 2). Literally, this indicates the latest time by which we must reach Event 11 if we are to complete the project on time. Similarly, for Event 10, its LFT is 52 (62 – 10). The LFT for Event 9 requires more thought, since there are two routes we must follow to reach this from Event 11. As with the EFT calculation, when faced with a choice we identify the route with the longest duration: here K and M. Event 9 will then have an LFT of 47.

Activity 13.6

Calculate the LFTs for the rest of the network.

Figure 13.10 shows the LFT information. Once again the only parts we need to be careful about are the points where there are multiple routes through the network.

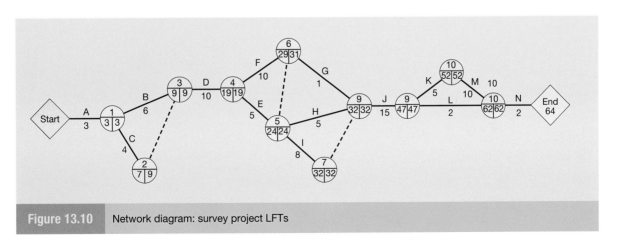

Figure 13.10   Network diagram: survey project LFTs

Identify the critical path through the network

The last part of the analysis now requires us to determine what is known as the *critical path* through the network. We can now use the EFT and LFT information to determine those activities whose completion dates are, literally, critical to the project being completed on time, and those activities which are non-critical. Consider Activity A. This starts on Day 0, takes three days to complete and must be completed on Day 3 (the LFT), otherwise the entire project will be delayed. Activity A is therefore designated a critical activity. Similarly, Activity B is critical. The earliest it can start is Day 3, it takes six days to complete and must be completed by Day 9. However, Activity C is non-critical. Its earliest start time is Day 3, it takes four days and must be complete by Day 9 (the LFT for Event 3).

However, this effectively gives us two days spare (or two days float time as the terminology of project planning has it). We literally have two days flexibility with activity C, which could be used to alter exactly when it starts, when it finishes or how long it takes. If C takes five days rather than the estimated four, it will not affect the completion date of the project. If Activity B, on the other hand, takes a day longer than expected, it will delay the project.

Activity 13.7

For the remaining activities in the project determine whether they are critical or non-critical and, for the non-critical activities, determine the float associated with each.

We can summarise the information associated with each activity as shown in Table 13.5.

Table 13.5   Critical and non-critical activities

Activity	Duration	EST	EFT	LFT	Float
A	3	0	9	9	0
B	6	3	9	9	0
C	4	3	7	9	2
D	10	9	19	19	0
E	5	19	24	24	0
F	10	19	29	31	2
G	1	29	30	32	2
H	5	24	29	32	3
I	8	24	32	32	0
J	15	32	47	47	0
K	5	47	52	52	0
L	2	47	49	62	13
M	10	52	62	62	0
N	2	62	64	64	0

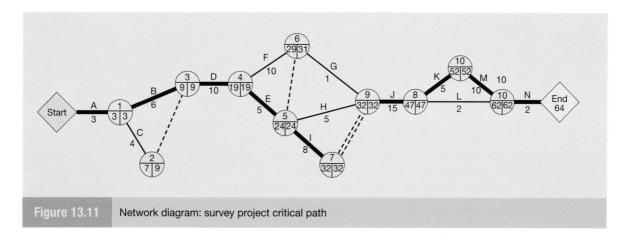

Figure 13.11 Network diagram: survey project critical path

This shows for each activity its duration, its earliest start time, EST, which is the EFT of the preceding event, its EFT, its LFT and the float time associated with it (the difference between LFT and EFT). Activity D, for example, has an EST of nine and an EFT of 19 (given its duration of 10 days). However, we also see that the LFT for activity D is the same as its EFT. This indicates that this activity has zero float time. Activity F, on the other hand, has two days float time. Its EST is 19 and it also takes 10 days, so its EFT is 29. However, its LFT is 31, indicating we have two days flexibility with this particular activity. It is evident that, by definition, critical activities have zero float whereas non-critical activities have positive float time. We can now indicate what is known as the critical path through the network by marking the critical activities, as in Figure 13.11. Such a path is continuous and the length of this path (in time) shows the duration of the project.

Using the Network Diagram

It is by now clear how useful the completed network diagram and the information it contains can be to the project manager. We are now able to:

● determine the project duration;
● prioritise between activities and their relative importance;
● assess the impact on the project duration of any changes in activity duration;
● use the diagram as a monitoring tool to check actual progress against planned as the project develops.

To illustrate we shall consider one or two examples.

● As project manager you are approached by the person responsible for printing the questionnaire: Activity H. This individual indicates that if you are willing to pay the workforce a bonus they can complete this activity ahead of schedule and take only three days to complete this, rather than the estimated five. What would your reaction be? Based on the diagram we know that Activity H is non-critical and we have three days float associated with it. Completing this activity early will be of no benefit in terms of completing the entire project any earlier. If the activity had been a critical one then we would have considered the option of reducing its duration. If, for example, the same offer had been made regarding data entry, Activity K, then the project manager would need to weigh up the extra costs with the time saved in completing the entire project.

- The Computing Services Department, which will be responsible for data entry, is understaffed and the departmental manager is trying to plan staff requirements over the next few months. You are approached as project manager and asked exactly when you will require the data-entry staff to be available for your project. From the diagram we see that – as long as everything goes according to plan – the data-entry activity, K, is scheduled to start on Day 47 and end on Day 52. This is when these staff will be needed. From the Computing Services Department manager's perspective, this indicates that it will serve no purpose having these staff available early: this will not help completion of this project. From a resource management viewpoint, project plans offer considerable potential.

- Part way into the project, you have reached the stage of having just completed activities A, B, C, D, E with F partly completed. However, it is now Day 26 and you should have reached this stage of the project by Day 24. Once again, the diagram will help you plan through the consequences of this delay. Other things being equal, and unless we take some positive action, such a delay clearly means the entire project will be delayed by two days. It is a straightforward matter to recalculate start and finish times for the activities still to be completed and communicate these as appropriate (for example to the data-entry staff). However, we can also evaluate our options in terms of trying to claw back some of this lost time. Activities I, J, K, M and N are all critical and still have to be undertaken. We would need to review urgently the estimated durations of these to see if the time taken for any of these activities can be reduced. Such information may well help us determine whether incurring extra costs – by paying the data-entry staff overtime, for example, to complete this activity early – is worthwhile in the context of the overall project objectives and resource allocation.

The network diagram that we have developed offers the project management a valuable tool not only in managing the project to ensure it is completed on time but also as a planning tool to resolve problems that, inevitably, will occur during the life of the project.

Precedence Diagrams

The network diagram we have developed is technically known as an activity-on-arrow diagram, since we use arrow-type notation to show sequencing through the network, and we associate a particular activity (and its duration) with a particular arrow. This type of diagram is particularly easy to sketch (rather than draw) and is helpful in initial project planning. Computer packages which provide project-planning support more usually adopt the use of what is known as a *precedence diagram*, using precedence activities, shown in Figure 13.12.

It can be seen that an activity is denoted using a box, with various parts of the box containing the information relating to that activity (notably its duration, the EST, EFT, LST, LFT and float). Each activity has its box and the boxes can then be linked together with lines to show dependencies and the critical path. Figure 13.13 shows the precedence diagram for the survey project. You should study it carefully. The critical path is

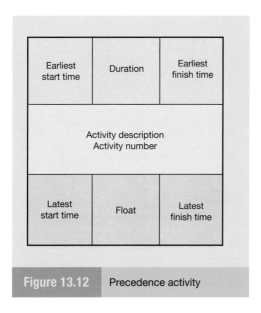

Figure 13.12   Precedence activity

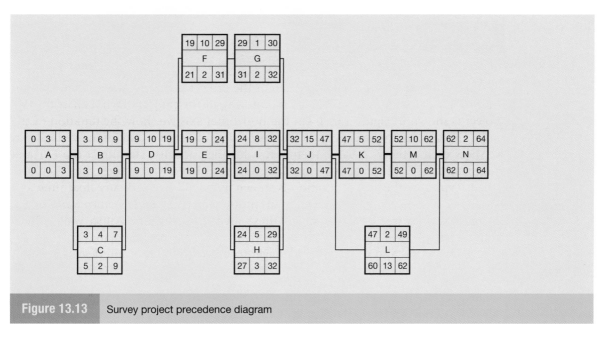

Figure 13.13   Survey project precedence diagram

denoted by the bold lines linking boxes. Although the layout of the diagram looks different from our earlier arrow network, it contains exactly the same information and can be used in the same way. For manual use, the activity-on-arrow is probably easier. For formal use, the precedence diagram is more likely to be encountered, if only because it will be computer-generated.

Gantt Charts

A further development we can introduce, based on the diagram and the information we obtained in Table 13.5, is to produce what is known as a *Gantt chart*, which presents the information in the network diagram in a different way. This is particularly useful in

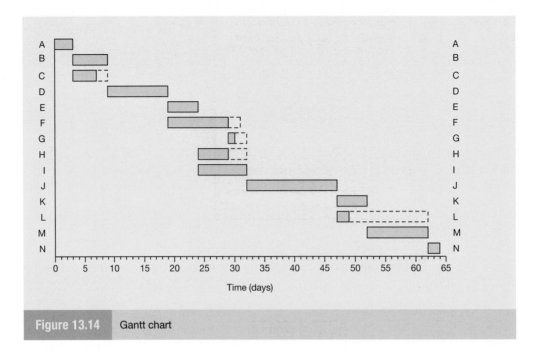

Figure 13.14   Gantt chart

meeting one of the requirements we had of the project planning model: that it would serve as a useful tool in the constant monitoring of the project. Such a chart for this project is shown in Figure 13.14. On the horizontal axis we show the duration of the project in days, up to the expected completion date of 64 days, and on the vertical axis we show each activity. A bar is then drawn for each activity, starting at the EST and ending at the EFT. If the activity has float time associated with it then the LFT is also added. Typically, the actual duration is shown as a solid bar with any float time as a dotted bar. It is easy to picture such a chart in the project manager's office wall (indeed many of you may well have seen one of these already on someone's office wall without realising what it was). The chart shows clearly the sequencing of activities and the critical activities, and also enables the manager to monitor progress and deviations from the project plan at a glance. For example, it is now very evident that Activity L, debriefing the interviewers, can take place any time between Day 47 and Day 62. Such an activity can be completed at the convenience of those involved. It will also be evident that, although the Gantt chart presents the same information as the network diagram, for many managers it will be seen as much more user-friendly.

QMDM IN ACTION

Cap Gemini Ernst & Young – contingency planning in project management

Cap Gemini Ernst & Young's client was a leading mobile phone company. The client had launched a major project to replace their billing and administration system. The timescale for this was particularly aggressive and given that the system was critical to the business and the possibility of a delay in its delivery, a contingency planning project was commissioned. This project was to run in parallel with the replacement project. In the event of a delay it was proposed to extend the operational life of the existing system although this would then raise issues over its capacity to handle existing levels of business growth.

Much of the client's billing and administrative work took place on an overnight basis. Cap Gemini Ernst & Young developed a model of the system's overnight batch processes with simulation built into the model to allow for uncertainty.

Three key factors were assumed to influence the amount of work required of the system and its level of utilisation: the size of the customer base, the number of calls being made by customers, and end-user generated activity. Cap Gemini Ernst & Young analysed the relationship between overnight batch job times and these key influences. The performance relationships were built into a spreadsheet model. Because of uncertainty and variability in predicted job times and significant variation in the levels of daily activity, model experimentation was carried out using simulation. This allowed a picture of overnight system performance to be built up and the probability of batch failure to be assessed for forecast levels of monthly business activity. Finally, the model was used to evaluate the impact of a number of potential contingency measures on the system life expectancy.

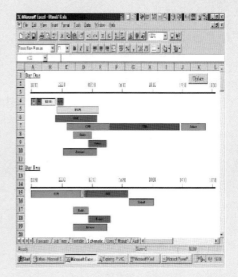

The benefits are as follows:

● An objective assessment of the system's life expectancy.

● Identification of the key influences affecting overnight system performance.

● An assessment of the effect of alternative contingency measures on the system's life expectancy.

I am grateful to Cap Gemini Ernst & Young for permission to use this case study and to reproduce the figure shown. Further case study applications are available through their website: www.uk.capgemini.com/services/consulting/or/success_stories

Uncertainty

It will be evident that, no matter how useful the model we have developed, the accuracy of the model will only be as reliable as the information which has gone into it: the estimated duration of each activity. No matter how much effort has gone into producing such estimates, it is clear that these must be seen as uncertain to a lesser or greater extent. Although we can use the model to help us assess the effects of such uncertainty on a piecemeal basis (what is the effect of Activity J, for example, taking 17 days rather than 15) this is clearly unsatisfactory. However, under certain assumptions we can incorporate uncertainty over activity durations into the model explicitly. The extension of the basic model in this way is technically a complex one and we shall present only the key parts of the development.

We begin by assuming, realistically, that for any particular activity we could produce not one estimate of its duration but three:

● an *optimistic estimate* (OD), which is the minimum time this activity would take to complete if everything went exactly as expected without any difficulties or problems whatsoever;

- a *most likely estimate* (MD), which is the most likely duration, assuming normal conditions;
- a *pessimistic estimate* (PD), which is the expected duration if major difficulties are encountered.

Although we could produce three such estimates for all the activities making up the project, we shall do so only for three to help keep the principles manageable: E, J and M.

Activity	OD	MD	PD
E	4	5	8
J	12	15	25
M	8	10	15

That is, for activity E, for example, the OD estimate is four days, the MD estimate five days and the PD estimate eight days. Using the three estimates for each activity we can now calculate an estimated duration for each activity using the formula to give a weighted average:

$$\text{Expected duration} = \frac{\text{OD} + 4\text{MD} + \text{PD}}{6}$$

Notice that the most likely estimate is given a large weight in the calculation and that the pessimistic and optimistic estimates have equal weights. This then gives, for the three activities:

Activity	OD	MD	PD	Expected duration
E	4	5	8	5.33 days
J	12	15	25	16.17 days
M	8	10	15	10.5 days

We could now rework the network diagram incorporating these durations and assessing the impact this will have on the project duration. In some cases the critical path itself may alter as a result of these calculations: in others (as this one) it does not, although the overall project duration time is now 66 days rather than 64. However, this hardly seems worth the effort, since all it provides is a variant of the original critical path network. We can use such estimates, however, to assess probabilities in the context of the project duration. For example, we may wish an answer to the question: how likely is it that the project will be completed no later than Day 60 – at least six days ahead of schedule? To answer this we return to the Normal distribution. Without proof we state that:

- if there are a large number of activities on the critical path
- if the duration of each activity is independent of other activities

Table 13.6	Estimated durations	
Activity	Estimated duration	Variance
A	3	0
B	6	0
D	10	0
E	5.33	0.44
I	8	0
J	16.17	4.69
K	5	0
M	10.5	1.36
N	2	0
Total	66	6.49

then the overall duration of the project will follow a Normal distribution. Such a distribution has:

- a mean equal to the total of the expected durations of the activities on the critical path
- a variance equal to the sum of the variances of the activities on the critical path.

We should remember that variance is the square of the standard deviation. For our revised problem, the critical path is as before and the estimated duration for each activity is shown in Table 13.6. We note that for those critical activities which have only one duration (as opposed to three) the estimated duration remains the same as in the original problem. The mean of the distribution is then 66 days. The variance of each activity is given by the formula:

$$\text{Variance} = \frac{(PD - OD)^2}{36}$$

and is shown in the table. For those activities with only one duration estimate then the variance by definition is zero. The total variance for all activities on the critical path is then 6.49. Given that the variance is the square of the standard deviation, this means we have a standard deviation of:

$$SD = \sqrt{6.49} = 2.55 \text{ days}$$

We therefore have a Normal distribution showing the project duration with a mean of 66 days and a standard deviation of 2.55 days. Using the principles of the Normal distribution we can calculate a Z score for this distribution and, using probability tables, determine the relevant probability. We require:

$$Z = \frac{X - \text{Mean}}{SD} = \frac{60 - 66}{2.55} = -2.35$$

which, from the table in Appendix B, gives a probability of 0.0094. That is, there is a probability of only around 1 per cent that this project will be completed at least six days

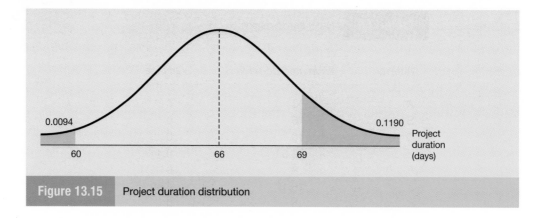

Figure 13.15   Project duration distribution

ahead of schedule. Similarly, if we wanted to know the probability of the project being completed no more than three days late we have:

$$Z = \frac{X - \text{Mean}}{\text{SD}} = \frac{69 - 66}{2.55} = 1.18$$

giving a probability of 0.1190 or around 12 per cent. However, this is the probability in the area of the tail of the distribution and we require the area up to the tail, since we are asked the probability that the project will be completed no more than three days late. This probability is then (1.0 – 0.119) or 88 per cent. The general principles of this approach are shown in Figure 13.15 and can clearly be used to quantify the uncertainty over the exact durations of activities. In this example we have introduced uncertainty with only three activities; the method is readily extended to all activities where uncertainty might apply.

Project Costs and Crashing

We have seen that the project-planning model we have developed can be used to help the project manager prioritise, particularly if parts of the project have not gone to plan and delays have occurred. So far, the project manager has been able to identify critical activities and assess subjectively whether reductions in the duration of these might be possible and worthwhile in terms of trying to bring the whole project back on schedule. For some projects it may also be possible to add detailed cost information to the project-planning model and to use this to help prioritisation. This is achieved through the introduction of what are known as *crash costs* and *crash times*. Consider Activity K, data entry. We can visualise that this activity has been costed in terms of its resource implications: staff costs, machine time and so on. Let us assume that this cost has been put at £1000. Such a cost is referred to as a normal cost, since it is linked to the estimate of the activity duration of five days, referred to as normal time. Clearly, for this activity, it might be possible to reduce the duration. However, this almost inevitably will incur additional costs: paying the data-entry staff overtime, using computing facilities at peak times, delaying other projects. Let us assume that we could reduce the duration of this activity to three days but at an additional cost of £500. This second duration and cost are known as crash time and crash costs respectively. However, what the project manager now has is information on the cost of reducing overall project duration – since Activity K is critical. On a daily basis we can reduce the project completion date at an extra cost of £250 per day for a maximum of two days. That is, the project could be completed in 62 days rather than the current 64 days. Obviously management would need to determine whether this extra cost and the reduction in completion date was worthwhile in the context of the overall project.

This principle of crashing, however, can be taken one stage further. It would clearly be possible to establish a crash time and a crash cost for several of the activities. Consider the data shown in Table 13.7.

This shows for several activities the normal times and costs and the crash times and costs. Activity B, for example, could be reduced by one day at an extra cost of £300.

Activity 13.8

Consider the information in Table 13.7. How could this be used by the project manager to prioritise which activities should be crashed?

Clearly, the options we face in terms of crashing – and thereby reducing the overall project completion time – are several. The first decision we can make is a simple one: there is no point incurring extra costs to reduce the completion time of a non-critical activity. Activity H is non-critical and therefore should not be crashed. All the other activities are critical, however, and it will be worthwhile calculating the crash cost per day's reduction in duration for each of them. This is shown in Table 13.8. We see, for example, that Activity B has a crash cost per day of £300 and Activity J of £1800, where each cost is calculated by taking the extra costs incurred in crashing this activity and dividing by the reduction in the number of days duration for that activity. It is clear that we can now use these daily costs to prioritise. Other things being equal, Activity D is the one which should be crashed first, although the decision to crash at all is still a subjective one.

Table 13.7	Crash times and crash costs			
	Normal		**Crash**	
Activity	Time (days)	Cost (£s)	Time (days)	Cost (£s)
B	6	1 200	5	1 500
D	10	3 800	7	4 500
H	5	750	4	850
J	15	11 000	10	20 000
K	5	1 000	3	1 500
M	10	3 000	7	3 900

Table 13.8		Crash cost per day				
	Normal			**Crash**		
Activity	*Time (days)*	*Cost (£s)*		*Time (days)*	*Cost (£s)*	*Crash cost per day (£s)*
B	6	1 200		5	1 500	300
D	10	3 800		7	4 500	233
H	5	750		4	850	–
J	15	11 000		10	20 000	1 800
K	5	1 000		3	1 500	250
M	10	3 000		7	3 900	300

Worked Example

Your company has decided to run a short management training course on project management. You have been asked to project manage the initiative. You have identified the key activities required for the project, shown in Table 13.9.

Table 13.9	Key activities for planning management training course		
Activity	*Description*	*Duration (weeks)*	*Preceding activity*
A	Agree course outline and publicity	4	–
B	Identify suitable tutors	2	A
C	Agree detailed course structure	6	B
D	Circulate publicity and application forms	6	A
E	Agree contract with tutors	2	B
F	Select participants	1	C, E
G	Send confirmation to participants	2	D
H	Agree teaching material	2	F, G
I	Prepare teaching material	5	H
J	Prepare venue for event	1	G
K	Run programme	–	I, J

For certain activities there is some uncertainty as to the exact duration and you have provided alternative duration figures:

Activity	*Optimistic*	*Most likely*	*Pessimistic*
A	3	4	6
B	2	2	10

Table 13.10	Costs of activities	

Activity	Extra cost (£s)	Minimum possible duration
A	1000	2
B	750	1
C	300	3
D	1200	8
E	100	1
G	1500	1
H	200	1

In addition, you have made estimates of the costs of the various activities, as shown in Table 13.10.

To put our project plan together we can start with the relevant network diagram, shown in Figure 13.16 in precedence activity form (you may wish to produce your own activity-on-arrow diagram for this problem). The overall project duration is 20 weeks, with critical activities shown as A, B, C, F, H and I. Other activities are non-critical and float time is shown for each in the relevant precedence box.

We know, however, that for two activities, A and B, uncertainty about the expected durations exists. We can now obtain the expected duration of the project (from the expected duration of all activities on the critical path) as 22.34 weeks. More usefully though, with the project variance at 10.92 and the standard deviation at 3.30, we can

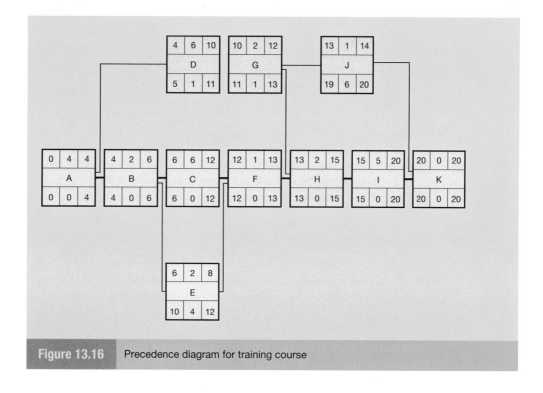

Figure 13.16 Precedence diagram for training course

determine a range of completion dates and the associated probability:

- a 90 per cent probability that the project will be completed within 26.6 weeks
- a 95 per cent probability that the project will be completed within 27.8 weeks
- a 99 per cent probability that the project will be completed within 30 weeks.

We can also apply the crashing information to the problem. From the information given we can calculate the crash cost per week for each activity:

Activity	Crash cost per week	Maximum possible time saved
A	500	2
B	750	1
C	100	3
D	1200	1
E	100	1
G	750	2
H	200	1

Recollect that only critical activities are worth considering for crashing. The current critical activities are A, B, C, F, H and I. It looks tempting to say we can crash C by three weeks at a cost of £300. However, closer inspection of Figure 13.6 reveals that we have limited float time with activities D and G. In fact, for these two activities combined, we have only one week of float time available (since G has an EFT of 12 while F currently finishes in week 13). So, we can only crash Activity C by one week before D and G also become critical. Visual inspection of the crash costs indicates the next option is to crash Activity H by the one week, available at a cost of £200. Activity A is the next possibility, at a cost per week of £500, but it would probably be sensible to determine what our available budget was for such crashing before completing the rest of the calculations.

Summary

In this chapter we have examined the issues and problems that typically arise for managers who have the responsibility for controlling a project. We have also developed a model – usually referred to as the critical path model (CPM) – which allows us to identify discrete activities which make up the project and use these to represent the project diagrammatically. With additional information about linkages between the different activities and their durations we can use this model to identify the critical path: the key activities which directly affect the overall duration of the project. We have also seen that the basic model can be extended to incorporate uncertainty through what is known as the project evaluation and review technique (PERT). This allows a manager to quantify the likelihood of a given completion date for the project.

We cannot finish this chapter, however, without repeating the message that project management involves far more than simply applying these models and using the information they generate. Project management calls upon a whole range of skills on the part of the project manager, many of them 'people' skills relating to teamwork, motivation, control and delegation. These are far more important than the simple quantitative models that we have developed. Such models can, however, provide valuable information to the project manager to assist in this wider management task.

Useful online resources

Detailed below are some internet resources that may be useful. Many have further links to other sites. An updated version is available from the accompanying website (**www.pearsoned.co.uk/wisniewski**). In addition, I would be grateful for details of other websites that have been found to be useful.

www.apm.org.uk/ – Association for Project Management

www.allpm.com/ – Project Managers' Homepage

www.projectmanagement.com/ – ProjectManagement.com

www.mapnp.org/library/plan_dec/project/project.htm – Project management

www.pmi.org – The Project Management Institute

www.startwright.com/project1.htm – Project management tools

www.mindtools.com/pages/main/newMN_PPM.htm – Project planning and management tools

QMDM IN ACTION
Central Regional Council, Scotland

At the time of this application in the UK there were two major levels of local government. There were district or borough councils, covering a reasonably concentrated area and typically responsible for local services such as leisure and recreation, local authority housing, and environmental services (street cleaning and refuse collection). Then there were the regional, or county, councils, which typically covered a geographical area consisting of several district councils. The regional councils had differing responsibilities, typically for regional economic development, regional transport, social services provision, primary and secondary education, and local policing.

Central Regional Council (CRC) in Scotland covered the areas of Clackmannan District Council, Falkirk District Council and Stirling District Council. The area covered is around 263 000 hectares and the council served over a quarter of a million citizens and had 13 000 employees. The area covered is particularly diverse, ranging from modern industrial

complexes like Grangemouth through to areas of outstanding natural beauty like Loch Lomond and the Trossachs. Employment, social and leisure patterns are equally diverse.

At the time of this application the majority political group in CRC issued a manifesto, *Challenge to Action*, which outlined overall policies and objectives for the region to which CRC would work over the coming years. There was a view that CRC was not a particularly policy-driven organisation, that the organisation's priorities did not always match the political priorities of elected representatives and that the existing decision-making structures and systems were not always adequate. *Challenge for Action* addressed a number of key issues but indicated a strong desire to establish a corporate system for policy planning and performance management (PPPM) so that CRC policies were clearly linked to the budgetary allocation process. As part of this it became clear that individual departments would need to establish a clear departmental

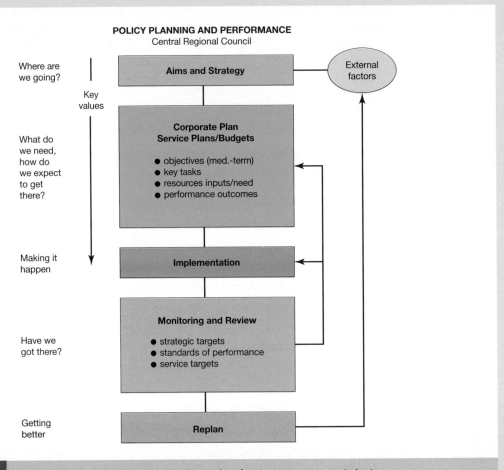

POLICY PLANNING AND PERFORMANCE
Central Regional Council

Where are we going?

Key values

Aims and Strategy

External factors

What do we need, how do we expect to get there?

**Corporate Plan
Service Plans/Budgets**

- objectives (med.-term)
- key tasks
- resources inputs/need
- performance outcomes

Making it happen

Implementation

Have we got there?

Monitoring and Review

- strategic targets
- standards of performance
- service targets

Getting better

Replan

| **Figure 13.17** | Central Regional Council: policy planning and performance management chart |

strategy, consistent with the organisation's corporate strategy; would need to translate strategic objectives into targets and actions; and would need to establish a monitoring and review process to assess progress in terms of strategic achievement. An overview of this process is shown in Figure 13.17.

As part of this process, CRC developed a corporate statement of strategic objectives and adopted key values of:

- closeness to the customer
- communications
- management devolution: ensuring decisions are taken by the right people at the right time.

The organisation recognised that, for many employees, such an initiative would require both a culture change and the development of new management skills and competencies. To help support this development process, CRC allocated some £500 000 for

an employee training and development strategy. As part of this development process it was decided that around 100 of the senior managers in CRC from the level of the chief executive downwards would attend a management development programme to help support the strategic planning process at both corporate level and individual department level. After initial discussions with a number of external training and development organisations, CRC appointed a specialist management development unit at Stirling University as the training and development provider for the programme. The overall structure of the programme consisted of a two-day programme on service-oriented strategic management and a two-day programme on performance management. At the end of this, a comprehensive review was planned to consider further development and training needs. Participants on the first part of the programme were deliberately mixed from different departments and functional areas within CRC. The second part of the programme was designed for participants drawn from the same department.

It was felt desirable to initiate the programme as soon as possible. However, the programme itself was required to be tailored to the specific needs, objectives and culture of CRC, which had implications for the time required for programme development. At the same time, because of the short timescale, the senior managers attending the programme needed to be informed as soon as possible when the programme would take place, given the complex logistics of ensuring attendance and availability. An added problem was that the whole initiative was taking place either side of the Christmas period, with obvious complications in terms of holiday arrangements for participants and key personnel. At an early stage it was decided to draw up an informal project plan for the initiative so that key events and dates could be identified and communicated to all concerned. A simplified network diagram is shown in Figure 13.18 and the Gantt

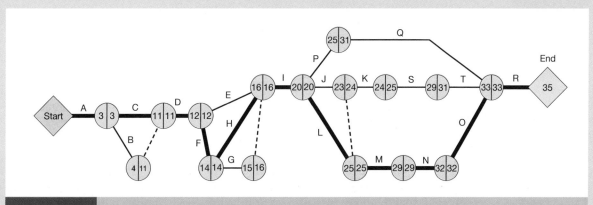

Figure 13.18   Central Regional Council: network diagram with critical path (times shown are in weeks)

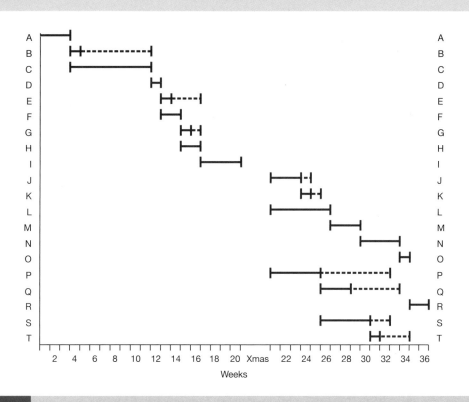

Figure 13.19   Central Regional Council: Gantt chart

chart in Figure 13.19. The project-planning approach not only helped the project team identify clearly, and in advance, the key tasks, events and personnel relevant to the initiative but also helped ensure that the complex organisational logistics of the programme were properly determined in advance.

I am grateful to Mr R Fairweather, former Training and Development Adviser, Central Regional Council, for providing this application.

This application relates to the local government structure prior to reorganisation in 1996/1997.

Exercises

1 Consider the situation of waking up in the morning and going to the kitchen to make yourself a cup of tea or coffee. Identify the various activities you would need to complete for this project and determine the dependencies between each activity. Use this information to construct a network diagram. When you have your result, try following the sequencing you have identified to make yourself a cup of tea or coffee and see if it works.

2 A business organisation is trying to improve staff morale and motivation and has decided to replace the existing staff canteen with a modern cafeteria. The works department has drawn up a detailed list of the various activities that will need to be completed, together with an estimate of how long each activity will take and the sequencing of activities. This information is shown in Table 13.11.

Table 13.11	Cafeteria project			
Activity		Duration	Preceding activities	Personnel required
A	Purchase construction materials	12 weeks	–	3
B	Purchase catering equipment needed for new cafeteria	3 weeks	–	2
C	Appoint supervisory architect	2 weeks	–	1
D	Clear site	3 weeks	–	3
E	Produce final building details	8 weeks	C, D	1
F	Prepare site for construction	3 weeks	E	2
G	Construct cafeteria	12 weeks	A, F	5
H	Install utility services	4 weeks	G	2
I	Install catering equipment	4 weeks	B, H	2
J	Decorate internally	2 weeks	B, H	2
K	Stock cafeteria	4 weeks	I, J	1
L	Hire catering staff	8 weeks	–	2
M	Train staff on site	2 weeks	I, L	3

(a) Using this information construct a network diagram for the project.

(b) Identify the critical path.

(c) Determine float times for all activities.

(d) To try to keep the project within budget it has been decided that ideally no more than five personnel should be involved in the project at any one time. Is this feasible?

3 A large banking organisation is installing a network of automated teller machines (ATMs) for use by its customers in a large town. These machines are installed in an exterior wall of the bank and allow customers to withdraw cash from their accounts. A number of major activities that have to be completed have been identified, along with estimates of the duration of each activity and the normal cost of each activity. Crash times and costs have also been estimated. The relevant information is shown in Table 13.12.

Table 13.12	ATM project				
Activity	Preceding activities	Normal duration (weeks)	Normal cost (£s)	Crash duration (weeks)	Crash cost (£s)
A	–	9	900	3	6 300
B	–	7	2 800	5	4 000
C	A	12	8 400	6	13 800
D	A	10	7 000	6	16 600
E	B	12	7 200	4	12 800
F	C, E	6	3 000	4	4 600
G	C, E	7	4 900	6	6 800
H	F	14	4 200	10	6 200
I	G, D	8	3 200	3	6 700
J	H, I	3	1 500	–	–

(a) Construct a network diagram using this information.

(b) Determine the critical path.

(c) Determine the expected normal completion time for the project.

(d) The bank has decided that in terms of increased customer satisfaction and new accounts it is worth up to £1000 a week to reduce the completion time of the project. Determine by how many weeks it would be cost-effective to reduce the completion date.

4 In the project detailed in Table 13.13, activity labels indicate the major activities to be completed in a project.

The duration of each activity and cost of each activity have been identified, on both a normal basis and a crash basis.

(a) Construct a network diagram for this project.

(b) Identify the critical path, the normal completion time and the normal cost of the project.

(c) By successively crashing activities, find the shortest possible time for the project as a whole and calculate the associated cost.

Table 13.13	Project					

Activity	Preceding activities	Normal duration (weeks)	Normal cost (£s)	Crash duration (weeks)	Crash cost (£s)
A	–	10	2000	4	2600
B	–	2	500	–	
C	A, B	3	1500	1	2000
D	A	12	3000	4	4600
E	C, D	5	900	3	1200
F	E	3	700	–	
G	E	5	1110	3	1340
H	C, D	9	2500	4	4000
I	F, G	16	4200	6	5200
J	H, I	2	400	–	–

5 You have been appointed secretary of a student group which has an annual programme of invited speakers from the business world. The group has suffered from a membership decline over the last few years and you are keen to reverse this trend by planning a more ambitious programme of guest speakers. Table 13.14 shows the individual activities you have determined make up the project and the estimated duration.

Table 13.14	Programme project		

Activity		Preceding activities	Duration (days)
A	Book individual dates for programme	–	2
B	Contact key speakers to agree availability	A	20
C	Arrange sponsorship to help with costs	–	15
D	Send out membership renewal details	–	5
E	Membership renewals returned	D	15
F	Send reminder notice to those who have not renewed membership together with list of key speakers	B, E	5
G	Membership renewals returned	F	15
H	Compile membership list	G	5
I	Print detailed programme	B, C	5
J	Mail final programme to members	I, G	5

(a) Estimate the overall completion time for the project.

(b) Construct a Gantt chart for the project.

6 A project comprises the activities shown in Table 13.15, which also shows the duration of each activity.

Table 13.15	Activities and duration of project			

		Duration in weeks		
Activity	Preceding activity	Optimistic	Most likely	Pessimistic
A	–	2	3	3
B	–	10	12	15
C	A	4	5	8
D	B	2	2	2
E	A, D	3	3	3
F	B	3	4	5
G	C, E, F	8	10	20
H	G	2	3	5
I	G	2	2	2
J	H	4	5	10
K	I, J	2	4	6

(a) Construct a network diagram for this project and determine the expected completion time together with the critical path.

(b) Determine the probability that the project will take longer than 50 weeks.

(c) Determine the probability that the project will take less than 42 weeks.

7 A firm is making minor alterations to its automated stock-handling system in one of its warehouses. The relevant information relating to this project is shown in Table 13.16.

Table 13.16	Activities relating to stock-handling system			

Activity	Expected time (weeks)	Preceding activities	Extra crash costs (£s)	Crash time (weeks)
A	3	–	6 000	2
B	2	A	–	–
C	8	–	16 000	5
D	1	C	–	–
E	6	B, D	18 000	4
F	4	C	20 000	2
G	5	E, F	15 000	4
H	1	E, F	–	–
I	1	G	–	–
J	5	G	5 000	3
K	6	H, I	12 000	3

The table shows the activities that must be completed, their expected duration times in weeks, and the activities that must precede each activity shown. Also detailed in the table are potential time savings for some activities and the extra costs that would be associated with such time savings.

(a) Construct a suitable diagram to determine the completion time of this project. The diagram should clearly show the critical path and all appropriate times.

(b) The warehouse manager has expressed concern about the disruption caused during the project and has indicated that an extra £25 000 of funding for the project would be available if the overall completion time could be reduced. Using the principles of crashing, determine by how much it would be feasible to reduce the overall completion time and which activities would be affected.

8 For a particular project the information in Table 13.17 has been obtained.

Table 13.17	Project information				
Activity	Preceding activities	Normal time (days)	Crash time (days)	Normal cost (£s)	Total crash cost (£s)
A	–	3	1	900	1700
B	–	6	3	2000	4000
C	A	2	1	500	1000
D	B, C	5	3	1800	2400
E	D	4	3	1500	1850
F	E	3	1	3000	3900
G	B, C	9	4	8000	9800
H	F, G	3	2	1000	2000

(a) Construct a network diagram for this project showing EFTs, LFTs and the critical path.

(b) The company concerned has indicated that it would like the project completed in no more than 16 days. Determine the additional cost of achieving this.

(c) What is the minimum possible time for completing the project?

14 Simulation

Learning objectives

By the end of this chapter you should be able to:

- describe the features of a simulation approach in business
- construct a simulation flowchart
- complete a manual simulation
- interpret information generated from a computer simulation

We have developed and used a number of quantitative models through the text. These models have had one key feature in common: they are primarily deterministic. That is, they are concerned with finding the specific solution to the problem as formulated, very often with this solution being seen as the 'best' or optimal solution. There are very many situations in business decision making, however, where it may be unrealistic to expect there to be an optimum solution. One group of models – simulation models – are concerned with this type of situation and differ from most other quantitative models in that they are primarily descriptive rather than deterministic: they are concerned with describing in modelling terms the business problem we are investigating rather than finding the solution to such a problem. Simulation models typically generate additional information about the problem – frequently information that no other model can produce – and this information must then be assessed and used by the decision maker as appropriate.

The Principles of Simulation

Consider the following scenario. The manager of a small supermarket is reviewing policy in terms of the number of checkouts that are available at any one time for serving customers. The manager has recently received a number of complaints from customers that they have to wait for an unacceptably long time at the checkout before being served by the checkout operator. That is, they have to wait in a queue of customers before receiving service and that the time they have to wait is unacceptable. Naturally this is a potentially serious situation for the manager.

Activity 14.1

As supermarket manager what action would you consider taking?

It is evident that one option that would be seriously considered would be the possibility of increasing the number of checkouts that were in use at any one time. Consider the logic of the situation which the manager faces. A number of customers will be in the supermarket at any one time and will be wandering around completing their shopping. When they are finished they will make their way to the checkout to pay for their goods and will leave the store. The number of customers who can be served in a given period of time will, then, be largely determined by the number of checkouts in use at any one time. In principle, the more checkouts in use then the shorter the time a customer is likely to have to wait before service. Naturally having more checkouts in use will not guarantee that every customer will receive faster service – we are in the realms of 'on average' once again.

Activity 14.2

If the solution to the problem is this simple and obvious why, as customers, do we always seem to face long queues in supermarkets?

Clearly, although in principle the manager has a simple solution to the problem, a number of other factors will have to be considered. Foremost of these is likely to be the issue of the extra cost incurred by opening additional checkouts – in particular the manager will want to know how cost-effective the decision will be. The difficulty is clear. Opening an extra checkout will cost money: in terms of the equipment that has to be made available, the staff who have to be employed and the training that has to be provided. These costs have to be weighed against the impact such a decision will have on the size of the queues in the store and the length of time that customers have to wait. What is clearly required is some sort of analytical approach to assist the manager in reaching a decision about whether to bring additional checkouts into use and if so how many. Even so, the decision as to how many checkouts to have open will to some extent still remain a subjective one.

It is not difficult to see that in reality the problem would be much more complex than the one we have described. Patterns of customer behaviour are likely to complicate matters: the fact that the store will be busier at some times of the day than at others, will be busier on some days than on others, that the number of customers will not only vary during the day/between days but also be uncertain and so on. We face a technically complex situation. It may also have occurred to you that even if we can develop a suitable quantitative model for such a situation the model is unlikely to be able to produce an optimal solution, simply because, from the manager's perspective, there will be no ideal solution to the problem. From the customers' viewpoint, of course, the ideal solution is to ensure there are sufficient checkouts in use so that a customer never has to wait for service. In practice, however, this would be too costly for the store. We can readily envisage that under such a situation many of the checkouts would be unused for large parts of the day: although customers would not have to wait for service, it is likely that checkouts would need to wait for customers! The manager, then, faces a trade-off situation: trying to reach some compromise between the amount of time customers spend in the queue and the 'waste' of resources tied up in underutilised checkouts. Even in this simple situation it is easy to see that the manager is trying to reconcile two conflicting objectives:

- minimising the time customers spend queuing
- minimising the resources the store requires.

The manager's difficulty is the absence of any hard, quantitative information about alternative trade-off positions. That is, what would happen to the length of time spent in the queue if an extra checkout were in use, or two extra checkouts, or three and so on.

This example typifies the problem that many managers in many different organisations face, a problem that is generically referred to as the *queuing problem*. In such a problem some service is provided (in our example service at a checkout). In other examples this service might relate to a service provided to a customer, a service that takes place on a production line, or a service that occurs in a stock-control system. The rate at which such a service can be provided is typically subject to variability. At the other end of the queuing system we typically have arrivals: of customers, production items, stock items, vehicles, aircraft, computer jobs and so on. Once again the rate of arrivals will be subject to variability. The manager involved then has the task of trying to balance the service rate and the arrival rate. Clearly, if the service rate is lower than the arrival rate then a queue will form: of customers at a checkout, of items on a production line, of stock items at the delivery depot. Too high a service rate and the queue disappears but the manager will be left with the resources committed to providing the service being underutilised: waiting for arrivals to serve at certain times.

In principle, of course, returning to the supermarket problem, the manager could experiment. For one week the manager could add an extra checkout to those in use and measure the effect this has on customers' queuing time, on costs, on profits and so on. A second week's experiment would have a different number of checkouts again. In principle, over time, we could then begin to see the impact different numbers of checkouts had on the key parameters of the problem. This would then help the manager assess an acceptable trade-off position between the two different objectives. It is also evident, however, that for a variety of reasons such experimentation is simply not possible in the real business world. The practicalities of such experimentation would be prohibitive. It is in situations like this that simulation models come into their own. Using principles primarily of logic and observation – and supported by computer technology – we can develop a simple descriptive model of such a situation that will, literally, simulate the situation we are keen on investigating. Effectively such a model allows us to experiment and observe the results in terms of key parameters without actually having to do such experimentation for real.

Decision-making software in the fast lane

By Alan Cane

In the heat of Formula One motor racing, success and failure are separated by hundredths of a second and a poor decision on the part of either driver or pit crew is punished immediately and irrevocably. A good decision, on the other hand, can lead to victory. In the 2005 F1 Grand Prix at Monte Carlo, Kimi Raikkonen was leading the race when an accident brought the safety car into play. Conventional wisdom at Monte Carlo, where the narrow streets make overtaking almost impossible, dictates that cars should head for the pits for refuellling and new tyres whenever the safety car is deployed. But the McLaren software said otherwise and Raikkonen continued to circulate, posting some super fast laps and eventually winning the race by a comfortable margin.

The McLaren strategists, based not at the trackside but in the company's technology centre just outside London, had just 10 seconds after the safety car was deployed to act on the various scenarios presented by the software.

Business strategists have, hopefully, a little longer to make the right decision. But the repercussions of their decisions can be just as devastating. Large pharmaceutical companies, for example, regularly spend almost a billion dollars developing a new drug and the success rate can be as low as one in 20. With such vast sums, finely judged and timely decisions can be worth small fortunes.

Here too, technology can help: "If the company can make the right decision a day earlier, it saves it $1m," says Simon Williams, chief executive of SmithBayes, a UK company that has developed software to make business decision-

making easier, faster and more accurate. What distinguishes SmithBayes Playmaker software from other decision support systems is its heritage. It was conceived and nurtured in the high-speed world of Formula One racing. It combines a number of mathematical techniques, including Monte Carlo (the casino, not the Grand Prix) simulations, with advanced visualisation.

MacLaren's engineers have been developing the software for eight years and using it to help with race strategy for six. The system is capable of analysing 8m scenarios for each race based on 3,000 variables. It recalibrates the race strategy every two seconds based on what is happening on the track and other information including, for example, informed guesses about competitors' intentions: "The whole platform embraces uncertainty rather than being based on hard data," Mr Williams says, which is why he believes it is well suited to analysing the business world. Monte Carlo methods, for example, are used when a solution depends on a large number of variables. All the big F1 teams use systems of this kind. But McLaren has gone further than the others in seeking to open its technology to business use.

"We had worked in financial markets and we saw that, over time, the pace of change meant that people that made faster, more precise decisions, held an advantage. We felt that held true across many business sectors."

Furthermore, in terms of business analysis, Mr Williams explains: "We believed it was pointless focusing on decimal places on what were essentially guesses and better to focus on flexibility and agility. As in sport, the organisations that can

respond to change with better insight, faster and with more precision have an advantage. We believe that agility will be a key element of competitive advantage for the next 10 years."

MacLaren gave SmithBayes access to its technology in exchange for a 40 per cent equity stake in the newly formed company. The motor racing group is no longer involved, however, following a management buy-out late last year, the financial details of which are not being disclosed. MacLaren will continue to use the core technology to support its racing programme but SmithBayes is entirely responsible for developing the business logic and marketing outside the motorsport arena. The underlying architecture has beeen re-engineered and rebuilt on .net3 to run on the Microsoft's Vista operating system.

So who could make use of the software? Customers are unwilling to be named because of the competitive advantage they hope the system will yield but any big company facing difficult business decisions based on inadequate data could benefit, Mr Williams says, giving as an example an aerospace manufacturer planning a new engine with four technical options to choose between.

"This is a big decision. The company is betting on a technological horse today that will have an impact on its engine development cycle for 10 years; the engines themselves will be on aeroplanes for a further 30 years, so it's a 40-year business decision." Mr Williams says that, for a 5 per cent price premium, the SmithBayes software provides a way to keep a final decision on three of the four technologies open for three years.

SmithBayes says it has four large customers and two smaller ones after six months or so of marketing. The system costs £50,000 a year for the core application plus £1,000 a month per seat. Customers are typically opting for five to six seats to begin with, representing an expenditure of about £100,000-£120,000 a year – small beer if the software brings the claimed advantages.

McLaren, meanwhile, is fine-tuning the core technology to continue to support its race strategies. But computers don't win races on their own. After a poor 2006, it must be hoping that its drivers, current world champion Fernando Alonso and rookie Lewis Hamilton, will be equal to the challenge.

Source: *Financial Times*, 28 February 2007.

Simulation is seen by some organisations as a key competitive edge.

Business Example

To illustrate the principles and to help us develop a specific model we shall consider the following problem in detail. The manager of a local hospital is under pressure from patients, medical staff and politicians to extend the range of medical services offered to the local population. The problem, as ever, is one of limited and scarce resources and these must be prioritised. One particular medical service is currently under serious evaluation. The typical situation encountered by the hospital is as follows. An individual may visit his or her family doctor or general practitioner (GP). After an initial examination the GP may decide to refer the patient to the hospital, where he or she can be examined by an appropriate specialist and where use can be made, as necessary, of specialist equipment. Typically, the patient will be referred to the hospital by the GP and will stay in the hospital a few days until the appropriate examinations and tests have been completed. On completion of the examinations, the patient will typically be discharged as not at risk or will be moved to another part of the hospital to await specialist treatment.

The hospital manager is currently trying to assess how many beds to make available for this particular unit. Naturally, this will be only one of many related decisions about resource allocation but it will enable us to focus easily on the principles of the simulation model. Some limited information has been obtained on the number of patients per day likely to be referred to the unit. This information is shown in Table 14.1.

This indicates that, on any given day, the unit could expect up to four new patients to be admitted. Also shown are the percentage frequencies associated with each number

Table 14.1	Patient referrals per day

No. of patients	Percentage frequency
0	30
1	25
2	20
3	15
4	10

Table 14.2	Patients' length of stay

Length of stay (days)	Percentage frequency
1	10
2	10
3	30
4	30
5	10
6	10

of patients. So, for example, there is a probability of 30 per cent that on any given day no new patients will be admitted and a probability of 10 per cent that four new patients will be admitted. Naturally, from the manager's perspective, this variable is beyond control – the decision to refer a patient is taken by the GP, not by the manager (you will realise that this is the same situation the supermarket manager faces in terms of how many customers will use the store at any one time). Similar information is available on the length of time patients stay in the unit before discharge (either back home or to another part of the hospital for treatment). This is shown in Table 14.2.

We see that length of stay could be anywhere between one and six days. Once again this variable is beyond the control of the manager – it will be a medical decision made by the specialist.

We now see clearly the problem facing the manager regarding the decision over how many beds to put into the unit. On the one hand, if too many beds are made available then it is likely that some of these will remain unused for long periods – a waste of scarce resources. On the other hand, too few beds and the unit will run the risk of having all beds in use when another patient is referred and not being able to cope with that patient. In fact this situation is typical of many to which simulation is applied and is often referred to, logically, as a queuing problem. The problem is clearly compounded by the uncertainty over the number of patients that could be expected on any one day and over the length of time they will need to stay in the unit. It is also evident that there will not be any ideal solution to the manager's dilemma as to how many beds to make available, only compromise and subjective preference. What the manager is lacking is information on the likely consequences of alternative decisions.

Activity 14.3

From the two tables calculate the mean number of arrivals per day and the mean length of stay. How could this information be used to decide how many beds to have in the unit? What problems would using this approach have?

Developing the Simulation Model

Clearly, we could use basic statistical information to try to help us with this problem. The mean number of arrivals per day is calculated at 1.5 and the mean length of stay at 3.5 days. We might be tempted simply to multiply the two together – to get 5.25 – and say that five or six beds would be adequate on average. The problem with this of course relates to the consequences of the arrival rate or the service rate not being average. All we would need in such a situation is to have three or four days when we have an above-average number of arrivals or three or four days when we have a below-average rate of service and we would have problems. We might also think about trying to use the variability information – perhaps through a standard deviation – although again it is not clear how this could be done. The simulation approach is to try to develop a descriptive model which will mimic the behaviour of the unit.

In order to develop the model for use we need to describe accurately the key elements of the process for this problem – remember that a simulation model is descriptive in essence. For this unit we might describe the situation in a number of stages. Before doing so it will usually be necessary to decide on a set of 'rules' that govern key parts of the process. In practice these will already be in place for the particular problem under examination. In our case we will impose the following rules:

- any patient due for normal discharge from the unit is discharged at the start of the day;
- new patients seeking admission to the unit do so at the start of the day;
- if a new patient seeks admission and the unit is full then an existing patient is moved to an adjacent unit. The patient who will be moved in this way will be the patient who is scheduled for the earliest discharge.

These 'rules' are to some extent arbitrary and we could develop a marginally different simulation model if we allowed different rules to operate. They will suffice for our purpose, however, as they allow us to describe the operation of the unit in the following sequence of events.

1 The unit 'opens' at the start of the day.
2 Patients due for discharge leave the unit.
3 Any new patients are admitted to the unit.
4 If empty beds are available new patients are allocated to them.
5 If empty beds are not available, existing patients are discharged early to an adjacent non-specialist ward. These beds are then used for new patients.
6 The unit 'closes' at the end of the day.

What we have is a simple verbal description of the operation of the unit. The purpose of this verbal description is to provide a detailed – and hopefully realistic – description of the sequence of events in this situation. Clearly, in this example we have a simple process to describe. The more complex the situation under investigation, the more complex and detailed the description will need to be. The key point is that the description should represent accurately the stages of the service process.

A Simulation Flowchart

It may also be desirable – and for larger simulation models essential – to show this process in diagrammatic form through a simulation flowchart. Such a flowchart is shown in Figure 14.1. The diagram will need careful consideration but it shows the sequencing of key events and activities and the decisions that need to be taken at various stages of the process. The flowchart represents the process of the management

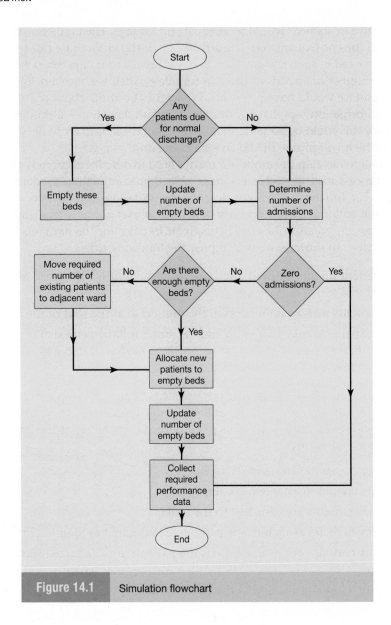

Figure 14.1   Simulation flowchart

of the unit for one day. The flowchart starts at the beginning of the day. Note that conventionally the oval shape is used to denote the start and end events. We then assess whether any existing patient is scheduled for normal discharge today (remember the rules we imposed earlier). If the answer is 'yes', then we need to empty these beds and keep track of how many empty beds we now have. If the answer is 'no', then clearly these actions are not required. Note again that conventionally we use a diamond-shaped box whenever a 'decision' takes place (or a question has to be answered) and a square box to denote some action being taken. We then move to determine the number of admissions today. If we have zero admissions then effectively the simulation for that day is at an end. If we do have some number of admissions, however, we first need to check if we have sufficient empty beds for these admissions. If the answer is 'yes', we allocate patients to empty beds and update the information we have about beds still vacant (for use at the start of the next day's simulation). If the answer is 'no' then we must effect the policy of moving existing patients to an adjacent ward to free up sufficient beds for the new admissions. Finally, no matter which route we took through the flowchart we need to collect data on the performance of the unit during today before ending today's simulation. Clearly we can then repeat this process for the next day and the next and so on.

The amount of detail we show in the flowchart is to some extent subjective, as long as it serves to describe accurately the process in the model. Like the network diagrams we introduced in Chapter 13, simulation flowcharts can take some getting used to but they are an excellent way of both describing a situation and indeed checking that we have got the description right (since if we find ourselves going down part of the flowchart we did not expect, it signifies the flowchart does not model the situation accurately). We can now begin to use the sequencing detailed in the flowchart to use the model and to start to generate management information.

Activity 14.4

Consider the last action in the flowchart of collecting performance data. What measures of performance would you want data collected for?

QMDM IN ACTION
Cap Gemini Ernst & Young – simulating airport management

Cap Gemini Ernst & Young's client was an airport operator. The client had initiated a major programme to investigate the use of IT throughout the business. Part of the project involved examining and improving the passenger 'experience'. As we all know from our own experiences as passengers, at an airport passengers have to move through several different stages or processes: parking the car, checking in, passport control, etc. Some of these processes are the responsibility of the client, and some are the responsibility of other businesses such as the airlines using the airport. The client was interested in simulating the passenger flow through the airport to allow it to investigate the effect that changes to the various processes might have.

A simulation model of the airport processes from the passengers' perspective was developed using specialist simulation software.

Cap Gemini Ernst & Young developed a simulation model for the key processes. The model was designed from the outset as a management support tool and the visual aspects of the model were impor-

tant in this respect. The model allowed for various process inputs to be set, such as passenger arrival rates, availability of key resources and process or throughput times, so that the effect of resourcing decisions could be investigated. The model allows managers to visualise (and quantify) the impact of decisions such as opening or closing additional check-in facilities or passport control desks. In addition, the model allows managers to identity those parts of the airport system where delays occur because of a mis-match between passenger flows and resource availability.

The figure on the next page shows a screen shot from the simulation model. The screen shows the arrival of passengers at the check-in area, where two airlines are processing passengers.

The benefits are as follows:

- A management tool to test 'what-if' scenarios for airport resource management.
- The ability to assess the effect of changes in key variables such as passenger growth and technology improvement on passenger flow.

● Demonstrating the importance of seeing the business as a complete set of inter-related processes.

I am grateful to Cap Gemini Ernst & Young for permission to use this case study and to reproduce the figure shown. Further case study applications are available through their website: www.uk.capgemini.com/services/consulting/or/success_stories Copyright is held by Cap Gemini Ernst & Young.

Using the Model

Before we can begin to use the model we must consider what information the manager will want from it. In this case we shall assume that two key performance measures are required:

● the level of utilisation of the resources, beds, over the period of the simulation;
● the rate at which existing patients were discharged early from the unit because of shortage of beds.

and that in addition we shall want data on:

● the number of admissions over time;
● patients' length of stay over time.

In practice of course the information required might be far more detailed than this. We shall also assume that the manager has already decided that somewhere between five and ten beds will be allocated to the unit. We therefore require the model to simulate these alternatives and generate information on the likely consequences – in terms of our performance measures – from each simulation. Let us see how we can use the model to simulate the unit's performance with five beds.

It is evident that we will need to simulate two key characteristics: the rate of daily admissions to the unit and the rate of daily discharges. As far as the manager is concerned, both of these events are variable and – within the limits set – are unpredictable. Consider the manager's position in terms of admissions. At the start of any given day the manager has literally no idea how many patients will seek admission (apart from knowing that it must be between zero and four). However, in the long run, the manager does expect the distribution of admissions to follow that shown in Table 14.1. The same logic applies to the length of stay of patients. It seems that somehow we should be able to use the probability information to help simulate this situation, although it may not be clear how.

The use of random numbers

In fact we simulate the variability in key variables through the use of what are known as *random numbers*. Consider the approach we could take for determining the number of admissions on a particular day. We could take 100 slips of paper and on each write one number from 1 to 100. If we put these slips into a bag we could then choose entirely at random one slip of paper from all those available. If the slip of paper had a number in the range 1 to 30 (since there is a probability of 0.3 from Table 14.1 that there are no admissions on a particular day) we could assume that zero patients were admitted that day; if it had 31 to 55, that one patient was admitted, and so on for the rest of the distribution. Clearly, in the long run, we would expect the number of slips of paper we drew from the bag which fell into each category to follow the probability pattern (assuming that we replaced the slip of paper in the bag after use). We could also undertake a similar process for determining the length of stay of patients once admitted.

Although this approach is logical, it is somewhat tedious and time-consuming. We can replicate this process, however, in one of two ways. We can use pre-calculated tables of random numbers or we can obtain random numbers directly from a computer system. Effectively what both these methods do is mimic the process of us choosing a slip of paper at random. Such a set of computer-generated random numbers is shown in Table 14.3.

By definition the sequence of numbers in the table is entirely random and shows no pattern. There are a few points we need to make about the use of such tables before proceeding.

- We can start to use the table from any point. We do not have to start with the top-left corner but could start from anywhere in the table.

- When using such tables, in order to ensure complete randomness we must use the numbers in strict sequence. That is, if we started at the top-left corner (although we could decide to start anywhere in the table) with 90, we must move in sequence either by row or by column. We cannot jump about the table for the next random number needed.

- We should use a separate, and different, table for each variable in the problem we want to simulate. However, to keep things simple for our purposes we shall use just

Table 14.3		Random numbers							
90	5	62	24	73	50	13	27	86	6
7	78	18	44	51	70	99	82	77	36
67	87	7	25	47	61	15	72	68	69
77	21	29	91	20	38	78	60	27	13
6	36	25	48	91	80	11	38	33	20
46	78	70	13	92	6	91	40	55	80
20	9	87	48	56	20	11	87	62	2
65	6	0	62	57	53	86	10	78	30
2	5	16	39	36	27	10	59	13	89
13	90	20	24	48	22	73	53	59	64

the one table for both admissions and length of stay. We shall start admissions at the top-left corner with 90 and move down the column. For length of stay we shall start at the bottom-right corner with 64 and move up the column.

● To keep the random numbers to two digits (rather than three) the first possible random number is zero. This means we can expect numbers to occur between 0 and 99. The corresponding tables for admissions and length of stay will then be as shown in Tables 14.4 and 14.5 respectively.

Beginning the simulation

We are now in a position to begin the simulation, following the structure of the flow-chart. Remember that we are assessing the performance of the unit with five beds. At the start of the simulation, therefore, all five beds will be empty and we will have no patients for discharge that day. We now need to simulate the number of patients being admitted on Day 1, and to do this we must use the random numbers shown in the table. From the selected starting point of the table for admissions we have a random number of 90. From Table 14.4 we see that this corresponds to four patients admitted on that day. Since we have five empty beds we can allocate each of these four patients

Table 14.4	Admissions and random number range	
No. of patients	Percentage frequency	Random number range
0	30	00–29
1	25	30–54
2	20	55–74
3	15	75–89
4	10	90–99

Table 14.5	Length of stay and random number range	
Length of stay (days)	Percentage frequency	Random number range
1	10	00–09
2	10	10–19
3	30	20–49
4	30	50–79
5	10	80–89
6	10	90–99

to one empty bed. This leaves us with one empty bed and brings us to the end of Day 1. To summarise we then have at the end of Day 1:

Bed 1 Occupied
Bed 2 Occupied
Bed 3 Occupied
Bed 4 Occupied
Bed 5 Empty
4 patients admitted
0 patients discharged early

Before proceeding to simulate Day 2 we will make a slight alteration to the flowchart. We will now simulate the length of stay required for each patient at the time of their admission. Clearly this is not what would happen in practice but it will make the simulation more manageable and it will not actually affect any results. We require four random numbers for the four patients and these will be 64, 89, 30 and 2. Using these in turn for the four patients we then have:

Day 1

	Length of stay	Due for discharge beginning of day
Bed 1 Occupied	4 days	5
Bed 2 Occupied	5 days	6
Bed 3 Occupied	3 days	4
Bed 4 Occupied	1 day	2
Bed 5 Empty		

4 patients admitted
0 patients discharged early

We can now move on to simulate Day 2. We start this by checking whether any existing patients are scheduled for discharge (remember the decision rule that discharges would take place at the start of the day). The patient in Bed 4 is due for discharge (admitted on Day 1 for one day). So we know that on Day 2 we will have two beds available for any new patients. To simulate arrivals we take the next random number in sequence, 7, which equates to zero admissions on Day 2. The position at the end of Day 2 is then:

Day 2

	Length of stay	Due for discharge beginning of day
Bed 1 Occupied	4 days	5
Bed 2 Occupied	5 days	6
Bed 3 Occupied	3 days	4
Bed 4 Empty		
Bed 5 Empty		

4 patients admitted
0 patients discharged early

The position for Day 3 follows the same logic. There are no discharges due today and the next random number, 67, indicates two admissions and that they will stay for five and three days respectively (using the random numbers 80 and 20 respectively). We then have:

Day 3

	Length of stay	Due for discharge beginning of day
Bed 1 Occupied	4 days	5
Bed 2 Occupied	5 days	6
Bed 3 Occupied	3 days	4
Bed 4 Occupied	5 days	8
Bed 5 Occupied	3 days	6

6 patients admitted
0 patients discharged early

At the end of Day 3 the unit is full, although one patient is scheduled for discharge at the start of Day 4. On Day 4 we encounter a capacity problem for the first time. Three patients require admission today (random number 77) but we have only one free bed, Bed 3. Accordingly we must implement the specified policy of moving two existing patients to other wards; freeing Beds 1 and 2. The three new patients have a scheduled length of stay of two, four and three days respectively. At the end of Day 4 we then have:

Day 4

	Length of stay	Due for discharge beginning of day
Bed 1 Occupied	2 days	6
Bed 2 Occupied	4 days	8
Bed 3 Occupied	3 days	7
Bed 4 Occupied	5 days	8
Bed 5 Occupied	3 days	6

9 patients admitted
2 patients discharged early

The principles of the simulation approach are also becoming evident. As we progress on a day-by-day basis we simulate arrivals and discharges as they might happen in real life. This allows us to assess the impact of a particular decision – having five beds – on the performance criteria.

Activity 14.5

Complete the simulation for Days 5 to 10. When using the random number table for arrivals, jump to the top of the next column to continue, and for discharges jump to the bottom of the next column.

By the end of Day 10 we have the following situation:

Day 10

	Length of stay	Due for discharge beginning of day
Bed 1 Occupied	4 days	12
Bed 2 Empty		
Bed 3 Empty		
Bed 4 Empty		
Bed 5 Empty		

12 patients admitted
2 patients discharged early

It is also evident that as we progress through the simulation we can determine the use of beds on a day-by-day basis. Any day a bed remains unoccupied is effectively a waste of that resource. Similarly, we can monitor our other key measure of performance: the rate at which patients were discharged early because there were no empty beds for new admissions. Although the manual simulation process is not difficult, it is tedious, and it is clear that we would require the simulation to cover several hundred, perhaps thousand, days before we regard the results as a reliable indicator of what might happen in the real world. (In fact the comparison between simulation and taking a sample of observations in statistical inference is a valid one.) Clearly, in practice, simulation has to be undertaken by using one of the specialist simulation packages that are available or building an appropriate model in a spreadsheet. Table 14.6 shows the results of such a simulation on this problem.

The computer simulation was run for 1000 days with five beds available. The information provided shows the following:

- The total number of patients admitted over this period. This would provide the manager with an indication of demand and would also indicate the trend of demand in the context of the information in Table 14.1.

- The average number of patients admitted. Although this is simply 1401/1000 it also serves as a check on the randomness of the simulation process. Remember from Table 14.1 the probability distribution in terms of patient arrivals. This has a mean number of patients per day of 1.5, which we would expect the simulation to approach. In this instance we see that the mean number of patients in the simulation is slightly below the 'population' mean.

Table 14.6	Computer simulation results

End of this simulation with five beds available for 1000 days

Total number of patients admitted	1401
Mean number of patients admitted per day	1.40
Total number of patient days required	4869
Mean length of stay (days)	3.48
Mean bed occupancy	79%
Number of early discharges	584
As % of total admissions	42%

● The total number of patient days required. This is the total length of stay for all patients and could provide the manager with information on staffing levels required in the unit.

● Mean length of stay in the simulation is 3.48 days. Again from Table 14.2 we would expect this to approach 3.5 in the long run.

● Mean percentage bed occupancy at 79 per cent. This is an indication of the level of utilisation of the key resource under investigation.

● Early discharges were 584 patients. Although bed occupancy at 79 per cent gives the impression of spare capacity, it is now clear that there were frequent occurrences when the unit was full and existing patients had to be moved to adjacent wards.

● As a percentage of total admissions we see that early discharges were 42 per cent.

It is evident from this example that simulation is an extremely useful source of information – information that may not be available from any other source. To reinforce the use of simulation, however, it is also clear that the model does not suggest a solution to the manager's problem of how many beds to allocate to the unit. The manager must decide whether the trade-off between bed occupancy and early discharges – at 79 per cent and 42 per cent respectively – is acceptable. What is also clear is that the manager would wish to see comparable results for the other available options: six beds through to ten beds. Once again such information is readily generated from the simulation model. The only amendment we require is to increase bed capacity from five to six, then to seven and so on.

Activity 14.6

In the context of the two key performance criteria – percentage bed occupancy and percentage of early discharges – what would you expect to happen to these two values if we increase the number of beds to six?

Table 14.7 shows the summary results for all the bed options obtained from the computer simulation. It is evident that as we increase the number of beds available then we see an improvement in the percentage of patients discharged early: this falls from 42 per cent for five beds to 2 per cent for ten beds. However, we see a marked – and

Table 14.7	Computer simulation results					
	5 beds	*6 beds*	*7 beds*	*8 beds*	*9 beds*	*10 beds*
Total number of patients admitted	1401	1483	1455	1516	1434	1478
Mean number of patients admitted per day	1.40	1.48	1.46	1.52	1.43	1.48
Total number of patient days required	4869	5217	5085	5287	4955	5174
Mean length of stay (days)	3.48	3.52	3.49	3.49	3.46	3.50
Mean bed occupancy	79%	76%	68%	63%	54%	51%
Number of early discharges	584	471	253	162	47	23
As % of total admissions	42%	32%	17%	11%	3%	2%

simultaneous – deterioration in the other measure of performance. Percentage bed occupancy falls from 79 per cent to 51 per cent. Once again we must stress that simulation is basically a what-if model. It does not indicate which of the bed options is 'optimal' but simply quantifies the likely outcomes of alternative decisions. However, it is also clear that the manager is now in a far better position to rationalise the decision that must be taken.

Although such simulated outcomes are not guaranteed, we know the likely results of the alternative decisions for this situation, and the manager can assess qualitatively the trade-off that will be acceptable. It can also be instructive to show the results of such simulations graphically when they have been repeated many times. Clearly, if we repeated the simulation for five beds we would expect similar but not identical results (just as would happen in real life). Figure 14.2 shows the results of repeating

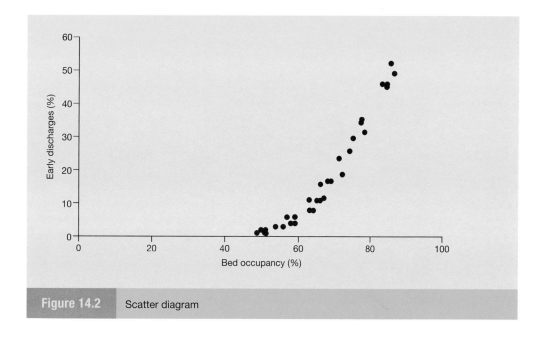

| Figure 14.2 | Scatter diagram |

the simulation of each bed option five times and plotting the results for the two performance criteria in a scatter diagram. The (non-linear) relationship between the two parameters is clearly shown and it is evident that the manager could use this to assist decision making, as it enables us to quantify the expected trade-off between the two objectives. For example, we see from the diagram that a bed occupancy performance of 80 per cent is linked to an early discharge performance of around 40 per cent. If the manager is under pressure to reduce the early discharges, say to 20 per cent, it is evident that, other things being equal, this will require additional resources (more beds) and that the consequence of this will be a reduction in bed occupancy to around 70 per cent.

Worked Example

A large utility company (electricity, gas, telecoms) based in Scotland is reviewing its customer service strategy. Although many of its domestic customers pay their utility bills indirectly through banks and by post, a considerable number still prefer to pay directly at one of the company offices. The company has been considering for some time whether it should offer a drive-in pay facility at selected sites: that is, establishing a system whereby customers can drive up to a special kiosk, hand over their bill and a cheque for payment, be issued with a receipt and then drive away, all without leaving the car. Under consideration is the establishment of a number of these kiosks at a number of company sites and the operation of this drive-in system from 4.30 pm to 6 pm each weekday – peak travel times during the afternoon/evening, a time that the marketing director thinks will be popular for this type of facility.

The provisional design of the pay-in facility will provide an off-street area where cars can queue while waiting for service at the kiosk, and the kiosk itself. The intended system and its layout are shown in Figure 14.3. Cars will enter from the public road, form a queue waiting for service (if necessary), take their turn at paying their bill and then exit back onto the public road.

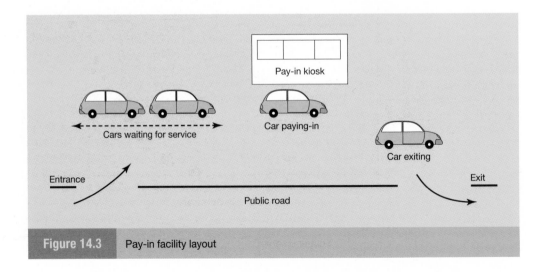

| Figure 14.3 | Pay-in facility layout |

Some initial data has been obtained relating to the likely number of cars that can be expected during this 90-minute period and the time it is likely to take to serve each car/customer at the kiosk.

No. of cars arriving in any one-minute period	Probability
0	0.55
1	0.33
2	0.10
3	0.02
4	0

Time taken to serve a customer/car (minutes)	Probability
up to 1	0.81
1 to under 2	0.14
2 to under 3	0.04
3 to under 4	0.01
over 4	0

The first set of data shows the expected number of cars arriving in any given one-minute period. This data has been obtained through a mixture of market research and observing similar drive-ins at other organisations (such as burger bars). There is some concern about the reliability and accuracy of this data, given that this would be a completely new venture for the company. The second set of data shows how long it is expected to take to service each car that arrives at the kiosk. This data is seen as more reliable, since it is based on the company's own performance at its traditional paying-in offices. Another area of concern relates to the amount of space this facility will physically take up. At some sites the amount of space available for vehicles queuing while waiting for service is limited, and the local managers have indicated that they do not want to be faced with a problem of cars queuing back onto the public road. Not only will this cause annoyance to other passing motorists (with subsequent adverse perceptions of the company), it might also get the company into trouble with the local police. We have been asked to advise on the initiative.

Given the uncertainties that exist over arrivals, service times and possible queue lengths, it appears that simulation would offer a useful management approach to the situation. Not only would this allow us to simulate the existing initiative in terms of its overall performance, we could do some what-if analysis on the two data distributions (arrivals and service times) and we could also simulate the performance of different designs – for example that of a two-kiosk operation. Clearly, any sensible simulation will need to be computer-based, but we might wish to explain the principles, so that management are aware of the approach, using a few iterations of a manual approach. Using the random numbers from Table 14.3, say Row 6 for arrivals and Column 10 for service times, we would simulate the first 10 minutes of the operation as shown in Table 14.8.

Over this first 10 minutes, eight cars have used the service, each of them taking up to one minute to be served. The maximum number of cars in the queue (waiting for an earlier car to finish paying and exit) was one. Naturally, all we are trying to do with this data is ensure the principles of the simulation approach are understood by the relevant managers, so that they are then in a position to understand, and evaluate, the output we get from a computer-based simulation. The output from this is shown in Table 14.9.

We see that two simulations have been run: one for the single kiosk situation we have described, the second for a scenario where we have two kiosks in operation but still only one queue of cars. From the first simulation we have output which is helpful

Table 14.8	Simulation of first 10 minutes

Minute	No. of cars arriving	Size of queue on arrival	Time taken to service
1	0	0	–
2	1	0	1
3	1	0	1
4	0	0	–
5	2	0	1
6	0	1	1
7	2	0	1
8	0	1	1
9	1	0	1
10	1	1	1

Table 14.9	Computer simulation output for 2500 days

	Simulation Single kiosk queue	Simulation 2 Two kiosks, single queue
Mean no. of cars in the system	3.0	0.87
Mean time in the system	5 minutes	1.45 minutes
Mean time in the queue	3.75 minutes	0.20 minutes
Probability of waiting in a queue	0.75	0.21
Mean time taken to pay bill	1.24 minutes	1.26 minutes
Maximum queue size	7	2
Mean no. of cars per 90-minute period	55	56

in evaluating the impact of this initiative. We see that with a single kiosk the maximum size of queue we have encountered is seven. Given management concern about the available space for queuing cars, this will help them evaluate any potential problems with cars queuing on the adjacent public road. If necessary we could also obtain output from the simulation in terms of the frequency of this queue size occurring (after all, this queue size might have occurred only once in the course of the whole simulation run – some 2500 days of 90 minutes per day). We also see that, on average, a car will be 'in the system' for five minutes. ('In the system' effectively means from the time it arrives to the time it exits, so includes both queuing time and time being served.) Again, management can evaluate whether they feel that customers might think this is too long to wait and so may be deterred from using the new system. We also see that of this five minutes some 3.75 minutes will be spent waiting their turn for the kiosk with the remainder of the time spent actually being served. We also see that there is a probability of 0.75 that a car will have to queue before service (i.e. that the kiosk is not free when the car arrives at the site). Again, management might wish to take some subjective view as to whether the fact that three-quarters of cars will not get immediate service is likely to be detrimental. We can also infer from this that the kiosk will be busy 75 per cent of the time (as will the member of staff inside the kiosk) and hence the member of staff concerned will be 'unused' 25 per cent of the time on average or for 22 minutes out of the 90 each day. Again, management might wish to consider the efficiency implications of this. Finally, we see that an average of 55 cars per 90-minute period each day are likely to use the new system. Given that we can quantify the likely cost to the company of the new initiative, again management can assess whether the cost is worthwhile in terms of the customer benefit.

The simulation output from a situation where we have two kiosks providing service shows some results which are similar and some which are quite different. We note, for example, that the average number of cars per 90-minute period is effectively the same (after all the arrival rate of cars has not changed). Similarly, the average time taken to serve each car is also about the same (since this has not changed either). What has changed are the other performance statistics. The maximum queue size has dropped sharply from seven to two, while the total time each car typically spends in the system has also fallen sharply from five minutes to 1.45 minutes (with the time spent actually queuing falling from 3.75 minutes to only 0.20 minutes). Similarly the probability of a car arriving and having to queue has fallen from 0.75 to 0.20. Adding an extra kiosk has dramatically altered the performance we can offer the customer, with (almost) instantaneous service being available. Again, management would have to decide whether this service improvement was cost-effective. We could also advise management that, based on the simulation, it looks highly unlikely that any increase in kiosks beyond two would be worthwhile in terms of reducing waiting time further (since service time would remain unaffected).

Hedge funds eye glamour of movie land

Matthew Garrahan in Los Angeles

Aside from the size of their respective bank balances and a shared fondness for extravagant cars, Hollywood film executives and hedge fund managers would seem to have little in common. After all, hedge funds like to invest in volatile quoted vehicles whereas Hollywood studios put their money into film franchises that can be exploited by their quoted parents. But after a spate of deals that have seen private equity and hedge funds pour money into film production "slates", the two industries are increasingly finding common ground.

The latest example of Hollywood courting the world of high-margin investment came this week when the Paramount studio, a subsidiary of Viacom, struck a $300m financing deal with Dresdner Kleinwort, the investment bank. Under the agreement, Dresdner arranged the funding, which mostly came from hedge-fund and private equity investors. The deal followed similar slate arrangements between rival studios and financial partners, with Warner Brothers, Fox and Universal among those to have bought in outside backers.

Co-financing is not a new phenomenon. High net worth individuals keen on a slice of Hollywood glamour have long associated themselves with the industry by funding film productions. But the interest shown by hedge funds and private equity firms is relatively new, and has been driven on by the need for those investors to find new homes for excess cash. "Private equity and hedge funds are awash with capital and are looking to invest in different asset classes," says Laura Fazio, managing director and head of media, global banking, at Dresdner Kleinwort.

Hollywood has never been an easy place to make money. Over-paid stars, poor accounting practices and box-office flops have historically been enough to deter seasoned financial investors. However, investing in a slate of films helps investors offset the risk of backing a box-office dud. "[Hedge funds and private equity] look at a slate as a portfolio investment, similar to investing in a basket of stocks," says Bill Block, chief executive of QED, which sells and distributes film projects in the US and in international markets.

When the average cost of a film was $40m, says Ms Fazio, co-financing "wasn't as high a priority. But with average budgets having grown to $75m, studios have been more motivated to bring in outside financing partners. Most of the studios are releasing 8–16 films a year which represents a sizeable capital investment."

Like other deals, though, returns will be determined by the success of the films on the slate. Relativity Media, a broker, has enjoyed success with its two Gun Hill Road funds. The first fund raised $600m for investment in 18 projects being developed by Sony Pictures Entertainment and Universal Pictures. An additional $700m was raised for Gun Hill Road II.

The marriages between hedge funds and Hollywood have not always worked, however. Warner Bros' recent $530m six-picture deal with Virtual Studios, a hedge fund backed vehicle, produced Poseidon, the year's biggest box-office flop. Equity holders in the movie are believed to have had the value of their investments written down to zero. Other deals have also struggled. Legendary Pictures, founded by Thomas Tull, whose background is in private equity, invested in Warners' Superman Returns, The Lady in the Water and The Ant Bully. All three films produced below-par box-office returns.

But such setbacks have not deterred risk-loving hedge funds. Using a computer model known as a Monte Carlo simulation, fund managers can analyse data from historical slates to estimate returns from unmade films.

Source: *Financial Times*, 9 October 2006.

Even Hollywood makes use of business simulation!

Summary

In this chapter we have introduced the principles of simulation modelling as an aid to decision making. We have seen that simulation models are descriptive and frequently based on logic rather than mathematics. They can produce information on the likely outcomes from alternative decisions. As such they can be particularly useful to management when multiple objectives, or qualitative objectives, are being sought. Because the models are built primarily on logic and a description of the key elements of the problem, they can prove attractive to management and decision makers who are unfamiliar with formal quantitative models.

Simulation is a very flexible model and has been developed and applied across a variety of business problems. It is evident from the simple example used in this chapter that the model could readily be developed to become more complex, and hence realistic.

We could add staffing levels to the model, budget allocations, equipment and the like. Equally we could use such a simulation model to assess the impact of changes in the arrival and service rates brought about by some separate management initiative. For example, we might be able to introduce some sort of appointments system for certain patients which might affect the arrivals distribution. The simulation model would allow us to quantify the effects of this on our performance parameters. Equally, medical specialists may be considering altering their diagnosis and treatment methods, which will have a knock-on effect on the service rate (the length of stay).

In one sense, the usefulness of simulation is limited only by the extent to which our imagination and knowledge limit our ability to develop a realistic descriptive model of some situation. One of the difficulties in using this approach, however, is that it requires the use of computer resources and, in many cases, the support of a computer specialist to help develop the computer model to generate the information required. Although considerable progress has been made in this area – to the extent that you no longer need a working knowledge of computer programming as such – the degree of computer-modelling skills needed is still at a high level. One interesting development has been that of the availability of what is known as 'visual interactive simulation', which makes use of the potential graphics capabilities of modern computer technology to use symbols and graphics to mimic the process under investigation rather than the use of statistics and probability distributions.

Useful online resources

Detailed below are some internet resources that may be useful. Many have further links to other sites. An updated version is available from the accompanying website (**www.pearsoned.co.uk/wisniewski**). In addition, I would be grateful for details of other websites that have been found to be useful.

> **www.scs.org/** – The Society for Modelling Simulation International
> **www.simul8.com/** – Simul8
> **www.solver.com/simulation/monte-carlo-simulation/tutorial.htm** – Simulation tutorial

QMDM IN ACTION
University Hospital of Wales

Regardless of the quality of health care provided, a trip to a hospital in the UK can be a particularly traumatic experience. This has little to do directly with concerns about medical treatment, diagnosis of an illness or medical matters in general, but rather with the fundamental question: will I be able to get a parking place? Most people who have visited a hospital – either as a patient or as a visitor – will doubtless know of the frustrations of trying to find a convenient parking place. A large number of such hospitals were built to cater for a geographical distribution of the population that has since changed markedly: the reason why many older hospitals are located in city and town centres where space generally is at a premium. Even many of the more 'modern' hospitals were built at a time when private cars were not creating the problems they are at present.

The University Hospital of Wales is an out-of-town hospital with 800 beds, typically with around 750 in-patients, up to 1000 people as out-patients on an average weekday and around 4000 working on the site. Although it was built in 1970, much of the hospital design – particularly car park provision – was planned in the late 1950s so it is perhaps not surprising that with only around 1500 car parking places, problems arise. A detailed study was conducted on the traffic using the site. The purpose of the study was to identify arrival patterns and length-of-stay patterns and facilitate the development of a computer-based simulation model designed to evaluate alternative policies in terms of car parking provision. The initial investigation revealed that over 7000 vehicles entered the site per day on average,

with around 37 per cent of this traffic related to staff and around 35 per cent to patients and their visitors. Almost 13 per cent of those using the site were doing so as a short-cut en route to elsewhere. The survey also revealed very different profiles in terms of arrival times for different groups of car users.

Figure 14.4 shows the patterns of arrivals for staff, visitors to in-patients and out-patients. An ogive was also produced showing the length of stay of staff and visitors (see Figure 14.5). It can be seen that approximately 50 per cent of visitors stay less than one hour on site, whereas over 70 per cent of staff stay longer than this. These different arrival times and length-of-stay patterns have clear implications for different parking requirements of different groups. The survey data was then used as the basis for developing a

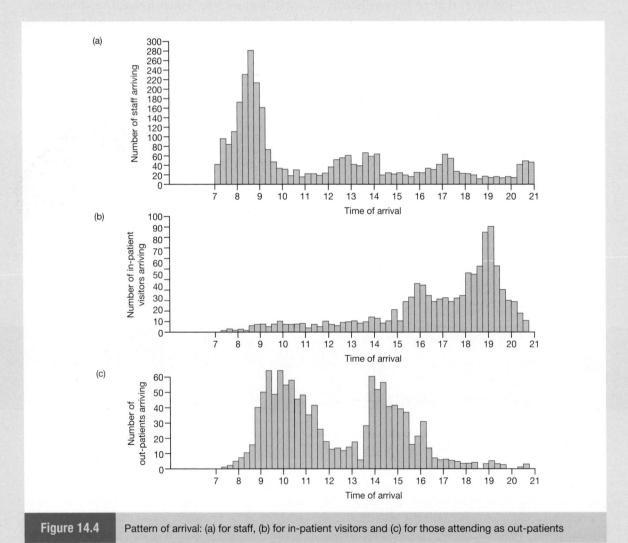

Figure 14.4   Pattern of arrival: (a) for staff, (b) for in-patient visitors and (c) for those attending as out-patients

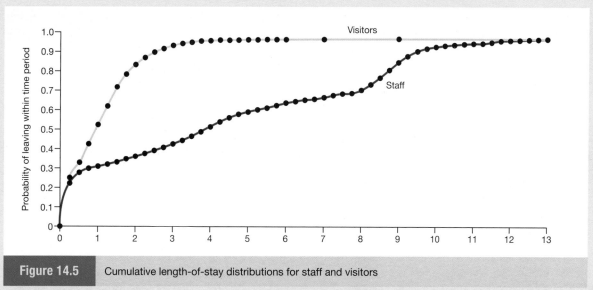

Figure 14.5   Cumulative length-of-stay distributions for staff and visitors

Taken from 'Patients, Parking and Paying', B Moores, C Bolton and A Fung, *Operational Research Insight*, **1**(2), 1988. Copyright held by the Operational Research Society.

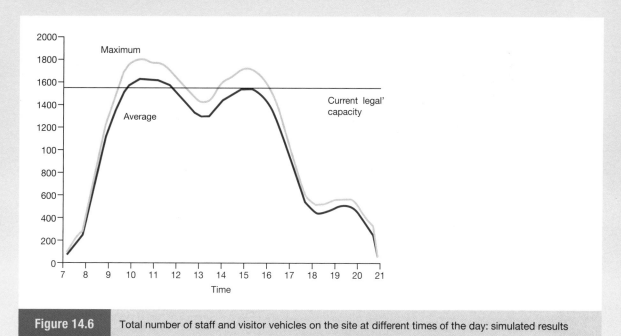

Figure 14.6   Total number of staff and visitor vehicles on the site at different times of the day: simulated results

The above application is based on the article: 'Patients, Parking and Paying', B Moores, C Bolton and A Fung, Operational Research Insight, **1***(2), 1988, pp 9–13. Copyright is held by the Operational Research Society.*

computer-based simulation. Using the arrival distributions and the length-of-stay distributions, parking behaviour on site was simulated a large number of times. From these results the pattern during the day of the average number of vehicles on site and the maximum number was produced. This is shown in Figure 14.6. The simulation reveals the overall pattern of demand for parking and the need, at certain times of the day, for additional parking capacity or for measures to restrict the inflow of vehicles onto the site. The simulation also allowed detailed 'what-if' analysis to be undertaken in terms of a financial evaluation of the impact of introducing some type of payment system for using parking facilities – an obvious attraction to a health care organisation perennially facing resource problems.

Taking the risk out of uncertainty

Risk and uncertainty are constant ingredients of business. But there are statistical ways to try to ascertain, and hence overcome, them.

By Kiriakos Vlahos

The business environment in which companies operate is becoming increasingly complex and uncertain due to the globalisation of business and the rapid introduction of new technologies. Most business decisions are taken with incomplete knowledge about how the future will evolve. For example, when a company introduces a new product, there are uncertainties about the market potential of the product, competing technologies that may be available in the future, development costs and the price that the product will command in the marketplace.

Of course companies can take a number of steps, including market research and building prototypes, to reduce the magnitude of the uncertainties. But decisions cannot be postponed indefinitely (what is often known as "analysis paralysis"), and at some point companies need to act accepting a certain level of risk. Other types of business decisions with highly uncertain returns include: ● entering a new market, for example, Russia, where currency and political risks are very large ● investment in a new plant ● choosing between R&D projects ● oil exploration ● engaging in lawsuits.

Figure 1: Merck's Market Research Model

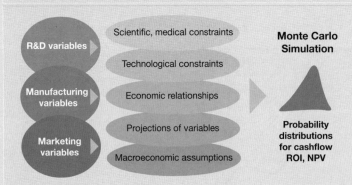

Risk analysis at Merck

Merck & Co Inc. invests about $2bn in R&D and capital expenditure annually. Most of this investment goes into long-term, risky projects that are impossible to evaluate using traditional cash flow analysis.

The reason is that the uncertainties are so wide as to make single-point estimates of the various uncertain parameters nonsensical.

Instead Merck developed sophisticated risk analysis models based on Monte Carlo simulation. These models assign probability distributions to the various input parameters and produce a range of possible outcomes in a probabilistic form.

The Research Planning Model. Bringing new drugs to the market is a very long-term and unpredictable process. Only 1 in 10,000 explored chemicals becomes a prescription drug. Development of the Research Planning Model started in 1983 and by 1989 it was used to evaluate all significant research and development projects over a 20-year horizon.

Figure 1 provides a diagrammatic explanation of the model's operation. The major inputs to the model are probability distributions of R&D, manufacturing and marketing variables. The model takes into account a number of medical and technological constraints as well as macroeconomic assumptions. It then uses simulation to compute probability distributions of the cash flow and the return on investment from specific projects.

The Revenue Hedging Model. This model helps develop hedging strategies by simulating Merck's net position and US dollar cash flows. It takes into account expenditure, local currency revenue and exchange rate projections over a five-year planning horizon.

All these inputs are expressed as probability distributions. The model then evaluates the impact of different hedging strategies and provides assessments of the currency risks that the company faces. The model is now used continually in order to fine tune the hedging programme in response to changing market conditions.

But how comfortable is senior management with the use of these and other sophisticated decision-support models? According to Judy Lewent, CFO of Merck, these models do not make decisions. Instead, they provide management with assessments of risk and return based on their (the managers') own judgments of the future developments in the market.

"Quantitative approaches do not daunt our CEO, Roy Vagelos, or other senior managers here. They don't view our models as some black box that completely ignores the great wisdom of management and tries to mechanise the decision making of the business. They understand both the potential and their limitations."

Most personal decisions also involve risk. For example, if you are considering taking an MBA, you will be faced with uncertainty about the market for MBAs a year or two down the road, the incremental benefits to your career prospects, and your ability to finance the costs.

Risk analysis

There is a big difference between *naive decision making* under uncertainty, which ignores uncertainties and is based on a single view of the future, *educated guesses*, which are based on gut feeling, and taking *calculated risks*. Risk analysis aims to achieve the last of these: to guide the decision makers into taking calculated risks. Risk analysis helps to:
● test the sensitivity of the rate-of-return/NPV calculations to the main assumptions ● identify the main uncertainty drivers, i.e. the parameters that have a make-or-break effect on the project ● calculate bounds to the possible project outcomes, allowing a foresight of circumstances that may have catastrophic consequences ● gain better perception of risks and their interactions ● think of ways of managing risks and reducing risk exposure with hedging instruments ● anticipate risks and create contingency plans.

Merck, one of the largest pharmaceutical companies in the world, uses risk analysis extensively (*see*

Figure 1). Judy Lewent, CFO of Merck, in an interview with Harvard Business Review, aptly summarised the benefits of risk analysis: "What is the payoff of all this sophistication? In short, better decisions."

Techniques

Today, managers have access to a range of techniques and tools for carrying out uncertainty and risk analysis. The main ones are briefly described below:
● *Sensitivity analysis* is the starting point for any type of uncertainty analysis. In its simplest form it involves asking "what-if" questions. For example, what if interest rates increase to 10 per cent? Or what if the market share drops to 5 per cent? Spreadsheets make it particularly easy to explore this type of question. In addition, they provide a facility for semi-automated sensitivity analysis, calculating important outputs (profit, rate-of-return, and so on) for a range of values of input parameters.

This facility is called *what-if tables* and depending on the number of inputs you may have one-way, two-way and three-way/what-if tables. As an example, in *Figure 2*, a small airline examines the sensitivity of profits to the capacity utilisation of aircraft and hours flown. More exotic ways of presenting sensitivity analysis

results have been developed, including *tornado diagrams* and *spider plots*. *Figure 3* shows an example of a tornado diagram. The aim of sensitivity is to understand and challenge the assumptions.
● *Scenario analysis* is used in different contexts with different meanings. Michael Porter in his book *Competitive Strategy* defines scenarios as "discrete, internally consistent views of how the world will look in the future, which can be selected to bound the possible range of outcomes that might occur". Although there are more profound uses of scenario analysis, in the context of risk analysis managers may try to develop a pessimistic and an optimistic view of the future and test the business project against each. This will provide a range of possible outcomes as well an opportunity to think about strategies for dealing with downturns.
● *Decision analysis*. Both sensitivity analysis and scenario analysis, in the form described above, take no account of the relative likelihood of different events. For example, a simplistic scenario analysis may provide a range of possible outcomes for profit, but it tells you nothing about how likely are particular values in that range. Decision analysis and Monte Carlo simulation (*Figure 4*) assign probabilities to

Figure 2

Two way what-if table.
It presents the sensitivity of the annual profits (in $) from a new plane to the capacity utilisation and the hours flown per year.

| | | Hours flown | | | | |
		800	900	1000	1100	1200
	50%	16080	23115	30150	37185	44220
	55%	30552	39396	48240	57084	65928
	60%	45024	55677	66330	76983	87636
Capacity	65%	59496	71958	84420	96882	109344
utilisation	70%	73968	88239	102510	116781	131052
	75%	88440	104520	120600	136680	152760
	80%	102912	120801	138690	156579	174468

Figure 3: Tornado diagram

It investigates the sensitivity of profits to a number of uncertain variables. For each variable the low value corresponds to profits resulting for a pessimistic value and the value for an optimistic value everything else kept at base values. The length of the line is an indication of the relative importance of the uncertainty in each variable in affecting profits.

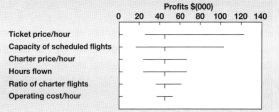

Profits $(000)

Ticket price/hour
Capacity of scheduled flights
Charter price/hour
Hours flown
Ratio of charter flights
Operating cost/hour

Figure 4: Overview of Monte Carlo simulation

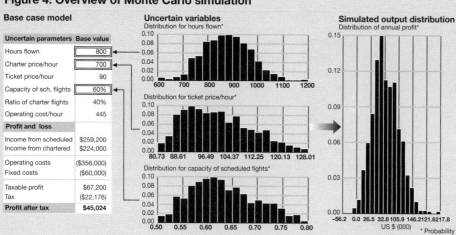

Base case model

Uncertain parameters	Base value
Hours flown	800
Charter price/hour	700
Ticket price/hour	90
Capacity of sch. flights	60%
Ratio of charter flights	40%
Operating cost/hour	445
Profit and loss	
Income from scheduled	$259,200
Income from chartered	$224,000
Operating costs	($356,000)
Fixed costs	($60,000)
Taxable profit	$67,200
Tax	($22,176)
Profit after tax	**$45,024**

Uncertain variables
Distribution for hours flown*
Distribution for ticket price/hour*
Distribution for capacity of scheduled fights*

Simulated output distribution
Distribution of annual profit*
US $ (000)
* Probability

the various possibilities. Decision analysis involves the graphical representation of business problems using decision trees and influence diagrams. It is particularly suited to *multistage* problems in which different decisions are taken at different times as the various uncertainties get resolved.

Monte Carlo simulation

This technique is named after the roulette wheels in Monte Carlo, viewed as devices for generating random numbers. It has been used in other scientific fields for a long time, but it was David Hertz of consultants McKinsey & Co who suggested the use of Monte Carlo simulation for the evaluation of capital investments in an article published by the Harvard Business Review in 1979.

At that time, building a simulation model was a very laborious exercise involving low-level computer programming. Today, many packages are available that allow powerful risk analyses to be carried out with minimal effort using widely available spreadsheet technology, and this has made the technique very popular. One such package is RISK, published by Palisade.

The basic steps required for carrying out risk analysis are illustrated

in *Figure 4* and explained below:
● *Step 1:* Build a base case cashflow model for the investment you are evaluating, usually in a spreadsheet. The main inputs of such a model are costs, sales and price projections, interest rates and so on. The main outputs are the revenues, the year-by-year cash flow, rate of return, and net present value of the investment.
● *Step 2:* Model the uncertainty about the main inputs of the model using probability distributions. This can be done simply by typing appropriate formulae in the cells containing the inputs. For example, a formula such as UNIFORM(800, 1100) specifies that the value of the cell is drawn from a uniform distribution between 800 and 1,100.

But where do these distributions come from? In some cases, for example in oil exploration, they may come from the analysis of historic or experimental data. In others they could reflect managerial judgments (for example, about sales of a new product) or expert opinion (about interest rates).
● *Step 3:* Specify the relationships between input variables. In many cases uncertain variables are not independent. For example, different fuel prices are known to be correlated. Also, market price and size

should be related. These relationships require careful thought. Try to model them by including the correlation coefficient in the specification of the model. Most risk analysis packages provide facilities for the specification of the correlation matrix between the uncertain variables.
● *Step 4:* Run the simulation. What happens during the simulation is the following. The software package repetitively draws samples of all input parameters specified as probability distributions in a way that reflects the likelihood of each value being selected. For each set of sampled inputs it then calculates the outputs. At the end of the simulation the calculated outputs are analysed and presented in a probabilistic form. For example, in *Figure 4* you can see the resulting distribution of annual profit values. This distribution is taking into account the uncertainty in all input parameters as well as their interdependence.

The Monte Carlo approach to risk analysis is based on brute force. The same calculation is repeated a number of times for different values of the uncertain inputs. Like most other sampling techniques the results depend on the specific values that happen to be selected. To reduce the impact of chance on the results, a "sufficient" number of iterations need to be carried out. Although it is difficult to predetermine what a sufficient number of iterations will be, there are some practical guidelines that help address this problem.

For example, start with a relatively small number of iterations, say 100, and then double them and observe the impact on the results. Repeat that process until there is little change in the shape and values of the output distributions. Some software packages automate this process by monitoring the convergence of simulation results.

Evaluating the simulation results

How do we use the results of a simulation exercise? Traditional cash flow models come up with a single number (NPV) that tells us whether or not we should proceed with a certain project. It is certainly more difficult to interpret a probability distribution about NPV or the rate of return. How do we use the information that the expected rate of return is 20 per cent but there is a 10 per cent chance that it will be below 5 per cent?

The information generated by risk analysis is much richer than that generated by static cash flow models, but it takes some understanding of probabilities and a lot of common sense to make good use of it. And in any case the results of a static cash flow model are likely to be misleading. Here is a list of questions you should ask yourself that will help you to evaluate properly the results of a risk analysis exercise: ● what is the range of possible values for the main outputs? ● what is the expected rate of return? (It may well be different from the one you get from cash flow modelling using expected values of the input parameters) ● what is the downside of this investment? ● how could I cope with the downside? ● is there any combination of uncertainties that result in catastrophic consequences? ● which are the main uncertainty drivers causing the variation in profits? ● what can I do to reduce these uncertainties? ● how does the risk–return profile of this project compare to other alternatives?

Risk analysis does not provide simple answers. Instead it provides a means of exploring the trade-off between risk and return. It is also an iterative process. Once you have identified the main uncertainty drivers you need to think about ways to reduce these uncertainties by taking advantage of various hedging opportunities or using better forecasting techniques, market research, and so on. But risk analysis is certainly a valuable tool for coping with a world in which just about everything is uncertain.

Summary

Most business decisions, such as launching a new product, are taken with incomplete knowledge about how the future will evolve. There is a big difference between naive decision making, educated guesses and calculated risks. Risk analysis aims to achieve the last of these. The main tools are sensitivity analysis (what-if questions, what-if tables), scenario analysis and decision analysis. Some understanding of probabilities and a lot of common sense is required to make good use of a simulation exercise.

Source: *FT Mastering Management Part 5*, 24 November 1995.

 Exercises

1 An investigation is being carried out into a local authority's housing policy. The local authority has a limited supply of housing which it owns and lets. It receives requests for housing from a number of individuals and families throughout the year. Some of these applications come from those who have moved into the area, others from single-parent families, married couples who have separated and so on. With the limited housing stock at its disposal, the authority is unable to allocate every applicant a house or flat immediately, and inevitably a waiting list has developed. Elected officials are expressing concern over the size of this waiting list and have told the housing manager to review the existing situation and to class all such applications into one of two categories: urgent and non-urgent.

Urgent cases include those who are homeless at the time of the application and other needy applicants such as those who are victims of domestic violence, those facing eviction from their existing accommodation, and those in substandard housing. Non-urgent cases are subdivided into general applications and those from disabled individuals who have special accommodation requirements.

Once classified as urgent, an application goes to the top of the housing waiting list (or straight into accommodation if available) provided no other urgent case is already on the list. If this is the case, then the latest urgent case goes to the highest place on the list following all other earlier urgent cases. Non-urgent cases are allocated housing points by the housing manager. These points depend on the circumstances of the applicants, with points allocated depending on the number of children in the family, the gender of the applicant, age, income level and whether the applicant is disabled. Housing points allocated to an applicant can vary from zero (the lowest) to 100 (the highest). After all available accommodation has been allocated to urgent cases, remaining vacant housing is allocated to those applicants with the highest number of points.

Applications for housing can be anything up to five per day. Only limited information is available and this is shown in Table 14.10.

Table 14.10	No. of applications for housing	
Case type	% of applicants	Number of working days to obtain housing
Urgent	5	3
Non-urgent		
General	80	18
Disabled	15	27

Elected officials are pressing for the disabled to be automatically classed as urgent cases. You have decided to carry out a simulation of the existing system to be followed by a simulation of the policy of classifying all disabled applications as urgent.

(a) Draft a short report to elected officials indicating why you think simulation would be suitable for this investigation.

(b) In addition to the information currently available, what other information would you require to enable you to undertake the simulation?

(c) Assuming that such information is available, construct a flowchart for the current policy and the suggested new policy.

2 You are currently employed by a high street bank and have been asked to investigate the bank's policy in one particular area of its operations, that relating to small loans to individual customers. The loans in question are usually short-term and requested for financing the purchase of domestic household goods such as TVs, DVD players, hi-fi systems and the like. The manager responsible for these loans has been asked by head office to recommend a suitable maximum amount that should be available each week. The manager has asked you for advice in this matter and you are considering the use of simulation to assess alternatives.

The information you currently have is limited, but from past records you have noted that the number of customers requesting a loan could be up to five on any one day. Table 14.11 shows the historical distribution of customer requests. You have also determined that the amount customers wish to borrow could vary up to £2000 (the bank's maximum under its current policy) with the full distribution as shown in Table 14.12. When requesting such a loan a customer is given a risk rating on the basis of their past banking history, their income level, credit status, etc., with this rating varying between one and three (with one indicating the lowest-risk customer) (see Table 14.13). As long as sufficient funds are available on a weekly basis, loans are allocated on a first-come, first-served basis.

However, if the demand for loans exceeds the supply of funds, the bank has a policy of allocating the following week's funds on a risk-priority basis. So, for

Table 14.11	Bank simulation: customer distribution

No. of customers per day	Probability
0	0.10
1	0.20
2	0.30
3	0.15
4	0.15
5	0.10

Table 14.12	Bank simulation: loan requested

Amount borrowed	Proportion of customers
up to £750	5%
between £750 and £1000	15%
between £1000 and £1500	20%
between £1500 and £2000	60%

Table 14.13	Bank simulation: priority rankings

Priority rankings	Proportion of customers last year
1	25%
2	70%
3	5%

example, if a priority I customer is unable to get a loan this week because all funds have been allocated, that customer will have priority over any risk 2 or 3 category customers the following week. At present the bank makes £20 000 per week available for these loans but is keen to assess whether this sum should be altered.

(a) Develop a suitable simulation flowchart for modelling this situation.

(b) For the current policy of allocating £20 000 of funds each week, simulate the bank's operations for 10 days (the bank has a five-day week). Use the random number table shown in Table 14.14.

Table 14.14		Random numbers							
79	9	44	11	1	50	70	41	6	80
10	47	52	40	59	89	29	95	72	63
77	92	48	85	56	27	5	42	10	55
18	30	52	55	58	85	96	64	92	84
39	28	97	93	78	82	15	59	48	19
35	41	6	1	53	68	32	61	14	29
69	23	19	38	99	59	31	42	79	29
43	72	10	19	16	49	99	82	68	92
60	17	99	24	55	38	54	19	95	87
91	23	97	93	39	64	60	73	29	81

(c) Explain how you would use your model to assist management decision making.

(d) Comment on any assumptions you have had to make to develop the simulation model and the effect these might have on the model's validity.

3 A utility company is currently reviewing its manpower requirements in the domestic-appliance servicing department. One feature of the servicing work relates to domestic central-heating systems. For an annual fee, a trained engineer will undertake a safety check on a customer's domestic central-heating system. As part of the check the engineer will inform the customer of any repair work that needs to be completed, although this work is not done at the time. The majority of such safety checks take place in the autumn of each year. Last year, in one geographical area served by an engineering team, the demand for such servicing was as shown in Table 14.15.

Table 14.15	Gas simulation: service demands
No. of safety checks per day	*No. of days*
up to 100	10
between 100 and 125	25
between 125 and 150	30
between 150 and 175	20
up to 200	15

Typically, gas domestic central-heating systems fall into two types: small-bore and large-bore systems. Approximately 25 per cent of engineer visits are to small-bore systems, although this percentage is increasing slowly over time. Depending on the type of system to be checked, some variability occurs in how long each service check takes. Information from last year is shown in Table 14.16.

Table 14.16	Gas simulation: servicing time		
Small-bore system		**Large-bore system**	
Time required	Probability	Time required	Probability
up to 45 minutes	0.50	up to 35 minutes	0.40
between 45 and 50 minutes	0.25	between 35 and 40 minutes	0.40
between 50 and 55 minutes	0.15	between 40 and 45 minutes	0.10
up to 60 minutes	0.10	between 45 and 50 minutes	0.10

Naturally, the engineer does not know in advance how long a particular service check will take. The times shown in this table include the engineer's travel time, rest breaks and so on. Engineers typically work an eight-hour shift and are allowed to travel home after completing their last job that day. If, as sometimes happens, an engineer has to work beyond the eight-hour total to complete a job then an overtime payment of £15 per hour or part hour is paid. Normal pay rates for engineers are £10 per hour. The company is trying to review the number of engineers who should be in the team covering this area.

(a) Produce a simulation flowchart for this situation.

(b) Using the random numbers in Table 14.14 simulate this situation for 10 days for a given number of engineers in the team.

(c) Draft a report to management explaining why you think funding should be made available to develop a computer-based simulation model for this problem.

15 Financial Decision Making

Learning objectives

By the end of this chapter you should be able to:

- explain the principles of interest-rate calculations
- explain the difference between nominal and effective interest rates
- calculate the net present value
- evaluate investment alternatives using different methods
- calculate and explain the internal rate of return
- evaluate alternative replacement decisions

Many of the models we have developed in earlier chapters have used financial information as part of the decision-making process, although frequently this has simply been one source of information used. In this chapter, however, we focus specifically on the use of financial information and we shall introduce a number of techniques applied specifically to the evaluation of such information. At the heart of most of these is the principle of interest and interest-rate calculations. This leads into an examination of the principles involved in assessing the value of money over time and seeing how this information can be used to evaluate alternative financial decisions. A word of caution is necessary before we start, however. The financial decision area is a veritable mine-field in the real world, hedged as it is with tax implications, depreciation allowances, investment and capital allowances and the like. This is one area in particular where the financial expert is needed. Nevertheless, the principles of such financial decision making are established through the concepts of interest and present value – two concepts which we detail in this chapter.

Shareholders need better boards, not more regulation

From Prof Theo Vermaelen

Sir, Prof Eric De Keuleneer blames the "dramatic lowering of ethical standards in the financial sector" for all types of evils, such as the fact that acquirers on average lose money in acquisitions (*Letters*, January 8).

Why do many bidders lose money in acquisitions? While bankers can advise companies, it is ultimately the chief executive who makes the decision. So, one explanation could be that some chief executives do not care too much about shareholder value and benefit personally from becoming bigger (through higher salaries, acquisition bonuses, prestige).

Alternatively, it could be that many chief executives simply do not want to learn finance and rely on their advisers for the valuation of acquisition targets. Whatever the reason, I do not think that the problem can be cured by regulation of the financial sector.

What we need is better governance; that is, board members who defend shareholder interests and understand finance, in particular the subtleties of discounted cash flow valuation techniques.

Theo Vermaelen,
Professor of Finance,
Insead, 77305 Fontainebleau,
France

Source: *Financial Times*, 11 January 2008. © Professor Theo Vermaelen.

A plea for those at the top to better understand financial statistics.

Interest

Most of the principles of financial decision making are based on a simple concept: that of *time preference*. Other things being equal, we would prefer to receive a sum of money now rather than that same sum at some time in the future. Offered a simple choice between receiving £500 now or £500 in one year's time the choice is clear: we would take the money now. The reasons for this are several.

● The future is uncertain, the present less so.
● Inflation will erode the purchasing power of a future sum of money.
● Our personal cash flow might be such that we need the money now.
● There is an opportunity cost involved in waiting to receive the sum of money, since if we took the money now we could invest it or we could use it to purchase goods and services from which we derive satisfaction now.

This last point is particularly relevant for financial decision making, since it leads directly into the issue of interest. Consider your local bank. It approaches you, the customer, with the offer that if you deposit your savings of £500 with the bank for a year, at the end of that time the bank will return £500 to you. Clearly such an offer is totally unattractive, given the 'sacrifice' you have to make over the next 12 months: going without the £500 for one year. The bank has to offer you some inducement to part with your cash. Such an inducement is the interest it is willing to pay. In effect, the bank will offer to pay you not £500 in a year's time but £500 plus a financial reward.

Interest-rate calculations are straightforward but they lead us into some important areas, so we shall take some time to explore their principles. Let us consider the sum of money you have available, £500, and denote this as the principal, P. The bank offers to pay you interest on the amount you give them at a rate of 8 per cent per year (per annum, or p.a.). At the end of the year your savings with the bank would be worth:

$$£500 + 8\%(£500) = £500 + £40 = £540$$

If we denote the rate of interest as a decimal, we can generalise this as:

$$500 + 0.08(500) = 500(1 + 0.08)$$

or denoting the rate of interest as r:

$$P(1 + r)$$

If you left your savings in the bank for a second year you would have:

$$540(1 + 0.08)$$

but since:

$$540 = 500(1 + 0.08)$$

this gives:

$$500(1 + 0.08)(1 + 0.08) = 500(1 + 0.08)^2$$

It is easy to see the pattern and what the calculation for year 3 would be:

$$500(1 + 0.08)^3$$

or in general:

$$P(1 + r)^t$$

where t is the number of periods for which we wish to calculate the interest payment. In fact this formula can be used in a variety of ways. If we denote V as the value of a sum of money in the future, we have:

$$V = P(1 + r)^t$$

but we can rearrange this as:

$$P = \frac{V}{(1 + r)^t}$$

to show the sum we must invest now, P, in order for this to increase to V in t periods of time at a rate of interest, r. Similarly, we can obtain:

$$r = \sqrt[t]{\frac{V}{P}} - 1$$

to determine the rate of interest which will increase a given principal to a known future sum after t periods. To illustrate, consider the following example. A small company knows that in five years a piece of equipment will need replacing. The best estimate is that at that time the equivalent equipment will cost £30 000. The company has the option of investing a sum of money now at a rate of interest of 6 per cent per annum to fund the equipment purchase.

Activity 15.1

How much does it need to invest now in order to be able to purchase the equipment in five years?

Using the second formula we have:

$$P = \frac{V}{(1 + r)^t}$$

with V = 30 000, r = 0.06 and t = 5 giving:

$$P = \frac{30\ 000}{(1.06)^5} = \frac{30\ 000}{1.3382} = £22\ 418$$

as the sum that must be invested now. This sum, £22 418, will have increased to £30 000 in five years at a rate of interest of 6 per cent. Consider a variant on this problem. The company has decided that its current cash flow will not allow such an investment to be made at present. The maximum amount the company can afford at the moment is £20 000.

Activity 15.2

What rate of interest is required if the company's investment is to grow sufficiently to purchase the equipment in the future?

Using the third formula we have:

$$P = 20\ 000$$
$$V = 30\ 000$$
$$t = 5$$
$$r = \sqrt[t]{\frac{V}{P}} - 1$$
$$= \sqrt[5]{\frac{30\ 000}{20\ 000}} - 1$$
$$= 1.084 - 1 = 0.084$$

or a required rate of interest of 8.4 per cent. Clearly, if the company cannot find such an investment opportunity, it will have to budget for a shortfall in the money it has available for purchasing the replacement equipment in the future.

Nominal and Effective Interest

The formulae we have developed have been shown for periods of a year or more. In practice they can be used for any calendar period: quarters, months, days. For example, consider a credit card company charging interest on the amount of outstanding debt that you owe. Such an interest charge will typically be calculated monthly. The formulae can be used, as long as we divide the annual rate of interest by 12 and multiply the number of time periods by 12. However, it is more instructive to consider the difference between what is known as the nominal rate of interest and the effective. Consider a situation where you invest £500 in a savings account which adds interest at the end of every month, and that the current annual rate is 9 per cent. After five years we calculate the account will be:

$$V = 500(1 + 0.09/12)^{60} = 500(1.0075)^{60} = £782.84$$

You will be able to see that if the interest had been calculated annually the sum would have been £769.31. The rate of interest quoted – 9 per cent per annum – is generally referred to as the *nominal* rate of interest. The rate actually earned, which is more than 9 per cent per annum, is known as the *effective* rate or the *annual percentage rate* (APR) frequently seen quoted in financial advertisements. The APR can be calculated using the formula:

$$APR = \left(1 + \frac{r}{t}\right)^{t} - 1$$

where r is the nominal rate and t the number of periods during the year when interest is calculated. Here this would give:

$$APR = \left(1 + \frac{0.09}{12}\right)^{12} - 1$$
$$= 1.094 - 1$$
$$= 0.094$$

or 9.4 per cent as the APR. The APR is a quick and easy method of comparing different options when the frequency of interest calculations might vary. For example, you are thinking of investing a sum of money for a 10-year period. One investment firm is offering a rate of interest of 6.4 per cent with interest added quarterly. A second is offering

I am confused about the meaning of different quoted interest rates – e.g. APR, AGR, AER. Please explain?

By Sarah Ross

You are not alone in your confusion, particularly because banks and credit card companies have different ways of calculating and applying rates. Things should improve a bit in the future since, from March, banks have to include an "honesty box" in all credit card marketing which gives consumers clear information on what annual percentage rates and other charges they will pay. All companies will have to use one method of calculating annual rates on cards rather than the two used up until now.

APR (Annual Percentage Rate) is the term used on a fixed repayment

schedule – for example a fixed rate loan involving fixed repayment amounts. It means the customer will know the number of repayments, the repayment amount and the time period for the repayments.

AER or EAR (Equivalent Annual Rate) is quoted for overdrafts so that (in theory) customers can compare rates across institutions. The calculation does not include fees, which are quoted separately.

Barclaycard says the main difference between APR and AER (or EAR as it prefers to call it) is that EARs are a "cut-down" version of an APR applicable to overdrafts

(because an overdraft does not have key features needed to do a full-blown APR calculation). They also say they have never heard of AGR although they guess it may be a reference to an annual gross rate on a savings product. That would be the rate, gross of tax, on a product which paid interest annually.

In the savings world, the term AER (Annual Equivalent Rate) is used and is the same as EAR, that is, the annualised gross rate to show the effect of compounding interest (even though in fact interest may be paid monthly or quarterly).

Source: Financial Times, 7 April 2004, FT.com site.

Confused by rates? You're not the only one.

6.2 per cent added monthly. Which is preferable? By calculating and comparing the APRs we see that option 1 has an APR of 6.56 per cent and option 2 has an APR of 6.38 per cent. Option 1 is therefore to be preferred.

Present Value

We can also use these basic principles to introduce a particularly important concept in financial decision making: that of *present value*. Using the formula we have developed, we are able to calculate what a sum of money now would be worth at some time in the future. For example, £1000 now would grow to £1050 in one year at a rate of interest of 5 per cent, to £1102.50 in two years and so on. Consider this information from a slightly different perspective. If you were offered £1000 now or £1050 in one year, which would you prefer? If we make a number of heroic assumptions, the answer will be that you are indifferent between the two; you have no preference. The logic behind this is that if you took the £1000 now it would only be worth the same as the £1050 in one year's time anyway. Effectively what we have done is to calculate the value now of a future sum of money. The £1000 is denoted as the present value of £1050 in one year's time. Of course it is also the present value of £1102.50 in two years' time. As we indicated, such indifference is based on a number of assumptions. In particular that:

- we ignore the effects of inflation;
- there is no risk involved in waiting;
- interest rates will remain stable.

In more complex applications it is possible to incorporate the relaxation of such assumptions into the calculations, but for our purposes we shall ignore them as they do not alter the fundamental principles involved. In general the present value of a future sum is given by:

$$PV = \frac{V}{(1+r)^t} \text{ or } V \times \frac{1}{(1+r)^t}$$

with r generally referred to as the discount rate and the term $1/(1+r)^t$ as the discount factor. Pre-calculated tables of discount factors are available. Present value is particularly important in the area of investment appraisal, which we shall turn to shortly. For the present we shall illustrate its use with a simple example. Some years ago you invested a sum of money into a scheme which guaranteed a return of £5000 at a specified future date. That date is six years from today. However, you really would like to get your hands on the money now if at all possible because you want to buy a car. A friend has indicated that he is willing to give you £3500 now in return for your savings scheme. That is, he will give you £3500 and you sign over your rights to the £5000 return in six years' time. Should you take his offer? To help make a decision we can apply the present value principles. Let us assume that current interest rates are 7 per cent per annum and you believe they will remain at that level for the next six years.

Activity 15.3

Calculate the present value of the £5000 and decide whether you would take up your friend's offer.

The present value of the £5000 is then:

$$PV = \frac{5000}{(1.07)^6} = £3332$$

That is, £5000 in six years' time has an equivalent value of £3332 today. If offered £3332 today or £5000 in six years' time you would not be bothered which you received (other things being equal). However, your friend is actual offering you £3500 not £3332. In this case you are being offered more than the present value of your investment. Other things being equal, you should take your friend's offer. Of course, the catch lies in the term 'other things being equal'. We would clearly want to consider all other factors in the situation as we usually do with all our models. In particular we might wish to consider the assumption about the rate of interest remaining at 7 per cent and the effect this has on our decision.

Activity 15.4

Recalculate the PV if the interest rate is 5 per cent.

Logically at a different rate of interest the PV of the future sum will alter. In general, if the rate of interest is higher, the PV falls and vice versa. In this case the PV increases to £3731. Your friend's offer is now less than the PV based on a discount rate of 5 per cent and should not be accepted. This may well explain of course why your friend is making such an offer. He may well have a different view from yourself about future interest rates. If he believes interest rates will fall – and they do – he will stand to gain from the transaction.

Inflation

As we indicated, one critical assumption in the calculations relates to that of zero inflation. In practice, if we have a view about future levels of inflation we can take this into account by using as the discount factor not the actual rate of interest but the real rate of interest, where:

Real rate of interest = Actual rate – Rate of inflation

So, if the actual rate of interest is 7 per cent and we anticipate a rate of inflation of 2 per cent, the real rate of interest is 5 per cent. Again, different perceptions of the future rate of inflation can explain differences in behaviour and choice.

Investment Appraisal

Present value is particularly useful when it comes to evaluating alternative projects in financial terms. To illustrate this, and introduce related methods, we shall develop an example. A printing firm is reviewing its current production facilities. Some of its printing equipment has reached the end of its useful working life and the firm is considering replacing this with the latest computer-based equipment. Such equipment will be costly but the firm expects to be able to reduce its staffing levels to compensate. Two options are currently under review.

Option A   Under Option A the firm will purchase a standard piece of equipment at a cost of £12 000 payable now. Over the next five years, however, the firm expects to be able to reduce its staffing costs by £4000 per year in the first three years and then by £3500 in year 4 and £3000 in year 5. At the end of the five years the equipment would have reached the end of its life and would need replacing.

Option B   Under Option B the firm would purchase a slightly more sophisticated piece of equipment for an initial cost of £15 000. In the first two years staff cost savings are estimated to be £4500 and £5000 respectively. In year 3, however, the equipment would need major refurbishment at an additional cost of £5000. Staff cost savings in years 3, 4 and 5 would be £5500, £6000 and £6500. At the end of the five years the equipment would have reached the end of its life and would need replacing.

The firm is seeking advice, in financial terms, as to its recommended decision. Clearly the firm faces two alternative decisions (actually three, since it could decide to buy neither machine) with different financial consequences. It will help if we summarise the financial information we have in tabular form. Table 15.1 shows the cash flow of the two options. For each option we show the cash outflows (expenditure) and the cash inflows (income or cost savings), with the net cash flow being the difference between the two. We see that Option A generates a positive net cash flow at the end of the five years of £6500 and Option B of £7500. On the face of it, Option B looks preferable since it generates a higher positive cash flow. However, there are a number of different approaches we could take in terms of identifying a preference for either option.

Payback method

The first of these is the payback method. This is particularly simple and measures the number of time periods, years in this case, it would take to recover the cost of the investment. Effectively the payback method determines when the net cash flow turns positive. In the case of Option A this occurs at the end of year 3, so this option would have a payback period of three years. In the case of Option B the net cash flow turns

Table 15.1   Cash flow projections

| Period | Option A | | | Option B | | |
	Cash outflow	Cash inflow	Net cash flow	Cash outflow	Cash inflow	Net cash flow
0 (now)	12 000		−12 000	15 000		−15 000
1		4 000	4 000		4 500	4 500
2		4 000	4 000		5 000	5 000
3		4 000	4 000	5 000	5 500	500
4		3 500	3 500		6 000	6 000
5		3 000	3 000		6 500	6 500
Total	12 000	18 500	6 500	20 000	27 500	7 500

positive between years 4 and 5. If we assume a constant stream of cash flow in year 5 the exact payback period would be four years eight months. On this basis, Option A would be preferred since it has a shorter payback period and will pay back the original investment in a shorter time.

Although crude and simple, the method does have the advantage of weighting early positive cash flows at the expense of later ones. Given that, in principle, cash flows at later periods are more uncertain and hence riskier, the payback method adopts a relatively 'safe' approach. However, it does have obvious disadvantages. It ignores the total profitability of projects and it ignores cash flows after the end of the payback period.

QMDM IN ACTION
Cap Gemini Ernst & Young – cost–benefit analysis

Cap Gemini Ernst & Young's client was a group of companies in the heavy buildings material business. The client had recognised the need for an IT system that would allow it to streamline business process across the group's companies. A joint client/Cap Gemini Ernst & Young team was required to undertake a scoping exercise to assess whether a bespoke system should be developed or whether a specific off-the-shelf system would meet the client's needs. To enable the comparison to be made cost and benefit information for the two options for each of the companies was pulled together into a summary model. This model then provided the basis for the client's capital expenditure proposal allowing the different IT options to be assessed.

Working closely with the company financial directors and other members of the joint team, one of the Cap Gemini Ernst & Young consultants developed a spreadsheet-based cost/benefit model.

The spreadsheet-based model used the incremental costs and benefits of the different IT options.

The model manipulated the cost/benefit streams over time into a format that was suitable for input into the client's own capital expenditure appraisal model. A common template was used across the companies to ensure that a consistent approach was used to collect the necessary data. A workshop was also organised to ensure that the quantification of expected benefits was also consistent.

The benefits are as follows:

● The development of a management tool to identify and quantify the expected benefits from the IT options.

● Generating summary financial information in the format required by the client's own capital expenditure appraisal model.

I am grateful to Cap Gemini Ernst & Young for permission to use this case study and to reproduce the figure shown. Further case study applications are available through their website: www.uk.capgemini/services/consulting/or/success_stories

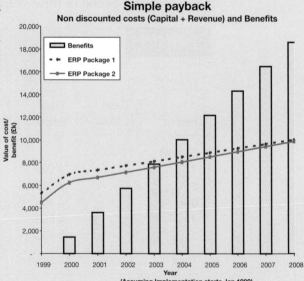

Simple payback
Non discounted costs (Capital + Revenue) and Benefits

Rate of return

The second method calculates a rate of return on projects, showing annual profit as a percentage of capital investment. In the case of Option A the total profit is £6500 and over a five-year period this gives an annual profit of £1300, which as a percentage of the total investment, £12 000, gives 10.8 per cent as a rate of return on the investment. For Option B we would obtain a return of 7.5 per cent on investment, and Option A would be preferred as it gives the higher return. Although the calculation relates profit to the size of the investment, it clearly does not take the timing of the returns into account, simply preferring those projects which have a higher overall return regardless of when in time this return occurs.

Net present value

The final method brings us back to the concept of present value. Clearly, given the timings of the cash flows of the two projects, we ought to assess the present values of the two alternatives to help us choose between them, something neither of the other two methods considered. To apply this method we need to establish a discount rate, which we will set at 8 per cent. This might, for example, represent the real cost of capital for the company. Table 15.2 shows the calculation for Option A.

Table 15.2	Net present value: Option A				
Period	Cash outflow	Cash inflow	Net cash flow	Discount factor	Present value
0	12 000		–12 000	1.0000	–12 000
1		4 000	4 000	0.9259	3 703.60
2		4 000	4 000	0.8573	3 429.20
3		4 000	4 000	0.7938	3 175.20
4		3 500	3 500	0.7350	2 572.50
5		3 000	3 000	0.6806	2 041.80
Total	12 000	18 500	6 500		2 922.30

In addition to the cash flows the discount factor is shown, together with the net cash flow for each period multiplied by this factor (the present value of each of these cash flows). The column total that we obtain, £2922.30, is the net present value for this option. That is, assuming a discount rate of 8 per cent, the sum of £2922.30 now and the stream of cash flows as shown for Option A over the next five years are seen as being identical. Such a calculation weights individual cash flows using the present-value principle. We could repeat the calculation for Option B to help choose between them. Other things being equal, a higher net present value (NPV) is the preferred option.

Activity 15.5

Calculate the NPV for Option B at a discount rate of 8 per cent. Which option would you recommend?

The NPV for Option B is calculated at £2683.85. On this basis, Option A would be recommended since it generates the higher NPV. The reason for this is clear. Although Option B generates a higher net cash flow, much of this occurs some years in the future. By definition, the opportunity cost of such future sums is high and the NPV takes the timings of the cash flows into account, giving more priority to those early on in the life of the project.

In practice, the NPV method is the one to be favoured in project appraisal, although the first two methods do have their uses. However, the one problem with the NPV method is that it assumes a particular, constant discount rate. We have seen earlier how a different rate may well affect the decision we take. Higher rates, other things being equal, lead to a lower NPV and vice versa. To avoid this problem, a method which relates to NPV is often used.

Internal rate of return

This method calculates what is known as the internal rate of return (IRR). Effectively this is the discount rate for a given project which will give an NPV of zero, and each

Terra Firma sued over 'modelling flaw'

By Megan Murphy in London

The pressure-cooker working environment of Guy Hands' Terra Firma may have driven two executives to conceal a critical error in the cash flow projections for the collapsed television rentals business Boxclever, a court was told on Monday. Natixis, the French bank, is suing the private equity firm for allegedly producing a flawed financial model for Boxclever during a £750m ($1.5bn) refinancing in 2002. The company defaulted on the debt less than a year after the deal closed.

Joe Smouha QC, Natixis's lawyer, compared the alleged modelling blunders to the rogue trader scandal at Société Générale, suggesting that high-earning bankers paralysed by "fear of failure" might have dug themselves deeper into a hole. "What this case is about is what life is really like in the City, where enormous amounts of pressure are put on individuals," Mr Smouha told the High Court.

The high-profile dispute, originally scheduled to start last month, poses a threat to more than Terra Firma's reputation. Natixis, which once held £200m worth of Boxclever notes, has already settled a related lawsuit against two other financial institutions that worked on the securitisation: Germany's WestLB and the Canadian lender CIBC. Terra Firma, as the only remaining defendant, faces a pay-out of tens of millions of pounds if it loses the case.

Natixis's case now centres on whether two Terra Firma executives, Paul Spinks and Quentin Stewart, knew the financial model for the Boxclever deal was flawed but failed to raise the alarm. Like most securitisations, the financing was based on a complex model of future cash flows, such as rental income from customers. Natixis claims Mr Spinks introduced a crucial error into those projections, leading to an overstated calculation of Boxclever's "net present value".

While Natixis bought £200m worth of Boxclever debt based on an estimated net present value of £943m, the real NPV was as much as 44 per cent lower, the French lender said. Mr Smouha claimed the Terra Firma team working on the securitisation was under constant pressure to close the transaction. With the private equity firm in the midst of launching its first fund, a failure to complete the Boxclever deal would have been "disastrous", Mr Smouha said.

Terra Firma denies wrongdoing and says Mr Spinks and Mr Stewart had no motive for concealing an obvious modelling flaw that would have destroyed their careers and the firm's reputation.

The case continues.

Source: Financial Times, 5 February 2008.

NPV calculations can be very contentious.

project will have a different IRR. It may seem odd that we would want to calculate such a result, but logic will help us see why. Consider Option A. At a rate of 8 per cent it has a positive NPV. If this rate increases, the NPV will fall. We repeat this process until we find the rate – the IRR – which gives a zero NPV. We now have a yardstick with which to assess the project. As long as the actual discount rate is lower than the IRR then we know the project will have a positive NPV. In other words, the IRR method removes the need to justify a specific discount rate and simply requires us to assess whether we think it will ever exceed the IRR during the life of the project.

There are a number of ways of determining the IRR for a project. One method uses a formula. To use this requires us to calculate the NPV for a project at two different discount rates, preferably one with a positive NPV and one with a negative. For example, for Option A we already have:

$$NPV_1 = £2922$$
$$r_1 = 8\%$$

If we were to repeat the calculation for, say, r = 20% we would obtain an NPV of –£681. If we denote:

$$NPV_2 = -£681$$
$$r_2 = 20\%$$

then the formula for estimating the IRR is given as:

$$IRR = r_1 + (r_2 - r_1)\frac{|NPV_1|}{|NPV_1| + |NPV_2|}$$

where $|NPV|$ is the absolute value of the NPV figure. We would then have:

$$IRR = 8 + (20 - 8)\frac{2922}{2922 + 681} = 17.73\%$$

That is, a discount rate of 17.7 per cent would give Option A an NPV of zero. Logically, as long as the discount rate in the real world is below the IRR, we know that Option A will have a positive NPV. If management are convinced that over the life of this project the discount rate will not rise above 17.7 per cent, they know the project will continue to have a positive NPV.

Activity 15.6

Calculate the IRR for Option B.

Using a second rate of 20 per cent we calculate the IRR for Option B at 14.9 per cent. The IRR is another method for choosing between projects. We made our earlier decisions, based on the NPVs, assuming a discount rate of 8 per cent. It is unlikely that this would remain constant over the life of the project. However, we know that as long as the discount rate does not exceed 17.7 per cent then Option A will generate a positive NPV. For Option B, however, the IRR is lower, so a smaller rise in the discount rate would turn the current positive NPV into a negative. Option B is more 'at risk' from an increasing discount rate than is Option A.

We should note that the formula we have used provides an estimate of the IRR. The reason for this is somewhat technical but basically relates to the fact that the formula allows us to calculate a linear approximation to the IRR when, in practice, the relationship is a non-linear one. Generally, the loss in accuracy is small and irrelevant for the

Lex: Internal rate of return

Imagine an investment that requires a payment of $5,000 up front and then produces positive cash flows of $3,000 in years two to 10. At a 10 per cent discount rate, this project will have a positive net present value of just over $11,160 and an internal rate of return of 59 per cent.

Now assume the investor can sell out at fair value in year three, receiving $14,605 (the NPV of the cash flows in years four to 10). The project's overall NPV remains exactly the same. But the IRR more than doubles to 120 per cent even

though no extra value has been created.

This is hardly news. But all too often, it creeps into practice: IRR is the private equity industry's main yardstick for judging performance, raising funds and rewarding managers. Indeed, the sector makes much of its superior, 25 per cent, returns. Yet as the example shows, such IRR-based numbers can be artificially boosted by extracting cash early through trade sales, listings or recapitalisations. Indeed, the theoretical investor could

accept as little as $5,000 in year three, thereby destroying considerable shareholder value, and still trumpet an IRR of over 59 per cent.

IRR calculations implicitly assume that interim cash flows are reinvested at the original IRR. It would be more realistic to assume, as NPV does, reinvestment at the cost of capital. Because it is intuitive and easy to calculate, IRR will remain popular. But it should not be used in isolation and investors should recognise its flaws.

NPV vs IRR DURING AN EARLY EXIT
Scenarios

	Investment	Years 2–3	Sale Year 3	Years 4–10	NPV	IRR
1. Hold	–$5,000	$3,000 pa	No	3,000 pa	$11,161	59%
2. Sale at "fair value"	–$5,000	$3,000 pa	$14,605	0	$11,161	120%
3. Sale below "fair value"	–$5,000	$3,000 pa	$5,000	0	$3,944	60%

Source: *The Real Cost of Capital*, by Tim Ogier and John Rugman, p 180.

Source: *Financial Times*, 1 June 2005.

The IRR, like any statistics, doesn't always tell the full story.

use to which the IRR is put. A more accurate estimation can usually be provided by developing a small spreadsheet program which allows for iterative calculations. If we were to do this we would find the IRR for Option A to be 17.29 per cent and for Option B to be 14.16 per cent.

Replacing Equipment

Every business organisation is periodically faced with decisions about the replacement of equipment. On a production line the decision relates to a robot-controlled machine tool, in an office to the photocopier, in many organisations to the company car, in a hospital to a specialised brain scanner. The decision for the manager relates to staying with the existing equipment – and probably incurring additional costs in terms of maintenance and repair – or buying a replacement, which requires a hefty initial investment.

Obviously there will come a point with any piece of equipment where it will be cheaper to buy new equipment than to keep incurring the expense of repairing the old. Naturally, any such decision will not be made purely on a comparison of these costs. Other factors will need to be taken into account: whether the company's cash flow will finance a replacement this year, whether the capital budget has sufficient funds for the new equipment, whether the general manager will sanction such an investment, whether quality is adversely affected to the point where the decision has to be made. One approach that can be developed is to assess the financial information available in terms of keeping the existing equipment and determining when these costs are at a minimum in terms of the replacement decision. Consider the following example. An organisation has bought a piece of equipment for £50 000. The value of the machine – in terms of its potential resale value – decreases over time as the equipment gets older, but the organisation's accountant has estimated that the resale values will be as shown in Table 15.3.

That is, after one year the equipment will have dropped in value to £20 000 and to £1000 by the end of year 7. (If you have ever bought a new car you will know the feeling of such 'depreciation'.) Clearly, this loss in value over time represents a 'cost' to the organisation: at the end of every year it has 'lost' a sum of money that it could have had by selling the machine one year earlier.

The other obvious cost that the organisation will incur by keeping the machine will be the running costs: operating costs, energy costs, maintenance and repair. For this piece of equipment the estimated running costs over the next seven years are shown in Table 15.4.

As we might expect, the running costs associated with the equipment increase over time as the equipment ages. It seems logical to try to assess when the equipment should be replaced by seeking to determine when these costs are at a minimum (remember the approach in Chapter 12 on stock control). The approach we can develop is to calculate the total costs incurred by keeping the equipment a certain length of time and comparing the average annual cost of the various replacement options. For example, at the end of year 1 the costs we have incurred (as a result of deciding not to replace the equipment) are:

Loss of resale value: £30 000 (50 000 – 20 000)

Running costs: £7000

giving total costs of £37 000. This is the total cost of deciding not to replace before the end of year 1. Since the machine has had a useful life of one year then the average total

Table 15.3	Resale value
	Value (£s)
Now	50 000
End year 1	20 000
End year 2	15 000
End year 3	12 000
End year 4	10 000
End year 5	9 000
End year 6	5 000
End year 7	1 000

Table 15.4	Resale value and running costs (£s)	

Year	Resale value	Running costs
1	20 000	7 000
2	15 000	7 700
3	12 000	8 500
4	10 000	9 500
5	9 000	10 500
6	5 000	13 000
7	1 000	18 000

cost will be £37 000/1 or £37 000. For year 2 a similar approach can be taken. Since the equipment had an initial value of £50 000, the loss in resale value of not replacing in either year 1 or year 2 is:

Loss of resale value: 50 000 − 15 000 = 35 000

Running costs: 7000 + 7700 = 14 700

giving a total cost over the first two years of £49 700 and an average cost per year of £24 850 (49 700/2). Clearly, we can repeat these calculations for each further year we keep the equipment.

Activity 15.7

For years 3 to 7 calculate the average total cost incurred by not replacing the equipment.

Table 15.5 shows the detailed calculations.

Table 15.5	Average cost (£s)					

Year	Value	Running costs	Value cost	Cumulative running costs	Cumulative total cost	Average cost
1	20 000	7 000	30 000	7 000	37 000	37 000
2	15 000	7 700	35 000	14 700	49 700	24 850
3	12 000	8 500	38 000	23 200	61 200	20 400
4	10 000	9 500	40 000	32 700	72 700	18 175
5	9 000	10 500	41 000	43 200	84 200	16 840
6	5 000	13 000	45 000	56 200	101 200	16 867
7	1 000	18 000	49 000	74 200	123 200	17 600

The column headed Value cost indicates the cost incurred by keeping the equipment to that time in terms of the resale value, and is calculated as £50 000 less that year's resale value. The next column – Cumulative running costs – shows the total running costs incurred up to that point. The Cumulative total cost is the sum of the previous two columns. The last column – Average cost – is the Cumulative total cost divided by the number of years the equipment has been in use. We see that these average costs are at their lowest at the end of year 5. This is when, other things being equal, this equipment should be replaced.

Present value

This decision, however, does not take the time value of money into account. It is evident that we could use the discounting principles introduced earlier to examine the average cost expressed in present-value terms rather than money terms. Let us first consider the resale value. By the end of year 1 the resale value is £20 000. However, because this is in the future its present value will be lower. Assume the organisation's cost of capital is 5 per cent per annum calculated on a monthly basis. The discount factor will then be:

$$\frac{1}{(1.00417)^{12}} = 0.9513$$

and the present value will then be £20 000 × 0.9513 = £19 027. The corresponding value cost will be:

£50 000 – £19 026 = £30 974.

Activity 15.8

Calculate the discount factors for the remaining years and the value cost each year in present-value terms.

Table 15.6 shows the value cost each year in present-value terms.

Table 15.6   Value cost in present-value terms (£s)

Year	Value	Discount factor	Present value	Value cost at present value
1	20 000	0.9513	19 026	30 973
2	15 000	0.9050	13 575	36 425
3	12 000	0.8609	10 330	39 668
4	10 000	0.8189	8 189	41 809
5	9 000	0.7791	7 011	42 987
6	5 000	0.7411	3 706	46 294
7	1 000	0.7052	705	49 295

Clearly, discounting has the effect of increasing the value cost. The same calculation can be undertaken on running costs. However, it is more realistic here to assume that running costs are incurred through the year rather than at the end of the year. The discount factor for the first year will then be calculated as:

$$\frac{1}{(1.00417)^{6}} = 0.9753$$

We use a discount factor for six months to allow for the fact that running costs will average at half their end-of-year amount. This will give a present value for the annual running costs of £6827. The calculation for year 2 will be the same but using (6 + 12) as the exponent for the discount factor.

Activity 15.9

Calculate the present value for running costs for years 2 to 7.

Table 15.7 shows the running costs expressed in present-value terms together with the cumulative running costs.

Table 15.7   Running costs in present-value terms (£s)

Year	Running costs	Discount factor	Present value	Cumulative present value
1	7 000	0.9753	6 827	6 827
2	7 700	0.9278	7 144	13 971
3	8 500	0.8826	7 502	21 473
4	9 500	0.8396	7 977	29 450
5	10 500	0.7987	8 387	37 837
6	13 000	0.7598	9 878	47 715
7	18 000	0.7228	13 011	60 726

The same logic can now be applied as before. We can calculate the total costs each year (value cost plus cumulative running costs) but with this expressed in present-value terms. This total cost can then be averaged over the life of the equipment to assess what time period represents the least-cost replacement. Table 15.8 shows the summary results.

Table 15.8   Total costs in present-value terms (£s)

Year	Value cost at present value	Cumulative running costs at present value	Total cost	Average cost
1	30 973	6 827	37 800	37 800
2	36 425	13 971	50 396	25 198
3	39 668	21 473	61 141	20 381
4	41 809	29 450	71 259	17 815
5	42 987	37 837	80 824	16 165
6	46 294	47 715	94 009	15 668
7	49 295	60 726	110 021	15 717

This indicates that the optimal replacement occurs at the end of year 6. Clearly, as with any present-value calculation, the result is based on the assumption that the cost of capital at 5 per cent will remain constant. It is evident, however, that this basic model is easily updated to allow management to perform 'what-if' analysis in terms of changes to the key parameters.

Worked Example

A company, WWE, has decided to install a new networked computer system. Initial discussions with the preferred supplier have indicated that WWE faces two basic options:

Option 1   WWE can purchase the system outright for an initial sum of £45 000. This sum includes a maintenance contract from the supplier for the first 12 months. At the end of the first year (and at the end of each subsequent year) WWE can purchase an annual maintenance contract for £2500. At the end of five years the system will be obsolete and will have a scrap value of £1000.

Option 2   Alternatively, WWE can lease the system from the computer supplier. WWE will pay £12 000 now and a further £12 000 per annum at the end of each subsequent year. So, the second lease payment will be due at the end of the first year (to pay for the system through year 2) and so on. At the end of five years the system will be scrapped, but its scrap value will go to the supplier not to WWE. The leasing fee also includes maintenance.

Assume again, the group's current cost of capital is 10 per cent.

Quite simply, which of the two alternatives should WWE choose?

It is usually essential to draw up a table of the timings of any cash flows in this sort of problem. As we have seen with NPV calculations, the timings are at the heart of the calculations. The cash flows for the options are shown in Table 15.9.

Note that in this case the 'year' refers to the end of the year shown. In this case, both projects generate negative cash flows, since we are not relating the project to any income generation or cost savings. At face value, the leasing option looks more expensive, generating a larger negative cash flow than purchasing outright. However, these

Table 15.9	Cash flow of Options 1 and 2	
	Option 1: Purchase	*Option 2: Lease*
Now	−45 000	−12 000
end of Year 1	−2 500	−12 000
end of Year 2	−2 500	−12 000
end of Year 3	−2 500	−12 000
end of Year 4	−2 500	−12 000
end of Year 5	+1000	
Total cost	−54 000	−60 000

		Purchase		Leasing	
Year	Discount factor	Net cash flows	Present value	Net cash flows	Present value
0	1.0000	−45 000	−45 000	−12 000	−12 000
1	0.9091	−2 500	−2 272.75	−12 000	−10 909.20
2	0.8264	−2 500	−2 066.00	−12 000	−9 916.80
3	0.7513	−2 500	−1 878.25	−12 000	−9 015.60
4	0.6830	−2 500	−1 707.50	−12 000	−8 196.00
5	0.6209	+1 000	+620.90		
Total		−54 000	−52 303.60	−60 000	−50 037.60

Table 15.10   NPVs for both options

totals ignore the timings of these flows and it is apparent that we must determine the relevant NPVs. The appropriate calculations are shown in Table 15.10.

In Table 15.10 the two series of net cash flows have been discounted at 10 per cent. For the purchase option the NPV is −£52 304. Similarly, the figure for the leasing option is −£50 038. Comparison of the two NPVs reveals that the leasing option has the lower negative value. This indicates that, other things being equal, the leasing option is to be preferred. The present value of the cash outflows is smaller than that of the alternative – purchase.

Naturally, in practice, we would not recommend that the decision be taken simply on the basis of the NPV calculations. We would need to assess other factors in reaching the decision: tax allowances, the likely rate of inflation and so on, as well as a view as to whether the rate of interest used to calculate the NPVs will remain constant at 10 per cent. This last point is critical for NPV calculations. Should the rate of interest/cost of capital change over this period then the present values will also change and possibly the recommendation we would make. We might wish to undertake some sensitivity analysis on the two options to see how sensitive the decision is to interest rate changes. Such analysis reveals that we would prefer to lease, based on this information, for any interest rate of 6.85 per cent or higher. If the rate fell below this figure, the NPV of the buy option would fall below that of the lease option. Management could be asked to indicate their expectations of future interest rate changes to help them evaluate their decision.

Summary

Although financial decision making in the real world is an area where financial experts must be involved because of the complexity of the tax and legal systems that surround these decisions, in principle the decisions revolve around the calculations of interest and present value in their many forms. At the heart of these calculations is the fundamental principle of the time value of money. The concept of interest is a critical one both to individuals and to business organisations. We have shown in this chapter how

Project approval: The key criteria

The concepts of net present value and discounted cash flow, as well as some more esoteric approaches, are detailed here.

By Adam Farkas

Capital budgeting decisions

Corporate managers are continuously looking for tangible and intangible assets that can increase the value of their company and result in an increase of shareholders' wealth. Capital budgeting is concerned with identifying and valuing potential investment opportunities to enable the management to make sound investment decisions.

The concept of present value (PV) and net present value (NPV) form the basis for the valuation of real assets and investment decision making. In this section, we have to develop these concepts into managerial decision-making tools that are widely used by corporations for the analysis of real assets with expected multi-period pay-off. Essentially, the method makes a comparison between the cost of an investment and the present value of uncertain future cash flows generated by the project. There are (at least) four major steps in a discounted cash flow analysis for a proposed project.

First, assuming that the project is all equity financed (i.e. all the necessary capital is provided by the shareholders), forecasts are needed as to what the expected incremental cash flows would be to the shareholders if the project was accepted. Second, an appropriate discount rate should be established that reflects the time value and risk of the project, and therefore can be used for the calculation of the present value of expected future cash flows. Third, based on the value additivity of present values,

the NPV of the project is to be calculated. Finally, a decision needs to be made on whether to go ahead with the project or not.

Estimating incremental after-tax cash flows

Before starting to build the actual cash flow model of the project and doing the forecasting exercise, some significant technical decisions must be made. The analyst has to decide how to treat inflation. The cash flow model can be built in nominal terms or in real terms (i.e. net of inflation). Both approaches have advantages and disadvantages from practical aspects, but the important point is to be consistent throughout the model. Then, an appropriate forecasting time horizon needs to be selected. Occasionally this can be easy, because the economic life of assets under consideration is known, but at other times an arbitrary decision is necessary.

The incremental cash flows that companies forecast consist of four elements. The first is the cash flow from operations (i.e. the cash flow generated by sales less expenditures related to the operation of the project). The second is the cash flow from capital investments and disposal. The third results from changes in working capital (net changes in short-term assets and liabilities). And last there are the additional corporate tax payments of the company resulting from the implementation of the project.

If the project is not expected to continue operations after the end of

the forecasting horizon, the salvage value of assets needs to be estimated. If management expects the project to last longer than the forecasting horizon, a continuation value for the project has to be established. The salvage or continuation value with its tax implications is then entered into the valuation model as the last expected cash inflow from the project.

Estimating the discount rate

The concept of present value includes the notion of the opportunity cost of capital. The appropriate discount rate, or the cost of capital, must first of all compensate shareholders for the forgone return they could achieve on the capital market by investing in some risk-free assets. It has also to compensate them for the risk they are undertaking by investing in this project rather than in a risk-free financial asset. Thus, the cost of capital is determined by the rate of return investors could expect from an alternative investment with a similar risk profile. Fortunately, the rich menu of traded financial assets provides managers with the opportunity to estimate the right rate.

Calculating net present value

Once the cash flow forecasts are finalised and the appropriate discount rate is established, the calculation of a project's NPV is a technical matter.

All future cash flows need to be discounted to arrive at their present values, and by adding them up, together with the present value of the necessary capital outlay, the NPV of the project is achieved.

By denoting the expected cash flow of the project in period t by C_t, and the present value of the necessary investment by C_0 (which has a negative sign), and the discount rate as r, the NPV of the project is:

$$NPV = C_0 + \frac{C_1}{(1+r)} + \frac{C_2}{(1+r)^2}$$
$$+ \cdots + \frac{C_n}{(1+r)^n}$$
$$= \sum_{t=0}^{n} \frac{C_i}{(1+r)^n}$$

Note that this traditional NPV model framework assumes that all future cash flows can be discounted by the same discount rate, which for some projects might be too restrictive. However, the model can accommodate discount rates that vary from period to period as well as cash flow profiles with more than one change in the sign.

Decision criteria

Based on the DCF analysis of project proposals, the decision criterion that follows is relatively straightforward. Assuming that the company operates in a capital market environment where access to capital is not limited, the management should accept all projects with positive net present values and thereby maximise the company's value.

Project analysis

Project analysis tools are widely used methods developed to provide managers with a deeper insight and better understanding of the financial aspects of investment projects, as well as to shed some light on the assumptions behind expected cash flow forecasts. They can enhance the confidence of managers in the DCF analysis and point out major risk factors that can potentially jeopardise the expected outcome of the investment.

Sensitivity analysis

Sensitivity analysis is a very useful tool to identify key variables or value drivers of projects and focus managerial attention on the most important components of forecasts that are underlying the expected incremental project cash flows.

The analysis is carried out by measuring the change in the value of the project after shifting the value of one underlying variable up or down, corresponding to a more optimistic or pessimistic forecast. The magnitude of the change in the net present value shows the sensitivity of the project to that particular underlying variable.

If, for example, the NPV proves more sensitive to the market share of the company and to the amount of fixed costs than to the price of the product, then management should focus on the reliability of market share estimates and fixed cost forecasts, as well as concentrate efforts during the implementation to improve these factors.

Break-even analysis

Break-even analysis goes one step further. It points out the critical value of each underlying variable at which the project's NPV is zero. Referring back to the previous example, it would tell management that if the market share of the product drops below, or the amount of fixed costs exceed, a certain level, which are called the break-even market share or break-even fixed cost, the company starts losing money on the project. The concept of financial break-even for investment projects is therefore looking at where the project recovers its opportunity cost as opposed to accounting break-even analysis, which focuses on historical costs.

Scenario analysis

The previous two project analysis tools are concerned with only one underlying factor at a time, thereby treating them as non-interrelated. However, companies often find that certain market events would result in a change of several underlying variables at the same time. If, for example, there is a threat of a new competitor entering an existing market then the market share of the company as well as the product price is expected to drop. Scenario analysis allows management to investigate the effect of potential future scenarios of events, which are translated into the DCF valuation model as consistent changes of various combinations of the underlying variables.

Alternative decision criteria

Companies of all sizes and sectors have long been using a number of other decision criteria to evaluate their capital investment projects either as a supplement to, or worse, as a substitute for the NPV rule. Let us briefly summarise how some of these criteria work and compare them with NPV.

Payback and discounted payback

The simple payback period of a project is defined as the expected number of years it takes for the company to recover its initial investment outlay by implementing the project. The decision criterion is then given as a maximum number of years, or cut-off period, above which capital investment proposals should be rejected. This implies that the shorter the payback period, the better the project is.

However, there are two major shortcomings to this rule. First, it fails to recognise the time value of money. No investors would be satisfied by investing £100 today and receiving exactly the same amount a year from now and nothing afterwards, even though the investment has a one-year payback period. Second, the rule disregards expected cash flows from the project after the cut-off period. It prefers projects with large pay-offs in the early years and perhaps nothing later to long-term projects with gradually increasing positive cash flows.

Companies often use the discounted payback rule to correct for disregarding the time value of money. This method involves the calculation of the payback period in terms of the present value of future cash flows generated by the project. However, the rule still does not give any weight to cash flows after the arbitrary cut-off date.

Therefore, its use should be restricted to comparing projects with very similar even cash flow profiles. One example could be parts of the property sector, where a number of investments are expected to produce long-term evenly distributed rental income.

Internal rate of return

The internal rate of return (IRR) of a project is defined as the discount rate that makes the project's $NPV = 0$, thus obtained by solving the following equation for r:

$$0 = C_O + \frac{C_1}{1+r} + \frac{C_2}{1+r}$$
$$+ \cdots + \frac{C_n}{(1+r)^n}$$

For most projects the IRR rule gives an identical answer to the question whether it should be accepted or rejected. However, for some others the use of IRR is not appropriate, or needs to be used with great care. These exemptions include projects where, instead of an initial investment, the cash flow of the project changes sign more than once over the forecasting period or when the company is ranking mutually exclusive projects because of either technical or capital constraints.

Profitability index

The profitability index (PI) of a project is defined as the ratio between the present value of future cash flows from the project and the initial investment (where C_O is assumed to be negative):

$$PI = \frac{\sum_{i=1}^{n} \frac{C_1}{(1+r)^n}}{-C_0} = \frac{PV}{-C_0}$$

The rule says that all projects with a profitability index higher than I should be accepted, which is identical to the outcome of applying the NPV rule, since if $PI > I$ it means that $PV > -C_0$, and thus $NPV > 0$. However, the profitability index is not useful when applied to ranking mutually exclusive projects since it captures the profitability, but not the scale, of projects.

Accounting measures

There are a number of accounting measures used in the process of investment decision making, such as the return on investment (ROI) or average book return on investment. The major problem with these measures in general is that they are based on book values that are often liable to arbitrary selection of accounting policies (for example on depreciation schedules).

In addition, book values and book income do not reflect the time value of money, therefore various adjustments are needed to arrive at meaningful results. This means the DCF analysis is clearly preferable to accounting measures in setting investment decision criteria.

Expanding the frontiers of capital budgeting criteria

As mentioned earlier, however, the assumptions underlying the DCF analysis represent a static approach to decision making, and can be very restrictive in some cases. The replacement of uncertain future cash flows by their expected value and the use of a single discount rate ignore the possibility of active managerial actions over the lifetime of the project.

For example, managers take actions aimed at cutting the losses due to unfavourable market events and retaining or improving profits following favourable changes. This can change the risk profile of the project. Also, the standard DCF analysis works in terms of making a decision now or never. It ignores the opportunity managers may take to delay some strategic decisions pending the outcome of future events.

To overcome these drawbacks, various attempts have been made to develop more sophisticated decision criteria and investment analysis methods. These include decision tree analysis, the use of certainty equivalent cash flows and the application of option pricing theory in the valuation of real assets. The application of these methods has proved to be a helpful complement to DCF analysis.

Summary

The basis for most investment decision making is present value (PV) and net present value (NPV). These are used to make a comparison between the cost of an investment and the present value of uncertain future cash flows generated by the project. At least four steps are involved: forecasting those incremental cash flows (which will require some technical decisions such as how to treat inflation); estimating the appropriate discount rate or cost of capital (determined by the rate of return investors could expect from another investment with a similar risk profile); using this information to calculate the net present value; and deciding whether the project should go ahead. Further illumination can be provided by sensitivity analysis (calculating the impact of changing one or more variables), break-even analysis (pointing out the critical value of each variable where the NPV is zero), and scenario analysis.

Other investment decision criteria include payback and discounted payback, the internal rate of return and the profitability index.

Source: *FT Mastering Management Part 2,* 3 November 1995.

interest payments can be calculated and evaluated. Equally, the ability to evaluate projects in financial terms is clearly important to any organisation. Because most project investments will have financial consequences over a period of time, it is necessary to allow for time preference in this financial evaluation. This can be achieved through the calculation of present values.

QMDM IN ACTION
Tomco Oil Inc.

As was discussed in the QMDM in Action in Chapter 6, the oil industry is one characterised by high levels of uncertainty and, linked to such uncertainty, high financial returns/high financial losses. Although one tends to think of the oil industry in terms of the large multinationals – Shell, BP, Exxon/Esso – the industry also contains many smaller, independent operators. Among these are the so-called wildcat operators – typically companies involved in exploration, drilling and production on a smaller scale and who have no pipeline or distribution systems of their own. For such companies the wrong decision about a particular operation can have fatal consequences for the organisation's survival.

One such operator is Tomco Oil, which was faced with a choice of two sites in Kansas, USA. It was seen in Chapter 6 that the sequential decision problem a company faces in such circumstances is typified by inadequate and uncertain information. Yet, based on this information, the organisation has to reach a decision about the likely financial consequences in terms of future cash flows. Figure 15.1 shows the various elements of the decision model and their interrelationship in this context. Tomco was faced with choosing between two sites: Blair East and Blair West. The available information on Blair East was less than that of the alternative site and this is reflected in the added complexity of the relevant part of the decision tree for Blair East, shown in Figure 15.2. While there were only five possible outcomes from the decision to develop Blair West, there were over 70 for Blair East.

To help assess the options, a financial evaluation was added to the model. For each outcome a financial contribution was calculated, consisting of the net cash inflows after deducting operating costs. Given that any given well is expected to have an economic life lasting a number of years, it is clearly appropriate to evaluate the options in terms of discounted cash flows rather than simple totals. This in itself required a detailed assessment of the future in terms of:

● future oil prices;

● estimates of oil reserves on the sites. These varied between 10 000 barrels and 40 000 barrels;

● annual oil production from each site;

● annual operating costs and taxes.

Table 15.11 shows the calculations for some of the options considered at a discount rate of 14 per cent.

The recommendation was made, at the end of the modelling process, to drill at Blair West. The president of Tomco later commented:

'Before we actually utilised decision-tree analysis to aid in our selection of drilling-sites, we were skeptical as to the applicability ... in oil exploration. (Such) analysis provided us with ... a clearer insight into the numerous and varied financial outcomes that are possible.'

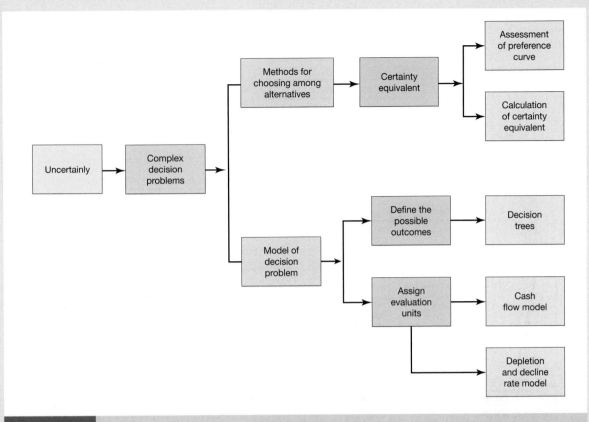

Figure 15.1   The structure of an integrated model of decision making under uncertainty

Reprinted by permission of J Hosseini. Taken from 'Decision Analysis and its Application in the Choice Between Two Wildcat Adventures', J Hosseini, *Interfaces*, **16**(2), 1986. Copyright held by the Operations Research Society of America and the Institute of Management Sciences.

Table 15.11   Calculation of net present value for a reserve of 10 000 barrels of capacity, pumped off at a 20 per cent depletion rate and discounted at 14 per cent

Year	Price ($)	Bbls.	Total ($)	Operating expenses ($)	Net cash flow ($)	NPV factor	Net present value ($)
1	29.00	2 000	58 000	11 630	46 370	0.877	40 666.50
2	29.00	1 600	46 400	11 630	34 770	0.769	26 738.13
3	30.74	1 280	39 347	12 238	27 019	0.675	18 237.83
4	32.58	1 024	33 362	13 852	19 510	0.592	11 549.92
5	34.53	819	28 246	14 683	13 563	0.519	7 039.20
6	36.60	655	23 973	15 564	8 409	0.456	3 834.50
7	38.80	524	10 331	16 497	3 834	0.400	1 533.60

Total net present value of cash flows $109 589.68

Reprinted by permission of J Hosseini. Taken from 'Decision Analysis and its Application in the Choice Between Two Wildcat Adventures', *Interfaces*, **16** (2), 1986. Copyright held by the Operations Research Society of America and the Institute of Management Sciences.

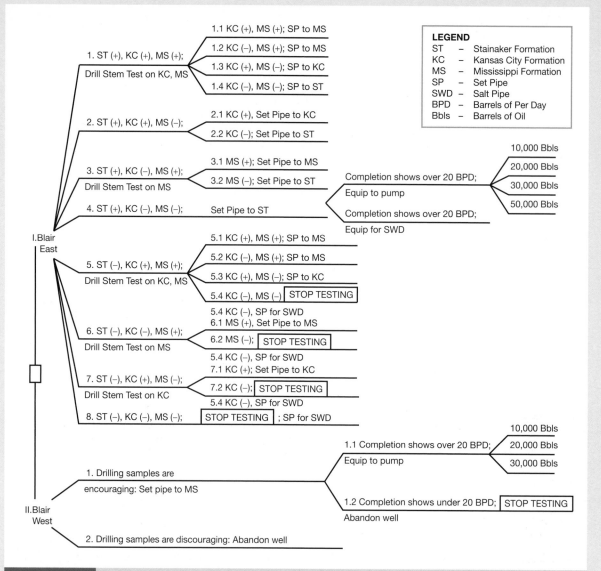

Exercises

1 You have the choice of investing a sum of money in four alternative schemes:

   (a) one which will pay 10 per cent per annum interest compounded daily;

   (b) one which will pay 10.25 per cent per annum interest compounded monthly;

   (c) one which will pay 10.5 per cent per annum interest compounded quarterly;

   (d) one which will pay 10.75 per cent per annum interest compounded annually.

   Which would you choose and why?

2 The company you work for is considering acquiring several of the latest generation desktop computers for use in an office. The company expects the equipment to have a useful life of three years. The finance director has asked you to recommend whether the equipment should be purchased outright or whether it should be leased from the supplier. If the equipment is purchased outright the total cost will be £4200. At the end of the three years it is estimated that the equipment will have a scrap value of £500. If the machine is leased then the rental charge will be £1660 per annum payable at the start of each year. The company's cost of capital is currently 10.5 per cent per annum.

   Draft a report advising the company whether it should purchase or lease the equipment and comment on any other factors the company may want to consider before making a decision.

3 A production company is considering purchasing a new piece of equipment for the production process for one of its products. The product itself is due to be withdrawn from the market in five years' time. The equipment will cost £600 000 and have a scrap value of £5000. Included in this price is a one-year service guarantee from the supplier of the equipment. Each additional year the equipment is in use the company will take out another service contract with the supplier at a cost of £7500.

   Calculate the net present value for this project assuming a cost of capital of 15 per cent. Explain how this calculation might help the company in its decision making.

4 A hospital has decided to replace an important piece of medical equipment at a cost of £30 000. The expected life of the equipment is five years and it will have a resale value of £4000 at this time. The hospital is trying to decide how to finance the purchase. One option is to buy the equipment outright. A second option is to obtain the equipment under a credit agreement with a finance company. Under this agreement the hospital will pay £10 000 now and £5500 at the beginning of each subsequent year. A third option is to enter into a leasing agreement. Under this agreement the hospital will pay an initial amount of £9000 at the start of the first year. At the start of each subsequent year another payment will be needed which will be the previous year's payment less 12 per cent. The current cost of capital for the hospital is 9 per cent.

   Which of the three options would you recommend?

5 A local authority is under severe financial pressure and is considering selling some of the land it owns to a building company. The building company is offering to pay £150 000 for the land now or a payment of £40 000 a year for the next five years.

(a) If the current interest rate is 8 per cent, which option would you advise the local authority to take?

(b) How would your recommendation be affected by changes in the interest rate?

(c) What other factors should the local authority take into account?

6 A large organisation is considering replacing part of its vehicle fleet with the latest equipment. Although such a decision is expensive, it is felt that the investment will be worthwhile in terms of generating future cost savings in repairs, maintenance and running costs and will also help improve the quality of service provided. The company's current cost of borrowing is 12 per cent per annum. Two suppliers have been asked to tender for the project. The relevant costs of the project and the corresponding savings (in terms of reduced costs, increased efficiency, etc.) are shown in Table 15.12.

(a) Which supplier would you recommend?

(b) Calculate the IRR for each supplier and explain how this could be used.

Table 15.12	Project costs and savings (£s)			
	Supplier A		Supplier B	
Year	Cost	Savings	Cost	Savings
Now	120 000	0	85 000	0
1	0	25 000	35 000	0
2	0	30 000	0	60 000
3	0	40 000	0	45 000
4	0	50 000	0	35 000
5	0	25 000	0	35 000

7 An organisation has recently purchased a company car for one of its senior managers at a cost of £25 000 and is trying to determine the most suitable time for replacement. It is estimated that the car will depreciate by £5000 in the first year, £2000 in each of the next two years and £3000 in each of the next two years. Running costs in the first year are estimated at £5000 and are estimated to increase by 15 per cent per annum thereafter.

(a) Determine a suitable time for replacing the car.

(b) The company has a capital cost for such projects of 5 per cent per annum and expects inflation to average 2 per cent per annum over the foreseeable future. Using present-value techniques determine a suitable replacement time for the vehicle.

Conclusion

We have now reached the end of a long, sometimes difficult, but hopefully productive journey. We set out with the intention of introducing a number of common and useful quantitative techniques and to illustrate these with their typical uses by a variety of business organisations. The purpose of doing this was to enable you to develop an awareness of such techniques, skills in their use, an understanding of their potential for the manager and an appreciation of their limitations. As we indicated at the very start of this text, such techniques are available as tools for the manager facing some decision problem. They do not offer instant solutions and they are not intended to be used in complete isolation. A sensible manager will assess the potential contribution such techniques can make in particular circumstances and weigh the information such techniques generate alongside that from other sources including personal experience and judgement.

As we have also indicated as we have progressed through the text, the techniques and models we have examined are capable of being developed and applied in far more complex ways than those we have illustrated. However, you should now be in a position to make a rational decision as to when to call in the 'experts' to put these techniques into practice and equally how to assess the results of their analysis in a reasonably competent way. No matter what the technical competence of the expert quantitative modeller, this is no substitute for the wider perspective that the competent manager must bring to decision making.

Appendix A
Binomial Distribution

	p =	0.01	0.02	0.03	0.04	0.05	0.06	0.07	0.08	0.09
n = 2	r ⩾ 0	1.0000	1.0000	1.0000	1.0000	1.0000	1.0000	1.0000	1.0000	1.0000
	1	.0199	.0396	.0591	.0784	.0975	.1164	.1351	.1536	.1719
	2	.0001	.0004	.0009	.0016	.0025	.0036	.0049	.0064	.0081
n = 5	r ⩾ 0	1.0000	1.0000	1.0000	1.0000	1.0000	1.0000	1.0000	1.0000	1.0000
	1	.0490	.0961	.1413	.1846	.2262	.2661	.3043	.3409	.3760
	2	.0010	.0038	.0085	.0148	.0226	.0319	.0425	.0544	.0674
	3		.0001	.0003	.0006	.0012	.0020	.0031	.0045	.0063
	4						.0001	.0001	.0002	.0003
n = 10	r ⩾ 0	1.0000	1.0000	1.0000	1.0000	1.0000	1.0000	1.0000	1.0000	1.0000
	1	.0956	.1829	.2626	.3352	.4013	.4614	.5160	.5656	.6106
	2	.0043	.0162	.0345	.0582	.0861	.1176	.1517	.1879	.2254
	3	.0001	.0009	.0028	.0062	.0115	.0188	.0283	.0401	.0540
	4			.0001	.0004	.0010	.0020	.0036	.0058	.0088
	5					.0001	.0002	.0003	.0006	.0010
	6									.0001
n = 20	r ⩾ 0	1.0000	1.0000	1.0000	1.0000	1.0000	1.0000	1.0000	1.0000	1.0000
	1	.1821	.3324	.4562	.5580	.6415	.7099	.7658	.8113	.8484
	2	.0169	.0599	.1198	.1897	.2642	.3395	.4131	.4831	.5484
	3	.0010	.0071	.0210	.0439	.0755	.1150	.1610	.2121	.2666
	4		.0006	.0027	.0074	.0159	.0290	.0471	.0706	.0993
	5			.0003	.0010	.0026	.0056	.0107	.0183	.0290
	6				.0001	.0003	.0009	.0019	.0038	.0068
	7						.0001	.0003	.0006	.0013
	8								.0001	.0002
n = 50	r ⩾ 0	1.0000	1.0000	1.0000	1.0000	1.0000	1.0000	1.0000	1.0000	1.0000
	1	.3950	.6358	.7819	.8701	.9231	.9547	.9734	.9845	.9910
	2	.0894	.2642	.4447	.5995	.7206	.8100	.8735	.9173	.9468
	3	.0138	.0784	.1892	.3233	.4595	.5838	.6892	.7740	.8395
	4	.0016	.0178	.0628	.1391	.2396	.3527	.4673	.5747	.6697
	5	.0001	.0032	.0168	.0490	.1036	.1794	.2710	.3710	.4723
	6		.0005	.0037	.0144	.0378	.0776	.1350	.2081	.2928
	7		.0001	.0007	.0036	.0118	.0289	.0583	.1019	.1596
	8			.0001	.0008	.0032	.0094	.0220	.0438	.0768
	9				.0001	.0008	.0027	.0073	.0167	.0328

p =	0.01	0.02	0.03	0.04	0.05	0.06	0.07	0.08	0.09
10					.0002	.0007	.0022	.0056	.0125
11						.0002	.0006	.0017	.0043
12							.0001	.0005	.0013
13								.0001	.0004
14									.0001

p =	0.01	0.02	0.03	0.04	0.05	0.06	0.07	0.08	0.09
n = 100 r ⩾ 0	1.0000	1.0000	1.0000	1.0000	1.0000	1.0000	1.0000	1.0000	1.0000
1	.6340	.8674	.9524	.9831	.9941	.9979	.9993	.9998	.9999
2	.2642	.5967	.8054	.9128	.9629	.9848	.9940	.9977	.9991
3	.0794	.3233	.5802	.7679	.8817	.9434	.9742	.9887	.9952
4	.0184	.1410	.3528	.5705	.7422	.8570	.9256	.9633	.9827
5	.0034	.0508	.1821	.3711	.5640	.7232	.8368	.9097	.9526
6	.0005	.0155	.0808	.2116	.3840	.5593	.7086	.8201	.8955
7	.0001	.0041	.0312	.1064	.2340	.3936	.5557	.6968	.8060
8		.0009	.0106	.0475	.1280	.2517	.4012	.5529	.6872
9		.0002	.0032	.0190	.0631	.1463	.2660	.4074	.5506
10			.0009	.0068	.0282	.0775	.1620	.2780	.4125
11			.0002	.0022	.0115	.0376	.0908	.1757	.2882
12				.0007	.0043	.0168	.0469	.1028	.1876
13				.0002	.0015	.0069	.0224	.0559	.1138
14					.0005	.0026	.0099	.0282	.0645
15					.0001	.0009	.0041	.0133	.0341
16						.0003	.0016	.0058	.0169
17						.0001	.0006	.0024	.0078
18							.0002	.0009	.0034
19							.0001	.0003	.0014
20								.0001	.0005
21									.0002
22									.0001

p =	0.10	0.15	0.20	0.25	0.30	0.35	0.40	0.45	0.50
n = 2 r ⩾ 0	1.0000	1.0000	1.0000	1.0000	1.0000	1.0000	1.0000	1.0000	1.0000
1	.1900	.2775	.3600	.4375	.5100	.5775	.6400	.6975	.7500
2	.0100	.0225	.0400	.0625	.0900	.1225	.1600	.2025	.2500
n = 5 r ⩾ 0	1.0000	1.0000	1.0000	1.0000	1.0000	1.0000	1.0000	1.0000	1.0000
1	.4095	.5563	.6723	.7627	.8319	.8840	.9222	.9497	.9688
2	.0815	.1648	.2627	.3672	.4718	.5716	.6630	.7438	.8125
3	.0086	.0266	.0579	.1035	.1631	.2352	.3174	.4069	.5000
4	.0005	.0022	.0067	.0156	.0308	.0540	.0870	.1312	.1875
5		.0001	.0003	.0010	.0024	.0053	.0102	.0185	.0313
n = 10 r ⩾ 0	1.0000	1.0000	1.0000	1.0000	1.0000	1.0000	1.0000	1.0000	1.0000
1	.6513	.8031	.8926	.9437	.9718	.9865	.9940	.9975	.9990
2	.2639	.4557	.6242	.7560	.8507	.9140	.9536	.9767	.9893
3	.0702	.1798	.3222	.4744	.6172	.7384	.8327	.9004	.9453
4	.0128	.0500	.1209	.2241	.3504	.4862	.6177	.7430	.8281
5	.0016	.0099	.0328	.0781	.1503	.2485	.3669	.4956	.6230

	p =	0.10	0.15	0.20	0.25	0.30	0.35	0.40	0.45	0.50
	6	.0001	.0014	.0064	.0197	.0473	.0949	.1662	.2616	.3770
	7		.0001	.0009	.0035	.0106	.0260	.0548	.1020	.1719
	8			.0001	.0004	.0016	.0048	.0123	.0274	.0547
	9					.0001	.0005	.0017	.0045	.0107
	10							.0001	.0003	.0010
n = 20	r ⩾ 0	1.0000	1.0000	1.0000	1.0000	1.0000	1.0000	1.0000	1.0000	1.0000
	1	.8784	.9612	.9885	.9968	.9992	.9998	1.0000	1.0000	1.0000
	2	.6083	.8244	.9308	.9757	.9924	.9979	.9995	.9999	1.0000
	3	.3231	.5951	.7939	.9087	.9645	.9879	.9964	.9991	.9998
	4	.1330	.3523	.5886	.7748	.8929	.9556	.9840	.9951	.9987
	5	.0432	.1702	.3704	.5852	.7625	.8818	.9490	.9811	.9941
	6	.0113	.0673	.1958	.3828	.5836	.7546	.8744	.9447	.9793
	7	.0024	.0219	.0867	.2142	.3920	.5834	.7500	.8701	.9423
	8	.0004	.0059	.0321	.1018	.2277	.3990	.5841	.7480	.8684
	9	.0001	.0013	.0100	.0409	.1133	.2376	.4044	.5857	.7483
	10		.0002	.0026	.0139	.0480	.1218	.2447	.4086	.5881
	11			.0006	.0039	.0171	.0532	.1275	.2493	.4119
	12			.0001	.0009	.0051	.0196	.0565	.1308	.2517
	13				.0002	.0013	.0060	.0210	.0580	.1316
	14					.0003	.0015	.0065	.0214	.0577
	15						.0003	.0016	.0064	.0207
	16							.0003	.0015	.0059
	17								.0003	.0013
	18									.0002
n = 50	r ⩾ 0	1.0000	1.0000	1.0000	1.0000	1.0000	1.0000	1.0000	1.0000	1.0000
	1	.9948	.9997	1.0000	1.0000	1.0000	1.0000	1.0000	1.0000	1.0000
	2	.9662	.9971	.9998	1.0000	1.0000	1.0000	1.0000	1.0000	1.0000
	3	.8883	.9858	.9987	.9999	1.0000	1.0000	1.0000	1.0000	1.0000
	4	.7497	.9540	.9943	.9995	1.0000	1.0000	1.0000	1.0000	1.0000
	5	.5688	.8879	.9815	.9979	.9998	1.0000	1.0000	1.0000	1.0000
	6	.3839	.7806	.9520	.9930	.9993	.9999	1.0000	1.0000	1.0000
	7	.2298	.6387	.8966	.9806	.9975	.9998	1.0000	1.0000	1.0000
	8	.1221	.4812	.8096	.9547	.9927	.9992	.9999	1.0000	1.0000
	9	.0579	.3319	.6927	.9084	.9817	.9975	.9998	1.0000	1.0000
	10	.0245	.2089	.5563	.8363	.9598	.9933	.9992	.9999	1.0000
	11	.0094	.1199	.4164	.7378	.9211	.9840	.9978	.9998	1.0000
	12	.0032	.0628	.2893	.6184	.8610	.9658	.9943	.9994	1.0000
	13	.0010	.0301	.1861	.4890	.7771	.9339	.9867	.9982	.9998
	14	.0003	.0132	.1106	.3630	.6721	.8837	.9720	.9955	.9995
	15	.0001	.0053	.0607	.2519	.5532	.8122	.9460	.9896	.9987
	16		.0019	.0308	.1631	.4308	.7199	.9045	.9780	.9967
	17		.0007	.0144	.0983	.3161	.6111	.8439	.9573	.9923
	18		.0002	.0063	.0551	.2178	.4940	.7631	.9235	.9836
	19		.0001	.0025	.0287	.1406	.3784	.6644	.8727	.9675
	20			.0009	.0139	.0848	.2736	.5535	.8026	.9405
	21			.0003	.0063	.0478	.1861	.4390	.7138	.8987
	22			.0001	.0026	.0251	.1187	.3299	.6100	.8389
	23				.0010	.0123	.0710	.2340	.4981	.7601

p =	0.10	0.15	0.20	0.25	0.30	0.35	0.40	0.45	0.50
24				.0004	.0056	.0396	.1562	.3866	.6641
25				.0001	.0024	.0207	.0978	.2840	.5561
26					.0009	.0100	.0573	.1966	.4439
27					.0003	.0045	.0314	.1279	.3359
28					.0001	.0019	.0160	.0780	.2399
29						.0007	.0076	.0444	.1611
30						.0003	.0034	.0235	.1013
31						.0001	.0014	.0116	.0595
32							.0005	.0053	.0325
33							.0002	.0022	.0164
34							.0001	.0009	.0077
35								.0003	.0033
36								.0001	.0013
37									.0005
38									.0002

	p =	0.10	0.15	0.20	0.25	0.30	0.35	0.40	0.45	0.50
n = 100	r ⩾ 0	1.0000	1.0000	1.0000	1.0000	1.0000	1.0000	1.0000	1.0000	1.0000
	1	1.0000	1.0000	1.0000	1.0000	1.0000	1.0000	1.0000	1.0000	1.0000
	2	.9997	1.0000	1.0000	1.0000	1.0000	1.0000	1.0000	1.0000	1.0000
	3	.9981	1.0000	1.0000	1.0000	1.0000	1.0000	1.0000	1.0000	1.0000
	4	.9992	.9999	1.0000	1.0000	1.0000	1.0000	1.0000	1.0000	1.0000
	5	.9763	.9996	1.0000	1.0000	1.0000	1.0000	1.0000	1.0000	1.0000
	6	.9424	.9984	1.0000	1.0000	1.0000	1.0000	1.0000	1.0000	1.0000
	7	.8828	.9953	.9999	1.0000	1.0000	1.0000	1.0000	1.0000	1.0000
	8	.7939	.9878	.9997	1.0000	1.0000	1.0000	1.0000	1.0000	1.0000
	9	.6791	.9725	.9991	1.0000	1.0000	1.0000	1.0000	1.0000	1.0000
	10	.5487	.9449	.9977	1.0000	1.0000	1.0000	1.0000	1.0000	1.0000
	11	.4168	.9006	.9943	.9999	1.0000	1.0000	1.0000	1.0000	1.0000
	12	.2970	.8365	.9874	.9996	1.0000	1.0000	1.0000	1.0000	1.0000
	13	.1982	.7527	.9747	.9990	1.0000	1.0000	1.0000	1.0000	1.0000
	14	.1239	.6526	.9531	.9975	.9999	1.0000	1.0000	1.0000	1.0000
	15	.0726	.5428	.9196	.9946	.9998	1.0000	1.0000	1.0000	1.0000
	16	.0399	.4317	.8715	.9889	.9996	1.0000	1.0000	1.0000	1.0000
	17	.0206	.3275	.8077	.9789	.9990	1.0000	1.0000	1.0000	1.0000
	18	.0100	.2367	.7288	.9624	.9978	.9999	1.0000	1.0000	1.0000
	19	.0046	.1628	.6379	.9370	.9955	.9999	1.0000	1.0000	1.0000
	20	.0020	.1065	.5398	.9005	.9911	.9997	1.0000	1.0000	1.0000
	21	.0008	.0663	.4405	.8512	.9835	.9992	1.0000	1.0000	1.0000
	22	.0003	.0393	.3460	.7886	.9712	.9983	1.0000	1.0000	1.0000
	23	.0001	.0221	.2611	.7136	.9521	.9966	.9999	1.0000	1.0000
	24		.0119	.1891	.6289	.9245	.9934	.9997	1.0000	1.0000
	25		.0061	.1314	.5383	.8864	.9879	.9994	1.0000	1.0000
	26		.0030	.0875	.4465	.8369	.9789	.9988	1.0000	1.0000
	27		.0014	.0558	.3583	.7756	.9649	.9976	.9999	1.0000
	28		.0006	.0342	.2776	.7036	.9442	.9954	.9998	1.0000
	29		.0003	.0200	.2075	.6232	.9152	.9916	.9996	1.0000

p =	0.10	0.15	0.20	0.25	0.30	0.35	0.40	0.45	0.50
30		.0001	.0112	.1495	.5377	.8764	.9852	.9992	1.0000
31			.0061	.1038	.4509	.8270	.9752	.9985	1.0000
32			.0031	.0693	.3669	.7669	.9602	.9970	.9999
33			.0016	.0446	.2893	.6971	.9385	.9945	.9998
34			.0007	.0276	.2207	.6197	.9087	.9902	.9996
35			.0003	.0164	.1629	.5376	.8697	.9834	.9991
36			.0001	.0094	.1161	.4542	.8205	.9728	.9982
37			.0001	.0052	.0799	.3731	.7614	.9571	.9967
38				.0027	.0530	.2976	.6932	.9349	.9940
39				.0014	.0340	.2301	.6178	.9049	.9895
40				.0007	.0210	.1724	.5379	.8657	.9824
41				.0003	.0125	.1250	.4567	.8169	.9716
42				.0001	.0072	.0877	.3775	.7585	.9557
43				.0001	.0040	.0594	.3033	.6913	.9334
44					.0021	.0389	.2365	.6172	.9033
45					.0011	.0246	.1789	.5387	.8644
46					.0005	.0150	.1311	.4587	.8159
47					.0003	.0088	.0930	.3804	.7579
48					.0001	.0050	.0638	.3069	.6914
49					.0001	.0027	.0423	.2404	.6178
50						.0015	.0271	.1827	.5398
51						.0007	.0168	.1346	.4602
52						.0004	.0100	.0960	.3822
53						.0002	.0058	.0662	.3086
54						.0001	.0032	.0441	.2421
55							.0017	.0284	.1841
56							.0009	.0176	.1356
57							.0004	.0106	.0967
58							.0002	.0061	.0666
59							.0001	.0034	.0443
60								.0018	.0284
61								.0009	.0176
62								.0005	.0105
63								.0002	.0060
64								.0001	.0033
65									.0018
66									.0009
67									.0004
68									.0002
69									.0001

Appendix B
Areas in the Tail of the
Normal Distribution

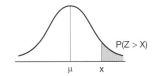

P(Z > X)

μ   x

Z	.00	.01	.02	.03	.04	.05	.06	.07	.08	.09
0.0	.5000	.4960	.4920	.4880	.4840	.4801	.4761	.4721	.4681	.4641
0.1	.4602	.4562	.4522	.4483	.4443	.4404	.4364	.4325	.4286	.4247
0.2	.4207	.4168	.4129	.4090	.4052	.4013	.3974	.3936	.3897	.3859
0.3	.3821	.3783	.3745	.3707	.3669	.3632	.3594	.3557	.3520	.3483
0.4	.3446	.3409	.3372	.3336	.3300	.3264	.3228	.3192	.3156	.3121
0.5	.3085	.3050	.3015	.2981	.2946	.2912	.2877	.2843	.2810	.2776
0.6	.2743	.2709	.2676	.2643	.2611	.2578	.2546	.2514	.2483	.2451
0.7	.2420	.2389	.2358	.2327	.2296	.2266	.2236	.2206	.2177	.2148
0.8	.2119	.2090	.2061	.2033	.2005	.1977	.1949	.1922	.1894	.1867
0.9	.1841	.1814	.1788	.1762	.1736	.1711	.1685	.1660	.1635	.1611
1.0	.1587	.1562	.1539	.1515	.1492	.1469	.1446	.1423	.1401	.1379
1.1	.1357	.1335	.1314	.1292	.1271	.1251	.1230	.1210	.1190	.1170
1.2	.1151	.1131	.1112	.1093	.1075	.1056	.1038	.1020	.1003	.0985
1.3	.0968	.0951	.0934	.0918	.0901	.0885	.0869	.0853	.0838	.0823
1.4	.0808	.0793	.0778	.0764	.0749	.0735	.0721	.0708	.0694	.0681
1.5	.0668	.0655	.0643	.0630	.0618	.0606	.0594	.0582	.0571	.0559
1.6	.0548	.0537	.0526	.0516	.0505	.0495	.0485	.0475	.0465	.0455
1.7	.0446	.0436	.0427	.0418	.0409	.0401	.0392	.0384	.0375	.0367
1.8	.0359	.0351	.0344	.0336	.0329	.0322	.0314	.0307	.0301	.0294
1.9	.0287	.0281	.0274	.0268	.0262	.0256	.0250	.0244	.0239	.0233
2.0	.0228	.0222	.0217	.0212	.0207	.0202	.0197	.0192	.0188	.0183
2.1	.0179	.0174	.0170	.0166	.0162	.0158	.0154	.0150	.0146	.0143
2.2	.0139	.0136	.0132	.0129	.0125	.0122	.0119	.0116	.0133	.0110
2.3	.0107	.0104	.0102	.0099	.0096	.0094	.0091	.0089	.0087	.0084
2.4	.0082	.0080	.0078	.0075	.0073	.0071	.0069	.0068	.0066	.0064
2.5	.0062	.0060	.0059	.0057	.0055	.0054	.0052	.0051	.0049	.0048
2.6	.0047	.0045	.0044	.0043	.0041	.0040	.0039	.0038	.0037	.0036
2.7	.0035	.0034	.0033	.0032	.0031	.0030	.0029	.0028	.0027	.0026
2.8	.0026	.0025	.0024	.0023	.0023	.0022	.0021	.0021	.0020	.0019
2.9	.0019	.0018	.0018	.0017	.0016	.0016	.0015	.0015	.0014	.0014
3.0	.0014	.0013	.0013	.0012	.0012	.0011	.0011	.0011	.0010	.0010

Appendix C
Areas in the Tail of the
t Distribution

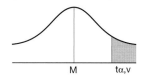

υ	α				
	0.10	0.05	0.025	0.01	0.005
1	3.078	6.314	12.706	31.821	63.657
2	1.886	2.920	4.303	6.965	9.925
3	1.638	2.353	3.182	4.541	5.841
4	1.533	2.132	2.776	3.747	4.604
5	1.476	2.015	2.571	3.365	4.032
6	1.440	1.943	2.447	3.143	3.707
7	1.415	1.895	2.365	2.998	3.499
8	1.397	1.860	2.306	2.896	3.355
9	1.383	1.833	2.262	2.821	3.250
10	1.372	1.812	2.228	2.764	3.169
11	1.363	1.796	2.201	2.718	3.106
12	1.356	1.782	2.179	2.681	3.055
13	1.350	1.771	2.160	2.650	3.012
14	1.345	1.761	2.145	2.624	2.977
15	1.341	1.753	2.131	2.602	2.947
16	1.337	1.746	2.120	2.583	2.921
17	1.333	1.740	2.110	2.567	2.898
18	1.330	1.734	2.101	2.552	2.878
19	1.328	1.729	2.093	2.539	2.861
20	1.325	1.725	2.086	2.528	2.845
25	1.316	1.708	2.060	2.485	2.787
30	1.310	1.697	2.042	2.457	2.750
40	1.303	1.684	2.021	2.423	2.704
50	1.299	1.676	2.009	2.403	2.678
∞	1.282	1.645	1.960	2.326	2.576

Appendix D
Areas in the Tail of the χ^2 Distribution

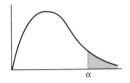

Degrees of freedom	Level of significance α		Degrees of freedom	Level of significance α	
	0.05	0.01		0.05	0.01
1	3.84	6.63	20	31.41	37.57
2	5.99	9.21	21	32.67	38.93
3	7.81	11.34	22	33.92	40.29
4	9.49	13.28	23	35.17	41.64
5	11.07	15.09	24	36.42	42.98
6	12.59	16.81	25	37.65	44.31
7	14.07	18.48	26	38.89	45.64
8	15.51	20.09	27	40.11	46.96
9	16.92	21.67	28	41.34	48.28
10	18.31	23.21	29	42.56	49.59
11	19.68	24.72	30	43.77	50.89
12	21.03	26.22	40	55.76	63.69
13	22.36	27.69	50	67.50	76.15
14	23.68	29.14	60	79.08	88.38
15	25.00	30.58	70	90.53	100.43
16	26.30	32.00	80	101.88	112.33
17	27.59	33.41	90	113.15	124.12
18	28.87	34.81	100	124.34	135.81
19	30.14	36.19			

Appendix E
Areas in the Tail of the F Distribution, 0.05 *Level*

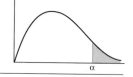

v_1 v_2	1	2	3	4	5	6	7	8	9
1	161.45	199.50	215.71	224.58	230.16	233.99	236.77	238.88	240.54
2	18.513	19.000	19.164	19.247	19.296	19.330	19.353	19.371	19.385
3	10.128	9.5521	9.2766	9.1172	9.0135	8.9406	8.8867	8.8452	8.8323
4	7.7086	6.9443	6.5914	6.3882	6.2561	6.1631	6.0942	6.0410	5.9938
5	6.6079	5.7861	5.4095	5.1922	5.0503	4.9503	4.8759	4.8183	4.7725
6	5.9874	5.1433	4.7571	4.5337	4.3874	4.2839	4.2067	4.1468	4.0990
7	5.5914	4.7374	4.3468	4.1203	3.9715	3.8660	3.7870	3.7257	3.6767
8	5.3177	4.4590	4.0662	3.8379	3.6875	3.5806	3.5005	3.4381	3.3881
9	5.1174	4.2565	3.8625	3.6331	3.4817	3.3738	3.2927	3.2296	3.1789
10	4.9646	4.1028	3.7083	3.4780	3.3258	3.2172	3.1355	3.0717	3.0204
11	4.8443	3.9823	3.5874	3.3567	3.2039	3.0946	3.0123	2.9480	2.8962
12	4.7472	3.8853	3.4903	3.2592	3.1059	2.9961	2.9134	2.8486	2.7964
13	4.6672	3.8056	3.4105	3.1791	3.0254	2.9153	2.8321	2.7669	2.7444
14	4.6001	3.7389	3.3439	3.1122	2.9582	2.8477	2.7642	2.6987	2.6458
15	4.5431	3.6823	3.2874	3.0556	2.9013	2.7905	2.7066	2.6408	2.5876
16	4.4940	3.6337	3.2389	3.0069	2.8524	2.7413	2.6572	2.5911	2.5377
17	4.4513	3.5915	3.1968	2.9647	2.8100	2.6987	2.6143	2.5480	2.4443
18	4.4139	3.5546	3.1599	2.9277	2.7729	2.6613	2.5767	2.5102	2.4563
19	4.3807	3.5219	3.1274	2.8951	2.7401	2.6283	2.5435	2.4768	2.4227
20	4.3512	3.4928	3.0984	2.8661	2.7109	2.5990	2.5140	2.4471	2.3928
21	4.3248	3.4668	3.0725	2.8401	2.6848	2.5727	2.4876	2.4205	2.3660
22	4.3009	3.4434	3.0491	2.8167	2.6613	2.5491	2.4638	2.3965	2.3219
23	4.2793	3.4221	3.0280	2.7955	2.6400	2.5277	2.4422	2.3748	2.3201
24	4.2597	3.4028	3.0088	2.7763	2.6207	2.5082	2.4226	2.3551	2.3002
25	4.2417	3.3852	2.9912	2.7587	2.6030	2.4904	2.4047	2.3371	2.2821
26	4.2252	3.3690	2.9752	2.7426	2.5868	2.4741	2.3883	2.3205	2.2655
27	4.2100	3.3541	2.9604	2.7278	2.5719	2.4591	2.3732	2.3053	2.2501
28	4.1960	3.3404	2.9467	2.7141	2.5581	2.4453	2.3593	2.2913	2.2360
29	4.1830	3.3277	2.9340	2.7014	2.5454	2.4324	2.3463	2.2783	2.2329
30	4.1709	3.3158	2.9223	2.6896	2.5336	2.4205	2.3343	2.2662	2.2507
40	4.0847	3.2317	2.8387	2.6060	2.4495	2.3359	2.2490	2.1802	2.1240
60	4.0012	3.1504	2.7581	2.5252	2.3683	2.2541	2.1665	2.0970	2.0401
120	3.9201	3.0718	2.6802	2.4472	2.2899	2.1750	2.0868	2.0164	1.9688
∞	3.8415	2.9957	2.6049	2.3719	2.2141	2.0986	2.0096	1.9384	1.8799

υ_2 \ υ_1	10	12	15	20	24	30	40	60	120	∞
1	241.88	243.91	245.95	248.01	249.05	250.10	251.14	252.20	253.25	254.31
2	19.396	19.413	19.429	19.446	19.454	19.462	19.471	19.479	19.487	19.496
3	8.7855	8.7446	8.7029	8.6602	8.6385	8.6166	8.5944	8.5720	8.5594	8.5264
4	5.9644	5.9117	5.8578	5.8025	5.7744	5.7459	5.7170	5.6877	5.6381	5.6281
5	4.7351	4.6777	4.6188	4.5581	4.5272	4.4957	4.4638	4.4314	4.3085	4.3650
6	4.0600	3.9999	3.9381	3.8742	3.8415	3.8082	3.7743	3.7398	3.7047	3.6689
7	3.6365	3.5747	3.5107	3.4445	3.4105	3.3758	3.3404	3.3043	3.2674	3.2298
8	3.3472	3.2839	3.2184	3.1503	3.1152	3.0794	3.0428	3.0053	2.9669	2.9276
9	3.1373	3.0729	3.0061	2.9365	2.9005	2.8637	2.8259	2.7872	2.7475	2.7067
10	2.9782	2.9130	2.8450	2.7740	2.7372	2.6996	2.6609	2.6211	2.5801	2.5379
11	2.8536	2.7876	2.7186	2.6464	2.6090	2.5705	2.5309	2.4901	2.4480	2.4045
12	2.7534	2.6866	2.6169	2.5436	2.5055	2.4663	2.4259	2.3842	2.3410	2.2962
13	2.6710	2.6037	2.5331	2.4589	2.4202	2.3803	2.3392	2.2966	2.2524	2.2064
14	2.6022	2.5342	2.4630	2.3879	2.3487	2.3082	2.2664	2.2229	2.1778	2.1307
15	2.5437	2.4753	2.4034	2.3275	2.2878	2.2468	2.2043	2.1601	2.1141	2.0658
16	2.4935	2.4247	2.3522	2.2756	2.2354	2.1938	2.1507	2.1058	2.0589	2.0096
17	2.4499	2.3807	2.3077	2.2304	2.1898	2.1477	2.1040	2.0584	2.0107	1.9604
18	2.4117	2.3421	2.2686	2.1906	2.1497	2.1071	2.0629	2.0166	1.9681	1.9168
19	2.3779	2.3080	2.2341	2.1555	2.1141	2.0712	2.0264	1.9795	1.9302	1.8780
20	2.3479	2.2776	2.2033	2.1242	2.0825	2.0391	1.9938	1.9464	1.8963	1.8432
21	2.3210	2.2504	2.1757	2.0960	2.0540	2.0102	1.9645	1.9165	1.8657	1.8117
22	2.2967	2.2258	2.1508	2.0707	2.0283	1.9842	1.9380	1.8894	1.8380	1.7831
23	2.2747	2.2036	2.1282	2.0476	2.0050	1.9605	1.9139	1.8648	1.8128	1.7570
24	2.2547	2.1834	2.1077	2.0267	1.9838	1.9390	1.8920	1.8424	1.7896	1.7330
25	2.2365	2.1649	2.0889	2.0075	1.9643	1.9192	1.8718	1.8217	1.7684	1.7110
26	2.2197	2.1479	2.0716	1.9898	1.9464	1.9010	1.8533	1.8027	1.7488	1.6906
27	2.2043	2.1323	2.0558	1.9736	1.9299	1.8842	1.8361	1.7851	1.7306	1.6717
28	2.1900	2.1179	2.0411	1.9586	1.9147	1.8687	1.8203	1.7689	1.7138	1.6541
29	2.1768	2.1045	2.0275	1.9446	1.9005	1.8543	1.8055	1.7537	1.6981	1.6376
30	2.1646	2.0921	2.0148	1.9317	1.8874	1.8409	1.7918	1.7396	1.6835	1.6223
40	2.0772	2.0035	1.9245	1.8389	1.7929	1.7444	1.6928	1.6373	1.5766	1.5089
60	1.9926	1.9174	1.8364	1.7480	1.7001	1.6491	1.5943	1.5343	1.4673	1.3893
120	1.9105	1.8337	1.7505	1.6587	1.6084	1.5543	1.4952	1.4290	1.3519	1.2539
∞	1.8307	1.7522	1.6664	1.5705	1.5173	1.4591	1.3940	1.3180	1.0214	1.0000

Appendix F
Solutions to Chapter
Activities

Note: if a particular activity does not have a solution shown here, the solution has been given in the chapter text following that activity.

Activity 2.1

(**a**) the number of private houses built last year
This will be discrete as only a whole number of houses can be built.

(**b**) the average price of a house
This is more problematic. The price will be measured in terms of a given number of £s. Financial data is technically discrete as it can take only fixed, numerical values. However, it is often treated as a continuous variable and we shall do so in this text.

(**c**) the number of people employed in the construction industry
Nominally, this will be discrete as we would normally think of counting the (whole) number of people employed. Even if we had fractions of people (perhaps representing those employed on a part-time basis) this would still be discrete (taking fixed, numerical values).

(**d**) the number of tonnes of concrete used in house construction
Technically continuous, as our measurement could, in theory, be to any required degree of accuracy.

(**e**) the different types of houses constructed
This would be an attribute variable.

Activity 2.2

25% can be expressed as 0.25 as a decimal or 1/4 as a fraction (i.e. we want to find 1/4 of the two original numbers). Using a pocket calculator it is easiest to use 0.25:

> We require $0.25 \times 12\,098$ which gives 3024.5
> and for 0.25×139.5 we get 34.875.

It is always a good idea when you are doing this sort of arithmetic (even on a spreadsheet) to have some mental idea as to the size of the number you should get as an answer. This will help you do a quick visual check as to whether the answer looks about right. Here we want 1/4 of each number. The first number is about 12 000 and mentally we can figure out that a quarter of this will be about 3000. Our calculated answer of 3024.5 is obviously in the right ballpark. Similarly a quarter of our second number, which is about 140, will be about 35. Get into the habit of doing this every time.

For the other calculations it is again best to convert them into decimals:

> 0.33
> 0.90
> 0.05 (take care over this one for 5%)
> 0.33
> 0.125
> 0.375

and using these in turn with each of the two original numbers:

> 0.33 gives 3992.34 and 46.035
> 0.90 gives 10888.2 and 125.55
> 0.05 gives 604.9 and 6.975
> 0.33 gives 3992.34 and 46.035
> 0.125 gives 1512.25 and 17.4375
> 0.375 gives 4536.75 and 52.3125.

Activity 2.3

(a) £1 078 245.7

(b) £1 078 250

(c) £1 078 000

(d) £1 100 000

Activity 2.4

(a) $100.2(34 - 7)/13$

The arithmetic order is to do the arithmetic inside the bracket first, then the multiplication, then the division. This gives:

> $100.2(27)/13$
> $= 208.108$
> $= 208.1$ (rounded)

(b) $0.5 - 0.8 \times 13 + 3$

Here, the arithmetic order is multiplication, addition, subtraction:

> $0.5 - 10.4 + 3$
> $= 0.5 - 7.4$ (taking care that $-10.4 + 3$ is done correctly)
> $= -6.9$

Note also that it would have been better to write (b) as:

> $0.5 - (0.8 \times 13) + 3$

(c) $(100 \times 2) - (5/2) \times 10$

Here we have two sets of brackets, so we need to do each of these first (it doesn't matter in what order), then the multiplication, then the subtraction:

$$(200) - (2.5) \times 10$$
$$= 200 - 25$$
$$= 175$$

Activity 2.5

(**a**) We wish to multiply two numbers so we must take their logs and add these together, then find the antilog.

log 1098.2 = 3.0406814
log 34 = 1.5314789
(log 1098.2) + (log 34) = 3.0406814 + 1.5314789 = 4.5721603
antilog(4.5721603) = 37 338.8

(**b**) We have:

log 345.6 = 2.5385737
log 23.7 = 1.3747483
log 109.3 = 2.0386202

giving

2.5385737 − 1.3747483 + 2.0386202 = 3.20244
antilog(3.20244) = 1593.84

(**c**) We take the log of 12.569, multiply by 5 and find the antilog:

log 12.569 = 1.0993007
multiply by 5 = 5.4965035
antilog(5.4965035) = 313 692.04

(**d**) We take the log of 156, divide by 8 and find the antilog:

log 156 = 2.1931246
divide by 8 = 0.274140575
antilog(0.274140575) = 1.88

Activity 2.6

(**a**) We require the sum of all the X values:

$$\Sigma X = 2 + 3 + 7 + 9 = 21$$

(**b**) Similarly, we require the sum of the Y values:

$$\Sigma Y = 10 + 12 + 14 + 18 = 54$$

(**c**) Here we require the sum of the X^2 values – that is, we square each X value and then add these resulting numbers together:

$$\Sigma X^2 = 2^2 + 3^2 + 7^2 + 9^2 = 4 + 9 + 49 + 81 = 143$$

(**d**) Here we find the total of the X values and square this total:

$$(\Sigma X)^2 = (21)^2 = 441$$

(**e**) This is the same as SY^2:

$$\Sigma Y^2 = 10^2 + 12^2 + 14^2 + 18^2 = 764$$

(**f**) We multiply each pair of Y and X values and then total:

$$\Sigma YX = (10 \times 2) + (12 \times 3) + (14 \times 7) + (18 \times 9) = 316$$

(**g**) $10! = 3\ 628\ 800$

(**h**) $3! = 6$

(**i**) $10! - 3! = 3\ 628\ 800 - 6 = 3\ 628\ 794$

Activity 2.8

We recognise this as a linear equation and following the steps set out we have the following:

Step 1

The price variable, P, corresponds to the X, horizontal, axis. It seems logical to set the minimum value for P at 0 (after all the firm cannot charge a negative price). The maximum value for P can logically be set at 20, since some mental arithmetic indicates that with P = 20 Q will equal zero and again negative values for Q have no business meaning. Accordingly, we have an X scale from 0 to 20.

Step 2

The Y (or Q) scale will go from 0 to 100, following on from the logic used in Step 1. Our two points will be:

P = 0, Q = 100
P = 20, Q = 0

Step 3

We need to ensure labels, scales, etc. are appropriately drawn.

Step 4

The two points, and the line joining them, are shown in Figure A.1.

From the graph we can determine Q when P = 7 as 65 (000). We can also determine that when Q = 40 (000) then P must be 12. Both results can also be confirmed directly from the equation.

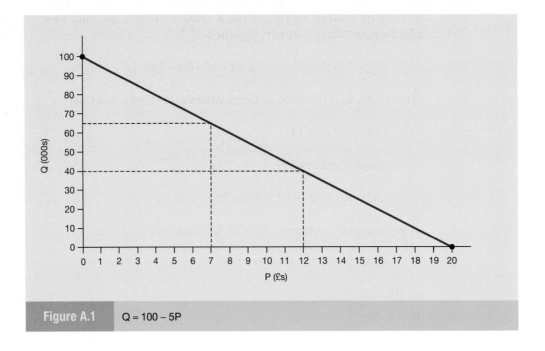

| Figure A.1 | $Q = 100 - 5P$ |

Activity 2.9

We calculate:

$$26\,000 \times \frac{100}{115} = £22\,609 \text{ (rounded)}$$

That is, the £26 000 is worth the same as £22 609 in 2007. After allowing for inflation over this period, we would be £2609 better off in real terms.

Activity 3.1

A retail organisation would probably be interested in reviewing such data as part of its overall strategic review. Changes in expenditure patterns and growth/decline in spending behaviour are clearly of critical importance to a retail organisation. From Table 3.1 itself a number of key points can be made:

- Overall, total expenditure has increased over this period by about 150 000 (£million).
- Over the expenditure categories shown, consumers' expenditure has changed in different ways.

However, it is also clear that without performing additional calculations it is difficult to assess relative changes over this period.

Activity 3.2

There are clearly a variety of bar charts we could use here and, again, until we produce them it is difficult to know which will best convey appropriate information. Figure A.2 shows the multiple bar chart for the various customer categories and for total sales. This is helpful in showing the relative importance of each category in the total. From the

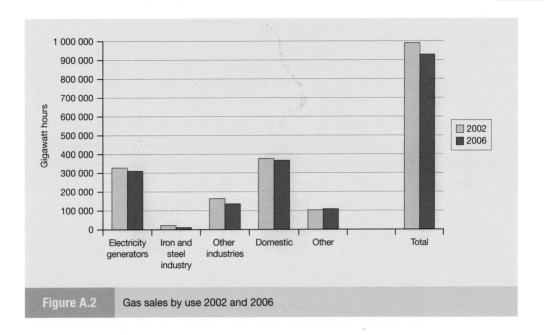

Figure A.2   Gas sales by use 2002 and 2006

Total we see that Gas sales have fallen over this 10-year period and that sales have fallen in each of the individual categories shown except for Other which shows a slight increase. We also see that Domestic sales is the largest category, closely followed by Electricity generators whilst Iron and steel is negligible.

Figure A.3 shows sales in each category as a percentage of total sales in each year. This gives a slight different picture. We see in percentage terms an increase in Electricity generators, Domestic and Other while Iron and steel and Other industries are taking a reduced share of total sales.

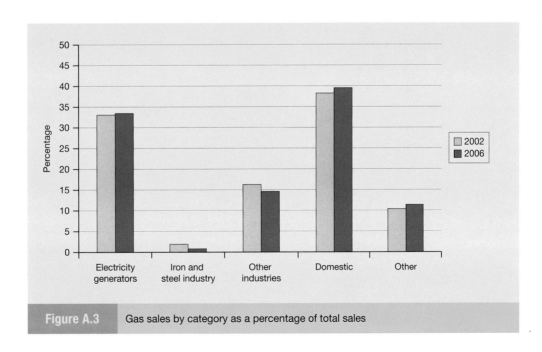

Figure A.3   Gas sales by category as a percentage of total sales

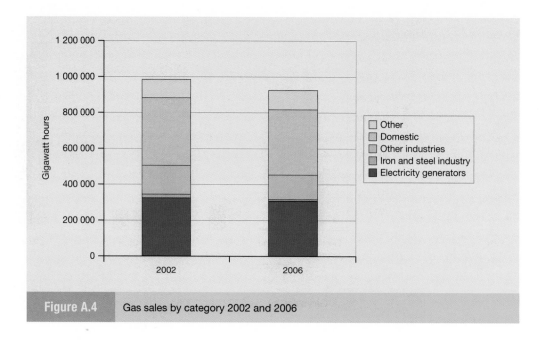

Figure A.4   Gas sales by category 2002 and 2006

Figures A.4 and A.5 show the component bar charts for the data. Your opinion may be different, but they really don't help to understand the data or the changes over this period and I wouldn't use them (although of course I didn't know that until I saw them).

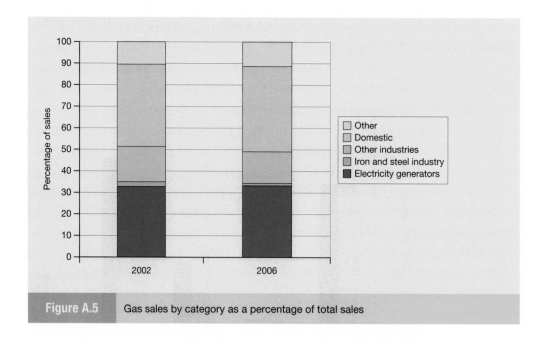

Figure A.5   Gas sales by category as a percentage of total sales

Figure A.6 shows the percentage change by category over the 10-year period. The diagram is effective at showing the very marked reduction in Iron and steel.

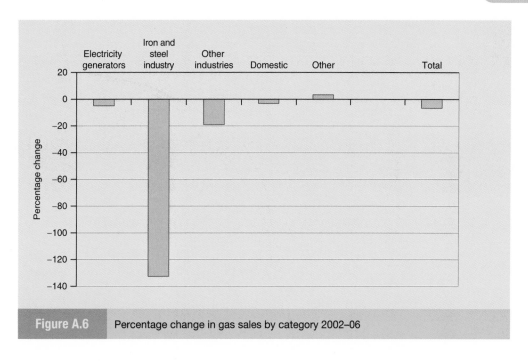

| Figure A.6 | Percentage change in gas sales by category 2002–06 |

Activity 3.4

The histogram is shown in Figure A.7.

As with the histogram for Region A (Figure 3.8), we need to adjust the frequencies for the last interval. As before, these are divided by two and a frequency of 3.5 should be plotted for the last interval. Comparing the histograms of the two regions we note that they give a very similar profile across the X axis, with both having a 'peak' in the 0–10 interval and then showing a tailing off effect as we move into higher profit intervals.

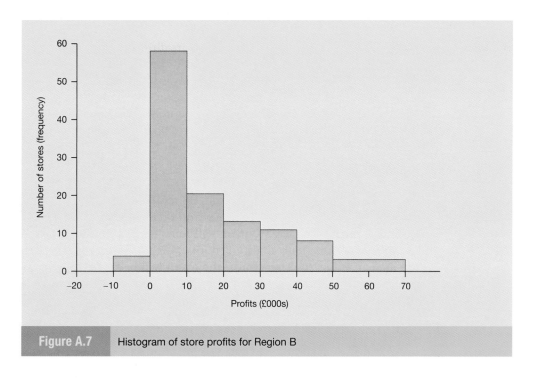

| Figure A.7 | Histogram of store profits for Region B |

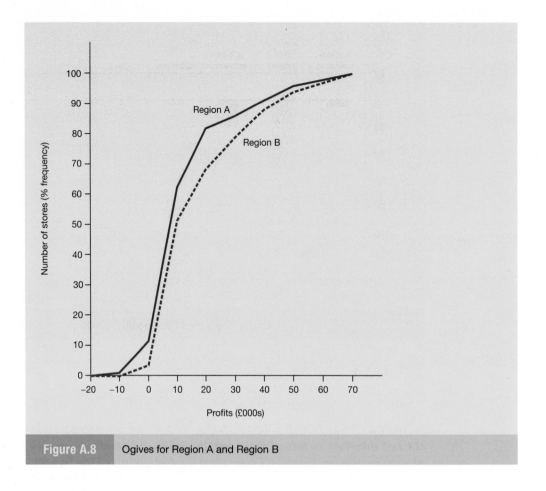

| Figure A.8 | Ogives for Region A and Region B |

Activity 3.5

Figure A.8 shows the two ogives. That for Region A, of course, is identical to that in Figure 3.12. We note that the two ogives are different and the implications of this need to be considered. We see that for Region B the ogive is below that for Region A. This implies that for any given profit level – say £30 000 – there is a smaller percentage of Region B's stores *below* this figure than Region A's. Conversely, there must be a higher percentage of Region B's stores *above* this profit. The implications of Region B's ogive being lower then is that, typically, its stores have higher profits than Region A's.

Activity 4.3

If one of the data items increases from 38 to 48 then the mean will increase (by 10/11 since we are adding 10 to the total, Σx, and there are still 11 numbers in the data set, n). However, the median for Month 1 will remain unchanged since in our ordered array we start at the smallest value and count along until we get to the sixth value, which is the median value. In other words, the mean will be slightly higher as a result, but the median will remain unchanged. This is a feature that will be helpful later.

Activity 4.6

The standard deviation for Month 2 works out at 3.3 days (the sum of the squared deviations is 122).

Activity 4.8

The various statistics are shown below:

	Before media campaign	After media campaign
Mean	234.2	277.5
SD	39.7	45.0
Min	173	204
Max	317	381
Range	144	177
Q1	205	241
Median	228	279.5
Q3	262	311
IQR	57	70
CofV	0.17	0.16
CofSk	0.47	−0.13

Note that figures have been calculated in an Excel spreadsheet and rounded.

All figures are in £s except for the Coefficient of Variation (CofV) and the Coefficient of Skewness (CofSk).

Let us examine the Before situation first. We see that there is a mean number of users of 234, although there is considerable variation around this, as shown by the standard deviation (calculated using the sample formula) of 40 and by the range of 144. The coefficient of variation indicates relative variability of 17 per cent around the mean. The median value is 228, slightly lower than the mean, implying a small number of high values in the data set. We see from the median that half the time the centre has less than 228 customers. The quartiles indicate that 25 per cent of the time there are less than 205 users and 25 per cent of the time there are more than 262. Half of the time, therefore, the centre has between 205 and 262 users.

After the campaign there are some interesting differences. The mean number of users per day has increased by over 40 (and we could use this to estimate the increase in revenue as a result). The median has increased by over 50, though, pushing it above the mean (as confirmed by the skewness coefficient, which is now negative at −0.13). This tends to imply that there are still some days where the number of users is quite low, although in general the campaign has pushed most days higher in terms of user numbers. This is confirmed by the minimum and maximum, with the former increasing by 20 and the latter by 60. Similarly, the upper quartile has increased more than the lower. In general, then, user numbers have typically increased after the campaign by about 40 per day, although we must be cautious about inferring cause and effect: we have no direct evidence that the media campaign has caused the increase in user numbers.

Activity 4.9

The mean for Region B is calculated as £16 776.86 (with Σfm at 2 030 000). Again note the difference between the mean calculated from the aggregated data and that for the raw data.

Activity 4.10

The two sets of calculations are shown in full:

| Region A | | | | |
m	f	fm	m^2	fm^2
−15 000	1	−15 000	225 000 000	225 000 000
−5 000	13	−65 000	25 000 000	325 000 000
5 000	56	280 000	25 000 000	1 400 000 000
15 000	22	330 000	225 000 000	4 950 000 000
25 000	5	125 000	625 000 000	3 125 000 000
35 000	6	210 000	1 225 000 000	7 350 000 000
45 000	5	225 000	2 025 000 000	10 125 000 000
60 000	5	300 000	3 600 000 000	18 000 000 000
Totals	113	1 390 000	7 975 000 000	45 500 000 000

Substituting into the formula we have:

$$\sqrt{\frac{\Sigma fm^2}{\Sigma f} - \left(\frac{\Sigma fm}{\Sigma f}\right)^2}$$

$$= \sqrt{\frac{45\ 500\ 000\ 000}{113} - \left(\frac{1\ 390\ 000}{113}\right)^2}$$

$$= \sqrt{402\ 654\ 867.257 - 151\ 311\ 770.695}$$

$$= 15\ 853.8$$

For Region B we have:

| Region B | | | | |
m	f	fm	m^2	fm^2
−15 000	0	0	225 000 000	0
−5 000	4	−20 000	25 000 000	100 000 000
5 000	58	290 000	25 000 000	1 450 000 000
15 000	21	315 000	225 000 000	4 725 000 000
25 000	13	325 000	625 000 000	8 125 000 000
35 000	11	385 000	1 225 000 000	13 475 000 000
45 000	7	315 000	2 025 000 000	14 175 000 000
60 000	7	420 000	3 600 000 000	25 200 000 000
Totals	121	2 030 000	7 975 000 000	67 250 000 000

Substituting into the formula:

$$\sqrt{\frac{\Sigma fm^2}{\Sigma f} - \left(\frac{\Sigma fm}{\Sigma f}\right)^2}$$

$$= \sqrt{\frac{67\ 250\ 000\ 000}{121} - \left(\frac{2\ 030\ 000}{121}\right)^2}$$

$$= \sqrt{555\ 785\ 123.967 - 281\ 463\ 014.821}$$

$$= \ \ 16\ 562.67$$

Note again the difference between the standard deviation based on the raw data and that for the aggregated data.

Activity 4.11

From Table 3.4 we have:

MI = 61

LCL = 0

CF = 4

CW = 10 000

F = 58

$$\text{Median} = 0 + (61 - 4)\frac{10\ 000}{58} = £9828$$

It is always worthwhile looking at your solution to see whether it looks 'sensible' in the context of the problem (it is not unknown in exams, for example, to see a negative standard deviation – think about it). Here the median item is item number 61, which must be close to the upper limit of the median interval (0 < 10 000) so the answer of 9828 at least appears to be in the right numerical area.

Activity 4.12

For Q1 we have:

Quartile item = 28.25

LCL = 0

CF = 14

CW = 10 000

F = 56

So that:

$$Q1 = 0 + (28.25 - 14)\frac{10\ 000}{56} = £2545$$

and for Q3:

> Quartile item = 84.75
>
> LCL = 10 000
>
> CF = 70
>
> CW = 10 000
>
> F = 22

giving:

$$Q3 = 10\ 000 + (84.75 - 70)\frac{10\ 000}{22} = £16\ 705$$

Activity 5.1

'Common sense' would tell us that there is a one in six chance of throwing the die and showing a six. This would be a theoretical probability since we know that there are six possible outcomes (the numbers 1 to 6) but only one of them can occur, and that each of them has the same chance of occurring (1/6).

However, consider the scenario that we have been throwing the die and noting which numbers are shown. We have done this 100 times and, as yet, have never thrown a six. We pick up the die one more time to throw. What would you say the probability is of throwing a six next time (assuming the die has not been tampered with in any way)?

The answer will depend on which of the three approaches to probability you adopt. On a strictly theoretical basis the answer must still be 1/6. On an empirical basis you might say the answer is 0 since a six has never appeared. On a subjective basis you might say the answer is 1 (or close to it) – that is, you're certain a six will appear because it hasn't been thrown for such a long time and has to appear sooner or later.

Activity 5.11

The mean and standard deviation are easily calculated:

> Mean = np = 50 000(0.12) = 6000
>
> Standard deviation = $\sqrt{npq}$ = $\sqrt{(50\ 000)(0.12)(0.88)}$ = 72.7

Potentially, these results and the principles of the Binomial could be used in a number of ways. First, by estimating the likely number of returns we can determine what these returns will cost us in postage, handling, etc. We also know that this cost has to be recouped from somewhere, so we can build this likely cost into the calculations for the profit margins we need to realise on the sales we achieve (estimated at 44 000). Equally, we can use this information for production and ordering. If we anticipate sales of 44 000 from orders of 50 000, there is clearly no point producing 50 000 items, as we will at some time have 6000 unsold items on our hands. We could also do some 'what-if' analysis around the problem. Clearly, the orders of 50 000 and the return rate of 12 per cent are not guaranteed outcomes – they are based on empirical observations. We could readily use the Binomial to determine the consequences of the number of orders differing from 50 000, and equally for the return rate to differ from 12 per cent to assess the consequences on our production decision and our profit.

Activity 5.13

Using the Z score formula we have:

Machine 1

$X = 475, Z = -2.5$

$X = 505, Z = 0.5$

$X = 518, Z = 1.8$

Machine 2

$X = 745, Z = -0.33$

$X = 725, Z = -1.67$

$X = 759, Z = 0.60$

Activity 7.17

We can treat the age distribution from government statistics as our expected (E) distribution. If our sample were representative then we should have a distribution by age group like the one in the government statistics. The sample we have obtained is clearly the observed (O) distribution. As with all these types of test, the null hypothesis is that $O = E$ (that is, that our sample distribution is representative, based on the government statistics). Presumably, it is important for the market research company to know whether or not the sample is representative so let us choose $\alpha = 0.01$. The calculations are then:

Observed	Expected	$(O - E)$	$(O - E)^2$	$(O - E)^2/E$
54	65	−11	121	1.86
63	60	3	9	0.15
167	190	−23	529	2.78
85	75	10	100	1.33
131	110	21	441	4.01
500	500	–	–	10.14

Notice that the expected frequencies total to 500 (the sample size). We have obtained a calculated χ^2 of 10.14. We have 4 degrees of freedom and from Appendix D we obtain a critical statistic of 13.28. Given the calculated statistic is less than the critical we have no reason to reject the null hypothesis. Remember that this is that $O = E$, so we cannot reject the hypothesis that the sample is representative compared with the government statistics.

Activity 8.3

The relevant information for the construction of a control chart is that we anticipate an average of 12 customer complaints per day averaged over 14 days (the sample period of two weeks). This would give warning limits of:

$$12 \pm 1.96 \, (5/\sqrt{14}) = 12 \pm 2.62$$

and action limits of:

$$12 \pm 3.09 \, (5/\sqrt{14}) = 12 \pm 4.13$$

One of the implications of these calculations, amongst others, is that a reduction in the mean number of customer complaints is not necessarily an indication that the number of complaints is falling. A reduction in one two-week period, for example, to 11 complaints would still be within the warning limits and could not be taken to indicate that the mean number of complaints had actually fallen (we would explain the reduction through the concept of sampling variation). The relevant control chart, with the first seven sets of results also plotted, is shown in Figure A.9. Our commentary on these results might be as follows.

We observe that in period 3 the result of 14.8 exceeds the upper warning limit. We would take this as evidence that the process might be out of control and we should obtain another sample as soon as is practical. We also observe that from period 3 onwards a clear downward trend is evident and although this is, by period 7, still within the warning limit we might anticipate period 8 being below the lower warning limit. In one sense this is not a problem for the supermarket since it implies a declining

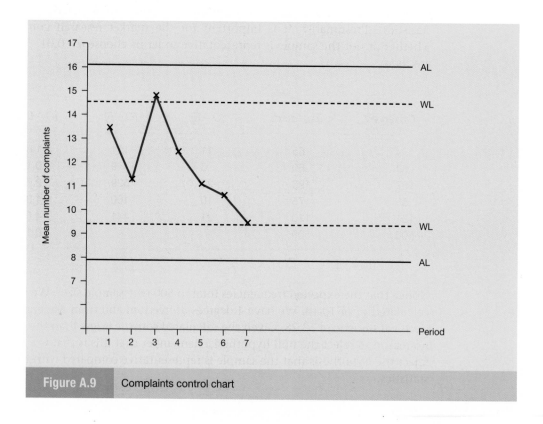

Figure A.9   Complaints control chart

mean number of complaints. However, the store manager would still be advised to try to assess why this trend was occurring. Is it linked to some management initiative intended to improve customer satisfaction? Is it linked to a customer care training programme introduced by the store? Is it linked to a change in the way customers are encouraged to complain (perhaps deliberately or accidentally the store has made it more difficult for customers to make complaints)?

Activity 10.2

Graphical solutions to Activity 10.2 are shown in Figure A.10.

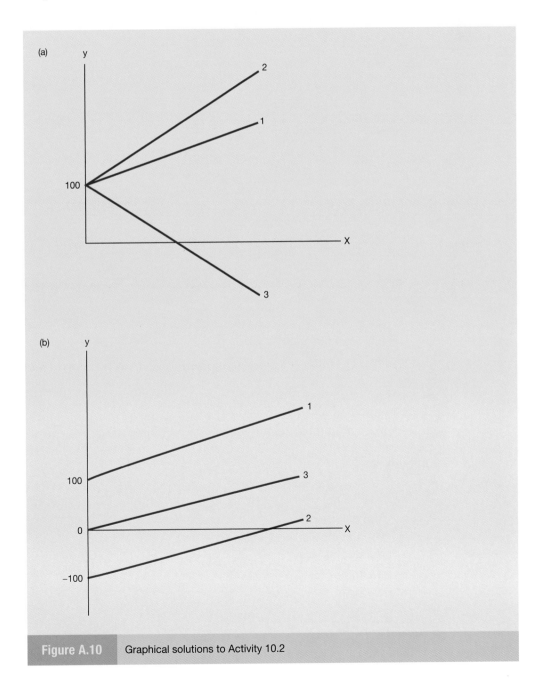

Figure A.10   Graphical solutions to Activity 10.2

Activity 10.9

The regression results using T = 1 to 22 are:

```
SUMMARY OUTPUT
```

Regression Statistics

Multiple R	0.994007162
R Square	0.988050238
Adjusted R Square	0.987452749
Standard Error	224.5747276
Observations	22

ANOVA

	df	SS	MS	F	Significance F
Regression	1	83401049.42	83401049.42	1653.673444	1.05187E-20
Residual	20	1008676.165	50433.80827		
Total	21	84409725.59			

	Coefficients	Standard Error	t Stat	P-value	Lower 95%	Upper 95%
Intercept	17475.88149	99.11996694	176.3104048	2.1285E-33	17269.12087	17682.64212
X Variable 1	306.8961745	7.546865304	40.66538385	1.05187E-20	291.1536894	322.6386596

This confirms a forecast for the trend in 2007 IV (T = 24) of 24 841.4. We also see that r^2 at 0.99 is higher than that for the model for Scenario A, implying a better fit of the regression line to the data. This would also be confirmed by comparing the two prediction intervals for Scenarios A and B. The trend forecast for Scenario B is statistically 'better', although whether it provides a better forecast in a business context is another matter, since both forecasts imply that the respective trend will remain unchanged.

Activity 11.2

We have a formulation:

Minimise $0.85H + 1.1C$

such that $4H + 2C \leqslant 20\ 000$

$1H + 3C \leqslant 15\ 000$

$1H \leqslant 4000$

$1C \leqslant 4500$

$1H \geqslant 2000$

$1C \geqslant 2500$

$H, C \geqslant 0$

Further Reading

Detailed below are articles and books which will help develop your knowledge and understanding of chapter topics. The list is periodically updated on the companion website.

Chapter 1

'L.L. Bean improves call centre forecasting', B.H. Andrews and S.H. Cunningham, *Interfaces*, **25** (6), 1995, pp 1–13.

'Quality management at Kentucky Fried Chicken', U.M. Apte and C.R. Reynolds, *Interfaces*, **25** (3), 1995, pp 6–21.

'Affairs of the heart', T. Bailey, A. Glaskin and D. Knowles, *Operational Research Insight*, **4** (3), 1991, pp 15–19.

'Consolidating and dispatching truck shipments of heavy petroleum products', D.O. Bausch, G.G. Brown and D. Ronen, *Interfaces*, **25** (2), 1995, pp 1–24.

'That was the idea that was', S. Crainer, *Management Today*, May 1996, pp 38–44.

'The impact of tourism', J. Fletcher and M. Baker, *Operational Research Insight*, **7** (4), 1994, pp 6–11.

'Operational research can do more for managers than they think!', L. Fortuin, P. van Beek and L. van Wassenhove, *Operational Research Insight*, **5** (1), 1992, pp 3–8.

'Keeping Scotch off the rocks', H.G. Jones, *Operational Research Insight*, **4** (1), 1991, pp 15–18.

'The Use of Quantitative Modelling Methods in the UK', B. Lehaney, S. Warwick and M. Wisniewski, *Journal of European Business Education*, **3** (2), 1994, pp 57–71.

'Go with the flow: modelling bed occupancy and patient flow through a geriatric department', S. McClean and P. Millard, *Operational Research Insight*, **7** (3), 1994, pp 2–5.

'Staffing the front office', C. Richardson, *Operational Research Insight*, **4** (2), 1991, pp 19–22.

'Coldstart: Fleet assignment at Delta Air Lines', R. Subramanian, R.P. Scheff, J.D. Quillinan, D.S. Wiper and R.E. Marsden, *Interfaces*, **24** (1), 1994, pp 104–20.

'Operational research: a toolkit for effective decision-making', A. Wiseman, *Management Accounting (UK)*, **66** (11), 1988, p 36.

'Does Anyone Use the Techniques We Teach?', M. Wisniewski, K. Kristensen, H. Madsen, P. Ostergaard, C. Jones, *Operational Research Insight*, **7** (2), 1994, pp 2–7.

'The Use of Quality Management Techniques in Denmark, Scotland and the UK', M. Wisniewski, K. Kristensen, H. Madsen, P. Ostergaard, C. Jones, *Journal of European Business Education*, **5** (1), 1995, pp 41–51.

Chapter 2

Foundation Quantitative Methods for Business, M. Wisniewski, Pitman Publishing, 1996, ISBN 0273607650.

Chapter 3

Considerable insight into the use of a variety of diagrams (good and bad) can be had through examination of business newspapers and magazines and government statistical publications. Amongst the more useful are:

> *Financial Times* newspaper
> *The Economist* magazine
> *Annual Abstract of Statistics*
> *Economic Trends Annual Abstract*
> *Monthly Digest of Statistics*
> *Regional Digest of Statistics*
> *Social Trends*

'The tools of quality – Part IV: histograms', Anon. *Quality Progress*, **23** (9), 1990, pp 75–8.

'British Rail InterCity strategic planning', B. Ball, *Operational Research Insight*, **4** (2), 1991, pp 2–5.

'Do computers imp[rove sales? A large insurance company assesses the impact of portable computers on the performance of its salesforce', D. Johnson and M. Whitehorn, *Operational Research Insight*, **7** (1), 1994, pp 8–15.

'Testing times in the coal industry', I. Turner, *Operational Research Insight*, **4** (2), 1991, pp 10–13.

'Maximising market effectiveness: achieving sales', G. Wills, S.H. Kennedy, J. Cheese and A. Rushton, *Management Decision*, **28** (2), 1990, pp 163–85.

'Boxplots', R. Allan Reese, *Significance*, September 2005, pp 134–5.

Chapter 4

'Promoting efficiency in the NHS: Problems with the Labour Productivity Index', J. Appleby, *British Medical Journal*, 313, 1996, pp 1319–21.

'Affairs of the heart', T. Bailey, A. Glaskin and D. Knowles, *Operational Research Insight*, **4** (3), 1991, pp 15–19.

Chapter 5

'Of calls and callers – establishing the resource requirements of a telephone desk', M. Gering, *Operational Research Insight*, **9** (3), 1996, pp 2–5.

'Operating margins – it's a gas!', G. Jack, *Operational Research Insight*, **4** (2), 1991, pp 6–9.

'Modelling age and retirement in manpower planning', J. P. K. Mohapatra, P. Mandal and B.K. Purnendu, *International Journal of Manpower*, **11** (6), 1990, pp 27–31.

Chapter 6

'A case analysis of the cost and value of marketing information', D.T. Brownlie, *Marketing Intelligence and Planning*, **9** (1), 1991, pp 11–18.

'The value of decision analysis at Eastman Kodak', R.T. Clemen and R.C. Kwit, *Interfaces*, Sept/Oct 2001, pp 74–92.

'Revisiting decision trees', S. Coles and J. Rowley, *Management Decision*, **33** (8), 1995, pp 46–50.

'Use a decision tree to recalculate control limits', C. Cullen, *Quality*, **35** (1), 1996, pp 20–22.

Decision Analysis for Management Judgement, P. Goodwin and G. Wright, John Wiley and Sons, 1991.

'How Bayer makes decisions to develop new drugs', J.S. Stonebraker, *Interfaces*, Nov/Dec 2002, pp 77–90.

Chapter 7

'Out-patient queues at the Ibn-Rochd health centre', M. Babes and G.V. Sarma, *Journal of the Operational Research Society*, **42** (10), 1991, pp 845–5.

'Doing the splits: using CHAID to identify customer segments', S. Baron and S. Worrall, *Operational Research Insight*, **9** (2), 1996, pp 21–5.

'Giving benefit to the buses. Evaluating strategies to encourage the use of public transport', S. Clark and R. Pretty, *Operational Research Insight*, **7** (2), 1994, pp 23–6.

'What practitioners need to know about . . . t tests', B. Hagin, *Financial Analysts Journal*, **58** (3), 1990, pp 17–20.

Chapter 8

'Using process control chart techniques to analyze crime rates in Houston, Texas', E.A. Anderson and J. Diaz, *Journal of the Operational Research Society*, **47** (7), 1996, pp 871–81.

'Are you getting the most out of your control charts?', A.J. Barnett and R.W. Andrews, *Quality Progress*, **27** (11), 1994, pp 75–80.

'Get control of your control charts', M.P. Boccacino, *Quality Progress*, **26** (Pt. 10), 1993, pp 99–102.

'Seven basic quality tools', C.C. Carter, *HR Magazine*, **37**, Jan 1992, pp 81–3.

'The rights and wrongs of control charts', R. Caulcutt, *Applied Statistics*, **44** (3), 1995, pp 279–8.

'Managing by fact', R. Caulcutt, *Significance*, March 2004, pp 36–8.

'Control charts in practice', R. Caulcutt, *Significance*, June 2004, pp 81–4.

'Using quality's tools: what's working well?', J. Ceridwen, *Journal for Quality and Participation*, **15** Mar 1992, pp 92–9.

'Practical implementation of statistical process control in a chemicals industry', S.S. Chaudry and J.R. Higbie, *International Journal of Quality and Reliability*, **6** (5), 1989, pp 37–48.

'Safety and total quality management', S.L. Curtis, *Professional Safety*, **40** (1), 1995, pp 18–20.

'Using the cause-and-effect diagram to manage conflict', D. Donndelinger and B. Van Dine, *Quality Progress*, **29** (6), 1996, p 136.

'Statistical process control in marketing and finance', J. E. Duarte, *CMA Magazine*, **65** (4), 1991, pp 20–3.

'Applying statistical process control to safety', P. Esposito, *Professional Safety*, **38** (12), 1993, pp 18–23.

'Successfully implementing SPC in integrated steel corporations', C.R. Harris and W. Yit, *Interfaces*, **24** (5), 1994, pp 49–58.

'Quality tools for improvement', M.K. Hart, *Production and Inventory Management Journal*, **33** (Pt. 1), 1992, pp 59–63.

'Quality statistical process control at Cherry Textron', J. Heinricks and M.M.K. Fleming, *Industrial Management*, **33** (3), 1991, pp 7–10.

'A graphical exploration of SPC – Part 1', R.W. Hoyer and W.C. Ellis, *Quality Progress*, **29** (5), 1996, pp 65–73.

'A graphical exploration of SPC – Part 2', R.W. Hoyer and W.C. Ellis, *Quality Progress*, **29** (6), 1996, pp 57–64.

Quality Planning and Analysis, J.M. Juran and F.M. Gryna, McGraw Hill, 1993.

'Making sense out of two Pareto charts', R.S. Kenett, *Quality Progress*, **27** (5), 1994, pp 71–3.

'Quality tools are applicable to local government', J.M. Kline, *Government Finance Review*, **9** (Aug), 1993, pp 15–19.

'Simple tools solve complex problems', B. Rudin, *Quality*, **29** (4), 1990, pp 50–1.

'The tools of quality Part II: cause and effect diagrams', S. Sarazen, *Quality Progress*, **23** (Pt. 7), 1990, pp 59–62.

'Statistical quality control in nursing homes', J.F. Schnelle, D.R. Newman and T. Fogarty, *Health Services Research*, **25** (4), 1990, pp 627–37.

Chapter 9

'Time-series forecasting', C. Chatfield, *Significance*, September 2005, pp 131–3.

'Analytical MS/OR tools applied to a plant closure', D.W. Clements and R.A. Reid, *Interfaces*, **24** (2), 1994, pp 1–43.

'Judgement or models: the importance of task difference', M. Lawrence and M. O'Connor, *Omega*, **24** (3), 1996, pp 245–54.

'Exponentially weighted moving average control schemes', J.M. Lucas and M.S. Saccucci, *Technometrics*, **32** (1), 1990, pp 1–13.

'Monitoring measurable process data. Why not use the EWMA chart?', C.R. Superville, *Quality Progress*, **28** (7), 1995, p 144.

'Judgemental and statistical time series forecasting: a review of the literature', R. Webby and M. O'Connor, *International Journal of Forecasting*, **12** (1), 1996, pp 91–118.

Forecasting methods for Management, S.C. Wheelright and S. Makridakis, John Wiley and Sons, 1985.

Chapter 10

'L.L. Bean improves call centre forecasting', B.H. Andrews and S.H. Cunningham, *Interfaces*, **25** (6), 1995, pp 1–13.

'Forecasting Sales with Trend Models – Coca Cola's Experience', N. Carroll Mohn, *Journal of Business Forecasting*, **8** (3), 1989, pp 6–8.

'Corporate modelling at RAC motoring services', S. Clarke, A. Hopper, A. Tobias and D. Tomlin, *Operational Research Insight*, **9** (3), 1996, pp 6–12.

Chapter 11

'Global supply chain management at Digital Equipment Corp.', B.C. Arntzen, G.G. Brown, T.P Harrison and L.F. Trafton, *Interfaces*, **25** (1), 1995, pp 69–93.

'Bags you choose, Optimising blood package usage in a regional Transfusion Centre', B.M. Baker, *Operational Research Insight*, **6** (3), 1993, pp 3–7.

'A history of mathematical programming in the petroleum industry', C.E. Bodington and T.E. Baker, *Interfaces*, **20** (4), 1990, pp 117–27.

'The Kellogg company optimizes production, inventory and distribution', G. Brown, B. Vegus, K. Wood, *Interfaces*, **31** (6), 2001, pp 1–15.

'Optimization of the production planning and trade of lily flowers at Jan de Wit company', J.V. Calxeta-Filho, J.M. van Swaay-Neto and A. de Padua Wagemaker, *Interfaces*, **32**, 2002, pp 35–46.

'Tea company steeped in OR', N. Chakravarti, *OR/MS Today*, April 2000.

'Orange harvesting scheduling management', J.V. Caixeta-Filho, *Journal of the Operational Research Society*, **57**, 2006, pp 37–42.

'Using mathematical programming to help supervisors balance workloads', J.R. Grandzol and T. Traaen, *Interfaces*, **25** (4), 1995, pp 92–103.

'Exploiting the scraps: an LP model improves the efficiency of aluminium recycling', M. Hasan and I. Osman, *Operational Research Insight*, **9** (3), 1996, pp 13–18.

'Contracting for coal', J. Hobbs and A. Neebe, *Operational Research Insight*, **8** (1), 1994, pp 28–32.

'Getting the mix right', A. Jacques, D. Eldridge, P. Danielsen and S. Brown, *Operational Research Insight*, **6** (1), 1993, pp 15–19.

'Keep the coffee coming', D. Reis, *Operational Research Insight*, **4** (3), 1991, pp 7–9.

'Led by LP! optimising feed and product mix at Brunswick Smelting', G. Warren, J. Bhadury and J. Hemingway, *Operational Research Insight*, **7** (3), 1994, pp 12–21.

Mathematical Programming: Optimization Models for Business and Management Decision Making, M. Wisniewski and T. Dacre, McGraw Hill, 1990.

'Optimizing Pilot Planning and Training for Continental Airlines', G. Yu, J. Pachon, B. Thengvall, D. Chandler and A. Wilson, *Interfaces*, **34** (4), 2004, pp 253–64.

Chapter 12

'Ford-Otosan optimizes its stocks using a six-sigma framework', M. Denizel, U. Ekinci, G. Ozyurt and D. Turhan, *Interfaces*, **37** (2), 2007, pp 97–107.

'Stock control: opportunities beyond the textbook', I. Fleming, *Operational Research Insight*, **5** (4), 1992, pp 9–11.

'Allocating warehouse stock in a retail chain', R.M. Hill, *Journal of the Operational Research Society*, **40** (11), 1989, pp 983–91.

'Getting control of Just-in-Time', U. Karmarkar, *Harvard Business Review*, Sep-Oct 1989, pp 122–31.

'Inventory Decisions in Dell's Supply Chain', R. Kapuscinski, R.Q. Zhang, P. Carbonneau, R. Moore and B. Reeves, *Interfaces*, **34** (3), May–June 2004, pp 191–205.

'Does manufacturing need a JIT revolution?', P.H. Zipkin, *Harvard Business Review*, Jan–Feb 1991, pp 40–50.

Chapter 13

'Critical path analysis with a spreadsheet', B. Baker, *Operational Research Insight*, **9** (2), 1996, pp 9–12.

'Plan for supply chain agility at Nokia: lessons from the mobile infrastructure industry', J. Collin and D. Lorenzin, *International Journal of Physical Distribution and Logistics Management*, **36** (6), 2006, pp 418–30.

'London Ambulance Service computer-aided despatch system', M. Hougham, *International Journal of Project Management*, **14** (2), 1996, pp 103–10.

Chapter 14

'Right on Queue', D. Atkins *et al.*, *OR/MS Today*, April 2003, pp 26–29.

'Out-patient queues at the Ibn-Rochd health centre', M. Babes and G.V. Sarma, *Journal of the Operational Research Society*, **42** (10), 1991, pp 845–55.

'The simulation of New Street station', O. Bird, G. Lee, P. Watson, R. Brooks and A. Tobias, *Operational Research Insight*, **7** (4), 1994, pp 27–31.

'On the waterfront', P. Danielsen, D. Eldridge and S. Brown, *Operational Research Insight*, **4** (1), 1991, pp 8–14.

'The growing need for renal services', R. Davies and J. Flowers, *Operational Research Insight*, **8** (2), 1995, pp 6–11.

'A little knowledge can be dangerous: handle simulation with care', J.R. Evans, *Production and Inventory Management Journal*, 2nd quarter, 1992, pp 51–4.

'The TARDIS simulation: Evaluating equipment replacement strategies in the electrical distribution industry', J. Freeman and M. North, *Operational Research Insight*, **7** (3), 1994, pp 22–7.

'A hospital capacity planning model', D. Gove and D. Hewett, *Operational Research Insight*, **8**(2), 1995, pp 12–15.

'A call center uses simulation to drive strategic change', R.M. Saltzman and V. Mehrota, *Interfaces*, May/June 2001, pp 87–101.

Chapter 15

'Net present value: an old tool finding use in assessing public sector capital expenditures', F. Blanchard, *Project Management Journal*, **26** (1), 1995, pp 41–6.

'Risk and capital budgeting: avoiding the pitfalls in using NPV when risk arises', D. Brookfield, *Management Decision*, **33** (8), 1995, pp 56–9.

'The applicability and usage of NPV and IRR capital budgeting techniques', C.S.A. Cheng, D. Kite and R. Radtke, *Managerial Finance*, **20** (7), 1994, pp 10–36.

'Watch for pitfalls of DCF techniques', C.W. Chow and A.H. McNamee, *Healthcare Financial Management*, **45** (4), 1991, pp 34–44.

Index